Guide to

Linux Networking and Security

Nicholas Wells

THOMSON

COURSE TECHNOLOGY

Australia • Canada • Mexico • Singapore • Spain • United Kingdom • United States

THOMSON

COURSE TECHNOLOGY

Guide to Linux Networking and Security

is published by Course Technology

Senior Editor:
William Pitkin III

Senior Editor:
Lisa Egan

Product Manager:
Amy M. Lyon

Developmental Editor:
Deb Kaufmann

Production Editor:
Aimee Poirier

Technical Editor:
Edward Sawicki, Accelerated
Learning Center

Senior Manufacturing Coordinator:
Laura Burns

MQA Technical Leaders:
Nicole Ashton and John Bosco

Product Marketing Manager:
Jason Sakos

Associate Product Manager:
Tim Gleeson

Editorial Assistant:
Nick Lombardi

Cover Design:
Janet Lavine

Text Designer:
GEX Publishing Services

Compositor:
GEX Publishing Services

Disclaimer
Course Technology reserves the right to revise this publication and make changes from time to time in its content without notice.

ISBN 0-619-00094-5

TABLE OF
Contents

CHAPTER TWELVE
Network Intrusion Detection   **527**

APPENDIX A
Linux Certification Objectives   **567**

APPENDIX B
Command Summary   **593**

GLOSSARY   **603**

INDEX   **626**

Preface

From obscure beginnings in large offices and laboratories, networked computers have become part of the daily routine of most people in the industrialized world. We share email with friends, use credit cards and ATMs through worldwide financial networks, conduct business online, and check out the latest movies, weather, and sports scores via a dozen different Internet services. Linux has been part of the Internet for nearly a decade, offering low-cost, stable support for every major Internet protocol and service. More recently, with the growing support of many third-party software companies, Linux is being used as a server in local networks providing file and print services, databases, intranets, and many other services.

All of this networking is occurring despite growing public fears about the dangers of placing so much information on public networks. The anonymity of using computers on a worldwide network, and the horror stories in the newspaper, make many people think twice before trusting these machines with their finances or other personal information. Stories of corporate malfeasance, invasion of privacy, threats to our civil rights, and continuous public attacks by malicious "hackers" all give us pause. And yet few would sacrifice the benefits that technology offers solely because dangers lurk in the shadows.

Instead, information technology professionals use robust systems such as Linux, with appropriate security measures and a good dose of pragmatic paranoia, to keep things running smoothly and securely.

As you prepare yourself to participate in this drama, you're certain to find it interesting, fast-paced, and full of colorful characters, both among the attackers and the usually less-conspicuous experts who block their antics and sometimes send them to jail.

In writing a single volume covering Linux networking and security, compromises were required to make the result manageable for readers. Some instructors or advanced students may decry the lack of depth on a favorite topic or a software utility that is not even mentioned. Yet those who have just completed a course on operating systems or beginning Linux administration are likely to feel overwhelmed at times by the hundreds of new terms and concepts that are presented in quick succession. With classroom support for the more adventurous, this book should nevertheless provide a solid and well-organized introduction to all of the key topics in these important but complex fields.

This book is the second in a set, the first being *Guide to Linux Installation and System Administration*. To get the most from this volume, you should be comfortable with Linux. You should have installed it before, and have experience using a Linux graphical environment to execute programs, and preferably a Linux command line to explore common system utilities, manage user accounts, and use a Linux file system. With that foundation, this book teaches you the basics of networking, specifically Linux networking, and of network security. One aim of the material presented is to prepare you to pass a Linux certification exam, to demonstrate to potential employers that you have mastered important theoretical and practical knowledge about Linux-based networking and security.

Several certification programs for Linux are currently available. This book and its companion volume, *Guide to Linux Installation and System Administration*, provide more than enough material for you to pass both the SAIR/GNU Linux Certified Administrator (LCA) certification program and the Linux Professional Institute (LPI) Level 1 certification. Two other Linux certifications are not covered explicitly. The Linux+ certification from CompTIA (see *www.comptia.com*) is a less technically demanding program that this book and its companion should also prepare you for. The Red Hat Certified Engineer certification is a more demanding program that may require additional study of Red Hat Linux before taking the hands-on certification exam.

The Linux Professional Institute (LPI) is sponsored by several major vendors, including Caldera International, Hewlett Packard, and IBM. It is a nonprofit organization that operates with a board of directors who gather input from members of the Linux community to develop overall certification goals, testing objectives, and future plans. LPI has planned a three-level certification program. The first level, addressed by this book, consists of two tests aimed at basic Linux proficiency.

The Sair/GNU certification effort was started by Tobin Maginnis, a professor at the University of Mississippi. With cooperation from leading free software enthusiasts, his organization created the LCA testing objectives and testing program. To obtain LCA certification, you must pass a series of four tests. The material in the first two tests is covered in *Guide to Linux Installation and System Administration*. This book, *Guide to Linux Networking and Security*, addresses the material in the last two tests. Appendix A provides the most current information about the LPI and LCA certification objectives available at the time of this writing, with references tying each objective in both programs to sections of this book or its companion volume. We realize that the exams may be updated in the future. For updated certification mapping information, please go to *www.course.com/networking*.

The Intended Audience

This book is intended for students and professionals who need to understand basic computer networking and security technology in the context of a Linux-based server. Though it begins with theoretical discussions of networking (in Chapter 1) and security (in Chapter 7), the focus is practical, with hands-on descriptions of many utilities and Web sites used by working system administrators. This book is ideal as the text for introductory courses on networking so long as students have some background in operating systems and are comfortable with a Linux or UNIX command line. The text and pedagogical features are designed to provide an interactive learning experience, so that further self-study of Internet and computer industry resources will prepare readers for more advanced education or work assignments in network administration and network security management. Each chapter includes Hands-on Projects that lead readers through various tasks in a step-by-step fashion. Each chapter also contains Case Projects that place readers in the role of problem solver, requiring them to apply concepts presented in the chapter in a situation that might occur in a real-life work environment.

Chapter Descriptions

Individual chapters discuss the following topics:

Chapter 1, "Networking Fundamentals," introduces networking technology, including the hardware components of networking and basic networking theory. It also introduces the basic networking protocols used in Linux.

Chapter 2, "Configuring Basic Networking," describes how networking devices are utilized in Linux and how to use both command line and graphical utilities to configure network addresses and basic routing. Basic command-line utilities used to test networks are also presented.

Chapter 3, "Configuring Client Services," describes how to set up name resolution, dial-in network access, and remote graphical access using the X Window system. Basic concepts behind Web browsers and email clients are also explained, and commonly used products are reviewed.

Chapter 4, "Configuring Simple Network Services," shows how to set up a Linux superserver to handle a variety of incoming network service requests. Some of the more basic services are described, along with key administrative functions that can rely on networking, such as logging and printing.

Chapter 5, "Configuring File Sharing Services," discusses four file sharing technologies that are supported on Linux: the Network File System (NFS), NetWare's NCP file sharing, File Transfer Protocol (FTP), and the Server Message Block (SMB) protocol used by Microsoft Windows systems.

Chapter 6, "Configuring Major Network Services," discusses four network services for which Linux is well-known: Domain Name Services (DNS), dynamic packet routing, email service using `sendmail`, and Web services using the Apache Web server.

Chapter 7, "Security, Ethics, and Privacy," introduces the second half of the book by describing the landscape of network security and its relationship to ethics in the profession of system or network administrator. Privacy of personal information as a legal issue and a concern for network administrators is also discussed.

Chapter 8, "Making Data Secure," discusses data encryption technologies, illustrating basic concepts and describing what protocols are currently used to secure network data. Commonly used Linux encryption tools are also covered in some detail.

Chapter 9, "User Security," describes how network administrators can safeguard user account information and help end-users act wisely to add to system security. Software tools and security policies designed to aid user security are presented.

Chapter 10, "File Security," discusses how to keep track of changes in important system files that may indicate that someone has attacked your server. Special utilities and cryptographic techniques are presented to help you safeguard these files.

Chapter 11, "Network Security Fundamentals," builds on user and file security to introduce network security, including concepts such as firewalls and using special routing techniques to protect internal networks.

Chapter 12, "Network Intrusion Detection," continues the discussion of network security by focusing on the attackers' techniques and how they can be successfully overcome using intrusion detection systems and various vulnerability assessment utilities.

Appendix A, "Linux Certification Objectives," provides a list of the objectives for SAIR/GNU Linux and Linux Professional Institute (LPI) certification programs, with references from each objective to the section of this book or its companion volume that cover the material in that objective.

Appendix B, "Command Summary," provides a table with all Linux command-line utilities, server daemons, and graphical programs described in this book and in the companion volume on installation and system administration.

Features

To aid you in fully understanding networking concepts, this book includes many features designed to enhance your learning experience.

- **Chapter Objectives**. Each chapter begins with a detailed list of the concepts to be mastered within that chapter. This list provides you with both a quick reference to the chapter's contents and a useful study aid.

- **Illustrations and Tables**. Numerous illustrations of networking concepts, protocol layouts, and security methods help you to visualize and better understand technical concepts. In addition, the many tables included provide concise references on essential topics such as command options and online information resources.

- **Chapter Summaries**. Each chapter's text is followed by a summary of the concepts introduced in that chapter. These summaries provide a helpful way to recap and revisit the ideas covered in each chapter.

- **Key Terms**. All of the terms within the chapter that were introduced with boldfaced text are gathered together in the Key Terms list at the end of the chapter. This provides you with a method of checking your understanding of all the terms introduced.

- **Review Questions**. A list of review questions is included to reinforce the ideas introduced in each chapter. Answering these questions will ensure that you have mastered the important concepts.

- **Hands-on Projects**. Although it is important to understand the theory behind the Linux operating system, nothing can improve upon real-world experience. To this end, along with thorough explanations, each chapter provides numerous Hands-on Projects aimed at providing you with practical implementation experience and real-world solutions.

- **Case Projects**. Located at the end of each chapter are several cases projects. To complete these exercises, you must draw on real-world common sense as well as your knowledge of all the technical topics covered to that point in the book. Your goal for each project is to come up with answers to problems similar to those you will face as a working network administrator.

Text and Graphic Conventions

Wherever appropriate, additional information and exercises have been added to this book to help you better understand the topic at hand. Icons throughout the text alert you to additional materials. The icons used in this textbook are described below.

 The Note icon draws your attention to additional helpful material related to the subject being described.

 Tips based on the author's experience provide extra information about how to attack a problem or what to do in real-world situations.

 The Caution icon warns you about potential mistakes or problems and explains how to avoid them.

 Each hands-on activity in this book is preceded by the Hands-On icon and a description of the exercise that follows.

 The Case Project icon marks case projects, which are more involved, scenario-based assignments. In these extensive case examples, you are asked to implement independently what you have learned.

Instructor's Materials

The following additional materials are available when this book is used in a classroom setting. All of the supplements available with this book are provided to the instructor on a single CD-ROM.

Electronic Instructor's Manual. The Instructor's Manual that accompanies this textbook includes:

- Additional instructional material to assist in class preparation, including suggestions for classroom activities, discussion topics, and additional projects.
- Solutions to all hands-on activities and end-of-chapter materials, including the review questions and case projects.

ExamView®. This textbook is accompanied by ExamView, a powerful testing software package that allows instructors to create and administer printed, computer (LAN-based), and Internet exams. ExamView includes hundreds of questions that correspond to the topics covered in this text, enabling students to generate detailed study guides that include page references for further review. The computer-based and Internet testing components allow students to take exams at their computers and also save the instructor time by grading each exam automatically.

PowerPoint presentations. This book comes with Microsoft PowerPoint slides for each chapter. These are included as a teaching aid for classroom presentation, to be made available to students on the network for chapter review, or to be printed for classroom distribution. Instructors, please feel at liberty to add your own slides for additional topics you introduce to the class.

Figure files. All of the figures and tables in the book are reproduced on the Instructor's Resource CD, in bitmap format. Similar to the PowerPoint presentations, these are included as a teaching aid for classroom presentation, to make available to students for review, or to be printed for classroom distribution.

Read This Before You Begin

The Hands-on Projects in this book help you to apply what you have learned about Linux networking and security. The following section lists the minimum hardware and software requirements that allow you to complete all the Hands-on Projects in this book. In addition to the following requirements, students must have administrator privileges on their workstations in order to complete many of the projects.

Although this book includes a copy of Red Hat Linux 7.3 Publisher's Edition, the Linux certification programs that the book tracks are not focused on Red Hat Linux, and the information in the book applies in most cases to all current versions of Linux, such as Caldera, SuSE, Debian, TurboLinux, Corel Linux, Mandrake, and many others. The exceptions occur in some of the utilities used as examples and in the location of certain files in the directory structure. In these cases, Red Hat is referenced particularly to give readers notice that non-Red Hat systems may differ. In particular, many of the projects rely on Red Hat Linux. Doing this allows the projects to be more complex than would be possible if they were aimed at the lowest common denominator among all versions of Linux.

Minimum Lab Requirements

- **Hardware:**
  - Each student workstation and each server computer requires at least 64 MB of RAM, an Intel Pentium or compatible processor running at 200 MHz or higher, and a minimum of 1.5 GB of free space on the hard disk. More hard disk space is useful, but 1.5 GB will allow all the critical network services to be installed.

  - The computer should also have a network card. Ethernet is assumed throughout the book, but others such as Token Ring will work equally well.

  - Many Hands-on Projects assume that all workstations are networked together. This can be done with simple Ethernet hubs. No particular cabling system or speed requirements apply, so long as the workstations can communicate with each other to experiment with networking and security protocols and utilities.

  - Several Hands-on Projects assume that student workstations can access the Internet to research topics and products. Care should be taken that security is not compromised in allowing workstations to access the Internet through a larger organizational LAN, since the tools and techniques used in the Hands-on Projects, if taken to extremes, are likely to make administrators on the LAN quite unhappy.

- RED HAT LINUX 7.3 PUBLISHER'S EDITION

This book includes a copy of the Publisher's Edition of Red Hat® Linux® from Red Hat, Inc., which you may use in accordance with the license agreement. Official Red Hat® Linux®, which you may purchase from Red Hat, includes the complete Red Hat® Linux® distribution, Red Hat's documentation, and may include technical support for Red Hat® Linux®. You also may purchase technical support from Red Hat. You may purchase Red Hat® Linux® and technical support from Red Hat through the company's web site (www.redhat.com) or its toll-free number 1.888.REDHAT1. There is a sticker on the top of the envelope containing the Red Hat® Linux® CD-ROMs (this sticker may also be on the inside back cover of the text). By ripping this seal, you agree to the terms listed above.

ACKNOWLEDGMENTS

It's much easier to be an expert when you have other experts backing up your work. To that end, I express my heartfelt appreciation for the many experts who made this project roll forward so smoothly.

The Senior Editor for this series of books is Will Pitkin, whose association I was pleased to enjoy as we exchanged woes about preparing books while going to graduate school (he to business, me to law). At least I only had one to do, instead of the entire Course Technology Networking Series to worry about, as he does. I fear I didn't make enough trouble with my deadlines, but I hope my project manager, Amy Lyon, will still know how much her upbeat attitude and pleasant notes were appreciated. Most of my interaction as an author was with the development editor, Deb Kaufmann. Deb smoothed over the rough edges of my writing, catching those points where I didn't really mean to say *that*, and deftly coordinated the work of everyone else I dealt with to lessen my load. And so, for the hundredth or so time, Thanks, Deb.

Course Technology really puts together a great team to make every book the best it can be. I was able to contribute this time by recommending a longtime colleague and friend, Ed Sawicki, as the technical editor for this project. Ed repaid me by significantly enhancing the technical precision of this volume, all the while adding anecdotes and opinions from his years of experience teaching similar material himself. In dozens of places, I've slipped his recommendations and observations into the text as my own. For the rest of the Course team I can take no credit, but only act as beneficiary. Aimee Poirier was the Production Editor, ironing out the final syntactic kinks (and nonsense that I missed earlier). Nicole Ashton, Chris Scriver, and Serge Palladino in the MQA department (quality assurance) carefully tested all of my assertions and procedures, hoping to save readers the trouble I occasionally caused them. Their work is all much appreciated. Their pride in a quality job is obvious.

Beyond Ed and the staff at Course Technology, my editors recruited several instructors to review the material as writing progressed. I considered their input invaluable in tailoring the material presented here to the needs of students based on their many years of experience in the classroom. My thanks to each of them:

Denny Brown	Ozarks Technical Community College
Rick Menking	Hardin-Simmons University
Doug Montgomery	Madison Area Technical College
Chris Spreitler	Vatterott College

I wish to thank more generally those instructors and readers who gave such a positive reception to the first volume of this set, *Guide to Linux Installation and System Administration*. After the tremendous effort required by so many people to prepare each of these books, strong feedback from readers is just the sort of encouragement one needs before doing a second volume.

But the biggest thanks go to the person who said the least, who listened to arcane networking details and security stories with a pleasant nod, who watched the little ones for "just a few more minutes," night after night, after just having watched me finish another sleepless semester of law school: The biggest thanks are reserved for my wife, Anne.

NETWORKING FUNDAMENTALS

After reading this chapter and completing the exercises you will be able to:

♦ Explain the purposes and development of computer networking

♦ Identify common types of networking hardware

♦ Describe how networking software operates

♦ Understand when popular networking protocols are used

♦ Define network routing and describe the purpose of popular routing protocols

In this chapter, you will learn basic information about computer networks—knowledge that will prepare you to support and use networking within the Linux operating system. This chapter describes the purposes and development of networking, then outlines the physical components that make up a network: the cables and computer parts that make it work. The second part of this chapter describes networking software in general terms and introduces you to the protocols—rules of operation—used by the most popular types of networks. Although this chapter does not explain networking hardware and protocols in great depth, it does give you a foundation for configuring Linux networking in the next chapter. You will learn more about networking protocols as specific services are configured later in this book.

THE DEVELOPMENT OF NETWORKED COMPUTERS

In the broadest sense, you could say that computer networking developed in response to the human need to communicate and share information, and to do it easily and quickly. The need to share information and resources is also essential for businesses and organizations. Although the earliest computers in the 1940s and 1950s were too expensive for anyone to worry about networking (who could afford *two* of them?), and the first PCs in the 1980s had no networking capability, it wasn't long before computers became popular in large companies and on university campuses, and the demand for networking increased.

Connecting computers and related devices in a local area network (LAN) provides several advantages, including:

- Being able to share information instantly without converting it to a transportable format such as a floppy disk or printout

- Automating some data-processing tasks that involve multiple computer systems

- Making more efficient use of resources; networking allows multiple people to use a computer, printer, or other resource even from a distance

This chapter focuses primarily on technology commonly used for **local area networks (LANs)**—networks within a relatively small space, such as an office or a building. **Wide area networks (WANs)**—networks spanning more widely separated geographical locations—often use different technologies. Details of wide area networks are beyond the scope of this book, though they become important as you learn more about Linux system administration, networking, and security.

Three historical trends have contributed to the multitude of network-capable systems you work with today:

- Networking capability was added to personal computers as the usefulness of networking became apparent and its cost dropped

- Network server computers based on UNIX became less expensive

- The Internet grew explosively and became widely accessible

Most of the larger computers connected to the Internet, even early on, were running the UNIX operating system. Because Linux is modeled on UNIX, the networking standards used by the Internet from its inception were also built into Linux from *its* inception. When designers of other operating systems (such as Microsoft Windows or Macintosh OS) want to include Internet features, they must do so by adding UNIX features (Linux features). Linux, you might say, has native support for the Internet.

As you probably know, the **Internet** is a collection of many networks around the world that are linked via high-speed connections. Communications on the Internet are based on specific protocols or rules of communication. Once the Internet became widespread enough that the average businessperson and student had access to it, organizations also began using Internet protocols to share information internally with employees, customers, and others. An **intranet** is a network within an organization that uses Internet protocols as the basis for sharing data and information. On an intranet, employees can use a Web browser (software available on any computer system) to access information on the organization's central Web server. This is much more efficient and cost-effective than earlier information-sharing systems.

Network Types

There are three general configurations in which computers can share information and resources: terminal connections, client-server computing, and peer-to-peer computing. Each of these types is explained in the following sections.

Terminals Tie Many People to One Computer

The terminal connection model was the earliest type of computer network, though terminals are still used by millions of users around the world. A **terminal** consists of a keyboard and screen that allow users to access a remote central computer, but has no computing ability on its own (see Figure 1-1). (For this reason, sometimes you hear them called **dumb terminals**.) Some terminals use a graphical user interface; many do not. Figure 1-1 shows several terminals connected to a single computer. The terminals send keystrokes to the computer; the computer sends responses to each terminal according to the keystrokes it receives from that terminal. Think of a terminal as being, in a sense, part of the remote computer.

CPU

Terminals

Figure 1-1   Terminals allow multiple users to interact with a single computer at the same time

Unless you are working in a large company or organization that uses "real" terminals (as opposed to personal computers), you might think you'll never see what a terminal looks like. Actually, most personal computers can emulate a terminal so that you can connect to another computer and enter commands for that computer at your "terminal." **Terminal emulation** is the term used to describe a program that acts like a terminal in letting you connect to another computer. For example, the Windows operating system includes a program called HyperTerminal that lets your personal computer act like a terminal to connect to a remote computer. Several terminal emulation programs are available for Linux. The `xterm` program is the most widely used example. It lets you open a command-line window within a Linux graphical environment. The command-line window acts like a terminal in letting you interact with the host's resources. This type of program is also called a **pseudo-terminal**, and is referred to among Linux devices as `pty`. For example, the first pseudo-terminal window that you open is `pty0`, the second, `pty1`, etc.

Other terminal emulation programs for Linux include `minicom` and `seyon`. These programs let you dial in to a remote computer and act as a terminal to that host.

Client-Server Computing

Suppose now that instead of a terminal being dumb, it was "smart." That is, when the terminal received data from the central computer, it had the capability to process it in some way before sending its next request. This is the idea behind the **client–server** model of computing. In client-server computing, the client is analogous to a terminal, but the client has a CPU and runs its own programs. The client initiates a request to a server, then processes the information it receives from the server. A **server** is a computer or a software program that provides information or services. A **client** is a computer or software program that requests information or services from the server and then processes or acts on the information it receives. For example, when you use a Web browser, you are acting as a client. You request information from a Web server somewhere on the Internet. The server returns that information to your client program—your Web browser. Figure 1-2 shows this interaction.

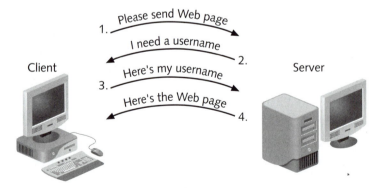

Figure 1-2   Client-server interaction to retrieve a Web page

Throughout this book you will see the terms client and server hundreds of times. An important point to remember is that your Linux system can act as a client *or* a server, depending on the software that you choose to run, and on the functions of that software. In fact, a single Linux system might act as a client for some programs and a server for other programs at the same time.

A Linux system can even act as both client and server to *itself.* This is a harder concept to follow, but it's one that you'll be seeing a lot in future chapters. Remember that Linux is a multitasking operating system. Suppose that one task running on your computer is a Web server, running in the background, and another task on the same computer is a Web browser. You enter a command in the browser requesting data from your own computer. The transfer of data from Web server to Web browser is a client-server network transaction, even though the data never leaves your computer.

Peer-to-Peer Networking

The idea of a computer acting as both a client and a server brings us to the idea of a peer-to-peer network. Most operating systems used today, including Linux and Windows NT/2000/XP, can run client programs *and* server programs; they do not rely on a centralized server to provide access to data or other resources (such as a shared printer). This type of networking is called **peer-to-peer networking**. Each computer on the network is a *peer* or equal to the other computers and has the ability to initiate communications, respond to requests for information, and interact with users independent of other computer systems. While a client-server model is centralized, peer-to-peer networking is decentralized, meaning that any host can communicate with any other host, and can share its resources as it chooses.

Linux is thought of as a peer-to-peer operating system, but it has client-server programs running on it. Thus, you have a centralized architecture for a particular service overlaid on a more general peer-to-peer network. For example, all users obtain Web pages from a single Web server, but all the computers can communicate with each other independent of the "server."

In some situations, a server is a dedicated system that can act *only* as a server. One example of this is a computer running the NetWare operating system. NetWare is a server operating system; it can't be used effectively as a client. Conversely, older versions of Windows, such as Windows 3.1, are client operating systems—they can not "serve" data to another computer.

When you study networking computers running Linux or Microsoft Windows, most of what you learn is focused on peer-to-peer networking. This is because the computers running Linux or other popular operating systems are powerful enough to act as independent systems, rather than as simply dumb terminals.

Of course, the system administrator may set up one Linux computer as "the server," but you should understand that the designation "server" is not based on running Linux—Linux can always act as a client as well, if it has a client program installed on it. A Linux computer may be called a server because it has a server software program installed on it (such as Web server software) and it has the hardware features that make it robust enough to handle the demands of being a server (which are generally much higher than those required of a client).

It's important that you understand the distinction between a terminal connection to a remote system, client-server computing, and peer-to-peer networking. Table 1-1 should help solidify these concepts.

Table 1-1   Comparing three networking models

	Terminal Connection	Peer-to-Peer Networking	Client-Server Computing
Focuses on the networking arrangement	Yes	Yes	No
Focuses on the application being used	No	No	No
Can I download data?	No	Yes, from any peer to any peer	Yes, client can download from server
Can I operate independently?	No; terminal has no intelligence	Yes	Yes; both client and server have intelligence but are designed to be used as a set

CREATING A NETWORK

To learn about the components that make up a modern network, let's suppose that you work in a small medical office that wants to network its computers. You want to use a server running Linux to hold everyone's files and give everyone access to a shared printer. Figure 1-3 shows the systems that are involved in this project.

You have two related questions to answer:

1. What pieces of equipment will you use to connect the computers into a network?

2. What software will you use to make the network function as you intend, enabling the transfer of files and other types of information on the network?

We'll take up the first question in this section, and begin exploring the second question later in this chapter and continuing throughout this book!

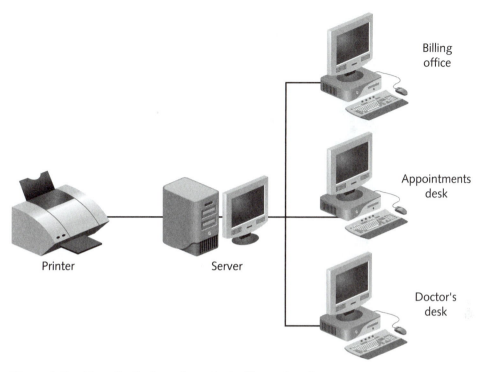

Figure 1-3   Hypothetical small medical office network

The basic hardware needed to network computers includes **network interface cards** (**NICs**, sometimes also called network adapters or network cards) and cables. Figure 1-4 shows a couple of typical NICs. Each node on the network must have a NIC, and (unless the network is a wireless one) a cable that connects the NIC to the network. (A **node**, or **host**, is any device directly connected to the network, such as a workstation or server.) Generally, NICs are installed in a PCI slot on the motherboard and have an external connection for the network cable. In addition, for this small office LAN, you probably want a hub or a switch to connect the three computers with the server. A **hub** is a wiring center that allows cables from multiple computers to be combined in a single network connection. Rather than run cables from each of the three computers to the server, you can connect all three to a hub within the office, then run one cable from the hub to the server room, as shown in Figure 1-5. A hub is inexpensive and normally is not intelligent (that is, it doesn't have a CPU, just a few electronics to merge signals from multiple cables onto a single cable). You can also use a **switch**, which is similar to a hub but more intelligent (it has a CPU and can make decisions about whether or not to allow network traffic to pass) and more efficient (its ability to make decisions makes for less traffic on the network).

Figure 1-4   Typical NICs

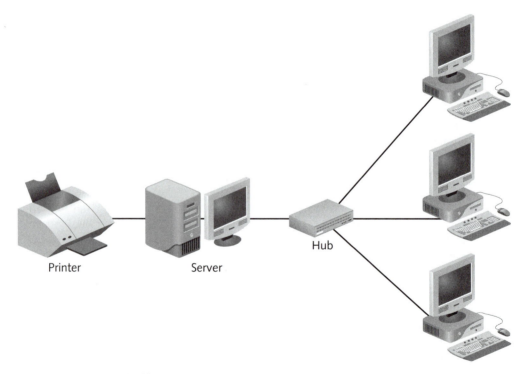

Figure 1-5   A small office network with hub

The work of physically connecting computers via cables and other devices is not part of Linux networking training. Of course, someone must do that work before you can network with Linux; but because Linux supports so many different technologies, it's likely that you're already working in an organization or computer lab of some sort where the networking hardware has been installed and configured. To be thoroughly versed in networking, you may want to learn more than just the Linux software covered in this book. For a more detailed discussion of networking hardware (and the protocols discussed later in this chapter), review a book such as *Network+ Guide to Networks* by Tamara Dean, published by Course Technology, Inc.

Networking Technologies

Before you buy any network hardware for your medical office network, you must decide what type of networking technology you will use. The most widely used technology is called Ethernet. **Ethernet** is a networking standard developed in the 1970s by Xerox, Intel, and Digital Equipment Corporation (now part of Compaq Computer Corp.). Ethernet is an international standard that has been revised several times. The version that people generally refer to when talking about Ethernet is called 802.3, because it adheres to the 802.3 networking standard of the IEEE (Institute of Electrical and Electronics Engineers).

There are currently three variations of Ethernet, with differences based primarily on speed: 10 Mb/s Ethernet, 100 Mb/s or Fast Ethernet, and Gigabit Ethernet. An important consideration for most networks is speed or **bandwidth,** the amount of information that a network technology can transmit. It is usually expressed in bits per second (bps). Low-speed transmissions use kilobits per second **(Kb/s)**. One Kb/s is 1,000 bits per second. Standard Ethernet NICs can transmit at either 10, 100, or 1,000 megabits per second **(Mb/s)**. One megabit is one million bits. So Ethernet can transmit roughly 100 million bits of data per second. Other abbreviations indicate still faster networks. One gigabit per second **(Gb/s)** equates to 1,000 Mb/s. One terabit per second **(Tb/s)** equates to 1,000 Gb/s. 1 Gb/s and 10 Gb/s Ethernet (called **Gigabit Ethernet**) are currently available, with higher speeds under development. Setting up a 10/100 Mb/s Ethernet network is relatively inexpensive—the cost for Ethernet cards, cable, and a hub or switch is less than $200. Similar hardware for Gigabit Ethernet, however, costs 5 to 10 times that much.

It's important that the networking cards installed in computers on the same network use the same version of Ethernet. Otherwise the network cards won't be able to communicate with each other.

Another popular networking technology is **token ring**. Token ring network technology uses a **token**—an electronic number that is passed from computer to computer—to identify which computer on the network has the right to send out data at that moment.

Token ring can have higher data **throughput** (the amount of data that can be transferred at a given time) than Ethernet, but it can be more difficult to expand a token ring network, it is not as fast as the latest Ethernet technology, and token ring equipment may be more expensive than Ethernet.

A token ring network segment cannot use hubs in the same way that Ethernet does. Each computer in a token ring network must be wired to a hub called a **multistation access unit (MAU)**. A MAU is an intelligent hub—it passes the token between computers to facilitate network traffic. Multiple parts of a token ring network can be tied together by connecting several MAUs.

A third type of network technology is **Fiber Distributed Data Interface (FDDI)**, a highly reliable 100 Mb/s technology that is not installed much now because it's slower and more expensive than newer Ethernet technologies. Another networking technology that is not as popular as it once was is **ARCnet**, a reliable but slower token-passing technology.

Asynchronous Transfer Mode (ATM) is a high-speed, very reliable, and very expensive technology used for Internet backbones and other specialized high-speed networks. ATM operates at 155 Mb/s, with 622 Mb/s ATM under development. Broad acceptance of Gigabit Ethernet will probably limit the spread of ATM.

A final network technology that is rapidly gaining popularity is the **wireless LAN (WLAN)**, which, as the name implies, doesn't use cables or wires to connect nodes to the network. Wireless LANs are popular where networking cables are difficult or impossible to install, such as outdoors or in historic buildings, or in situations where many of the clients are mobile, such as on college campuses. Computers or devices on the network use wireless NICs with an antenna to send and receive data via radio signals or infrared light. Wireless LANs can be set up in a peer-to-peer arrangement, in which each computer communicates directly with the others, or the NICs can communicate with an access point that is connected to a server or to a regular wired LAN. Figure 1-6 shows how the medical office could be set up with a WLAN. Radio-based WLANs have some disadvantages, however. They tend to be less secure than other types of networks, because communications can be more easily intercepted, and they can have problems with bad signal quality between floors or when surrounded by too much concrete, metal, or devices generating electromagnetic interference.

For reference, Table 1-2 lists popular network technologies and shows their relative speeds. Remember as you review this table that new products are arriving every month. New network technologies don't appear often, but faster and cheaper devices do.

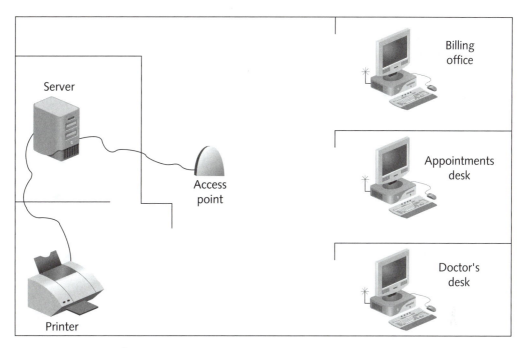

Figure 1-6 A wireless LAN (WLAN)

Table 1-2 Major networking technologies for local area networks

Technology	Speed	Comments
Ethernet	10 Mb/s or 100 Mb/s	Inexpensive and easy to install
Gigabit Ethernet	1 Gb/s or 10 Gb/s	Quite expensive; Linux has relatively few drivers for these cards
Token ring	4 or 16 Mb/s	Some networks can run at 20 or 40 Mb/s
Fiber Distributed Data Interface (FDDI)	100 Mb/s	Highly reliable, but not installed much now because it's slower and more expensive than newer Ethernet technologies
Asynchronous Transfer Mode (ATM)	155 Mb/s	Expensive and specialized. 622 Mb/s ATM is under development.
Wireless LAN (WLAN)	11 Mb/s	802.11b (Wi-Fi) networks are popular; newer 802.11a products will operate at 54 Mb/s

Cabling a Network

The network technologies mentioned above (except for wireless LANs) use a variety of types of cable. The primary cable types are unshielded twisted pair (UTP), shielded twisted pair (STP), fiber optics, and coaxial cable. These types of cable are shown in Figure 1-7 and described below.

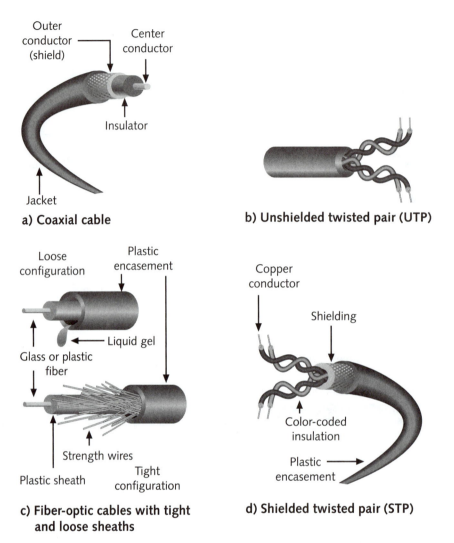

Figure 1-7   Networking cables

- **Unshielded twisted pair (UTP)** is made up of several pairs of wires encased in plastic insulation. UTP comes in six categories, with Category 6 (CAT 6) being the highest quality and highest speed. CAT 5 and CAT 6 UTP cable are most widely used with Ethernet networks. Even the fastest UTP (CAT 6) is relatively inexpensive, and so may be a good compromise between getting *very* expensive wiring (like fiber-optic cable) and having a reasonable path for upgrading. If you install CAT 5 or CAT 6 UTP cables on an Ethernet 10/100 network, for example, you could later upgrade the Ethernet cards to Gigabit Ethernet without rewiring the office. UTP cables are susceptible to interference from other electrical signals, and may also be less secure because Ethernet (for which they are often used) allows a person to add a computer at any point to see all the traffic on the network. (We'll return to this topic in detail later in the book.)

- **Shielded twisted pair (STP)** is very similar to UTP but includes a metallic shielding around each pair of wires. This protects the network signal from outside electromagnetic interference, but also makes STP cables more expensive than equivalent-quality UTP. STP is not used much except in environments where a lot of interference is expected from other electrical or electronic equipment; even then, because the industry has focused more effort on UTP, the availability of higher-quality cables (like CAT 5 and CAT 6) and filters to get rid of interference mean that UTP may still be a better choice.

- **Fiber-optic** cable is a specialized, high-end networking solution that uses light pulses rather than electrical pulses to transmit data. It is capable of extremely fast transmission speeds and is immune to electromagnetic interference. Fiber-optic cable is the most secure system, nearly impossible to eavesdrop on, and it will undoubtedly support increasing network speeds in the future. However, it is much more expensive than the other wiring types. Not only is the cable itself expensive, but installation is expensive as well. Special rules apply to how fiber optics can be bent, cut, and connected to computers; it's difficult to work with. Fiber is also not adaptable to many types of networking. Although many types of networking technologies can use fiber-optic cables—FDDI, Ethernet, and ATM—not every technology you might want to use supports fiber-optic cabling. Some software you wish to use may also not support fiber-optic devices. Newer plastic fiber-optic cables may eventually make fiber easier to work with and less expensive.

- **Coaxial cable (coax)** was a popular network cabling medium, but now has been overtaken by UTP. An early implementation of 10 Mb/s Ethernet, 10Base5, uses thick coax (sometimes called ThickNet); another early 10 Mb/s Ethernet implementation, 10Base2, uses a smaller coax cable sometimes called ThinNet. Coax is also used for video signals and for **cable modems**.

Choosing Cable

Your first reaction might be to just choose the fastest, cheapest, best cable available. But trade-offs must always be made in such decisions. How you decide to cable a network deserves a separate analysis from choosing the type of network technology you want to use. This is because cables are part of the infrastructure of an office, separate from your computer equipment and the networking cards you choose to install. Depending on the environment, cabling an office may cost more than the computers you install in that office, so making a wise choice—one that can let you upgrade your computer equipment later without rewiring—is very important.

As with choosing networking technologies, choosing transmission media means making trade-offs between a variety of characteristics. For example:

- Cost of the cable/media itself

- Cost of installing the media because of limited or difficult access

- Maximum speed

- Typical speed

- Susceptibility to interference from nearby electrical devices

- Ability to expand the network capabilities over time (scalability)

- Availability of skilled technicians to install and maintain a new system (assuming you don't have the time or expertise to do everything in-house)

If you have a legacy system (existing wiring) to deal with, you might need to look at issues such as these:

- Do I have any existing cable that I could use to save time and money by not rewiring the building or the rooms where the network will operate?

- Will the existing cabling handle the amount of network traffic that I foresee for the next 6 months, 2 years, 5 years?

- Do the computers I intend to use on the network have the hardware and software to utilize the existing cables?

- If I have to rewire, what characteristics must guide my decision: cost, transmission speed, scalability, or others?

Last Mile Options

In addition to LAN cabling options, there is what is called the **last mile connection**, or the connection between your LAN and the Internet or other high-speed network. This refers to the connection that begins at the home or office, goes through the local neighborhood, and ends at an Internet service provider (ISP) or other fast service provider. The connections that make up the nation's data-transmission infrastructure are generally very fast and well established, but the last mile connections that link these high-speed transmission lines to the home or office vary tremendously in speed and availability. Table 1-3 shows some of the last mile connections currently available. Cost increases proportional to speed in these options; a dial-up modem can cost as little as $50, and a fiber-optic OC connection can cost millions.

Table 1-3   Last mile connections

Transmission Type	Speed	Typical Use/ Comments	Time to Transmit Contents of One 680 MB CD-ROM (Hours:Minutes)
Dial-up modem	56 Kb/s	Home	26:53
Integrated Services Digital Network (ISDN)	128 Kb/s	Home or office; used for modem connectivity	12:5
Cable modem	5 Mb/s to 512 Mb/s	Home	3:2 to 0:18
Digital Subscriber Line (DSL)	128 Kb/s to 1.544 Mb/s	Home; a relatively new digital telephone service that can be added to existing telephone lines in some areas	12:5 to 0:58
T-1	1.544 Mb/s	Home	0:58
T-3	44.736 Mb/s	Large companies, ISP	0:2
OC-1	52 Mb/s	ISP to regional ISP	8 seconds
OC-256	13.271 Gb/s	Major Internet backbone; uses fiber-optic cable	Less than 1 second

In addition to these wired last mile technologies, watch for wireless broadband solutions such as **fixed wireless** transmission to become increasingly popular. Fixed wireless uses transceivers mounted on buildings to transmit at up to 11 Mb/s over a distance of up to 18 miles, and are cheaper to install than fiber-optic systems. By using wireless towers on your buildings, you avoid paying the telephone company for expensive dedicated connections between offices. Wireless broadband connections may be appropriate when you would otherwise pay thousands of dollars per month in fees for renting telephone lines. Wireless broadband requires special hardware, software, and expertise; Linux is generally not a part of these solutions. Despite high speed and *comparatively* low cost (they still cost thousands of dollars to install), there must be a clear line of sight between sender and receiver, rain and fog can disrupt transmissions, and transmissions may be susceptible to eavesdropping by determined parties who have access to expensive equipment. Of course, after reading this book, you will know how to protect all of the data on your network from eavesdroppers!

So far we've seen many of the components that would likely be used to create a small office network. You must select a networking technology, which defines the types of NICs you install and, to some extent, the cabling you use. The combination of Ethernet NICs and UTP cable is a common choice for a small office network. How you cable the network depends on the environment you're working in—you might even elect to use WLAN hardware to avoid most of the cables. Finally, last mile technologies allow you to get an Internet connection at your home or office.

Before we turn to the software aspects of networking, let's consider how data moves on a network and the physical arrangement, or topologies, of networks.

How Data Is Transferred on a Network

Data is transferred across a network as a series of electronic or light pulses. These on/off pulses are interpreted as digital data, bits and bytes. These bits and bytes are organized into packets to be sent over the network. A **packet** is a general term that refers to a collection of data with identifying information that is destined for or coming from a network. For example, a Web page may be sent across the Internet as many packets, each with information describing the server that the page came from and the client computer that receives the page. Packets are of different sizes depending on the network type being used. The maximum size for a packet is called the **Maximum Transfer Unit (MTU)**. The default MTU for Ethernet is 1,500 bytes. The MTU for FDDI is 4,470 bytes. A packet can be smaller than the MTU, but it can't be larger. If more data must be sent, additional packets are used.

Each packet is organized into a header and payload. The **payload** is the data that needs to be transferred from one computer to another. The **header** is a collection of information (in a very structured format) that defines how the parts of the network should treat the packet. For example, a header identifies a sequence number for a large data transfer, indicates the type of application sending the data, and declares the total size of the data transfer.

Ethernet transmits data packets using a system called contention. That simply means that all the nodes on the network (all the network cards, specifically), *contend* for access to the network: each sends out data packets whenever it needs to, leading to *collisions* among the network packets. A **collision** is when two or more Ethernet packets attempt to use an Ethernet cable at the same time. Without exploring the technology deeply here, we can tell you that Ethernet has methods of detecting collisions to improve throughput on the network. A network engineer can run tests to determine how many collisions are occurring. If too many collisions are occurring (more than about 15% of the network packets), a device on the network may have a misconfigured network card or the network may simply be too busy, causing all network traffic to slow down significantly.

Throughput refers to how much payload information can be transmitted on a network. A busy network might end up sending so much system management data (such as packet headers) that its throughput is choked off. Users don't care much about bandwidth; users care about getting their files downloaded or their email messages sent: that's throughput.

Remember that a byte consists of 8 bits, so a 10 Mb/s network can handle 1.25 *megabytes* (MB) of data per second, including all the overhead needed to correctly process the application data being sent.

Network Topologies

Networked computers are arranged logically and physically into topologies. A **topology** is the shape or ordering of the connections between systems. Three topologies are commonly used:

- A **bus topology**, in which computers are connected along a single line, as shown in Figure 1-8

- A **star topology**, in which multiple computers connect to a single center point, usually a hub or switch, as shown in Figure 1-9

- A **ring topology**, in which computers are linked into a circular shape, as shown in Figure 1-10

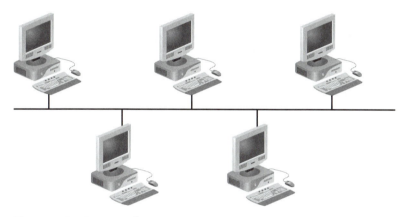

Figure 1-8   Bus topology

The topology is largely determined by the networking technology you choose. For example, if you choose to use token ring networking, you cannot use a bus topology. You must use a ring or a star because of the way that the token is passed between computers. Ethernet, on the other hand, typically uses a bus topology.

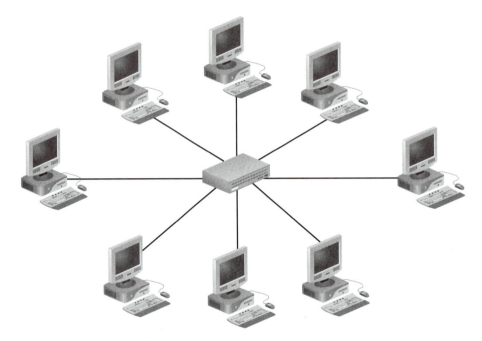

Figure 1-9   Star topology

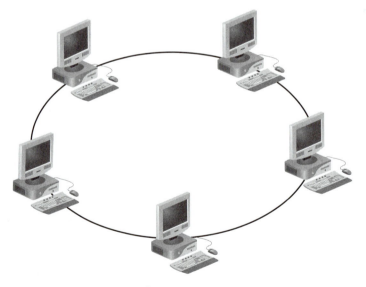

Figure 1-10   Ring topology

Using a hub in an Ethernet network makes it look like the diagram of a star topology because all the wires run to a single point. But because a hub is simply a wiring concentrator, Ethernet remains a bus topology; you can unplug or add computers without affecting others on the network. The important lesson here is that the physical layout of a network may not match the logical layout exactly.

You can use different technologies within the same network by dividing the network into segments. A network **segment** is a part of a network whose traffic has been isolated from other parts of the network, so that packets generated by hosts within the segment are only "seen" by other hosts within the same segment unless they are destined for a host outside the segment. When a large network is broken into segments, the amount of network traffic on each part of the network (each segment) is greatly reduced. Networks are typically built using multiple segments, for several reasons:

- Each segment can choose the network technology most appropriate to its needs, based on factors such as cost, speed, compatibility with existing equipment, etc. For example, if a manufacturing company already has network cables installed in its offices, it might choose to install a small wireless network on the factory floor to avoid the need to run wires in that area. The wireless network would use a different network technology and thus be a separate segment.

- Each segment can often be configured and managed separately, allowing different features to be implemented as needed. For example, the security level for Internet access might be more restrictive for one segment used by data-processing staff than for another segment used by market research staff.

- The network traffic from each segment can be isolated so that the entire network doesn't require a higher bandwidth. For example, suppose one department of a company transfers a lot of files and wants a very fast network, but another department does relatively little networking. If all the computers are on a single segment, everyone must have the high-speed networking equipment. If the departments are broken into separate segments, only those who need fast equipment must install it.

- A single network segment normally would not have more than 30 to 40 computers. Using multiple segments allows you to create larger networks.

Parts of a network are connected using several different devices. You've already seen how hubs and switches can connect nodes to a network. More complex devices are needed to connect multiple segments of a network. You can't simply wire together cables from an Ethernet card and a token ring card, for example: they don't speak the same electronic language. A **router** is a device that connects multiple network segments, translating data formats as needed. For example, one part of an office might have computers with token ring network cards all wired to a MAU. To connect that network segment to another part of the office running Ethernet, you must have a router that can "speak" both Ethernet and token ring. When data from the token ring network reaches the router, it can be sent out on the Ethernet segment, and vice versa. Figure 1-11 illustrates this arrangement.

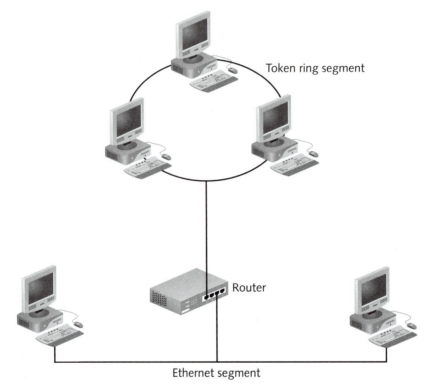

Token ring segment

Router

Ethernet segment

Figure 1-11   A router connects different network technologies

 Another network device used to connect segments is a **bridge**. A bridge works by examining the address of every packet to let segments share data.

The router in this example has both a token ring network card and an Ethernet network card. A router can also be used to connect two segments of the same type. Remember the reasons for creating separate segments, such as limiting the network traffic within each segment. You could create two large Ethernet segments connected by a router in order to isolate the network traffic generated by each of the two segments.

A router can be a specialized device that only routes network traffic. Cisco is the best-known maker of network routers. Routers intended to handle huge traffic loads can cost tens of thousands of dollars; you can also purchase a simple but robust router for a few hundred dollars. Often, however, a regular computer is used as a router. In particular, a

Linux computer makes a great router. If you install two Ethernet cards in a computer running Linux and then set up routing software (as you'll learn in Chapter 6), you have a low-cost, very effective router.

Connecting Multiple Networks

A task that faces nearly every network administrator is the connection of existing net-works. For example, suppose that your small business currently has two networks. On the manufacturing floor are a dozen or so computers networked using token ring. The business office has nearly 50 computers connected using Ethernet over CAT 6 UTP cable. The various vice presidents have decided that they want to be able to share information between the two networks so that they can update marketing information and parts ordering in real time as manufacturing events take place. So you need to connect the token ring and Ethernet networks. In addition, the VPs want everyone in the company to have Internet access. Figure 1-12 illustrates the end result you're trying to achieve.

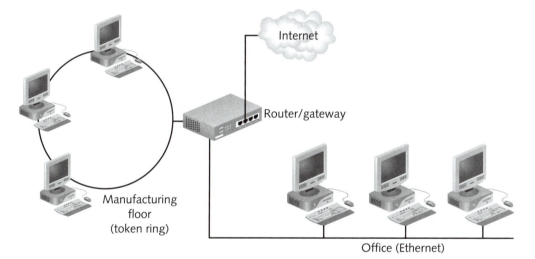

Internet

Router/gateway

Manufacturing
floor
(token ring)

Office (Ethernet)

Figure 1-12   A router between segments and an external gateway to the Internet

To connect the two segments in the office, you would use a router. To connect to the Internet, you would use a gateway. A **gateway** is like a router in that it transfers net-work traffic between network segments, but a gateway has more intelligence than a router: it may translate data at a more complex level than a router, which simply passes data packets between segments.

NETWORKING SOFTWARE

All of the networking hardware you've been learning about isn't much use without the software to control it and connect it to applications that you want to use on your network. That software begins with a network-capable operating system—Linux is one good example. But the operating system is composed of many pieces that perform different networking tasks.

Modern networking is built around the idea that you need different tools for different tasks, and that those tools should be modular and interchangeable. For example, developers could have built networking software in which a single massive program did all the networking that you expected to ever need. The problem (to call it such for a moment) is that we keep inventing new things. If a single networking program tried to handle everything, you'd be in trouble every time a new networking card appeared, or every time a new method of communication was needed—everything would need to have been included in The Networking Software.

Instead, you'll soon see that networking is built on a veritable alphabet soup of networking tools. Most of these tools are protocols. A **protocol** is a formalized set of rules for communication. In diplomatic circles, a person from one country learns how those from another nation act in order to communicate effectively with them. In the same way, a computer protocol allows one computer or device to communicate effectively with any other that uses the same protocol. Each protocol was designed for a specific purpose—that's why there are so many of them.

Before exploring the multitude of protocols, let's step back and look at some conceptual models of networking.

Conceptual Models of Networking

When networks first began to be developed, there were no standards for communication between computers. To identify the levels of communication needed for networking, the ISO (International Organization for Standardization) developed the **Open Systems Interconnect (OSI) model.** The OSI model is a theoretical model of network communications. It uses seven layers to represent how information travels from the application you use to the networking hardware, and then to a similar application on another computer. Figure 1-13 shows the OSI model.

- The *Physical layer* manages sending information over a networking media, such as a cable.

- The *Data Link layer* manages the physical layer by watching for errors and managing hardware address information (such as the hardware address of each Ethernet card).

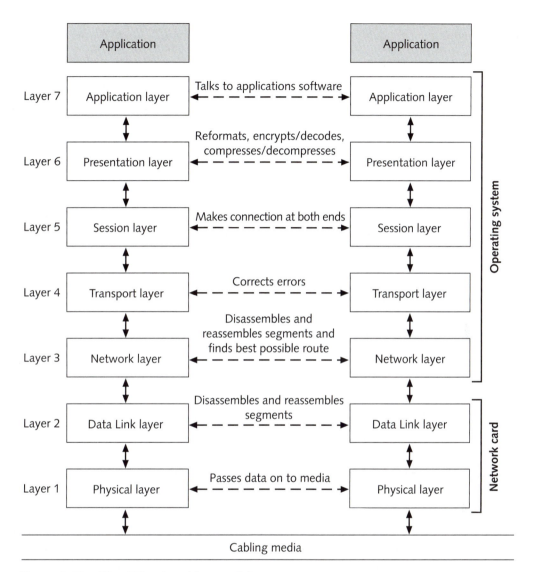

Figure 1-13 The OSI networking model

- The *Network layer* finds the best route for packets that must be transferred between different networks. The Network layer gets the data from both the Physical and Data Link layers so that it can "translate" between different network types.

- The *Transport layer* sets up connections between specific computers across the network. To do this, it watches for lost pieces of data, checks for flow of information, and rearranges data that is received out of order.

- The *Session layer* manages network connections at a more abstract level than the transport layer, allowing a user to stop and restart network activities.

- The *Presentation layer* handles data representation issues such as whether compression or encryption are added to the data to be sent over the network.

- The *Application layer* communicates with any application that wishes to use the network. The Application layer generates the data to be transported based on requests from a "real application" such as a Netscape Web browser. It then uses protocols from the lower layers to move that data across the network to another application that can understand what is being sent.

You can also use the OSI model to conceptualize how data is transmitted over the Internet. However, the model doesn't translate exactly. Another networking reference model, the **Internet model** (or **TCP/IP model**), is more often used to describe Internet communications. Linux design focuses on Internet-style communications, so understanding the Internet networking model is important for understanding Linux networking. The Internet model uses four layers, and each layer has specific protocols associated with it:

- The *Application layer* includes protocols like HTTP for Web browsers, SMTP for email, and FTP for file transfers.

- The *Transport layer* creates connections between two computers so that information from an Application layer protocol can be exchanged. Protocols that you'll read about later in this chapter from this layer include ICMP, TCP, and UDP.

- The *Internet layer* provides delivery of data packets from the Transport layer. The most important protocol in this layer is IP.

- The *Link layer* manages the physical networking hardware. It includes protocols such as Ethernet, token ring, DSL, and ISDN.

Figure 1-14 shows the layers of the Internet model with the principal protocols used in each. The protocols taken as a whole are sometimes referred to as the TCP/IP suite of protocols, hence the alternate name of the model given above: the TCP/IP model. Above the networking layers in the figure are applications that rely on the networking protocols; below are the physical cables used to transmit the data.

Before exploring specific protocols, let's walk through how these layers operate in general terms using an example.

1. An application, such as a Web browser, wants to send a piece of data via HTTP. The data is generated by the application and passed to the transport layer.

2. The Transport layer—TCP in this case—adds a header that describes the information being sent and identifies a session so that TCP can keep track of whether the packet is received or not. The packet is then passed to the Internet layer.

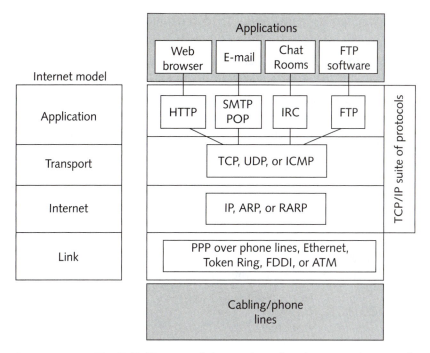

Figure 1-14 The TCP/IP suite of protocols within the Internet networking model

3. The IP stack adds a header that identifies the computer to which the data is being sent, the protocol that should be used to read the packet once it is received, and a few other items. The packet is then passed to the Link layer.

4. The Link layer—Ethernet in this example—locates the MAC address and the physical address of the NIC of the computer that the packet is addressed to, then adds its own header information and sends the packet out "on the wire" as a series of electrical impulses.

5. The Link layer on the Web server sees that the packet indicates its MAC address as a destination, so it grabs the packet, examines its Ethernet header information, then passes it to the Internet layer on the server.

6. The Internet layer examines the IP header data, notes that the packet was sent using TCP, and passes the packet to the TCP stack.

7. The TCP stack removes the TCP headers, examines them, sends back a packet to the client saying that this packet has been received correctly, then passes the packet to the Web server, which is registered to handle all HTTP packets.

8. The Web server reads the payload of the packet, prepares a response to the client request, and starts the whole process again.

Before going on, a few comments are in order about layers in general.

The software for maintaining each protocol is often called a **protocol stack**. A protocol stack is software designed to receive data in a specific format from a higher-level protocol and transmit it to a lower-level protocol as the lower-level protocol requires.

Transport-layer protocols can be connectionless or connection-oriented. A **connectionless** transport protocol sends each packet without regard to whether any other packet was received by the remote computer that it was sent to. It just "throws them over the wall" and hopes for the best. If a part of the transfer is lost en route, the computer receiving the data must request that the lost information be sent again. Another name for connectionless is **stateless**, because no information is maintained about the "state" of the ongoing transmission.

Conversely, some Transport-layer protocols are **connection oriented**, or **stateful**. In these protocols, the protocol software maintains information about which packets have been correctly received by the destination computer. If an acknowledgment of a packet is not received saying "Yes, I got it," then the packet will be resent.

Popular Protocols

Most of the protocols that you'll learn about in this book are closely tied to the Internet. Internet protocols are first proposed by an experienced software developer or engineer. That person writes a document called a **Request For Comments (RFC)**. The RFC defines the protocol or other technical advance. Other experts around the world comment on the information in the RFC document, which is then revised several times to build on the suggestions received. Eventually, many people come to rely on the RFC as the standard definition of the new protocol. All RFC documents are available (and searchable) on the Web site *www.rfc-editor.org*. More than 3,000 RFCs are included on this site. As a Hands-On project at the end of this chapter, you'll explore this site.

Let's look at some of the popular protocols in more detail so that you'll understand their use as you learn about configuring networking on Linux in the next chapter. We'll start with the lowest level: the hardware.

 Remember that this chapter provides only an overview with a few key networking details, just enough to get you started without overwhelming you with new terms at the outset.

As you would likely guess by now, each type of hardware has its own protocol to manage communication with other hardware of that type. For example, a token ring network card "speaks" the token ring protocol, so it can send bits of data over a cable to other token ring cards. Because Ethernet is the most widely used protocol, this book focuses on Ethernet hardware.

Throughout this book you will see notes about using other types of networks, such as token ring, ATM, or FDDI. In addition, specific sections in later chapters are devoted to dial-up connections using modems.

Every Ethernet card has a unique address assigned by the manufacturer, called its **Media Access Control (MAC) address**, or simply its **hardware address**. Each manufacturer of Ethernet cards has a different range of numbers assigned to ensure that every Ethernet MAC address in the world is unique. When one host on an Ethernet network wants to communicate with another host, it must obtain the MAC address of the destination Ethernet card. To obtain this MAC address, a host broadcasts a message to the entire network segment using the **Address Resolution Protocol (ARP)**. The message says, in effect, "I need the MAC address of the computer having the IP address aa.bb.cc.dd." (We'll get to IP addresses shortly.) All of the hosts on the network segment see the ARP request; the host that has the requested IP address responds with its MAC address directly to the computer that sent the ARP request (the source host). The source host then stores, or caches, that correspondence between MAC address and IP address so that it won't need to repeat the ARP request later on. With the correct MAC address available, the Link layer can prepare packets from the IP stack and send them out on the network via the Ethernet card.

Some Internet-layer protocols use the hardware MAC address of an Ethernet card as part of their addressing system (for example, NetWare's IPX). This makes it easier to configure these systems, but also makes them much less flexible in adapting to a worldwide network using a variety of hardware types.

We haven't looked at the headers for an Ethernet packet because that is beyond what we'll be exploring in this book. But they are similar in design to the IP headers, with **source** and **destination addresses** (MAC addresses instead of IP addresses), and various flags to help Ethernet determine how to process the packets.

The Internet Protocol

The **Internet Protocol (IP)** is the foundation for transporting data across most Linux networks as well as the Internet. Although IP was designed decades ago and has in some ways been stretched past its original design, it still serves well, as millions of systems around the world rely on it.

When learning about a new protocol, reviewing the structure and components of the header for that protocol can tell you a lot about how it's used and what it is capable of. The IP header is shown schematically in Figure 1-15. Each row is 4 bytes (32 bits). A typical IP header is 20 bytes long though. Because the options field at the end is optional, the length can vary. Each of the fields is described here. Note that we've only described in detail the fields that are of use in setting up Linux networking—some other fields are more relevant to specialized routing issues that you might face in learning about Cisco routers, for example. You won't actually have to assemble any of the information in these fields, but you can understand networking better if you know what is being transmitted across the network and why each piece of information is useful.

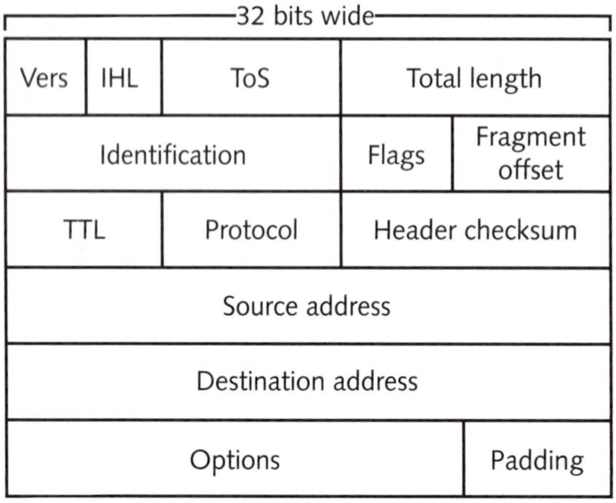

←——————32 bits wide——————→			
Vers | IHL | ToS		Total length	
Identification		Flags	Fragment offset
TTL	Protocol	Header checksum	
Source address			
Destination address			
Options			Padding

Figure 1-15   The header fields of an IP packet

The *Version Number* field identifies the version of the IP protocol that was used to create this packet. The version number is currently 4. (We'll briefly mention a newer version—IPv6—later in this section.)

The *IP Header Length (IHL)* field defines how many bytes are part of the header, normally 20. This field is used in conjunction with the Total Length field. The number of bytes in the header is removed and analyzed; the remaining bytes of the packet are payload.

The *Type of Service (ToS)* field is used to designate how the packet should be processed (routed). Some options include maximizing throughput, maximizing reliability, and minimizing cost. Unfortunately, few network routers are able to do anything with these bits. Most are not capable of keeping track of which route provides the highest reliability, lowest cost, etc. As a result, this field is normally ignored.

The next three fields are used together: *Identification, Flags,* and *Fragmentation Offset.* These fields allow IP packets to be routed on networks that have a smaller MTU than the network that created the packet. For example, suppose you are using an Ethernet network with an MTU of 1,500 bytes. You exchange information with another Ethernet network in a distant office, but to reach that network, your data must pass through two routers and an intermediate network that uses an MTU of 256 bytes. Figure 1-16 shows a schematic representation of this situation.

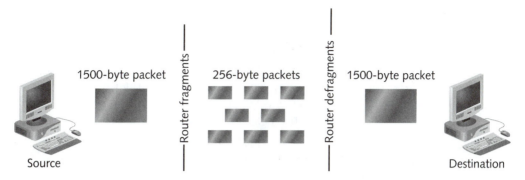

Figure 1-16   Fragmentation occurring when an intervening network has a smaller MTU

Each IP packet from your network must be broken into pieces in order to be transmitted on the intermediate network; this is **fragmentation**. The Identification field provides each packet with a unique number so that the pieces of that packet can be reassembled. The Flags signal when more pieces of the indicated packet are still to arrive. The Fragmentation Offset identifies where in the original packet the current piece fits.

Fragmentation occurs regularly on larger networks with many diverse segments. However, you should keep in mind that fragmentation is a necessary evil: though it allows us to share data between networks with different packet sizes, it also adds a significant amount of overhead, including:

- Space wasted in partially filled packets—because the payload size of an IP packet may not match exactly the payload size of the smaller packets

- Extra data needed to send multiple headers—one for each fragment of the original IP packet

- CPU time spent breaking a packet into pieces and then correctly reassembling it

The lessons then are that you must understand fragmentation well to avoid networking headaches, and that if you can design networks to minimize fragmentation, everyone will be happier.

Time To Live (TTL) is an attribute of a data packet, but it's not really about how long a packet can live; rather it indicates how many routers the packet can go through before it is discarded. When a packet is sent to a remote computer, it passes through multiple routers to reach its destination. Each router on the path decrements the TTL field by one. If the packet has not reached the destination network after passing through about 64 routers, the last one will see that the TTL field is zero and drop the packet rather than continue to route it. (You can alter the Linux default TTL of 64.) This prevents network congestion caused by packets that keep looping around looking for the right network.

The *Protocol* field indicates which Transport-layer protocol should receive the payload of the IP packet. A numeric code identifies the protocol. You'll be working with three

Transport-layer protocols: TCP, UDP, and ICMP, though several other specialized routing protocols are also supported.

The *Header Checksum* field is used to ensure the integrity of the header information. By using this field as a mathematical check of the contents of the other fields, the system receiving the packet can tell whether any data in the header has become corrupted. (If part of the payload is corrupt, the Transport or Application layer must determine that; IP just hands the payload to the next layer without checking it.)

The *Source Address* and *Destination Address* fields indicate the IP address of the computer that created the packet (the source) and the computer to which the packet is being sent (the destination). The next section describes IP addresses in detail.

Options can be used for debugging, but are not often used at all. The *Padding* field simply indicates that some additional space may be part of the header because the header must have a length that is a multiple of 4 bytes (32 bits). In other words, the header must end on a 32-bit boundary. The Padding field contains zeros.

IP Addressing

IP works by assigning a unique address to every computer on the Internet. By referring to its IP address, you can instantly contact any computer that is connected to the Internet or an intranet, no matter where it is located. (So long as your routing is set up correctly, as described later!)

IP addressing is a numbering scheme that allows each computer, printer, or other device on an IP network such as the Internet or an intranet to have a unique ID number. By referring to that ID, you can communicate with any system on the Internet. Unfortunately, the addressing scheme was developed before the Internet was as popular as it is today, and so IP addressing is stretching to keep up. IP addressing is a complex topic, but one that you must understand well to use Linux networking.

Both an IP address and a MAC address are assigned to each NIC. The IP address is a worldwide address that can be used with any type of networking technology; it is passed around the Internet and used to identify a host. A MAC address is part of an Ethernet card. It is used within a single network segment to locate a host. ARP maps an IP address to a MAC address for "final delivery" of a packet that has arrived at its destination network.

As you may already know, IP addresses are assigned by a central Internet authority to ensure that each network node has a unique address. If you simply choose an IP address out of the air, you're likely to make someone, somewhere, very mad. ISPs are assigned large blocks of addresses that they can then assign to their customers. Your school or organization probably has a block of addresses assigned. The system administrator can assign you an address from that block. Of course, in a lab environment that is cut off from all other networks, you can use whatever IP addresses you choose.

1

An IP address is assigned to each network card in a computer or network device. Each address is 32 bits long, made up of four 8-bit numbers separated by periods. The largest possible 8-bit number is 11111111, or 255 in decimal, and the largest possible IP address in decimal is 255.255.255.255. You've probably seen many of these addresses: for example: 192.168.12.254 is a valid IP address. The **dotted–quad notation** shown here—four numbers separated by periods—is commonly used to write IP addresses.

An IP address has two parts, though you wouldn't know by looking at it. The first part of the address is a **network ID** and the last part is a **host ID**. Each network on the Internet has a unique ID, and within each network, each host has a unique ID. Setting off the network as a separate ID makes it possible to find computers all over the world. A simple way to view this is to think of the first three numbers as the network ID and the last number as the host ID, so 192.168.12.254 consists of a network ID: 192.168.12.0, and a host ID, 254. Whenever you refer to a network ID, you should use a full IP address (all four numbers), but fill in the host ID portion with all zeros. In this case, the last number is the host ID, so in stating the network ID, you would insert a zero in that place. The computer named by this address uses the full IP address of 192.168.12.254; other computers on the same network segment would have a different last number. One might use the address 192.168.12.34, for example.

In olden times (10 or 15 years ago), IP addresses were divided into classes. An **IP address class** is a grouping of IP addresses according to how large a network the IP address represented. Classes A, B, and C were used, as described in Table 1-4. (Classes D and E were also defined for special purposes beyond what we're exploring in this introductory chapter.)

Table 1-4   IP address classes A through C

IP Address Class	Address Range	Subnet Mask	Number of Networks in the Class	Number of Hosts Possible in Each Network of the Class
A	1.0.0.0 to 126.0.0.0	255.0.0.0	126	16,777,214
B	128.0.0.0 to 191.255.0.0	255.255.0.0	16,384	65,534
C	192.0.0.0 to 223.255.255.0	255.255.255.0	2,097,151	254

Along with IP address classes, a **subnet mask** was used to denote how many bits of the IP address were part of the network ID: any bit set in the subnet mask was part of the network ID. Of course, because classes used predefined network ID lengths, this was somewhat redundant, and a default subnet mask was often used without a second thought. The subnet mask was written after the IP address, if at all, with a preceding slash: 192.168.111.45/255.255.255.0.

Some numbers are missing from Table 1-4. As part of the design of IP addressing, some addresses were reserved for special purposes. To begin with, you should learn these special addresses, because, unlike IP classes, these conventions are still used:

- Any address beginning with 127 (127.0.0.1 is normally used) is called the **loopback address**. It is used only within a computer for testing the network stacks. No packet with a 127 address is ever sent out of the local computer.

- When an IP address has all zeros for its host ID portion, the address refers to the network as a whole.

- Several address ranges are designated for private networks, including any address beginning with 192.168. Whenever you use these IP addresses, packets are never routed outside of your local network segment. This means these addresses are appropriate for small internal networks that don't need to connect to the Internet. (You don't need an assignment or permission to use a private IP address on your local network segment.) Most of the examples in this book use a private network IP address.

A special type of class-based address is used to create a supernet. A **supernet** is an IP address that would be in one of the classes such as B or C, but its network mask identifies it as having a smaller network ID than the corresponding class would have. For example, the IP address and mask 192.168.12.1/255.255.0.0 define a class C address (as Table 1-4 indicates), but the network mask indicates that the network ID includes only the first 16 bits. So this "class C" network supports 65,534 hosts. We won't be using supernets, but you need to be aware of them. They're very useful for configurations in which you want to group together networks to minimize extra networking traffic caused by excess routing information being passed around the network.

Although class-based IP addresses were used for years, as it happened, there are not that many networks that have 16 million hosts, or even 65,000 hosts. But we're running short of addresses for networks with 254 hosts. The more modern technique does not use network classes. Instead, it simply defines a network prefix length: the number of bits (out of 32) that compose the network ID. The remaining bits are the host ID. The shorter the network prefix, the more hosts the network can have (because more bits are available to provide a unique host ID). The formula for determining how many hosts a network can have is shown here. N is the number of hosts and L is the network prefix length:

$$N = 2^{(32-L)} - 2$$

Two possible hosts are subtracted from the total because if the host ID is all zeros, the address refers to the network itself, and if the host ID is all ones, the address refers to the local broadcast address (as described later in this section). As an example of using the above formula, you could specify that an IP address consisted of 28 bits for the network ID and 4 bits for the host ID. This would define a network that could have 14 hosts: $2^{(32-28)} - 2 = 2^4 - 2$, so 2 x 2 x 2 x 2 - 2 = 14.

Most networks use one of a few standard network addressing systems, so you rarely need to get out your calculator. But you must still determine how large the network ID and host ID are based on the networking space assigned to you by your ISP and the number of hosts you want to support in each segment of your network. In addition, the networking software must have some way to know what part of an IP address is the network ID and what part is the host ID. Two methods are used to show this:

- A **network address mask** is a series of numbers that looks like an IP address but contains 1s for the network ID portion of the address and zeros for the host ID portion of the address. (Yes, this is just like a class-based subnet mask, under a different name.) For example, the network address mask 255.255.255.0 has 24 bits of 1s, so it indicates a 24-bit network ID, and 8 bits of 0s, for an 8-bit Host ID. You need to provide a network mask when you configure networking, although a default may be provided by the network configuration tool.

- A prefix length indicator written after a computer's IP address indicates the number of bits used for the network ID. This notation method for network prefix length is called **Classless Inter-Domain Routing (CIDR) format**. For example, 192.168.12.254/24 indicates that 24 bits of the address are the network ID and the remaining 8 bits are the host ID. You should become familiar with these conventions so that you understand their meaning when you see them.

You can use either an address mask or CIDR format to indicate a classless address. You will see examples of both throughout this book. Because class-based addresses formed the basis of the Internet for years, network configurations based on them are still common. However, a subnet mask is only intended for calculating a network ID on the local network segment, while a network prefix length (network address mask) is intended to follow an IP address wherever it goes, so that the address can be correctly interpreted without class-based defaults. Every router, for example, examines the network prefix length for each packet it routes. To help you become familiar with the standard network IDs, Table 1-5 shows commonly used prefix lengths with corresponding network masks.

Table 1-5 Host IDs with varying network prefix lengths

Maximum Number of Hosts	Network Prefix Length	Corresponding Address Mask
2	/30	255.255.255.252
6	/29	255.255.255.248
14	/28	255.255.255.240
30	/27	255.255.255.224
62	/26	255.255.255.192
126	/25	255.255.255.128
254	/24	255.255.255.0
510	/23	255.255.254.0
1,022	/22	255.255.252.0
2,046	/21	255.255.248.0

Broadcast and Multicast Addressing

In the list of special IP addresses in the previous section, recall that when the host ID is all ones, the IP address refers to a broadcast message for the entire network being referred to. This is often called the **broadcast address** for that network. That is, if a computer sends a packet to a network such as 192.168.12.0/24, and the host ID contains all ones, the packet is delivered to all hosts on that network. The broadcast address for this example network is 192.168.12.255/24.

A broadcast message of this type is used chiefly for system administration purposes, such as informing everyone that a server is about to shut down. It is also used by some specialized software for broadcasting other messages. (Novell NetWare servers use this type of networkwide broadcast, for example.) When a packet has a destination address that matches the network ID, every host on the network grabs that packet and passes it to the higher levels of the networking stack (IP, then TCP or UDP, etc.). Normally, of course, a host grabs only packets that have its own host ID as the destination address; other packets are ignored.

Using a network ID to broadcast a message works with any network; you can use broadcast-capable software to send a broadcast message to a network anywhere on the Internet. But more often, a system needs to send a broadcast message to everyone on *its own* network. For that purpose, a special **local broadcast IP address** is used: 255.255.255.255. Any packet that has this IP address is picked up by every host on the network. It is also *not* routed outside the network, because then every host on other networks would think it was a broadcast message for them.

Broadcast messages have been used since IP first became popular. Another special type of IP addressing has great promise, but is not yet widely used. This is **multicasting**, an IP addressing system in which one computer can address a packet to multiple specific hosts. To understand why this is valuable, consider this example: You have created a large report that you need to distribute to 5,000 servers around the world. You can't use a broadcast address because most of those servers are located on separate networks in different parts of your organization. You would have to send 5,000 separate transmissions, one to each server. If the report is 22 MB in size, that totals 110,000 MB, or 110 GB of data that must be transmitted. But what if you could send a single copy of the report to the Internet with a list of all the destination IP addresses? Each router that intercepted the packets composing the report could determine whether hosts on its network were part of the destination group and pass those packets on as needed. The report would be replicated (duplicated) at points near the destination servers, instead of being sent entirely from a central source. This is the idea behind multicasting.

True multicasting is not supported by the Internet as a whole. It requires special applications at the source and destination computers, updated network stacks to process multicast IP addresses, and routers that understand multicasting options. A specialized multicast system can be built, but at this point, multicasting is not as widespread as it is likely to become in the next five years. Because multicasting makes much more efficient use of network bandwidth and also allows "pushing" data to subscribers (as the example above describes), both businesses and technical experts continue to work for wider availability of multicast capabilities.

IPv6

The current version of IP (IPv4) supports roughly 3.7 billion unique addresses. That must have seemed more than sufficient when IPv4 was developed. But because of the incredible growth of the Internet and the many new types of devices that are connecting to the Internet (such as personal digital assistants), IPv4 is fast running out of address space. To cope with that, and a few other technical limitations that we haven't touched on in this discussion, a new version of IP has been developed by a group of Internet engineers. The new version is called IP version 6, or **IPv6**.

The most interesting feature of IPv6 for most users is that it uses 128 bits per IP address, rather than 32 bits. Because each additional bit doubles the number of possible addresses, IPv6 supports over 100 undecillion addresses (that's a 1 followed by 38 zeros). It also has numerous enhancements to make multicasting more workable, to allow dynamic configuration of networks, and to allow routers to make more intelligent routing decisions.

IPv6 doesn't throw IPv4 out the window; it just extends its technology and usefulness. ISPs will still assign IP addresses, network and host IDs will still be used, and networks will still become overburdened and slow because of too much traffic. But IPv6 prepares the Internet for the next several years by upgrading and fixing technical issues that were making it harder to keep networks properly configured and running well. Because IPv6 provides so much capability for dynamic configuration and intelligent routing, it requires more sophistication in the infrastructure components of the Internet—the massive routers that keep network traffic moving as well as the simpler components within organizations. In addition, networking software must be upgraded to support IPv6. Beyond the IP stack itself, upper- and lower-layer stacks (Ethernet, TCP, etc.) must undergo major revisions to truly benefit from what IPv6 can offer. This takes a great deal of time and effort.

Despite the fact that we're speaking of IPv6 in the future tense, in fact, IPv6 is up and running now. You can read all about it, install it on your Linux system, and try it out. But you'll be in the minority. Because of the differences between IPv4 and IPv6, IPv6 defines several methods of tunneling over an IPv4 network. **Tunneling** refers to packaging one type of packet from a network layer within another type of packet from the same layer; in this case, packaging an IPv6 packet inside a few IPv4 packets. Islands of IPv6 are cropping up as people experiment and switch over to the newer, more powerful protocol. Over time, the backbone of the Internet will change to IPv6 and eventually islands of IPv4 will remain, transmitted around the Internet by IPv6. To learn more about IPv6 and how you can begin to use it, visit the Web site *www.6bone.net*. That site also has a link to the Linux IPv6 site, *www.bieringer.de/linux/IPv6/*. Linux already has networking stacks for IPv6 ready to download and install, but you won't be working with them in this book.

Transport Protocols

In the Internet networking model, the Internet layer focuses on routing packets between different hosts and network segments. IP includes fields to handle packet fragmentation, to identify the source and destination host addresses, and to mark the time to live (TTL) of a packet.

Transport protocols focus on providing a foundation for applications to operate. They may begin by establishing a session. A **session** is a connection between two hosts, through which the destination host is expecting a stream of packets from the source host.

ICMP

Most transport protocols focus on providing a networking mechanism for applications. The application can hand a collection of data (such as a file) to the transport protocol stack and let the stack worry about getting it across the network to the destination host.

But the **Internet Control Message Protocol (ICMP)** serves a slightly different purpose. Because IP is designed for efficiency, it has no provision for handling problems with transmissions at the Internet layer. ICMP is an integral part of the operation of IP; it is the protocol that IP uses to describe error messages such as congested routers that can't handle traffic, a host that cannot be located on the network, or packets that cannot be routed correctly. ICMP is a minimal protocol; it provides a small number of codes to identify the information that it carries. The data (payload) in an ICMP packet includes the first 64 bytes of the IP data being described in the ICMP message. The header of an ICMP packet includes the following fields, as shown in Figure 1-17:

- *Type* and *Code* (one byte each) to identify the message being sent
- *Checksum* to verify the integrity of the ICMP packet
- *Sequence number* to order a series of ICMP packets

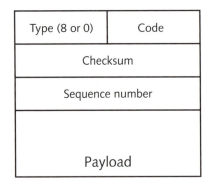

Figure 1-17   Structure of an ICMP packet

Without providing an exhaustive list of the types and codes used by ICMP, a few examples include Destination Unreachable, Router Advertisement, Time Exceeded,

Timestamp, and Traceroute (a utility you'll see later in this book). If a Destination Unreachable Type is used, the Code field can contain additional information, such as Net, Host, Protocol, or Port Unreachable, Fragmentation needed but not possible, or Destination Network or Host Unknown.

Most of these ICMP messages are handled directly by IP; you won't deal with them until you start troubleshooting networking problems. The most common use of ICMP, however, is via `ping`. `ping` is an administrative utility that uses the Echo and Echo Reply message types within ICMP to test whether a host is reachable and alive (listening to network traffic). We'll explore `ping` in detail beginning in Chapter 2. On most systems, including Linux, the `ping` command can include numerous parameters to test for various issues such as timing, routing, and packet fragmentation.

Name Services

Beyond the numeric addresses assigned to a computer for IP, you're probably familiar with more readable names such as yahoo.com or amazon.com. These are called domain names. A **domain** is a collection of computers, usually on the same network, that can be accessed using a common name (often a name based on an organizational affiliation such as a company or school).

Because humans find *www.ibm.com* much easier to comprehend and remember than 129.42.17.99, name services were developed to map domain names assigned to groups of computers to IP addresses. A **name service** is an Application-layer software program that lets a computer provide a name and receive back an IP address, or provide an IP address and receive back a name. (This process is also called **name resolution**.) A **name server** is a computer running name-service software that can translate from IP addresses to names and vice versa. For example, when you enter the name *www.bn.com* in your Web browser, the first thing the Web browser does is to send a request to the name server saying "what is the IP address of the server *www.bn.com*?" When the name server responds, the Web browser can initiate a network connection using that IP address.

The name service used by the Internet is called **Berkeley Internet Name Domains (BIND)**. A shorter name that you may have heard is simply **Domain Name Service** for the software or a **Domain Name Server** for the computer running the software; both are abbreviated as **DNS**. To complete configuration of a network so that users can easily access other systems, you must configure the name service in addition to the networking protocols and their addresses. Chapter 2 describes how to configure the client portion of DNS so that a Linux system can access another DNS server; Chapter 6 describes how to set up the DNS software that comes with Linux to make your own DNS server.

Transmission Control Protocol

The **Transmission Control Protocol (TCP)** is the workhorse of the Internet. Nearly all of the services you are likely to use regularly on the Internet rely on TCP as their transport protocol. These include HTTP (the Web), SMTP (email), FTP (file transfers), and Telnet (used to control a computer remotely). Although IP is efficient for packet delivery, it doesn't provide the reliability that an application needs. TCP is used on top of IP because it provides a connection-oriented session that guarantees delivery of each data packet (or at least provides notice when a packet cannot be sent). For example, if you request a Web page, TCP manages the request so that each packet of the Web page arrives, lost packets are re-requested, and all the packets are assembled into the correct order.

TCP provides transport services to applications using ports. A **port** is a number that is associated with a network-capable application. By using ports, TCP can work with many sets of data while keeping track of which packets should be handed off to which applications. For example, Web server software is typically assigned port 80. When your Web browser sends a TCP packet requesting a page, it uses the IP address of the Web server machine to get the packet to the right computer; it also uses the port 80 designation to reach the right application running on that machine. The Web server software "listens" at port 80, waiting for TCP packets that are addressed to that port. Each connection created using TCP between a sending port on one host and a receiving port on another host is called a **socket**. A socket is a communications channel between two applications; it allows them to communicate over a network.

 A port in Linux can be any number from 1 to 65,536. Ports numbered below 1,024 are reserved for use by network services such as the Web, email servers, and FTP servers.

A port is also used on the client system—the one running the Web browser. The port on the client end is not predefined. The Web browser simply uses any available port number and includes that number in the TCP packets. So the details of a packet include a source port and a destination port. The source port identifies which application should receive the response when the Web server (in the previous example) sends back data.

The structure of a TCP packet header is shown in Figure 1-18. Each of the fields is described below.

- *Source port* is the port assigned to the application that created this data.

- *Destination port* is the port assigned to the application that should receive this data (we hope that an application will be waiting to receive it!).

- *Sequence number* identifies the position within the stream of data for the data in this packet. This allows the TCP stack on the destination computer to reassemble packets in the correct order (because of routing, the packets could arrive out of order). It also allows TCP to see if any packets are missing and request that they be re-sent.

- *Acknowledgment number (ACK)* confirms that a specific packet was received correctly.

1

```
┌──────────────32 bits wide──────────────┐
├────────────────────┬───────────────────┤
│    Source port     │     Dest. port    │
├────────────────────┴───────────────────┤
│           Sequence number               │
├────────────────────┬───────────────────┤
│                    │     TCP header    │
│        ACK         │      length       │
├────────────────────┼───────────────────┤
│       Flags        │      Window       │
├────────────────────┼───────────────────┤
│     Checksum       │   Urgent pointer  │
├────────────────────┼───────────────────┤
│     Options        │      Padding      │
└────────────────────┴───────────────────┘
```

Figure 1-18   The fields in the header of a TCP datagram

- *TCP header length* defines the length in bytes of the TCP header information. The TCP header is variable because of the options field (though that field is rarely used).

- *Flags* contains codes that indicate special actions such as starting or ending a TCP connection (you may have heard of the ACK and SYN flags). This part of the header also defines the length of the TCP header, which can vary based on the number of options included with the packet.

- *Window* refers to the sliding window size, which defines how many packets the receiving computer is ready to receive and process.

- *Checksum* provides a mathematical method of verifying the integrity of the data contained in the TCP packet. Unlike IP, the checksum in TCP is used to verify the integrity of the payload data, not just the header.

- *Urgent pointer* indicates a range within the payload of the packet where urgent data begins.

- *Options* can define special actions for the TCP stack, but this field is very rarely used.

- *Padding* is used, as in IP, to fill the header up to a 32-bit boundary.

Remember that payload is a flexible term: it refers to whatever a specific protocol needs to transmit. That is, the full TCP packet, both headers and payload, becomes the payload portion of an IP packet. The IP stack takes the TCP packet, adds its own IP header, and passes it on to Ethernet (or another Link-layer protocol stack). At the destination computer, the IP stack strips off the IP headers, examines them to find that TCP is the indicated protocol for the payload, and then hands the payload off to the TCP stack. The TCP stack then does the same thing, reviewing the TCP headers and handing the remaining payload to an application-level protocol.

UDP

Whereas TCP is used for guaranteed connections to a destination, the **User Datagram Protocol (UDP)** provides fast, connectionless service at the Transport layer. Like IP, UDP does not provide an acknowledgment of each packet received, it may drop packets or duplicate them along the way, and packets are not ordered. But UDP also has low overhead: 8 bytes per header instead of 40 bytes, plus no network traffic is used for sending acknowledgments. UDP provides a service similar to IP in scope, but with the addition of port numbers, so that data can be sent between specific applications, as with TCP. UDP is used when the applications themselves are able to tell whether packets are missing and order them correctly.

 Packets sent using a connectionless protocol such as UDP are also referred to as **datagrams**.

Examples of applications that use UDP include name servers (described later in this chapter) and network management utilities, where overhead needs to be low.

The UDP header includes only four fields. No options are available, so no padding is needed:

- *Source port* to identify the application that is sending the data

- *Destination port* to identify the application that should receive the data

- *Message length* to indicate how many bytes are in the packet

- *Checksum* to correct for network transmission errors

Application Protocols

The protocols we've looked at so far are used to transfer data across a network at one level or another. Application protocols have a purpose directed more specifically at something a user would want to do. Table 1-6 lists many of these application protocols that you will install and configure throughout this book, along with their commonly used port numbers.

Many other protocols exist, of course. But remember that many of the other popular protocols that you may have heard of, or even have used, are not necessarily Application-layer protocols, and so are not included in this list. A few are mentioned in the next section.

Table 1-6   Application protocols commonly used in Linux

Protocol	Purpose	Commonly Used Port
File Transfer Protocol (FTP)	Transfer of (often large) files from a dedicated FTP server to a single remote user	20 (data) 21 (control information)
Network News Transport Protocol (NNTP)	Transfer of large numbers of small newsgroup postings from central news servers to other news servers and end users	119
Simple Mail Transport Protocol (SMTP)	Transfer of (usually small) email messages from one host to another	25
Domain Name Service (DNS)	A special network service designed to provide applications with a mapping from domain name to IP address and vice versa	53
Hypertext Transport Protocol (HTTP)	Transfer of usually small files from a Web server to a single remote client	80
Post Office Protocol 3 (POP3)	Transfer email messages stored on a server to a client for viewing	110

When we speak of the TCP protocol, we are describing a system of transferring information using various header fields and systems of initiating connections, terminating connections, acknowledging packets, etc. But when we describe HTTP—an application protocol—we are defining the commands that a Web browser and Web server can send to each other. For example, one common HTTP command is GET. A valid HTTP command looks like this example:

```
GET /index.html HTTP/1.1
```

A Web browser initiates a network connection with the Web server, then sends the above HTTP command. The text of the command becomes the payload of the TCP packet, which is then passed to lower network stacks. On the Web server, when the packet reaches the TCP layer, the TCP header is removed and the TCP payload—the HTTP command itself—is handed to the Web server, which examines the command to check for valid HTTP format and then responds.

Similarly, the email protocol SMTP has a structured system of messages (we'll see the details later) that tell an SMTP-capable email server program how to interpret email message information. The nice part about working with application protocols is that the commands are more or less human-readable, as the GET example in HTTP illustrates.

ROUTING CONCEPTS

Most of the discussion so far in this chapter assumes that you are working with a single network segment. Many new issues arise when you need to connect multiple network segments, a more common situation than a single, isolated network segment.

To illustrate some of the issues that arise with connecting network segments, consider the network segments shown in Figure 1-19. Each network segment has a network ID assigned to it. To send packets from Host A to Host B requires that the packets pass through two network segments.

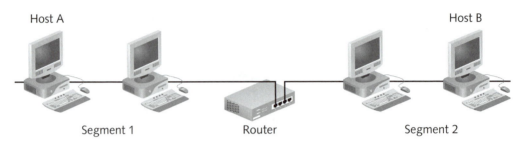

Host A   Host B

Segment 1   Router   Segment 2

Figure 1-19   Multiple network segments with a router

In Figure 1-19, suppose Host A wants to send a packet to Host B. The IP packet contains a destination IP address that refers to a different network from the one that Host A is located on. Because of this, the network stacks on Host A know that the packet must be sent to a router—a computer that is connected to more than one network and can forward packets between networks. To **forward** a packet is to transmit it onto a different network than the one where it originated. A router is sometimes called a gateway, though gateway has another more specific meaning as described previously, which you will explore in later chapters.

When you configure Linux networking, you specify the IP address of a computer that can act as a **default router** to other networks. (This is also called the **default gateway** in some Linux documentation.) This is the router used when a packet is addressed to a host that is outside the source host's network. The default router may be connected to just one other network, as in Figure 1-19, or it may provide access to the entire Internet. In any case, the packet from Host A isn't destined for Network A, so it has to go to the router for further processing.

The **default route** is an IP address configured on a host computer that identifies the computer that packets should be sent to when their network is not otherwise known to the host. In Figure 1-20, you see two networks inside an organization, connected by a router. For Host A, the router is configured as the default gateway: packets addressed to the other internal network are sent on by the router to that network. For the router itself, Host G is an upstream router, or a gateway to networks beyond the organization. Host G is connected only to the router and to the Internet. If a packet arrives at the router and is destined for neither network segment X nor segment Y, it is sent by the router to Host G for further routing onto the Internet, where it is eventually routed to its correct destination.

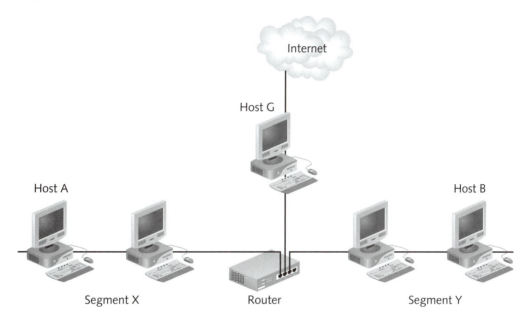

Figure 1-20 A router with a separate gateway to the Internet

Routers use a routing table and a routing algorithm (also called a routing engine) to decide where to send packets. A **routing table** is a listing that contains at least three things:

- The network ID for which a route is being stored, which lets the router identify the network IDs it knows how to reach

- The network interface through which the network ID can be reached. For example, some networks might be reachable through the Ethernet card, others through a dial-in modem connection to the Internet

- The IP address of the upstream router that handles the listed network ID; this field is called the gateway in the output of several Linux commands, because it provides a gateway to other networks

Routing tables may contain additional information to help make the best routing decisions. The **routing algorithm** or **routing engine** is software that determines how to process a packet that is sent to the router. The routing engine uses the routing table as data to help make a good routing decision. Routing tables are populated (filled with entries) in two ways.

- Manually, by a system administrator (such as you) entering a route by which packets can reach a named network ID. This can be done in Linux using the **route** command or a variety of graphical tools that we'll begin exploring in Chapter 2.

- Automatically, by a protocol designed specifically to keep track of how packets are flowing through a network and report that information to a router. The most commonly used routing protocols within organizational networks are the **Routing Information Protocol (RIP)** and the **Open Shortest Path First (OSPF)** protocol. Routing table entries are cached so that they are available for use in routing future packets.

As you configure Linux networking on your system in Chapter 2, you will learn how to use the `route` command to set up manual routes. Every system must act as a router at some level because it must know how to handle packets sent to IP addresses outside the local network. A typical host has a very basic routing engine and expects only manually configured routing table information.

Linux can also act as an automatic router. You might think of this as a "real" router because its goal is to forward traffic between network segments rather than just routing the packets generated by a single host. The Linux program `routed` uses RIP to gather routing information automatically. In later chapters you'll learn more about routing protocols and setting up Linux routing.

 Linux can even be optimized as a dedicated router. In fact, the Linux Router Project provides a complete Linux operating system configured as a router on a single diskette. (See *www.linuxrouter.org*.)

CHAPTER SUMMARY

- ❐ By networking computers, users can work more efficiently by sharing data instantly, automating tasks, and using expensive resources more efficiently.

- ❐ A terminal acts simply as a remote keyboard and monitor for a system, while client-server computing assumes that both systems are intelligent. Although many Linux programs use client-server techniques, Linux is designed for peer-to-peer networking.

- ❐ Networking hardware uses various technologies such as Ethernet to send electrical signals over transmission media—cables or wireless systems. Each collection of data is called a packet (or a datagram for connectionless protocols such as UDP).

- ❐ Bandwidth of various types of physical networking ranges from just a few Kb/s to several Gb/s, though throughput—the amount of useful data received by a remote user—is a better measure of the value of a network in the eyes of most end users.

- ❐ Network topologies define the physical and logical layout of a network. Bus, star, and ring network designs are common choices.

- ❐ Many types of transmission media are available, such as UTP, fiber optics, and wireless systems.

❑ Modern networks use different layers of software to handle the different aspects of managing a network connection. Software that handles a networking task is designed around a protocol, or well-defined communication system for that task.

❑ The OSI and Internet models are two important conceptual layered models of networking.

❑ Protocols are defined by RFC documents, which are created by technical experts and posted on the Internet for review and comment.

❑ Networking protocols can be connection-oriented (stateful) or connectionless (stateless). Connection-oriented protocols like TCP provide guaranteed delivery of data between two hosts.

❑ IP is focused on unreliable packet delivery based on source and destination IP addresses. It is connectionless.

❑ IP addressing can be defined with or without using address classes (A, B, C). When classes are not used, a network prefix length must be specified. In either case, an IP address always consists of a network ID and a host ID.

❑ Fragmentation allows packets with different MTU sizes to be routed across intermediate networks. But fragmentation introduces several inefficiencies and so should be avoided whenever possible.

❑ IPv6 will provide more addresses and many additional features as it is rolled out in the next few years to replace the existing IPv4 infrastructure of the Internet.

❑ Broadcasting and multicasting provide special methods of sending IP packets to multiple hosts simultaneously, although multicasting is not well supported on the Internet at this time.

❑ Name services convert between IP addresses and human-readable domain names such as *www.whitehouse.gov*. Linux uses BIND as its name service to create DNS servers.

❑ TCP, UDP, and ICMP are Transport-layer protocols. TCP provides guaranteed delivery; UDP is a faster protocol for when guaranteed delivery is not needed; ICMP provides error message delivery for IP plus the `ping` utility for testing.

❑ Many application protocols are used as part of network-aware programs, such as Web servers and email servers. These protocols are command oriented rather than consisting of fields within packet headers as lower-layer protocols do.

❑ Routers move packets between network segments. Each router maintains a routing table to identify how to reach various network IDs. The routing table is filled either by manual entries or by automatic entries generated by a routing protocol such as RIP or OSPF.

KEY TERMS

Address Resolution Protocol (ARP) — A protocol that broadcasts a message to an entire network segment in order to obtain a host's MAC address.

ARCnet — An older token-passing network technology that has lost a great deal of its former popularity. ARCnet is reliable, but slower than more modern networking technologies like token ring or Ethernet.

Asynchronous Transfer Mode (ATM) — A networking technology used for the Internet backbone or other specialized high-speed networks. It is fast (currently 155 Mb/s with 622 Mb/s under development) but also expensive.

bandwidth — The amount of information that a network technology can transmit; usually expressed in bits per second (b/s).

Berkeley Internet Name Domains (BIND) — The name service used by the Internet.

bridge — A network device used to connect segments so they can share data. A bridge works at the OSI Data Link layer, examining the address of every packet to facilitate network communications.

broadcast address — An IP address in which the host ID consists of all ones that causes the packet to be sent to every host on the named network.

bus topology — A network topology design in which computers are connected to a single length of cable.

cable modem — A device that supports high-speed networking through a cable television connection with the cable TV company acting as the ISP.

client — A computer or software program that requests information or service from a server and then processes or acts on the information it receives.

client-server — A model of computing in which information is shared between networked systems by multiple clients requesting information from a server.

coaxial cable (coax) — A network transmission media (a cable) made up of a single thick copper wire encased in thick plastic and foil layers of insulation. Coax is used mostly for video signals, though many people now have Internet access available via a cable modem using coax cable.

Classless Inter-Domain Routing (CIDR) format — A method of indicating the network prefix length of an IP address by writing it with a slash following the address, e.g. 192.168.14.45/24.

collision — When two or more Ethernet packets attempt to use an Ethernet cable at the same time.

connectionless — A protocol that sends packets without regard to whether they are correctly received by the destination computer. IP and UDP are examples. *See also* stateless.

connection-oriented — A protocol that keeps track of which packets have been correctly received by the destination computer, resending those that are not received, managing the flow of packets, and reporting errors. *See also* stateful.

datagram — A network packet sent over a connectionless protocol such as UDP.

default gateway — *See* default router.

default route — An IP address configured on a host computer that identifies the computer to which packets should be sent when their network is not known to the host.

default router — The router to which a packet is sent if a host has no idea where else to send it. Also called the *default gateway*.

Digital Subscriber Line (DSL) — A relatively new digital telephone service that can be added to existing telephone lines in some areas, used for relatively fast Internet connections.

domain — A collection of computers, usually on the same network, that can be accessed using a common name.

Domain Name Server (DNS) — The software or the computer running the software that provides a name service for network-connected computers. In Linux, a DNS server runs BIND.

Domain Name Service (DNS) — The name normally used to refer to the name service used by the Internet (BIND).

dotted-quad notation — A method of writing IP addresses as four numbers separated by periods.

dumb terminal — *See* terminal.

Ethernet — An international networking standard developed in the 1970s by Xerox, Intel, and Digital Equipment Corporation (now part of Compaq Computer Corp.).

Fiber Distributed Data Interface (FDDI) — A networking technology that uses fiber-optic cable in a dual ring topology. It is highly reliable, but not installed much now because it is slower and more expensive than newer Ethernet technologies.

fiber optic — A network transmission media (a cable) made of glass or plastic to transmit light signals; it is capable of extremely fast transmission speeds, immune from electromagnetic interference, and highly secure. It is also very expensive to install.

fixed wireless — A wireless network communication technology that relies on small transceivers mounted on buildings; it is normally used to connect multiple offices in the same city.

forward — To send a packet onto a different network than the one where it originated.

fragmentation — The process of breaking up an IP packet into multiple smaller packets for transmission on a different type of network.

gateway — Generally, a router that can forward packets to other network segments. Also, the default router that acts as a "gateway" or exit point to reach networks outside of a local segment. Also, more technically, a system that can translate between protocols at the Transport and Application layers of a network.

Gb/s — Gigabits per second. 1 Gb/s is 1,024 Mb/s or roughly a billion bits per second.

Gigabit Ethernet — An Ethernet networking technology that can transmit data at either 1 Gb/s or 10 Gb/s.

hardware address — *See* Media Access Control (MAC) address.

header — Highly structured information within a packet that defines how the network stacks should handle the packet.

header checksum — A numeric code within an IP packet header used to ensure the integrity of the header information.

host — *See* node.

host ID — The part of an IP address that designates the host to which the address refers within a certain network.

hub — A device used as a wiring center that allows cables from multiple computers to be concentrated into a single network connection.

Integrated Services Digital Network (ISDN) — A type of telephone service that provides digital signals for higher-speed network connectivity than standard modems.

Internet — A collection of many networks around the world that are linked together via high-speed networking connections.

Internet Control Message Protocol (ICMP) — A protocol used by IP to transmit control and error data about IP traffic on a network. Most widely known as the basis of the `ping` utility, which uses ICMP Echo and Echo-request commands.

Internet Protocol (IP) — The foundation protocol for transporting data across most Linux networks as well as the Internet.

intranet — A network within an organization that uses Internet standards as the basis for sharing information, usually via Web browsers.

Internet model — A conceptual model of networking that divides protocols into four layers based on their function. This is the model used by Linux.

IP addressing — A numbering scheme that allows each computer in the world that wants to use the Internet (or just IP) to have a unique ID number.

IP address class — A grouping of IP addresses. Classes A, B, and C are commonly referred to, each defining a set of networks with a specific maximum number of hosts.

IPv6 — The new version of IP that uses 128 bits for addresses instead of 32 bits, and adds numerous other features including dynamic configuration capabilities, better security options, and more intelligent packet routing. Using IPv6 requires many changes to other protocols, as well as generally more sophistication in networking hardware and software.

Kb/s — Kilobits per second. 1 Kb/s is 1,024 bits per second.

last mile connection — The connection between a LAN within a home or office and the Internet or other high-speed network.

local area network (LAN) — A network within a relatively small space such as an office or a building.

local broadcast IP address — The special IP address 255.255.255.255, used to broadcast packets to all hosts on the local network segment.

loopback address — Any IP address beginning with 127 (127.0.0.1 is normally used). This address is used only within a computer for testing the network stacks. No packet with a 127 address is ever sent out of the local computer.

Maximum Transfer Unit (MTU) — The maximum size for a packet on a given type of network.

Mb/s — Megabits per second. 1 Mb/s is 1,024 Kb/s or roughly one million bits per second.

Media Access Control (MAC) address — A unique address assigned to (and programmed into) each Ethernet card in the world.

multicasting — An IP addressing system in which one computer can address a packet to multiple specific hosts.

multistation access unit (MAU) — A device that acts like a switch or intelligent hub for a token-ring network, passing the token between computers to facilitate network traffic.

name resolution — The process of converting a domain name into a corresponding IP address.

name service — An Application-layer software program that lets a computer provide a name and receive back an IP address, or provide an IP address and receive back a name.

name server — A computer running name service software that can translate from IP addresses to names and vice versa.

network address mask — A series of numbers that looks like an IP address but contains 1s for the network ID portion of the address and zeros for the host ID portion of the address. A network address mask is basically a subnet mask used for classless IP addressing.

network ID — The part of an IP address that designates the network to which the address refers.

network interface card (NIC) — A hardware device used to connect a computer to a network.

node — A device on the network, such as a workstation, server, or printer.

Open Shortest Path First (OSPF) — A protocol that automatically fills routing tables with information about how to reach networks.

Open Systems Interconnect (OSI) model — A reference model that divides networking into seven conceptual layers, each assigned a specific task. The OSI model is the basis for much of modern networking theory and system design.

packet — A small collection of data with identifying information (headers) that is destined for or coming from a network.

payload — The data that a network packet is transferring. Packets are divided into a header and payload.

peer-to-peer networking — A model of networking in which all computers on the network are *peers* and have the ability to initiate communications, respond to requests for information, and interact with users independent of other computer systems.

ping — An administrative utility that uses the Echo and Echo Reply message types within ICMP to test whether a host is reachable and alive (listening to network traffic).

port — A number that is associated with a network-capable application.

protocol — A formalized system of rules for communication.

protocol stack — The software for maintaining a network protocol. A stack may refer to a single protocol capability or to the collection of protocols supported by a host or server.

pseudo-terminal — A command-line window acting as a terminal in letting a user interact with a host's resources. These are referred to within Linux as `pty` devices.

Request For Comments (RFC) — A document describing a protocol or other technical advance, written by a technical expert and posted on the Internet for review. It then becomes the accepted definition for the protocol or standard it describes.

ring topology — A network topology design in which multiple computers are linked into a circular shape.

router — A device that connects multiple network segments, translating data formats as needed by forwarding packets between segments; also the software program on a computer used for this purpose.

routing algorithm — Software that determines how to process a packet that is sent to the router for forwarding; also called a *routing engine*.

routing engine — *See* routing algorithm.

Routing Information Protocol (RIP) — A protocol that automatically fills routing tables with information about how to reach networks.

routing table — A listing within a router containing network IDs, the network interface by which packets can reach that network, and the IP address of the next router to which the packet should be sent.

segment — A part of a network whose traffic has been isolated from other parts of the network to improve the efficiency of the network as a whole. Each segment's network traffic is only "seen" within that segment unless it is destined for a host outside the segment.

server — A computer or software program that provides information or services of some type to clients.

session — A connection between two hosts, where the destination host is expecting a stream of packets from the source host.

shielded twisted pair (STP) — A type of network transmission media (a cable) made up of several pairs of wires encased in foil-wrapped insulation to block interference by electromagnetic radiation.

socket — A communications channel between two applications that need to communicate via a network; created using a protocol such as TCP.

source and destination addresses — Fields within an IP packet that indicate the IP address of the computer that created the packet (the source) and the computer to which the packet is being sent (destination).

star topology — A network topology design in which multiple computers connect to a single center point, usually a hub or a switch.

stateful — A connection-oriented protocol; one that maintains information about the state of the network transmission so that it can adjust or correct its behavior as needed to ensure success of the overall transmission.

stateless — A connectionless protocol; one that maintains no information about the state of the ongoing transmission that allows it to track packets after each is sent.

subnet mask — A set of numbers similar in appearance to an IP address that are used to denote how many bits of an IP are part of the network ID: any bit set (1, not 0) in the subnet mask is part of the network ID; used for class-based IP addressing.

1

supernet — An IP address that would be in one of the classes such as B or C, but whose network mask identifies it as having a smaller network ID (and thus potentially more hosts) than the corresponding class would have.

switch — A device used to connect other networking devices (such as hosts or printers) into a larger network using built-in intelligence to decide which network packets should be sent to which parts of the network.

Tb/s — Terabits per second. 1 Tb/s is 1,024 Gb/s or roughly a trillion bits per second.

TCP/IP networking model — *See* Internet model.

terminal — A screen and keyboard attached to a computer, usually at a distance from the computer. Multiple terminals attached to the same computer allow multiple people to access the computer at the same time; also known as *dumb terminal.*

terminal emulation — A software program that allows a personal computer (or other intelligent device) to act like a terminal in connecting to another computer.

throughput — The amount of useful payload information that can be transmitted on a network.

Time To Live (TTL) — A counter within an IP packet header that determines how many hops (routers) a packet can pass through before being discarded as "destination unreachable."

token — An electronic code that is passed from computer to computer to identify which computer on the network has the right to send out a data packet at that moment. Used by certain types of networks such as token ring.

token ring — A popular networking technology that uses a token—an electronic number that is passed from computer to computer—to identify which computer on the network has the right to send out data at that moment.

topology — A shape or ordering applied to the connections between systems on a network.

Transmission Control Protocol (TCP) — A widely used connection-oriented Transport-layer protocol. TCP is the transport mechanism for many popular Internet services such as FTP, SMTP, and HTTP (Web) traffic.

tunneling — The process of packaging a packet of a given Network-layer protocol within another type of packet from the same layer; for example, IP within IP or IPX within IP.

Type of Service (ToS) — A field within an IP packet used to designate how the packet should be processed (routed). Rarely used at this time.

User Datagram Protocol (UDP) — A fast, connectionless Transport-layer protocol.

wide area network (WAN) — A network spanning more widely separated geographical locations.

wireless LAN (WLAN) — Wireless network designed to be used within a small radius of a central transceiver.

REVIEW QUESTIONS

1. By maintaining state information, the _____ protocol is able to _____.

    a. TCP; guarantee packet delivery by tracking packet acknowledgments

    b. ICMP; report errors in IP transmissions

    c. TCP; avoid the need to use a checksum field

    d. IP; retransmit packets that are dropped by routing processes

2. Forwarding packets refers to:

    a. transferring them from the segment on which they originate to a different segment to which they are addressed

    b. storing packets in a router until they are requested by the destination host

    c. caching packet IDs to prevent fragmentation

    d. configuring an Ethernet card to handle multiple network data types on the same local network segment

3. Each Ethernet card has a number assigned to it by the manufacturer: this is called the:

    a. NIC Header checksum

    b. Ethernet cyclic redundancy check

    c. Data Link protocol

    d. Media Access Control (MAC) address

4. A token ring MAU would be equivalent to:

    a. a header checksum field in an IP packet

    b. using fiber-optic cable for best network performance

    c. a hub used on an Ethernet network

    d. a numeric code used to identify which computer can transmit data

5. Assuming you have moved into a new building that already contains CAT 5 UTP cable to each office, which of the following network technologies might you choose to set up the new network?

    a. FDDI, because the cost of existing cabling could be deducted from the total cost of the project

    b. a wireless system, in case we needed to expand the network to off-site locations

    c. not Ethernet, because the star configuration required for Ethernet would not be feasible using UTP cable

    d. Ethernet, because the existing cable could provide a high-speed network without the expense of rewiring

6. Each entry in a routing table consists of at least the following three items:

   a. a network ID, a checksum, and the interface through which the network can be reached

   b. a default fault for the local network segment, a header for the routing protocol being used, and optional flags

   c. a network ID, a network interface, and the IP address of the next hop router

   d. a network ID, a network interface, and a routing engine

7. Which of the following IP addresses indicates a 24 bit network ID with a CIDR-format network prefix?

   a. 192.168.14.5/24

   b. 192.168.14.8/255.255.255.0

   c. 192.168.14.0/8

   d. 192.168.14.24/255.255.240.0

8. Name services such as DNS are used to:

   a. translate between human-readable domain names and IP addresses

   b. translate headers between levels of the network architecture

   c. assign packet IDs to each session initiated by the TCP stack

   d. locate services available on the worldwide Internet

9. A default route is normally defined at the same time Linux networking is configured on any host. This allows Linux to:

   a. accumulate routing table information passed on by a routing protocol such as RIP

   b. avoid duplicate packets being sent to the local segment and to the correct remote segment

   c. respond automatically to ISP requests for routing information

   d. act as a router, sending packets addressed to other segments to the "gateway" out of the local segment

10. Multiple segments on a large network are defined so that:

    a. A single large segment does not have to bear all the network traffic of an entire organization.

    b. Parts of a network can be configured with different networking hardware or security features.

    c. Routers can defragment packets more efficiently because the segments are smaller.

    d. a, b, and c

    e. only a and c

    f. only a and b

11. If an IP stack does not have the MAC address of the system it needs to communicate with, it must:

    a. Send the packet in question to the default router, which has the MAC address for the system noted in the destination IP address.

    b. Consult the routing engine tables to obtain the correct IP address, which includes the MAC address as well.

    c. Consider fragmenting the packet so that it can travel across intermediate network segments without the use of standard IP header information.

    d. Use ARP to obtain the MAC address directly, caching it for future communications with the same remote system.

12. System administrators commonly use the `ping` command, which is:

    a. a method of accessing the echo/echo reply functions within ICMP

    b. a keep-alive option dedicated to Web server performance enhancement

    c. the UDP equivalent of TCP connection-oriented state information

    d. discouraged because of the extra load it places on intermediate network segments

13. A packet for any networking layer below the application layer consists of:

    a. a collision field and a header checksum field

    b. a header and payload

    c. both TCP and UDP capabilities

    d. fragmentation offsets, if required by intervening segments with a smaller MTU

14. The broadcast IP address for a local network is:

    a. a method of distributing a packet from one source host to multiple, specifically named destination hosts

    b. 255.255.255.255

    c. dependent on the routing protocol

    d. the appropriate network prefix with the Host ID set to all zeros

15. Ports are used by TCP and UDP to:

    a. attach security information to lower-level IP packets

    b. autoconfigure TCP header information

    c. identify a remote host by a specific Ethernet hardware address

    d. provide an application-to-application path for network packets

16. Some applications prefer to use UDP instead of TCP, even though TCP provides guaranteed packet delivery, because:

    a. UDP has lower network overhead, with smaller packet headers and less computation for packet tracking.

    b. UDP is able to interact more directly with the IP protocol, thus providing better throughput than TCP.

    c. UDP is a more secure protocol for Internet traffic.

    d. UDP prevents fragmentation by creating smaller default packets for IP to hand off to the local network segment.

17. The TTL field in an IP packet is used to:

    a. hold a "hop counter" that is decremented each time a packet passes through a router

    b. hold a countdown timer; when the timer reaches zero the packet is discarded

    c. keep track numerically of a sequence of packets that were fragmented to pass through an intermediate segment with a smaller MTU

    d. identify the upper-layer protocol that the payload should be handed to after IP packet headers are stripped off for processing

18. A dumb terminal is called "dumb" because it:

    a. typically has no sound capability

    b. is not connected to the Internet

    c. cannot understand natural language queries

    d. does not have a CPU that can process data received from another computer

19. The software that provides network protocol capabilities on a system is called, in general terms:

    a. the protocol stack

    b. the routing engine

    c. the routing algorithm

    d. the fragmentation offset

20. Connectionless protocols are used when:

    a. Error correction is not needed.

    b. Guaranteed delivery of packets is managed by an application rather than a Transport-layer network protocol.

    c. Full state information must be maintained for network connection.

    d. IPv6 may be required at a future date.

21. A network's topology defines its:

    a. logical and physical layout

    b. networking layers

    c. application port configurations

    d. IP addressing headers

22. An intranet differs from the Internet in that:

    a. One is open-standards based, the other uses no open-source software.

    b. One can route packets by default, the other requires dedicated routing protocols

    c. One is used privately, within an organization; the other is public and worldwide.

    d. One is based on IP, the other uses proprietary protocols.

23. The chief advantages of using fiber-optic cable include:

    a. ability to upgrade the cabling to new topologies as faster networking technologies make FDDI obsolete

    b. limited bend radius and high tensile strength

    c. low cost compared to CAT 6 UTP

    d. impervious to electromagnetic interference and difficult to eavesdrop on

24. Terminal emulation is available in many operating systems via:

    a. popular software programs like minicom in Linux or HyperTerminal in Windows

    b. hardware add-ons such as firewire cards.

    c. dumb terminals in the typical computer lab.

    d. the IP and TCP networking stacks.

25. A CIDR-formatted address indicates:

    a. The information has been cached as a MAC address.

    b. A broadcast address must be used to reach the host.

    c. A network prefix length has been appended to the IP address.

    d. A subnet mask has been appended to the IP address.

HANDS-ON PROJECTS

Project 1-1

In this project you review RFC documents for some of the protocols described in this chapter. To complete this project you need a Web browser with an Internet connection.

1. Start your Web browser and point to the address *www.rfc-editor.org*.

2. Click the link to search for an RFC.

3. Search for RFC number 792.

4. Click on the result returned by your search to view RFC 792.

5. After RFC 792 is downloaded, browse through it. What are the purposes of this protocol as outlined in the Introduction? How many message types are supported by this protocol (check page 36)?

6. Press the browser's **Back** button twice to return to the Searching and Retrieving screen.

7. Enter **HTTP** in the search text field.

8. On the right side, select **Search: RFC**; **RFC Contents via: HTTP**; and **Show Abstract: On**.

9. Click **Search**.

10. Review the results screen. Select one that looks interesting and click on its link to read more about it. RFC 2616 is the main HTTP protocol definition standard.

Project 1-2

In this project, you calculate the address size needed for a small network. You need a pencil and paper to complete this project.

1. For this project, suppose you anticipate a network segment size of a maximum of 50 hosts. Using the formula given in the chapter, find the number of binary bits required to represent that many hosts by seeing what power of 2 will reach or exceed 50.

   a. You find that 2^6 $(2 \times 2 \times 2 \times 2 \times 2 \times 2) = 64$. $64-2 = 62$. The Host ID for your segment needs to be 6 bits long. 7 bits will provide space for 128-2=126 hosts, more than you need; 5 bits will only allow 32-2 = 30 hosts, which is not enough.

   b. Because 6 bits are needed for the host ID, 32-6, or 26 bits of a 32-bit IP address remain for use as the Network ID. So you will add a /26 after the IP address to indicate the network prefix length.

   c. Suppose that you are using a private network address, 192.168, as your IP address range. A sample address might be 192.168.1.104/26. By reviewing the bit values in the last number, 104, you see that they are

      0 1 1 0 1 0 0 0

The left-most two bits are part of the network ID. Only the last 6 bits form the host ID. The host ID here includes bits valued at 8 and 32, so the host ID value is 40.

2. Refer to Table 1-4 and determine what classful-style subnet mask would correspond to a 26-bit network prefix length.

Project 1-3

In this project, you research networking hardware on the Web. To complete this project you need a Web browser with an Internet connection.

1. Start your Web browser and point to the address *www.warehouse.com*.

2. Place your mouse pointer over **Networking** on the left side of the screen, then click **Cabling Products**.

3. Look for an Ethernet cable such as CAT 5. Click the **More Info** link below it. (Try searching for product DCA7284 or for Ethernet Cable if nothing appropriate appears.)

4. Review the Overview product page, then click the **Specifications** link.

5. Move your mouse back over **Networking** on the left side of the screen, then select **Networking** in the pop-up window.

6. Choose **Token Ring**. Review the list of products that appears.

7. Find the search text field in the upper-left corner of the Web page. Enter **Cisco** and click **GO**.

8. Choose two products that are widely different in price. Can you identify the chief reasons for the price difference?

CASE PROJECTS

You have been asked to consult for a medium-sized federal government agency. The agency is opening a new office in your town because their current office (also in your town) is severely overcrowded. You are told that they will be renting space in a standard office building. The building is about eight years old and was originally wired with UTP cable, though you aren't told any more details about the state of the existing wiring.

1. Some pieces of this puzzle are still missing. What questions will you want to ask of the agency directors and of the technical people assigned to the project before beginning your analysis for network design? If some of that information is not directly available from them, what steps will you take to obtain the data you need to make a solid analysis of the situation and create a preliminary design?

2. What assumptions might you make about this project based on who your client is? How will those assumptions fit into your design?

3. After turning in your first draft, you are informed that this office will be hosting a Web site that will contain a publicly downloadable video clip library and photo archive from government projects that the agency has directed over the past 10 years or so. How will your network design need to change? If a great deal of change is needed, how might you have planned your original design to make it fit the new requirements more easily? What trade-offs does that force you to make?

4. Visit the site *www.6bone.net* and review the description documents regarding IPv6. Does IPv6 sound like a good fit for this project? Why or why not?

2

CONFIGURING BASIC NETWORKING

> **After reading this chapter and completing the exercises you will be able to:**
>
> ♦ Describe how networking devices differ from other Linux devices
>
> ♦ Configure Linux networking using scripts and text-mode utilities
>
> ♦ Configure Linux networking using popular graphical utilities
>
> ♦ Effectively use networking utilities to test a network and troubleshoot networking problems
>
> ♦ Understand the IPX and AppleTalk protocols

In this chapter, you learn how the networking principles in Chapter 1 are implemented in Linux, and how to configure Linux networking. That configuration can be accomplished using simple command-line tools or any of several graphical utilities; modern Linux distributions typically include at least one such tool.

In the second part of this chapter, you will learn about the basic networking utilities—most of which are command line-tools—and how to test and troubleshoot a network using these tools. Finally, you will learn a little more about other protocols that are occasionally used in Linux to connect with other types of networks. These protocols include IPX and AppleTalk.

UNDERSTANDING NETWORK DEVICES IN LINUX

The design of the Linux operating system is based on the concept of the computer as a collection of devices. Information is stored on a hard disk device, output is written to a video card device, input is read from a keyboard device, and so forth. Devices in Linux are typically accessed via the /dev subdirectory of the file system, where hundreds of device names are listed. Not all devices named are actually present on your system; the name is there for convenience in case you install a corresponding device. For example, the device name /dev/sda is included on your system even if you do not have the SCSI device installed to which this name refers.

If you have a device installed, you can begin using it as soon as you install software that knows how to communicate with the device. This software may be a specific **device driver**, such as a driver for a Zip drive, or it may be a more general-purpose program, such as a terminal-emulation program that uses a set of standard commands to communicate with modem devices via a serial interface.

You might think that Linux networking devices would appear in the /dev directory and be configured similarly to other devices. However, Linux networking devices differ from most other devices in several ways:

- Networking devices are not shown in the /dev directory, and in fact do not "exist" on the system until an appropriate device driver is installed in the Linux kernel.

- Networking in Linux is handled directly by the Linux kernel, rather than by other programs.

- A networking device in Linux can refer to software that manages networking functionality.

Physical networking devices are easy to identify: routers, hubs, NICs, etc. But it may help you to think of a networking device in Linux as a named channel over which network traffic can pass. Some Linux networking devices refer to physical Ethernet cards; others refer to logical networking channels, such as the loopback interface, which you'll learn about later in this chapter. The overall network configuration may include multiple levels of networking devices, like the layers of an onion, or more appropriately, layers of cladding on a cable!

Because networking is handled in the Linux kernel, all device drivers for networking are actually kernel modules. **Kernel modules** can be loaded or unloaded while Linux is running, but most system administrators configure their system so that the networking modules are loaded immediately at system startup.

Although networking-related kernel modules are commonly loaded at boot time, you can also recompile the Linux kernel with the networking modules compiled into a monolithic kernel. This doesn't really save any space or improve performance, but sometimes makes troubleshooting certain problems or configuring complex networks easier. We have assumed that you will be loading all the networking components as modules unless specially noted.

 If you need to recompile your kernel, make sure you have the kernel source code installed (for Red Hat 7.3 install the kernel-source package from CD 2). Then change to the /usr/src/linux directory and use the make menuconfig or make xconfig command to get started. Directions are provided in Wells, *Guide to Linux Installation and Administration* (ISBN 0-619-00097-X), Chapter 4, or the kernel-HOWTO document on *www.linuxdocs.org* or *www.linuxhq.com*.

Table 2-1 is only a partial list of networking devices used by Linux. For example, ATM networking is not mentioned because ATM support in Linux is a fairly recent development and is not likely to be widely used.

Table 2-1 Examples of Linux networking devices

Device Name	Description
eth0	First Ethernet NIC
tr0	First token ring NIC
ppp0	Point-to-Point Protocol
slip	Serial Line Internet Protocol
plip	Parallel Line Internet Protocol
arc0	ARCnet
fddi0	FDDI NIC
dlci0	Frame Relay NIC
ippp0	Integrated Services Digital Network (ISDN) modem

The device name referred to throughout most of this chapter is eth0. The "eth" refers to Ethernet; the "0" is the number of the first Ethernet card; thus, eth0 is the name of the first Ethernet card installed in a host. You may well have two or more Ethernet cards installed in a system (a router, for example). The second Ethernet card is eth1, and so on.

 The latest release of the Linux kernel—the 2.4 series at this writing—uses a new system for handling all devices that resembles what has always been done with networking devices. The system is called the **Device File System (DevFS)**. It allows more flexibility (and expansion) of the devices that Linux can name and recognize.

To establish networking in Linux, your first step after installing a networking card (which won't be covered in this book) is to make Linux recognize that card, or realize that a networking device is installed on the system. To do this, you load the appropriate module into the Linux kernel. The process in simplest terms is as follows:

1. Use the **modprobe** command to load a kernel module.

2. If you have loaded the correct module, it will locate and recognize the networking card you have installed in your system. A corresponding device name will be created within the Linux kernel.

3. If you have loaded an incorrect module, or not included command-line **parameters** that let the kernel module locate and recognize the networking hardware, you will see an error message when the module attempts to load. No networking device will be created and you will need to try the process again, starting at Step 1.

Installing network devices, as you might guess, can be a very frustrating process. Fortunately, this is becoming much less so, because the networking driver modules in Linux are continually improving, and because modern Linux distributions include software that detects what networking hardware you have installed and loads the correctly configured module for you. You'll walk through both methods later in this chapter.

Having a networking card recognized by the Linux kernel establishes the lowest layer of the networking model. In the Internet model discussed in Chapter 1 and used throughout this book, that is the Link layer. If you're using an Ethernet card, for example, loading the correct Ethernet card driver module means that Linux "knows how" to communicate over that Ethernet card, can access the Ethernet card's MAC address, and so forth. All that then remains is to configure the higher-layer protocols (including IP) so that applications can use them to transmit data properly over the Ethernet card.

Installing other Linux networking devices uses the same basic process: locate the correct kernel module and load it. The kernel module then recognizes the hardware it is designed to operate and creates an appropriate network device in the Linux kernel. Some examples are given in the list of device names in Table 2-1 and described in more detail here:

- **Point-to-Point Protocol (PPP)**: Using this protocol allows a host to tie directly to a single computer, making a network of two systems. PPP can operate over several types of hardware. The most common use of PPP is to create a network connection over a modem to reach an Internet Service Provider (ISP). Depending on the type of connection you have, you might have something like PPP over Ethernet. For example, if you are using a Digital Subscriber Line (DSL) or a cable modem from your telephone or cable television company (acting as your ISP), you might be connecting a special modem to your Ethernet card and creating a PPP connection to the ISP. PPP is covered in detail in Chapter 3.

2

- **Serial Line Internet Protocol (SLIP)**: You can use this protocol to transmit network data over a serial port, rather than a special networking cable. SLIP is used with a serial modem to connect to an ISP, but has been superceded by PPP, which is more flexible. SLIP is still fully supported in Linux.

- **Parallel Line Internet Protocol (PLIP)**: Similar to SLIP, this protocol is the basis for a networking device that uses a parallel port to transmit network data. PLIP allows you to connect two computers using an inexpensive parallel cable, and creating a network without any additional network cards. The data throughput rate can reach about 20 Kb/s (similar to the speed of a standard modem connection).

- **Integrated Services Digital Network (ISDN)**: This is a special type of telephone service that is widely used in Europe. ISDN is available in much of the United States, but is less favored now that DSL and cable modems provide faster service for lower cost. (ISDN provides 128 Kb/s bandwidth, compared to speeds up to 10 times that or more for DSL and cable modems.) ISDN cards work like modems, using a PPP-type networking device. Linux has very strong ISDN support. Detailed information, including a list of ISDN hardware supported by Linux, is available at *www.isdn4linux.de/faq*.

- Several other types of high-speed networking connections are supported by Linux, though a complete explanation of them is beyond the scope of this book. For example, you can use a **Frame Relay** card to connect to an ISP using a **T-1** line from your telephone company. T-1 provides a speed of 1.544 Mb/s, usually for a few hundred dollars per month. A **T-3** line provides 45 Mb/s, but usually costs many thousands of dollars per month.

Most of the discussion to this point has been conceptual. Let's sit down at a keyboard and see how it all works.

PREPARING TO CONFIGURE NETWORKING

When you installed Linux—whichever version you used—you might have entered some networking information as part of the installation procedure, even without understanding what it all meant. For example, you might have entered an IP address, a name server address, and a hostname. In this section, you'll work from the ground up, creating a network configuration using the command-line utilities that the installation program would have used for you in the background.

You may not have entered any network information during your Linux installation either because you didn't use networking (your system was standalone) or because you used Dynamic Host Configuration Protocol (DHCP), which automatically assigned an IP address to your system. DHCP is described in Chapter 3.

Although you may have networking already running, we'll assume that you don't, or that you don't mind having it unavailable for a while as you learn the ins and outs of the networking tools. In order to show you concrete examples of networking commands throughout this chapter, we will invent a networking scenario. You'll need to modify the commands to fit your own network, but the scenario should make it easier to see how the networking commands are really used.

Suppose that you have a small network of five computers, or hosts, labeled A through E. Host A has a modem and connects the network to the Internet. (You'll see how that's done a little later, in Chapter 3.) Host B has two Ethernet cards and acts as a router to other networks in our organization. Hosts C, D, and E are clients, in that they are not configured to provide services to any other systems. Figure 2-1 shows a diagram of the hypothetical network you'll be working with.

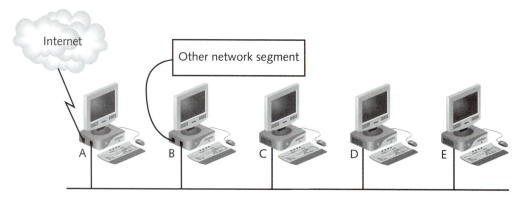

Figure 2-1 A simple networking scenario

Adding a Kernel Module

To create a networking device within the Linux kernel, you must add the correct module to your kernel, as described previously. When you do that, the module locates the Ethernet card (or other type of card, such as Token Ring, ISDN, etc.) and creates the appropriate device name. You can then refer to that device name for configuration in the sections that follow.

All of the available kernel modules for networking devices are included in your Linux system, normally in a subdirectory under **/lib/modules**. The exact location varies according to your Linux system, and the kernel version you are using is usually one of the subdirectory names. Red Hat Linux 7.3, for example, stores the network card drivers in **/lib/modules/2.4.7-10/kernel/drivers/net**. Within that directory are other subdirectories for special types of network drivers, such as **irda** (infrared), **wireless**, and **appletalk**. In total, over 150 kernel modules are included. Similarly, Caldera OpenLinux eDesktop 2.4 includes the kernel modules in **/lib/modules/2.2.14/net**.

When loading a kernel module, you don't need to use the entire directory name; the `modprobe` command is aware of the location of the modules on your system. You also don't need to include the ".o" file extension that you see in the filenames within the modules' subdirectories. All you need is the name of the module, as shown in the examples that follow.

Deciding Which Module to Use

Given that Red Hat 7.3, as one example, includes over 150 network card drivers, how do you know which module to use, other than simply trying them all? The module names are certainly not self-explanatory (for example, you see drivers named `at1700`, `e100`, `ni5010`, and `sis900`). The easiest solution to this dilemma is to ask someone (including the manufacturer or a technical support representative) which Linux kernel module supports your network card, or else use the feature of `modprobe` that lets you check each driver until one works. That's described below.

If you know which module to use, simply use the `modprobe` command with that module name:

```
modprobe 3c59x
```

The `modprobe` command automatically loads any other modules that are prerequisites for the networking module you have selected (including multiple levels of prerequisites) and then loads the module itself. The module initializes itself within the Linux kernel by searching for and identifying the physical hardware that it will operate with (the Ethernet card, for example). If everything is successful, the command prompt returns after the `modprobe` command with no additional output. No news is good news.

You can use the `lsmod` command to list the modules that are loaded in your kernel at that moment. Simply enter `lsmod` at any command prompt. If the module that supports your networking hardware was loaded and was able to find the networking hardware, you should see it listed after running `lsmod`. (The name of the module as listed by `lsmod` is the same name you used with the `modprobe` command above.)

If the module has a problem because it cannot initialize itself and find the hardware it expects to find, then you see an error message. If you see an error message, you don't yet have a valid networking device that you can set up with an IP address.

You may be familiar with the `insmod` command, which you can use to insert a module into a running Linux kernel. The `insmod` command certainly can do the job, but `modprobe` is better because it automatically handles checking all the dependencies and then uses `insmod` itself in the background. If you execute `insmod` directly, you have to figure out all the dependencies yourself, which may require that you load several modules manually and in the correct order.

Problems with installing a new module are of two types: either you've chosen the wrong module, or you've chosen the correct module but have not provided the information that the module needs to load the driver and use the hardware correctly.

For the first problem, you can try using the -t option of modprobe. This option instructs modprobe to try every driver in a directory that you name until one of them works (a "brute force" method of solving the problem). To install a network driver using this method in Red Hat Linux, use this command:

```
modprobe -t kernel/drivers/net
```

Be certain to search the Web sites of your network card manufacturer and your Linux vendor for information that may help you configure the card quickly or more appropriately for your needs. Red Hat Software provides a very useful hardware compatibility list that includes both certified hardware (which Red Hat has tested) and all compatible hardware (not tested in-house but expected to work). Visit *hardware.redhat.com*, choose the type of information you want (Certified, Complete List, etc.), and review the information on the product you are interested in. The information includes comments and an "ease of installation" rating, plus the specific kernel module that supports that network card.

For the second problem (choosing the right module, but not providing the correct or necessary parameters), you need to provide hardware details to the module so that it knows how to operate the hardware or where to find the hardware in the system. For modern hardware, such as PCI-style network cards, this is not often needed. For older ISA network cards, it's not uncommon that the modprobe command requires you to provide a hardware interrupt number, a memory address (sometimes referred to as the I/O port of the card), or other details before the network card can be initialized by the appropriate kernel module.

Suppose that you know your Ethernet card is configured to use Interrupt 15 (IRQ 15) and a memory address of 300. You can include that information as part of the modprobe command, instructing the kernel module how to access the hardware. For example, to specify IRQ 15 and memory address 300, you use a command such as this one:

```
modprobe ne2000 irq=15 io=0x300
```

Unfortunately, if not surprisingly, the author of every networking kernel module decides individually what parameters to use for that module. While most use the same abbreviations for IRQ and memory address, as shown in the previous example command, each kernel module may differ in what optional parameters it supports. These module parameters can become very important even if you don't appear to need them the first time you use modprobe. Some special features of the network card may be activated via a module parameter at the time the module is installed.

Some network cards require that you use special software provided by the manufacturer to set or view the card settings (such as IRQ). While this is easier than moving tiny jumpers around on the card itself to configure such settings, the programs provided by the manufacturer invariably run on DOS or Windows. In this case, you may be able to install the card and the software on a computer running that operating system, configure the card, then move the card to the system running Linux. Alternatively, if you have access to a single-disk version of DOS, you may be able to boot the Linux system from that DOS diskette, then run the network card configuration program. Remember that this procedure is typically only needed for older cards, and that Linux is continually gaining support from hardware vendors. If possible, you may choose to invest in a new Ethernet card.

To learn about the parameters that may be applicable to the module you need to use, you can refer to the kernel documentation at *www.linuxhq.com/kernel/v2.4/doc/networking/ net-modules.txt.html*. This document includes a list of all valid parameters for over 50 networking modules.

Once you know which kernel module is needed for your networking hardware, you want that module to load each time you boot the system. Some versions of Linux automate that process for you. For example, Red Hat Linux detects when a needed module is not loaded and loads it for you. Other systems rely on a configuration file in /etc that lists the name of each module to be loaded at boot time. In either case, you need to specify any module parameters (such as an IRQ number) that should be included when the module is loaded by the system.

In Red Hat Linux, you must include an **options** line in the file /etc/modules.conf for each kernel module that requires kernel parameters when loaded. (The configuration file is /etc/conf.modules in some Linux distributions.) Two sample lines within /etc/modules.conf might look like this, depending on the networking hardware that you are using:

```
alias eth0 3c59x
options 3c59x irq=15 io=0x300
```

We're hoping, of course, that you've only skimmed through most of this section because your Linux system automatically detected and installed the correct kernel module. That's likely the case, especially if you're using a PCI network card. Linux vendors are working diligently to remove the headaches of hardware configuration.

CONFIGURING NETWORKING WITH COMMAND-LINE UTILITIES

Most Linux distributions use a very similar set of commands and scripts to configure networking. In fact, the two core command-line programs are the same on all versions of Linux: **ifconfig** and **route**.

Using `ifconfig` to Set Up Network Interfaces

The `ifconfig` utility configures a networking interface within the Linux kernel. This command is used by the system-startup scripts at boot time, though you can use it to manually reconfigure the network if needed. The parameters used by `ifconfig` include, at a minimum, a network interface (such as eth0) and the IP address assigned to the interface. These two pieces of information allow packets to be sent. Additional parameters that you can configure using `ifconfig` include the broadcast address, the MTU (the maximum size of packet that the interface supports), and various special features such as point-to-point connections and IPv6 addressing (which you won't be concerned with here).

When you are working at a command line in Linux, you can enter the `ifconfig` command with an interface name such as `eth0` to see the status of that interface. You can also use `ifconfig` by itself—without any parameters—to see the status of all the configured network interfaces on your system. The output from the command `ifconfig` looks like this:

```
eth0 Link encap:Ethernet HWaddr 00:10:5A:9E:9D:6F
     inet addr:192.168.100.10 Bcast:192.168.100.255 Mask:255
     .255.255.0
     UP BROADCAST RUNNING MULTICAST MTU:1500 Metric:1
     RX packets:421 errors:0 dropped:0 overruns:0 frame:0
     TX packets:19 errors:0 dropped:0 overruns:0 carrier:0
     collisions:0 txqueuelen:100
     RX bytes:49814 (48.6 Kb) TX bytes:1434 (1.4 Kb)
     Interrupt:11 Base address:0x1400

  lo  Link encap:Local Loopback
      inet addr:127.0.0.1 Mask:255.0.0.0
      UP LOOPBACK RUNNING MTU:16436 Metric:1
      RX packets:52 errors:0 dropped:0 overruns:0 frame:0
      TX packets:52 errors:0 dropped:0 overruns:0 carrier:0
      collisions:0 txqueuelen:0
      RX bytes:3428 (3.3 Kb) TX bytes:3428 (3.3 Kb)
```

If you haven't configured any network devices, you see nothing. But more likely, you see at least a listing for the localhost, or loopback device, as indicated by the `lo` in the leftmost column of the output. (The rest of the fields are explained in a moment.)

The `lo` notation is the name of the **loopback** network device, a special "logical" device (it doesn't physically exist) that is used to move packets within a host, such as between a client and server running on the same computer. It also serves a useful function for testing networking without needing to have another computer to which you have true network access. The loopback device is called `lo` within the Linux kernel (compare this to `eth0` for the Ethernet card). The typical address for the loopback device is 127.0.0.1. Recall from Chapter 1 that any IP address beginning with 127 is reserved for use within a single host. The name **localhost** is assigned to address 127.0.0.1, but you often hear the device (loopback) and the name (localhost) used interchangeably.

The fields of `ifconfig` output are described here, though some are only mentioned briefly because their true usefulness is beyond the scope of our discussion.

- `Link encap`: The type of networking being used, such as PPP or Ethernet (as given in Table 2-1)

- `HWaddr`: The hardware address of the NIC (for example, the Ethernet card's hardware address, as used by ARP)

- `Inet addr`: The IP address assigned to the network interface, with its broadcast address (`Bcast`) and network mask (`Mask`) following on the same line

- Flags indicating the status of the network interface, including `UP` to indicate a running interface, `BROADCAST` and `MULTICAST` to indicate that those types of addressing are supported, or `LOOPBACK` to indicate that the device is used for internal networking only

- On the same line as the flags is the `MTU` (the maximum size of packet that the interface supports) and the **metric** (a preference value for routing through this device); the MTU for Ethernet always defaults to 1500, though you could change it to avoid fragmentation if most of your traffic had to pass through a network segment with a smaller MTU; the metric at this point always is 1, as explained further in the next section discussing the `route` command

- The `RX packets` and `TX packets` lines represent the number of packets that have been received and transmitted, respectively, over the interface; the first number is the total figure, with separate indications of erroneous packets indicated afterwards

- A specific error is listed on the next line: the number of `collisions` (remember that Ethernet packets collide if multiple NICs try to use the cable at the same instant)

- The `txqueuelen` parameter indicates how many packets the network interface can store for transmission while waiting to actually send the packets on a busy network.

- The `RX bytes` and `TX bytes` are similar to the `RX` and `TX packets` lines, but here the numbers measure how much information has been transmitted. In the example above, the figures show the number of bytes, followed by a summary in Kb.

- Finally, some hardware-specific information is provided: the IRQ (labeled Interrupt) and memory address (labeled Base address) used by the card. That may seem superfluous to you now, because you already have the Ethernet card configured, but the `ifconfig` command simply reports back the information that the kernel is maintaining on that network interface! This is useful data when you run a router with multiple Ethernet cards and need to see which NIC is referred to for each reported network interface.

By specifying an interface such as `eth0` in the `ifconfig` command, you can start an interface working ("bring it up") or stop it ("take it down"). To do this, you add **up** or **down** after the interface name. For example, to stop the Ethernet interface, enter this command:

```
ifconfig eth0 down
```

To start it again, enter this command:

```
ifconfig eth0 up
```

You shouldn't need to use this command directly (as explained in the next section). If you do, note that you still need to set the route manually for the interface to work as expected with other computers on the network. The basic syntax of an `ifconfig` command looks like this:

```
ifconfig device ip_address netmask address broadcast address
```

A real example might look like this:

```
ifconfig eth0 192.168.100.1 netmask 255.255.255.0
    broadcast 192.168.100.255
```

Using the `route` Command

The second core networking command is **route**, which lets you view or configure the routing table within the Linux kernel. The routing table tells the IP networking stack where to send packets that aren't part of the local network. In fact, it even includes the local network, as you'll see.

As with `ifconfig`, the `route` command is executed by your Linux system at boot time when networking is initialized. You can always use it manually to view or change the configured routes. But you shouldn't plan on needing `ifconfig` and `route` regularly except to see a quick list of how the kernel is currently configured.

Using the `route` command with no parameters displays the kernel routing table. Sample output is shown here:

```
Kernel IP routing table
Destination     Gateway          Genmask         Flags Metric Ref Use Iface
192.168.100.0   *                255.255.255.0   U     0      0   0   eth0
127.0.0.0       *                255.0.0.0       U     0      0   0   lo
default         192.168.100.5    0.0.0.0         UG    0      0   0   eth0
```

Let's walk through each part of this output, which is labeled by the utility itself as the "Kernel IP routing table." The output for this host consists of three lines (after the column headings):

- A line defining where to send traffic for the 192.168.100.0 network (that's the network associated with the IP address of the `eth0` device)

- A line defining where to send traffic for the 127.0.0.0 network (that's the localhost or loopback network address)

- A line defining where to send any packet with a destination address on a network other than the two just mentioned; those packets must go to the gateway, since this system doesn't know how to reach any other networks

Now let's look at the columns in the output of the **route** command:

- **Destination**: The network to which the routing table entry applies. If the destination address of an IP packet is part of the network listed on a line, then that entry will be used to route the packet.

- **Gateway:** The computer that should receive a packet destined for the specified network. Because this output is from a host (not a machine acting as a dedicated router), the Gateway field contains either an asterisk (*) to indicate that the network is the one the host is a part of (no routing is needed) or the default gateway (send all nonlocal traffic to the named IP address).

- **Genmask:** Specifies the network mask used to identify the network ID portion of any IP address that is part of the destination network identified on that line.

- **Flags:** Nine single-letter flags indicate information about this routing table entry. The **U** indicates that the route is Up; the **G** indicates that the route refers to a gateway. Most of the other flags (all of which you can view in the **route** command's online man (manual) page by entering **man route**) are used for dedicated routers, not single hosts, and refer to how the route was created or updated using routing daemons. (A **routing daemon**, as you'll learn in Chapter 6, is a program that automatically generates routing table entries based on information received over the network via protocols dedicated to routing information.)

- **Metric:** The number of hops (how many routers) needed to reach the specified network. (Not used by the Linux kernel.)

- **Ref:** How many references are made to this route. (Not used by the Linux kernel.)

- **Use:** The number of times this route has been looked up by the routing software. This gives a rough measure of how much traffic is headed for the specified network.

- **Iface:** The network interface on which packets destined for the specified network should be sent.

The online manual pages cover nearly all Linux commands, configuration files, and programming functions. You can access them from any command line by entering the man command followed by the command name or the configuration file name.

As with `ifconfig`, you shouldn't plan on using `route` to set up your routing table; let the scripts described in the next section or the graphical tools do it for you. But for the sake of completeness, a sample command to add a route might look like this:

```
route add -net 192.168.100.0 netmask 255.255.255.0 dev
    eth0
```

This example adds a route to reach the network 192.168.100.0 by specifying the network mask for that network and the device to which packets should be sent in order to reach that network: `eth0`. Another example is shown below. This command adds a default gateway route, which indicates that traffic to any network for which a route has not been set up should be sent to the gateway system, which knows what to do with it.

```
route add default gw 192.168.100.5
```

As you work with more complex networks than those described so far, you'll find it helpful to be familiar with the output and the options of the `route` command. At times you may need to modify or add routes to make your Linux system function as desired within a larger network that has multiple gateways or uses network prefixes that require manual configuration.

For example, suppose your organization has two Ethernet network segments. Your segment includes a connection to the Internet, but the other segment is not permitted to access the Internet. Your network is 192.168.10.0; the other segment is 192.168.20.0. A router, Host R, connects the two segments. The router has two network interfaces, 192.168.10.1 and 192.168.20.1. Figure 2-2 shows this scenario. You are sitting at Host A; the Internet connection is through Host G (192.168.10.5); you want to connect to Host B, which is located on the other network: 192.168.20.0.

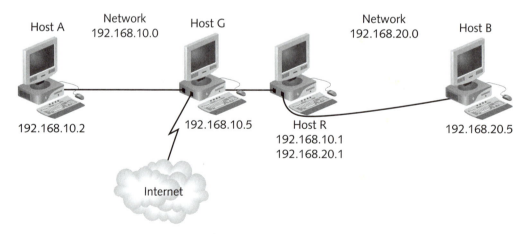

Figure 2-2 A network with a routing problem

Suppose that you use standard commands to set up your network connections. You also set up the default gateway to have nonlocal traffic routed to Host G, the Internet gateway. Your routing table will look something like this:

```
192.168.10.0  *                   255.255.255.0 U    0 0   0 eth0
127.0.0.0     *                   255.0.0.0     U    0 0   0 lo
default       192.168.10.5 0.0.0.0              UG   0 0   0 eth0
```

However, this arrangement is very inefficient for reaching Host B, if indeed you can reach it at all. Because a packet destined for network 192.168.20.0 isn't included in the routing table, that packet is sent to the Internet gateway. If the other network segment (containing Host B) had an Internet connection, the packet would likely find its way back to that network (slowly). What is needed is a route specifically for network 192.168.20.0, so that traffic destined for that network goes to Host R to be routed immediately to that network; other traffic—traffic that belongs to neither local network—can still go to the default gateway route (Host G in this example). The following command would add the needed route:

```
route add -net 192.168.20.0 netmask 255.255.255.0 gw
     192.168.10.1 dev eth0
```

This results in a routing table that looks like this:

```
192.168.10.0  *              255.255.255.0 U  0 0 0 eth0
192.168.20.0 192.168.10.1 255.255.255.0 U  0 0 0 eth0
127.0.0.0     *              255.0.0.0     U  0 0 0 lo
default       192.168.10.5 0.0.0.0         UG 0 0 0 eth0
```

In the next chapter, you'll learn about using names instead of relying on IP addresses, as we have so far.

As you study the previous example, notice that Host B does not have the same problem; its default gateway is configured as Host R. There is no place else for traffic to go, because there are not two "escape hatches" out of that network segment. This is a very simplified example, but should illustrate some of the issues that arise in complex networks, where you want network packets to take the most efficient path possible to reach any given host.

Using ARP

In Chapter 1 you learned about the Address Resolution Protocol (ARP), which the networking stacks use to obtain the hardware address of a computer they need to send a packet to. Now that you are more familiar with the **route** command, you can try the **arp** command, which displays the **arp cache**, a mapping of IP addresses to hardware addresses. The **arp** command is used mainly for troubleshooting network connectivity.

The protocol ARP is used in four ways (or with four acronyms, you might say):

- Regular ARP is used when a host has an IP address and needs to know the hardware address of the host with that IP address. The first machine broadcasts a message: "Who has this IP address? Tell me your hardware address!" The machine with that IP address responds with its hardware address, which is then cached (stored) for future use.

- **Reverse ARP (RARP)** is used when a host that has no local storage (often called a diskless workstation) knows its hardware address but has "forgotten" its IP address. It relies on another system having cached that information and providing it back to the host.

- **Inverse ARP (InARP)** is used when one host knows the physical address of another host, but needs its IP address. (This is like RARP, but for a different host.)

- **Proxy ARP** is the term used when a host responds to a request for *another* host's hardware address. Normally, a host only responds if someone is asking for its own hardware address. Linux automatically does proxy ARP in some routing circumstances.

The Linux `arp` command lets you view the ARP table within your system and add or delete entries manually. Changing the table is rarely necessary, but viewing it with the command `arp -a` (for "all") is instructive. Most ARP entries are dynamic and are discarded if not referenced within two minutes. One reason to add a hardware address manually is that you can make the entry static (so it is not dropped from the ARP cache); you can also specify when proxy ARP is to be used.

The relationship between the hardware addresses that ARP maintains and the routing tables is especially important for you to understand. Think back to the previous scenario in which a packet from Host A needs to reach Host B by going through Host R instead of to the default gateway, Host G. If the packet itself always has the destination IP address of Host B, how does Host A get the packet into the hands of Host R, which sees that the destination IP address belongs on the other network segment and route it accordingly? Recall that routers do not "look at" every packet on the Ethernet cable; they only review those packets that are addressed to them, so the router (Host R) does not automatically "see" the packet from Host A that is addressed to Host B.

The answer to this dilemma is that Host A leaves the destination IP address for Host B intact, but at the lower level of networking—the Link layer—instead of using the MAC address of Host B (which Host A might have trouble obtaining anyway), Host A attaches the hardware address of the router, Host R, which it can obtain by sending an ARP query on its local network segment. Once Host R sees that the packet contains its own MAC address, it grabs it and has a look. It then discovers that the packet's destination IP address is not Host R, so it assumes the packet must be routed. Host R consults its routing table, obtains the MAC address of Host B from ARP, and sends the packet onward with the destination IP address of Host B still intact, *plus* the MAC address of Host B, which Host R was able to obtain. That's a long process to describe; Figure 2-3 may help illustrate this basic two-step routing example.

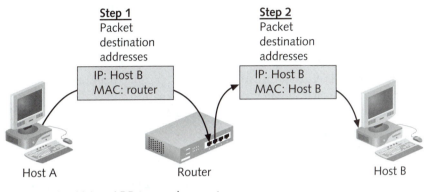

Figure 2-3   Using ARP to reach a router

System Networking Scripts

As we've alluded to, you don't really use `ifconfig` and `route` to set up Linux networking. Linux vendors have provided numerous scripts and configuration files to make complex networking easier to set up and to make starting and stopping networking smooth on all Linux systems. The networking scripts follow the model used for most system services on UNIX-based computers. You'll see many more examples of these scripts in coming chapters.

The simplistic view is that networking on nearly every Linux distribution is controlled or managed by a single script: **/etc/rc.d/init.d/network**. Assuming that you have a network card installed, you can start up networking with the following command:

```
/etc/rc.d/init.d/network start
```

Using this command stops networking:

```
/etc/rc.d/init.d/network stop
```

The beauty of this system is evident when you compare it to the system for setting up networking in Microsoft Windows operating systems. In Linux, you never need to reboot the system to make changes to the networking configuration. The only time you must shut down is when you're exchanging hardware in the back of the computer (and for some systems, not even then!). In Linux, you can make whatever changes you want to the network configuration files, then use the above two commands to make them active. If you're impatient, most Linux systems even support this command to do it all at once:

```
/etc/rc.d/init.d/network restart
```

Some Linux vendors use a slightly different directory structure, but the principle still holds. For example, Debian Linux uses the script /etc/init.d/ network. Also, /etc/init.d is a standard location that is provided as a symbolic link in Red Hat Linux.

Elegant though it may be, this grand network script begs the question: How does it do all of this? The answer is that more scripts and configuration files lie behind the scenes. All of these are located in the directory **/etc/sysconfig**, under the subdirectories network-scripts and in the file networking.

The network-scripts subdirectory contains scripts that start and stop individual network interfaces. In that directory you see two main scripts called **ifup** and **ifdown**. These are used to control more common interfaces such as localhost and Ethernet. Other specialized scripts may also be found in that subdirectory for interfaces such as IPv6, PPP, or ISDN.

A question should be forming in your mind: Why use a script instead of just the up and down options with ifconfig? The short answer is this: the scripts can be much more intelligent in handling the network interfaces. For example, they can check whether a firewall configuration needs to be adjusted, whether a wireless interface is involved, whether default routes must be updated, and so forth. You can obtain the more complex answer if you have any experience with shell scripts: open the files in a text editor and study them.

Scripts that control individual network interfaces do not contain the actual configuration data. That information is stored in separate files in the /etc/sysconfig/ network-scripts subdirectory according to the name of the interface. The file you're most likely to see is /etc/sysconfig/network-scripts/ifcfg-eth0, which contains information to configure the first Ethernet interface. The contents of that file are shown here:

```
DEVICE=eth0
BOOTPROTO=static
BROADCAST=192.168.100.255
IPADDR=192.168.100.10
NETMASK=255.255.255.0
NETWORK=192.168.100.0
ONBOOT=yes
```

If you are using DHCP to obtain IP address information, your ifcfg-eth0 file will look different from the one shown here.

With this file, you can finally see how the data to configure the interface is actually stored. If you were to change the IP address in this file and use the command /etc/rc.d/init.d/network restart, the IP address of your system would be changed. Most Linux systems add graphical configuration utilities to let you change IP addresses, add network interfaces, and so forth. Behind the scenes, those utilities are changing the data files and using the system scripts that control networking.

2

To see the flexibility and usefulness of this system and its many scripts and configuration files, consider how you would manually add a new interface. Suppose that you needed to assign an additional IP address to your Ethernet card. This is called **IP aliasing**, and occurs when a single physical interface has more than one IP address assigned—a feature that is useful when hosting multiple Web sites on a single machine, for example. IP aliases are referred to by adding a number to the physical interface name. So, if the interface is eth0, the first additional IP address would refer to `eth0:0`, the second to `eth0:1`, and so on.

To create the IP alias you need, you would simply create a new file in the `/etc/sysconfig/network-scripts` directory with the name `ifcfg-eth0:0`. The easiest way would be to copy the existing file `ifcfg-eth0`. Then change the values of the `DEVICE` and `IPADDR` lines to refer to `eth0:0` and the new IP address. Now restart networking to make the additional IP address automatically active. Every time you start up Linux, the additional IP address will be started. To stop this, delete the additional file that you created and restart networking. This experiment is one of the Hands-on Projects at the end of this chapter.

Configuring Networking Using Graphical Tools

A good system administrator knows how things work "under the hood," rather than just relying on the basic tools. By knowing about the networking scripts and the `ifconfig` and `route` commands, you'll have a better grasp of how to diagnose any problems that arise on your network. Once you understand those things, however, there's no reason not to use the tools that make life easier. Every major version of Linux includes graphical utilities to help you set up and manage networking. This section describes the utilities included with some popular versions of Linux.

Using Red Hat Linux Graphical Utilities

Red Hat Linux previously used a program called **LinuxConf**, which was a utility that seemed to include everything but the kitchen sink, including many networking configuration options. The latest Red Hat release, 7.3, has introduced the new **Red Hat Network Administration Tool**. It provides an attractive graphical interface (much superior to LinuxConf) in which you can manage hardware devices (that is, the kernel modules used to access them), including parameters needed for each one, plus the network addresses you want to support on those devices.

You can start the Network Administration Tool from the graphical menu of the Gnome desktop in Red Hat Linux by choosing Programs, System, and then Network Configuration. You can also start the program from a command line by entering the utility name: **neat**. Figure 2-4 shows the main screen of this utility.

In this section we only explore the Hardware and Devices tabs. Hosts and DNS will be covered later

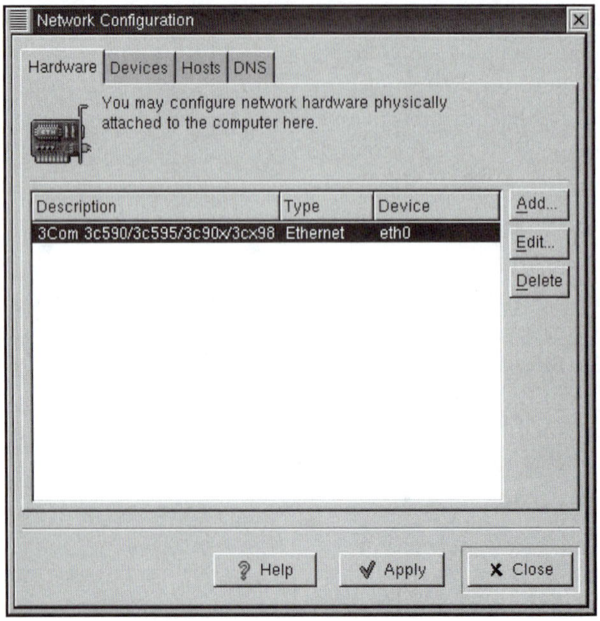

Figure 2-4   The main screen of the Red Hat Network Configuration utility

The fields in the Hardware tab show you a description of the hardware based on which network cards the installed kernel module supports. The type of hardware is displayed along with the device name that is assigned to the hardware and kernel module.

If you choose Edit to the right of the list, you see the different parameters that this module might include. Figure 2-5 shows the Network Adapters Configuration dialog box. Generally, no parameters are needed for this particular example. If they were, you could enter them in this dialog box.

Clicking the Add button in Figure 2-4 opens a dialog box in which you can select the type of hardware for which you want to add support to the kernel. The supported options are Ethernet, Token Ring, ISDN, and Modem. Linux supports many other types of networking (DSL, ATM, etc.), but the options shown are the ones you can manage using this utility. To configure others you must use the command line.

Moving to the Devices tab (Figure 2-6), you see a list of each Linux networking device name and the type of hardware driver associated with it. You use the Add button on the Devices tab to configure many types of networking interfaces, though again, not nearly as many as Linux actually supports. Taking a standard Ethernet card as an example, choosing Edit, then selecting the Protocols tab displays the settings used for that Ethernet device (also shown in Figure 2-6). The settings are divided into three tabs, which let you perform tasks such as determining whether the device is started at boot time, deciding whether nonroot users can activate and deactivate the device, setting up IP aliases, and configuring what protocols the device uses, among others.

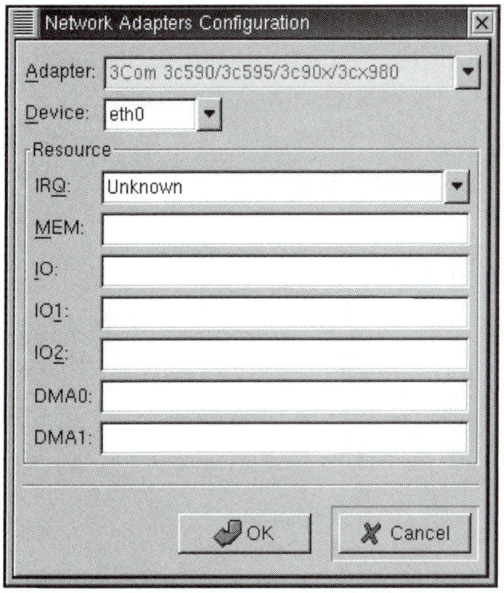

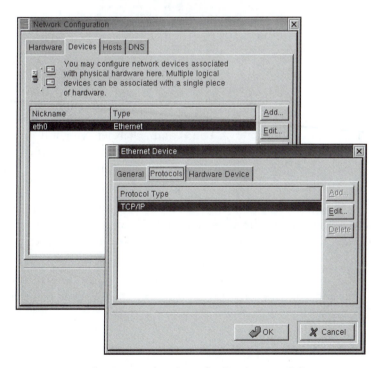

Figure 2-5   The Network Configuration dialog box in the Red Hat Network
                 Configuration utility

Figure 2-6   The Protocols tab under Devices => Edit

On this system, only TCP/IP is installed (AppleTalk, IPX, and other Link-layer proto-cols are not installed). Because of this, the Add button is not available. You can edit the TCP/IP protocol, however, by clicking the Edit button and using the TCP/IP tab in the dialog box that appears, as shown in Figure 2-7. You'll recognize the IP address, mask, and default gateway fields from our discussions in Chapter 1.

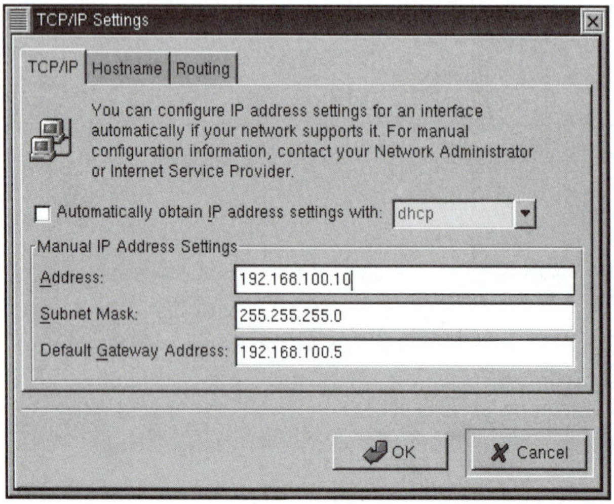

Figure 2-7   The TCP/IP Settings dialog box

As in other dialog boxes, a discussion of some parts of this dialog box has to wait until later. You'll learn about DHCP for automatic IP address assignment and the Hostname tab later in this chapter and in Chapter 3. The Routing tab lets you add routes to the kernel routing table. You should only need to do this if you have nonstandard routing needs caused by working on a large network with multiple gateways or points through which you can reach the Internet.

After you make any changes in the dialog boxes of the `neat` utility, use the OK button to close each dialog box. Then use the Close button and confirm that you want to save your changes and update the system with the new information you've entered.

A less glamorous utility is also provided in Red Hat Linux. The `netconfig` program operates in text mode and lets you enter the most basic IP address information for the default network interface. You can start this utility from any command line. The main data entry screen is shown in Figure 2-8.

Using Webmin in Caldera OpenLinux

Several Linux distributions, such as Caldera OpenLinux eDesktop 2.4, use **Webmin** to manage many system functions, including network configuration. Any user can start Webmin by choosing System, then Webmin from the main KDE graphical menu. Webmin operates in a browser. You select the features you want to configure, view the current settings, and enter any new settings in a form on a Web page. Scripts that are part of the Webmin package make changes in your system configuration files.

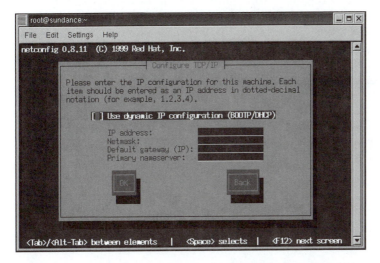

Figure 2-8   The `netconfig` text-based utility in Red Hat Linux

To start using Webmin you must log in with a username and password. By default, only the root user has access to Webmin, so log in using the username **root** and your Linux system's root password. The first screen that appears includes Webmin configuration options that let you set up which users can access Webmin, which hosts you can connect to Webmin from, and options such as the color scheme, logging standards, language, and many others. Figure 2-9 shows this screen.

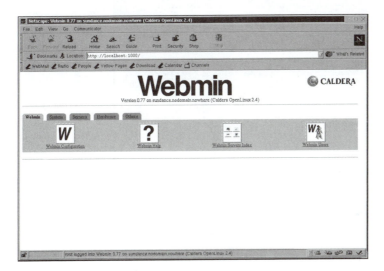

Figure 2-9   The initial screen of Webmin

To review the network configuration settings, choose the Hardware tab. From the Web page that appears, choose Network Configuration. The Network Configuration page appears with four more options (Figure 2-10). On this screen, choose Network Interfaces. A list of all the configured network interfaces on your system appears. Figure 2-11 shows the list of network interfaces on our system. From this Web page you can activate or deactivate network interfaces, add or remove interfaces, and configure the parameters of each interface.

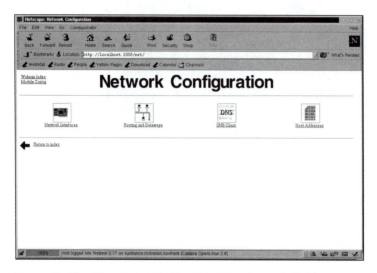

Figure 2-10   The Network Configuration page in Webmin

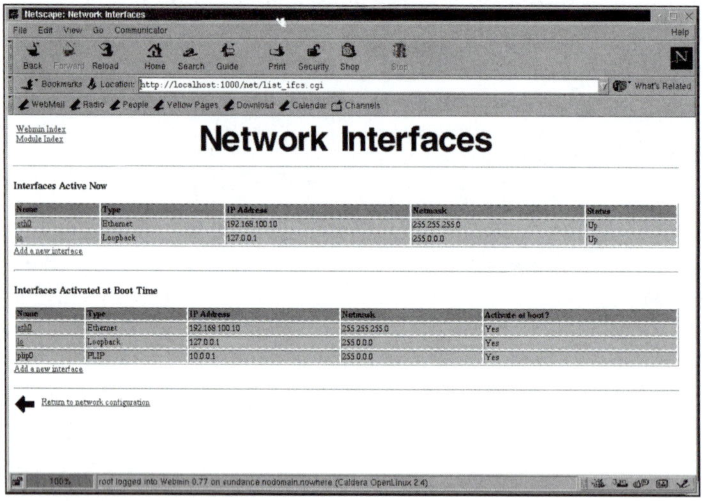

Figure 2-11   The list of network interfaces in Webmin

As with Red Hat Linux, networking is probably already set up on your system because of the autodetection done during installation. You can review the information and features in this Webmin screen to see how Webmin handles the functionality you've learned about, such as IP addresses, kernel devices, and even IP aliasing.

You can select an interface from the list of Interfaces Active Now to change the current settings of a network interface, which brings up the Edit Active Interface page shown in Figure 2-12. On this page you can view and alter settings such as the IP address, network mask, and broadcast address. You can also choose the Add Virtual Interface link to add another IP address to the physical interface you have selected (using IP aliasing, as described previously). To start or stop the interface you selected, use the Up and Down buttons in the Status field. Once you have made any desired changes, click the Save button to update this active interface. If you don't want to execute your changes, use the Back button of your browser or choose the Return to network interfaces link on the Web page.

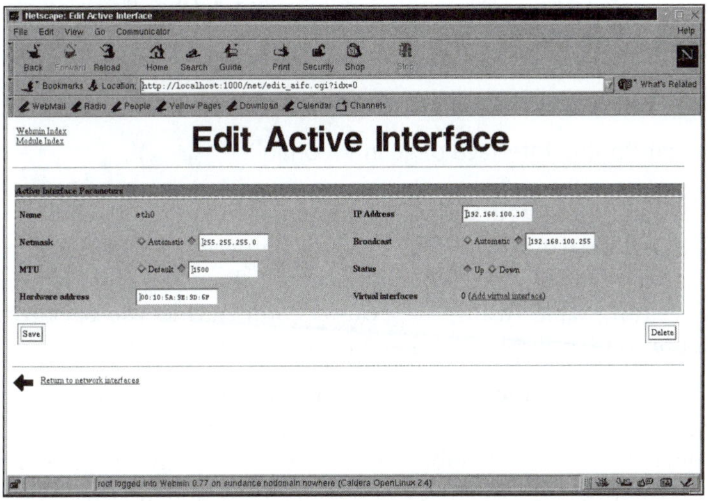

Figure 2-12   The Edit Active Interface page in Webmin

If you select an interface from the bottom list of Interfaces Activated at Boot Time (Figure 2-11), the Edit Bootup Interface page appears, as shown in Figure 2-13. Because this page controls the initial settings for network interfaces, you normally use this page instead of simply editing the active interface settings. Some types of information, however, are only shown in one screen or the other. For example, you choose whether to have an interface activated at boot time only in the Edit Bootup Interface page; you set the current status of an interface—up or down—only in the Edit Active Interface page. Within the Edit Bootup Interface page, you can choose the appropriate button at the bottom of the Web page to either save the information you have entered (choose Save), or save it but also apply it to the current activated settings (choose Save and Apply). Either button returns you to the list of networking interfaces shown in Figure 2-11.

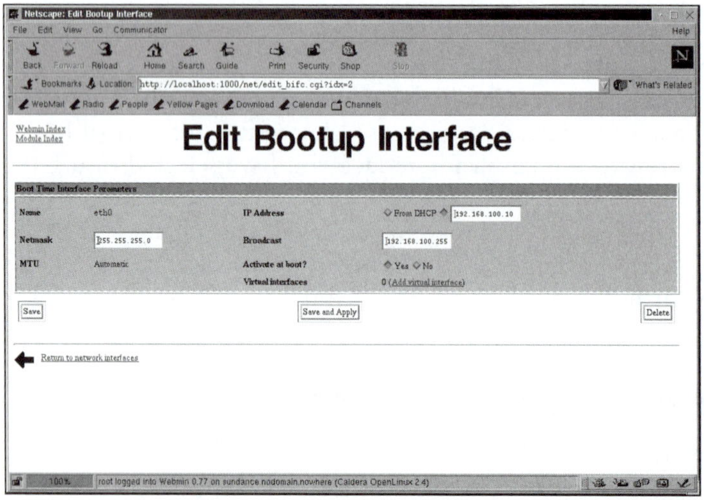

Figure 2-13 The Edit Bootup Interface page in Webmin

Returning to the Network Configuration page shown in Figure 2-10, you see additional buttons used to set up networking: Routing and Gateways, DNS Client, and Host Addresses. The last two of these are treated in Chapter 3; Routing and Gateways sets up part of the kernel routing table (using the `route` command in the background). The page shown in Figure 2-14 is displayed when you choose this button.

This page actually only handles the default route; routes for other networks are configured behind the scenes as part of the network interface setup. For example, if you configure an `eth0` device with the IP address 192.168.100.5 and a network mask of 255.255.255.0, the network 192.168.100.0 is automatically added as part of your routing table by the scripts that set up networking. This automation is helpful, though for complex networks, it may not be sufficient to configure your network in the most effective way. That's why we thought you should know about the basic theory of routing (Chapter 1) and the `route` command (earlier in this chapter).

In the Routing and Gateways page of the Webmin utility you indicate the address of the default router, if you have one, and the device through which that default router should be accessed. If you are on a standalone network segment without connections to other networks, a default router is not necessary.

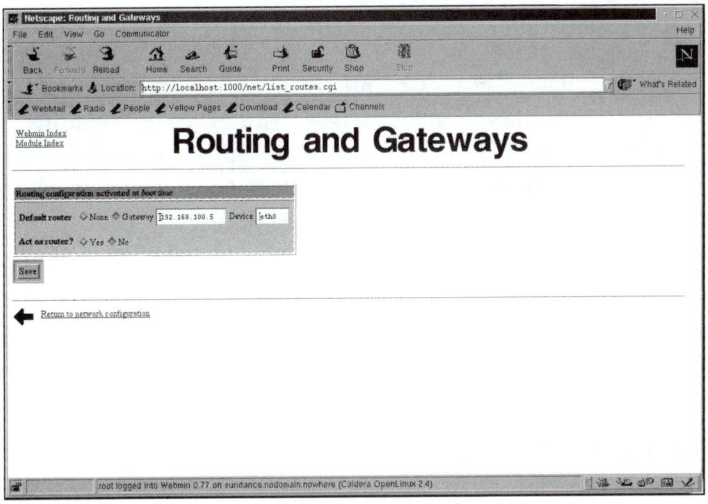

Figure 2-14   The Routing and Gateways page in Webmin

You can also specify here that you want the local machine to act as a router. This is a simple method of routing between networks. It merely says to Linux: "If you see any packets from other computers that aren't destined for the network that they came from, see if you have a routing table entry that can get them to the correct place." The technical term for what the `Act as router? Yes` button does would be "Enable IP Forwarding." **IP forwarding** assumes that you have more than one network interface (for example, two Ethernet cards or an Ethernet card and a modem–based connection to the Internet). When network packets arrive on one of the interfaces, Linux sends them out on the other interface only if IP forwarding is enabled. If it is not, no packets can cross the line, so to speak, between the two interfaces.

Within any recent version of Linux (using a 2.2 or 2.4 kernel), you can enable IP forwarding from the command line by writing a "1" to the appropriate kernel configuration file within the `/proc` directory. Specifically, use this command to see the current setting on your system:

```
cat /proc/sys/net/ipv4/ip_forward
```

Use this command to set the value to 1.

```
echo 1 > /proc/sys/net/ipv4/ip_forward
```

Remember that filenames in the `/proc` subdirectory represent information within the kernel; these filenames do not represent data stored on your hard disk.

A final thought about using graphical tools to set up Linux networking: beyond the two utilities described here, several other graphical networking tools are available for various versions of Linux. For example, the **YAST2** utility is used in SuSE Linux; older versions of Red Hat Linux used the LinuxConf or netconf utility; older versions of Caldera OpenLinux used the COAS administration utility; the Gnome and KDE desktops have various system configuration utilities available as well. The point to remember is that a graphical tool can help you configure networking, but you should still understand what's happening in the background and how to dig deeper into the system in case troubleshooting becomes necessary (it will!). Keep your eyes open for the tools that you prefer to use and that save time in the types of networking environments where you find yourself working.

USING BASIC NETWORKING UTILITIES

With basic networking running smoothly on your Linux system, you're ready to begin exploring the utilities and applications that make it useful. This section provides a description of three popular utilities that you should become familiar with as troubleshooting and informational tools. For each, a brief summary and a few examples are provided. To learn more, you should experiment with these utilities (the projects at the end of this chapter are a good place to start), and also review the online man page documentation when questions arise about how to use them.

The Telnet Remote Login Utility

Telnet is a terminal-emulator program. It allows you to log in to a remote computer as if you were sitting at that computer's keyboard. Once you are logged in, you can view any files that your user account permits you to view. You can also execute any command, including changing or deleting files, or restarting the system.

Telnet is a convenient and powerful part of Linux, but a dire warning is in order: Telnet is not encrypted or encoded to prevent eavesdropping. Everything you do in Telnet can easily be viewed by anyone connected to the same network. In fact, in Chapter 11 we'll see how to do this using utilities included with Linux. Instead of Telnet, you should use the ssh—secure shell— utility, which will be described in more detail in Chapter 11. Until then, consider Telnet a temporary measure and use it with caution, assuming that any information you type (including passwords) may fall into the hands of others.

To use Telnet, you must have a Telnet client that requests a connection to a computer and a Telnet server that accepts and manages that connection. The details of setting up clients and servers are discussed in Chapters 4 and 5. Many Linux systems already have a Telnet server running (though this is considered a security risk). All Linux systems have a Telnet client installed, as do most Windows systems.

The `telnet` command in Linux requires you to enter the hostname or IP address to which you wish to connect. If a connection can be made—that is, if a Telnet server on that host accepts your client's request for a connection—then you are prompted to enter a username and password. Once logged in, you see a command prompt as if you were sitting at the remote computer.

If you want to try a Telnet session from Windows, launch the Telnet program included with some Windows versions or obtain a free Telnet program. (You can search on a site such as *www.tucows.com* for free Windows Telnet client software.) Graphical Telnet programs generally ask for the following information:

- The remote host to which you want to connect. For this field you can enter an IP address or a host name.

- The port number to which you want to connect. By default, the Telnet port—23—is used. You can choose other ports for testing or experimentation as you learn about other services.

- The type of dumb terminal that you want the software to emulate. A standard choice would be a **VT100** terminal. Hundreds of dumb terminal models exist, but VT100 is the most widely supported.

- Username and password. You may be asked to enter a username and password, which is sent to the remote host as part of your login. The Telnet program typically requests that this information be saved, so you don't have to enter it each time you connect to the same remote host. Figure 2-15 shows a Telnet session being started in the Windows Telnet program. (Depending on your version of Windows, the program may differ slightly from that shown in the figure.)

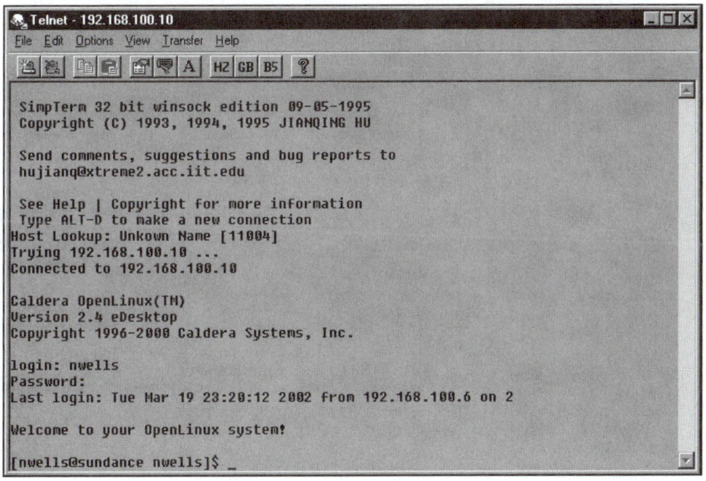

Figure 2-15   The Windows Telnet program with a session in progress

Using `ping` for System Testing

In Chapter 1 you learned about the `echo` message type in the ICMP protocol. ICMP is used to send status or error messages about an IP connection; `echo` is used to send test packets to see whether a remote host can be reached. The utility that you use to send ICMP echo packets is called `ping`.

To use `ping`, just include the hostname or address of the host that you want to contact. For example:

```
ping 198.60.22.20
```

This command sends a series of 64-byte packets to the host with the IP address 198.60.22.20. If the host is reachable via whatever routers are between you and it, the IP stack on that host responds with a message saying "I'm here," and your system prints a message on your screen to show that the remote host is "alive." Another packet is sent every second until you stop the `ping` program. The resulting listing looks like this:

```
PING 198.60.22.20 from 64.24.90.213 : 56(84) bytes of data.
64 bytes from 198.60.22.20: icmp_seq=0 ttl=244 time=319.537
   msec
64 bytes from 198.60.22.20: icmp_seq=1 ttl=244 time=299.984
   msec
64 bytes from 198.60.22.20: icmp_seq=2 ttl=244 time=299.994
   msec
64 bytes from 198.60.22.20: icmp_seq=3 ttl=244 time=300.008
   msec
64 bytes from 198.60.22.20: icmp_seq=4 ttl=244 time=280.005
   msec
64 bytes from 198.60.22.20: icmp_seq=5 ttl=244 time=280.006
   msec
64 bytes from 198.60.22.20: icmp_seq=6 ttl=244 time=279.998
   msec
-- 198.60.22.20 ping statistics --
7 packets transmitted, 7 packets received, 0% packet loss
round-trip min/avg/max/mdev =
279.998/291.298/319.537/10.805 ms
```

When you press Ctrl+C to end the `ping` program, it calculates the statistics that are printed at the end of the listing. It's common to use a series of `ping` commands to test networking. By using these commands in the order given here, you can identify at what point a problem occurs.

The `ping` command on a Windows system simply sends four echo packets and then stops; note that in Linux, `ping` continues until you press Ctrl+C.

- Ping `127.0.0.1` to check that the internal networking stacks are functioning and that networking is enabled in the Linux kernel.

- Ping your own IP address to check that your networking card is configured as expected.

- Ping the IP address of another host on your local network segment to check that your Ethernet card and cable are functioning correctly.

- Ping the IP address of a host on another network segment close by to check that the default gateway or basic routing tables (depending on the complexity of your network) are correctly configured.

- Ping an IP address beyond your organization to check that distant routers are able to work with those in your organization in getting traffic to and from the Internet or other distant networks.

You can also use `ping` with a hostname, as we did in the example above. Ping your own hostname to see that it can be resolved (converted into an IP address). Then ping the hostname for another host on your local network segment, then of a distant host or Internet site. We will explore this more in Chapter 3; the basic idea is the same: ping to hosts further and further away from your system. If something stops working, you know where the error occurred. For example, if you can ping other hosts within your local network segment but not on any other segments, you know that your packet cannot get outside the local segment. This might be caused by bad cabling between segments, a lack of IP forwarding at the router, a bad routing table entry, a firewall entry blocking your traffic, or a few other things. But at least you know where to start looking.

Regarding pinging Internet sites, you should be aware that several types of system attacks in the past have relied on the `ping` command. One example is the "flood ping," which sends many `ping` commands in rapid succession from multiple hosts, overwhelming the server that tries to respond to them. Another example is the "ping of death," in which a single `ping` command with a very large payload is sent to a server; the payload over-flows the memory space allocated to receive ICMP packets and corrupts other parts of the server's memory. Because of attacks like these, a number of hosts on the Internet completely block pings originating from anywhere outside their organization. That is, if you try to ping a site where the system administrator has blocked all ping packets, you will get no response because the server simply drops ICMP echo packets without responding. This isn't very neighborly of them, but to be fair, the `ping` command can put a strain on a network and has been used for some types of malicious attacks; you should use it sparingly on other peoples' systems. To avoid wasted time because of sys-tems that don't respond to `ping`, find a few Internet sites (universities are a good bet) that do respond, then get in the habit of using one of those for a quick test.

Notice now the parts of the `ping` output from the listing shown previously. They include:

- The number of bytes sent in the packet. You can change this using a parameter of `ping`, should you ever need to.

- The hostname (if you included one) and IP address of the host you are pinging.

- A sequence number, starting with 0. ICMP assigns the number and simply keeps counting up sequentially.

- The Time To Live (TTL) of the ICMP packet. This is the number of routers that the packet can pass through before being discarded. The default here—224—is quite high, indicating that you *really* want to reach the host.

- The time elapsed between sending the ICMP echo packet and having it returned. In this example you see a time of about 280 milliseconds (shown as msecs). On fast connections, you often see times below 100 milliseconds; try pinging within your local network and you often see times in the teens. Note that `ping` waits one second between each packet sent, even though the response comes back in much less time.

- The statistics shown after you press Ctrl+C include minimum, maximum, and average time to get a response, plus the number of packets for which no response was received (typically zero percent if you reached the host at all).

The `ping` command has numerous command-line options that let you set parameters such as the number of packets to send before automatically stopping, the time to wait between each packet (the default is one second), the size of packet to send (the default is 64 bytes), and other specialized features that are useful for debugging routing problems. For example, the `-R` option lists all of the intervening routers that your ping packet passed through to reach the destination host. (This is similar to the `traceroute` command described next.)

Using `traceroute` to Examine Routing Patterns

When the information provided by `ping` is not enough to help you figure out a routing problem, `traceroute` is the logical next step. The **traceroute** command carefully tracks each router (each hop) between you and a destination host. This lets you see exactly where the packets are going and how long each hop takes. Sample output from the command `traceroute 198.60.22.77` is shown here:

```
1 192.168.100.5 (192.168.100.5) 2.922 ms 9.798 ms 19.928 ms
2 wdc2-dial7.popsite.net (64.24.80.232) 219.817 ms 199.408
  ms 199.944 ms
3 wdc2-dial7.popsite.net (64.24.80.232) 199.930 ms 209.430
  ms 199.942 ms
4 wdc2-core1.popsite.net (64.24.80.225) 199.995 ms 199.461
  ms 199.923 ms
5 wdc1-core1-p1-0.starnetusa.net (64.24.80.1) 200.004
  ms 199.437 ms 189.952 ms
6 wdc3-core1-pos2-0.starnetusa.net (216.126.145.122)
  199.987 ms 199.401 ms 199.952 ms
7 jsy1-core1-a3-0-2.starnetusa.net (216.126.145.105)
  220.021 ms 949.325 ms 900.048 ms
8 chi1-core1-s4-0.starnetusa.net (216.126.145.113) 1619.974
  ms 3579.417 ms *
```

```
 9 * sjc1-core1-a3-0-2.starnetusa.net (216.126.146.18)
   2045.692 ms 319.424 ms
10 pao1-core1-p6-0.starnetusa.net (216.126.145.97) 360.012
   ms 319.415 ms 339.969 ms
11 xmission-paix.xmission.com (198.32.176.42) 289.961
   ms 1049.435 ms 949.921 ms
12 xmission-paix.xmission.com (204.228.132.29) 819.957
   ms 309.562 ms 309.941 ms
13 core-border.xmission.com (166.70.4.10) 309.973
   ms 309.580 ms 309.887 ms
14 ftp.xmission.com (198.60.22.77) 309.989
   ms 319.627 ms 309.934 ms
```

Each line is numbered. In this example, it took fourteen hops to get from our system to the server *ftp.xmission.com*. The IP address is shown for each router along the way, along with a hostname for that machine if `traceroute` can find one. Three timing values are shown after the IP address for each router. `Traceroute` sends three "probe packets" and shows the length of time that each took to respond. If an asterisk (*) appears in the listing, the router did not respond within the default time limit of five seconds. `Traceroute` tries a maximum of 30 hops to reach a destination, though you can change that number using a command-line parameter.

`Traceroute` relies on the `ttl` field and ICMP "packet timed out" messages to move step-by-step through the Internet to reach the host you are interested in. Because not all systems follow standard practices in using these features, some lines of the `traceroute` output may contain nothing but three asterisks. In most cases, however, `traceroute` is a very useful tool for diagnosing problems such as the following:

- Where a packet stops. You try to reach a certain host, but because of bad routing information, it reaches a certain point on the Internet and doesn't go any further. The output of `traceroute` shows you the last router reached by the packet.

- Where a packet slows down. Your connectivity to a certain site seems unusually slow. `Traceroute` indicates the time to receive a response from each router. The one that takes an inordinate amount of time to respond deserves special attention. (You'll learn in the next chapter how to find out who to call.)

Other problems are possible, of course, but these are two common uses for `traceroute`. Command-line options in `traceroute` include setting the maximum number of routers to try, limiting the time to wait for each response, and indicating that packets cannot be fragmented, which can help you diagnose problems related to packet fragmentation between different types of networks (as discussed in Chapter 1).

Troubleshooting Network Connections

This may surprise you, but you have learned enough already about Linux networking to troubleshoot a variety of problems. Networking can become very complex, and we have not yet delved into many of the hardware issues that could arise (such as cabling problems). Table 2-2, however, lists some common networking problems that you can diagnose and troubleshoot with the tools covered so far. We will expand this list with other troubleshooting tables as you learn more about different aspects of networking, such as DNS in Chapter 3.

Table 2-2   Basic networking troubleshooting review

Trouble	Things to Check
Networking doesn't appear to function at all	Use the `ifconfig` command to see whether networking is up and running; if not, try the network script in `/etc/rc.d/init.d`. (Remember to check things that seem too obvious: Is the cable plugged into the Ethernet card? Is an Ethernet card installed? Is the cable plugged into the wall or a hub?)
The network script doesn't appear to work	Use the `lsmod` command to see whether any network modules are installed in the kernel. If not, use `modprobe -t` as described in this chapter or a graphical utility to install the right kernel module for your networking card.
Can't ping any other systems on the local network segment	Check the cables; check with `ifconfig` whether a valid IP address has been assigned; check the routing tables to see that a route is listed for the local network
Can't ping any system on another segment within the organization	Check the cables at the hub or server room; Check with `ifconfig` to see if a valid IP address is assigned and how that address compares with those of the other network segment (is there a conflict?); does the routing table include a route for the other network that refers to an intermediate router if necessary?
Traffic to another segment seems very slow	Check the routing table to see whether the most direct route is defined; check whether another system has the same IP address assigned; review the output of the `ifconfig` command to see whether a large number of collisions are occurring—if so the network may be overloaded; check `ifconfig` output to see whether a large number of errors are occurring—if so the NIC may be defective; review whether fragmentation problems between the two segments could be slowing down traffic; use `traceroute` to see at what point along the way the transmission slows down significantly

OTHER NETWORKING PROTOCOLS

In later chapters, you will learn a lot about many different protocols designed for different types of information sharing. But two lower-level protocols deserve mention in the same context as the discussion of TCP/IP and routing. These are IPX and AppleTalk.

IPX and Linux

The **Internetwork Packet Exchange (IPX)** protocol was designed by Novell, Inc. based on an older protocol called the Xerox Network System (XNS) protocol. IPX was the dominant protocol on local area networks from about 1985 through the mid-1990s.

2

In the early 1990s, many companies replaced IPX with IP, because IP is the protocol of the Internet and is perceived as a superior network protocol. Novell's products, in fact, now boast "Pure IP" capability, even though IPX has distinct advantages over IP when running a smaller network.

IPX support in Linux is very dependable; most Linux IPX software was created by a former Novell engineer. Not much development work is going on any longer, however, because of the lack of demand. If you work with NetWare networks, you can use Linux to communicate with NetWare servers as a client, act as a NetWare file or print server, or route IPX network traffic. This section describes the basics of IPX; Chapter 5 describes the additional software you can use to emulate a NetWare client or server. For complete information on setting up IPX on Linux, review the IPX HOWTO document, which you can find at *www.ibiblio.org/mdw/HOWTO/IPX-HOWTO.html*.

IPX avoids all of the addressing challenges of IP, such as the need to assign and manage IP addresses and the shortage of IP addresses around the world. It does this by using the hardware address of the network card (the MAC address of an Ethernet card, for example) as the address of the host (called the node ID within the IPX addressing scheme). Each network segment is assigned a network ID by an IPX router—frequently the one built into every NetWare server. Each host is uniquely identified by an IPX address consisting of the network address followed by the node ID (the MAC address of the host). This arrangement does lack some of the flexibility of IP, and it's perhaps not as suitable for a worldwide network, but it is a lot easier to manage for a network of a few hundred or perhaps even a few thousand systems.

To handle routing, IPX uses two additional protocols: the Routing Information Protocol (RIP) and the **Service Advertising Protocol (SAP)**. These protocols help an IPX-based server gather information about other systems' network addresses and available network services. These protocols regularly broadcast information, so they tend to stress a network with a large number of hosts. But again, they do their job without much work from a system administrator.

IPX hosts can automatically "configure themselves" by looking for packets broadcasted from IPX servers and IPX routers. You can make Linux an IPX-capable client in this way, or you can make Linux an IPX router or IPX server. IPX must be enabled in the Linux kernel, which normally means recompiling the kernel. Do not expect IPX to be part of your Linux system, because relatively few Linux users need this functionality.

Once IPX is enabled in the kernel, you can review IPX status by viewing the IPX information files in the directory **/proc/net**. A set of utilities for managing IPX is available, as described in the IPX HOWTO document referred to earlier. These include:

- **ipx_configure** enables or disables automatic IPX configure via broadcast information from an IPX server on the same network.

- **ipx_interface** lets you add, delete, or check IPX interfaces manually, much like the **ifconfig** command for TCP/IP.

- `ipx_internal_net` helps you set up an internal IPX network, similar to the loopback device. This is used in IPX networks as part of the routing mechanism to set what is called the "primary interface."

- `ipx_route` manually modifies the IPX routing table, much like the `route` command for IP.

The IPX protocol on Linux is quite flexible. You can use IPX over a PPP connection; you can also connect two IPX networks over an IP connection like the Internet.

Apple Networking and Linux

Another well-designed but less-popular networking system is that of the Apple Macintosh. Anyone who has used the Macintosh may wonder about the complex maneuvers needed to set up a PC network (running Windows or Linux). A Mac provides true plug-and-play networking. But as with IPX, that simplicity doesn't scale to something like the worldwide Internet, so AppleTalk is used on a limited number of computers at this point.

AppleTalk is the name of the networking protocol used by Macintosh computers. On Linux you can install the **Netatalk** package to allow Macintosh computers to recognize Linux (have it show up on the Mac desktop as an available shared resource). Another program called **afpfs** lets Linux users access Macintosh resources. However, afpfs is not currently being developed and is not therefore supported by the latest Linux kernels (2.4).

Netatalk has a lower level of automation than TCP/IP. As with IPX, you need to recompile the Linux kernel to include Netatalk support. You also need to compile the Netatalk software and edit several configuration files to set up security and define the parts of your Linux file system that you want to share with Macintosh users on your network. To get started, carefully review the Netatalk HOWTO document and download the appropriate software as directed. See *www.anders.com/projects/netatalk/* for the details.

 You may find a prepackaged version of Netatalk for your Linux system. Although you still need to update your kernel, this can save a lot of effort in compiling and configuring the rest of the Netatalk package. You can begin by searching for Netatalk on *rpmfind.net*, which lists several dozen packages for different Linux distributions.

CHAPTER SUMMARY

- Linux networking devices are created directly in the Linux kernel when a kernel module supporting a type of networking is loaded.

- Many types of networking are supported in Linux, though the most widely used for standard LANs is Ethernet.

2

❑ The **modprobe** command is used to add a networking module to the Linux kernel. The currently-loaded kernel modules can be listed using the **lsmod** command.

❑ Sometimes installing a kernel module requires that you include parameters to help the module locate or operate the networking hardware.

❑ The **ifconfig** command sets up a networking interface in the Linux kernel or displays the current setup for all configured interfaces.

❑ The **route** command establishes entries in the kernel IP routing table or displays the current routing table entries.

❑ The **arp** command lets you view the hardware address entries in the system's ARP cache. These entries are used by IP to route a packet to its final destination correctly.

❑ A number of networking scripts are used to streamline the configuration of Linux networking, making it more flexible and robust. The main networking control script is **/etc/rc.d/init.d/network**, or a script in a similar location.

❑ Networking configuration parameters are stored in files within the **/etc/sysconfig/ network-scripts** subdirectory. These files can be edited directly, but are usually modified using a configuration tool of some sort, such as Webmin.

❑ IP aliasing occurs when multiple IP addresses are assigned to the same physical network interface (such as a single Ethernet card).

❑ Red Hat Linux includes a powerful Network Administration Tool; Caldera uses the Webmin browser-based interface to configure networking; SuSE uses YaST. Other Linux versions use a variety of graphical tools to configure networking.

❑ Enabling IP forwarding allows Linux to move packets between multiple network interfaces on the same host, effectively permitting a system to act as a router.

❑ The **telnet** utility lets you connect to a remote host as if you were sitting at that host, but Telnet is not secure or encrypted and must be used with caution.

❑ **Ping** is a utility that uses the ICMP **echo** command to check whether a remote host is accessible and alive. Ping is a widely used tool for testing network connections, though some systems on the Internet do not respond to **ping** because of previous attacks that used this utility.

❑ The **traceroute** command displays each of the intervening routers between your host and another host you wish to contact. **Traceroute** provides information that helps troubleshoot problems connecting to a remote host or with slow connections.

❑ IPX is a useful protocol that originated with Novell's NetWare operating system. It is supported in Linux, though not widely used.

❑ AppleTalk is supported in Linux via the Netatalk package, which you can add to Linux so that a Macintosh computer can see and access Linux resources.

KEY TERMS

/etc/rc.d/init.d/network — The main networking control script in Linux. The exact location of this script may vary within different Linux systems, though this is a standard location for it.

/etc/sysconfig — Directory in which networking configuration files and scripts are stored, specifically in the subdirectory **network-scripts** and the file **networking**.

/lib/modules — Directory in which all of the available kernel modules for Linux are stored.

afpfs — A software package that lets Linux users access Macintosh resources. This software is still available for download but, because it is not currently being developed, is not supported by the latest Linux kernels (2.4).

AppleTalk — The networking protocol used by Apple Macintosh computers. AppleTalk is supported in Linux via the Netatalk package.

arp — A command that displays or alters the contents of the arp cache. Used mainly for troubleshooting network connectivity.

arp cache — A list of IP address-to-hardware mappings maintained by the ARP protocol to assist in routing packets.

device driver — Software installed in the Linux kernel that knows how to communicate with a physical or logical device. A logical networking device is used to create a communications channel that any program can use for networking.

Device File System (DevFS) — A system for handling all devices in Linux kernels beginning with version 2.4. This system is a good example of what has always been done with networking devices.

eth0 — The device name in Linux for the first Ethernet card installed in a host.

frame relay — A technology used to provide dedicated high-speed Internet connectivity via telephone wires.

ifcfg-eth0 — A file, usually located in **/etc/sysconfig/network-scripts/**, that contains information to configure the first Ethernet interface.

ifconfig — The interface configuration utility that configures a networking interface within the Linux kernel or that lists all currently configured network interfaces.

ifdown — Script used to shut down individual networking interfaces. Generally used by other scripts such as **/etc/rc.d/init.d/network** rather than directly by a user.

ifup — Script used to start individual networking interfaces. Generally used by other scripts such as **/etc/rc.d/init.d/network** rather than directly by a user.

insmod — Command used to install a module into a running Linux kernel. It may include parameters that provide additional information to the module being installed.

Internetwork Packet Exchange (IPX) — A protocol designed by Novell, Inc., based on an older protocol called the Xerox Network System (XNS) protocol. IPX was the dominant protocol on local area networks for many years and is fully supported in Linux. It uses the network hardware address as a host ID, thus simplifying network configuration.

2

Inverse ARP (InARP) — A method of using ARP that allows one host to obtain the IP address of another host when it knows the physical address.

IP aliasing — A networking feature that allows a single physical interface to have more than one IP address assigned to it.

IP forwarding — A feature of Linux networking that instructs the Linux kernel to send network packets out on whichever network interface the routing tables dictate. Without IP forwarding, packets arriving on a given network interface can only be sent out on the same interface.

kernel modules — Parts of the Linux kernel, such as device drivers, that can be loaded or unloaded while Linux is running using a command such as `modprobe`.

LinuxConf — The utility that was used in Red Hat prior to version 7.2 to configure networking. Though it is still included in Red Hat, `neat` is now more popular.

`lo` — Device name of the loopback network device.

localhost — The name assigned to the loopback device, corresponding to IP address 127.0.0.1. Often used interchangeably with the term *loopback device*.

loopback device — A special "logical" network device used to move packets within a single host. The IP address of the loopback device is 127.0.0.1. Often used interchangeably with the term *localhost*.

`lsmod` — Command used to list the modules that are loaded in your kernel at that moment.

metric — A value assigned to a network interface to guide dynamic routing decisions about when to use that interface. A higher metric means an interface is less likely to be used if other interfaces are also available.

`modprobe` — The command to load a kernel module while automatically checking for and loading dependent modules.

`neat` — The command-line invocation of the Red Hat Network Administration Tool.

Netatalk — A software package for Linux that allows Macintosh computers to recognize Linux (have it show up on the Mac desktop as an available shared resource).

Parallel Line Internet Protocol (PLIP) — A protocol that relies on a parallel port to transmit network data, often to connect two computers in a simple, inexpensive network.

parameters — Command-line information provided when loading a kernel module to help the module locate and recognize the hardware it is designed to work with.

`ping` — The utility used to send ICMP echo packets for network testing.

Point-to-Point Protocol (PPP) — A protocol that allows a host to tie directly to a single computer, making a network of two systems. PPP is used most often with a modem providing the underlying physical connection to the second computer.

proxy ARP — The feature of ARP that allows a host to respond to a request for *another* host's hardware address. Normally, a host only responds to an ARP request if its own information is being requested.

Red Hat Network Administration Tool — A graphical interface provided in Red Hat Linux that is used to manage hardware devices (the kernel modules used to access them), including parameters needed for each device, plus the network addresses associated with them. It can be started from the command line using `neat`.

Reverse ARP (RARP) — A method of using ARP that allows a host (generally one that has no local storage, such as a diskless workstation) to retrieve its IP address by sending out its own network hardware address.

`route` — A command that displays or configures the routing table within the Linux kernel.

routing daemon — A program that automatically generates routing table entries based on information received over the network via protocols dedicated to routing.

Serial Line Internet Protocol (SLIP) — A protocol that relies on a serial port as the underlying physical connection used to transmit network data, usually over a modem to an ISP.

Service Advertising Protocol (SAP) — A protocol used on IPX networks to distribute information about what network services are available on each server within a network.

T-1 — A high-speed transmission format (1.544 Mb/s) available through your local telephone company, usually for a few hundred dollars per month.

T-3 — A high-speed transmission format (45 Mb/s) available through your local telephone company, usually for several thousand dollars per month.

Telnet — A terminal emulator program that allows a user to log in to a remote computer as if sitting at that computer's keyboard.

`traceroute` — A command used to list each router (each hop) that a packet passes through between a source host and a destination host.

VT100 — The most widely supported dumb terminal standard.

Webmin — A browser-based utility that can manage many system functions, including network configuration. Included by default with Caldera OpenLinux products.

YAST2 — A utility provided in SuSE Linux that includes network configuration tools.

REVIEW QUESTIONS

1. A key advantage of IPX over IP is that:

   a. IPX does not require configuration of a host ID because it uses the network hardware address.

   b. Even IPv6 does not provide as large an address space as IPX.

   c. Linux has stronger support for IPX than for ICMP.

   d. IPX routing relies on RIP instead of just the `route` command.

2. Networking devices differ from other Linux devices in that:

    a. Networking devices use a different set of major and minor device numbers than devices that do not rely on kernel modules.

    b. Networking devices can transmit data much faster than other types of devices.

    c. Networking devices are not directly visible in the /dev subdirectory, but are created on the fly when a networking device module is loaded into the kernel.

    d. Networking devices can only be accessed via shell scripts.

3. Modprobe is preferable to insmod for loading modules because:

    a. Modprobe allows you to include module parameters on the command line and insmod does not.

    b. Modprobe loads any dependent modules automatically before the requested module.

    c. Insmod is not supported in all versions of Linux, but modprobe is.

    d. Insmod can interfere with operation of the ifconfig command on token ring systems.

4. From the Hardware tab in WebMin, what is the next step to reconfigure the IP addresses of a network interface?

    a. Choose the Network Configuration icon.

    b. Choose the Network Interfaces icon.

    c. Select the hardware interface for which you want to enter new IP addresses.

    d. Select whether you want to modify the active interface parameters or the boot-up interface parameters.

5. Which of the following directories is most likely to contain kernel modules for networking devices?

    a. /lib/modules/networking

    b. /etc/sysconfig/network-scripts

    c. /proc/sys/net

    d. /lib/modules/2.4.7-10/kernel/drivers/net

6. When using telnet you might refer to VT100 because it is:

    a. a standard protocol designation used by Telnet

    b. the port used by default to connect to the Telnet server

    c. the most commonly used terminal emulation standard

    d. the speed at which terminal emulator connections are typically handled

7. In which circumstance would kernel parameters most likely be needed to make a NIC function correctly in Linux?

   a. You are using an older, used ISA NIC that has a special feature allowing automatic IRQ mapping in software.

   b. You are using a brand-new PCI NIC that is identical to an established model.

   c. The documentation with your new NIC explains that Windows-based software is provided to help you configure the card.

   d. You want to do IP aliases and IP forwarding on your network.

8. Explain the difference between the TX packets and TX bytes lines in the output of `ifconfig`.

9. Which is not a valid `ifconfig` command?

   a. `ifconfig eth0 up`

   b. `ifconfig eth0 192.168.100.1 netmask 255.255.255.0 broadcast 255.255.255.0`

   c. `ifconfig`

   d. `ifconfig eth0 if-up`

10. Which information field is not part of the output of the route command?

    a. the gateway to reach the specified network

    b. the MAC address of the interface used to transfer packets to the specified network

    c. the interface through which the specified network can be reached

    d. the network address to which each routing table entry applies

11. Which statement is true about the following command:

    ```
    route add -net 192.168.20.0 netmask 255.255.255.0
    gw 192.168.10.1 dev eth0.
    ```

    a. It is valid and defines the router that can reach network 192.168.20.0.

    b. It is valid and defines a default gateway for all traffic not destined for network 192.168.20.0.

    c. It is invalid because it does not specify the host IP address of the source of the packets to be routed.

    d. It is invalid in format because it lacks needed dashes before command-line options.

12. The `plip` networking device refers to:

    a. Protocol Layer Internet Proxy activity

    b. ProxyARP Layered Internet Protocol transmissions

    c. Parallel Line Internet Protocol support

    d. multiple, parallel SLIP channels

13. Distinguish between RARP and InARP.

14. You would use the `arp` command to:

   a. send a hardware address to a remote host per an ARP protocol request

   b. turn on and off ARP functionality for your network

   c. collect hostname-to-IP address mappings for each of the hosts on your local network

   d. view or modify the arp cache containing hardware address to IP address mappings

15. Scripts such as `/etc/rc.d/init.d/network` and their corresponding data files are used to control networking because:

   a. using `ifconfig` and `route` is too complicated for the average user

   b. the `ifconfig` and `route` commands alone don't complete the network configuration

   c. using scripts allows flexibility and power in managing multiple interfaces, firewall settings, and peripheral requirements that involve many diverse parts of Linux

   d. by relying on scripts, graphical utilities can create a more user-friendly environment that makes system administrators more efficient

16. The correct device designation for an IP alias to the first Ethernet card is:

   a. `eth00`

   b. `eth0:0`

   c. `Ethernet II`

   d. `eth1:0`

17. In the Red Hat Network Configuration Utility (`neat`), the Hardware tab includes:

   a. a list of all networking hardware for which a module is currently installed

   b. a list of all available networking modules in Red Hat Linux

   c. a list of parameters that are available for currently installed modules

   d. the IP addresses of each installed hardware interface

18. The loopback device is assigned the IP address:

   a. 255.255.255.0

   b. 127.0.0.1

   c. 127.0.0.0

   d. any IP address beginning with 192.168

19. IP forwarding is enabled by which command:

   a. `ifconfig eth0 ip_forward`

   b. `arp ip_forward`

   c. `route add default ip_forward -net 192.168.10.0 netmask 255.255.255.0`

   d. `echo 1 > /proc/sys/net/ipv4/ip_forward`

20. Which utility cannot be used to configure network interfaces?

    a. YAST2

    b. netconf

    c. COAS

    d. ping

21. Telnet is considered dangerous because:

    a. It provides access to networking stacks, which only the root user should have access to.

    b. It transmits data—including passwords—without encrypting them, so anyone on the network can see them by using special software.

    c. It causes an increased number of Ethernet collisions by ramping up network traffic with broadcast messages to the local network segment.

    d. It requires that a user provide a password to gain access to a remote system.

22. Ping is used to test networking connections by:

    a. trying to contact systems that are progressively further from your host to see if any networking problems occur

    b. flooding the network with traffic to see if it has sufficient bandwidth

    c. testing whether remote servers are configured to respond to ICMP echo-request packets

    d. noting the route that packets take when responding that they are "alive"

23. `Traceroute` is a useful troubleshooting tool because:

    a. All data sent by `traceroute` is fully encrypted, so it can be used safely on open networks.

    b. It reports the ARP cache of each system it contacts.

    c. It reports each router that a packet passes through to a destination IP address, along with the time needed to reach that router.

    d. It uses UDP to report errors generated by the IP stack of intermittent routers that may be misconfigured and slow down packets as they traverse large networks.

24. If you cannot ping a host on a different segment of your local network, you probably wouldn't bother checking:

    a. the cable connections at the hub or in the server room

    b. whether `ifconfig` indicates that the host has a valid IP address that does not conflict with any other host on the network

    c. whether the routing tables of the host and the router include the proper entries to tie the segments together

    d. whether the `ping` command was subject to fragmentation by the router in trying to reach the other segment

25. Define what the Netatalk package does for a Linux system.

HANDS-ON PROJECTS

In the following projects you experiment with the networking configuration of your host. You must be aware that changing your IP address causes your networking to cease functioning correctly. It may also cause someone else's networking to cease functioning! Check with your instructor or system administrator before completing these projects. In addition, note that we have used standard file locations when discussing networking files. Some Linux systems may place these files in slightly different subdirectories. You should be able to locate them by exploring the /etc subdirectory or asking someone who is familiar with your Linux distribution.

Project 2-1

In this project, you explore the Address Resolution Protocol on your host. To complete this project, you should have a network connection configured with at least one other host on the network. An Internet connection is used for the last part of the project, but is not strictly necessary.

1. From any Linux command line, enter this command:

   ```
   arp -a
   ```

   This displays the contents of the ARP cache on your Linux system. The result may be nothing—the cache is probably empty at this point if you have not done any networking in the last few minutes. Each entry is saved only for about two minutes.

2. If the ARP cache is not empty, note the contents carefully. See if you can identify a neighbor on the network (in your computer lab, for example) that is not listed in the output of the command. Obtain that neighbor's IP address.

3. Ping your neighbor using a command such as this (substitute the neighbor's IP address for 192.168.100.45):

   ```
   ping 192.168.100.45
   ```

4. Run the **arp** command a second time:

   ```
   arp -a
   ```

   Do you see your neighbor's system listed (as indicated by an IP address that you recognize)?

5. Ping an Internet site such as 155.99.1.2 or 192.20.4.70.

6. Run **arp -a** again. Why is no additional entry included for the new site that you pinged?

Project 2-2

For this project you need a running Linux system with Internet access on which you can log in as **root**. You should open a command-line window to complete this project.

1. Obtain the IP address of a host (not your own) within your computer lab or your organization, but not on the Internet.

2. Execute the **traceroute** command using this IP address and note the times displayed for reaching each point on that route to that host.

3. Locate a business that is headquartered or located near you, such as a bank in your city or the local government Web site. (Don't choose your own school or organization. You may want to ask your instructor for a suggestion or use an Internet search site to help you find the Internet address for the entity you select.)

4. Use a **traceroute** command to see how packets reach that site from your host. If your system has DNS configured already, feel free to use a command such as this, rather than using only an IP address:

   ```
   traceroute www.uva.edu
   ```

For some sites, you may see a number of asterisks instead of the times you expect to see. Review the man page for **traceroute** to learn what these indicate.

5. You are likely to see a long list of unusual names for the routers that the packets pass through to reach someone's site close to you. Can you identify where these routers are physically located by their names (that is, which city and state they are located in)? In Chapter 3 you will learn about the **whois** command to help you do this.

6. Why might a packet travel so far to get across town? How could the routing be improved?

Project 2-3

For this project you need a running Linux system with Internet access. You should open a command-line window to complete this project. After each step shown, make a note about what its successful completion indicates about your network. To complete the last few steps (as indicated) you need to have **root** access and your instructor's permission, as these steps may create a heavy load on your network.

1. Run the **ifconfig** command to view your networking devices. See that you have both **lo** and **eth0** devices configured.

2. Ping your loopback device using its IP address.

3. Ping your own IP address.

4. If you are working in a classroom or computer lab, ask your neighbor for his or her IP address, then ping their host.

5. If your instructor gives you permission to continue, make sure you are logged in as **root**.

6. Use the **ping** command with the **-f** option, for flood. This sends pings (ICMP echo-request packets) as fast as possible. Each period that is printed on your screen after you execute this command indicates one dropped packet (because the host being pinged cannot respond quickly enough).

7. If possible, have your neighbor try to complete a networking task such as opening a browser window and viewing a graphically intensive page. The flood ping places a heavy load on the network and should be used with caution. This is why some system administrators block pings, and why you will want to learn in Chapter 11 how to do the same yourself.

Project 2-4

For this project you need an Internet connection and a Web browser.

Suppose you have an Intel NIC, model i82557 (Ether Express Pro 100). You want to know if it is compatible with Linux, and what kernel module supports this card in case it doesn't configure automatically when you install Linux.

1. In your Web browser, visit *hardware.redhat.com*.

2. Choose **Hardware Compatibility List**.

3. Choose **Complete Listing**. You could also choose Certified Hardware, which would provide you with more information about using this card with Linux, based on tests by Red Hat Software, Inc., but since you don't know if the card is even compatible with Linux, your best bet is to start with the complete hardware listing.

4. From the drop-down list of hardware manufacturers at the bottom of the page that appears, select **Intel**. You don't need to click anything else; choosing a manufacturer automatically goes to the next Web page.

5. A list of categories for Intel appears showing all the types of hardware that Intel manufactures. Select **Network Device/Controller**.

6. Among the 30 or so entries that appear for Intel NICs, locate your model, **i82557** (Ether Express Pro 100). Make certain you are looking at a line that refers to the x86 architecture (a standard PC) rather than the Alpha architecture (a different type of CPU). Click the link.

7. Is this card supported in Linux? If so, what kernel module supports this card? What caveats apply when using this card in Linux?

Project 2-5

For this project you need to be connected to an Ethernet network and have the permission of your instructor and a static IP address assignment to use when creating an IP alias. (You cannot create an IP alias if you are using DHCP to obtain an IP address for your host.) You must be logged in as **root** to complete this project.

1. Run the **ifconfig** command to see that you have **eth0** configured.

2. Change to the directory **/etc/sysconfig/network-scripts**:

   `cd /etc/sysconfig/network-scripts`

3. Copy the configuration file for the eth0 interface as a basis for creating a new interface called **eth0:0**, which is an IP alias to the same physical Ethernet card.

   `cp ifcfg-eth0 ifcfg-eth0:0`

4. Open the file **ifcfg-eth0:0** in a text editor.

5. Change the **DEVICE** parameter from **eth0** to read instead **eth0:0**.

6. Change the **IPADDR** parameter to reflect the new IP address provided by your instructor. Remember, if you simply choose a random IP address, you may cause networking problems for others in your lab or on the Internet.

7. Restart networking by running the network script with start and stop (or restart on some Linux distributions):

   `/etc/rc.d/init.d/network stop`
   `/etc/rc.d/init.d/network start`

8. Run the **ifconfig** command. Notice that you now have a new interface, **eth0:0**.

9. Ping the IP address of **eth0**. Ping the IP address of eth0:0. In later chapters you will learn how you can use an IP alias to make management of multiple Web sites easier.

10. Return to the **/etc/sysconfig/network-scripts** directory if you have left it:

    `cd /etc/sysconfig/network-scripts`

11. Delete the file you created, confirming the deletion if prompted:

    `rm ifcfg-eth0:0`

12. Restart networking a second time:

    `/etc/rc.d/init.d/network stop`
    `/etc/rc.d/init.d/network start`

13. Run the **ifconfig** command to verify that you once again have only two networking devices: **lo** and **eth0**.

CASE PROJECTS

You have been hired as a consultant by the law firm of Snow, Sleet, and Hale, based in Fairbanks, Alaska. The firm has been in business for many years, but is just now realizing the need to upgrade its information technology infrastructure. The firm consists of three offices, two in Fairbanks and one in Juneau. The Fairbanks headquarters is the largest, with 40 attorneys plus support staff of paralegals, secretaries, librarians, and others. They are divided into two practice groups, one for environmental work and another for energy work relating to oil, natural gas, hydrothermal, and hydroelectric. The work of the two groups doesn't intermingle much, though the attorneys from the two groups occasionally have a common client. All staff members share email, of course, and occasionally need to access the same files. The managing partner tells you that she isn't ready to provide Internet access to the company as a whole. (A few attorneys have a private modem connection for legal research, but you needn't be concerned about that yet.) The second Fairbanks office is located about two miles away from headquarters. It consists of 10 lawyers who also do energy work, almost exclusively for a large company that occupies the same building. The Juneau office is relatively new and focuses on government-related work at the state capitol. It consists of 7 lawyers and a few support staff.

Based on the volume of network traffic you anticipate over the next four years or so, you have already decided on using standard 100 Mb/s Ethernet cards in each computer, with new CAT 6 cabling throughout the office. You have also planned for a high-speed connection between all three offices (don't worry about the specifics of the connection at this point).

1. Your immediate question is how to set up the three offices to make the best use of the network bandwidth so that everyone has fast access to the information they use most, with perhaps slower access to information they need less often. Diagram the network segments as you would arrange them, noting your reasons for the arrangement. Within the parameters described above, you can assume a physical arrangement of personnel within each office so that it suits your plan. Try to plan for the placement of hubs and routers, as well as how segments are arranged. Consider also these questions: Why might you consider or avoid IPX as a network format? What questions would you ask the managing partner about future growth plans before solidifying your network arrangement? What contingency plans could you make based on her responses? This scenario leaves many questions unanswered that will be addressed in future chapters. What additional questions come to mind that you may not have adequate information to answer yet?

2. As law firms are wont to do, Snow, Sleet, and Hale has merged with another firm: Sand & Son, located in Amarillo, Texas. Sand & Son is an energy law firm of 10 attorneys serving mainly oil companies. The two firms have several common clients and feel the merger will strengthen their position among clients seeking energy law specialists. Sand & Son has a fairly new office network for its 10 lawyers and staff. It runs on Token Ring at 4 Mb/s. They have no Internet access. Assuming that you set up a high-speed network connection between Texas and Alaska, how will you incorporate Sand & Son into the existing corporate network? How will the need to integrate this office affect existing network topology? Will you need additional routers? Will you need to reconfigure anyone's IP addresses? What about possible packet fragmentation and slow data transfers between offices? What other problems might the Token Ring network pose?

3. One year later, the managing partner concedes to your recommendation. The entire firm must have Internet access to work effectively for their clients. Make some simple assumptions about the costs of different types of connections such as a modem or a T-1 line, then consider questions such as these: How can you add Internet access to your network design? How many connection points do you anticipate? What new problems arise because of how you set up the segments and routing? Would you have been better off setting things up differently initially if you had known that this requirement would come up, or would that have made things too inefficient in the intervening year?

CONFIGURING CLIENT SERVICES

After reading this chapter and completing the exercises you will be able to:

♦ Configure DNS name resolution

♦ Configure dial-up network access using PPP

♦ Understand client services such as DHCP and LDAP

♦ Use remote graphical applications and remote dial-up authentication

♦ Use common client tools such as Linux Web browsers and email clients

In this chapter, you move to the higher conceptual levels of networking—beyond the level of the TCP/IP protocol. Here you will use applications that rely on the networking technologies you learned about in Chapters 1 and 2.

The first part of this chapter describes tasks that must be accomplished prior to using common networking applications. For example, you learn about setting up DNS name resolution, so you can use names instead of IP addresses to refer to hosts on the network.

In the second part of the chapter, you learn about specific Linux client services that let you view Web pages, run graphical applications, get your email, or remotely execute Linux commands on another computer.

SETTING UP NAME RESOLUTION

In Chapters 1 and 2, you might have recognized that most of the discussion left out an important part of networking: the system that lets you use a name like *www.yahoo.com* instead of an IP address like 143.13.55.12. Unless you're in the habit of memorizing your credit card numbers, IP addresses alone are probably not how you want to refer to hosts on the network. (Or on the Internet; imagine the advertisement for a new movie: "See us online at http://178.43.231.27"!) Although Chapter 1 mentions the domain name server, DNS, we omitted details to avoid piling on too much at one time. Now we pick up that discussion again.

The domain name service is implemented by a domain name server, which you will learn to set up on Linux in Chapter 6. The purpose of a domain name server is expressed by this exchange: A client sends a request to a DNS server saying, "I need to contact domain name X; what is the corresponding IP address?" The DNS server then responds (if it can) with the IP address. A client may also send an IP address to a DNS server and ask for the corresponding domain name. This is a security feature called **reverse DNS** that you'll learn more about in Chapter 6.

The term **domain name** loosely refers to the name of multiple hosts on the Internet that are referred to collectively, such as *ibm.com* or *utah.edu*. But let's look more precisely at the terms used by DNS. In Chapter 1 you learned that a domain is a collection of computers that can be accessed using a common name; a logical grouping of hosts. Domains have several levels. The most widely known top-level domain is probably .com, which refers to commercial addresses in the U.S. Table 3-1 shows some top-level domains (but not all—over 200 different countries each have a top-level domain name).

Table 3-1 Examples of top-level domains

Top-Level Domain Name	Example	Description
.com	www.ibm.com	Commercial organization (business)
.gov	www.state.gov	U.S. federal government
.edu	www.ucla.edu	Postsecondary educational institution
.mil	www.army.mil	U.S. military
.org	www.un.org	Organization, usually nonprofit or otherwise not a business
.net	www.internic.net	Networking service
.us	www.co.arlington.va.us	Geographical domain that coexists with other domains in the U.S.; used by most state governments
.jp	www.sony.jp	Japan
.it	www.maserati.it	Italy
.de	www.bmw.de	Germany

New top-level domain names have been debated for several years. The new domains .biz, .info, and .name were recently added, with others under consideration. You can see a discussion of top-level domains by visiting *www.rfc-editor.org* and reviewing RFC-1591 and RFC-3071. To see all the country-specific codes, visit *www.iso.org* and do a Standards Search for ISO-3166.

3

Within a top-level domain, an organization also has its own domain or domains. For example, IBM Corporation controls the *ibm.com* domain. IBM may also make smaller (sub) domains, such as *marketing.ibm.com* or *engineering.ibm.com*. You should think of a domain name as corresponding roughly to a network ID, or part of a network ID, because a domain contains multiple hosts. (Of course, many domains also refer to hosts in multiple networks.) The organization that controls a domain (such as ibm.com) decides all of the subdomains within that domain.

Each host on a network is also assigned a name, called its **hostname**. The hostname is arbitrary, although sometimes a system administrator assigns one to you. Many administrators use a series of related words to name their servers, such as the names of plants, cities, planets, bands, inventors, poets, etc.

When you combine a hostname with the name of the domain of which the host is a part, you create a **fully qualified domain name (FQDN)**. A common example would be *www.ibm.com*. This FQDN refers to the host called *www* within the domain *ibm.com*. Some FQDNs may be much longer; schools often have labs within departments within colleges, so a FQDN might be *edison.tomahawk.ucc.cs.utah.edu*. The first word (edison) is the hostname; the rest is the domain of which the host is a part. The parts of the FQDN are always separated by periods.

You can refer more casually to a name such as *www.ibm.com* as the name of the server, but you should understand the precise terms described above. You will learn more about how domain names are organized in Chapter 6. For now, you'll learn how to set up Linux so that it can query a DNS server to resolve a domain name into an IP address. **Resolving** is the process of converting a domain name to an IP address, or vice versa.

Configuring the DNS Resolver Manually

The **resolver** is the client part of DNS: it makes requests to a DNS server so that other programs on your system can use the IP address of a given server to make a network connection. Networked programs such as a Web browser automatically use the resolver in Linux to resolve domain names into IP addresses.

If you included a DNS server address when installing Linux, the resolver should already be configured. You can test it by pinging another system using a hostname instead of an IP address. For example, enter `ping www.novell.com`.

The resolver is configured by a single file in Linux: **/etc/resolv.conf** (notice that "resolve" is missing an "e" in the filename). You configure the resolver by storing the IP address of one or more DNS servers in the **resolv.conf** file, preceded by the keyword **nameserver**. A keyword is simply a word to which the program reading the configuration file attaches a special meaning. You must obtain these addresses from a system administrator or an ISP that maintains a DNS server. You can use any DNS server on the Internet that allows you access, but the closer the server is to your local network segment, the faster the responses are to resolver requests. You can include up to three DNS servers in **resolv.conf**, each on a separate line. The resolver tries to reach each of the servers in the order you list them until a request succeeds.

You can also include other items in **resolv.conf**, such as the domain name of which your host is a part. This information guides the resolver in determining exactly what hostname it should resolve. Because a DNS server often maintains information for a number of domains (including the domain name that you are coming from), it can make many searches quicker. You can include multiple domain names to search using the **search** keyword. They must all be on a single line or only the last one is used. On most Linux systems you can list up to six domains to search.

The format of **resolv.conf** entries is straightforward, as shown in this example:

```
domain xmission.com
nameserver 198.60.22.2
nameserver 10.21.105.1
```

You can change the **resolv.conf** file in any text editor. This configuration file is checked before each query, so if you make a change in **/etc/resolv.conf**, you don't need to take any other action for the change to take effect.

The **search** line in **/etc/resolv.conf** is optional. If you don't include it, the resolver uses your local domain name when trying to resolve the name in question to an IP address. You can also review the man page for **resolv.conf** to learn about the **options** keyword, which you can include to control things such as the length of time that the resolver waits for a response from a name server and the number of retries it makes before giving up. Another option, **rotate**, causes the resolver to use each of the listed name servers in turn instead of always trying the first one listed. This spreads the load out among several name servers, which may be appropriate in some settings.

Linux includes a number of utilities for researching DNS problems. These include dnsquery, nslookup, dig, whois, and host. Because these utilities report a lot of complex information from a DNS server, we'll postpone describing them until we've walked through configuring a Linux DNS server in Chapter 6.

The hosts File

The DNS resolver is actually the more complicated way to convert an IP address to a domain name. The simpler method is to store the IP addresses and corresponding domain names in a text file on your host. This file is called **/etc/hosts**. By default, it contains only the hostname **localhost** and your own host's name (on some versions of Linux). All of the possible names that can be used to refer to the listed IP address are included on the same line, separated by spaces. A sample file from Caldera OpenLinux is shown here:

```
# Do not remove the following line, or various programs
# that require network functionality will fail.
127.0.0.1          sundance xmission.com localhost
```

When you have a small network, you can create a **hosts** file that contains each host and the IP address of that host. By installing that file in the **/etc** directory of every host, you avoid the need for a DNS server. Each time the resolver needs to convert a domain name to an IP address, it can find the needed information on the local hard disk without relying on a network connection, which is much slower.

For some networks, IP addresses are assigned dynamically using a protocol such as DHCP, described later in this chapter. If a host does not have an IP address permanently assigned to it, you shouldn't try to use the /etc/hosts file to provide an IP address for a hostname.

However, even if you have a small network and want to include the names and IP addresses of all local hosts in the **/etc/hosts** file, you may want to have nonlocal domain names resolved by a request to a DNS server. You can configure this in two ways. The older method is to set up the **/etc/host.conf** file to specify the order in which the resolver should consult resources to resolve the hostname to an IP address. This file typically contains a single line:

```
order hosts,bind
```

This line tells the Linux resolver to check the **/etc/hosts** file first when a domain name must be resolved to an IP address; if the domain name is not listed in **/etc/hosts**, the resolver uses the configuration in **resolv.conf** to query a DNS server. (Remember, DNS servers use the BIND protocol; hence the word **bind** in the **host.conf** file.) If you wanted to check the DNS server first, you would switch the order of the words in **/etc/host.conf**. That would be unusual, however, except when testing your configuration.

More common than using **/etc/host.conf** in current Linux distributions is using the **/etc/nsswitch.conf** file. This file functions much like **/etc/host.conf** but is used by a number of different programs, not just the resolver. It also includes more options for where information can be obtained, rather than just **/etc/hosts** or a DNS server. A sample **nsswitch.conf** file from Red Hat Linux is shown below. The file from other versions of Linux is very similar; we've used the Red Hat example because it includes comments that help you understand the possible entries in this file.

```
#
# /etc/nsswitch.conf
#
# An example Name Service Switch config file. This file
# should be sorted with the most used services at the
# beginning.
#
# The entry '[NOTFOUND=return]' means that the search for
# an entry should stop if the search in the previous entry
# turned up nothing. Note that if the search failed due to
# some other reason (like no NIS server responding) then
# the search continues with the next entry.
#
# Legal entries are:
#
#         nisplus or nis+  Use NIS+ (NIS version 3)
#         nis or yp        Use NIS (NIS version 2), also
#                              called YP
#         dns              Use DNS (Domain Name Service)
#         files            Use the local files
#         db               Use the local database (.db)
#                              files
#         compat           Use NIS on compat mode
#         hesiod           Use Hesiod for user lookups
#         [NOTFOUND=return] Stop searching if not found so
#                              far
#

# To use db, put the "db" in front of "files" for entries
# you want to be looked up first in the databases
#
# Example:
#passwd:    db files nisplus nis
#shadow:    db files nisplus nis
#group:     db files nisplus nis

passwd:     files nisplus
shadow:     files nisplus
group:      files nisplus

#hosts:     db files nisplus nis dns
hosts:      files nisplus dns

# Example - obey only what nisplus tells us...
#services:  nisplus [NOTFOUND=return] files
#networks:  nisplus [NOTFOUND=return] files
```

3

```
#protocols:   nisplus [NOTFOUND=return] files
#rpc:         nisplus [NOTFOUND=return] files
#ethers:      nisplus [NOTFOUND=return] files
#netmasks:    nisplus [NOTFOUND=return] files

bootparams: nisplus [NOTFOUND=return] files

ethers:       files
netmasks:     files
networks:     files
protocols:    files nisplus
rpc:          files
services:     files nisplus

netgroup:     files nisplus

publickey:    nisplus

automount:    files nisplus
aliases:      files nisplus
```

The line beginning with `hosts:` controls how the resolver converts hostnames to IP addresses. Using the above example, it first looks in the local file (for hosts:, the local file is `/etc/hosts`); then it tries NIS+, which is not configured by default, so it generally won't yield any information; finally, it uses the information in `/etc/resolv.conf` to contact a DNS server to resolve the hostname.

 The **Network Information System (NIS)** protocol, or more commonly now, the more advanced **NIS+,** lets hosts share configuration information across a network, so that only one master configuration file need be supported for a number of hosts. Linux supports NIS and NIS+, but they are not discussed further in this book. To learn more about them, search for the NIS HOWTO document at *www.linuxdocs.org*.

Configuring the DNS Resolver Graphically

If you're trying to avoid using a text editor to configure Linux, you can use a number of graphical utilities to complete this task, including those described in Chapter 2 for network configuration.

In Red Hat Linux, the same Network Administration Tool you used in Chapter 2 also manages the contents of the `/etc/hosts` and `/etc/resolv.conf` files. To use it, start the program by choosing Programs, System, Network Configuration from the Gnome desktop menu. When the main program window appears, choose the `Hosts` tab. From this tab you can use the `Add` button to enter new combinations of IP addresses and Hostnames to store in your `/etc/hosts` file. Remember that any names you store here can be accessed without contacting a DNS server, but they also won't be updated if an IP address on the network changes (unless you modify the `/etc/hosts` file yourself).

To configure the `/etc/resolv.conf` file, choose the DNS tab. This tab displays your hostname and domain name (which is just extracted from your FQDN), plus the contents of your `/etc/resolv.conf` file. The hostname of your system is physically stored in the file `/etc/sysconfig/network`. The network script, `/etc/rc.d/init.d/network`, uses it from there. You can modify it by entering a new value in the hostname or domain fields of the DNS tab.

 Don't casually modify your hostname or domain name. That information is probably also stored on a DNS server somewhere. If you change it, other systems may not be able to reach you, and you may not be able to reach others because they think you are not who you say you are!

The three possible DNS servers are listed in the Primary, Secondary, and Tertiary (Third) DNS fields. You can enter IP addresses here as needed. The `search` line in `resolv.conf` is controlled by the DNS Search Path section of the window. You add to the list by entering a domain name in the Search Domain field, then choosing the Add button. Once you have one or more search paths (domains) listed, you can use the Edit, Delete, Up, and Down buttons to modify the contents of the list and the order in which the resolver uses them. None of the options described in the `resolv.conf` man page can be added to the file using this graphical screen. For reference, Figure 3-1 shows the DNS tab.

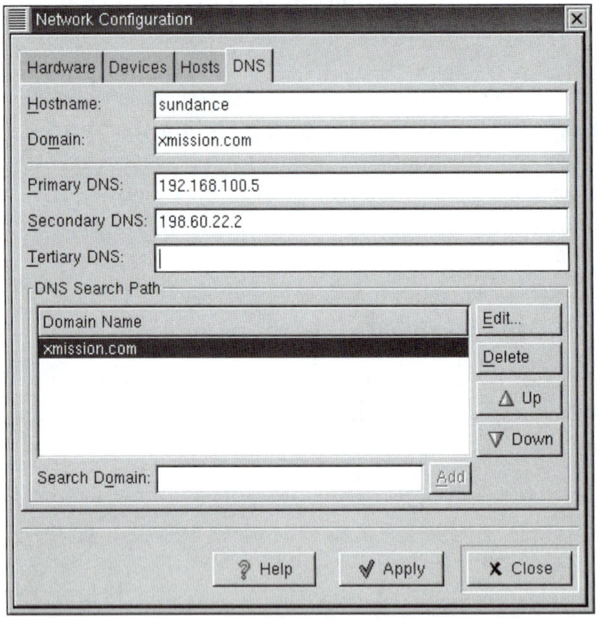

Figure 3-1   The DNS tab of the Red Hat Network Configuration Tool

To set up the `resolv.conf` and `hosts` files in Webmin, choose the Hardware tab after starting the Webmin interface. From among the icons that appear on the Hardware tab, shown in Figure 3-2, choose Network Configuration. On the Network Configuration page shown in Figure 3-3, you can choose either Host Addresses or DNS Client. If you choose Host Addresses, you see a list of the IP addresses and associated hostnames that are stored in `/etc/hosts`. You can click on an address to alter it, or click Add a new host address to create a new entry in the `hosts` file.

3

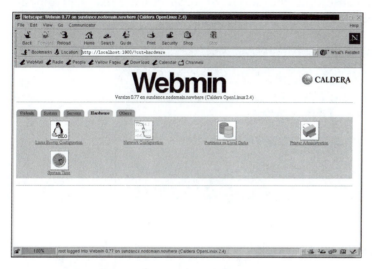

Figure 3-2   The Hardware tab in Webmin

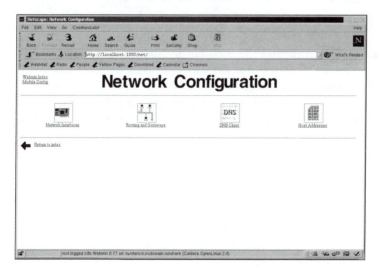

Figure 3-3   The Network Configuration page in Webmin

If you choose DNS Client, you see a Web page with a list of DNS servers and search domains (corresponding to the Search Path list in the Red Hat tool or the **search** line within /etc/resolv.conf). See Figure 3-4. You can click in the list of search domains to edit the list. You also see a set of drop-down boxes that indicate the order in which the resolver should use the methods outlined in this section. By default the /etc/hosts file is used first (listed in the drop-down box as Hosts), followed by NIS, then DNS servers referred to in resolv.conf (and configured on this same page). The information in the series of drop-down boxes corresponds to the /etc/host.conf file, or the /etc/nsswitch file on most modern Linux systems.

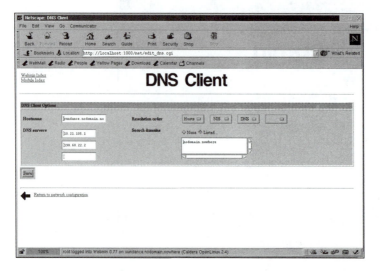

Figure 3-4   The DNS Client Web page in Webmin

Graphical tools such as Webmin and the Red Hat Network Administration Tool include sections where you can define entries for the /etc/hosts file and specify the order to try to resolve domain names. You can also find many other tools such as LinuxConf and YaST2 that can help you configure the resolver. Although the /etc/resolv.conf file is simple enough to set up, because many versions of Linux use /etc/nsswitch, a graphical utility can be a safer way to configure the resolver until you are comfortable with how your distribution is set up.

DIAL-UP NETWORK ACCESS USING PPP

In Chapter 2 you learned about PPP, the Point-to-Point Protocol, one method of making a network connection between two hosts. Because PPP is widely used to connect to the Internet via modem, it deserves special attention. Fortunately, Linux vendors have also given it special attention and provided a number of easy-to-use graphical tools for setting up PPP connections.

3

PPP differs from traditional dial-up terminal connections. When you call in to a remote computer using a terminal emulator program such as **minicom**, the program simply sends characters over the modem to be interpreted by the Telnet server on the remote computer. In contrast, using PPP establishes a low-level network protocol over which other programs can communicate with the remote computer independent of one another. PPP includes features that make it more secure, flexible, and dependable than a terminal emulation setup. Of course, that's exactly why people use PPP; it allows your computer to download files, run multiple networking programs simultaneously, run graphical programs, and in general act like an independent node on the network rather than a terminal to a distant CPU.

Setting up PPP used to be quite a challenge. It involved the following steps:

1. Identify your modem's serial port and make certain it functions correctly, perhaps by using a program such as **minicom** to call a remote computer and test the modem.

2. Set up a **ppp-options** file to instruct the PPP daemon (the PPP server) how to operate.

3. Create a script for the **chat** program. The **chat** program uses this script to send commands to the modem. The script tells **chat** to watch for text such as "ssword" coming in on the modem. This would indicate that a password is being requested by the remote computer, and **chat** should respond accordingly.

4. Have the script launch the PPP server program, **pppd**, using the correct options file and command-line parameters.

Using a **chat** script and a PPP options file was considered challenging under ideal conditions. Troubleshooting it was difficult, and the interaction of multiple components (the modem, **chat**, **pppd**, the remote computer's login program, and the remote computer's **pppd**) made it generally an unpleasant topic among new users of Linux.

In addition, standard PPP was not secure because the username and password you used to connect to the remote computer were stored in the **chat** script file, then passed over the modem to the remote computer. Two advances improved the security of PPP. One is the **Password Authentication Protocol (PAP)**, which stores pairs of usernames and passwords in a file (**/etc/ppp/pap-secrets**) that only the root user can access. They are still passed over the modem (where others might be able to eavesdrop), but at least they are more secure on the local host. The more advanced type of security is called **Challenge Handshake Authentication Protocol (CHAP)**. CHAP never sends your password across the modem to the remote computer. Instead, the remote computer selects a random string, encrypts it with a user's password and sends it to the host that is trying to authenticate for PPP. The host uses the password stored in the CHAP file (**/etc/ppp/chap-secrets**) and sends back the random string. By showing that it can decode the string, it demonstrates that it has the correct password for the user.

Most ISPs provide PPP connections, and nearly all of these ISPs use PAP or CHAP, rather than the older-style scripts.

PPP Connections Using wvdial

In response to the difficulty of using PPP, several new projects have appeared in recent years that make it easy to connect using PPP. One of these is a text-mode utility called **wvdial**. This program detects how to configure the modem and how to respond to queries from the remote server to establish a connection with the basic information you provide (such as the phone number of the ISP, the username, and the corresponding password). You can learn more about the WvDial project by visiting *http://open.nit.ca/* under the Project Info list. **wvdial** is installed by default on most versions of Red Hat Linux, but it is not part of Caldera OpenLinux. Use the **locate** command to see if **wvdial** is installed on your system.

One advantage of **wvdial** is that you can easily use it from a command line on a server without using a graphical interface. To use **wvdial**, first run the **wvdialconf** program. This program finds your modem and detects how to operate it (whether it uses standard commands or not, for example). It then creates the configuration file that the **wvdial** program uses to actually connect to a remote host. The format of the **wvdialconf** command includes the name of the configuration file to be created, as shown here:

```
wvdialconf  /etc/wvdial.conf
```

After running **wvdialconf**, open the **/etc/wvdial.conf** file in a text editor and enter your ISP information (phone number, username, and password). Then you can connect to your ISP by executing **wvdial** (with no options). The Defaults section shown in the sample file below defines the ISP information. Every line except the username, password, and phone was generated by **wvdialconf**. If you run the **wvdialconf** program again, it checks and updates the information within **/etc/wvdial.conf**, but doesn't disturb the details you entered.

```
[Dialer Defaults]
Modem = /dev/ttyS2
Baud = 115200
Init1 = ATZ
SetVolume = 1
Dial Command = ATDT
Init4 = ATM1L2
Username = nwells
Password = secretpassword
Phone = 703-437-0900
Stupid mode = 0
```

Because many people work with multiple ISP accounts, you might use a more complex `wvdial.conf` file than the previous example. `wvdial` lets you set up multiple ISP accounts in the `wvdial.conf` configuration file and choose which connection you want to initiate each time you start the program. For each account, the file can contain a `Dialer` section; you connect to that account by entering `wvdial` followed by the account name. For example, within `wvdial.conf`, one section might look like this:

```
[Dialer usnet]
Username = nwells@nd.us.net
Password = topsecretpassword
Phone = 801-997-5599
Inherits = Dialer Defaults
Stupid mode = 0
```

The `Stupid mode = 0` setting in the last line indicates that `wvdial` should start PPP immediately after the remote server answers, without waiting for specific instructions to start it. A few ISPs require this setting in order to connect successfully, but by default it is not used. To connect using the settings in this section, enter this command:

```
wvdial usnet
```

PPP Connections Using rp3

Red Hat Linux uses a utility called **rp3** (for Red Hat PPP) to configure PPP connections and manage their use. You can set up a dial-up connection to reach your ISP from a Red Hat Linux system in either of two ways: choose Dialup Configuration from the Gnome Programs submenu under Internet, or enter the command **rp3-config** from any graphical command line.

The first time you use this tool, or anytime you add a new account, you see a "wizard" interface that asks you questions about the ISP to which you want to connect. You set up an account for each ISP so that you can choose which connection to initiate simply by referring to an account by name. The information you enter is stored in the **rp3** configuration files. You can also use the tabs and buttons within **rp3-config** to modify the configuration of your dial-up accounts directly. Figure 3-5 shows the **rp3-config** main window with a single account configured and the Advanced configuration tab selected after the Edit button has been pressed.

Most users never need to access the advanced configuration screen, nor do they need to use the Modems tab in Figure 3-5. These features are useful, however, both to troubleshoot problematic dial-up connections and to make the best use of the modem hardware you have. Because modern PPP dialers are able to autodetect information about your modem and about the request being made by the ISP server that you dial into, little remains to be done to configure an ISP account beyond providing a phone number, username, and password. Features such as modem volume and automatically reconnecting if the dial-up connection is dropped are the types of things that are configured in these tools.

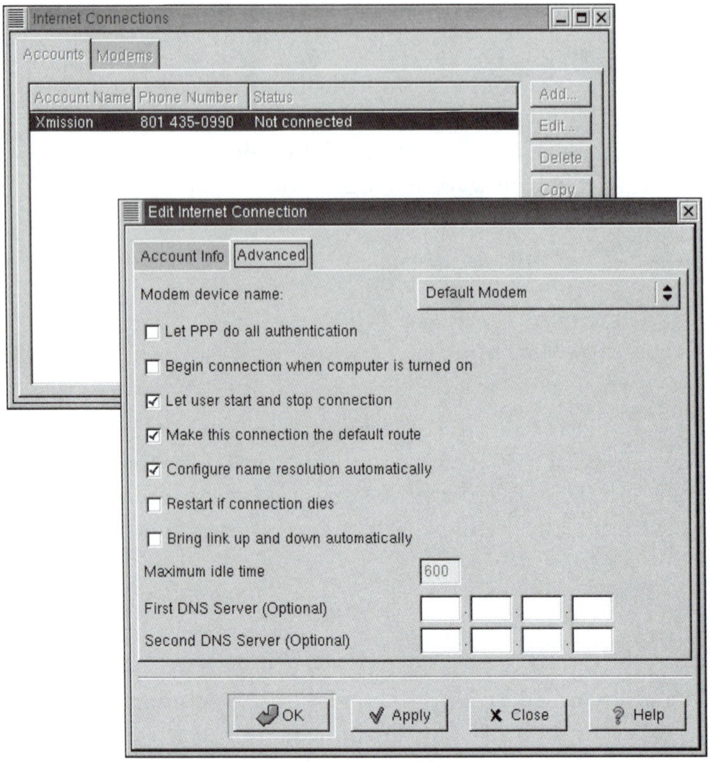

Figure 3-5   Advanced account configuration within `rp3-config`

Once you have set up at least one account using `rp3-config`, you can connect using that account by either entering `rp3` at any command line or choosing RH PPP Dialer on the Programs menu under Internet in Gnome. You are presented with a small window containing a list of all the network interfaces, including `loopback` for localhost and `eth0` for Ethernet (if you have an Ethernet card installed). The account name that you configured in `rp3-config` is included in the list. Select the name of the account you want to activate, and choose OK to dial in to that ISP and activate the network connection. The `rp3` program manages the connection, including executing the correct `route` commands to send packets to the Internet.

 As an experiment, try running the `ifconfig` command at a command line after connecting via a dial-up account. Notice the `ppp0` network interface and the IP address assigned to that interface. (The IP address was probably assigned randomly by the ISP server.)

PPP Connections Using KPPP

Most vendors of Linux (except for Red Hat) rely on KDE as a graphical environment. KDE includes a utility called **KPPP** that lets you configure ISP accounts and connect to them using PPP. Previous versions of KPPP used a single multitab dialog box to set up accounts and launch a connection. But security concerns related to the necessity of root access for certain tasks have led the designers of the latest versions of KPPP to use the same model as `rp3` in Red Hat: you first create an account, then use the KPPP dialer to launch a connection using that account.

Within Caldera OpenLinux, for example, you use the COAS administration tool within the KDE Control Center to define an ISP account. This is done by choosing COAS, then Network, then Internet Provider in the KDE Control Center. On the window that appears, check the Use dial-up networking box at the top of the screen, then select User defined from the list of providers and click the Details button. Within the dialog box that appears, enter a name for the account in the Name field. You could use your ISP's name for this. Next, enter the telephone number to reach the ISP as well as the DNS server information provided by the ISP (if any—if you don't enter this, it may be configured automatically via DHCP as the PPP connection is established, as described later in this chapter). Close the dialog box. The name that you entered for the account does not appear anywhere, but it has been saved. Finally, if you are the only user on this host or you want all users to be able to start the dial-up connection, check the Save authentication information box and enter the username and password for the ISP account that you defined.

With an account defined, you can start the KPPP program by choosing Kppp on the Internet submenu of KDE. The KPPP window displays a Connect to field that lists the account name you entered. Make sure that name is selected, then choose the Connect button to establish the dial-up connection. You can also choose the Show Stats button to see networking statistics about the connection. Figure 3-6 shows the Internet Provider page within the KDE Control Center, with the KPPP window to the left of the Control Center. The Show Stats window is below the main KPPP window.

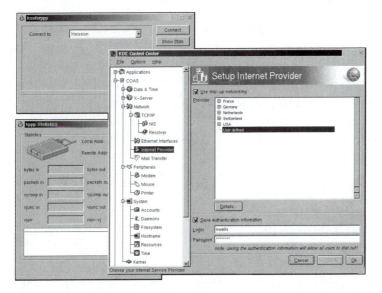

Figure 3-6   Dialog boxes for setting up an account and starting a connection using KPPP in OpenLinux

Automating PPP with `diald`

Many users who rely on a modem for a dial-up connection must balance the hassle of starting and stopping their connection (even using a convenient program like `rp3` or a script) with the need to keep down ISP charges or keep a home telephone line open for other uses. Moreover, when a modem is used to connect several users on a LAN to a single Internet connection, those users may not know how to make the connection or have access to the computer where the modem is located.

The `diald` program lets a dial-up connection remain active only when needed, disconnects after a specified period of inactivity, and automatically reconnects when anyone makes a request to an Internet site. Although this is a highly useful set of features, the program only recently became stable enough to use on production systems, so you won't find it included with most Linux distributions. You can learn more by visiting *diald.sourceforge.net*. "Stable," however, does not mean easy to use. `diald` competes well for the title of most opaque configuration (though Procmail likely wins, as you'll see later in this chapter).

`diald` works by setting up a "fake" network interface (a proxy interface) as the default gateway. Whenever network traffic is routed to that interface, `diald` establishes a PPP connection and changes the default gateway to that network interface. `diald` monitors the packets that are coming to the proxy interface to determine whether they warrant starting the dial-up connection. You can set configuration parameters such as how long the connection should remain active without any activity or when the connection should not be established even if network traffic appears to justify it.

The difficulty in using `diald` is that it relies on the "old-fashioned" method of configuring PPP: using login scripts, `chat` scripts, and manually configured security files (such as `/etc/ppp/chap-secrets`). In addition, `diald` uses a number of complex text-based configuration files to set its operating parameters. The program is flexible and powerful, but challenging to set up unless you feel quite comfortable with all the topics discussed in chapters 1 and 2, plus PPP dial-up scripting.

The easiest way to set up `diald` is to locate an RPM or Debian format software package for your version of Linux (check *rpmfind.net*). Such a package includes configuration files designed to interact with other parts of your specific Linux distribution. However, because few preconfigured packages are available for `diald`, you may need to download the source code, compile it, and configure the following files in `/etc/diald/`:

- `diald.conf`: Contains all standard operation parameters. Note that in the `diald` documentation, this file is often referred to by its name in previous versions of `diald`, which was `diald.options`.

- `standard.filter`: Indicates how different types of network traffic are handled, i.e., whether they cause the connection to come up or keep it up once established.

- **diald.connect**: Contains the instructions for starting a PPP connection using a script written for the **chat** program located in **/etc/chatscripts**.

- **ip-up** and **ip-down**: These optional scripts are executed each time the link is initiated or dropped.

- **addroute** and **delroute**: These scripts reset routing if anything more complex than a single interface is being managed by **diald** (in which case the routing changes made by **diald** are adequate, and these additional scripts are not needed).

Man pages are provided for the **diald** program and several of the supporting programs (such as **diald-control**). You can learn more by reviewing either the FAQ file under the Documentation link on *diald.sourceforge.net* or the **diald** HOWTO document, available on *www.linuxdocs.org*. (This second document includes example scenarios for connecting within recent versions of Debian, Slackware, and SuSE Linux.)

Using DHCP

The **Dynamic Host Configuration Protocol (DHCP)** lets you configure a service that automatically hands out IP addresses to clients on a network. DHCP is backward-compatible with the **BOOTP** system that has long been used by diskless workstations to obtain network configuration instructions. Using DHCP can drastically reduce the administration needs of a network, though it's not appropriate for all networks. Linux provides excellent support for DHCP as both a server, using the **dhcpd** daemon, and as a client, using any of several packages. The most popular Linux DHCP clients are **dhcpcd**, **dhclient**, and **pump**.

The DHCP server is installed by default on many Linux systems. Configuring this server involves creating an **/etc/dhcpd.conf** file (the location may vary among Linux versions). This file instructs the DHCP server which IP address ranges are available for DHCP clients that request an address. It also may define addresses of DNS name servers, a broadcast address, a maximum time that a client can use the address, and many other options. Each time a client requests an IP address, the DHCP server is said to **lease** the address to the client for a specified time. After that time, the client must request a renewal of the lease, which may involve getting a different IP address. Once configured, however, the whole arrangement is transparent to the user on the client host. A sample **dhcpd.conf** file is shown here:

```
# Sample /etc/dhcpd.conf
default-lease-time 600;
max-lease-time 7200;
option subnet-mask 255.255.255.0;
option broadcast-address 192.168.1.255;
option routers 192.168.1.254;
option domain-name-servers 192.168.1.1, 192.168.1.2;
option domain-name "mydomain.org";
```

```
subnet 192.168.1.0 netmask 255.255.255.0 {
    range 192.168.1.10 192.168.1.100;
    range 192.168.1.150 192.168.1.200;
}
```

This file defines two ranges of addresses within the 192.168.1.0 network. Within these ranges, IP addresses are randomly assigned to any client that requests an address. You can tie a specific IP address to a specific host by using the MAC address of that host's Ethernet card. That portion of the configuration file looks like this:

```
host haagen {
    hardware ethernet 08:00:6b:3a:29:7f;
    fixed-address 192.168.1.5;
}
```

Many additional options are supported by dhcpd. You can refer to the man page for a list of these. Once you have the DHCP server configured, you can start it using the standard script in /etc/rc.d/init.d.

A DHCP client can run any operating system. So long as it "speaks" DHCP, it can obtain an IP address from the Linux DHCP server. Windows DHCP clients, however, do not follow the DHCP standard, and require that you add a route so that they can use the Linux DHCP server (change the dev from eth0 to match your networking device as needed):

```
route add -host 255.255.255.255 dev eth0
```

Configuring a Linux DHCP client is quite easy. Most Linux distributions install one of the DHCP clients by default and include graphical tools to configure it. The configuration tools rely on changing the /etc/sysconfig/network file and the ifcfg-eth0 file. In Red Hat Linux, you can configure an interface to use DHCP to acquire an IP address using the Red Hat Network Configuration Tool. Within this tool, choose the Devices tab, then select the device that you want to configure for DHCP, for example, the eth0 device. Then choose Edit. When the Ethernet Device dialog box appears, choose the Protocols tab, then select TCP/IP from the list of protocols shown, and choose the Edit button. In the dialog box that appears, you see a list of address fields. Above those fields is a checkbox labeled "Automatically obtain IP address settings with," followed by a drop-down list box. Choose dhcp from this list, then close all the dialog boxes. When you close the main window of the Network Administration tool, confirm that you want to save your changes. DHCP is now activated. Figure 3-7 shows the dialog boxes used in Red Hat to configure DHCP.

A similar process is used in Webmin, YaST, and other network configuration utilities. After DHCP is configured, it can take a minute or two for the DHCP client to obtain an IP address and activate the network interface. If you execute ifconfig and see 0.0.0.0 for the IP address, DHCP has not yet obtained an IP address. Wait a few moments and try ifconfig again to see whether a valid IP address is shown.

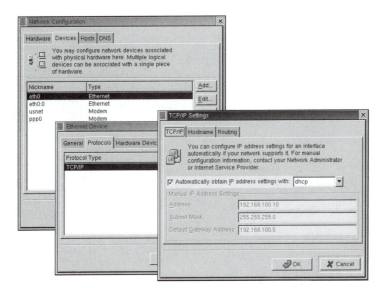

3

Figure 3-7   Using the Red Hat Network Configuration Tool to configure an interface to use DHCP

UNDERSTANDING LDAP

On a single host, you can easily review the contents of configuration files or a graphical utility to learn about your system. On larger networks, knowing "what's out there" can become a real problem. Both system administrators and users often need to know more about a network resource than is readily apparent. These resources might include users (user accounts), services provided by hosts, printers, and many others.

The solution to this lack of information is to create a **directory service**: a database of information about network resources (or other resources) that can be accessed by people all over the network. Several international standards have emerged for creation of just such a directory. One of these is **X.500**. A popular commercial implementation of a directory service is Novell Directory Services (NDS) and eDirectory. Another similar model is the Lightweight Directory, which you can access using the **Lightweight Directory Access Protocol (LDAP)**. While LDAP is too large a topic to explore in depth here, a review of its core concepts can prepare you to retrieve the LDAP documentation and begin using this system. Linux typically uses the free **OpenLDAP** server. You can learn about that server and LDAP in general by visiting *www.openldap.org*.

Directories such as X.500 and LDAP are organized as inverted trees of information. Each level of the tree consists of **objects**, or **nodes**. At the bottom of the tree, the objects are **leaf objects**; at a higher level they are **container objects**, because they contain other objects (below them in the tree). Figure 3-8 illustrates how these objects types are used in a Novell Directory Services tree. Each object is created based on a **class**; the class defines the type of resource that the object represents, such as a printer, a user, or a company. Each class has a definition that includes **attributes** to specify information about that type of object. Each leaf object in the tree has a name, called its **common name**. The **schema** is the collection of all the possible object classes and their attributes that the directory supports. The directory tree itself contains data mapped out using those classes and attributes.

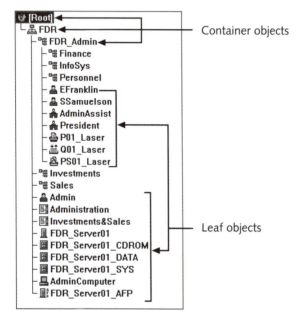

Figure 3-8 Container and leaf objects in a Novell Directory Services tree

To use a directory, you use client software (the **ud** program is one text-mode LDAP client in Linux) to traverse the tree, looking for the information you need within the database. For example, think of the top of the tree as having a label; call it Top for our purposes. Underneath Top are a number of other objects, each representing a country; these are objects with a class of country. Each country object has useful attributes that define a country, such as name, principal languages, international telephone codes, etc. When you see the object named Latvia, you can use your LDAP client to query the attributes of that country object.

More likely, you will continue down the tree. Each country object is a container that holds many organization objects. An organization object has certain attributes, including a name, and is also a container that may contain resources such as user objects, printer objects, group membership objects, and many other classes of objects.

You are not allowed to read all parts of the worldwide LDAP tree, but by having access to parts of it, you could gather information in a structured way. You could also add your own information for your own use or for access by those to whom you want to provide it.

You refer to an object in the directory tree using a formalized set of identifiers. For example, a user named Luis Rodriguez working at IBM in Mexico might be referred to using this designation:

```
cn=Luis Rodriguez, o=IBM, c=MX
```

3

This is the **distinguished name (DN)** of the user-class object representing this person. The DN is the complete path to an object within the directory tree. The *cn* in the above text stands for common name; the *o* for organization, the *c* for country. Once you knew how to refer to this object (perhaps by browsing the directory tree until you found it), you can query for the attributes of the object to learn Luis's email address or phone number, if he had made those publicly readable. Figure 3-9 shows how a portion of an LDAP directory tree might appear.

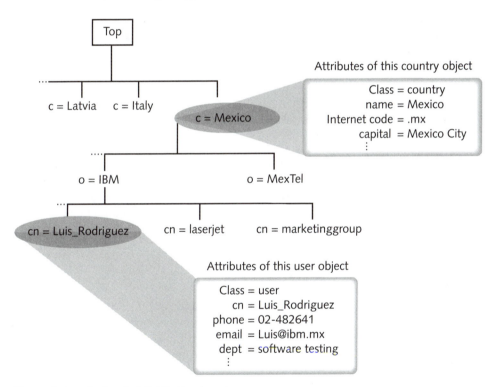

Figure 3-9   A simple LDAP directory tree

You should get the sense from this brief outline that directory services are a very large topic. LDAP is just one of the available directory services, though it continues to grow in popularity. The OpenLDAP server included with most Linux distributions lets you set up a local directory service so that users on your network can query for information from the worldwide LDAP database or a local resources database that you establish. When the server doesn't know a piece of information, it connects with other LDAP servers around the world to present a single logical database to client users. You should explore your Linux distribution to see what LDAP software is installed or available. For example, in Red Hat Linux, the OpenLDAP and OpenLDAP-client packages are installed by default in some configurations. These provide both the client and server software. You must still configure the server before use, but you can immediately begin experimenting with the client using the following command to refer to a remote LDAP server (before you get your own set up):

```
ud -s root.openldap.org
```

 Other LDAP clients include `ldapsearch` (text mode), KLDAP for KDE, and GQ for Gnome.

Once **ud** starts, enter **help commands** to see the available commands; don't expect to get far until you have reviewed the ud man page or explored other LDAP documentation, such as the LDAP HOWTO on *www.linuxdocs.org*. The OpenLDAP-clients package includes many other command-line utilities to help you access and manage LDAP information.

 Some other programs can be used to access LDAP information. For example, Netscape Communicator can access a roaming user profile or address book information from an LDAP server. For the user profile, open the Preferences dialog box on the Edit menu in Communicator, choose Roaming User (Roaming Access in the Windows version of Netscape), then Server Information. In the LDAP fields you enter the LDAP server to query and the full distinguished name of your user-class object. (You must set up this object and include profile information in it before you can use this feature.)

RUNNING APPLICATIONS REMOTELY

Once you have a network connection to a system running Linux, you can execute programs remotely in several ways. This section explores running both graphical and text-based programs remotely, normally between two Linux hosts, but in some cases between a Windows host and a Linux host (as explained in the XDMCP section).

 When using any of the technologies described in this section, remember that they are not considered secure. That is, if you are using them across a network on which you don't trust all of the users, you should worry that your passwords may be grabbed, or that your applications may be viewed as you work. The so-called r-utilities are considered particularly insecure. Graphical remote execution using X, however, can be done using the `ssh` secure shell program to create a completely secure connection. (The secure shell is described in Chapter 11, though using it for remote X applications is beyond the scope of this book. See the `ssh` documentation for more information or visit either *www.ssh.com* or *www.openssh.org*.)

Using X for Remote Graphical Applications

The flexibility of the Linux graphical environment—the X Window System or just X—was always the Achilles heel of Linux installation. However, X provides a feature that few other systems can emulate: it separates the computational aspects of a program from collecting keystrokes and displaying program output. This allows you to run the program on one host but collect input (keyboard and mouse) and display output on a different computer. This is very similar to the terminal concept described in Chapter 1, except that the program is graphical (and the whole system much more complex!).

For example, suppose you have a program installed on host paris, but you are working on host rome. You don't want to install the program on rome, but you need to use it. X allows you to log in to paris and start the program with an additional instruction: "Display the program on rome and get input from rome." The program then starts running on paris but appears on the screen of rome. If the computer is powerful enough, dozens of users can log in to paris and launch programs that are displayed on computers across the network. This setup is illustrated in Figure 3-10.

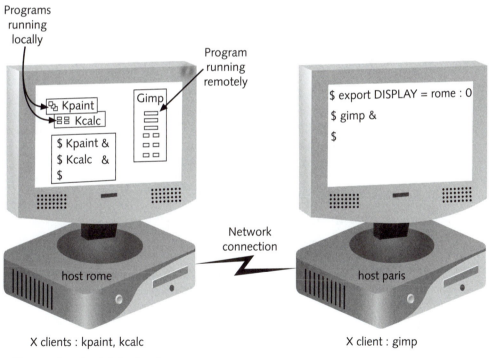

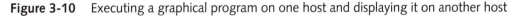

Figure 3-10   Executing a graphical program on one host and displaying it on another host

To begin using remote X execution, you must learn two terms that may be counter-intuitive:

- The program running on a host is the **X client**.

- The screen, keyboard, and mouse of the system where the program is remotely displayed are those of the **X server**.

Each system uses an environment variable called **DISPLAY** that contains a hostname and a screen number to define where each X client should display its windows and collect its input. Normally, your **DISPLAY** variable contains only a **sequence number** and perhaps a **screen number** (both zero), and so by default X displays programs on your local host. (Some systems might have multiple displays, in which case the zeros would not always be used for the local host.) The results of the **echo** command to show the variable's value indicate this. (Here only a sequence number is shown; your system may display **:0.0** for both a sequence number and a screen number.)

```
echo $DISPLAY
:0
```

You can change the **DISPLAY** variable manually. Suppose you log in to rome using a program like Telnet and then enter these commands (in the default Linux bash shell):

```
DISPLAY=rome.mynet.com:0.0
export DISPLAY
```

Now every graphical program is displayed on rome rather than paris. You can also include the display information on the command line when you start a graphical program. The format of this option is the same for all graphical programs. For example, instead of starting the **gimp** graphical program like this:

```
gimp &
```

Start it with the **--display** option, like this:

```
gimp --display rome.mynet.com:0.0 &
```

The **--display** option overrides the **DISPLAY** environment variable.

 Each user on a system has a different set of environment variables, so all users can log in and have the programs they run displayed on different remote hosts.

Before an X client can display its windows on a remote host, the remote host must be configured to allow other computers to use its X server. You can do this in two ways: one easy and insecure, the other more difficult, but more secure.

3

xhost Authentication

The easy method is to use the **xhost** program on the host where you want the X client to display its output, specifying the host that is allowed to use the local X server. To use **xhost**, you include the hostname of the computer that you want to allow to display. For example, if you are logged in on host rome and want to allow X clients from host paris to use rome as an X server (to display on and get input from rome), this command sets that up:

    xhost +paris.mynet.com

When you are finished running the program, you can remove paris from the list of authorized hosts using this command:

    xhost -paris.mynet.com

 You commonly see xhost used without a hostname, as xhost +, which allows any host to use your system as an X server. This is highly insecure and allows anyone to start a program and have it show up on your screen. It also allows a clever user to capture the keystrokes you are entering as you work. Use xhost — to disable all access, then use specific hostnames to add hosts that you want to allow to use your system as an X server.

These steps summarize the process of remotely executing a graphical program:

1. Open a command-line window on your host.

2. Enter the **xhost** command with the name of the host that will run the X client.

3. Log in to the remote host.

4. Start the program with the **--display** command-line option referring to your host (or set the **DISPLAY** environment variable if you intend to run multiple programs).

5. The X client program appears on your local screen.

 You will quickly notice that the X protocol uses a lot of network bandwidth. Various compression methods can ease this, but be aware that running graphical applications remotely uses much more bandwidth than running text applications remotely.

xauth Authentication

Even when used with a hostname, the **xhost** command is not terribly secure because it permits *any* user on the named host to use your host as an X server. The **xauth** system prevents that problem by requiring that an X client present a specific token (a long number) to the X server in order to be granted access to use that X server. The common term for a numeric token of this sort is a **cookie**, and the **xauth** system uses a number that is also called the **MIT Magic Cookie**. The `xauth` process works like this:

1. Suppose you start a program on host paris that is to be displayed on host rome (rome is running the remote X server). The program you execute on paris examines the **.Xauthority** file in your home directory on paris to see whether a token is given for the remote host rome.

2. Assuming that a token is available (you must put it there yourself, as we'll show you next), it is sent to rome using the X network protocol, as paris tries to initiate a connection to use the X server on rome.

3. The X server on rome looks in *its* **.Xauthority** file for a token that corresponds to host paris. If it finds one, it allows the connection to proceed. If not, the connection is refused and the program on paris will not run (because it has been instructed to use rome for its display and rome won't allow that).

The .**Xauthority** files mentioned in this process are stored in a user's home directory. So each user must have the necessary tokens to use another user's X server. Of course, the most common situation is that you have accounts on two systems and you copy the token between your home directories so that you can run and display programs on any of the systems to which you have access. In any case, **xauth** is designed to be a user-to-user security system, rather than a host-to-host security system.

To use the `xauth` security method, you must start the X Window System with the option `auth--` and the name of the authority file to use, `$HOME/.Xauthority`. This is the normal authority file by default in most modern Linux systems, but if yours uses a different authority file, you should examine the `startx` script that is typically used to launch X. Alternatively, if you are running with a graphical login, the configuration you need to alter is in the display manager file. For example, the .`Xauthority` file is specified in Red Hat Linux as part of the `gdm.conf` file in `/etc/X11/gdm`.

You can see the .**Xauthority** file in your home directory using the `ls -a` command (it's a hidden file). To view or alter the file's contents, you use the **xauth** program, which you can start from any command line. From the **xauth** prompt, you enter commands to manage the tokens stored for your use on the X server. A few helpful commands include **help** to show all the **xauth** commands, **list** to list all the tokens currently stored, and **add** to place a token into the authority file for use by a remote host.

The authority file should always include a token for the host where you are working. A new token is generated each time you log in to X. If your file doesn't include a token for your local host, use the **generate** command within **xauth** to create one. Below, you see **xauth** launched, followed by the **list** command to show all the known tokens on host rome.

```
[root@rome root]# xauth
Using authority file /root/.Xauthority
```

3

```
xauth> list
rome.xmission.com/unix:0  MIT-MAGIC-COOKIE-1
   6da29c0a7399aa179c90cba39426dd5f
rome.xmission.com:0  MIT-MAGIC-COOKIE-
   1  6da29c0a7399aa179c90cba39426dd5f
xauth>
```

If you have a file like this one and you want host paris to be able to use rome as an X server (that is, to display programs on it), you must get the information from this file into the `.Xauthority file` on paris. Once you have done this, paris has a valid token to send to rome so that rome can allow paris to connect for remote program display.

You can accomplish this in several ways, from writing down the information on a piece of paper (which is rarely done by Linux pros) to using a program like `telnet`, `rlogin` (described later in this chapter), or `ssh` (described in Chapter 11) to log in to one machine while sitting at the other, then copy and paste the information between two windows. For example, you could follow these steps:

1. Open two Xterm windows in your graphical environment on the X server host (the host that you want to display programs—rome in the previous example).

2. In the first window, start `xauth` and use `list` to display the known tokens.

3. Switch to the other window and log in to the remote host on which you will run the X client programs (paris in the previous example).

4. Start `xauth` on the remote system.

5. In the first window, click and drag on the line containing the token for the X server host.

6. Switch to the second window, type `add`, then choose Paste from the Edit menu of the Xterm window. The text of the token is pasted on the line containing the `add` command.

7. Make sure the `add` command has the correct format, then press Enter. Use `list` to make sure the token is included correctly.

8. Type `exit` in both windows to close the `xauth` program.

As a review of what you've already learned, think about why you can log in as part of Step 3 above, even though you don't have access for graphical program display. What are the differences between these two things?

The `add` command referred to looks something like this (with the token taken from your own file):

```
add rome.xmission.com:0  MIT-MAGIC-COOKIE-1
   6da29c0a7399aa179c90cba39426dd5f
```

Don't be surprised if the remote display of graphical applications doesn't work correctly on your first attempt. The many components of X can make it difficult to configure. If you are having problems, be certain that your `DISPLAY` variable is correctly set. Check with your system administrator to see if X was started with the `-nolisten tcp` argument, which stops it from listening for remote connections. Make certain that the host-name you have specified is reachable on the network (try `ping`, for example). Check again that the tokens in the two `.Xauthority` files match and that some problem such as an expired token is not interfering with your efforts. Finally, review the man pages (for X, `xauth`, etc.) and HOWTO documents related to X to see what else might be preventing your setup from functioning as expected.

Using XDMCP for Remote Graphical Terminals

Many Linux systems are now configured during installation to use a graphical login screen automatically, so users never see text-mode displays. The graphical login screen is presented by a display manager. The commonly used programs are **xdm**, **gdm**, and **kdm** (for X generally, Gnome, and KDE, respectively). You can typically explore the config-uration files for these programs in the subdirectories of `/etc/X11`. These files tell the display manager what login screen to display, how to respond to shutdown commands, and many other options.

One feature of a display manager is its ability to display the login screen on a remote com-puter so that a user can begin running Linux programs without first logging in using Telnet or another text-based program. The display manager presents a login screen, the user logs in, and the Linux desktop (Gnome, KDE, or another interface) appears, ready for the user to launch programs graphically. This capability is especially useful when you are running X server software on a non-Linux computer. For example, many users running Windows have an X server program such as X-Win32 or Hummingbird Exceed. This program allows a program (an X client) running on a remote Linux system to be displayed on a Windows desktop and collect its keyboard and mouse input from that system.

To have a graphical login display appear on an X server, you must configure the display manager control protocol, **XDMCP**. XDMCP is not a secure protocol, so it is turned off by default on most Linux distributions. To enable it, you must change the configuration so that the components of X and the display manager can utilize network connections. This is not especially difficult, but the process varies among Linux versions because each sets up X configuration in a slightly different way. The following steps outline how to enable XDMCP on Red Hat Linux 7.3. We have also included comments that should assist you on other versions of Linux, but because of the limited time we can devote to XDMCP here, you are advised to review the HOWTO documents for XDMCP, XDM, and X if you have difficulty making this process work.

1. Make the X Font Server, `xfs`, utilize a network connection. Open the file `/etc/X11/fs/config`. Comment out the `no-listen=tcp` line, and add the line `port=7100`. On other systems, you might instead need to alter the

3

line in `/etc/rc.d/init.d/xfs` that begins with `daemon` so that the port specified is 7100 instead of −1.

2. Allow hosts to communicate with the display manager. Open the file `/etc/X11/xdm/Xaccess` and remove the comment sign (#) from the line starting with "*" and indicating "any host can get a login window."

3. Enable the XDMCP protocol within the display manager configuration file. Open the `file /etc/X11/gdm/gdm.conf`, find the `Enable` line within the `[XDMCP]` section, and change it from `False` to `True`. Be certain that a line within this section indicates `Port=177`.

4. Be certain that the file permissions (the mode) of `/etc/X11/xdm/Xsetup_0` is 755.

5. Be certain that the file `/etc/X11/XF86Config` includes the line `FontPath "unix/:7100"`

6. Restart the X Windows system to be certain the configuration files have been reread.

7. On the remote X server (including a Windows host running X-Win32 or similar program), provide the hostname or IP address of the Linux host, or use the XDMCP-broadcast method to try to reach the Linux display manager. If all works as it should, the X server displays a Linux-like graphical login screen after a few moments.

Using r-Utilities for Remote Execution

Many Linux programs allow you to access remote hosts to run programs, transfer files, or perform other functions. The **r-utilities** (r is for "remote") were designed to accomplish the same thing within a trusted network environment. Of course, few of us dare assume that any network is trustworthy any longer, and so the r-utilities have fallen on hard times. Just keep in mind that they were designed to be convenient, not secure, and use them only when you are working behind a strong firewall and trust everyone on your network.

The r-utilities let you learn about or execute a program on another host. They are intended to allow a user who has accounts on multiple systems to access his or her account on other systems easily without resorting to a Telnet login to the other hosts. The r-utilities thus assume that you have an account on a remote system that matches your username on the local host. If that's not the case, you can specify a different login name to use on the remote host. A simple configuration file on the remote host lists remote hosts and users who are allowed to run r-utilities using that user's account. The basic r-utilities and their functions are presented in Table 3-2.

Table 3-2 Commonly used r-utilities

Utility Name	Description
rwho	List the users that are logged in on all hosts attached to the local network (hosts that have the r-utilities networking features activated)
ruptime	List all hosts attached to the local network (that are using r-utilities) with the uptime for each
rlogin	Log in to a remote host; very similar to telnet, but uses the r-utilities authentication methods (the .rhosts file) described below
rsh	Execute a command on a remote computer without logging in
rcp	Copy one or more files between different computers (the local computer and a remote computer or between two remote computers)

The r-utilities rely on Remote Procedure Call (rpc) networking, which you will learn about in more detail in Chapter 5 as part of the Network File System discussion. You must have rpc and the portmapper application installed in order to use r-utilities.

A few examples should clarify how this works. Suppose you have a user account named nwells on host stockholm and a user account nicholas on host oslo. (You could use full domain names and access hosts on different network segments, but considering the security hazards of these utilities, let's stay close to home for this example.) The r-utilities networking support (rpc) is enabled, and the r-utilities packages are installed on both systems. (For example, a daemon called rlogind listens for network connections from the rlogin utility—check your system scripts in /etc/rc.d/init.d to see if this and other r-utilities are installed.)

Whenever you are logged in to stockholm, you can enter the **rlogin** command with the -l option to specify the account name on oslo that you want to use. You are prompted for the password to that account. The initial exchange looks like this:

```
[nwells@stockholm nwells] rlogin -l nicholas oslo
password:
[nicholas@oslo nicholas]
```

Once logged in to oslo, you can enter commands and otherwise act as if you were sitting in front of oslo. You enter the **exit** command to terminate the **rlogin** session.

While **rlogin** is great when you need to work with interactive programs on a remote host, you can use the **rsh** command to execute a program on a remote host without logging in, or **rcp** to copy files between two hosts.

You could continue to use the -l option and enter a password with every command, but these utilities offer convenience—and security risks. You can set up a configuration file on oslo that allows you to run **rsh** and **rcp** without ever entering a password. If you have root access to oslo, you can create a file called **/etc/hosts.equiv** that contains all the hosts and usernames that are permitted to access this system using r-utilities. As an individual user you can create a hidden file in your home directory called **.rhosts** containing a list of hosts and usernames that you want to permit to access your account without a password. A sample **.rhosts** file on oslo might look like this:

```
stockholm nwells

helsinki wells
```

With this file in place, let's review a couple of examples showing what you can do with the **rsh** and **rcp** commands. While logged in to stockholm, you can display a list of the processes running on oslo without ever "logging in" to oslo by using this command:

```
rsh oslo ps aux
```

The output from this command is displayed on your screen on stockholm. If you want to store the results in a file on oslo, the command would include a redirection operator enclosed in quotes so that your local shell doesn't interpret it and create the file on stockholm:

```
rsh oslo ps aux '>' processlist
```

The **rcp** command lets you copy files between any two computers that are running the r-utilities. You simply include the hostname as part of the file specification. For example, while logged in to stockholm, you can copy a file named **processlist** from oslo to stockholm using this command:

```
rcp  oslo:processlist  /home/nwells/
```

You can also copy between two other computers (not the one you are sitting at). For example, while logged in at stockholm, you could copy a file from oslo to helsinki with this command (assuming the .rhosts file on helsinki is configured with your stockholm information):

```
rcp  oslo:processlist  helsinki:/temp/processlist_backup
```

To learn more about the r-utilities, start by reviewing the man pages for **rlogind** and **rshd**.

Using UUCP for Remote Access

Before the Internet was established and (relatively) secure, system administrators needed a simple but reliable method of transferring email between sites using a modem. The **Unix to Unix Copy Protocol (UUCP)** system was designed to meet that need. UUCP is an old protocol, but it's actually seeing renewed interest on some fronts because it provides a very inexpensive transfer of email over modem between multiple email servers, all without the security concerns that the Internet presently poses. If you have any sort of volume on your email server, consider sticking with the Internet and implementing the security measures detailed in later chapters. However, UUCP is still an ongoing part of Linux that some users may find valuable.

UUCP is implemented as several subprotocols, each assigned a code letter. The different protocols are designed to use different transport media (modem, Ethernet, etc.) and thus have different characteristics. For example, the version designed for Ethernet (UUCP "i") uses TCP as a transport protocol and so has no error correction; the version designed for modem-based transfers (UUCP "g") implements its own error-correction scheme. UUCP transfers are handled via a set of structured commands regarding data transfer and the two hosts' ability to handle the outgoing and incoming data.

A number of commands are part of the UUCP software package. One of them is called **uucp** and allows a user to copy any file between two UUCP-capable hosts without relying on UUCP's automatic transfer of email files that occurs at regular intervals. Most UUCP commands, however, are included in scripts that control the processing of email on a system that relies on UUCP to transfer email. Popular email servers like **sendmail** are UUCP "capable," though not configured to use it by default.

Newsgroup posting also can rely on UUCP. For most news servers, however, the volume of newsgroup posting would rule out this solution.

UUCP in Linux is typically not installed by default, nor used or understood by many system administrators. If you have an interest in using this old standby, review the UUCP HOWTO document on *www.linuxdocs.org*. It provides guidance on using the Taylor UUCP package, which is the most popular Linux version of UUCP. This package lets you use either Ethernet or modem connections to transfer email, newsgroup postings, or regular files.

WEB AND MAIL CLIENTS

Most computer users have some experience with the World Wide Web and with electronic mail (email). This section describes the client programs available in Linux for using these two services.

Popular Linux Browsers

The earliest graphical Web browser, NCSA Mosaic, was not an overly complex program when it first appeared in the early 1990s. It selected a display font, inserted graphics, and displayed the resulting Web page based on the HTML codes that the page contained. Mosaic was freely available, and its code became the basis for all modern browsers, from America Online to Netscape Communicator to Microsoft Internet Explorer.

Things quickly became much more complex, however, as formatting options expanded, plug-in modules for multimedia extensions were developed, and security concerns evolved. Almost every browser remains free as a method of promoting the company that makes it.

Dozens of browsers are available for Linux. For example, the file-browsing applications in the KDE and Gnome graphical desktops can also browse Web documents.

Unfortunately, the complexity of a Web browser has overtaken the ability of most free software team's ability to keep up. More problematic is the lack of Linux support from vendors of popular add-on modules—called **plug-ins**—for things like video clips or other multimedia products. Still, using the popular graphical browsers in Linux lets you view nearly every page on the Web. The exceptions are the growing number of Web pages designed specifically for Internet Explorer. When viewing these pages in some other browser, such as Netscape Communicator (on Linux or Windows), you normally only see a blank screen. The three most popular browsers on Linux are described here.

Lynx is a text-based browser. It supports fill-in-forms but can cause problems with tables, Java, and a host of other advanced features. Lynx is nevertheless a great tool for the text-oriented Linux user, partly because it is so fast, and partly because you aren't bothered by any flashing advertisements while you search Web pages for the information you need.

Lynx is installed by default on many popular Linux distributions. It is a small program compared to the following two Linux browsers, and can be run from any command-line window. Figure 3-11 shows a Lynx screen. Compared to graphical browsers, Lynx keyboard commands take more practice to use effectively, but again, using the program to navigate Web pages becomes very fast once you are comfortable with Lynx.

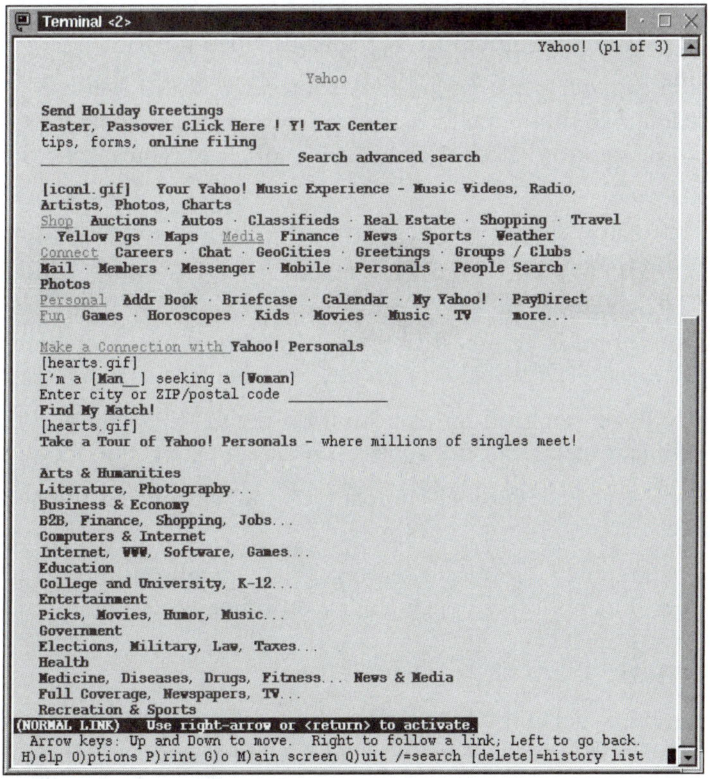

Figure 3-11   The Lynx text-based Web browser

To start Lynx, enter lynx on any command line, followed by a Web page address. For example:

```
lynx www.yahoo.com
```

or

```
lynx http://www.yahoo.com
```

Use the up and down arrow keys to move between links on the Web page. When a link you want to jump to is selected, use the right arrow to go there (like clicking on it in a graphical browser). Use the left arrow key like the back arrow in a graphical browser. To move between screens of text without reference to links on the page, use the Page Up and Page Down keys. Many other keys for different browser functions are displayed at the bottom of the Lynx screen. To exit Lynx you can use the **q** key (then confirm with **y**) or just press Ctrl+C.

The Netscape Communicator browser is included in many Linux distributions, including Caldera OpenLinux and Red Hat Linux (though Mozilla is the default; Netscape is on the Programs menu, under Internet). Netscape on Linux is substantially similar to Netscape on Windows, though the version numbers are different. Netscape on Linux includes an email client (described in the next section), a newsgroup viewer, complex configuration options (see the Edit menu, Preferences item), security options for e-commerce, and support for plug-ins like Flash, Adobe Acrobat, and various video formats.

Though the **Mozilla** browser began as an open source version of Netscape Navigator, it has since been redesigned substantially. Red Hat Linux includes Mozilla as the default browser on the Gnome desktop. Mozilla operates like other graphical browsers that you may have used.

In addition to the basic browsers included as part of the Gnome and KDE desktop environments, some of the many other browsers available for Linux include the following. These are taken from a long list of Web applications on the site *www.linuxapps.com*:

- *Opera*: A very popular graphical Linux browser created by a commercial group but available for free use (with advertisements).

- *dillo*: A very small graphical browser built on the GTK+ graphical libraries (Gnome-compatible). Does not support frames, Java, etc. but is only 200K.

- *Galeon*: A full-featured, Gnome-compatible browser built on the Mozilla display engine.

- *SkipStone*: A graphical browser based on GTK+ graphical libraries and the Mozilla code, but with few dependencies on other system libraries.

Understanding Email

Email is one of the most widely used Internet services in the world and is a large topic to study. In Chapter 6 you will learn how to set up a basic email server in Linux. In this section we present a few basic ideas and introduce you to some of the email reading programs on Linux.

The protocol by which email is transferred on the Internet is called **Simple Mail Transport Protocol (SMTP)**. It uses TCP port 25 by default. Email-related programs are divided into three categories:

- **Mail Transfer Agent (MTA)**: A program that moves email messages from one server on the Internet to another. When we use the term email server, we generally mean an MTA.

- **Mail Delivery Agent (MDA)**: A program that places email in a user's mailbox so that it can be read.

- **Mail User Agent (MUA)**: A program that displays and manages email messages for a user.

The process of sending and receiving email works something like this:

1. You use an MUA (Mail User Agent—an email client like those we'll describe below) to create an email message.

2. The MUA hands the message to an MTA (Mail Transfer Agent).

3. The first MTA contacts the MTA of the recipient of the message. (This is done through DNS, as you'll see in Chapter 6.) The message is transferred between the MTAs using SMTP.

4. The recipient MTA hands off the message to the MDA (Mail Delivery Agent), which uses a set of rules to deliver the message to the mailbox of the recipient user. In many cases, the MTA acts as the MDA, placing the message directly in the mailbox.

5. When the user is ready to read email, he or she starts an MUA, which accesses the mailbox and displays the messages that have been received.

One assumption behind this process is that email servers are always available—always turned on. Users can come and go as they choose, but the server is always available to accept a message that might arrive from another server.

On every Linux system, if you have a user account, you have an email account as well. Your email is placed in the **/var/spool/mail** directory in a file corresponding to your username. So if your account name is nwells, your email inbox file is /var/spool/mail/nwells. Placing messages in this file is done by whatever MDA or MTA you are using. No special action is required to make email "work" on Linux. In fact, even if you are not running any sort of email server, many system administration programs "send" messages to the root user by writing directly to the mailbox file /var/spool/mail/root. You can open this file in any text editor to see the raw format of Internet email messages. Once the messages are stored in that file, the user can use an MUA to read the message.

When you create additional email folders (beyond your default inbox), they are separate files in your home directory. Messages in these folders are not stored in /var/spool/mail.

Because many of us don't leave our computers on all the time, we rely on a remote email server to receive our messages. This might be a central email server for an organization or a server at an ISP site. When we feel like it, we turn on our computer and use an MUA (an email client) to retrieve our email messages. We typically do this in one of three ways:

- Use the **Post Office Protocol, version 3 (POP3)** via a POP3 server (acting as an MDA) to download all the messages to our own computer.

- Use the **Internet Mail Access Protocol (IMAP)** (again, using an IMAP server acting as an MDA) to view messages on the remote server, never storing them on our local computer.

- Use a Web browser to view, delete, and create messages that are stored on a remote server.

When you use POP3 to download messages to your own host, you can indicate whether the messages should be saved on the email server or deleted. Normally you would choose to delete them so that they don't continue to take up space on the email server. You might choose not to delete them on the server if you are working on a system that you don't normally use for email.

Once the email messages are downloaded, you can read them at any time (without a network connection), extract attached files, back up the messages to another location, or delete them.

When you use IMAP to view email messages on the remote email server, no storage space is required on your local computer, and the messages can be backed up or otherwise managed by a system administrator for all of the users who have email on that server. The advantage to this is that people are unlikely to "erase their mailbox" and lose all of their messages because they are always controlled by the system administrator. A user can always download files attached to messages or print the messages on paper if needed.

The downsides of IMAP, however, are that a system administrator who has a technical problem loses everyone's email, not just one person's! In addition, because users' local hard disks never run out of space when they keep lots of old messages (because the messages are never downloaded to the local hard disk), using IMAP places a burden on the system administrator to encourage people to clean out their mail boxes if the server starts to run low on disk space.

This potential downside of IMAP must be balanced, however, with an organization's policies regarding email. For example, a company may have an explicit policy that management is allowed to review any email sent or received by an employee using company equipment. IMAP makes this straightforward to implement.

Many users now rely on email that they access via a Web browser, using the same concept as the IMAP model. A Web-mail program on the email server constructs Web pages that present lists of email messages, the text of a selected message, etc. The user clicks on links within the page that cause the Web browser to send requests to the email server such as "Send a list of message titles," "Display message number 127," or "Send the file attached to message 73." These are the same type of messages that an IMAP email client would send to an IMAP server.

You can view email without using POP3 or IMAP. If you log in to the host on which the messages are stored (where the MDA has placed them), either directly or using `telnet`, `ssh`, etc., then you can use an email client that simply reads your mailbox file in `/var/spool/mail`. Later in this section you'll learn about email clients that read email in just this way.

Using an Email Filter: Procmail

One special MDA you should be aware of is **Procmail**. While POP3 and IMAP servers simply deliver email as requested by a POP3 or IMAP-capable email client, Procmail acts as a filter, typically in conjunction with an MTA, though it can act alone on a mailbox that is already full of messages. Procmail processes email based on characteristics that you define. Typically, it is used to delete unwanted messages automatically or store specific message types in different mail folders. Procmail is difficult to configure, but it is a great way to delete junk email and autosort your mailbox if you have a large number of incoming email messages.

Procmail is installed by default on many Linux systems and is available in convenient `rpm` or `deb` package format if you need to install it. Procmail can be started manually, but more commonly it is configured to operate as part of an email server on the same system, filtering messages as they are placed in your inbox file. Procmail checks for both a system-wide Procmail configuration file, **/etc/procmailrc**, and a per-user configuration file, **.procmailrc**, stored in a user's home directory. Each of these files can contain **recipes**, or formulas for examining an email message and taking an action if it matches certain criteria. In most configurations, such as for Red Hat Linux, Procmail is installed by default and begins working as soon as you create a `.procmailrc` file. This means that you should not create a file of that name in your home directory until you have completed all the recipes you want to use and carefully reviewed them, perhaps saving your work under a different name until you are ready to activate the recipes.

 Many users create each recipe in a separate file and then refer to them within `.procmailrc` using the INCLUDERC directive. This allows you to disable or modify each recipe quickly and individually without examining an entire `.procmailrc` file.

The first part of a `.procmailrc` file contains environment variables to guide Procmail's work. For example, you might include the MAILDIR variable to specify a working directory for Procmail; all nonabsolute paths in the `.procmailrc` file then refer to that directory.

The format for a Procmail recipe is daunting at first glance, but need not be complicated when you first use the program. The syntax of each recipe is as follows:

```
:0<flags>: <lockfile>
* <condition-character> <condition-1>
* <condition-character> <condition-2>
* <condition-character> <condition-N>
<action-character><action >
```

Each recipe starts with a colon followed by a zero. A flag may follow to indicate a special type of recipe. The second colon tells Procmail to "lock" the message so that more than one process can't try to alter it at the same time. A default `lockfile` name is used for this purpose unless you specify one. Locking is a good precaution on busy systems, but it does add a fair amount of overhead when you have many recipes or many messages for Procmail to process.

Within the recipe, one or more conditions are listed, each starting with an asterisk. If no conditions are listed, all messages "match" and the recipe is applied to them. If multiple conditions are listed, a message must match all of them for the recipe to be applied. After checking the conditions, matching messages are processed according to the action character and action. This action line is often just the name of a file where the message should be stored (or `/dev/null` if the message should be discarded). If the action delivers the message to another user or to a mailbox file, no other recipes are examined for that message. If the action does not deliver the message, the remaining recipes are checked for a match against the message until one recipe delivers the message.

An email folder or inbox is nothing more than a text file containing email messages. You don't need to do anything special to create a new email folder; just use an existing or new filename.

More than a dozen possible flags are listed in the **procmailrc** man page, but basic recipes don't need any flags. Likewise, you won't need a lot of characters in condition lines. These conditions let you do things like check the size of a message (in bytes) or negate a condition (a condition is satisfied if it *does not* match the description on that line). The condition itself uses regular expression matching to check all the text within a message. To use Procmail effectively, you should be quite familiar with using regular expressions. For example, suppose you keep getting junk email from the domain *getrichquick.com*. To match any email with a From: header that included the word *getrichquick*, you could use this condition line:

```
* ^From: *getrichquick*
```

The ^ character ties the "From" text to the beginning of the line. You could check multiple headers for an address:

```
* ^(To|Cc|From) *caldera.com
```

Following one or more conditions, you specify the action to take on matching messages. If no action character is specified, the email is saved to the filename given. You can add a "!"

to send the message to the named email address, or a "|" to pipe the message text to another program. You can also use { } to enclose additional recipes for nested processing.

 Be very careful about simply sending messages to /dev/null as your action. Instead, write junk email to a file and check a few times to see if good email is being discarded because of an imprecise recipe. Once you have determined that the recipe is reliable, you can change it to delete messages permanently by using /dev/null instead of a filename.

A small sample .procmailrc file is shown below, based on Red Hat documentation. It sets a variable for the file where junk email is stored (to be checked and then deleted if no good messages are caught in the Spam Web). Three types of messages are caught in this set of recipes: those with no valid To: header, those with more than 15 recipients (this may delete good email!), and those without a valid Message-ID header. Of course, you could create more specific filters to catch the type of spam you are receiving, either based on the From: header, the Subject: header, or other characteristics that you notice about the junk email.

```
SPAM=discard
0:
* To??^$
$SPAM
:0:
*
^(To|CC):.*,.*,.*,.*,.*,.*,.*,.*,.*,.*,.*,.*,.*,.*,
$SPAM
:0:
* ^Message-Id:.*<[^@]*>
$SPAM
```

Linux E-Mail Clients

The most basic Linux email client (MUA) is called **mail**. You can use the **mail** program to send an email message from the command line or to read all the messages stored in your local mailbox. **mail** only reads local files; it doesn't use POP3 or IMAP.

To use **mail** to send a message from the command line, use the **-s** option to indicate a subject, followed by the email address of the recipient. For example, enter a command like this:

```
mail -s "Question about your schedule" tom@mail.house.gov
```

You then enter the text of the message on multiple lines as needed, pressing Ctrl+D when you have finished. If you enter the command **mail** without anything after it, the **mail** program displays all of the messages in your email inbox and starts its interactive mode. You can enter **?** to see a list of commands.

Two other text-based email clients that have been around for years are **pine** and **elm**. Both of these operate on locally stored mailbox files, but are very fast and powerful at managing your email if you don't rely on viewing attached graphics files. System administrators who prefer a command-line interface typically use **mail**, **pine**, or **elm** for their email. These programs are not installed by default on most systems, but are available for you to install, either from the CD that accompanied your Linux product or by downloading the software package or source code.

It's not uncommon for an organization to require all personnel to use a particular email system, such as Lotus Notes or Microsoft Exchange. It's also not uncommon to see a second computer in the system administrator's office that is running Windows and is used solely for company email. This is less so nowadays because most systems can deliver email via a Web browser, but you should be aware of the possibility. If you have email messages arriving on two computers, check them both regularly so that users don't feel you are ignoring their requests for help.

You can start both **elm** and **pine** from any command line. The first time you run them they set up directories to hold their files. Somewhat cryptic messages at the bottom of the screen indicate the keys to use for core functionality, with a help screen available listing all the possible commands. Figure 3-12 shows a screen from **elm**. Messages are listed with a few commonly used commands below. Single-key commands make **elm** efficient once you have memorized the keystrokes you need.

```
 root@sundance:/mnt/cdrom/RedHat/RPMS                          _ □ ×

 File   Edit   Settings   Help

           Mailbox is '/var/spool/mail/root' with 16 messages [ELM 2.5 PL6]


   0   1    Mar 25 * Anacron          (17)   Anacron job 'cron.daily'
   0   2    Mar 25 * root             (19)   LogWatch for sundance
   0   3    Mar 23 * Anacron          (17)   Anacron job 'cron.daily'
   0   4    Mar 23 * root             (19)   LogWatch for sundance
   0   5    Mar 21 * Anacron          (17)   Anacron job 'cron.daily'
   0   6    Mar 21 * root             (19)   LogWatch for sundance
   0   7    Mar 19 * Anacron          (17)   Anacron job 'cron.daily'
   0   8    Mar 19 * root             (37)   LogWatch for sundance
   0   9    Mar 18 * Anacron          (17)   Anacron job 'cron.daily'
   0  10    Mar 18 * root             (19)   LogWatch for sundance


    You can use any of the following commands by pressing the first character;
 d)elete or u)ndelete mail,  m)ail a message,  r)eply or f)orward mail, q)uit
  *To read a message, press <return>.  j = move down, k = move up, ? = help

 Command: ▮
```

Figure 3-12   The Elm text-mode email reader

Many administrators are big fans of either **pine** or **elm**. If you answer hundreds of questions coming in on a company "info" email address, the speed and efficiency of **elm** make it a good choice. You might consider switching to Netscape if you need to use a POP3 client instead of directly logging in to the email server.

Despite the advantages of `elm`, most Linux users prefer to use a program such as Netscape Communicator or Mozilla to graphically view and manage their email messages. Both programs assume you are using POP3 or IMAP to retrieve messages that have been stored on a remote email server. Within either program, you must first set up the email accounts that you want to access. In Netscape Communicator, you choose Preferences from the Edit menu, then choose Mail Servers under the Mail & Newsgroups category. Figure 3-13 shows this configuration screen.

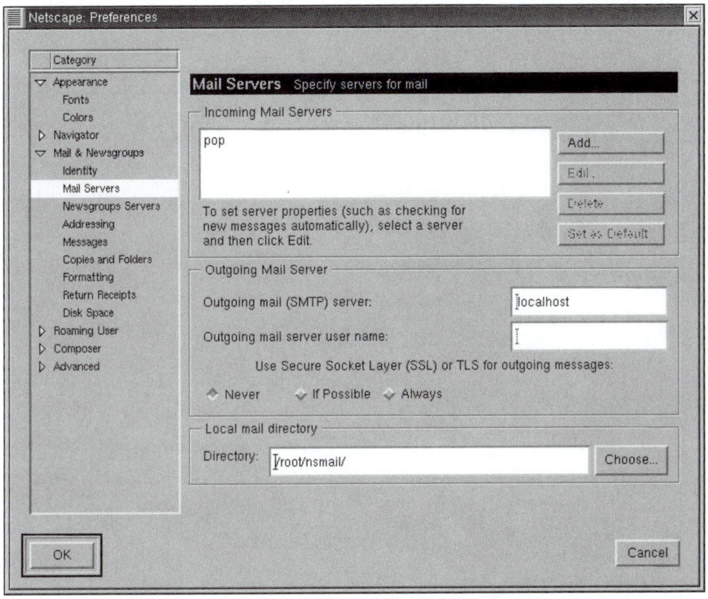

Figure 3-13   Setting up email accounts in Netscape Communicator

In Netscape Communicator, you can set up a single POP3 account or multiple IMAP accounts by providing the server information that Netscape needs to contact that server: its hostname and your account username and password. You also specify other details about sending out new messages, either through the remote email server or using a local service (such as a local copy of `sendmail`). If you are using a remote POP3 server, it's normally easier to use that server to send out messages unless you are already comfortable setting up an email server locally (see Chapter 6).

Once you have configured your accounts, you can choose Messenger from the Communicator menu in Netscape. This opens an attractive three-part window listing mailboxes (you can add additional ones), a list of messages, and the text of a selected message. Netscape stores email messages locally in the `~/nsmail` subdirectory.

The Netscape email system is similar to the Mozilla model, though Mozilla provides an Account Setup Wizard the first time you open the Email window (by choosing Mail from the Tasks menu). The Wizard lets you fill in information about the email account such as the type (POP3 or IMAP), the username and password, and the servers that Mozilla should query to check for mail and send out new messages.

Other graphical email programs are available for Linux. Two examples are the **Balsa** program included with Gnome and the **Kmail** program included with KDE (both are included on the Internet submenu by default, under the names Balsa and Mail client, respectively). These programs are attractive and capable, but because Netscape and Mozilla provide such rich and full-featured email systems integrated with a popular browser, most users who prefer a graphical email program choose Netscape or Mozilla.

 You may have noticed that `elm` and `pine` are not used for POP3 and IMAP accounts; the fancy graphical programs are used mainly for POP3 and IMAP accounts. However, other simpler programs are available for POP3 and IMAP as well. The **fetchmail** program is one example that has been popular with Linux users for years. It is not installed by default on most systems, but is widely available.

CHAPTER SUMMARY

- ❏ The client portion of the domain name service (DNS) is called the resolver. It is configured by placing the IP address of name servers in the `/etc/resolv.conf` file. Several graphical utilities are available to help with configuration.

- ❏ A fully qualified domain name (FQDN) consists of a hostname plus the domain of which the host is a part. The term domain name is also used casually to refer to FQDNs.

- ❏ The `/etc/hosts` file can also be used to resolve between a domain name and an IP address. The `/etc/host.conf` or `/etc/nsswitch.conf` files determine the order in which the resolver looks to various sources to resolve IP addresses.

- ❏ PPP is a popular method of making network connections via a modem. Configuring PPP connections is now easily done using a variety of graphical utilities such as `rp3-config` and KPPP.

- ❏ PPP security is typically provided by the Password Authentication Protocol (PAP) or the Challenge Handshake Authentication Protocol (CHAP).

- ❏ The `wvdial` utility can configure and manage a PPP connection from the command line.

- ❏ The `diald` program automates use of a dial-up connection via PPP, connecting automatically when network traffic requires the connection, and dropping the connection when traffic drops off.

- ❏ The Dynamic Host Configuration Protocol (DHCP) allows clients to configure IP networking automatically by receiving network address information from a DHCP server, which hands out (leases) addresses to clients on a network.

3

❏ Most versions of Linux include the **dhcpd** server and at least one of the three common DHCP clients: **pump**, **dhcpcd**, and **dhclient**. The DHCP client is normally configured using a graphical interface such as YaST in SuSE Linux or the Red Hat Network Administration Tool.

❏ The Lightweight Directory Access Protocol (LDAP) provides a directory service that lets users query a worldwide database for information on resources (companies and individuals). Each object within the hierarchical LDAP database is composed of attributes that describe the characteristics of the resource that the object represents.

❏ The OpenLDAP server is provided with most Linux distributions. The **ud** program is a text-mode LDAP client.

❏ X can execute graphical programs remotely by referring to the **DISPLAY** variable or the **--display** command-line option. Two methods of authenticating users who want to remotely display applications include **xhost** and **xauth**, the latter being much more secure.

❏ XDMCP lets users on remote X servers obtain a graphical login screen and begin using X clients on Linux without first logging in to Linux using a program like Telnet.

❏ The r-utilities provide a convenient way to execute commands on, or copy files between, remote hosts when working in a trusted network environment. The **/etc/host.equiv** and **.rhosts** files control access to remote hosts using r-utilities.

❏ The Unix to Unix Copy (UUCP) protocol was designed to facilitate inexpensive transfers of email messages between servers in the days before Internet connectivity was widespread. It is being used again for low-volume email servers to avoid security fears associated with the Internet.

❏ Many Web browsers are available for Linux. The most popular are the text-mode browser, Lynx, and the graphical browsers Mozilla and Netscape Communicator. Most other Linux browsers do not have full capabilities for the latest HTML documents, XML, Java, etc.

❏ Internet email relies on a Mail Transfer Agent (MTA), typically called a mail server, to move messages between hosts on the Internet. A Mail Delivery Agent (MDA) may process mail as it is delivered to a user's mailbox file. Finally, a user relies on a Mail User Agent (MUA) to read messages and send new email.

❏ MUAs can either read local mail files (including the default mailbox in **/var/spool/mail/username**), or an MUA can use the POP3 or IMAP protocols to retrieve messages from a central server.

❏ The Procmail program processes email messages using recipes, which may result in email being moved to new email folders or discarded.

❏ Many other Linux email clients are popular, including the text-based programs for reading local mail files: **elm** and **pine**; the POP client **fetchmail**; graphical programs such as those provided in Netscape Communicator and Mozilla; plus standalone graphical programs like Kmail and Balsa.

KEY TERMS

.procmailrc — The configuration file for individual Procmail users. *See also* /etc/procmailrc.

.rhosts — A file stored within a user's home directory to determine who is allowed to access that user's account via r-utilities commands such as **rsh** and **rcp**. *See also* /etc/hosts.equiv.

.Xauthority — The file that contains tokens (cookies) used by the **xauth** security system for displaying graphical programs.

/etc/host.conf — The file that specifies the order in which the resolver should consult resources to resolve the hostname to an IP address.

/etc/hosts — The file used to store IP addresses and corresponding domain names for hosts, usually those frequently accessed on a local network.

/etc/hosts.equiv — A system wide database of remote hosts and usernames that are permitted to access the host using r-utilities. *See also* .rhosts.

/etc/nsswitch.conf — The file that defines the order in which the resolver and many other programs use various local or network resources to obtain configuration information.

/etc/procmailrc — The system wide configuration file for Procmail. *See also* .procmailrc.

/etc/resolv.conf — The file that configures the Linux resolver.

/var/spool/mail — The default directory for email inboxes on most Linux systems.

attribute — A discrete data element that is part of an object within a directory service database such as LDAP.

Balsa — A graphical email client (MUA) provided with some releases of the Gnome desktop.

BOOTP — A protocol used by diskless workstations (prior to DHCP being available) that allowed them to obtain network configuration instructions.

Challenge Handshake Authentication Protocol (CHAP) — A security method used by PPP. CHAP maintains username and password data locally but never sends it to the remote computer.

class — A definition for a type of object within a directory service database such as LDAP. The class defines the attributes that an object consists of as well as its place within a directory service tree.

common name — The name assigned to a leaf object in a directory service database such as LDAP.

container object — Within a directory service database such as LDAP, an object that can have one or more subordinate objects "below it" in the data structure. *See also* leaf object.

3

cookie — A token, or long number, used as an identifier by a program such as a Web browser or the `xauth` X Window System security program.

dhclient — One of the most widely used Linux DHCP client daemons.

dhcpcd — One of the most widely used Linux DHCP client daemons.

dhcpd — The most widely used Linux DHCP server daemon.

diald — A program that manages PPP dial-up connections, initiating a connection only when needed by network traffic and disconnecting when the connection is no longer needed.

directory service — A database of information about network resources (or other resources) that can be accessed by people throughout a network.

--display — An option supported by all graphical programs that defines the X server on which the program's output should be shown and from which input should be collected. Overrides the `DISPLAY` environment variable.

DISPLAY — An environment variable that controls the display of graphical programs in X.

distinguished name (DN) — The complete path to an object within the directory tree, traversing (and naming) all the container objects above that object.

domain name — A name applied to multiple hosts on the Internet that are referred to collectively, such as *ibm.com* or *utah.edu*.

Dynamic Host Configuration Protocol (DHCP) — A protocol that allows a server to hand out IP addresses automatically to clients on a network.

elm — A powerful text-based email client (MUA) for reading locally stored email folders.

fetchmail — A basic POP3 client for Linux.

fully qualified domain name (FQDN) — The complete or official name of a network host including the name of the domain of which the host is a part. More casually, a domain name.

hostname – The name assigned to a host on a network.

Internet Mail Access Protocol (IMAP) — A protocol used to interact with a user's email messages that are stored on a remote server, as with many popular Web portals that allow email access via a Web browser.

Kmail — A graphical email client (MUA) provided as part of the KDE graphical environment.

KPPP — A utility within KDE that allows users to connect to an ISP graphically using PPP.

leaf object — Within a directory service database such as LDAP, an object that cannot have subordinate objects "below it" in the data structure. *See also* container object.

lease — The action a DHCP server takes in assigning an IP address to a client for a specific length of time.

Lightweight Directory Access Protocol (LDAP) — A protocol for accessing the lightweight directory service.

Lynx — A text-based Web browser.

`mail` — A very basic text-mode email client (MUA) for Linux.

Mail Delivery Agent (MDA) — A program that places email in a user's mailbox so that it can be read. This function is often subsumed by an MTA.

Mail Transfer Agent (MTA) — A program that moves email messages from one server on the Internet to another. Also called an email server.

Mail User Agent (MUA) — A program that displays and manages email messages for a user.

`minicom` — A terminal emulator program used to connect to a remote computer using a modem.

MIT Magic Cookie — The name given to a cookie used by the `xauth` program for X display authentication.

Mozilla — A very popular graphical Linux Web browser that began as an open source version of Netscape Navigator.

Network Information System (NIS) — A protocol that lets hosts share configuration information across a network, so that only one master configuration file need be supported for a number of hosts. *See also* NIS+.

NIS+ — A more advanced version of the NIS protocol. *See* NIS.

node — A data element within a directory service database such as LDAP. Also called an object.

object — A data element within a directory service database such as LDAP. Also called a node.

OpenLDAP — The most widely used LDAP server on Linux systems.

Password Authentication Protocol (PAP) — A security method used with PPP. PAP stores pairs of usernames and passwords in a local file and transmits them over the Internet for review by an ISP.

`pine` — A powerful text-based email client (MUA) for reading locally stored email folders.

plug-ins — Programming modules that add functionality to a Web browser, typically the ability to process multimedia formats.

Post Office Protocol version 3 (POP3) — A protocol used to download a single user's email messages that are stored on a remote email server.

Procmail — A special MDA (Mail Delivery Agent) that filters email messages.

`pump` — One of the most widely used Linux DHCP client daemons.

`rcp` — A utility that allows a user to copy files between two hosts. Either or both of the hosts can be remote to the host on which `rcp` is executed.

recipe — A formula used by Procmail to filter or examine an email message and take an action if it matches the given criteria.

resolver — The client portion of DNS, which makes requests to a DNS server so that other programs on a host can use the IP address of a named server to make a network connection.

resolving — The process of converting a domain name to an IP address, or vice versa.

reverse DNS — A method of using DNS in which a client sends an IP address to a DNS server and requests the corresponding domain name.

rlogin — A utility that allows a user to log in to another host, much like the telnet command.

rp3 — (for Red Hat PPP) A utility in Red Hat Linux that graphically presents dial-up accounts to permit easy connections using PPP.

rp3-config — A graphical configuration tool in Red Hat Linux that allows users to easily set up dial-up accounts. Typically used together with **rp3**.

rsh — A utility that allows a user to execute a command on a remote host without logging in to that host.

r-utilities — (for "remote utilities") Programs that allow a user to access remote hosts to run programs, transfer files, or perform other functions within a trusted network.

saucer — Client software for Linux that is used to browse an LDAP directory service tree.

schema — The collection of all the possible object classes and their attributes that a directory service supports.

screen number — A number used as part of the **DISPLAY** environment variable for remotely running graphical programs. Most systems have only a single X Window System session, referred to as screen number 0. The screen number is the second zero (the first is the sequence number) in the standard format **:0.0**.

sequence number — The sequential number of the screen on which a graphical program is displayed. Used as part of the **DISPLAY** environment variable for remotely running graphical programs. Its value is zero (indicated by :0) except on multimonitor systems.

Simple Mail Transport Protocol (SMTP) — The protocol by which email is transferred on the Internet.

Unix to Unix Copy (UUCP) — A system used to transfer email between servers via a modem.

uucp — A program that allows users to transfer files between two computers using a modem.

wvdial — A text-mode utility that allows users to configure and initiate dial-up connections easily using PPP.

X client — A graphical program running on a host. *See also* X server.

X server — The screen where a graphical program is remotely displayed (and the keyboard and mouse of that system). *See also* X client.

X.500 — A widely known international standard for a directory service.

xauth — A security system for managing the display of graphical programs on remote computers by sharing a numeric token called a cookie; also the program used in Linux to manage this security system and the numeric cookies associated with it.

XDMCP — A protocol that allows remote hosts to use X running on a Linux system to provide a graphical login display.

xhost — A program that can control access by X clients to an X server for display of graphical programs. **xhost** is not a secure system.

REVIEW QUESTIONS

1. Based on the top-level domains you have learned about, which is not a correctly formed FQDN?

   a. ftp.state.va.us

   b. red.marketing.lockheed.com

   c. www.ge.dns

   d. www.af.mil

2. The Linux resolver:

   a. resolves an FQDN to an IP address and vice versa

   b. resolves conflicts between multiple IP addresses on the same host

   c. resolves contention between Ethernet packets using a network cable

   d. resolves authorization issues for X clients using **xauth**

3. Which is not a valid configuration file discussed in this chapter?

   a. `/etc/host.conf`

   b. `/etc/nsswitch`

   c. `/etc/resolve.conf`

   d. `/etc/hosts`

4. Two widely used PPP authentication (security) mechanisms are:

   a. PAP and POP3

   b. CHAP and UUCP

   c. DHCP and IMAP

   d. PAP and CHAP

5. To use the **wvdial** utility, you would first use this program to create a basic configuration file:

   a. `ppp-options`

   b. `rp3-config`

   c. `diald`

   d. `wvdialconf`

6. Before initiating a dial-up connection using `rp3` or KPPP, you must:

   a. Create a valid chat script.

   b. Create all necessary `diald` configuration files.

   c. Define accounts using `rp3-config` or KDE tools.

   d. Use `wvdial` to check the `ifconfig` settings for `ppp0`.

7. Commonly used Linux DHCP clients include:

   a. `dhcpd`, `pump`, and `dhclient`

   b. `dhcp.conf`, `dhclient`, and `fetchmail`

   c. `dhcpd`, `pump`, and `bootp`

   d. `dhcpcd`, `dhclient`, and `pump`

8. Which statement is valid?

   a. A DHCP lease can assign an IP address based on a MAC address.

   b. A DHCP server requires a valid Linux DHCP client to request an IP address.

   c. DHCP is not compatible with Windows clients.

   d. Addresses assigned by DHCP include only the host IP address and netmask.

9. If you were working with an LDAP database, the following would be best described as what: `cn=Tomas_Trevino.o=Ferrari.c=Italy`.

   a. a FQDN

   b. an object class

   c. an object's common name

   d. an object's distinguished name

10. Describe at least one advantage and one disadvantage of using `xauth` instead of `xhost`.

11. The `DISPLAY` environment variable:

    a. is used only by `xhost`, not by `xauth`

    b. must be used in conjunction with the `--display` command-line option

    c. is only used when connecting via Telnet or `ssh`

    d. often includes a screen number and sequence number with the hostname

12. If you have installed and configured r-utilities, including a host and username in your `.rhosts` file allows a person using the `rcp` command on another host to:

    a. copy files to or from your home directory without entering a password

    b. also use `rlogin` without entering a password

    c. execute the command if `/etc/host.equiv` also lists the remote host

    d. view the output of the `rlogind` daemon

13. The advantage of CHAP over PAP for PPP is that:

    a. CHAP is much faster than PAP over slow modem connections.

    b. CHAP never sends passwords over the network, but PAP does.

    c. CHAP can be configured graphically, but PAP cannot.

    d. CHAP is only useful for terminal programs like minicom, not for PPP.

14. The function of `diald` is to:

    a. Automatically initiate and drop dial-up connections to match network traffic.

    b. Automatically detect and configure modems and account settings for dial-up connections.

    c. Automatically set up routes and IP addresses provided by a remote (ISP) host.

    d. Create a secure dial-up environment in which UUCP can operate.

15. The `/etc/hosts` file is checked before contacting a DNS server only if:

    a. The `/etc/host.conf` or `/etc/nsswitch` file says to use `/etc/hosts` first.

    b. A DNS server cannot be contacted.

    c. The `search` keyword in `/etc/resolv.conf` indicates a local domain name.

    d. A graphical tool was used to configure both `/etc/resolv.conf` and `/etc/hosts`.

16. Which browser is text-based rather than graphical?

    a. Mozilla

    b. Opera

    c. Galeon

    d. Lynx

17. Which protocol is used to transfer messages between two MTAs?

    a. SMTP

    b. POP

    c. IMAP

    d. PPP

18. Netscape Communicator can be used as an:

    a. MTA

    b. MUA

    c. MDA

    d. MTU

3

19. Setting up an email account for a Linux user requires:

    a. nothing; all users automatically have email inboxes in `/var/spool/mail`

    b. setting up a valid MUA with a local inbox file

    c. configuring the MTA to recognize each user on the system

    d. using either POP3 or IMAP to download messages from a remote server

20. A key difference between POP3 and IMAP is that:

    a. POP3 can be used on DHCP-capable systems, but IMAP should not

    b. POP3 downloads all messages, but IMAP does not

    c. POP3 support is available in Netscape, but IMAP is not supported

    d. POP3 is considered secure; IMAP is not

21. The Procmail program uses recipes to:

    a. Define which users can access email remotely using POP3.

    b. Automate downloading of messages using either POP3 or IMAP.

    c. Take actions on (filter) messages based on their content.

    d. Configure basic MTA functionality.

22. Each object within an LDAP directory service database:

    a. is based on a class, which defines the attributes of that object

    b. must be a leaf node to have valid attributes

    c. includes an organization and country code

    d. is referred to using a FQDN or, more commonly, a domain name

23. Describe the difference between the terms X Client and X Server when using X to display programs remotely.

24. To enter IP addresses of DNS servers in Webmin, you use what?

    a. the DNS Client icon within the Network Configuration page

    b. the Host Addresses icon within the Network Configuration page

    c. you cannot configure DNS server details in Webmin

    d. the tertiary DNS field

25. Three text-based Linux email clients are:

    a. `mail`, `elm`, `pine`

    b. `mail`, `procmail`, `kmail`

    c. MTA, MDA, MUA

    d. POP3, IMAP, SMTP

HANDS-ON PROJECTS

Project 3-1

To complete this project you need a functioning Linux system with the Lynx browser installed (on some systems it is not installed by default). You should also have Internet access and permission to write files on the local system. You do not need root access.

1. Open a command-line window within Linux.

2. Lynx has several dozen command line options controlling its functions. Start the Lynx browser with the **–dump** option to dump the referenced Web page to STDOUT. Include a redirection operator to store the Web page to a file. Here is an example, but you can choose any URL you wish:

   ```
   lynx -dump http://www.linuxapps.com > ~/linuxapps_home.html
   ```

3. Use **–dump** again, but instead of storing the results to a file, pipe them through another Linux command. For example, search for a specific word with `grep`. Here is one example that searches the home page of the FreshMeat Open Source developer site for the word `Webmin`. If a Webmin update is listed on the FreshMeat home page, a line of text will be printed on your screen, otherwise, nothing will appear:

   ```
   lynx -dump http://www.freshmeat.net | grep Webmin
   ```

4. Start Lynx again with the following URL:

   ```
   lynx www.yahoo.com
   ```

5. Use the **Page Up** and **Page Down** keys to look through the document.

6. Press the **/** (forward slash) key to initiate a search. Type the word **movies**.

7. Press **Enter** or the **right arrow** key to jump to the selected Movies link on this Web page.

8. After scanning the page, press the **left arrow** key to move back to the previous page (like the Back button in a graphical browser).

9. Press **Ctrl+C** to exit Lynx.

Project 3-2

To complete this project you need a working Linux system.

1. Log in to Linux and open a command-line window.

2. Enter the following command to send an email message to your own user account (substitute your username as indicated).

   ```
   mail -s "An email test" username
   ```

3. When you press **Enter** after the above command, you do not see a new command prompt. Instead, you enter the text of your message on the blank line, pressing **Enter** as needed for new lines of the message. Press **Ctrl+D** when you have finished entering the text of your message.

4. Use whichever email client you prefer to view the email message that you just sent to yourself.

5. You can use `mail` to send thousands of messages with a single command. Suppose you have created a file called `namelist` containing thousands of email addresses, one per line, and another file called `message_file` containing the text of an email message you want to send to each email address. The following command sends the contents of `message_file` to every email address in `namelist` by using the `cat` command within single backquotes to effectively insert the entire contents of `namelist` as a parameter specifying email recipients for the `mail` command:

   ```
   mail -s "Association Newsletter for August" 'cat namelist'
   <message_file
   ```

Project 3-3

To complete this project you need a Web browser with access to the Internet. This project focuses on how you can learn more about a topic in this chapter, using LDAP as an example.

1. Open your browser and go to the site **www.rfc-editor.org**.

2. Choose the **RFC Search** link at the top of the page.

3. Enter **LDAP** and choose **RFC** as the search area. When the list appears, review the titles. Select any that look interesting and review them.

4. Now go to the page **www.linuxdocs.org**.

5. Enter **LDAP** as a search term.

6. From the results that appear, choose the **LDAP Linux HOWTO** document.

7. Can you find the section that describes how to use LDAP for the Netscape Address Book?

8. Now go to the page **www.linuxworld.com**. This is a commercial online Linux magazine.

9. Review the titles of the articles that appear. Choose one that looks like it would contain an introduction to LDAP. Click on that link and review the article.

10. Finally, go to the page **www.openldap.org**.

11. Choose the link to the **Admin Guide** and review the contents. Do you see the different components of the Linux OpenLDAP server listed here?

Project 3-4

To complete this project you need root access to a Linux system that can reach the Internet. For each of the `ping` commands described in this project, you only need to let two or three response lines of `ping` appear before pressing `Ctrl+C` to interrupt `ping` and continue with the next step.

1. Open a command line window.

2. Choose a site that allows you to ping it and execute the `ping` command to see that it is alive. We've used the University of Utah as an example:

   ```
   ping www.utah.edu
   ```

3. As the ping packets are returned, note how the domain name and a corresponding IP address for the site are shown on each line. Write down the IP address.

4. Open the **/etc/hosts** file in a text editor and add a line like this one to the end of the file. Then save the file. (Use the domain name and IP address that you used in steps 2 and 3 if you prefer.)

   ```
   155.99.1.2      www.utah.edu
   ```

5. Ping the same site again. This time the IP address is being taken from the `/etc/hosts` file instead of DNS. Do you know why?

   ```
   ping www.utah.edu
   ```

6. Open **/etc/hosts** again and change the IP address that you entered in step 4. Save the file again. For example, change the line to read like this:

   ```
   155.99.255.255       www.utah.edu
   ```

7. Ping the site a third time. This time it doesn't work, showing you that the `hosts` file is being referenced instead of a DNS server.

8. Open **/etc/hosts** a final time and delete the line that you added.

9. Ping the site a final time. Because a reference to the site is not included in `/etc/hosts`, the resolver must use a DNS server to obtain an IP address, so `ping` works correctly again.

   ```
   ping www.utah.edu
   ```

Project 3-5

To complete this project, you need a working Linux system with a graphical (X) display, and a friend in your classroom or lab with a similar system. You will work as a team on this project.

1. Log in to Linux. Instead of using the **xauth** command interactively as the chapter text describe, use command-line options. Start with the **list** option (no dashes) to dump to the screen the cookies stored in your **.Xauthority** file.

   xauth list

2. Now use the **extract** option to create output in the **cookielist** file that can be merged into another **.Xauthority** file. You must include the display for which cookies are being extracted, which would be **:0** on most systems.

   xauth extract cookielist :0

3. Give this file to your trusted friend (email it, use FTP, copy it to a diskette, or whatever means you prefer).

4. Move to your friend's computer and copy the file containing the cookie from your system into your friend's home directory. (The easiest way to transfer the file if you don't have all your networking services already set up is to use the **mcopy** command to transfer to the file to a floppy disk and then from floppy disk onto the other host.)

5. On your friend's computer, execute this command, inserting the filename containing the cookie from your system. This command merges the **xauth** cookies from the named file into the **.Xauthority** file on your friend's system.

   xauth merge cookielist

6. On your friend's system, execute this command to start a graphical program. You can use any graphical program that is installed, but be certain to substitute your own hostname where the command says hostname. (You might try **xcalc** or **netscape** if **kpaint** is not installed.)

   kpaint --display *hostname:0.0*

7. You and your friend should see the program appear on your system.

8. Move back to your system and execute this command, substituting the program name if you used a different program in step 6.

   ps aux|grep kpaint

9. You see that the program that appears on your system's screen is not running on your system; it is running on your friend's system.

10. Close the program by pressing **Ctrl+C** on your friend's system or choosing **Exit** from the **File** menu on your screen.

11. Though you trust your friend, the next time you log out of X and log in again, a new **xauth** cookie is generated automatically, so your friend will not be able to use your system as an X server unless you hand over your cookie again.

CASE PROJECTS

You are still consulting for the law firm of Snow, Sleet, and Hale in Alaska. The firm is doing well, with very little employee turnover. Because of the static nature of the network information, you are considering taking some steps to reduce the burden on their system administrator.

1. Would you consider relying on an /etc/hosts file instead of a DNS server for the firm? For just one office? What are the costs and benefits of doing this?

2. Would you consider using DHCP instead of assigning IP addresses statically? Would you do this throughout the firm? If so, would you use a separate DHCP server in each office? What are the trade-offs you must consider in deciding this?

3. The firm has been using a proprietary email system but is considering relying solely on Internet email in the future. Describe how you might set up their email system so that they can reliably and securely exchange email within the company and also have access to the Internet. Although you have not studied email servers yet, consider what you have learned in this chapter to decide how the benefits and features of the following protocols might be relevant: POP3, IMAP, PPP, UUCP. Where would you store email for each office? How would you allow users to download or view it? How would you transfer messages between offices and to and from the Internet? Based on your initial plan, can you foresee cost, performance, or security concerns that may arise initially, or that may arise as the volume of email increases (as it always does)?

CHAPTER

4

USING SIMPLE NETWORK SERVICES

After reading this chapter and completing the exercises you will be able to:

♦ Configure "superservers" to handle multiple network services

♦ Set up administrative services like logging and printing

♦ Use simple network information services like `finger` and `talk`

♦ Understand basic mailing list and news server configurations

The Linux services that you have learned about so far have been mostly client-oriented, such as email clients, Web browsers, and the DNS resolver. In this chapter you begin to learn about server software that runs on Linux. This chapter explores a number of network services that are part of most Linux systems, including both administrative services that help to maintain a working server and specialized information services for users or system administrators. The services described in this chapter are not the "famous" ones, like Web, FTP, and email (those are covered in Chapters 5 and 6). Instead, the administrative services in this chapter include things like logging, printing, time services, and network management.

The basic information services described in this chapter will help you understand how Linux network services operate. You learn here about `finger`, `talk` (which is like Internet chat), and `whois`. In addition, you learn how to set up mailing lists to manage email in a large group, and the core concepts behind setting up a news server to facilitate newsgroup postings by the users on your network.

165

THE SUPERSERVERS

You have learned that Linux is a peer-to-peer operating system—it can be used as both client and server, even at the same time. But a Linux system is still more likely to be used (and heavily relied upon) as a dedicated server, providing services such as Web, email, and various file- and print-sharing options. In fact, a typical computer running Linux acts as a server for many different protocols or services, all running concurrently.

This is not always the case. A particularly busy server might be dedicated to just one task, such as transferring email, responding to DNS queries, or routing packets between multiple network segments.

As you learned in Chapter 1, applications communicate with other systems on a TCP/IP-based network (such as the Internet) by using ports. Many port numbers are predefined for standard services; others are used ad hoc. For example, you can decide to set up a Web server that listens to port 8008 instead of port 80, the default. The catch is simply that you must tell users that their client software must refer to port 8008 (for example, use a URL like this: *www.myserver.com:8008*). The mapping of services to default port numbers is done via the **/etc/services** file. The /etc/services file in the latest release of Red Hat Linux contains over 500 lines. A few lines from /etc/services are shown here. You should recognize these services: FTP (data and control ports), Telnet, and SMTP (email).

```
ftp-data    20/tcp
ftp-data    20/udp
ftp         21/tcp
ftp         21/udp
telnet      23/tcp
telnet      23/udp
smtp        25/tcp    mail
smtp        25/udp    mail
```

Each line in /etc/services consists of a service name, a port/protocol block, any aliases (alternative names) for the service, and finally an optional comment (none are included in these sample lines). Many different programs refer to **/etc/services** to determine which port to use for a particular network service. Although most services use either TCP or UDP as a transport protocol, **/etc/services** includes a line for both. Most of the services you need are already included in **/etc/services**, but you can use any text editor to add a line if needed. You can learn about the preassigned ports by reviewing the **/etc/services** file in detail or by visiting *www.iana.org/assignments/ port-numbers*. Port numbers from 1 through 65535 are possible, matching the two bytes available in a TCP packet for the port number. The port numbers 1 through 1024 are reserved for use by servers or the root user; clients use whichever ports are dynamically assigned to them by Linux. Port numbers above 1024 are used by default.

On a Linux system providing many services, however, it could be wasteful of such resources as system memory to have 30 different services running at the same time; client requests for each service are unlikely to arrive regularly. The solution is the **superserver** (also called a **metaserver**), which listens on multiple network ports and starts the appropriate service when a client connection arrives for that port. The most widely used superserver program is called **inetd**, for Internet daemon. Another superserver that is gaining in popularity is **xinetd**, for extended Internet daemon. **xinetd** is used by default on Red Hat Linux.

Both **inetd** and **xinetd** are configured using a text file in /etc. This file indicates which ports the superserver should listen to and which program the superserver should start if a packet arrives on one of those ports. **xinetd** has a more developed configuration model and better security, though **inetd** is perfectly adequate when used in conjunction with certain security measures you'll learn about shortly.

Using xinetd

The **xinetd** program is a revised version of **inetd** that focuses on creating a more secure environment, and happens to be more sound in its configuration architecture as well. **xinetd** as shipped with Red Hat Linux (which does not include **inetd**) includes a configuration file /etc/xinetd.conf that refers to the contents of the /etc/xinetd.d directory. Within that directory, each service is configured by a separate file. A sample file, /etc/xinetd.d/wu-ftpd, is shown here:

```
# default: on
# description: The wu-ftpd FTP server serves FTP
   connections. It uses \
#      normal, unencrypted usernames and passwords for
   authentication.
service ftp
{
        socket_type        = stream
        wait               = no
        user               = root
        server             = /usr/sbin/in.ftpd
        server_args        = -l -a
        log_on_success     += DURATION USERID
        log_on_failure     += USERID
        nice               = 10
        disable            = yes
}
```

The format of each file in /etc/xinetd.d names a service, as in the **service** line above. Brackets then enclose options that apply to that service. Some of these options match those described in the next section for the **inetd.conf** file, such as **socket_type**, **user**, and **server**. Several other options extend the functionality of **xinetd** beyond what the older **inetd** program offers. For example, various logging options are provided to determine what information `xinetd` writes to the system log when a connection is attempted, and several security options are available to control access to services. For example, the parameters `only_from`, `no_access`, `access_time`, and `deny_time` determine which hosts can access a service and when they can access it.

The extensive man page for `xinetd.conf` describes its available options. One particular option to note is the `disable` option. Several services in Red Hat Linux are fully configured but are disabled, so no connections are accepted. You can enable them by changing the line in the appropriate configuration file to `disable=no`.

You should also restart `xinetd` after making any changes to the configuration files within `/etc/xinetd.d` (or to `/etc/xinetd.conf` itself). You can use the script in `/etc/rc.d/init.d` or the `kill` command, but be careful with the `kill` command so that you send the right signal and don't simply stop the superserver. The authors of `xinetd` were wary of intruders changing access settings and then restarting `xinetd` using a standard `SIGHUP` restart signal. Instead, to restart `xinetd` you must send a `SIGUSR2` signal. Either of the following example commands can do this:

```
kill -SIGUSR2 'cat /var/run/xinetd.pid'
killall -USR2 xinetd
```

Using `inetd`

The `inetd` program is configured using `/etc/inetd.conf`. A few example lines from this file, taken from Caldera OpenLinux, are shown here. The six fields on each line are described below.

```
ftp     stream tcp nowait root /usr/sbin/tcpd in.ftpd -l -a
telnet  stream tcp nowait root /usr/sbin/tcpd in.telnetd
pop3    stream tcp nowait root /usr/sbin/tcpd ipop3d
imap    stream tcp nowait root /usr/sbin/tcpd imapd
telnet  stream tcp nowait root /usr/sbin/tcpd in.telnetd
```

- The far left field is the service name, which must correspond to a service name in `/etc/services`. The service name tells `inetd` which port to listen to.

- The next field is `stream` in all the example lines. This indicates the type of connection that is made. The other option is `dgram`, for datagram. You will see that TCP connections are `stream` and UDP connections are `dgram`.

- The next field is `tcp` in all the example lines. Most services use TCP as their transport protocol, but you will also see some services in `inetd.conf` that use `udp` in this field (such as NFS, which is described in Chapter 5).

- The fourth field is either `wait` or `nowait`. When a packet arrives at the port being listened to, this field determines whether `inetd` waits for that packet to be processed before watching that port again, or immediately hands the packet to a server and goes back to listening for more packets on that port. The value `nowait` is typical here, since it allows many more client requests to be processed in a shorter time.

- The next field indicates the user ID that `inetd` should use when it starts a server program to handle an incoming packet. For many services, this must be `root`, since the server is not designed to be run by anyone but root. If the server is capable of running as another user, however, you can improve your system security by creating a user account specifically for that server and entering that user name in this field instead of root.

- The final field, on the far right, indicates the program that `inetd` should launch when a packet arrives at the port specified by this service name. This is confusing at first because the program name in each case includes `/usr/sbin/tcpd`. For example, in the second line, the final field is `/usr/sbin/tcpd in.telnetd`. In this case this field is used to launch the Telnet server, `in.telnetd`, whenever a packet arrives on port 23.

TCP Wrappers

The `/usr/sbin/tcpd` portion of the last field is the security mechanism referred to a moment ago. For nearly every service managed by `inetd`, the program that `inetd` starts is `tcpd`. `tcpd` is a security program known as **TCP Wrappers** that examines the incoming network connection and compares it to a configuration file to determine whether the connection is allowed. If so, the "real" program is launched (`in.telnetd` in the previous example). If it is not allowed, the packet requesting a connection is simply dropped, as illustrated in Figure 4-1.

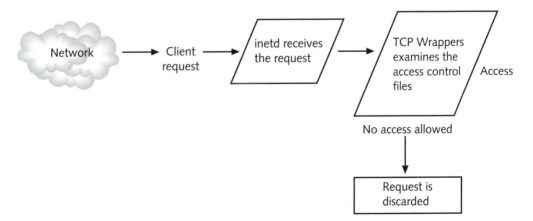

Figure 4-1   Processing incoming client requests through TCP Wrappers

TCP Wrappers—`tcpd`—is an application-level access control program. It is not a firewall in the traditional sense, because it operates at the Application layer of networking instead of a lower layer such as Transport or Internet. In theory, TCP Wrappers is not as secure as a firewall because the packet in question is already being examined by the software running on your system. That said, TCP Wrappers provides a good way to add security to a system that is already protected with a firewall. You should use both whenever you have any concerns about who accesses your Linux system.

TCP Wrappers is configured by two files: **/etc/hosts.allow** and **/etc/hosts.deny**. The interaction of these two files in controlling access to network services is shown in Figure 4-2. Getting started with these files is easy, but be aware that you should test the configuration carefully before relying on it. This flexibility in configuration means that you may not be configuring exactly what you *think* you are configuring! The format is simple. You list a service, followed by the hostname or IP address that should be allowed or denied access to that service. A few keywords are supported as well, such as **ALL** and **EXCEPT**. For example, suppose the `hosts.deny` file contains this line:

```
in.telnetd    ALL
```

And the `hosts.allow` file contains this line:

```
in.telnetd    192.168.
```

This indicates that only users whose IP addresses begin with 192.168 are allowed to access the Telnet server. Similarly, suppose the `hosts.allow` file contains this line:

```
in.telnetd    *.myplace.net EXCEPT ns.myplace.net
```

This indicates that users from the myplace.net domain name, except the name server (ns.myplace.net), are allowed to use Telnet. Of course, these examples only touch upon the complexity of the assignments you can create. The **ALL** and **EXCEPT** keywords (plus several others) can be used in the service name field as well to protect a number of fields at the same time. For example, the `hosts.deny` file can contain this line to block access to all services for all users:

```
ALL    ALL
```

Note that the default action of `tcpd` is to allow access. The `hosts.allow` file is checked first, and if an entry matching a pending connection request is found, the connection is accepted. If no entry is found, `hosts.deny` is checked. If an entry is found there, the connection is denied; otherwise it is accepted. The safest configuration you can make for TCP Wrappers is therefore to block all services to all users, then in `hosts.allow` you specifically allow any service you want users to have access to, with corresponding IP addresses, hosts, or even an **ALL** designation.

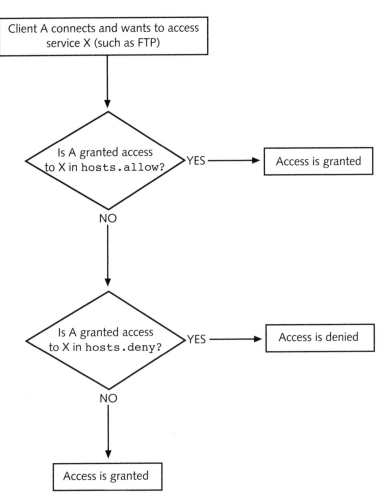

4

Figure 4-2   Controlling access via `hosts.allow` and `hosts.deny`

Whenever you make a change in the `inetd.conf` file, you must restart the `inetd` program using the system script with a command like this:

```
/etc/rc.d/init.d/inetd restart
```

You can also use either the `kill` or `killall` command to send a reinitialize signal to the daemon, causing it to reread its configuration file. An example of each command is shown here:

```
kill -HUP 'cat /var/run/inetd'
killall -HUP inetd
```

TCP Wrappers supports user-specific entries in the `hosts.allow` and `hosts.deny` files, as well as advanced options such as returning a message to the client initiating the connection. To learn about these options, carefully review the man page for `hosts.allow` and `hosts.deny` using this command:

```
man 5 hosts_access
```

 Another way to view this information is the `pinfo` command, which presents man pages in a color-coded format with hypertext links to other documents referenced in the man page. Use this command: `pinfo hosts_access`.

Services Beyond the Superserver

Many of the services described in this and later chapters do not rely on the super-server mechanism; they are designed to run standalone, without having multiple copies started by `inetd` or `xinetd` as new connections arrive. The best example of this is the Apache Web server (or its predecessors, such as CERN or NCSA). Apache was originally designed to run in either `inetd` mode (as a server launched by `inetd`) or in **standalone mode** (always running and watching port 80 itself, rather than letting a superserver watch the port for incoming requests).

 Newer versions of Apache no longer support `inetd`. They only run in stand-alone mode.

In other cases, servers such as SMTP or FTP that can be used with `inetd` or `xinetd` are used in standalone mode, because they are running on a server that is dedicated to that task, or on one that simply receives a heavy load of that type of traffic. If you anticipate a lot of FTP traffic, for example, it is more efficient to have the FTP server running continuously instead of using a superserver to manage the incoming requests. Security mechanisms in individual programs let you duplicate the features of TCP Wrappers in most respects.

Another important point to remember about the `inetd` program is that the default configuration on many Linux systems directs `inetd` to watch many ports. A more secure configuration is to disable *all* services that `inetd` provides (that is, comment out every line in `/etc/inetd.conf`). Once you have your system running smoothly, add services one at a time as you need them by removing the comment characters in `/etc/inetd.conf`. Do this after you have configured any necessary security settings and checked the stability of the server software that `inetd` launches. (This discussion refers to the second subject of this book, security, but is worth mentioning here because of the role that `inetd` plays in making many Linux systems insecure.)

By default, the configuration files located in */etc/xinetd.d/* in Red Hat Linux include the line `disable=yes` so that the service is not active (available to clients) until you manually alter this default setting.

Exploring Network Testing Services

The `inetd` and **`xinetd`** servers support several network services that are internal to the superserver—that is, no other server programs are launched. These services are used to test the network and the operation of the superserver, including experimenting with the security settings using a service that doesn't pose much threat. (Still, production sites normally shut down these services to avoid any possible security holes.) These services are typically disabled by default; to use them you must change the **`disable=yes`** line in the appropriate file in `/etc/xinetd.d` to **`disable=no`** or remove the comment character from the beginning of the appropriate line in `/etc/inetd.conf`.

Five of the testing services are described here. You can use any one of them (after enabling it) by using Telnet to connect to the indicated port. You can do this locally to explore how these function, or by connecting to any remote host on which the service is enabled and to which your host has been granted access. For example, this command starts the **`chargen`** service on the local host:

```
telnet localhost 19
```

 If your system is configured to block access to unnecessary services, you will receive an error when using the above telnet command to test `chargen`.

Some of the services described here are explored in a hands-on project at the end of this chapter.

- The **echo** service repeats back to you whatever you type. This shows you that a remote host is receiving correctly the information that you type. No password is needed, and no processing is done on the text; it is simply parroted back to you. The **echo** service uses port 7.

- The **chargen** service (for character generator) returns a stream of characters (the standard character set, in numeric order). **chargen** continues to issue this stream until you end the Telnet session. **chargen** uses port 19.

- The **discard** service is like `/dev/null`. Anything you send to the port is discarded without any processing. **discard** uses port 9.

- The **time** service returns a number corresponding to the current time and closes the connection. This number is returned in a program-readable format, which appears as unreadable characters if you use this service from a command prompt; it may be useful within a program to collect the time from another host. **time** uses port 37.

- The **daytime** service returns the current date and time in human-readable form, then closes the connection. For example, the response would look something like this: 02 APR 2003 23:17:02 EST. This service uses port 13.

USING ADMINISTRATIVE SERVICES

You can use services such as echo, chargen, and daytime to test networking. Other services are used to provide administrative services for Linux, such as logging and printing. This section describes how those services operate.

Logging with logd

You are probably already familiar with the Linux logging facility, controlled by the two daemons klogd and syslogd (for kernel messages and all other messages, respectively). These programs are managed using standard scripts in /etc/rc.d/init.d. The logging function is configured via the file /etc/syslog.conf. Multiple types of messages from multiple types of programs are generated on a typical Linux system and passed to syslogd; messages from the Linux kernel are processed via klogd. The syslog.conf file supports three basic options for how a message is handled. These can be combined as you choose:

- Write the message to a file.

- Print the message on the terminal of one or more named users or all users. (Users must be logged in to receive a message designated for this type of delivery.)

- Forward the message over the network to another Linux system, where it is processed according to the **syslog.conf** file on that system.

Here we focus on the last option. Log messages provide key information about how a system is operating and about how users are utilizing system resources. Sending some or all logging messages to another host can improve security because intruders can't change the log files to hide their tracks. Storing log entries remotely also lets you track what has happened when a system (or just a program) makes the original log files unreachable. (For example, suppose you have an isolated, unmanned system that mysteriously goes down. If the log entries were being sent over the network for remote storage, you might be able to get a good idea of the problem by reviewing the last few log entries; the log file on the unmanned system is unavailable until you fix it.)

The **syslogd** daemon uses port 514 to communicate with **syslogd** on another system. This port must be listed in /etc/services (it is by default). By default, syslogd does not support remote transfer of log messages. To enable this feature you must add the -r option to the command launching syslogd. You can best do this by editing the /etc/sysconfig/syslog file and adding the -r to the SYSLOG_OPTIONS line.

4

 The `syslogd` program sends kernel messages to a remote host if so configured in `/etc/syslog.conf`, as described below. You don't need to configure `klogd` specially.

Once you start `syslogd` with the **-r** parameter, it watches the correct port and accepts incoming connections from remote logging daemons. (You can check the man page for `syslogd` to see how to specify additional or multiple ports for `syslogd` to watch for incoming connections from remote `syslogd` daemons.) Remember that for `syslogd` to communicate remotely, you must allow UDP traffic destined for port 514 to pass through any firewalls between the host producing log messages and the host you intend to receive them.

Now turn your attention to the host receiving the log messages. To configure one host to send log messages to another host, use the "@" symbol on the far right of the appropriate configuration line in `/etc/syslog.conf`. For example, suppose you originally had a configuration line such as this, which causes all kernel messages to be stored in the `/var/log/messages` file:

```
kern.*          /var/log/messages
```

By changing the line as shown here, the messages are logged on the host london.myplace.net (typically in the file `/var/log/messages` on the remote host, but that depends on how `syslog.conf` is set up on the remote host).

```
kern.*          @london.myplace.net
```

As a final note, if you set up remote logging, you should review the options available for `syslogd` in the man page. For example, the **-s** option lets you specify domain names to be stripped off before logging an event, and the **-x** option indicates that hostnames should not be dereferenced for remotely logged events (to avoid a deadlock if the DNS server is unavailable). These and several other `syslogd` options are designed to make remote logging more effective.

Printing with `lpd`

Printing in Linux uses networking by default; it was designed with the assumption that many hosts would need to send print jobs to a single printer on the network. To configure printing to a remote host, you set up the appropriate entry in the `/etc/printcap` file (or more likely, use a graphical tool). For example, in Red Hat Linux, the **printtool** program provides a graphical interface in which you can create printer definitions and manage print queues. It also lets you restart the **lpd** print server by selecting a menu item.

After launching **printtool** in Red Hat Linux, you select the New button on the toolbar to create a new printer definition. To define a remote printer attached to a Linux host, choose the UNIX/LPD option. In the next screen, shown in Figure 4-3, you enter the hostname and the remote print queue name to which this printer definition should refer.

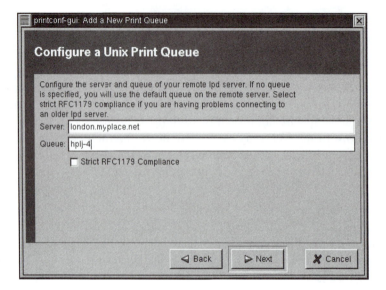

Figure 4-3   Using `printtool` to define a remote print queue

Many operating systems have a version of the `lpd` print server. Linux can print directly to UNIX, Windows, or other hosts running `lpd`. On the other hand, Windows includes a different print sharing protocol by default: Server Message Block (SMB, described in Chapter 5). It's normally better to use SMB to print to Windows hosts.

In order for this printer definition to print successfully, you must specify a print queue that is valid on the remote host. You must also be granted permission to print on the remote host, although by default, no restrictions are placed on who can print remotely. (Permissions are configured in `lpd` using the `/etc/lpd.conf` and `/etc/lpd.perms` files.) After you have set up a printer definition, it appears in the main window of the `printtool` program, as shown in Figure 4-4.

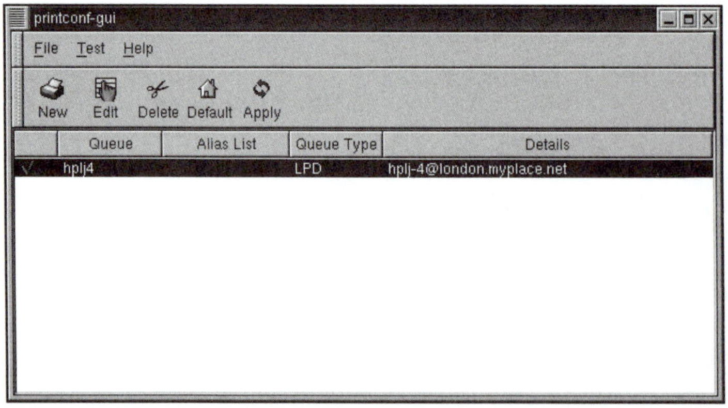

Figure 4-4   The main window of `printtool`

The printer definition resulting from using this graphical tool is shown here as it appears in the `/etc/printcap` file. Fortunately, most of us use graphical tools instead of creating such files in a text editor. The relevant lines begin with `:rm=`, defining the remote host to print to, and `:rp=`, defining the remote print queue to use. If you don't define a remote print queue when you create this printer definition, `lpd` uses the default print queue on the remote system.

```
hplj4:\
      :sh:\
      :ml=0:\
      :mx=0:\
      :sd=/var/spool/lpd/hplj4:\
      :af=/var/spool/lpd/hplj4/hplj4.acct:\
      :rm=london.myplace.net:\
      :rp=hplj-4:\
      :lpd_bounce=true:\
      :if=/usr/share/printconf/util/mf_wrapper:
```

After you have defined a printer, the `lpd` print server accepts print jobs (files to be printed), spools them to a directory, and sends them one at a time to the physical printer. Printing programs such as `lpr`, `lpq`, and `lpc` interact with the `lpd` print server.

Whenever `lpd` sees that a print job is destined for a remote printer, it uses port 515 to connect to the `lpd` program running on that remote host. Assuming that no firewall is blocking communication and that `lpd` is running smoothly on the remote host, the remote copy of `lpd` accepts the connection, processes the print job being sent, and spools it to a local file as if it had originated on the local host (using its own **printcap** printer definitions).

The `lpd` daemon is controlled using a standard script in `/etc/rc.d/init.d`. Note that some users can experience problems with `lpd` if basic networking is not configured correctly. For example, if the localhost interface does not have valid settings (as shown by the output of `ifconfig`), then printing may not function correctly.

Time Management with NTP

On many networks, maintaining a consistent time among all the hosts is important for the proper functioning of programs used on the network or to the users working with those programs. For example, if many users run a common program that manages money or handles a time-sensitive registration system, it is important that all hosts agree on the time.

The solution to this potential problem is to use a time-server daemon on one system so that all hosts on the network can obtain the time from the same place and stay synchronized. Time in Linux is managed using the **Network Time Protocol (NTP)**. The **ntpd** daemon implements this protocol. If you get involved in using NTP, you quickly see that timekeeping is a serious affair. Multiple layers of time servers (each called a **stratum**) provide time to hosts at lower levels. The top level (stratum 1) consists of several hundred servers all over the world that synchronize their computer clocks using input from an atomic clock or a satellite or radio connection. These servers are located in places like the National Institutes of Science and Technology (NIST) and the U.S. Naval Observatory (USNO).

Servers on stratum 2 receive the correct time by querying a stratum-1 server; stratum 3 by querying a stratum-2 server, and so on. A so-called NTP client is just like any other host running NTP except that no other hosts query it for the correct time. Figure 4-5 illustrates the basic structure of NTP server strata. On a LAN, NTP is designed to maintain correct time to within a few milliseconds. The NTP protocol is designed for precision of 232 picoseconds, but most computers can't maintain that precision. When time is truly critical, NTP's extensive documentation describes how to configure redundant servers and multiple network paths with cryptographic authentication to ensure that all systems receive the correct time via a known and reliable time server.

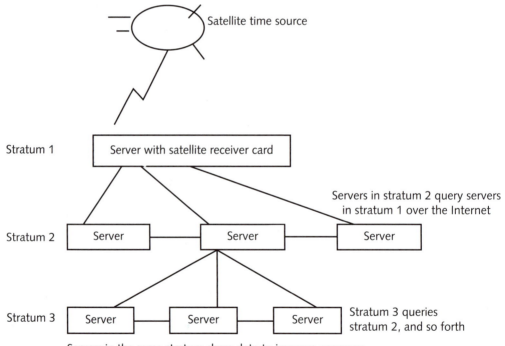

Figure 4-5   The structure of NTP time server strata

Despite the considerable power of the NTP protocol and the **ntpd** time server daemon, setting up a host to synchronize its time to another host's time is very easy. The **ntpd** program is installed on most Linux systems by default or is available as a prebuilt package. It is typically controlled by a script in **/etc/rc.d/init.d**. Before you can use ntpd, you must create a configuration file, /etc/ntp.conf. This file should contain at least the following two lines:

```
server time.server.com
driftfile /etc/ntp.drift
```

The **server** option specifies the server that **ntpd** should query for the correct time. It executes this query at regular intervals and resets the Linux system clock accordingly. If **ntpd** is shut down or restarted, it saves information in the file specified in the **driftfile** line in order to synchronize itself when it starts up again. Many options are supported on the command line when you launch **ntpd**; dozens more are configured within the **ntp.conf** file. A few versions of Linux have a default **ntp.conf** file installed that you can alter as needed.

 Note that the program name may be **xntpd** on some Linux systems.

A suite of utilities is provided with the **ntpd** server. For example, **ntpq** lets you query the time to see if the time server is functioning correctly. If the time stored in your host's hardware clock varies considerably from "true" time as determined by **ntpd**, the server may assume something is very wrong and simply stop working, writing a message to the system log (**/var/log/messages**). If this appears to be happening, research the problem beginning with the Quick Start section of the NTP documentation. (View the **quick.htm** file in your Web browser; in Red Hat Linux this file is located in **/usr/share/doc/ntp-4.1.1**.)

No man pages are provided for **ntpd**, but extensive documentation is available in the **doc/** directory. For example, in Caldera OpenLinux, the docs are in **/usr/doc/xntp-4.0.97**; in Red Hat 7.3 they are in **/usr/share/doc/ntp-4.1.1**. The NTP Web site, *www.ntp.org*, is an invaluable source of information for anyone who needs a time-synchronized server. Along with documentation, the author of NTP, David L. Mills, maintains lists of public NTP servers for stratum 1 and stratum 2 (visit *www.eecis.udel.edu/~mills/ntp/servers.htm* to access this list). For your network, you should choose a stratum-2 server that is geographically close to your site, then follow the "rules of engagement" provided on the NTP Web page closely to avoid overloading servers or offending the organization that is providing the public time server. A typical listing for a time server looks like this:

```
133.US PA fuzz.psc.edu (128.182.58.100)
     Location: Pittsburgh Supercomputing Center,
        Pittsburgh, PA
     Synchronization: NTP V3 secondary (stratum 2), DEC500
        0/200
     Service area: NSFNET, PSC region
     Access policy: open access, but please send a
        message to notify.
     Contact: noc@psc.edu
```

Understanding SNMP on Linux

The **Simple Network Management Protocol (SNMP)** is designed to give you feedback about how the components of your network are functioning. For example, you can use SNMP to determine whether routers are overloaded or whether software programs on remote servers have crashed. Using SNMP is a large and complex topic; you can research it further by visiting *http://linas.org/linux/NMS.html*. The link to the SNMP FAQ has a detailed discussion of the protocol, and the rest of the page describes numerous SNMP software tools that run on Linux. RFC 1067 is the basic reference document on SNMP (see *www.rfc-editor.org*).

SNMP uses a client-server architecture, but also uses other terms to describe its actions. An SNMP-aware program running on a host is called an **agent**. You configure the agent to watch for specific events on a host. Anytime such an event occurs, the agent collects the details. An SNMP **console** program gathers data from SNMP agents on the network for a system administrator's review. A console can also present SNMP data statistically as graphs or as summaries.

Benchmarking with NetPerf

A special aspect of network monitoring involves the performance of your network: how fast can it operate, and how much traffic can it really handle? The **NetPerf** benchmarking package can help you answer questions like these for numerous standard protocols.

Benchmarking is the process of comparing items by evaluating their performance on a fixed task. It's sort of like receiving grades for a final exam: everyone is asked to take the same test so the results can be compared and evaluated. This analogy, however, also points to the severe limitations of benchmarking: you may not get a good grade on a test because you didn't sleep well, had to miss class for an emergency, or simply have strengths in other areas. Likewise, benchmarking computer systems is subject to so many outside factors that many computer professionals don't give benchmarks a lot of weight. Still, just as grades (and certification tests) provide some measure of how well you have mastered material, benchmarks help you evaluate performance of technical systems.

The NetPerf program is one of many benchmarking suites. It is designed to measure performance of network connections, telling you how much data a connection can process (its throughput). You can learn more about NetPerf and download information on the NetPerf home page at *www.NetPerf.org*. NetPerf lets you easily test network speeds using the UDP and TCP transport protocols.

The NetPerf Web page includes a database of benchmark numbers from hundreds of systems running various operating systems. This database is useful for researching the performance that other Linux users have achieved using various hardware. The Other Resources link on the home page also provides access to information on benchmarking in general.

Allowing Dial-in Access with a PPP Server

In Chapter 3 you learned about setting up a Linux client to connect to a remote host using PPP, typically over a modem connection. The other side of that story is that a server somewhere must accept people calling in who want to connect using PPP. In this section you learn the basics of setting up such a service on Linux. The same program, `pppd`, is used for both the client and server sides of a PPP connection; the only difference is who calls whom, and how `pppd` is configured.

 Configuring a dial-in PPP server, especially for use by multiple modems, is a complex task. Your computer is basically becoming an ISP when you set this up. The information in this section should get you started.

When you log in to Linux from a command line (as opposed to a graphical login screen), a terminal program watches for your username and password, then passes them on to the login program, which starts a command shell if they are acceptable. The command-line environment for Linux includes multiple virtual terminals (usually six) that you can switch to using the key combinations Alt+F1 through Alt+F6. Each of those virtual terminals is monitored by a program called **getty** or something similar like **mgetty** or **mingetty**. These are different versions of a program that does the same thing: watches for someone logging in.

The **getty** program is managed by **init**, a master control program that the Linux kernel starts right after the system is started. The **init** program configuration is located in `/etc/inittab`. Part of this file includes configuration lines for each of the virtual terminals. A sample line from `/etc/inittab` is shown here:

```
1:2345:respawn:/sbin/mingetty tty1
```

To set up a PPP dial-in server, you must have a **getty**-type program that watches a modem; **mgetty** is typically used because it was designed with modems in mind. **mgetty** listens to a serial port instead of a virtual terminal. Whenever someone sends login information via the modem, **mgetty** verifies its validity, then starts **pppd** using the parameters that initializes a valid network device. For example, if you have **mgetty** installed on your Linux system, you can add a line like this one to the end of `/etc/inittab` to have **mgetty** watch the modem on the first serial port (device **ttyS0**) for incoming calls.

```
S1:2345:respawn:/sbin/mgetty -x 3 -s 57600 -D ttyS0
```

After making this change, you can restart the **init** program with this command:

```
kill -1 1
```

Or this command:

```
init 6
```

When another host calls the modem on your serial port, mgetty examines the characters sent by the remote host. If the host requests a PPP connection, mgetty starts pppd. To make this happen, however, you must configure mgetty to use the AutoPPP command by making certain that this line appears in the /etc/mgetty+sendfax /login.config file (this command is case sensitive):

```
/AutoPPP/ - a_ppp /usr/sbin/pppd -detach
```

You can include other options in the pppd command, but they are normally stored in the /etc/ppp/options file. The options file contains configuration parameters that apply to every copy of pppd running on your system. Each individual modem can also have a configuration file with parameters that only apply when pppd is used for that device. For example, a modem attached to the first serial port would use the file /etc/ppp/options.ttyS0. If you use a multiport serial card to attach multiple modems to your Linux system, you would create multiple options files, one for each modem device. This allows you to specify an IP address to use for each client that calls in. The main file, /etc/ppp/options, might look like this:

```
name sundance    # the name of my server
require-pap      # require PAP authentication
refuse-chap      # don't permit CHAP authentication
proxyarp         # let clients use proxy ARP
login            # authenticate the dial-
                    in user to the local /etc/passwd file
netmask 255.255.255.0
# send this network mask to the dial-in client
idle 600
# disconnect if this modem sits idle for 600 seconds
asyncmap 200a0000    # convert special characters XON, XO
                        FF, and ^]
crtscts          # Use hardware flow control
modem            # Use standard modem control signals
```

Some additional options are useful if Windows clients are dialing into your Linux PPP server. See the pppd man page for more information on those. To assign the IP address to a dial-in client, the /etc/ppp/options.ttyS0 file contains a line like this (remember to use only IP addresses that you have been assigned from your upstream ISP). This "range" causes the address 192.168.150.1 to be assigned to any client dialing into the modem on ttyS0.

```
192.168.150.0:192.168.150.1
```

PPP creates a single point-to-point connection between your host and the dial-in host. For any packets to reach the rest of the network, you must have IP forwarding enabled on your host, as described in Chapter 2.

If this basic configuration does not function for you, check the log files for `pppd` and `mgetty` (such as `/var/log/mgetty.log.ttyS0`) and review the documentation for `pppd` or the `PPP HOWTO` document on *www.linuxdocs.org*. PPP is complex, but provides a very useful service for many small and medium networks.

USING BASIC INFORMATION SERVICES

In this section you learn about a few additional services that provide simple network information or communications capability. As indicated in the text that follows, many of these services are not enabled by default after a standard Linux installation because they are not considered highly secure. You can change the settings to experiment with them or have them active as a regular part of your network.

Communicating with `talk`

Linux and UNIX systems had functionality like Internet "chat" long before chat was as popular as it is now. The **talk** program uses the **talkd** daemon to let you initiate a real-time conversation with another user who is logged in on a remote host that is also running the **talkd** daemon. The **talkd** daemon uses UDP on port 517 to communicate with remote hosts. You must enable this service in `/etc/inetd.conf` or in `/etc/xinetd.d/talkd` as appropriate; your Linux installation may not have this enabled by default. Be certain you restart the superserver if you make changes to its configuration file before trying out **talkd**.

To use **talkd**, use the **talk** program with the user name and host name that you want to contact. For example, suppose you are logged in as nwells at host london. Your friend is logged in as abutler on host dublin. You can enter the following command to initiate a chat session using **talkd**:

```
talk abutler@dublin
```

You do not use the fully qualified domain name (FQDN) because you're on the same local network as your friend, so Linux adds the domain name by default, yielding the correct FQDN for the remote host. If firewalls are not in the way, you can use `talkd` across the Internet to any host in the world using a FQDN.

When you enter the above command, the **talk** program "takes over" your window and displays messages as it tries to establish a connection with the remote user. Meanwhile, the **talkd** daemon on dublin checks whether abutler is logged in. If she is not, a message on london informs you of that, and you can press any key to exit **talk**. If she is logged in, however, **talkd** displays a message on her screen:

```
Message from Talk_Daemon@london.myplace.net at 22:52
talk: Connection requested by nwells@london.myplace.net.
talk: respond with: talk nwells@london.myplace.net
```

This message is repeated once per minute until abutler either responds with a `talk` command or nwells cancels the `talk` command with Ctrl+C. Assuming that abutler enters the `talk` command as prompted, the two-way communication is initiated and the command-line window on both screens is split, with you typing in the top half of the screen and abutler's responses appearing in the bottom half of the screen. Each line appears as soon as it is typed.

You can use Ctrl+P and Ctrl+N to scroll the text lines that have been entered either up or down, respectively, to review the conversation. If you want to stop people from bothering you with talk requests, use the **mesg** command to disable access to your command-line window:

```
mesg n
```

Using this command is a good idea anytime you are working with a full-screen program such as `elm` or `pine` for email.

If you generally work at a graphical display rather than a character-mode screen, you can still access `talkd` functionality using a graphical tool such as Ktalk (for KDE). (The actual program name is `ktalkdlg`.)

Linux also supports a number of popular chat-style systems for communicating across the Internet. Table 4-1 summarizes some of the programs that are available for various chat and messaging systems.

Table 4-1 Linux chat programs for various messenger systems

Program Name	Description
B-Chat	Yahoo! Messenger client for Gnome
EveryBuddy	A Universal Instant Messaging client supporting America Online Messenger (AIM), I Seek You (ICQ), Yahoo! Messenger and Microsoft Network Chat
Gabber	Client for the Open Source Instant Messaging system, Jabber
GAIM	AIM client for Gnome; plug-ins support ICQ, Yahoo! Messenger, Microsoft Network Chat, Internet Relay Chat (IRC), Jabber, Napster, and Zephyr
Kchat	A basic chat program for KDE (use with the `chatserver` package)
Kicq	A KDE client for ICQ chatting
Kit	AIM client for KDE
Kmerlin	A KDE client for Microsoft Network Chat
Kntalk	A KDE client for the `ntalk` chat protocol
Kopete	A plug-in based multiprotocol messaging client for KDE
Ksirc	IRC chat client for KDE
KYIM	A Yahoo! Messenger client for KDE
Licq	A widely used ICQ chat client
meko	Client for the Say2 chat protocol
Qirc	A basic IRC chat client
QtChat	A KDE client for Yahoo! Chat

Using `finger` to Collect User Information

For you to use `talk`, the user you want to contact must be logged in. The **finger** program provides a quick method of determining whether that is the case. The **finger** program uses the finger protocol via the `in.fingerd` daemon. `finger` also provides information such as how long a user has been logged in and the user's full name. Once **finger** is enabled in `/etc/inetd.conf` or `/etc/xinetd.d/finger`, the superserver watches for incoming finger queries on port 79 and sends them to the `in.fingerd` daemon.

You initiate a finger query from a command line using the username of the person you want to learn about and the hostname, if that user account is not on the same host you are working from. For example, if you want to learn about jthomas, who has an account on the same host where you are logged in, you can use this command:

```
finger jthomas
```

The resulting output from the **finger** program (via the `in.fingerd` daemon) looks like this:

```
Login: jthomas                          Name: Juan Thomas
Directory: /home/jthomas                Shell: /bin/bash
On since Wed Apr 3 19:41 (EST) on tty1  11 minutes 52
   seconds idle
On since Wed Apr 3 19:37 (EST) on pts/0 from :0
    56 minutes 44 seconds idle
On since Wed Apr 3 19:39 (EST) on pts/1 from :0
Mail last read Wed Apr 3 19:42 2002 (EST)
No Plan.
```

If jthomas is located on another host, include the hostname in "email" format, like one of these examples, depending on whether you are fingering the account from within the same domain or not:

```
finger jthomas@sophia
finger jthomas@sophia.myplace.net
```

In any case, the finger protocol must be enabled with `in.fingerd` running, and traffic to port 79 must be allowed by any intervening firewalls. The finger protocol is less used nowadays, partly because we have other methods of learning about each other via the Internet, and partly because **finger** has presented several gaping security holes in past years. Nevertheless, the real usefulness of **finger** is apparent when you learn what it can provide beyond the information shown already.

On a system supporting **finger**, any user can create a hidden file called **.plan** in his or her home directory. When **finger** is used, it sends the contents of the **.plan** file in addition to the account information. This lets a user provide information such as a mailing address using **finger**. The contents of two other files, **.project** and **.pgp**, are also sent in response to any **finger** request. The **.project** file is limited to one line, but the **.plan** file can be as long as you like. The **.pgp** file is used to provide an encryption key for the user account being queried (as described in Chapter 8). Sample `finger` output that includes a `.plan` file might look like this:

```
Login: jthomas                Name: Juan Thomas
Directory: /home/jthomas      Shell: /bin/bash
On since Wed Apr 3 19:41 (EST) on tty2  13 minutes 35
  seconds idle
No mail.
Plan:
123 Elm Street
Washington, DC 20023
```

If your system administrator likes `finger`, but you prefer that no one use it to learn about your activities, create a **`.nofinger`** file in your home directory and make it visible to the finger daemon. The `finger` program should then report nothing about you, including your existence as a valid user on the system. The following commands can set that up, but test this before relying on it for privacy if `finger` is active on your host:

```
touch ~/.nofinger
chmod o+x ~
chmod 644 ~/.nofinger
```

 The `.nofinger` file only works to block finger queries originating on systems other than your own.

As with `talk`, you can use a graphical client to execute a `finger` query. The **`kfinger`** program for KDE actually includes both `finger` and `talk` capabilities. `kfinger` is part of the kdenetwork package and therefore should be installed on any system with KDE. Figure 4-6 shows the main window of `kfinger`.

```
— kfinger                                     · □ ×
  File   Options   Help
  ▨  ▤  ▧ ⏱  nwells      ▾  localhost     ▾
 Login: nwells                Name: Nicholas Wells
 Directory: /home/nwells      Shell: /bin/bash
 Last login Wed Apr  3 22:59 (EST) on tty3
 No mail.
 Plan:
 123 Elm Street
 Arlington, VA  23109
 Fax: 312-541-1212




 Finger nwells@localhost  --   Thu Apr 4 21:31:56 2002
```

Figure 4-6   The main window of `kfinger`

Collecting Server Information with `whois`

Next, we return for a moment to the world of the DNS server. In order to maintain a semblance of order in the computer world, all domain names are registered, as noted in previous chapters. Previously, a single entity handled all registration, but now many companies register domain names. Information about each domain name is stored in a database maintained by the domain registrar. The **whois** utility queries that database to learn about a specific domain.

Learning about a domain is usually a two-step process. First, you use the **whois** command with the domain you are interested in. This causes **whois** to query the main **whois** server, called *whois.internic.net*. The results of this query tell you which registrar will have more detailed information about the domain you're interested in. For example, suppose you want to know about Brigham Young University's domain, byu.edu. You begin with a command to query the *whois.internic.net* server (shown in bold). The results are shown after the command:

```
$ whois byu.edu
Whois Server Version 1.3

Domain names in the .com, .net, and .org domains can now
be registered with many different competing registrars. Go
to http://www.internic.net for detailed information.

   Domain Name: BYU.EDU
   Registrar: EDUCAUSE
   Whois Server: whois.educause.net
   Referral URL: http://www.educause.edu/edudomain
   Name Server: NS1.WESTNET.NET
   Name Server: NS1.BYU.EDU
   Name Server: NS2.BYU.EDU
   Updated Date: 25-jan-2002

>>> Last update of whois database: Wed, 3 Apr 2002
    16:58:13 EST <<<

The Registry database contains ONLY .COM, .NET, .ORG, .EDU
domains and Registrars.
```

This is helpful, but not as detailed as you might like. Notice the lines in the output that refer you to the Registrar and another **whois** server. You can use that **whois** server in another **whois** command with the **-h** option to get further details about the domain. Here is the second step, with the output shown after the command. (You can see all the commentary as well as the details about the domain; notice carefully what you *cannot* use **whois** information for.)

```
$ whois -h whois.educause.net byu.edu
This Registry database contains ONLY .EDU domains.
The data in the EDUCAUSE Whois database is provided
by EDUCAUSE for information purposes in order to
assist in the process of obtaining information about
or related to .edu domain registration records.

The EDUCAUSE Whois database is authoritative for the
.EDU domain.

A Web interface for the .EDU EDUCAUSE Whois Server is
available at: http://whois.educause.net

By submitting a Whois query, you agree that this
information will not be used to allow, enable, or
otherwise support the transmission of unsolicited
commercial advertising or solicitations via e-mail.

You may use "%" as a wildcard in your search. For
further information regarding the use of this WHOIS
server, please type:help

_____


Domain Name: BYU.EDU

Registrant:
  Brigham Young University
  290 FB
  Provo, UT 84602
  UNITED STATES

Contacts:

  Administrative Contact:
  Kelly C. McDonald
  Brigham Young University
  Information Systems Services
  167 TMCB
  Provo, UT 84602
  UNITED STATES
  (801) 378-5025
  kcm@byu.edu


  Technical Contact:
  Brigham Young University
  159 TMCB
  Provo, UT 84602
```

```
UNITED STATES
(801) 378-7782
dnsmaster@byu.edu


Name Servers:
  NS1.BYU.EDU        128.187.22.200
  NS2.BYU.ED         128.187.22.202
  NS1.WESTNET.NET

Domain record activated:     19-Jan-1987
Domain record last updated: 14-Dec-2001
```

4

Now you have some truly useful information: the name, address, phone, and email address of a real person. You also have the IP addresses of the name servers for this domain, which you can use after reading Chapter 6 to glean further information about how this domain is configured or why it is not operating as expected.

The `whois` utility is straightforward and doesn't have other options besides `-h`. You can, however, use the command below to learn about extended queries you can make based on available information in the network information database:

```
whois help
```

Linux Telephony

A special type of "information service" that Linux can manage is your telephone system. The term **telephony** typically refers to having a computer interact with a telephone in such a way that it can be an answering machine, it can route and track calls, act as a voice recorder, and so forth. Millions of dollars are spent by companies each year to set up telephony systems to track incoming customer phone calls and manage employee use of extensive telephone switches. Linux has some support for special hardware cards that allow you to connect phone lines directly to your computer, then manage and track calls using Linux software.

Using Linux as a fax server is a simple but useful form of telephony, and Linux supports several free and commercial fax server packages. These include HylaFax, eFax, sendfax (with `mgetty`) and a number of graphical programs to configure and maintain these utilities.

The best place to begin exploring this still-emerging topic in the Linux world is *www.linuxtelephony.org*. This site is oriented to software developers, but it provides lists of hardware and software related to telephony to help a new user become acquainted with available technology. Choose Links for an especially helpful list of resources for Linux telephony and telephony in general. Table 4-2 lists a few telephony-related Linux software packages. Figure 4-7 shows a screen from gPhoneMan as an example of the information that telephony software can provide. You can learn more about this program and download a copy of it at *www.pvv.org/~skjelten/*.

Table 4-2   Telephony-related software for Linux

Package name	Description
KmsgModem	Retrieves messages and faxes from a U.S. Robotics (USR) Message Modem
KAlcatel	Manages Alcatel 50x and 70x mobile phones
Voxpak	Used to play, edit, and otherwise manage voice and fax messages
KMLOVoice	Processes voice messages received using the ELSATM MicroLinkTM Office modem
KAM2	An answering machine for ISDN cards
gPhoneMan	A generic phone manager for tracking calls (still in the early development stage)

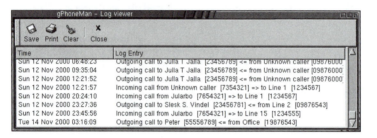

Figure 4-7   gPhoneMan tracks incoming and outgoing calls

A related but distinct topic that sometimes is categorized as telephony is the use of IP as a protocol and the Internet as a transport medium for long-distance telephone calls. This process is more commonly called **Voice-over-IP**, or **VoIP**. The idea is this: an Internet connection involves a local phone call but lets you connect to servers all over the world without additional charges via the routers that make up the Internet backbone. By digitizing a voice collected via a microphone and sending it as a stream of IP packets to a destination host, you can effectively "talk" to someone around the world without calling long distance. Of course, Internet packet routing was not designed for this type of real-time transfer, as the sound quality of many VoIP products demonstrate. However, many products are now available, including standalone Internet phones that plug into a standard phone jack but actually call a local ISP to complete long-distance calls. This technology continues to evolve and improve, especially with the increasing speed of the Internet backbone (reaching 600+ Gb/s in some places) and better last mile connectivity to homes using DSL, cable modems, and other broadband technologies. Also, the need to retool much of the Internet infrastructure to use IPv6 provides an opportunity for other new protocols like VoIP to gain a foothold over older, more established systems.

Linux software for VoIP includes the Kphone and linphone packages.

UNDERSTANDING MAILING LISTS AND NEWS SERVERS

In this section you learn more about sharing information with other users, either on your local network or around the world. Two popular methods of sharing information with a large group are mailing lists or newsgroups. Each is organized to fulfill different purposes, as you will see.

A **mailing list** enables a group of users to share information on an ongoing basis via email. Mailing lists are topically oriented. Some are designed to send announcements to members of the list, such as for Linux security issues, for new museum exhibits, or for class schedule changes. Others are designed to allow all members of the mailing list to send messages to each other, such as a list that includes all developers of a new software project, or all members of an extended family. The concept behind a mailing list is that when you send an email message (post it) to the email list, the **mailing list manager (MLM)** software sends your message to all users on the list. A single MLM can manage thousands of users subscribed to hundreds of different lists on a single Linux server.

You become a member of a mailing list by subscribing. When you subscribe, the mailing list software adds your email address to the list. You can unsubscribe later if you decide you no longer want to receive such messages. The sections that follow on specific mailing list packages describe how to subscribe and unsubscribe.

The advantage of mailing-list software is that it automates subscribing, unsubscribing, and sending all the messages so an individual doesn't have to spend the time to manage a (sometimes) huge list of users. Conversely, some email lists are moderated. A moderated email list is one that you can join only if the person managing the list (the list administrator) approves your subscription, or one for which each message posted to the list must be approved by or originate from the administrator. For example, on the Caldera-Security-Announcements mailing list, only the Caldera administrator can post messages to all users of the list.

A note of caution: Don't accidentally send a message to all members of a mailing list when you intend to send a message only to the administrator of the mailing list or to a single member of the list. Check the To: and CC: lines of your message before you send it!

Most MLM packages allow the owner of a list (a user designated as the manager of the list) to create digests—summaries of all messages posted to the list during a day or week. Users can elect to receive a digest instead of all the individual email messages. Archiving options are also provided, as well as commands to help users control what email they receive, such as suspending message delivery while on vacation.

Newsgroups differ from mailing lists in several ways. First, they are not email messages, so they are not handled by an email server using SMTP. Instead, newsgroup messages (postings) are transferred using the **Network News Transport Protocol (NNTP)**. Newsgroup postings are more like a giant bulletin board; instead of subscribing, you provide the name of a newsgroup server to a news client (as described in the sections that follow) and you may see hundreds of messages that you can read. Newsgroups are more free form than mailing lists—the term anarchy comes to mind. Although a few newsgroups dedicated to specific topics are moderated, most impose no control other than the flames (disparaging postings) between users.

 Internet newsgroups are also referred to as **Usenet news** or just net-news.

Below are descriptions of several popular software packages for setting up mailing lists and a discussion of setting up a server for newsgroups.

Using `majordomo` **for Mailing Lists**

One of the most widely used MLM packages is called **majordomo**. `majordomo` is a collection of Perl scripts that interact with the **sendmail** mail server to create automated mailing lists. `majordomo` may be installed on your system already, or you may be able to install it quickly using a software package such as **rpm** or **deb**. In either case, you need to configure `majordomo` before use by creating a user and group ID for `majordomo`, then using a program called **wrapper** (part of the `majordomo` package) to create a new mailing list with an administrative password, owner email address, and description.

 Visit *www.majordomo.com* to learn more about this program and download additional resources.

Instructions for configuring `majordomo` are provided in the documentation directory (for example, `/usr/doc/majordomo-1.94.5` in Caldera OpenLinux). Because `majordomo` configuration can be complex and may require that you alter the configuration of the **sendmail** email server, you should consider using a graphical tool to help you set it up.

For example, Webmin includes modules to configure `majordomo`. After launching Webmin, choose the Servers tab, then Majordomo List Manager. The first time you use this page you must designate which user manages `majordomo` by entering an email address in the Owner email address field. You can then begin creating mailing lists using the Add a new mailing list link. Figure 4-8 shows the page on which you add a new mailing list.

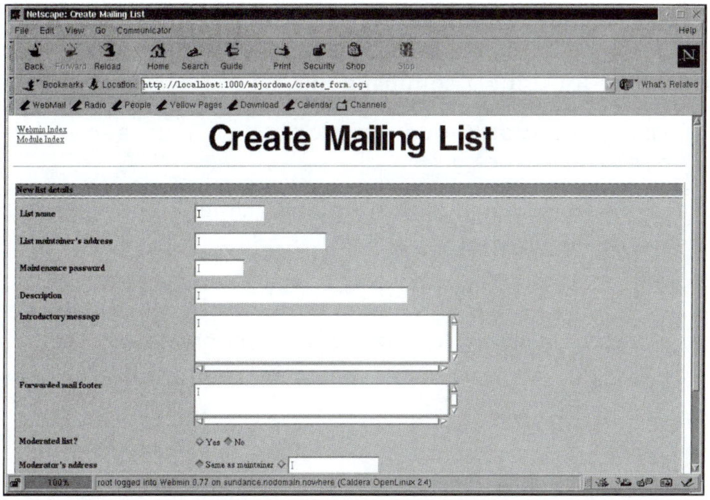

Figure 4-8 Adding a new mailing list to `majordomo` using Webmin

Each mailing list must have a person who acts as a managing user (also called the owner of the specific mailing list). When `majordomo` must report a problem, or when a user sends something to the "list owner" explicitly (using the email address of *listname-owner*), the message goes to the user name you specify in this field. You provide a password so that only the designated maintainer can alter the configuration of the list. You can also select to have the list be moderated and name the list maintainer or another user as the moderator.

Part of `majordomo` configuration involves setting up aliases within **sendmail** for the mailing lists you create. This allows anyone on the Internet to send a message to the list name as a regular email address and have **sendmail** correctly route the message to `majordomo`. For example, suppose you create a mailing list called linux-security on your host rome.myplace.net. Users all over the world can interact with that list by sending messages to linux-security@rome.myplace.net or linux-security-owner@rome.myplace.net.

If a user is unfamiliar with using an email server, a message addressed to majordomo@rome.myplace.net with **help** as the body of the message shows the format and commands that the user can send to interact with `majordomo`. Similarly, sending the word **list** as the body of an email message to majordomo@rome.myplace.net causes `majordomo` to send back a list of all the mailing lists being hosted on that server, so the user knows what addresses he or she can use to subscribe to a desired mailing list.

 Some MLMs require that commands appear in the subject of an email message; others (like `majordomo`) look in the body of an email message for the command text.

Once a mailing list is set up, the mailing list owner/maintainer can interact with `majordomo` using email messages. For example, the maintainer could approve a new person being added to the list using a command like this:

```
approve maintainer-password subscribe linux-security
    abutler@usnetworks.org
```

Some commands can be issued only by the list maintainer or moderator (and thus require that a password be included). Others are user commands, such as this one:

```
subscribe linux-security abutler@usnetworks.org
```

If no email address is included in the command, `majordomo` assumes that the email address of the sender (taken from the message headers) should be subscribed to the named mailing list.

Using Other Mailing List Managers

Although `majordomo` is widely used (and freely available), several other MLMs are also supported on Linux. These include:

- **LISTSERV** is the most widely used MLM in the world, with over 100 million subscribers being served. LISTSERV is a commercial product available from L-Soft (*www.lsoft.com*). Although LISTSERV is expensive to purchase, a trial version with reduced functionality is available as well. The advantages of LISTSERV include its scalability for huge mailing lists (numbering thousands of users or millions of email messages), flexible security features, and a Web-based configuration and maintenance interface. For subscribers, using LISTSERV is similar to the `majordomo` functionality already described. For example, you send email messages including a command such as `SUBSCRIBE linux-security`.

- **ListProc** is another commercial MLM that features graphical configuration tools, security enhancements such as password-protected postings, digests and archives, and special features like the ability to delete invalid email addresses. You can learn more about ListProc by visiting the ListProc home page at *www.listproc.net*.

- **SmartList** is a free MLM that works in conjunction with `procmail` (described in Chapter 3) and `sendmail` (described in Chapter 6). SmartList includes features such as remote list maintenance, archiving, and message digests.

- **Mailman** is a free MLM with many standard list management features. It is managed via a Web browser interface.

Most MLMs include functionality designed to reduce the occurrence of **spam**—unwanted advertisements sent to a large number of recipients (i.e., all the members of a mailing list). This is an important part of list management; mass emailers are always trying to find ways to reach more recipients, but an abundance of spam is the best way to offend list subscribers and make a mailing list worse than useless.

Understanding Linux News Servers

Newsgroup postings are passed around the Internet using NNTP. When you set up a news server, it receives news postings by getting a feed from another news server (generally a large ISP). Your news server downloads all the messages that the ISP news server has, and uploads messages generated by users at your site. As you probably know, there are thousands of newsgroups. Each can be included or excluded from your news server, either individually or by category. For example, many newsgroup postings include program files or pictures. You can exclude the newsgroups where these are posted to reduce the resources required by your news server.

The most widely used Linux news server software is **INN** (the news server daemon itself is `innd`). But for most networks, setting up a dedicated news server is not worth the effort. Unless many users (dozens or hundreds) need access to news postings, a better solution is to gain access to your ISP's news server. For reference, some potential problems associated with having your own news server include:

- You need a lot of network bandwidth and storage space. A full news feed can consume 250 GB of storage *each day*. A news feed that excludes binaries and pictures would consume around 2-3 GB each day. (Messages are typically stored for 10 days.)

- Configuration is difficult, including ongoing tuning requirements to keep the server functioning efficiently (and to avoid downtime from resource exhaustion).

- You may face policy questions regarding how newsgroups can be used within your organization, including issues such as which newsgroups can be accessed or the proper etiquette for postings to avoid complaints coming back to you as the administrator of the news server.

If you still feel that your organization should have its own news server, the good news is that some Linux distributions (notably Red Hat) include the Internet News server (INN) with most of the basic configuration already complete. This includes having a user account ("news") created for you; having the necessary configuration and spool directories set up (as described below); and having `cron` scripts to manage some basic aspects of the news server automatically, such as hourly uploads of newly created postings. Starting from this foundation, your first steps in setting up a news server would be:

- Check that the two packages `cleanfeed` and `inn` are installed on your system. (Use the `rpm -q` command if you have Red Hat, Caldera, Mandrake, or another rpm-based system.) Install them if they are not.

4

- Contact your ISP to discuss using their news server as a news feed.

- Plan your news server, focusing on what newsgroups to include, what local newsgroups you might create (for use only within your organization), and how to store articles (how long and in what format, as described below).

- Consider the policies that you want users to follow and how to inform them of these policies (and monitor or punish prohibited activity if necessary).

The configuration files for INN are stored in `/etc/news`. You can review example configuration files in the documentation for INN (in Red Hat, for example, see `/usr/share/doc/inn-2.3.2/`). Newsgroup postings are stored in the spool directory, typically `/var/spool/news`.

Even with a system like Red Hat Linux, where a lot of the work is done for you, you need to set up some information in the `/etc/news/inn.conf` file. For example, you must define parameters such as the address of the server that acts as your news feed, the address of your server, and your organization's name. A complete list of the many supported parameters is included in the man page for `inn.conf`.

To set up which newsgroups you want to include on your server, refer to the master list maintained by the Internet Software Consortium at *ftp://ftp.isc.org/pub/usenet/CONFIG/*. The newsgroups file contains a list of all standard newsgroups with a one-line description of each. The active file contains an abridged list of commonly included newsgroups. You should download both files and store them in `/etc/news`. (Download the compressed versions and then uncompress them.) Edit the active file to indicate which newsgroups you want to include on your news server.

Given the massive number of postings on a news server, the method you choose to store messages can greatly affect how you manage your system. By default, each message is stored in a separate file. A better solution is to configure the **compact news file system (cnfs)** method, which stores multiple messages in a single file. The file acts as a buffer; when the buffer becomes full, the oldest messages are deleted. This system lets you maintain messages for as long as possible without the risk of running out of disk storage and without administrator intervention to manage a large number of files.

As installed initially, INN allows all users with an account on the same host as the news server to access it. To allow other users on your network to access the news server, you need to configure the `/etc/news/readers.conf` file with details on who should be allowed to read the news. To enable this, be certain that no firewalls or similar obstacles block access to news (such as a proxy server that only allows HTTP to pass).

Two other news servers available for Linux are **C News** and **LeafNode** (see *www.leafnode.org*). Both programs are simpler to configure than INN, but are not intended for use on larger news sites.

Linux News Clients

Whether you set up your own news server or rely on your ISP's, Linux provides several good news clients that let you read newsgroup postings, either graphically or in text mode. Most full-featured Web browsers now include newsgroup browsing capabilities, but you can also choose from several standalone news readers.

To set up newsgroup access in the Netscape browser, choose Edit, then Preferences. Within the Preferences window, open the Mail and Newsgroups item on the left side. Choose the Identity category and enter at least your name and organization. Without having your name, news servers won't accept message postings from you. Next, go to the Newsgroups Servers category under Mail and Newsgroups. You must have at least one news server listed—use the Set as Default button to make your entry the server that Netscape uses. Ask your ISP for the correct server name of a news server you can access.

Once you have configured Netscape, you can begin viewing newsgroups by choosing the Communicator menu, Newsgroups item. Within the Message Center window, choose File, then Subscribe and select the newsgroups that you want to review from the dialog box that appears. Only messages for the newsgroups you select are downloaded to your system. After you have selected newsgroups to subscribe to, choose File, then Get New Messages to download messages for viewing in the main Newsgroup window.

Both Gnome and KDE support multiple graphical news readers. Some are focused on posting binary (program) files, such as Gnewspost and Knewspost. Others are more generic, for reading and posting standard text messages. Either the **Knode** news reader or `krn`, or both, come with most Linux distributions that include KDE. The initial configuration window that appears when you start using Knode is shown in Figure 4-9. For Gnome, the **Pan** newsreader is installed by default. The first time you use it, a set of configuration screens appears. Both Knode and Pan help you set up the same types of information that Netscape also requires before using newsgroups.

The most widely used text-mode news reader is probably `trn`, the threaded news reader. Because so many good graphical news readers are available, and perhaps because `trn` is so hard to learn, it is not installed by default on many systems. One example of the available graphical newsreaders is `krn`, a KDE-based newsreader.

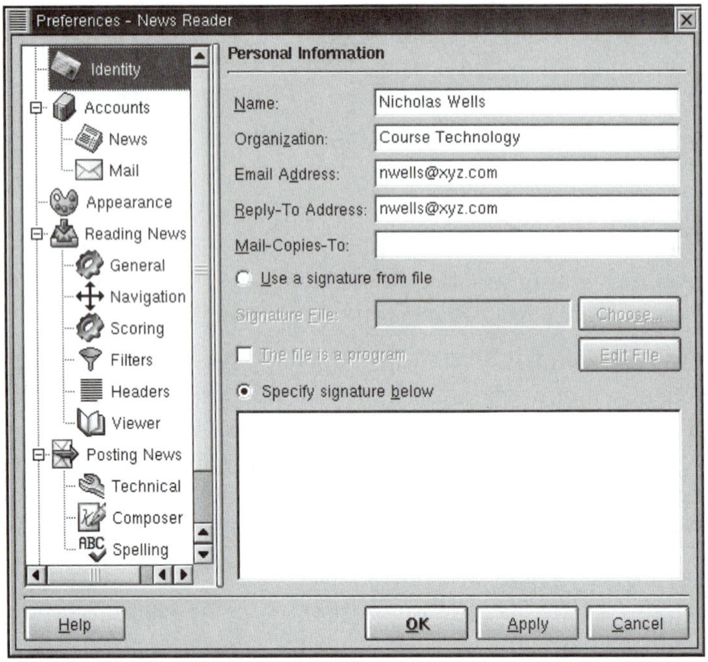

Figure 4-9 The initial configuration screen of the Knode news reader

CHAPTER SUMMARY

- The superservers, `inetd` and `xinetd`, listen to numerous network ports and start network services when needed to respond to an incoming client request.

- Application-level security is provided for `inetd` via TCP Wrappers—the `tcpd` program. `tcpd` uses `hosts.allow` and `hosts.deny` as configuration files to control access to services. The `xinetd` configuration files include security functionality similar to `tcpd`.

- Ports are mapped to service names by the `/etc/services` file.

- Some network services such as the Apache Web server and the `innd` news server are not designed to be run by a superserver and should always be run standalone.

- Network testing services such as `chargen` and `echo` are provided by `inetd`.

- System logging can be done remotely using `syslogd` by enabling another host to receive `syslog` messages across the network and specifying a host in `/etc/syslog.conf`.

❐ Linux can print across the network using `lpd`. Printer definitions that specify remote hosts cause a local copy of `lpd` to contact `lpd` running on a remote host and forward the print job to that host.

❐ Time management in Linux is provided via NTP and the `ntpd` daemon. Although complex setups are possible, a simple two-line configuration file permits a host to retrieve time synchronization data from a time server.

❐ SNMP provides detailed information about what is happening on hosts on a network. An administrator configures SNMP agents to gather information, which is then requested by an SNMP console that processes and displays that data for the administrator.

❐ NetPerf provides benchmarking service to help you determine how the throughput of your networking hardware compares with that of other systems.

❐ To configure Linux as a `PPP` server, use `mgetty` or a similar program to watch for incoming modem calls. `mgetty` launches `pppd`, which uses its option files to determine how to communicate with a dial-in client.

❐ The `talk` system lets users communicate in real time between two hosts. `talk` is generally used in text mode, but graphical clients are also available.

❐ Linux supports a number of chat-style messaging services such as Yahoo! Chat, America Online Instant Messenger (AIM), and Microsoft Network messaging.

❐ The `finger` program provides a small user account summary. If a user has created a `.plan` file, the contents of that file are also returned by the `finger` command.

❐ The `whois` command lets you query information about a domain name through the network information databases maintained by name registrars around the world.

❐ Linux telephony is a growing field that allows your computer to interact with voice telephone systems, acting as an answering machine and tracking or initiating calls.

❐ Voice-over-IP (VoIP) is a technology that allows you to make long-distance telephone calls by converting your voice to digitized packets transmitted via the Internet using IP.

❐ Mailing list management (MLM) software provides automated management of message delivery between a potentially large number of users. Popular MLM packages include `majordomo`, LISTSERV, and ListProc.

❐ Setting up a news server on Linux is possible, but maintaining such a server can entail a lot of work and system resources. A popular alternative is to use an ISP as a news server. Some versions of Linux include the INN news server with most configuration options preset.

❐ Many Web browsers include news-reading capability. Linux also supports a number of graphical and text-based news clients such as `krn` for KDE and `trn`, a text-based newsreader.

KEY TERMS

.nofinger — A file which, when created in a user's home directory, causes the **finger** program to display no information about that user.

.plan — A hidden file within a user's home directory, the contents of which the **finger** program displays when queried.

/etc/hosts.allow — Configuration file that defines services and hosts that should be permitted service by TCP Wrappers.

/etc/hosts.deny — Configuration file that defines services and hosts that should be denied service by TCP Wrappers.

/etc/services — Configuration file that maps service names to port numbers. Used by many programs, including the **inetd** and **xinetd** superservers.

agent — An SNMP-aware program running on a host. The client that collects data for analysis and transmission using other SNMP software.

benchmarking — The process of comparing performance by evaluating it against others performing the same fixed task.

C News — A Linux news server program designed for small networks with low newsgroup volume.

chargen — A network testing service provided by **inetd** on port 19. Whenever queried, **chargen** responds with a stream of characters (the standard character set, in numeric order).

compact news file system (cnfs) — A method of storing newsgroup postings within INN using a single file as a buffer for holding multiple individual postings.

console — The SNMP program that collects and analyzes data from SNMP agents on a network.

daytime — A network testing service provided by **inetd** on port 13. Returns the current date and time in human-readable form.

discard — A network testing service provided by **inetd** on port 9. **discard** acts like **/dev/null**. Anything sent to the service is discarded without any processing.

echo — A network testing service provided by **inetd** on port 7. **echo** parrots back whatever it receives.

finger — A program that provides brief information about a user.

getty — A program (and also a type of program) that monitors terminals for activity and processes it, generally to allow a user to log in.

in.fingerd — The Linux daemon that implements the finger protocol (using port 79).

inetd — The most widely used superserver program. *See also* **xinetd**.

init — The master control program that the Linux kernel starts right after the system is started.

INN — The most widely used news server software for Linux. Implemented by the innd daemon.

kfinger — A graphical version of `finger` (including `talk` protocol capability) for KDE.

Knode — A newsreader for KDE.

LeafNode — A Linux news server program designed for small networks with low newsgroup volume.

ListProc — A commercial mailing list manager (MLM). See *www.listproc.net*.

LISTSERV — The most widely used MLM in the world. A commercial product available from L-Soft (*www.lsoft.com*).

lpd — The standard Linux print server.

mailing list — A group of users who share information on an ongoing basis via email using special management software.

mailing list manager (MLM) — A software package used to create and manage mailing lists, including collections of user information and the messages those users send.

majordomo — One of the most widely used MLM packages. A free software package consisting of Perl scripts that interact with the `sendmail` email server.

mesg — Command that disables access to the command-line window so that `talk` or other programs cannot interrupt a work session.

metaserver — *See* superserver.

mgetty — A version of `getty` adapted to use with modems.

mingetty — A minimalist version of `getty`.

NetPerf — A benchmarking package that analyzes networking performance.

Network News Transport Protocol (NNTP) — The protocol used to transport newsgroup messages (postings).

Network Time Protocol (NTP) — A time management and synchronization protocol used by Linux. Implemented by the `ntpd` daemon.

ntpd — The Linux daemon that implements the NTP protocol. *See also* `xntpd`.

Pan — A newsreader for Gnome.

printtool — The graphical print configuration tool provided in Red Hat Linux.

Simple Network Management Protocol (SNMP) — A protocol designed to provide feedback about how the components of a network are functioning.

SmartList — A free mailing list manager that works in conjunction with `procmail` and `sendmail`.

spam — Unwanted advertisements sent to a large number of email or newsgroup recipients.

standalone mode — Using a network program without support from a superserver such as `inetd`.

stratum — A layer within the time server structure of NTP.

superserver — A program that listens on multiple network ports and starts appropriate network service daemons when a client connection arrives for that port. Also called a metaserver. The most widely used superserver program is `inetd`.

syslogd — The system logging daemon, which can use port 514 to communicate with syslogd on another system to provide remote logging capability.

talk — A program used with the **talkd** daemon to initiate and manage a real-time typed conversation with another user.

talkd — The daemon that implements the **talk** communication system.

tcpd (TCP Wrappers) — An application-level access control (security) program that examines incoming network connections when requested by a superserver, then compares the connection details to a configuration file to determine whether the connection is allowed.

telephony — Technology that lets a computer interact with a telephone in such a way that it can serve as an answering machine, call router, voice recorder, and so forth.

time — A network testing service provided by **inetd** on port 37. Returns a number corresponding to the current time in a program-readable format, which appears as unreadable characters on-screen.

trn — The threaded news reader, probably the most widely used text-mode news reader for Linux.

Usenet news — Another name for Internet newsgroups.

Voice-over-IP (VoIP) — Use of IP as a protocol for transport of digitized voice packets, often as a medium for long-distance telephone calls over the Internet.

whois — A utility that queries an Internet database to learn about the person who manages a specific domain.

xinetd — A superserver with extended configuration options. Standard on Red Hat Linux instead of the more usual **inetd** program.

xntpd — A daemon used on some Linux systems to implement the NTP protocol. *See also* ntpd.

REVIEW QUESTIONS

1. Which line would occur in the `/etc/services` file?

   a. `telnet 23/tcp`

   b. `telnet stream tcp nowait root /usr/sbin/tcpd in.telnetd`

   c. `in.telnetd *.myplace.net EXCEPT ns.myplace.net`

   d. `telnet localhost 19`

2. Linux port numbers reserved for use by system services and the root user include:

   a. all ports up to 65,535

   b. only those specified in `/etc/services`

   c. ports below 1024

   d. ports assigned by Internet authorities

3. The inetd superserver typically starts:

a. TCP Wrappers

b. an Internet service daemon such as `in.ftpd`

c. `pppd`

d. standalone services like a Web server

4. The `nowait` option within `inetd` or `xinetd` configuration indicates:

a. that ICMP packets should not respond to ping packets

b. that additional copies of a service daemon can be started without waiting for the current copy to finish processing

c. that TCP Wrappers should be used to process the client request

d. that the UDP transport protocol should be used for the client request

5. TCP Wrappers is configured using:

a. `/etc/hosts`

b. `/etc/inetd.conf`

c. `/etc/hosts.allow` and `/etc/hosts.deny`

d. `/etc/services`

6. Select the meaning of the `in.telnetd 192.168.0` line within `/etc/hosts.allow`:

a. Deny access to the Telnet service for all hosts on any network ID starting with 192.168.0.

b. Permit access to the Telnet service for all hosts on any network ID starting with 192.168.0.

c. Deny access to the Telnet service for any host except those on any network ID starting with 192.168.0.

d. Permit access to the Telnet service for all hosts except those on any network ID starting with 192.168.0.

7. To enable remote logging using `syslogd`, you must:

a. Use the `-r` option when starting `syslogd`.

b. Include port 514 in `/etc/services` and allow traffic for that port through firewalls.

c. use a @hostname designation within `/etc/syslog.conf`.

d. only a and b

e. answers a, b, and c

8. The `lpd` program allows Linux to:

    a. manage print queues on remote print servers

    b. print to remote printers when properly defined in `/etc/printcap`

    c. connect to remote hosts using a modem

    d. access control agents used by management protocols

9. Describe the arrangement of time servers in multiple strata as used for NTP.

10. An SNMP agent provides:

    a. detailed event information to an SNMP console

    b. analysis of multiple events from a range of hosts

    c. access to an SNMP console via a graphical interface

    d. configuration capability through either Gnome or KDE

11. Describe the purpose of benchmarking.

12. Which program is used to listen for modem connections and start `pppd` when needed?

    a. `init`

    b. SNMP

    c. `mgetty`

    d. `majordomo`

13. IP addresses are usually assigned to multiple modems connected to a dial-in PPP server using:

    a. the `/etc/ppp/options` file

    b. information in the `/etc/mgetty+sendfax` configuration files

    c. parameters included in `/etc/inittab`

    d. individual `/etc/ppp/options` files named for each device (such as `ttyS0`)

14. To prevent `talkd` from interrupting a work session, you:

    a. Create a `.nofinger` file in your home directory.

    b. Issue the command `mesg n`.

    c. Delete any `.plan` file in your home directory.

    d. Use a graphical program such a Ktalk to initiate the session.

15. Name three Linux clients used for messaging or chatting.

16. Which piece of information about the queried user is not included in a standard reply to `finger`?

    a. the contents of the `.pgp` file in the user's home directory

    b. the full name of the user whose account is queried

    c. the user's home directory

    d. the contents of the `.nofinger` file

17. The main `whois` server, whois.internic.net,

    a. is the only place on the Internet where information about domain maintainers is stored

    b. is replicated at various sites around the world

    c. can refer you to other `whois` servers that can provide specific information on domains not provided by whois.internic.net

    d. must be specified with the `-h` parameter of the `whois` command

18. Briefly explain the difference between Linux telephony and Voice-over-IP technology.

19. Which MLM can be configured using Webmin?

    a. `majordomo`

    b. SmartList

    c. LISTSERV

    d. INN

20. A moderated mailing list refers to one that:

    a. only accepts postings via newsgroups

    b. requires that a list moderator approve subscriptions and/or message postings

    c. has been configured using LISTSERV

    d. uses a filter to prevent spam

21. Linux news servers include:

    a. Knode, `trn`, and `pan`

    b. INN, NTP, and SNMP

    c. `trn`, `elm`, and `majordomo`

    d. INN, C News, and LeafNode

22. Network testing services provided by `inetd` include:

    a. `chargen`, `daytime`, `echo`, and `discard`

    b. `mesg`, `chargen`, and SNMP

    c. `daytime`, `time`, `date`, and `echo`

    d. `getty`, `mgetty`, and `mingetty`

23. Using a server in standalone mode refers to:

    a. relying on information in `/etc/services` so that `inetd` can initiate it correctly

    b. not using a superserver to control the server

    c. testing the server by connecting only to `localhost`

    d. relying on TCP Wrappers for security rather than built-in security functions

24. Which must be done as part of establishing a dial-in PPP server?

    a. Create an options file for pppd.

    b. Configure a `getty`-like program to monitor incoming modem calls.

    c. Establish AutoPPP to make `getty` launch `pppd`.

    d. Create a CHAP authentication file.

25. What does the term metaserver refer to?

HANDS-ON PROJECTS

Project 4-1

In this project you establish a time server using NTP. To complete this project you need root access to your Linux system and an Internet connection.

1. Log in as root and open a command-line window.

2. Be certain that the NTP server software is installed on your system. You can do this by looking for either `ntp` or `xntpd` in the directory `/etc/rc.d/init.d` or the corresponding system startup script directory on your version of Linux. Or, you can search for the NTP package. This command will find an `rpm` package on most `rpm`-based versions of Linux:

    ```
    rpm -qa | grep ntp
    ```

3. Open a Web browser and go to *www.ntp.org*.

4. Select the **Public NTP Servers** link.

5. Open the list of secondary time servers by clicking **Public NTP Secondary (stratum 2) Time Servers**. The list of servers is organized alphabetically, first by two-letter country code, then by state or province code. Locate the time servers in your state or province, or as close to you as possible. Carefully review the Access Policy field of each listing in your area to choose one that you can use.

6. Copy the information from the server you have selected. (Write it down or copy and paste it into a document that you can save.) The critical information is the IP address of the server and the email address of the administrator, since in most cases you want to send an email to that person informing them of your intention to use their time server.

7. Now configure your NTP daemon. See if you have an `/etc/ntp.conf` file already installed (both Red Hat and Caldera versions of Linux normally do). If you do, open it and find the **server** line (usually about the first noncomment line in the file—add it as shown below if you don't find one). Place the IP address of the time server after the keyword **server**. For example:

    ```
    server 140.162.8.3
    ```

8. If you don't have an `ntp.conf` file, open a text editor and create one with the following two lines, substituting the IP address of the server that you located above.

```
server 140.162.8.3
driftfile /etc/ntp.drift
```

Then create the `drift` file with this command:

```
touch /etc/ntp.drift
```

4

9. With NTP configured, you are ready to restart the `ntpd` or `xntpd` daemon. Use a set of commands like this to do so:

```
/etc/rc.d/init.d/ntpd stop
/etc/rc.d/init.d/ntpd start
```

10. Wait a moment for the server to attempt to contact the time server, then use the `ntpq` program to query the time server.

```
ntpq
```

11. You can use the `help` command at the `ntpq` prompt to see a list of ntpq commands. Then use **help *command_name*** to see a one-line description of any command. Use the `poll` command to query a time server from within the `ntpq` command:

```
poll 1
```

Project 4-2

In this project you use `whois` to look for information about a domain name. To complete this project you need a working Linux system and an Internet connection.

For this project, you are helping a friend set up the new computer lab at Alexandria High School in Northern Virginia. Since this will be a small lab, you want to have a couple of backup DNS servers that you can include in your configurations in case you need to stop your local DNS server for maintenance. You decide that Northern Virginia Community College (NVCC) probably wouldn't mind if you pointed to their site for your secondary and tertiary DNS servers.

1. You've seen two different URLs for the NVCC site. Try the first one, *nvcc.vccs.edu*, in a `whois` query. What result do you see?

2. If this didn't work, maybe you need to reference the `whois` server that is specific to the .edu domain. If you didn't do this in Step 1, use *whois.educause.net* and query again for *nvcc.vccs.edu*.

3. If this still didn't work, consider the address itself. It apparently refers to NVCC within some larger unit, vccs—probably the Virginia Community College System, or something like that. With this theory in mind, try a query to the Educause whois server using just *vccs.edu*. What results do you see?

4. You are concerned that the VCCS people may not have direct authority over the NVCC servers, so you decide to try the other NVCC address to see if you can locate someone at that school. Run a **whois** query for *nv.cc.va.us*. (You might want to view both *www.nv.cc.va.us* and *www.nvcc.vccs.edu* in your Web browser first to check that they are valid domains.) Where did you query for *nv.cc.va.us*? What result did you see, and why did you get that result?

5. Concerned that you haven't been able to find the contact person yet at NVCC, you decide to try the University of Virginia site, *uva.edu*. Make this **whois** query. Sometimes a query directly to *whois.internic.net* connects directly to another **whois** server such as *educause.net*. Other times you may need to specify Educause.net as your **whois** server.

6. From the information listed, obtain the IP addresses of the DNS servers and the name, phone, and email address of the contact person. You should check with the contact person as a courtesy before referencing their DNS servers.

Project 4-3

In this project you experiment with the **finger** protocol. To complete this project you need Red Hat Linux 7.3 installed and root access to the system.

1. Log in as root and open a command-line window.

2. Verify that the finger-server package is installed using this command:

   ```
   rpm -q finger-server
   ```

3. Enable the finger-server configuration in **xinetd** by modifying the **disable** line in /etc/xinetd.d/finger.

4. Also enable the **daytime** and **chargen** services by modifying the **disable** line in /etc/xinet.d/daytime and also within /etc/xinetd.d/chargen.

5. Restart **xinetd** to make your changes active.

6. Experiment with the **daytime** service by issuing a **telnet** command to the **daytime** port. Why might you want to use this network service?

   ```
   telnet 127.0.0.1 13
   ```

7. Experiment with the **chargen** service by issuing a **telnet** command to the **chargen** port. Why might this service be useful in testing your network?

   ```
   telnet 127.0.0.1 19
   ```

8. Use a text editor to create a **.plan** file within the home directory of your regular user account. Include information in the file such as a favorite saying or a list of your classes.

9. Set the permission of the **.plan** text file to **644** using **chmod**.

10. While still logged in as root, finger your regular user account. What information is returned by `finger`?

11. Find a friend in your classroom or computer lab who has participated in this project. Ask for their username and hostname, then finger that username and hostname. What result do you see?

Project 4-4

4

In this project you explore the `xinetd` superserver configuration. Because `finger` is a convenient method of doing this, you may find Project 4-3 useful as background before doing this project; however, note that the options used here are part of the `xinetd` configuration and are not specific to `finger`. To complete this project you need Red Hat Linux 7.3 installed and root access to the system. You should work as a team with another student to complete this project; designate one of your systems as client and one as root, then work together as directed.

1. Determine the IP address (or hostname if you have access to a DNS server) of the client system.

2. Log in as root on the server and open a command-line window.

3. If you have not already done so in Project 4-3, enable `finger` within the `/etc/xinetd.d` directory and restart `xinetd` to make that change take effect.

4. From the client, finger your regular user account on the server. You should see a basic `finger` reply.

5. On the server, edit the `finger` configuration file to add a `no_access` line that refers to the IP address of the client as in this example, but use the IP address for your client system:

   ```
   no_access = 192.168.100.10
   ```

6. Restart `xinetd` on the server, then finger your user account from the client. What is the result?

7. Add the following two lines to the `finger` configuration file on the server:

   ```
   log_type = FILE /tmp/fingerlog
   log_on_failure  += HOST
   ```

8. Restart `xinetd` on the server.

9. Create the log file using `touch`. How could you alter the `log_type` attribute to take advantage of the default system logging facilities? (See the `xinetd.conf` man page.)

10. Open a second command-line window and use this command to watch the log during the next few steps.

    ```
    tail -f /tmp/fingerlog
    ```

11. From the client, finger your user account on the server again. What result do you see on the client? On the server?

12. Add the following line to the `finger` configuration file, but using the client's IP address:

    ```
    only_from = 192.168.100.10
    ```

13. Restart `xinetd`, then go to the client and finger your user account on the server again. What result do you see on the client? On the server? Which takes precedence, the `only_from` attribute or the `no_access` attribute?

14. Delete from the finger configuration file the `no_access` line, save the file, and restart `xinetd`.

15. From the client, finger your user account a final time. What result do you see? How could you alter the logging done in this case?

16. Remove all of the extra lines from the `finger` configuration file and restart `xinetd`.

Project 4-5

In this project you learn more about some of the hardware options available to Linux as a dial-in PPP server. To complete this project you need a Web browser with Internet access.

1. Stallion Technologies and Sangoma Technologies have supported Linux users of their hardware for many years. Go to the Stallion Technologies Web site at *www.stallion.com* and look for the EasyIO multiport serial adapter on the Products page. This is a basic card that lets you attach either 4 or 8 modems through a single expansion slot. Stallion and others sell cards supporting 256 or more modems on a single card.

2. Review the information on EasyIO. What is the stated maximum data rate per port?

3. Assume that the EasyIO product sounds appropriate for your needs, but you don't know if it has Linux support. Return to the home page of Stallion Technologies and search for a Linux driver for EasyIO by using the **download** link.

4. Within the listed drivers for the EasyIO product, is the Linux operating system shown? If so, what is the filename of the driver software provided?

5. With EasyIO selected as the modem port card, you also want a high-speed card to connect your PPP server to the Internet via a T-1 line. Visit the Sangoma Web site at *www.sangoma.com* to explore their networking products.

6. Look for WAN Cards under the **Products** link. Can you see any cards that support T-1 connections?

7. Under Service/Support you see a link for WanPipe for Linux. What does this refer to? Are the T-1 cards supported in Linux or not?

8. If it appears they are, what is the filename for the latest WanPipe software for Red Hat Linux 7.3 running on an SMP server?

CASE PROJECTS

Returning once again to the law offices of Snow, Sleet, and Hale, you are thinking today about the services that the offices may need.

1. Of the basic network services you learned about in this chapter—`finger`, `talk`, `chargen`, `echo`, `daytime`, `discard`—which, if any, might be useful to the users on the law office network? Why did you select any that you did?

2. Lawyers use a lot of paper—even lawyers that specialize in environmental work. Nevertheless, why might you choose *not* to use `lpd` as your main remote printing mechanism for these offices? (Hint: think about the clients that are printing.)

3. Would a PPP dial-in server be of use to these offices, either to employees working from home, or as a connection between the different offices? What concerns would you have about using a PPP dial-in server for either use? If you feel that a PPP server is useful, what concerns would you have if the size of the firm doubled after you had set up the PPP server and dial-in clients?

4. A few attorneys have asked about using a mailing list to share information about legal topics and current clients of the firm. It does sound useful to you. Consider the following questions, including your reasons for each response: which MLM would you likely use? Where would you host the mailing lists? Who would you make the maintainer of various lists? What security concerns would these lists raise? Given what you know about the size of the law firm and the volume of messages that you think they would generate, would newsgroups be a better option than a mailing list?

5

CONFIGURING FILE SHARING SERVICES

After reading this chapter and completing the exercises you will be able to:

♦ Configure an FTP server for anonymous or regular users

♦ Set up NFS file sharing between Linux and UNIX systems

♦ Understand NetWare NCP-based file sharing

♦ Use SMB to share files and printers with Windows-based PCs

In this chapter, you explore different file sharing technologies that let you exchange information with computers running Linux and a number of other operating systems.

Each of the file-sharing methods described in this chapter has strengths and weaknesses; you will learn to decide which technology to use based on the operating systems you are working with and the differing needs of your network.

RUNNING AN **FTP** SERVER

The **File Transfer Protocol (FTP)** has been used for decades to share files between networked computer systems. It was part of UNIX in the 1960s. Since then client and server programs to implement FTP file sharing have been developed for almost all available platforms. Much of the value of FTP comes from the ability to share files between nearly any two computers. Another source of the ongoing popularity of FTP is that it is integrated into modern Web browsers. You may have downloaded information from an FTP server within a browser and not even realized it.

Remember from the discussion of network protocols in Chapter 1 that different protocols were designed to meet different needs. Some of the design characteristics of FTP are listed here:

- FTP was designed for efficient distribution of a single file to multiple remote clients.

- FTP operates in real time, so when you finish using FTP, you have downloaded a file or files on your local computer. (Compare this to email; when you press Send, the email message you created is not immediately delivered to the recipient.)

- FTP was designed to be used by the public. This is called **anonymous FTP**, because any user can log in anonymously (without a predefined user account on the FTP server) and download files.

- FTP is an effective protocol for transferring large files. In contrast, both HTTP and SMTP were designed for small files. Despite the popularity of email and Web browsing, FTP traffic still accounts for a large number of the packets traveling the Internet.

- FTP was not designed to be used as a "shared local disk." That is, many protocols (such as NFS, NCP, and SMB, described later in this chapter) were designed with the expectation that you would assign a local directory to the networked drive, so that when you looked at the contents of a certain local directory, you would really be looking at a network resource—a remote hard disk provided via the file-sharing protocol. FTP, on the other hand, was designed differently: you log in, download, and log out.

FTP servers are very popular for anonymous users: when you have files that you want to be available to anyone, FTP is the protocol of choice. Many servers on the Internet are dedicated solely to FTP traffic, providing a repository of downloadable Linux programs, NASA images, government documents, or the like. Although security holes have been discovered (and repaired) in FTP, it was designed with anonymous users in mind. You can also set up an FTP server that is only used by "known" users, or that supports both known and anonymous users.

Using an FTP Client

Accessing an FTP site requires an FTP client. Linux includes a text-mode FTP client that you can use from any command line. An FTP client session begins with the **ftp** command and the name of the server you want to contact:

```
ftp ftp.ibiblio.org
```

 The **ncftp** program is a newer and more refined text-mode ftp program. It is installed by default on many Linux systems, including Red Hat Linux, but the **ftp** program remains the old standby. You can try **ncftp** on your own after learning **ftp**; the commands are very similar.

If your system can connect to the FTP server (resolve the hostname, etc.), you are prompted for a username and password. For a public FTP site, you should enter *anonymous* as your username (the username **ftp** often works, as well). Then use your email address as your password. Some systems won't let you log in without entering an email address in a valid format, but most do not care what you enter. The information is logged, creating a record for the system administrator.

Once you have logged in, you typically see a welcome message followed by the **ftp>** prompt. From this prompt, you can enter commands to control interaction with the FTP server. Table 5-1 shows a list of often-used FTP client commands. When you are finished with the FTP client, enter **bye** to exit.

Table 5-1   Often-used commands in the text-mode FTP client

Command Name	Description
open	Initiate a connection to an FTP server
close	End an FTP connection
ls	List the contents of the current directory on the FTP server
pwd	Display the current directory you are working in on the FTP server
cd	Change to a new directory (follow the command with the directory name you want to switch to)
get	Download a file; include a filename after the command; regular expressions (such as ? and *) are not allowed (use mget)
mget	Download a set of files. Include a filename that may include regular expression characters (such as ? or *) after the command name. You are prompted to answer Y or N to each matching filename to say if you want to download it. To avoid this prompting, execute the prompt command.
put	Upload files to the FTP server. On most FTP servers this is only allowed for those with regular user accounts, not anonymous users. Include the name of the file you want to upload.

Table 5-1 Often-used commands in the text-mode FTP client (continued)

Command Name	Description
mput	Upload multiple files from your system to the FTP server. Include a regular expression pattern to define the files you want to upload. You are prompted to answer Y or N for each matching file (unless you have issued the prompt command).
lcd	Change the directory that you are working in on your local system (not on the FTP server); useful when you want to download files to a different directory than the one you were in when you started the FTP client
prompt	Turn off or on prompting for downloading or uploading multiple files; enter the command alone to toggle between off and on, or include either word after the command.
binary	Set the transfer mode to 8-bit. Everything but plaintext files should be transferred in binary mode, otherwise you lose part of every byte in the file. If you download a program and it won't even run, this is often the cause. The ascii command changes to 7-bit mode for text files, though you can use binary mode to download them as well.
bye	Exit the FTP client

If you prefer working in a graphical environment, you can use a Web browser to access FTP sites. For example, point your browser to *ftp://ftp.hq.nasa.gov*. The Web browser uses the name *anonymous* and your email address to log in to the server and displays the main directory. The browser also creates HTML "Web" pages from the FTP server file listings on the fly as you change directories. Depending on your browser, you can usually download a file by clicking on it and entering the location to save it in a dialog box. Figure 5-1 shows a browser being used to access the NASA FTP site.

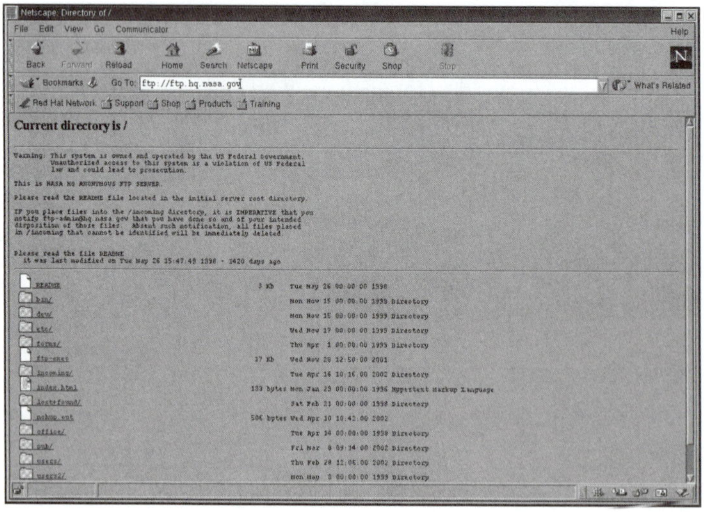

Figure 5-1 Using a browser to access a public FTP site

You can access FTP sites with real user accounts. Use the format *ftp://user-name@ftp.servername.com/*. The browser prompts you for a password after making a connection. But beware: as with any FTP client, your username and password are transferred without encryption across the network.

So far, you've used only the *anonymous* user account to access public FTP sites. If you have a user account on a remote server, and that server is running FTP server software, you can also log in with your user account and transfer files between your host and the remote host on which you have an account. Anonymous FTP servers restrict your access for security reasons, but when you log in using an FTP client to a server on which you have a regular user account, you can access all parts of the system, change filenames, upload, download, delete files—anything that you could do if you were logged in at the remote host using the same username. Of course, the FTP administrator may restrict which activities you can perform remotely, again for security reasons. You'll learn how shortly.

Using a browser as your FTP client limits you to basic directory listings and file downloads, but several graphical FTP clients provide much more complete FTP functionality. One good example is the **gFTP** program, shown in Figure 5-2. You enter the host that you want to connect to, plus your username and password, in the fields at the top of the window. You can select to transfer files with either FTP, HTTP, or SSH (described in Chapter 8). gFTP is not specifically oriented toward anonymous FTP users—it has a number of options that are useful for regular users who access their accounts on multiple Linux systems. The Bookmarks menu even has a list of numerous Linux-related FTP sites for immediate access. gFTP is installed by default on Red Hat Linux and is widely available for other platforms.

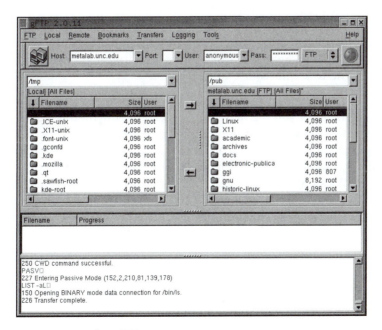

Figure 5-2   The gFTP program

Another popular graphical FTP client is **IglooFTP**, which you can download free from *www.iglooftp.com*.

Introducing FTP Servers

The most widely used FTP server on Linux is the Washington University FTP server, **wu-ftp**. (The name of the server daemon is `in.ftpd`.) On many Linux systems, the FTP server is installed and minimally configured by default. On Red Hat Linux, this server is in the package `wu-ftpd`. You can use this command to check which FTP-related packages are installed:

```
rpm -qa | grep ftp
```

Red Hat Linux also uses a separate package called `anonftp` to set up the `/var/ftp` directory for anonymous FTP users. Other distributions may have anonymous FTP directories configured at `/var/ftp` or `/home/ftp` as part of installing the FTP server software.

A protocol similar to FTP is **Trivial FTP (TFTP)**. This protocol is supported by the server `in.tftpd` and various TFTP clients. It provides basic FTP-like services for special-purpose computing situations where a full FTP configuration would take up too much memory or disk space. One example is when a diskless workstation needs to download its operating system from a server during the boot process. TFTP provides the workstation with the functionality to download the needed files.

Setting up the FTP server is done via a number of configuration files. (Are you beginning to see a pattern?) Table 5-2 lists the FTP server configuration files. By default, not all of these files are installed. The sections that follow walk through the different files and how you might choose to set up your FTP server.

In addition to these configuration files, you need to be aware of the **anonymous user home directory**. Whenever you log in to an FTP server anonymously, you are not permitted to see the entire file system of the remote computer. Instead, you are limited to a working area—a subdirectory—in which all the publicly downloadable files are stored. In most modern versions of Linux, this directory is either `/home/ftp` or `/var/ftp`. For this chapter, we'll assume you are using Red Hat Linux, which recently changed to using `/var/ftp,` to avoid placing anonymous FTP information in the same directory structure (`/home`) as that of regular users.

Table 5-2 FTP server configuration files

FTP Configuration File	Description
`/etc/ftpaccess`	The main FTP configuration file; to use this file, the FTP server must be launched with the –a option (as it is by default in most Linux distributions)
`/etc/ftpusers`	A list of user accounts that are not allowed to log in via FTP. This file includes administrative accounts by default (such as bin, daemon, news, mail). You can add any regular user accounts for which you want to block FTP access
`/etc/hosts.allow` and `/etc/hosts.deny`	Because the FTP server is typically started via the `inetd` superserver, you should set up host or domain-specific access controls for FTP in these files if you are using `inetd` (Recall TCP Wrappers from Chapter 4)
`/etc/inetd.conf`	If you are using the `inetd` superserver, enable FTP in this file by removing the # sign in front of the line for the FTP service
`/etc/xinetd.d/wu-ftpd`	For the `xinetd` superserver, set up host- and domain-specific access controls in this file. Also enable the service by changing `disable=yes` to `disable=no` and adding any logging attributes that you want to use

5

As you explore `/var/ftp`, you will see a number of directories, such as `/bin`, `/etc`, and `/lib`. These resemble the root of your file system, though these subdirectories don't contain many files. They contain only the files required by the FTP server to continue operating without looking outside the `/var/ftp` directory structure. In technical terms, the FTP server does a "change-root" operation when you log in as anonymous. This means that the server "thinks" that `/var/ftp` is the root of the file system—it can't access any other parts of the hard disk. So all of the libraries and other files that the server needs must be stored in the subdirectories of `/var/ftp`.

The key location for anonymous users is `/var/ftp/pub` (pub stands for public). This is the directory in which files for public download are stored. When you log in to a public FTP server such as *ftp.ibiblio.org*, you can immediately click on the `/pub` directory to begin exploring what is available for download.

FTP is normally controlled via the superserver (`inetd` or `xinetd`). You must enable the FTP service in either `/etc/inetd.conf` or `/etc/xinetd.d/wu-ftp`. Then restart the superserver to reread the configuration file. Once the superserver is watching for FTP connections, you can stop allowing connections using the command **ftpshut**. This command accepts parameters to define how long the server should continue accepting connections and to send a message to each connected user's screen. For example, to stop accepting FTP connections immediately and disconnect all FTP connection, use this command:

```
ftpshut now
```

A kinder method would be this command, which causes the FTP server to shut down at 9 P.M. and sends a warning message to all connected users:

```
ftpshut 21:00 "The FTP server will shut down at 9:00 pm.
Please complete your work and disconnect."
```

The `ftpshut` command creates a file called `shutmsg` in `/etc` or in `/var/ftp`. (The filename is defined by the `shutdown` directive in `/etc/ftpaccess`.) When the superserver starts the FTP daemon for an incoming connection, the daemon checks for the presence of the `shutmsg` file. If it exists, the daemon prints the contents of `shutmsg` and closes the connection immediately. So, to allow FTP connections again, just delete the `shutmsg` file:

```
rm /etc/shutmsg  /var/ftp/shutmsg
```

Setting Up FTP Configuration Files

The FTP server is configured using the **ftpaccess** file in the `/etc` directory. To set up an FTP server, you should think about the following three questions:

- Which users do you want to have access to the FTP server?

- When do you want them to have access ?

- What do you want them to be able to do?

The last question is hard to answer until you know what the options are—what the FTP configuration files allow—so let's start with the first question. FTP users are of three types:

- **Anonymous users**, as described already, use *ftp* or *anonymous* as their login name. They are placed in the `/var/ftp` directory and have limited access to the system.

- **Real users**, as described already, log in using a regular Linux user account. They can work in any directory of the file system that they could access when logging in normally to Linux. (You can restrict what they can do via FTP, however, to enhance your server's security.)

- **Guest users** have regular Linux user accounts, but are more restricted in what they can do while logged in using FTP. They often are not allowed to log in at all except using FTP, and their FTP actions are limited.

You define a guest user with the **guestuser** directive. For example, suppose you created a user account for a colleague named John Lin. His Linux account name is jlin. Use this line within `/etc/ftpaccess` to make him a guest user when he logs in using FTP:

```
guestuser jlin
```

Note that this does not prevent John from logging in normally and having access to the system. Typically, you would modify the entry for jlin in the `/etc/passwd` file after creating the account so that he had no regular login shell.

In addition to defining system users as guests for FTP purposes, you can create **classes of users**. This is optional, but it allows you to assign permissions within FTP based on a grouping that you define. Using classes can be confusing at first, because the named classes that you create are independent of the distinctions for anonymous, real, and guest users. For example, you could define all users who log in from a certain address as being in the class *office*, while all others are in the class *other* (the class definitions are checked in the order listed within the file).

```
class office   real,guest,anonymous   192.168.100.0/24
class other    real,guest,anonymous   *
```

You'll use these classes shortly to define specific access rights. First, however, consider the messages that you want users to see on their screens during different parts of their FTP session. You can define several different message files that are automatically displayed by the FTP server at different points. Table 5-3 summarizes these files. You can use any, all, or none of these. Several are defined by default in most FTP configurations.

Table 5-3   Message files defined in `ftpaccess`

Configuration Keyword	Description	Example
`banner`	Display the contents of the named file before prompting the user for a username and password; you must create the file in plaintext	banner /etc/ftpbanner.msg
`readme`	Print a message telling the user to read the contents of a file whose name matches the pattern given. The example will cause FTP to print a message stating "Please read the *file-name* file" if any file matching the pattern README* exists in the root directory (`/var/ftp`). The second example provides the same type of notice message if any file matching the name README* exists in any directory that the user changes into using the `cd` command. (The contents of the named file are not displayed; the user must open the file to view it.)	readme README* login readme README* cwd=*
`greeting`	Set how much information is displayed when first connecting to the FTP server (such as the data, time, and version of the FTP server software); options for this keyword include full, brief, or terse	greeting terse
`message`	Display the contents of the named file when the user logs in (using login, the first example) or enters a directory (`cwd=`, the second example)	message /etc/ftpwelcome.msg login message .message cwd=*

You can control which file actions an FTP user is permitted to perform using a series of directives naming the file action, followed by **yes** or **no**, followed by the classes of user to which the directive applies. You can use the predefined classes (real, guest, or anonymous), or you can use a class that you have defined, such as *office* and *other* in the previous examples. Table 5-4 shows how these directives are used.

Table 5-4   File action directives within `ftpaccess`

Command Keyword	Description	Example
chmod	Controls whether the user can change the file permission of files on the FTP server	`chmod no anonymous`
delete	Controls whether the user can delete/remove files on the FTP server	`delete yes class=office`
overwrite	Controls whether the user can overwrite existing files	`overwrite no anonymous,guest`
rename	Controls whether the user can change the name of files	`rename no anonymous,guest`
umask	Controls whether the user can issue the umask command to set the default file permissions assigned to file	`umask yes class=office`
compress	Controls whether the user can compress filesfor faster transfers; typically, all users are allowed to do this	`compress yes all`
tar	Controls whether the user can tar files together for more convenient multifile transfers; typically, all users are allowed to do this	`tar yes all`

It's normal to have several lines setting permissions for different groups using the directives in Table 5-4. In addition to these file-related directives, the **upload**, **noretrieve**, and **allretrieve** directives control how users can download and upload files. The syntax of these directives is more complicated than the syntax of those in Table 5-4. For the **upload** directive, the format is as follows:

```
upload root-directory upload-directory permission user-
ID group-ID umask directory-rights
```

An example is shown here:

```
upload /var/ftp /incoming yes ftp ftp 0666 nodirs
```

This example allows users to upload files in the `/incoming` directory. This directory name is relative to the `/var/ftp` directory, so it is actually `/var/ftp/incoming`. The **yes** indicates that uploading is permitted (you could have multiple upload directives setting **yes** and

no permission for various subdirectories). Files uploaded into the directory are assigned the user-ID of `ftp` and the group-ID of `ftp`, with the permissions of `0666`. (This mode indicates read and write permissions for all users, displayed as `rw-rw-rw-` and done using this command: `chmod a+rw filename`). Finally, no directories can be created (you could substitute the `dirs` keyword to permit directories to be created).

You can control downloading using the `noretrieve` and `allow-retrieve` directives. These directives have several alternate formats, so reviewing a couple of examples is the best way to see how to use it. For reference, the syntax of `noretrieve` looks like this (items in square brackets are optional—`allow-retrieve` syntax is similar to this):

```
noretrieve [relative|absolute] [user-class]
    filename|directory
```

The following example gives a directory name that is absolute (starting with the true root of the Linux file system. It prohibits downloading any file in the `/etc/` subdirectory by any guest or anonymous user.

```
noretrieve absolute guest,anonymous /etc
```

The following example includes only a list of filenames. No user is permitted to download any file with a name that matches either of the names given here.

```
noretrieve core stocks
```

You can effectively override the `noretrieve` directive using the `allow-retrieve` directive. It uses a very similar syntax, as this example line shows:

```
allow-retrieve relative class=office /pub/reports/
    summary.txt
```

This example lets any user in the *office* class download the named file, which is given relative to the FTP root directory, even if the `noretrieve` directive would otherwise block the download.

It is critical to remember that when working with FTP permissions such as `upload`, `allow-retrieve`, and all the items in Table 5-4, the user must have permission within the Linux file system *in addition to* the permission of the FTP server, or an operation is not permitted. For example, if you use an `upload` directive to permit a real user to upload files to the FTP server, but that user account does not have permission to create files in a particular directory, the FTP server does not override Linux security. A user must have both permission within the file system (as set using the `chmod` command) *and* permission from the FTP server in order to complete a task.

Once you have decided which capabilities you want users to have on your FTP server, you may also want to restrict access in other ways. The `limit` directive lets you limit the number of users that are logged in at one time, by class, and also lets you limit the days of the week and times of the day that they are permitted to log in. To limit the overall number of users allowed to log in, use the keyword **Any** with the **limit** directive. Here is an example:

```
limit other 50 Any /etc/ftplimit.msg
```

This example limits the number of users in the *other* class to 50 at a time. If one logs out, another can log in. The **Any** refers to the day and time; the limit always applies. The contents of the **ftplimit.msg** file are displayed for any user who is not allowed to log in because the limit is exceeded. You can use a time of day range, or a set of days of the week, instead of **Any**. For example, this line limits to 20 the number of users of class *office* that can log in on Saturday or Sunday:

```
limit office 20 SaSu /etc/ftplimit.msg
```

You can use the **file-limit** and **data-limit** directives to limit the number of files or number of bytes that a user can transfer in a single session. (The count for a user is reset when he or she logs out.) You can use the keywords **in**, **out**, or **total** to limit by uploading (**in**), downloading (**out**), or both combined (**total**). For example, the following line limits users of class *office* to downloading only 50 files per session:

```
file-limit out 50 office
```

The following line limits users in the *other* class to a total transfer (uploading and downloading) of about 100 MB:

```
data-limit total 100000000 other
```

To limit the time that a user can be logged in, use the **limit-time** directive. The following example limits anonymous users to 60 minutes per session.

```
limit-time anonymous 60
```

Because FTP is usually started from a superserver, you can use the access control mechanisms of TCP Wrappers or **xinetd** configuration files to allow or block access based on hostname, domain name, or IP address. FTP itself has a similar feature. This is useful if you are running FTP in standalone mode; it also may be more convenient if you are already working in the **/etc/ftpaccess** file. The **deny** directive denies access to specific hostnames, displaying the contents of the named file when access is denied.

```
deny hosta,hostb,hostc  /etc/ftpdeny.msg
```

Similarly, you can deny or allow access based on the username that is provided during log-in. These directives work together with the **/etc/ftpusers** file (see Table 5-2). That is, a user must *not* be listed in **/etc/ftpusers**, and must also have a user and group ID that are allowed by the directives **allow-uid**, **allow-gid**, **deny-uid**, and **deny-gid**. A typical setting is to block all user IDs between 100 and 65534. The command to do this is shown here. (This alone does not block anonymous FTP access.)

```
deny-uid %-99 %65534
```

You can also log all of the transfers that are managed by your FTP server. Transfers are logged to the file `/var/log/xfers`. The standard directive used in `ftpaccess` is:

```
log transfers anonymous,guest,real inbound,outbound
```

This directive causes both uploads and downloads (inbound and outbound) to be logged, no matter what type of user does the transfer. Software is available to analyze and create statistics from your `xfer` log file about how your FTP server is being used. For example, try the Ftp Logger perl script or the Flog program, both of which you can download from *linux.tucows.com*. Connection attempts that failed are also logged by the FTP server in the system log file, usually in `/var/log/messages`. Examining these messages lets you know if someone is trying to break in to your system via FTP.

A few final options are not part of the broader categories covered so far, but are part of nearly every `ftpaccess` configuration file. The `email` directive identifies where the FTP server should send messages when a problem arises or the server simply needs to notify the administrator of something. A typical line looks like this:

```
email root@myplace.net
```

Related to the limitation directives, the `loginfails` directive defines how many bad username and password combinations a user can enter before the connection is dropped by the FTP server. This slows down someone who is attempting to break in using FTP. The typical value is 5:

```
loginfails 5
```

A final directive that is included at the end of all default `ftpaccess` files is `passwd-check`, which defines how closely the FTP server pays attention to the password entered by an anonymous user. These users are asked to enter their email address as a password. The first parameter after the directive can be `none`, which ignores the password, `trivial`, which checks that it contains a "@" character, or `rfc822`, which checks for a correctly formed email address. The second parameter defines what action to take if the first parameter (if `trivial` or `rfc822`) is not met. It can be either `warn`, to simply tell the user that the password was not correctly formed, or `enforce`, to log the user out because a valid email address was not entered. The typical line looks like this:

```
passwd-check rfc822 warn
```

You can view the documentation for `wu-ftpd` in the `/usr/share/doc/wu-ftpd-2.6.1` directory. In the `examples` folder you can see the file `ftpaccess.heavy` for a more complex example file than is included below. A graphical tool called `kwuftpd` lets you create an `ftpaccess` file, but it doesn't help a great deal unless you already understand the options presented in the dialog boxes.

The man page for `ftpaccess` contains further details on the directives presented in this section, plus dozens of other more esoteric directives. The `ftpaccess` file is normally installed as part of an FTP server package. Part of the file included with Red Hat Linux 7.3 is shown below; you should recognize all of the directives included in this file.

```
email root@localhost

# Allow 5 mistyped passwords
loginfails 5

# Notify the users of README files at login and when
# changing to a different directory
readme   README*     login
readme   README*     cwd=*

# Messages displayed to the user
message /welcome.msg            login
message .message                cwd=*

# Allow on-the-fly compression and tarring
compress       yes          all
tar            yes          all

# Prevent anonymous users (and partially guest users)
# from executing dangerous commands
chmod      no     guest,anonymous
delete     no     anonymous
overwrite  no     anonymous
rename     no     anonymous

# Turn on logging to /var/log/xferlog
log transfers anonymous,guest,real inbound,outbound

# If /etc/shutmsg exists, don't allow logins
# see ftpshut man page
shutdown /etc/shutmsg

# Ask users to use their email address as anonymous
# password
passwd-check rfc822 warn
```

FILE SHARING WITH NFS

The **Network File System (NFS)** has been around almost as long as FTP, but its purposes are very different. NFS was part of a larger effort by Sun Microsystems to make multiple UNIX systems appear as a single large system. That is, hard disks located all over the local network (or even a remote network) would appear as if they were part of the local directory structure. So, for example, when you execute a command such as `ls /data/aircraft`, you might actually be viewing the contents of the

`/parts/data/reports/aircraft` directory on a host located in the next room or the next county.

System administrators regularly mount file systems to make an additional hard disk partition appear as if it were part of the local file system. For example, this command makes the contents of a Windows partition on the second hard disk appear as the directory `/mnt/windows` on Linux:

```
mount -t vfat /dev/hdb1 /mnt/windows
```

NFS can be used in the same way. It was designed for permanent, long-term connections that allow you to access remote file systems as part of your regular user environment. Organizations sometimes use NFS for actions such as maintaining a centralized `/home` directory on a main server and mounting each user's home directory automatically using NFS when the user logs in. This makes system administration and backup of all users' data easier. NFS is often used with the Network Information System (NIS) referred to previously and with the r-utilities. (NIS allows a single database of user information on the network to provide login information for multiple hosts.) You can imagine how NFS, NIS, and the r-utilities together allow a user on one host to act like all the network's resources were part of a seamless whole.

However, the types of security concerns that keep people from using the r-utilities also apply to NFS. NFS was designed with a trusted network in mind, and no one dares trust their network any longer. (NFS security is discussed later in this section.) NFS has other strikes against its widespread use as well. First, NFS on Linux can be slow unless it is well configured. The latest versions improve performance somewhat, but it remains an issue. NFS' method of operation also annoys users at times; if the server that you are connected to using NFS becomes unavailable, NFS simply waits, and waits, and waits. This quickly becomes frustrating for end users who wonder what is happening behind the scenes.

A final concern with NFS is its UNIX-centric nature. You can add NFS to a Windows server or to a NetWare server, but the performance is typically a disappointment. Additionally, you must pay extra to purchase the NFS software for Windows or NetWare, since it's not included with the operating system. You can obtain better results by adding Windows or NetWare capability (for free) to Linux.

With those caveats in mind, realize that NFS is not hard to use and can be very useful as a transfer mechanism, especially when you are working with multiple Linux systems. In fact, one of the popular uses of NFS is to install numerous Linux servers over a network connection, which is much easier and faster than hovering over each workstation and swapping CD-ROM discs. (We don't describe an NFS-based Linux installation in this book, but several Linux distributions support it, including Red Hat Linux. The documentation included on the Red Hat CD describes this process.)

5

NFS is a good way to share commonly used directories over a local network. For example, you might use NFS to share the /home directory, the /var/log directory, or the /var/spool/mail directory. By having the information from these directories in a single location, administration (such as backups) and security management can be simplified. Just be certain you have the network bandwidth to keep all the users on the network happy with the performance of these remote file systems.

Running the NFS Daemons

The NFS protocol is implemented by several daemons, each handling a different set of tasks. These daemons are not started up by default in Linux. You should start them yourself and set them to start automatically only after you have configured the NFS system as described in this section.

NFS communication is built on the **remote procedure call (rpc)** system. This system functions almost like a superserver: programs are assigned an rpc number. A program called **portmap** watches for rpc requests from programs like the NFS daemons, then maps them to TCP or UDP ports to use the network. If you are curious, you can view the rpc number mappings in /etc/rpc. The portmap program is started by default on your Linux system to handle any requests from programs like the NFS daemons. If the portmap daemon is not running, NFS does not work.

The r-utilities described in Chapter 3 also use rpc and the portmap program.

NFS itself uses the **rpc.mountd** daemon to make new connections—that is, to mount a remote file system. The **rpc.mountd** command checks all the relevant permissions to see whether the mount is permitted. Once a file system is mounted, the **nfsd** daemon handles file transfers based on the settings that the **rpc.mountd** daemon has validated. Some systems (including Red Hat Linux) add one or two peripheral programs to these two programs to help manage NFS-mounted file systems. The first is **rpc.rquotad**, which permits tracking user disk space quotas for remotely mounted file systems, just as you can on local Linux file systems. The second is **rpc.rstatd**, which helps manage NFS-mounted file systems when the remote NFS server crashes (or otherwise breaks its connection) and then comes up again.

All of these programs are normally started by a script in the /etc/rc.d/init.d directory. In some versions of Linux, they are listed individually by name, in others they are grouped for management by a few scripts. For example, in Red Hat Linux, when you execute /etc/rc.d/init.d/nfs start, three daemons are started: rpc.mountd, nfsd, and rpc.rquotad. You start the rpc.rstatd daemon using the nfslock script in the same directory.

The `portmap` program that controls network access by the NFS server uses the TCP Wrappers program. You use the `/etc/hosts.allow` and `/etc/hosts.deny` files that you learned about in Chapter 4 to define which hosts have access to NFS. Within these files, use the service name `portmap` (not one of the NFS-specific daemons).

Accessing Remote NFS File Systems

Acting as a client to an NFS server is straightforward: you use the `mount` command as you would for any local hard disk partition containing a file system you wanted to access. The only difference is the file system type you specify—plus a variety of options you can add when mounting an NFS file system.

You should already be familiar with the `mount` command and the use of the `/etc/fstab` file to define file systems for automounting or delayed mounting. If not, these `nfs` examples should help you. The basic format for a configuration line in `/etc/fstab` is:

```
host:directory    mountpoint nfs  options    0 0
```

You must create the mount point (a directory on your Linux system), and the host must have allowed mounting of the directory (you'll see how to do that next). The options are the interesting part. The `mount` man page lists about 20 options specific to NFS file systems, in addition to the many options that are applicable to all file system types. A few especially useful options are listed here:

- `rsize=8192,wsize=8192`—Used together, these options alter the default buffer size for NFS transfers. Using these options avoids the speed problems sometimes associated with NFS on Linux.

- `ro` and `rw`—You can mount a file system as read-only (ro) or read-write (rw).

- `hard` or `soft`—You can **hard mount** an NFS file system, which means your programs waits—without limit—for the NFS server to respond. If the remote server goes down and then comes up again a while later, your program will continue without a hitch. Alternatively, you can **soft mount** an NFS file system, which means that NFS waits for a while and then gives up. The documentation recommends not using the `soft` option unless the NFS server you are working with is quite unreliable.

- `noauto`—This option causes the NFS file system not to be mounted automatically at system startup.

We won't review all of the `mount` options and usage that you should already be familiar with, but consider this example line in `/etc/fstab` for an NFS file system.

```
rome:/home/public   /mnt/rome   nfs   rsize=8192,
    wsize=8192,rw,noauto 0 0
```

You could, of course, have many different NFS file systems in /etc/fstab, each listed on a separate line. As with other types of file systems, once you have this information defined in /etc/fstab, you can use both the mount command and the umount command with just the remote directory or the local mount point. All of the information in /etc/fstab is applied to the command. For example, if the information above is included on your system, you can issue this command to mount the NFS file system.

```
mount   /mnt/rome
```

Exporting Your File Systems Using NFS

To make parts of your file system accessible over the network to other systems, you must have the NFS daemons running (as described previously), and you must allow NFS traffic to pass between the two hosts (without a firewall blocking it). Beyond these requirements, you must set up the /etc/**exports** file to define which of your local directories you want to be accessible to remote users (that is, which directories are exported) and how each can be used.

Once you have /etc/exports carefully set up, run the **exportfs** command to activate the contents of /etc/exports, then start the NFS daemons using the scripts in /etc/rc.d/init.d.

The syntax of a line within /etc/**exports** is shown here. You can include multiple hostname(option) settings for the same directory, separating each by a space.

```
/directory-path    hostname(option,option,…)
```

The hostname can be defined in several ways. You can use a complete hostname to define a specific host; you can use a domain name to define all hosts within a domain; or you can use an IP address, either for a single host or for a network or part of a network. The exports man page lists all of the possible permutations.

An /etc/exports file can be as simple as this:

```
/projects
```

This /etc/exports file allows anyone who can reach your host via NFS to mount the /projects directory, since no hostname or access options are specified. Well, that's almost true. When you use an NFS client to access a remote file system, the NFS server must decide what user to treat you as, because you never "log in" or provide a password when you use the NFS client (as you saw in the previous discussion of the mount command). The default action is that the mount command sends your user ID and group ID on the client, then the NFS server uses the same user ID and group ID on the server system. Your file permissions match those of the corresponding user and group. This is designed for a situation where a single user has accounts on multiple systems, with the same user ID and group ID on each one.

This arrangement is not always easy to achieve, nor is it always appropriate. For this reason, you normally include options in `/etc/exports` to **map** incoming client user and group IDs to user and group IDs on the NFS server.

NFS uses a security concept called **squashing** to prevent a user from gaining access to a user account on the NFS server simply because the user has the same ID on the NFS client. The most important use of this is squashing the root account: you shouldn't have root access on the NFS server just because you have root access on an NFS client! Squashing of the root account is done automatically unless you use the `no_root_squash` option. One method of squashing incoming client user IDs is to define an anonymous user account and tell NFS to map all incoming users to that account. Thus, all NFS clients have access only to areas that you have specifically granted to this "anonymous" user. Reviewing a few examples should make the uses of this system apparent.

```
/ scout(rw,no_root_squash)
```
no space

This line shows a very trusted host, scout, for which squashing is not used (remember, `root_squash` is the default action). The root user can thus have root access to the `/` directory on the NFS server. This type of entry would be used for a trusted network in which a single system administrator wanted to have complete access to multiple hosts' file systems via NFS.

The next example assumes that everyone on the myplace.net domain has a user account with a matching user ID on the NFS server. They all are permitted to access the `/projects` directory, reading and writing according to the file permissions within `/projects` on the NFS server.

```
/projects *.myplace.net(rw)
```

In the following example, the `/pub` directory is available to all hosts (not naming any host is equivalent to using `*` as the hostname), but the hosts can only mount `/pub` in read-only mode. The `all_squash` option causes all users on client systems to be mapped to a "nobody" user on the NFS server. This means that even if they were able to somehow create a file on the NFS server (via a security hole of some type), it would have a user ID of "nobody" and thus be less harmful than a file created by a valid user.

```
/pub (ro,all_squash)
```

In a final example, users on train01 can access `/home/testing` on the NFS server, but all users on train01 are mapped to user ID 150 and group ID 100, which you need to define in `/etc/passwd` and `/etc/group` on the host running the NFS server. All of these users have read-write access, but can only act as the named user, providing a good margin of safety for what they are actually allowed to do.

```
/home/testing train01(rw,all_squash,anonuid=150,
    anongid=100)
```

Again, the man page for `exports` has examples and descriptions of many other options than those explored here. The basics of defining sets of hostnames, mapping users between systems, and controlling read-only or read-write access should get you started with NFS.

Remember to run `exportfs` after making any changes to `/etc/exports`. This activates your changes and also alerts you to any syntax errors in the file. (This program is run automatically each time you reboot your system.)

Avoid exporting `/` or `/etc`, or other sensitive directories on your system unless you are very confident in your `/etc/exports` configuration. Always export the smallest portion of your file system that satisfies the need of clients; don't just export `/` and assume everyone can find what they need. Such laziness invites trouble.

The security defined for NFS is similar to that for other services you are learning about: it has many layers. Don't let these layers confuse you as you try to control access while still letting some people use a service. NFS, for example, has the following layers of security, stated broadly:

- Does the firewall allow NFS traffic through? (You'll learn about firewalls in the second part of this book.)

- Does the `portmap` program block access to NFS because of TCP Wrappers configuration in `/etc/hosts.deny`?

- Does the NFS server allow the requesting hostname to connect?

- Does the NFS server permit the type of access that is wanted (for example, read-write access)?

- Do the `mount` options used on the NFS client include the type of access desired? (Even if the server allows read-write access, you could be mounting the file system as read-only for your own purposes.)

- Based on the user ID that a user is assigned by the NFS server, do the file permissions within the remote file system allow the user to perform the task desired? (You can have all possible access for a given user name, but still won't be allowed to explore other users' home directories, because you don't have file permissions in those areas.)

NetWare File and Printer Sharing

For many years, Novell **NetWare** was the premier network operating system, and it still provides excellent file- and print-sharing services. You can use NetWare protocols on Linux to act as a NetWare file and print server, or as a client to other NetWare servers.

These extensions to Linux provide access to only a small part of the functionality of NetWare servers. However, if you have NetWare on your networks, they let you at least transfer files easily and avoid having isolated islands of either Linux or NetWare on the network.

If you are familiar with Novell's product line, you'll be sorry to learn that the packages described here, while freely available, provide only NetWare 3.x support. Later versions of NetWare and related products that support the **Novell Directory Service (NDS)** network resource directory are not supported in Linux. Novell formerly licensed a fully NDS-compatible NetWare client and server, which were created and sold by Caldera, but those products are no longer available.

To use either the client or server tools for NetWare, you must have IPX installed on Linux, as described in Chapter 2. NetWare uses a transport protocol called the **NetWare Core Protocol (NCP)**. Because NetWare uses IPX, IP addresses are not used. Instead, each server is assigned a name. You refer to the server by name when requesting a connection. You must have a username and password on the server you are contacting (unless you are using NDS, which provides a networkwide single login, but the NetWare tools on Linux don't support NDS).

Learning NetWare is comparable to learning Linux or Windows networking. Rather than attempt to teach it thoroughly here, we present only an outline of NetWare functionality to help you see how the NetWare client and server tools are used.

NetWare is a dedicated network operating system. Rather than really acting as a client to other operating systems, it focuses on providing services to clients. In the context of Linux, these services are limited to file and printer sharing. Each NetWare server maintains a database of its resources called the **bindery**. Each database entry in the bindery is referred to as an object, and each object has a name and various properties associated with it. Recent versions of NetWare (since about 1993) have used NDS, but also provide **Bindery Emulation** to let clients that are not NDS-capable access NetWare services. Objects in the bindery include users, groups, and volumes. A **volume** in NetWare is equivalent to a file system in Linux.

Each file and directory in a NetWare volume can have a list of access rights associated with it. These are called the **trustee rights**. Any user on the server (listed in the bindery) can have specific access rights granted, and is called a **trustee** of the file or directory to which access has been granted. This is a much more detailed system than the three groups that Linux provides for file security—it's more like the file security of later Windows operating systems. For example, in NetWare, you can assign one user permission to see a file, another user permission to create new files, and a third user permission to delete a file. Groups of users can also be assigned specific access rights to a file or directory. Each file and directory has eight rights associated with it. Each file also has a number of attributes that can be set. You can explore these capabilities in the documentation for NetWare and in the Linux programs described in the sections that follow as much as your needs warrant.

Accessing NetWare Servers as a Client

The **ncpfs** package implements NCP and provides a number of client utilities to let you log in, transfer files, print, and so forth. The **ncpfs** package is not installed by default, but is included on CD 2 for Red Hat Linux, and is available for most other Linux systems. You need to install the **ipxutils** package before **ncpfs** on Red Hat Linux; other versions of Linux may place the needed IPX utilities in different packages. The **rpm** command informs you of dependencies when you install **ncpfs**.

The **ncpfs** utilities let you specify command-line parameters for the server you want to contact. You are then prompted for the username and password to use in contacting that server. Alternatively, you can create a **.nwclient** file in your home directory that contains default settings, such as the NetWare servers that you regularly contact, with your username and password for that server. For example, a simple **.nwclient** file might contain these lines, one for each of the three NetWare servers on your network:

```
mktg_server/nwells    marketingpassword
eng_server/nwells     engineeringpassword
print_server/guest    -
```

You should set the file permission of the **.nwclient** file to 0600 so that other users and groups cannot read them (use the command **chmod 0600 .nwclient**). Anyone who obtained the usernames and passwords in **.nwclient** could log in to NetWare as you.

Table 5-5 outlines the major utilities included with the **ncpfs** package. These utilities mirror, for the most part, the client utilities that Novell provided for older versions of NetWare running on DOS and Windows clients. The descriptions here refer to the basic features of NetWare outlined previously, but you should review the man pages for each utility you intend to use regularly. To use a number of these utilities, you must be logged in as the administrative superuser, SUPERVISOR, or in later versions of NetWare, Admin (these are equivalent to root in Linux).

If you already have an account on NetWare and simply need to access files on the NetWare server, focus on the two commands **nwauth** (to "log in") and **ncpmount** (to make a NetWare volume accessible as part of your Linux file system). Remember, these utilities attempt to glean information from the **.nwclient** file if you don't include all of the expected parameters.

Making Linux into a NetWare Server

Most Linux distributions include a package that lets your computer emulate a NetWare server. The Martin Stovers NetWare Emulator package (**mars-nwe**) provides several NetWare-specific protocols and lets any NetWare-capable client (including a Windows NetWare client) access the Linux system as if it were a NetWare server. In addition to the NCP transport protocol, **mars-nwe** provides the NetWare Routing Information Protocol (RIP) and the Service Advertising Protocol (SAP) that let Linux act as a peer with other NetWare servers and that let NetWare clients locate the Linux/NetWare server.

Table 5-5   NetWare client utilities in `ncpfs`

Utility Name	Description
nsend	Send a pop-up message to another user's workstation via the NetWare server; this is similar to using `talk` in Linux, but is unidirectional
nwauth	Log in (authenticate yourself) to a specific NetWare server by providing a valid username and password
nwbols	List bindery objects on the NetWare server
nwboprops	List the properties of a given bindery object
nwbpset	Set a value for a specific property within a bindery object
nwfsinfo	Display information about a NetWare server; you can use this command without first authenticating (using `nwauth`)
nwpasswd	Change your NetWare password (alters the password property of your user object in the bindery)
nwpurge	Purge deleted files from a directory; (NetWare saves all deleted files; until purged, they can be undeleted)
nwrights	Display your user's rights to a given file or directory
nwsfind	Search for a specific NetWare server by name and obtain information for reaching that server on the network
nwtrustee	List all the trustee assignments (file permissions) for a file or directory
nwuserlist	List all the users that are currently logged in to the named server
nwvolinfo	Show information about a given volume on a NetWare server
slist	List all the NetWare servers that are reachable on the network
ncpmount	Mount a NetWare volume within the Linux file system
ncpumount	Unmount a previously mounted NetWare volume
nwbocreate	Create a new object within the bindery of a NetWare server
nwborm	Remove an object from the bindery on a NetWare server
nwfsctrl	Issue control commands regarding the file system on a NetWare server
nwgrant	Grant access rights to a specific user for a specific file or directory
nwmsg	Send a broadcast message to all users who are logged in to the NetWare server
nwrevoke	Revoke a trustee assignment; that is, revoke a user's rights to access a given file or directory.mput

The `mars-nwe` package is included on Red Hat Linux CD 2. You can install it using a standard `rpm` command; it's not installed by default. On Red Hat, you need to install the `ipxutils` package before installing `mars-nwe`. Other distributions may have the needed IPX tools in different packages, but the `rpm` command should inform you of any missing dependencies when you try to install `mars-nwe`. After configuring the server, you can start it using the script in `/etc/rc.d/init.d`. To make `mars-nwe` start up each time you boot Linux, edit your run-level directories (such as `/etc/rc.d/rc3.d`) or use the configuration tool `chkconfig`. For example, this command alters the run-level directories in Red Hat Linux so that `mars-nwe` always starts at boot time:

```
chkconfig mars-nwe on
```

The `mars-nwe` package actually includes a number of separate server daemons, including `nwserv`, `nwconn`, `ncpserv`, and `nwbind`. You can review the contents of the `mars-nwe` package to see the various program names. All of these, however, are controlled using the `mars-nwe` script in `/etc/rc.d/init.d`.

 Notice that the package name and script name use a hyphen: `mars-nwe`. But several of the files in the package use an underscore: `mars_nwe`. Watch these carefully to avoid frustration!

You configure the functionality of `mars-nwe` using the `/etc/nwserv.conf` file. Getting the server up and running is not complicated, but the number of options in `/etc/nwserv.conf` can be intimidating at first glance. The file is organized into sections with a heading for each. You don't need to examine every configuration line to experiment with `mars-nwe`, but you should at least define the SYS volume (where the NetWare operating system is stored on each NetWare server), assign a server name and networking numbers, and designate the Linux user account that clients who log in to your NetWare server will be assigned.

The documentation in `/usr/share/doc/mars_new-0.99p120` provides complete information on setting up the `/etc/nwserv.conf` file. The best place to start, however, especially if you are already familiar with NetWare, is the default `/etc/nwserv.conf` file installed with the `mars-nwe` package. This file includes 881 lines in the latest version, most of which are explanations about how to set up the file. In fact, only 40 lines are not comments. And of those, only about 20 are options that you would need to review and possibly update before running your own `mars-nwe` server. The rest are debugging or esoteric options that can usually be left unchanged.

Once you have `nwserv.conf` set up, start `mars-nwe` with the script in `/etc/rc.d/init.d` and access your NetWare-on-Linux volumes from any NetWare-capable client on your network.

WINDOWS FILE AND PRINT INTEGRATION WITH SAMBA

In the previous sections of this chapter you've learned about file-sharing protocols that originated with UNIX and with Novell NetWare. Windows uses a file-sharing protocol called **Server Message Block (SMB)**. Later versions of Microsoft products use the name **Common Internet File System (CIFS)** for this protocol. SMB/CIFS builds on the **NetBIOS** name service. In roughly the same way that DNS is the name service for the Internet, NetBIOS is the name service for Windows systems. Of course, the methods used by NetBIOS differ from those used by DNS, but the principle of identifying numerous systems on a network is the same. Windows systems prior to Windows 2000 can locate each other using a **WINS** (Windows Internet Naming Service) server, which is like a DNS server on a Windows network. (That is, WINS implements "search and find" features of the NetBIOS protocol.) Newer versions of Windows use DNS.

To implement SMB, CIFS, and NetBIOS in Linux, you use the **Samba** suite of programs ("Samba" was chosen because the name resembles SMB but avoids using Microsoft's trademarked protocol name). The server portions of Samba allow a Linux system to appear in Windows networks (specifically on a Windows desktop) as if it were another Windows system. The client portions of Samba also let Linux access Windows systems that are configured to share their resources. Printers can also be shared in both directions.

To use Samba, be certain that the `samba`, `samba-common`, `samba-client`, and `samba-swat` packages are installed in Red Hat Linux, or similar packages in other versions of Linux. For example, in Caldera OpenLinux look for the four packages `samba`, `samba-doc`, `smbfs`, and `swat`. The easiest way to check for Samba on a system that uses `rpm` packages is with these two commands (in some systems the packages are named for the protocol, in some, for the suite of programs):

```
rpm -qa | grep smb
rpm -qa | grep samba
```

Strictly speaking, the `samba-swat` or `swat` package is optional. SWAT is a Samba configuration tool described later in this section, but if you're new to Samba, it's the best way to learn about the capabilities of Samba.

The Samba packages include a number of utilities; the major ones are covered in this chapter.

The history of Samba development is a fascinating story of a few software developers in Australia (led by Andrew Tridgell) who reverse-engineered Microsoft's networking system; they had no intention initially to create software that would allow UNIX and Linux users all over the world to interact with Windows systems. You can read the full story at *www.samba.org*.

Using Samba Client Utilities

The two main Samba client utilities let you access shared Windows resources as if yours were another Windows-based computer. Windows-based computers are not able to tell that you are running Linux.

The **smbclient** utility operates much like the FTP client. It is a command-line utility that lets you log in to a Windows host and interact using a series of commands much like the FTP commands.

To use the `smbclient` command, you need to know three things:

- The hostname or IP address of the Windows system you want to contact. Use this with the **-L** option.

- Your username on that host. Use this with the **-U** option.

- The workgroup that the host is a part of (the command may work without this, but you improve your odds on a large network by including it). Use this with the **-W** option.

The command format to use is shown here. Notice that the options are case sensitive. Windows normally refers to workgroup names, so you may avoid potential problems if you do the same:

```
smbclient -L hostname -U username -W WORKGROUP
```

After you enter this command, you may have to wait a minute while `smbclient` finds the Windows system. There may be a wait even on a very small network, and it may be longer if you have only recently started up one or both of the computers or are working on a larger network. At any rate, after a minute, you are prompted for the password (which does not appear on the screen as you enter it). The `smbclient` program then lists all the resources reported by the server you indicated. Sample output is shown here:

```
added interface ip=192.168.100.10 bcast=192.168.100.255
   nmask=255.255.255.0
Got a positive name query response from 192.168.100.6
   ( 192.168.100.6 )
Password: *******
Domain=[WELLS] OS=[Windows NT 4.0] Server=[NT LAN Manager
   4.0]

        Sharename       Type        Comment
        ---------       ----        -------
        ADMIN$          Disk        Remote Admin
        IPC$            IPC         Remote IPC
        C$              Disk        Default share
        D$              Disk        Default share
        E$              Disk        Default share
        F$              Disk        Default share
        V$              Disk        Default share
        G$              Disk        Default share
        HPLaserJ        Printer     HP LaserJet 4L
        print$          Disk        Printer Drivers

        Server                  Comment
        ---------               -------
        LONDON
        SUNDANCE                Samba Server
```

```
Workgroup                Master
---------                ------
WELLS                    LONDON
```

Each version of Windows has variations, but the basic method of creating a shared resource in Windows is to find the resource (hard disk, subdirectory, printer, etc.) in Windows (from My Computer or Windows Explorer, for example), then right-click on the item, and choose Properties. Within the Properties dialog box, choose the Sharing tab and set the appropriate fields to name the share and select who can access it. See your Windows documentation (or online help) for further information.

Each Windows resource that is available over the network is called a **share**. Once you have identified the share to which you want to connect, you can issue a second `smbclient` command to begin using it. (If you already knew the share name, of course, you could begin with this step.) The format of the server name and share name are peculiar to Windows networking. Start with a double forward slash, followed by the server name, then a single forward slash, then the share name. For example, to connect to drive D—share D$—use this command:

```
smbclient //london/D$ -U nwells
```

Once again, you must enter the password for the user, then you see the **smb** prompt:

```
smb: \>
```

At this prompt you can enter commands as you did in the FTP client. In fact, most of the commands you're likely to use are the same: `get`, `put`, `ls`, `pwd`, `cd`, `mget`, `mput`, and `prompt`. (See Table 5-1.) To exit `smbclient`, however, enter `exit`; `bye` doesn't work.

A few graphical tools are equivalent to `smbclient`, but the better way to graphically access Windows systems is to mount a Windows share as part of your Linux file system. This is done using the standard `mount` command using a file system type of `smbfs`—the SMB file system. When using a `mount` command to mount a Windows share, you include a username as an option with the `o` parameter. In some situations, you also want to include the password to fully automate the `mount` command during system startup, for example. The command would then look like this example, assuming you had already created a directory as the mount point:

```
mount -t smbfs -o username=nwells,password=coconuts
     //london/d$ /mnt/london_d
```

If Linux successfully makes a connection and the username and password are valid, the above command returns after a moment to the command line. At that point, you can access the directory `/mnt/london_d` as you would any other part of the Linux file system, including using any standard Linux graphical utilities to manage your files. Figure 5-3 shows a Linux desktop with the contents of a Windows share shown.

Figure 5-3   A mounted Windows share viewed within a Linux desktop

You can use additional options in your **mount** command. For example, you can mount the Windows share as read-only; define the user ID and group ID that all files will appear with in Linux; log in as a guest on Windows; or define the Windows workgroup name. Enter the command **man smbmount** to learn about these and other options.

In addition to accessing Windows files from Linux, you can print to a Windows printer. This is done using the **smbprint** command, but most users prefer that you define a regular Linux printer that routes print jobs transparently through to the Windows printer. The easiest way to do this is using one of the modern graphical printer tools. One good example is Red Hat's Printer Configuration Tool, which you can start by entering **printconf-gui** at a command line, or by choosing Programs, then System, then Printer Configuration on the Gnome menu. This utility lets you both create printer definitions that are stored in the **/etc/printcap** file (where all Linux printer definitions are stored) and also manage print queues once they are created.

Within the Red Hat Printer Configuration Tool, you can click the New button to begin creating a new printer definition. A series of dialog boxes guides you through the process. You can select Windows as the type of printer to which you want the printer definition to refer (as shown in Figure 5-4). This causes the utility to refer to **smbprint**. Then you enter the same information as when you use **smbclient** to access a Windows share. Note in the listing previously given from **smbclient** that a printer is listed: HPLaserJ. Refer to Figure 5-5 to see how the Windows information is included in the dialog box to define this Windows printer. After the configuration is complete, the printer appears in the list of available print queues. Any time a user sends a print job to that print queue, **smbprint** routes the print job to the appropriate Windows printer.

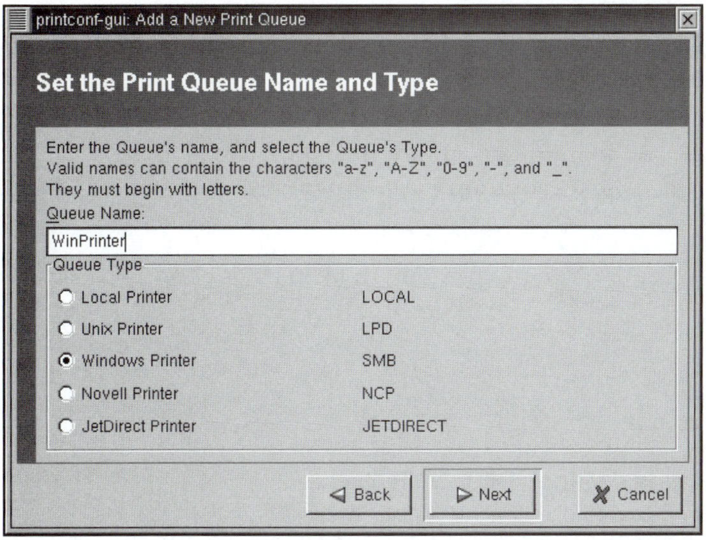

Figure 5-4 Selecting Windows as the printer type in the Red Hat Printer Configuration tool

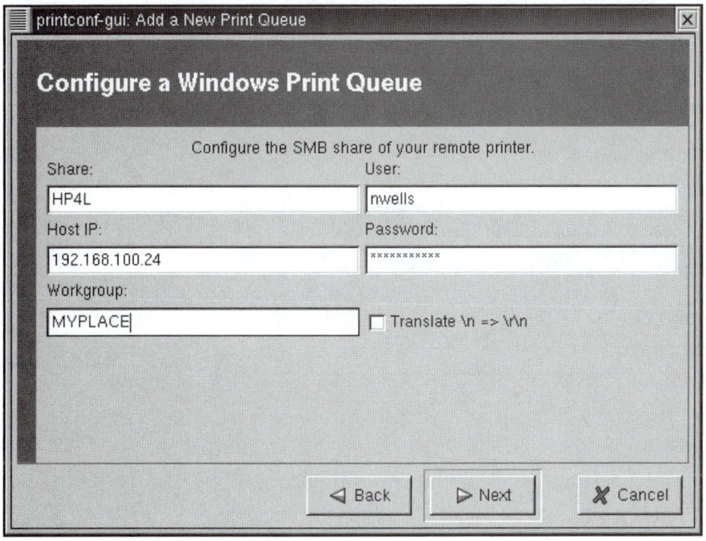

Figure 5-5 Entering information to permit printing to a Windows printer

If you're already experienced with Linux printing, you may wonder how this is done behind the scenes. The Printer Configuration tool creates a definition in `/etc/printcap` that looks like this. Note how the `lp` line pipes the print job to the **smbprint** command. Review the `printcap` man page for details on the other items shown in this file:

```
# /etc/printcap
#
# DO NOT EDIT! MANUAL CHANGES WILL BE LOST!
# This file is autogenerated by printconf-backend during
   lpd init.
#
# Hand edited changes can be put in /etc/printcap.local,
   and will be included.

HPLJ:\
     :sh:\
     :ml=0:\
     :mx=0:\
     :sd=/var/spool/lpd/HPLJ:\
     :af=/var/spool/lpd/HPLJ/HPLJ.acct:\
     :lp=|/usr/share/printconf/util/smbprint:\
     :lpd_bounce=true:\
     :if=/usr/share/printconf/util/mf_wrapper:
```

As part of the standard printer definitions, any printer tool can manage the print queues once this definition is created. For example, KDE includes a print job administration program. This program is available in Red Hat Linux by choosing KLpq on the Utilities menu; in Caldera OpenLinux, it appears as Printer Queue on the System menu. You can also start it from the command line using the command **klpq**. This program is shown in Figure 5-6. A print queue created to print to Windows is selected.

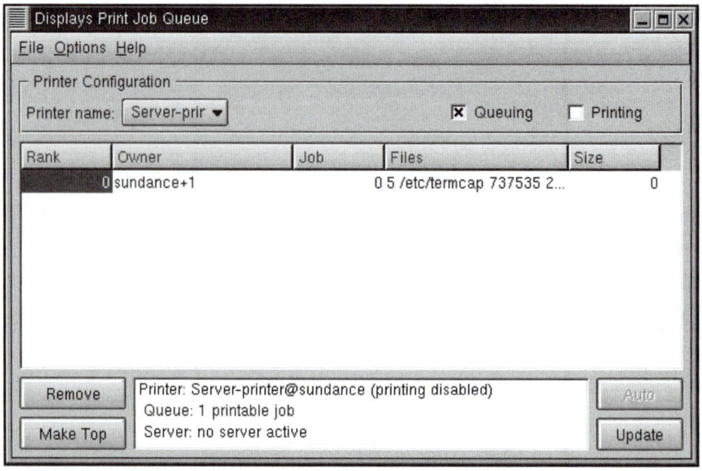

Figure 5-6   The KDE print job administration tool

We've covered the major Samba client tools, but you can learn more about them by using the command `rpm -ql samba-client` to see a listing of all the programs included in the Samba-client package. Check which are program files and which are man pages that you can read to learn more.

Setting Up a Samba Server

The Samba suite includes two server daemons: **nmbd**, which implements the NetBIOS name service, and **smbd**, which implements the SMB file and print sharing. Both of these daemons must be running to implement a Samba server, and both are managed using a single script in `/etc/rc.d/init.d`. On some systems, including Red Hat, the script is called **smb**; on others, including Caldera, it is called **samba**. As soon as you have configured Samba as described in this section, you can start the server using this script and use **chkconfig** to make it start automatically whenever you boot Linux.

Samba configuration files are typically stored in `/etc/samba`, though the location may vary in different Linux distributions. The main configuration file is **smb.conf**. A sample or default **smb.conf** file is provided. You need to review this file and add your own settings before running the Samba server. A very basic **smb.conf** file is shown here, though the sample file on your system is filled with comments explaining numerous other options.

```
[global]
workgroup = MYPLACE
netbios name = sundance
server string = Samba on Linux posing as Windows 2000
hosts allow = 192.168.100.
printcap name = /etc/printcap
load printers = yes
printing = lprng
log file = /var/log/samba.log
max log size = 0
security = user
encrypt passwords = yes
smb passwd file = /etc/samba/smbpasswd
socket options = TCP_NODELAY SO_RCVBUF=8192 SO_SNDBUF=8192
dns proxy = no

[homes]
comment = User home directories
browseable = no
writable = yes

[printers]
comment = Linux printers
path = /var/spool/samba
browseable = no
guest ok = no
printable = yes
```

The `smb.conf` file is divided into sections. The [global] section defines the overall operation of the server. Other sections define how the server handles shared resources: either the printers or specific file system "shares" (directories that you want to share). The [homes] and [printers] sections are standard names that refer to the home directories of each user who logs in and the Linux printers, respectively. You can create other sections to define other shares. Each line in the minimal `smb.conf` example file above is explained here:

- *workgroup = MYPLACE*: The workgroup of which your Samba server is a part.

- *netbios name = sundance*: The host name of your Samba server. This is normally the same as your Linux hostname, though it doesn't have to be, since NetBIOS and WINS servers operate independently of DNS. If they differ, however, be careful to keep track of them!

- *server string = Samba on Linux posing as Windows 2000*: This is the comment that appears in Windows when you access this Samba server. If you put something like "Windows XP" here, no one can tell you are really running Samba on Linux!

- *hosts allow = 192.168.100.*: Which hosts the Samba server allows to access the server. This definition specifies all hosts on the network 192.168.100.0. You can specify this field in various ways. This field does not substitute for a good firewall.

- *printcap name = /etc/printcap*: Defines where Linux printers are defined, so that Samba can obtain a list of the printer names to present to clients.

- *load printers = yes*: Printing is enabled by using **yes** here.

- *printing = lprng*: The printing system used on nearly all Linux systems is called `lprng`.

- *log file = /var/log/samba.log*: Samba sends log messages to this file. You can create per client log files using the `%m` option as well.

- *max log size = 0*: With the maximum log size set to zero, no maximum is imposed. If you include a number, it defines a maximum size for the log file in KB. You should use a log rotation plan to avoid having overly large log files.

- *security = user*: Require each user to provide a username and password before accessing the Samba server. Other security methods are described below.

- *encrypt passwords = yes*: User passwords must be encrypted for Samba to accept them. This is the standard choice because all newer Windows systems (Windows 98 and later) require encrypted passwords.

- *smb passwd file = /etc/samba/smbpasswd*: The list of user accounts to which Samba should refer.

- *socket options = TCP_NODELAY SO_RCVBUF=8192 SO_SNDBUF=8192*: How Samba uses TCP/IP for transporting data. The options shown here are a standard way to speed up transmissions. (You may recognize that they resemble the options used to speed up NFS as well!)

- *dns proxy = no*: Don't use DNS to resolve names; rely instead on Windows protocols.

- *[homes]*: Indicates the Windows share devoted to user home directories.

- *comment = User home directories*: The share's contents.

- *browseable = no*: The share cannot be located by "browsing"; you must know the name of the share that you want (your own home directory in this case).

- *writable = yes*: Users can create or update files in their home directories.

- *[printers]*: The printing management section of Samba.

- *comment = Linux printers*: The contents of this share.

- *path = /var/spool/samba*: A path where print jobs are spooled (stored).

- *browseable = no*: Printers are not browseable, you must know the name of the printer you want to access.

- *guest ok = no*: Guest users cannot print, only those who log in using a valid username and password.

- *printable = yes*: Yes, users can print!

Creating Samba Users

The user security model requires that each user must log in with a valid username and password before using a share on the Samba server. It's common to allow everyone with a Linux user account to also log in via Samba. Several utilities included with the Samba suite make this easy to implement. Assuming that you have created all your Linux user accounts, the following command creates a Samba password file for all your Linux users:

```
cat /etc/passwd | mksmbpasswd.sh > /etc/samba/smbpasswd
```

No passwords are transferred in this process; you must enter a password for each user (twice) using the **smbpasswd** command. For example, this command lets you set the Samba password for user nwells in the **smbpasswd** file:

```
smbpasswd nwells
```

User nwells can then use that password to log in from a Windows system.

If you add Linux users to your system after setting up Samba, you can add them to your **smbpasswd** file using the **smbadduser** command. This command takes the Linux username and the desired Samba username as arguments. (It's normal for them to be identical.) For example:

```
smbadduser abutler:abutler
```

You then must use **smbpasswd** to set a password for the new user before he or she can log in. If you prefer not to use the user security model described so far, consider one of these values for the "security =" setting.

- *security=share* means that all users who log in to your Samba server have the same access, which you define in your configuration. Normally you assign all Samba users to Linux user nobody, or a similar user account with few rights. This type of security is ideal for a Samba server that is acting solely as a print server.

- *security=server* is the same as *security=user*, except that you define another server that verifies the username and password. This system looks the same as *security=user* to the client, but lets you avoid setting up separate password files on every server if it doesn't make sense.

- *security=domain* lets you rely on a Windows NT domain server for user authentication. You still need to set up Linux user accounts before using this option, however.

Using SWAT to Configure SMB

The example **smb.conf** configuration file described previously contains only a fraction of the hundreds of options supported by Samba. Exploring them all can be a challenge, especially if you are new to Windows networking. Several graphical tools can help you configure Samba (check *www.kde.org* or *www.gnome.org*, for example), but the method of choice according to the developers of Samba is the SWAT tool. **SWAT** is a browser-based graphical interface that sets up the **smb.conf** file, restarts the Samba servers, and provides some status information on how the server is being utilized.

SWAT runs as a network service managed by the superserver. To use SWAT, the SWAT service must be included in your **/etc/services** file (it is on most modern Linux systems). The line in **/etc/services** should appear like this:

```
swat 901/tcp
```

You also must enable SWAT within your superserver configuration. Check either **/etc/inetd.conf** or **/etc/xinetd.d/swat** to make sure the service is enabled; the superserver can then start SWAT when a request arrives from your browser. You can use your browser from any system to reach SWAT and manage your Samba server. However, SWAT transfers are not encrypted, so unless you are using SWAT to manage Samba on the same machine, you risk exposing your root password to someone snooping around on your network.

To access SWAT once you have the network capabilities configured, launch your Web browser and enter the URL *http://localhost:901/* (assuming you are configuring SWAT on your own machine.) You are prompted for a username and password. You must enter the username **root** and the root password for your host. The initial SWAT page then appears, as shown in Figure 5-7.

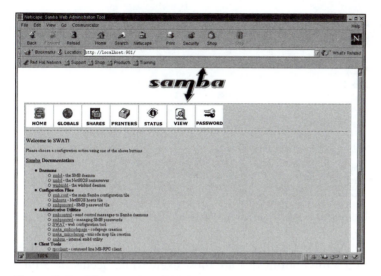

Figure 5-7   The opening SWAT page

    SWAT modifies your /etc/smb.conf. It may delete comment lines you have entered or rearrange the configuration lines in the file. If you have hand-edited /etc/smb.conf, make a backup copy of it under a different name before using SWAT.

The great advantage of using SWAT is that you can learn about Samba as you config-ure it. If you haven't already, you should use SWAT at least to check (and possibly mod-ify) the settings listed previously in the small example **smb.conf** file. Beyond that, you can view the SWAT pages to see what options are available. You begin using SWAT by selecting one of the buttons at the top of the page. For example, you can choose Globals to alter the global server configuration, or Home to set up home directory shares. A page full of options then appears. Figure 5-8 shows the Global options page.

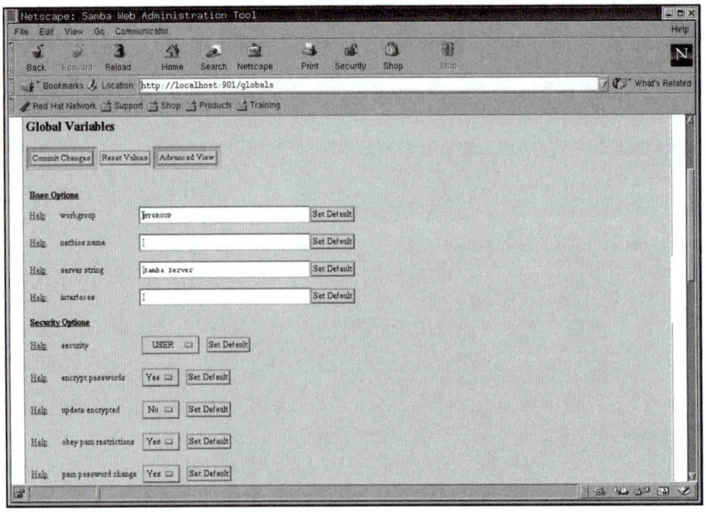

Figure 5-8   Global Samba options within SWAT

You can choose the Help link to the left of any option to see how it is used. Each Samba page initially includes the options that are most likely to be needed in a typical configuration. Review all of these options to consider what you might need to configure for your server. After you make changes, use the Commit Changes button at the top of each screen to update the Samba configuration file. When you're ready to explore in more depth, click the Advanced View button at the top of the page (each section has one) to expand the page, listing all the available options, including many that you will probably never need. But you can learn a lot by reviewing them!

> If you are curious, explore some of the 195 options included in the Advanced View of the Global section.

Within SWAT, you create new shares (directories that you want to make available to clients) using the Shares button at the top of the SWAT Web page. You enter a name for the new share and choose the Create Share button. You can then select the share from the drop-down list and click the Choose Share button to configure settings for that share.

The Status page shows you the state of the **smbd** and **nmbd** servers and lets you start or restart them using buttons on the Web page. Figure 5-9 shows this page. The bottom part of the page lists all the active client connections to the server.

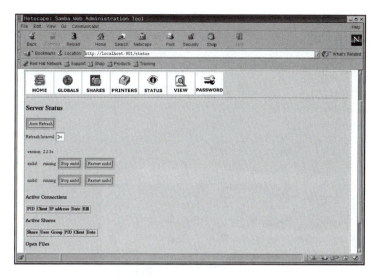

Figure 5-9   The SWAT Status page

The `smbstatus` command lets you see similar status information at any command line. A useful exercise is to review the files included with the various Samba packages to see what specialized utilities and documentation files are included.

Accessing Samba from Windows

Once you have a Samba server up and running, you can access Linux files and print to Linux printers from any Windows-based host. All you need is the correct Windows networking configuration and a valid username and password. Although Windows networking can use various low-level networking protocols such as TCP/IP, IPX, and others, Samba uses only TCP/IP. To reach a Samba server from a Windows host, therefore, you should use the Networking icon on the Windows Control Panel to be certain the following components are installed:

- *A network adapter*: Windows should be able to recognize your NIC and have a valid driver for it. The network card is listed in the resources of the network configuration dialog box.

- *TCP/IP*: You should configure TCP/IP so that you have a valid IP address.

- *NetBEUI*: The **NetBEUI** protocol implements NetBIOS functionality on Windows systems. Both this and TCP/IP can be added using the Add button within the Network Configuration dialog box. (In Windows NT look under the Protocols tab.)

- *Client for Microsoft Networks* must also be installed. Again, you can add this if it's not already listed.

From your Windows desktop, you access a Samba server by opening the Network Neighborhood (or My Network Places) icon and browsing to the appropriate work-group. For example, in Windows NT 4, you may have to choose Find, then select Computer on the Windows menu and search for either the Samba server's name or even its IP address before Windows can locate the server (this is true particularly when you have just started up Samba). Once you see an icon for the server, you can double-click it to see a list of shares (after entering your username and password). Then double-click on a share to view its contents. Figure 5-10 shows a Windows NT 4 desktop while working with a Samba server.

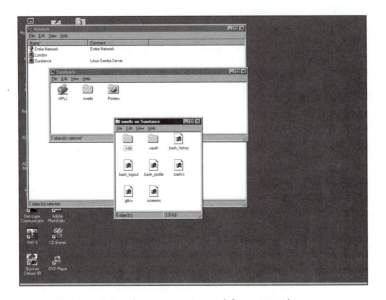

Figure 5-10   A Samba server viewed from Windows

Chapter Summary

- ❐ FTP is a widely used Internet protocol that was designed for efficient transfer of files (including large files) from a server to multiple clients at diverse locations.

- ❐ The anonymous feature of FTP makes it popular for public download archives. Many capabilities of the anonymous feature can be configured to control access to the FTP server.

- ❐ To access an FTP server, you can use the text-mode client, `ftp`, a graphical client such as gFTP or IglooFTP, or a Web browser.

- ❐ The standard FTP server is `wu-ftpd`. It is configured using `/etc/ftpaccess`, logs file transfers to `/var/log/xfer`, and usually relies on the access control mechanism of the superserver that launches it, though `ftpaccess` can also include host-based access controls.

5

❏ You can configure classes of users in `ftpaccess`, then assign permission to perform different file actions, or define other types of access limits using those user
classes.

❏ The Network File System (NFS) lets you access remote file systems as part of your
local directory structure by using the `mount` command to contact an NFS server.
Numerous options control how a client mounts an NFS file system; these options
are usually placed in the `/etc/fstab` file to simplify mounting and unmounting
operations.

❏ An NFS server consists of several possible daemons; at the least, `nfsd` and
`rpc.mountd` are required. NFS is not managed by a superserver, but instead uses
the `portmap` program in conjunction with the remote procedure call (rpc) system.

❏ An NFS server is configured using the `/etc/exports` file, which defines which
local directories are available for remote clients to mount. Each line in
`/etc/exports` also defines which hosts can mount the directory and how the
server should configure their access. This includes options such as user mapping and
read-only versus read-write access.

❏ NFS is prone to security holes, but it relies on several layers of security, including
the client `mount` command, the configuration of `/etc/exports`, and any restrictions in the `/etc/hosts.allow` and `/etc/hosts.deny` files using the
`portmap` daemon name.

❏ The NetWare network operating system can be emulated on Linux as a powerful
file-and-print server. The `mars_nwe` package provides this capability, though only
the older NetWare bindery is supported, not the newer NDS.

❏ The `mars_nwe` NetWare emulator is configured using the `/etc/nwserv.conf`
file. You must set up at least basic information such as the server name and the SYS
volume before using this program.

❏ Linux can access NetWare servers as a client using the `ncpfs` package, which provides a number of command-line tools to manage and access NetWare servers,
including the `ncpmount` command to make a NetWare volume appear part of the
local Linux directory structure.

❏ Windows networking uses the NetBIOS and SMB (also called CIFS) protocols,
both of which are implemented by the Samba suite in Linux.

❏ Using the Samba client utility `smbclient` and mounting Windows file systems of
type `smbfs` provide convenient access to shared resources. Most modern graphical
Linux printer management tools also let you use the `smbprint` utility to automatically print to Windows printers.

❏ A simple Samba server configuration in `smb.conf` involves defining the server
name, basic security options, and defining shares. Samba shares are viewed from
Windows just like any Windows server.

❐ SWAT provides graphical configuration and administration functionality for Samba. Though it is not secure for use across a network, SWAT makes it easy to learn more about Samba through listing all available options with online help.

❐ Multiple Samba security models are supported, including Windows NT domains and guest accounts, which often use Samba as a dedicated print server.

KEY TERMS

.nwclient — A configuration file used by the `ncpfs` package for client access to NetWare servers.

anonymous FTP — Using FTP for public access via a common username, without a user-specific account on the FTP server.

anonymous user home directory — The directory on Linux which anonymous FTP users can access for downloading or uploading files. Typically either `/var/ftp` or `/home ftp`.

anonymous users — Users logging in to an FTP server who do not have a regular Linux user account and are thus restricted to a specific area of the file system. *See* anonymous FTP.

bindery — A database of system resources stored on a NetWare server. Versions after NetWare 3 use the newer Novell Directory Service (NDS). *See also* Bindery Emulation.

Bindery Emulation — A system used by versions 4 and above of NetWare to simulate a bindery when the operating system actually uses NDS.

classes of users — The practice of defining groups of potential FTP clients within an FTP server configuration to aid efficient server configuration.

Common Internet File System (CIFS) — The latest extended version of the SMB protocol, used by recent Microsoft operating systems and provided in Linux via the Samba suite.

exportfs — A command used to activate the contents of `/etc/exports`.

exports — The `/etc/exports` configuration file defining file systems that NFS can make available to other hosts.

File Transfer Protocol (FTP) — A protocol used to share files between networked computer systems.

ftp — The most common text-based client program for accessing FTP servers.

ftpaccess — The main FTP server configuration file.

ftpshut — A command that causes the FTP server to stop allowing connections.

ftpusers — An FTP server configuration file listing user accounts that are not allowed to log in via FTP.

gFTP — A graphical FTP client. Installed by default on many Linux systems.

guest users — Users logging in to an FTP server who have a regular Linux user account, but are restricted in what they can do while logged in using FTP.

hard mount — A method of mounting an NFS file system that causes NFS to wait indefinitely for the NFS server to respond.

IglooFTP — A popular graphical FTP client.

map — To create a correspondence between a user ID on an NFS client and user permissions on an NFS server.

mars-nwe — Martin Stovers NetWare Emulator package; software for Linux that provides NetWare server capabilities.

ncftp — A text-based FTP client program similar to ftp, but newer and more refined.

ncpfs — A Linux software package that implements NCP and provides a number of NetWare client utilities.

NetBEUI — A protocol within Windows-based computers that implements NetBIOS functionality.

NetBIOS — A protocol that provides a network name resolution service, similar in concept to DNS. Used by Windows operating systems and provided as part of the Samba suite.

NetWare — A network operating system by Novell, an early market leader and still renowned for excellent file and print sharing services.

NetWare Core Protocol (NCP) — A transport protocol used by NetWare for file and print sharing.

Network File System (NFS) — A protocol used to share file systems on a network.

nfsd — A daemon that handles file transfers for a mounted NFS file system, based on the settings that the **rpc.mountd** daemon has validated.

nmbd — The daemon within the Samba suite that provides NetBIOS capability to Linux.

Novell Directory Service (NDS) — A network resource directory supported by later versions of NetWare but not by NetWare-related Linux tools.

nwserv.conf — A configuration file used to set up the **mars-nwe** NetWare emulator.

portmap — The program that watches for rpc requests (such as from NFS daemons) and creates the network connections to make them function.

real users — Users logging in to an FTP server who have a regular Linux user account.

remote procedure call (rpc) — A protocol used to allow programs to communicate over a network. rpc acts almost as a superserver, watching for network requests from rpc-capable programs and transferring them to the appropriate transport protocol (such as TCP or UDP).

rpc.mountd — A daemon used as part of NFS to make new connections, mounting a remote file system after checking relevant permissions to see if the mount is permitted.

Samba — A suite of programs for Linux and many UNIX operating systems that permits these systems to support Windows protocols such as SMB, CIFS, and NetBIOS.

Server Message Block (SMB) — The transport protocol used for file and print sharing by Windows systems and the Samba suite.

share — A Windows resource for shared use over a network.

smbclient — A utility that provides client access to Windows-based hosts or to Samba servers. Part of the Samba suite.

smbd — The daemon within the Samba suite that provides SMB capability to Linux.

smbfs — The file system type designation used to mount a Windows share as part of a Linux file system using the `mount` command.

smbprint — A command within the Samba suite that enables printing to a Windows printer over the network.

soft mount — A method of mounting an NFS file system that causes NFS to give up on an operation after waiting for a specified time.

squashing — A security concept used by NFS servers to prevent a user from gaining access to a file system on the NFS server simply by virtue of having the same user ID on the NFS client.

SWAT — A browser-based graphical configuration interface for setting up and managing the Samba SMB server.

Trivial FTP (TFTP) — A protocol similar to FTP, but designed for downloading an operating system over a network to boot a diskless workstation. Requires less memory and provides fewer features than standard FTP.

trustee — A user who is granted access to a file or directory on a NetWare server.

trustee rights — Access permissions assigned to a file or directory on a NetWare volume.

volume — A unit of storage in NetWare that is equivalent to a file system in Linux.

WINS — Acronym for Windows Internet Naming Service, a host locating service for Windows systems, similar in function to a DNS server. The Samba suite can act as a WINS server or client.

wu-ftp — The Washington University FTP server. The name of the server daemon is `in.ftpd`.

REVIEW QUESTIONS

1. Describe how the purpose of FTP differs from the purpose of HTTP and SMTP.

2. Which is not an FTP client program?

   a. `gftp`

   b. `ftp`

   c. `wu-ftpd`

   d. `ncftp`

3. Within the standard FTP client program, you would use the prompt command to:

   a. prevent being prompted for confirmation before downloading a set of files using mget

   b. cause the server to prompt you if you were about to exceed your time limit or download size limit

   c. turn off prompting of help screens for new users

   d. change the format of the default command-line prompt within the utility

4. Which is a correctly formed URL to reach an FTP site within a standard Web browser?

   a. *http://nwells@ftp.myplace.net/*

   b. *ftp://nwells@in.ftpd/*

   c. *ftp://nwells@ftp.myplace.net/*

   d. *http://ftp.myplace/*

5. Assuming the FTP server is running in standalone mode, which file lists user accounts that are not allowed to access the FTP server?

   a. `/etc/ftpusers`

   b. `/etc/hosts.deny`

   c. `/etc/shutdown.msg`

   d. `/var/ftp/pub/ftpusers`

6. Describe the difference between a real user and a guest user when configuring an FTP server.

7. A filename given after the banner directive in `/etc/ftpaccess` will:

   a. cause the FTP server to alert the user to the presence of the file after logging in

   b. display the contents of the file to the client before logging in

   c. display the contents of the file to the client after logging in

   d. display the contents of the file to the client upon entering the /etc directory

8. Which does not use rpc?

   a. NFS

   b. r–utilities

   c. `portmap`

   d. FTP

9. The two principal NFS daemons on Linux are:

   a. `rpc.mountd` and `nfsd`

   b. `portmap` and `rpc`

   c. `rpc.mountd` and `rpc.umountd`

   d. `fstab` and `exports`

10. Which is the valid line in `fstab` to configure mounting for an NFS file system on rome?

   a. nfs rome:/home/public /mnt/rome rsize=8192,wsize=8192,rw,noauto 0 0

   b. rome:/home/public /nfs/rome rsize=8192,wsize=8192,rw,noauto 0 0

   c. rome:/home/public /mnt/rome rpc rsize=8192,wsize=8192,rw,nfs 0 0

   d. rome:/home/public /mnt/rome nfs rsize=8192,wsize=8192,rw,noauto 0 0

   e. nfs:/home/public /mnt/rome nfs rsize=8192,wsize=8192,rw,noauto 0 0

11. Why is root squashing the default action on an NFS server?

12. Which is a validly formed configuration line in `/etc/exports`?

   a. `(ro,all_squash)`   `/pub`

   b. `portmap`   `o=ro,all_squash`

   c. `/pub`   `host1(ro,all_squash)`

   d. `/pub`   `host1=ro,all_squash`

13. How is `inetd` or `xinetd` configured to manage which hosts can access an NFS server?

   a. It isn't. NFS uses portmap, not the superserver, though `/etc/hosts.allow` and `/etc/hosts.deny` are still checked.

   b. It isn't. NFS uses host-specific configurations within `/etc/fstab` to control host access.

   c. By setting the appropriate host definitions for the nfsd daemon in `/etc/hosts.allow` and `/etc/hosts.deny`.

   d. By relying on the xinetd parameters within the nfs file in `/etc/xinetd.d.` configuration.

14. Which is the transport protocol used by NetWare servers?

   a. mars-nwe

   b. NCP

   c. NetBEUI

   d. NDS

15. NetWare client and server capabilities in Linux are provided by _____ and _____, respectively.

    a. mars–nwe, ncpfs

    b. ncpfs, mars–nwe

    c. ndsfs, mars–nwe

    d. RIP, SAP

16. The NetWare Server emulator on Linux is configured in the file:

    a. nwserv.conf

    b. nwbind.conf

    c. ncp.conf

    d. nds.conf

17. The Samba suite can act as a WINS server on a Windows network, which is roughly equivalent to a _____ server for a Linux-only network.

    a. SMB

    b. NetBEUI

    c. FTP

    d. DNS

18. Which choice contains only protocols supported by the Samba suite?

    a. CIFS, SMB, NetBIOS

    b. CIFS, SMB, DNS

    c. SMBD, NMBD

    d. SMB, SWAT, NCP

19. The smbclient program most resembles which other program in this chapter?

    a. `exportfs`

    b. `ftpshut`

    c. `ftp`

    d. gFTP

20. To see a list of file and printer shares available on an SMB server, you would include that server name with the _____ parameter of the _____ command.

    a. –S, smbfs

    b. –L, smbclient

    c. –S, smbclient

    d. –W, smbprint

21. To mount a Windows share as part of your Linux file system, you:

    a. Use the `mount` command with the `-t` parameter set to `smbfs`.

    b. Rely on a graphical utility for convenient access.

    c. Use `smbclient` to download the desired files.

    d. Make certain that the `smbpasswd` file was first properly configured.

22. Which security model within the SMB server of Samba is most like anonymous `FTP`?

    a. server

    b. share

    c. user

    d. domain

23. What is the principal concern with using SWAT to configure the Samba suite across a network connection?

24. From which page of SWAT can you restart the smbd and nmbd server daemons?

    a. Global

    b. Shares

    c. Home

    d. Status

25. Which choice correctly lists components that must be installed on a Windows-based host to access a Samba server running on Linux?

    a. Client for Microsoft Networks, NetBEUI, TCP/IP

    b. Client for Microsoft Networks, NetBIOS, NetBEUI, SMB

    c. NetBEUI, SMB, TCP/IP

    d. SMB, TCP/IP, WINS

HANDS-ON PROJECTS

Project 5-1

In this project you experiment with the FTP client program, `ftp`. We describe the steps needed to complete the procedure on Red Hat Linux 7.3, but the steps should be substantially equivalent on any Linux distribution using `wu-ftpd` as the FTP server. In particular, the `ftp` client program does not vary between distributions. Be aware that if you used a High Security setting when you installed Linux or otherwise set up firewalling, the procedure may not work. If you are in a safe lab environment, you can delete all firewall rules on the system and set all default firewall policies to ACCEPT by issuing the following commands while logged in as root:

```
ipchains -F
ipchains -P input ACCEPT
ipchains -P forward ACCEPT
ipchains -P output ACCEPT
```

For this project you should work in teams; one Linux system should be designated as the FTP server and the other as the FTP client. You should have root access to the FTP server system.

1. On the server, create a document tree for anonymous FTP testing using this command:

   cp -r /usr/share/doc/pam-0.75/* /var/ftp/pub

2. On the server, open the /etc/ftpaccess file in a text editor and change the **passwd-check** directive from **warn** to **enforce**. It should look like this:

   passwd-check   rfc822   enforce

3. Enable the FTP server by editing the /etc/xinetd.d/wu-ftp file (or the ftp service line in /etc/inetd.conf if you have a version of Linux that uses inetd).

4. Do you need to restart anything for this to take effect? What and why?

5. On the client Linux system, log in with the **ftp** command using the name of the server system. Enter **ftp** as the username when prompted.

6. When prompted for your password, enter your username again, not your email address.

7. Describe what happens.

8. Log out of the FTP client using the **bye** command, then start it again as in Step 5.

9. Use the username **anonymous** this time (it is equivalent to the username ftp).

10. When prompted, enter your email address correctly as the password.

11. Enter the **help** command to see a list of ftp commands. Do you recognize many of these from your previous work at the Linux command line?

12. Choose one that you haven't seen before and use the **help** command to see a one-line description of it. For example, if you want to learn about the **mdelete** command, enter:

    help mdelete

13. Change to the /pub/txt directory on the FTP server. (This assumes you copied the files from the **pam-0.75** directory in step 1.)

    cd pub/txt

14. List the files in that directory.

15. Choose a file and try to rename it with the **rename** command in ftp.

16. Why can't you do it? How could you make it possible for an anonymous user to do this? Do so and try again.

17. Log out from the client.

18. On the server, use the **tail** command to view the last few lines of the transfer log. What do you see?

19. Also on the server, use the **tail** command to view the last few lines of the system message log, **/var/log/messages**. What do you see? How does this relate to the steps you completed above?

Project 5-2

In this project you continue to experiment with FTP. The steps describe the procedure on Red Hat Linux 7.3, but they should be substantially equivalent for any Linux distribution using **wu-ftpd** as the FTP server. To complete this project, you should have the FTP server and client programs installed and have completed Project 5-1 so that you have a set of files in the **/var/ftp/pub** directory. Be aware that if you used a High Security setting when you installed Linux, or otherwise set up firewalling, the procedure may not work. If you are in a safe lab environment, you can delete all firewall rules on the system and set all default firewall policies to ACCEPT by issuing the following commands while logged in as root:

```
ipchains —F
ipchains -P input ACCEPT
ipchains -P forward ACCEPT
ipchains -P output ACCEPT
```

For this project you should work in teams; one Linux system should be designated as the FTP server and the other as the FTP client. You should have root access to the FTP server system.

1. On the server, add the following line to the **ftpaccess** file:

```
data-limit raw total 10000
```

2. Search the man page for **ftpaccess** to determine what the **raw** keyword after the directive means.

3. Save the **ftpaccess** file. Do you need to restart anything to have it take effect?

4. On the client, create a temporary directory and change into it.

```
mkdir ~/temp
cd ~/temp
```

5. Log in to the FTP server using the anonymous user.

6. Change to the **/pub/txt** directory on the FTP server.

7. Use the **prompt** and **mget** commands to download the entire contents of the **txt** directory. Were you successful?

8. Devise a test to determine whether you can complete the transfer of a file once you have started it if that transfer exceeds the data-limit setting on the FTP server. You may decide to copy a larger file from somewhere on your server to the `/var/ftp/pub` directory to use for this experiment.

9. Suppose you notice anonymous FTP users logging in multiple times simultaneously to be able to download many Linux files from your FTP server at the same time. This means a single person is using several of the limited number of connections you have allowed and "hogging the bandwidth." Review the man page to find the directive that lets you limit each host to a single simultaneous connection (or a specified number of connections) to your FTP server.

Project 5-3

In this project you experiment with the NFS protocol. The steps describe the procedure on Red Hat Linux 7.3, but they should be substantially equivalent for any Linux distribution. To complete this project, you should have the NFS daemons installed. Be aware that if you used a High Security setting when you installed Linux, or otherwise set up firewalling, the procedure may not work. If you are in a safe lab environment, you can delete all firewall rules on the system and set all default firewall policies to ACCEPT by issuing the following commands while logged in as root:

```
ipchains -F
ipchains -P input ACCEPT
ipchains -P forward ACCEPT
ipchains -P output ACCEPT
```

For this project you should work in teams; one Linux system should be designated as the NFS server and the other as the NFS client. You should have root access to both systems.

1. On the server, edit the `/etc/exports` file and add the following line, substituting the hostname of your client system where indicated:

    `/usr/share/doc     client_host(all_squash,rw)`

2. Also on the server, edit the `/etc/hosts.deny` file by adding this line:

    `portmap        client_host`

3. What steps need to be taken to activate these two changes? (e.g., `portmap`, TCP Wrappers, `nfsd`, `nfslock`, `xinetd`...?)

4. On the client, log in as root and create a mount point directory for the NFS server. Here is an example:

    `mkdir /mnt/server_hostname`

5. Edit the `/etc/fstab` file on the client by adding this line:

    `server_hostname:/usr/share/doc     /mnt/server_hostname`
    `nfs     o=ro, rsize=8192,wsize=8192 0 0`

6. Use the `mount` command on the client to mount the NFS file system you exported:

   `mount /mnt/server_hostname`

7. Why did it not work?

8. On the server, edit `/etc/hosts.deny`, removing your addition.

9. On the client, try the `mount` command again.

10. Change to the mount point directory that you created.

11. Noting that the directory is exported as `rw` on the server, create a new directory in that directory:

    `mkdir mydocs`

12. Give three reasons why this didn't work.

Project 5-4

In this project you experiment with printing using Samba. The steps describe the procedure on Red Hat Linux 7.3, but they should be substantially equivalent for any Linux distribution with a standard Linux distribution installed. To complete this project, you should have `lpd` installed and running, you should have Samba packages installed as described in the chapter text, and be familiar enough with the chapter materials to get Samba running as a server.

For this project you should work in teams; one Linux system should be designated as the Samba server and the other as the Samba client. Your team should have root access to both systems.

1. On the server, use a printer configuration tool to set up a local Linux printer definition. The easiest way is to start the `printconf-gui` program, choose **New**, select a **LOCAL** printer type, and enter a name such as **printer1** to identify the printer. Complete this step even though you may not have a physical printer attached to your Linux system.

2. Also on the server, stop `lpd` from attempting to send print jobs queued to your new printer definition to a physical printer, in case one does not exist. Use the `lpc` command, like this:

   `lpc stop printer1`

3. On the server, use the basic Samba configuration file shown in the chapter text, or similar settings, to get the Samba server up and running. Be certain you have a [printers] section. Create at least one user account to use for this project and assign it a password. You can use SWAT if you prefer that to hand editing the file.

4. On the client system, use the `printconf-gui` utility to define an SMB printer. Name the SMB printer definition printer2. Specify printer1 as the remote printer name on the Samba server; use the username, password, workgroup, etc. that you used to get the Samba server running.

5. On the client system, use the `lpr` command to print a text file to the SMB printer that you defined printer2. You can use a graphical utility with a print function if you choose, but many Linux graphical programs do not list the available printers, so it may be easier to just print from a command line using a command like this one:

```
lpr  -P printer2 /etc/termcap
```

6. Back on the server, use the `lpq` command to view the contents of the print queue for the local Linux printer that you defined printer1. The command looks like this (you might also choose to try a graphical printer manager in KDE or Gnome):

```
lpq -P printer1
```

7. This shows that you have effectively printed from a Samba client to a Samba server; both sides acted as if the other side were a Windows-based host. Now use `lprm` to delete the print job on printer1.

8. Using the `printconf-gui` utility, delete the printer definitions that you created on the client and server.

Project 5-5

In this project you experiment with Samba file transfers. The steps describe the procedure on Red Hat Linux 7.3, but they should be substantially equivalent for any Linux distribution with a standard Linux distribution installed. To complete this project, you should have Samba running as a server.

For this project you should work in teams; one Linux system should be designated as the Samba server and the other as the Samba client. Your team should have root access to both systems.

1. Make certain the Samba server is running.

2. Log in to the SWAT Web page for your Samba server, as described in the chapter text.

3. Within SWAT, alter the security method to be *share* and add a guest user account. To do this, click on the Globals icon and change the Security item in the Security Options section.

4. On the **Shares** page, define a share called **Pub**.

5. Switch to a command prompt and copy some files to the directory that you defined as the location of the share. (Use the `cp -r` command.)

6. Log in to the client system and create a download directory.

7. From within the download directory that you created, log in to the Samba server using `smbclient`.

8. Download a few files from your `/Pub` file collection.

9. How does this process differ from using anonymous FTP? Is it easier to set up for the administrator? Does it seem easier for the end user? Does it seem more or less secure? If more secure, why might you still not use Samba?

10. Log out of the `smbclient` program and return to the server.

11. Review the contents of the log files you specified in your Samba server configuration (probably located in `/var/log/samba`). What information is recorded?

CASE PROJECTS

Your work in Alaska has been such a success that word has spread. Island Associates, colleagues of Snow, Sleet, and Hale located in Los Angeles, want you to set up an FTP server for their maritime public records database, so that users around the country can download reports about how recently passed maritime laws might affect their rights.

1. They have given you the following rules for setting up the FTP server, based on their current Internet connectivity and security concerns.

   a. The individual reports are fairly small, but they don't think a user should be allowed to download more than 10 during one login session, or a maximum of 10 MB of data.

   b. Anonymous FTP access should be restricted to 30 minutes per session.

   c. They have been having trouble with a group of users originating at the no-law.org domain, so you should block all access to that domain.

   Write the `ftpaccess` lines that will implement these rules. You will need to refer to the `ftpaccess` man page for the correct directives and formatting. Don't include the entire `ftpaccess` file, only the lines used to set up these requirements.

   ```
   file-limit out 10 all
   data-limit out 10000000 all
   limit-time anonymous 30
   deny no-law.org  /etc/deny.msg
   ```

2. Island Associates also would like all 15 of their staff to have access to the reports posted on the FTP site. They should be able to view them as part of their local file system rather than having to download them using FTP. This prevents having 15 copies of each report, which might lead to individuals having different versions as the reports are updated. The office includes a central Linux server hosting the FTP server you created and several other network services. The server is *ftp.islandnet.com*. The office also has a Windows PC on each user's desk. Assume for a moment that each Windows PC has NFS client capabilities from previous configurations. Write out the configuration line(s) in `/etc/exports` to allow the users to mount/access the reports on the Linux server. Given that the reports are on the same server that is being used for anonymous FTP access, also write out a configuration for `/etc/hosts.allow` and `/etc/hosts.deny` to limit access to the server for NFS server. Did you place all the reports in a single directory? Did you use the same directory as you did for anonymous FTP downloads?

Why? Do you think you would use NFS if the Windows clients did not already have NFS clients installed? Why? If not, what would you use instead?

3. Island Associates has also asked for your help in setting up a small FTP server for reports originating from their branch office on Rarotonga in the Cook Islands. Because this will be a small server with limited resources, you decide to review other FTP servers to see how you can make the most effective use of the Rarotonga server. You are considering something that might combine several protocols, and maybe use Java or something similar to provide for remote administration of the server (the Cook Islands being a long flight from your office). Look up FTP servers on *www.sourceforge.net* or another Linux resources site that you prefer and write a brief report (1/2 to 1 page) on three programs that provide FTP server capabilities and would be worth reviewing as a selection for this project. Include the advantages and risks associated with each program.

5

CONFIGURING MAJOR
NETWORK SERVICES

**After reading this chapter and completing the exercises
you will be able to:**

♦ Expand the routing capabilities of your Linux server

♦ Set up your own DNS name server

♦ Configure a basic email server

♦ Understand how Linux can excel as a Web server

In this chapter, you continue to explore network services that are commonly used on Linux systems. The previous chapter focused on file-sharing services. In this chapter the focus is on the services for which dedicated Linux servers are often used: routing, DNS, email, and the Web.

In the first part of the chapter, you learn about creating a Linux router with dynamic routing tables, building on the concepts you learned in Chapters 1 and 2. You also learn about setting up a DNS server on Linux, so that you can resolve domain names without resorting to another DNS server on the Internet.

The second part of the chapter is devoted to email server and Web server configuration. Email servers are less ubiquitous than Web servers, but form a key part of Internet information sharing; the discussion here will get you started with a basic configuration. Linux has a long tradition as a Web server platform; you'll learn how to set up a basic Web server and explore some of the many additional technologies that are available to expand a Web server's capability on Linux.

DYNAMIC ROUTING WITH ROUTING PROTOCOLS

In Chapter 2 you learned how routing is configured in the Linux kernel using the `route` command. You learned that each entry in the routing table contains the following elements:

- The target network or host to which the routing table entry applies; that is, the network or host that you can reach using the information in the entry.

- The network mask to use when calculating addresses for the target.

- The address of the next hop router, or, more simply put, the system to which packets are sent that are destined for the target network or host. (A **hop** refers to passing through a router to reach a final destination.)

- The network interface on which packets should be sent to reach the target network or host. For example, if there are three Ethernet cards installed and a dial-up connection, this part of the routing entry would specify one of those four interfaces for each entry in the routing table.

The Linux kernel running on a given host uses the information in the routing table whenever packets arrive that have the host's MAC address (physical address of the network card) but another host's IP address. As long as IP forwarding is enabled, Linux routes packets to the next hop router until they eventually reach their destination.

The routing described thus far is called **static routing**. The routing table in your Linux kernel is assembled by entries in your start-up scripts or by `route` commands that you enter to update or modify the routing table. This is straightforward and effective for a small, reliable network, but static routing is not the best choice for larger networks and sometimes unreliable connections. In most routing situations, dynamic routing is used. **Dynamic routing** is the process of using a specialized routing protocol to build and modify routing tables automatically through a network based on information shared by the routers, without constant human intervention.

To see the value of dynamic routing, consider the networking configuration shown in Figure 6-1. Host Abe wants to reach Host Bill. If static routing is used, Router 1 would have an entry showing that the Ethernet card connected directly to Router 2 was the correct way to reach Host Bill. However, if something breaks the network connection between Router 1 and Router 2—for example the phone connection is broken, or someone unplugs the wrong network cable in a server room—Host Abe is unable to reach Host Bill, even though Host Bill *could* be reached via Router 3 and Router 4. With static routing, Router 1 can't find this out; a system administrator would need to learn of the problem, determine an alternate route, and enter the information at a command line. Later, when the problem was fixed, the original route directly to Router 2 would need to be entered in Router 1's routing table in order to keep the network operating as efficiently as possible.

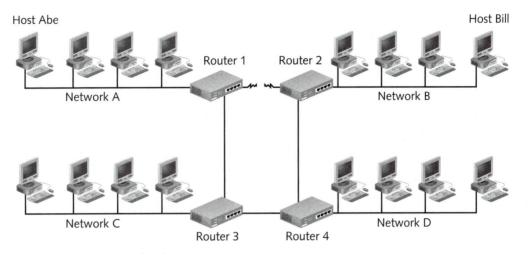

Figure 6-1   The need for dynamic routing

On the other hand, if all four of the routers in Figure 6-1 are using a routing protocol, they will exchange information often about the networks that they are capable of reaching. Before a minute had passed, Router 3 would have informed Router 1 that packets for network A should be sent to it, passed on to Router 4, and then Router 1. Even on a large network, a well-configured routing protocol would have reestablished the connection between Host Abe and Host Bill via another route within a minute or two, without any administrator having to take action.

Many routing protocols are available, but only a few are widely used. Routing protocols are divided into two categories: interior and exterior. While the difference can seem vague at the outset, loosely stated, **interior routing protocols** are those designed for routing packets among networks under your control; they route packets based on mathematical models (though you won't need any math to implement them). **Exterior routing protocols** are designed for routing packets between networks controlled by different organizations; they route packets based on administration policies, often controlled by how much a particular organization's routing information is trusted.

All routing protocols are designed to exchange information among routers. They use broadcast messages or other techniques to inform other routers of the networks that they know how to reach. For example, one router might send a message using a routing protocol that says, "I can reach network 198.60.12.0 in 5 hops." If another router sees that message and doesn't know how to reach the named network in 4 hops or less, it copies that information to its routing table. Then it can broadcast to other routers: "I can reach network 198.60.12.0 in 6 hops." (It adds one hop to reach the router that it received the information from.)

A packet typically passes through many routers (makes many hops) to reach its destination. You saw this when you experimented with the `traceroute` command in Chapter 2. In some routing protocols, the hop count is called the metric. In Chapter 2, however, you learned that a metric is an abstract numeric measure of how good a route is—a preference value as to whether a route should be selected if multiple routes are available.

All routing protocols have the same function: communicating among routers to find the most efficient route for network packets. Routing protocols are distinguished by the method they use to communicate routing information to other servers and the method they use to decide which route is best among several known routes. Several popular routing protocols are described in the sections that follow.

Routing Information Protocol (RIP) and `routed`

RIP, an interior routing protocol, is the oldest routing protocol still in common use. Its usefulness is limited to smaller networks or routing that is not highly complex. RIP does not provide support for classless IP addresses except in RIP version 2, and it can only handle routing with up to 15 hops between source and destination.

RIP defines the best route as the route with the lowest number of routers (hops) to reach the destination network. When RIP is started on a host (we'll call it Router 1), it broadcasts a request for routing information. Any router that receives the broadcast and is running RIP responds by sending all the entries from its routing table to Router 1. Router 1 populates its routing table with the entries it receives using a series of simple rules.

- If an entry refers to a network that is not in the routing table already, that route is added.

- If the **cost** (the number of hops) to reach a network is less via the information received from another router, Router 1 discards the route it has and substitutes the newly received route. (The cost of a route is a measure of how efficient it is; the route with the lowest cost should always be chosen, other things being equal.)

- If Router 1 receives a route with a cost of 15, the route is assumed to be unreachable and is deleted from Router 1's routing table.

RIP is implemented in Linux using the **routed** daemon, which is included with most Linux distributions. It is not installed by default in Red Hat Linux 7.3, but you can find the **routed** package on CD 3. To start **routed** after installing the package, use the script in `/etc/rc.d/init.d` or start it directly using the command:

```
/usr/sbin/routed
```

The **routed** daemon immediately begins broadcasting requests for routing information and assembling routing table entries. **Routed** needs no command-line parameters and requires no configuration file. If you choose to, you can create an **/etc/gateways** file that provides initial settings for `routed` to use. Each line in the file contains a routing table entry that looks like this example:

```
net 192.160.14.0 gateway 172.14.88.12 metric 1 passive
```

The `net` and `gateway` numbers refer to the network ID and gateway used to reach that network. The `metric` is an initial "hop" value for the route. The last word indicates that the router named here, 172.14.88.12, does not participate in RIP exchanges, probably because it is running a different routing protocol. If you were referring to another RIP-based router, you would use the word `active` instead.

The `routed` daemon is easy to configure and run, and is the choice of most network administrators who maintain routers on Linux networks. It is not a strong solution, however, for larger networks because of the limitations of RIP. As you can see in the `/etc/gateways` example line above, the network mask is not even provided, so any network using classless IP addressing (which is very common) is unable to use the routing information correctly. Using RIP version 2 solves this one problem, but the larger answer lies in using other routing protocols.

Open Shortest Path First (OSPF) and `gated`

The Open Shortest Path First (OSPF) protocol is an interior routing protocol designed to work effectively even in very large networks. OSPF uses a technique called flooding. A router running OSPF periodically floods the network with everything it knows about its neighboring hosts. Other OSPF routers see information coming from other routers and use this data to intelligently construct a "chart" inside the router that defines the best way to reach the various networks. It's as if OSPF tries to let each router take the pulse of distant networks so that OSPF can determine which route to use for the most efficient connection from point A to point B. To construct its virtual chart of networking connections, OSPF uses a mathematical technique formally called the Dijkstra Shortest Path First algorithm. OSPF is an open protocol (one everyone can use) that uses the Shortest Path First algorithm, hence the name of the routing protocol.

OSPF uses a metric, like RIP, but in OSPF the metric refers to how much better a given route is than other available routes to the same network. OSPF has no predefined limit on how many routers a packet can pass through to reach its destination. OSPF also lets you define authentication parameters to control which routers you accept routing data from, and lets you assign priorities to different routers on your network based on their capabilities (that is, you can send the most packets to the most powerful router on the fastest network connection available).

Relatively few Linux network administrators need to use OSPF. The larger, often nationwide networks for which OSPF was designed generally rely on dedicated router hardware such as that provided by Cisco Systems. Nevertheless, Linux does support OSPF using the **gated** daemon, which is included in many Linux distributions, including Red Hat 7.3 (on CD 2). It is not installed by default because, again, it is not often needed.

The `gated` daemon is a powerful tool that supports multiple routing protocols and can combine routing information provided by those protocols to make the most intelligent routing decisions. The home page for the `gated` daemon is *www.gated.org*. You can learn more about `gated` after installing the rpm for it by viewing the documentation provided at `/usr/share/doc/gated-3.6`. The `gated` daemon supports RIP (including RIP version 2), OSPF (as described above), and an external routing protocol called **Border Gateway Protocol (BGP)**.

BGP is designed for routing between major national networks. Initial configuration of BGP is not hard—that is, the configuration file is not long—but at this level, managing packet routing becomes very complex. In fact, some of the most highly specialized (and highly paid) Internet careers focus on the sometimes mundane task of keeping routers running efficiently.

 To use BGP, you must have an autonomous system number to identify your organization to others with whom you will be exchanging routing information. This number is included in the configuration file for `gated`. You obtain this number from the Internet Assigned Names Authority (IANA). To learn more, visit *www.iana.org*, select Protocol Number Assignment Services, and scroll down to the section on autonomous system numbers, which is labeled "AS Numbers (RFC 1930)."

You configure `gated` using the file `/etc/gated.conf`. The format is similar to other configuration files, with sections devoted to each protocol you want to support, and braces enclosing options for that protocol. To have `gated` run only RIP (not OSPF or BGP), use a simple `/etc/gated.conf` configuration file such as this example:

```
rip yes  {
     broadcast;
     interface 192.168.10.3
          version 2
          multicast
          authentication simple "noSecrets";
};
```

This file causes `gated` to use RIP version 2, which supports classless IP addresses. The `broadcast` keyword indicates that the router should actively broadcast the routes that it knows about—it should participate in propagating RIP information with other RIP-capable routers on the network. The `interface` line defines a networking interface using the IP address of that interface. For that interface, `multicast` refers to how information is sent back to other RIP routers that request information. The `simple authentication` line defines a basic scheme for identifying routers on a common network. Numerous other examples and tips are provided in the complete `gated` documentation.

Table 6-1 summarizes the routing protocols described in this section.

Table 6-1 Popular Routing Protocols

Protocol	Daemon	Comments
Routing Information Protocol (RIP)	`routed` or `gated`	The most basic interior routing protocol; of limited use because it does not support classless IP addresses
Routing Information Protocol (RIP) version 2	`routed` or `gated`	A popular interior routing protocol for small networks; supports classless IP addresses but does not scale well (for example, supports a maximum of 15 hops)
Open Shortest Path First (OSPF)	`gated`	The best choice for an interior routing protocol for small to large networks; scalable; distributes routing information by flooding the network periodically with all the routing information it has
Border Gateway Protocol (BGP)	`gated`	A widely used exterior routing protocol, used to route packets between organizations on the Internet and other very large networks; cannot be used until you obtain an autonomous system number from *www.iana.org*

6

SETTING UP A DNS NAME SERVER

In Chapter 3 you learned how to configure the DNS resolver using configuration files such as `/etc/resolv.conf`, `/etc/hosts`, `/etc/host.conf`, and `/etc/nsswitch.conf`. Most of the domain names that your resolver must convert to an IP address are not located in the `/etc/hosts` file, but must instead be determined by querying a DNS server. In this section you learn how to set up a DNS server on Linux.

DNS is central to the Internet. Every time someone enters a URL in a Web browser, a DNS server converts that name to an IP address, allowing the client system to send a packet to the Web server as requested. Understanding how DNS functions and setting up your own DNS server lets you participate in this service and provide this capability for your network without always relying on outside servers. The result is also faster service for users on your network.

The information in DNS can be thought of as an Internetwide inverted hierarchical tree, as Figure 6-2 illustrates. The very top of the tree is called root and is represented by a period: "." The root is typically only referred to in regard to the **root name servers**— DNS servers that the organizations that run the Internet have designated as a starting point for DNS queries. More commonly, you see the last part of domain names referred to as top-level domains such as .org, .com, .edu, and .net, along with many others.

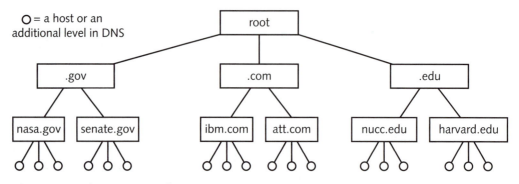

Figure 6-2 The structure of DNS

The steps below outline how the resolver on a host converts a domain name to an IP address. Note that every DNS server caches, or stores, every domain name-to-IP address resolution that it learns of. For this example, we will resolve the domain name *alpha.nasa.gov*. This process is also illustrated in Figure 6–3.

1. The resolver on the client queries the DNS server that is configured in the `/etc/resolv.conf` file (call this DNS server A). If the client cannot reach any of the name servers listed in `/etc/resolv.conf`, the client gives up and the name cannot be resolved.

2. DNS server A receives the query from the client and checks both its own databases (stored in files on the DNS server, as you will soon see) and the domains that it has previously learned about and cached in memory. Not finding the requested domain anywhere, it looks to its list of root name servers (stored in memory, but taken from the DNS server configuration files described below) and sends the query on to one of them.

3. The root name server receives the query and checks its cache. Seeing that it doesn't have the requested domain, it says to DNS server A, in effect, "I don't know the IP address of *alpha.nasa.gov*, but I do know about the DNS server for the .gov domain. Try asking there."

4. DNS server A then asks the .gov DNS server the same question. The .gov DNS server responds, in effect, "I don't know the IP address of *alpha.nasa.gov*, but I do know the DNS server for the *nasa.gov* domain. Try asking there."

5. DNS server A asks the DNS server for *nasa.gov*, which checks its database of DNS records and responds, "Certainly, the IP address of *alpha.nasa.gov* is 192.168.1.45."

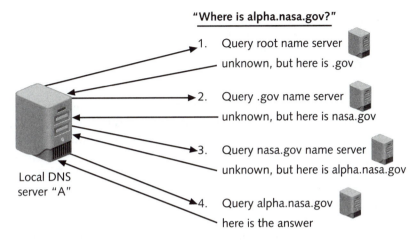

Figure 6-3   Resolving a domain to an IP address using DNS

Fortunately, the process is rarely this tedious, but you should understand the steps to query down the tree to find the needed information within the DNS database. The more normal process for this example would be shortened because DNS server A probably has cached the DNS server address for the .gov domain (it will after the first time someone on the network requests that a .gov address be resolved). The *nasa.gov* DNS server is also likely to have accumulated in cache most of the systems within the *nasa.gov* domain, even if they are not permanently stored on the DNS server that you queried. Finally, if our example domain were a Web site or some other frequently visited location, the next time a query arrived for the same domain name, DNS server A would respond immediately with the in-cache information that it collected in the first query.

One lesson from this process is that, even if you don't have your own domain name to maintain, you can speed things up for users on your network by setting up a caching DNS name server. When DNS query results are stored on a machine within your network, the average time required for each DNS query can drop substantially.

From the example steps given above, you also get a sense that for each domain, a specific server is designated to provide answers about that domain. The root DNS servers are operated by the Internet Engineering Task Force (IETF), but a commercial domain such as the *ibm.com* domain is managed and controlled by IBM Corp. Likewise, if you obtain your own domain name, *mysmallbusiness.com*, you are in charge of maintaining a master DNS server for that domain. If you don't maintain such a server, no one will be able to find your hosts and your domain name will have little value to you. The master DNS server for a domain is the DNS server that can provide official or authoritative information about that domain. Even though many other DNS servers might have cached the information you need, one server on the Internet is the master for each domain.

The **master DNS server** for a domain contains database files that provide IP addresses for every host in that domain that the administrator wants DNS clients to be able to locate. For small domains, it's common to ask your ISP to maintain your DNS information as part of the ISP's DNS server; it's very easy for a good ISP to simply store another domain's DNS database files. The only downside would be that you must have your ISP update the files anytime you make a change in the hostnames or IP addresses of your network.

In addition to a master DNS server, each domain should have at least one **slave DNS server**. The slave DNS server also contains the database files for all hosts in the domain, but it acts as a backup to the master DNS server in the event of hardware or software problems. One expert recommends having the slave DNS server for a domain as physically far away as possible from the master DNS server—in another country if possible. More realistically, you would create a slave DNS server on your ISP's server or at another office of your organization, which might be located in a different city.

For DNS servers, the terms primary and master are used together or interchangeably: the **primary master server**, the **primary server**, or **master server** all refer to the same thing. Likewise, **secondary slave server** and **secondary server** are used interchangeably. The keywords used in the configuration files, however, are `master` and `slave`.

Many advanced users understand that DNS is used to convert hostnames to IP addresses, also called **forward lookup**. A less familiar function of DNS is **reverse DNS**: using DNS to obtain the hostname that corresponds to an IP address (also called a **reverse lookup**). Reverse DNS is becoming increasingly important as a security measure on the Internet. In general terms, the problem that reverse DNS seeks to avoid is called **spoofing**: when a malicious user contacts a server posing as someone else. This is done by using special programs that place incorrect information in IP or TCP packets, or by intercepting someone else's network packets and substituting different information so that the results come to your own system.

Reverse DNS is one method of protecting against these types of problems. It works like this: Every request from a client on the Internet includes the IP address of that client as part of the network packet. Often, the request provides a hostname as well. The server receiving the request can query a DNS server to ask "what is the hostname that corresponds to this IP address?" If the hostname provided in the request does not match the hostname provided in the client request, or if the DNS server responds "I can't find any hostname for that IP address," then the request is ignored. Reverse DNS is also used to log information about requests. For example, later in this chapter you will learn about Web server logs. These logs can store the IP address of each host requesting a Web page, or they can use reverse DNS to store the hostname of every requester.

Reverse DNS operates in the same way as regular DNS, but incorporates the components of an IP address in the domain name. The numbers are also in reverse order and have a special code at the end to indicate a reverse DNS query. As an example, suppose your ISP has assigned you the network address 192.168.24.0. In addition to acting as the master DNS server for your domain name, your computer also must act as the master DNS server for the domain 24.168.192.in-addr.arpa. This is just your network ID (without 0, the host ID portion) plus in-addr.arpa. Just as with regular domains, a DNS server would locate this address by starting at the root name server, which would provide an address for the .arpa name server, and so forth until arriving at your DNS server as the master for your network address.

Historically, some system administrators would not bother with reverse DNS, because it was one more configuration file to update. Today, however, it is critical that you provide accurate reverse DNS records on your DNS server. If you do not, hosts on your network will be unable to contact some outside servers, because those servers cannot verify the identity of the host through a reverse DNS query.

Setting Up a Basic Name Server

The program that implements a DNS server is called **named**, the name daemon. This program is found in the BIND package on most Linux systems. BIND (Berkeley Internet Name Domains) is the name of a collection of programs that implement the DNS protocol. If you selected the name server component when installing Red Hat Linux, you also have: `bind-conf`, which provides a graphical configuration utility that is described later in this section; `bind-utils`, a collection of command-line utilities for querying name servers; and `caching-nameserver`, a set of simple configuration files that make **named** ready to run.

A **caching name server** is one that doesn't have any preconfigured information on domains (except localhost, as described below), but simply queries other DNS servers and caches the results. By running your own DNS server, you ensure that all queries are cached close to your users. If you normally connect through a modem, this can dramatically reduce the traffic over the modem compared with having all name servers on the remote side of the modem.

One program that can act *only* as a caching name server (it can't be a master server for a domain) is `dnscache`, part of the djbdns package. You can find this package at *http://cr.yp.to*. Because `dnscache` is much smaller and faster than **named**, networks that don't need to respond to outside DNS queries might choose `dnscache` instead of **named**.

On any Linux distribution, all you really need to get started is the **named** daemon. It is normally controlled via a system script in `/etc/rc.d/init.d`, though you must set up the configuration files as described below before starting it. Different versions of the **bind** package are available. An older version, 4, is still in widespread use.

You can recognize BIND version 4 by the version name on the **bind** package, but also because it uses the /etc/named.boot configuration file. The **bind** package then skipped to version 8, and version 9 is now available. Red Hat Linux 7.3 uses BIND version 9.2.0; you should use this version or a later version.

 Because BIND is so widely used and so potentially complex to configure, DNS servers are subject to frequent attacks by those trying to break into and/or sabotage your network. Using the latest software is one simple way to reduce the possibility of trouble. Later versions of BIND use the configuration file /etc/named.conf.

The basic /etc/named.conf file provided by the Red Hat caching-nameserver package is a good place to start. It is shown here:

```
// generated by named-bootconf.pl

options {
        directory "/var/named";
        /*
         * If there is a firewall between you and name
           servers you want
         * to talk to, you might need to uncomment the query
           -source
         * directive below.  Previous versions of BIND
           always asked
         * questions using port 53, but BIND 8.1 uses an
           unprivileged
         * port by default.
         */
        // query-source address * port 53;
};


//
// a caching only nameserver config
//
controls {
        inet 127.0.0.1 allow { localhost; } keys
        { rndckey; };
};
zone "." IN {
        type hint;
        file "named.ca";
};

zone "localhost" IN {
        type master;
        file "localhost.zone";
        allow-update { none; };
```

```
};

zone "0.0.127.in-addr.arpa" IN {
        type master;
        file "named.local";
        allow-update { none; };
};

include "/etc/rndc.key";
```

This file is divided into five sections: `options`, `controls`, three different `zones`, and an `include` line, which refers to the `rndc` security key file (discussed below). The only noncomment line in the `options` section is the `directory` line, which identifies where all the `named` files are stored. Each filename referred to in `named.conf` is relative to the directory `/var/named`. There are many other options you can include in this section, but only the `directory` line is critical at this point.

The `controls` section defines who can control the running name server using the `rndc` control program. Although you can start and stop the name server using the script in `/etc/rc.d/init.d`, the `rndc` control program is the preferred method of reinitializing the name server and handling various other administration tasks. You'll see how to use it shortly. `rndc` can control the name server remotely over a TCP network connection, but the `controls` section here permits only localhost to control the name server. In order to use `rndc`, an rndc key is used. The `control` section refers to this key, which is specifically named in the `key` section of the file (via the `include` line at the end). The contents of that file are shown here:

```
key "rndckey" {
        algorithm            hmac-md5;
        secret
"LfuzfpIleaIDuyqzTHrOGnuAZDtyOvuOvFbaHXPU0sizqgnQEAJpII0UK
   DIf";
};
```

In order to use `rndc`, the same key must be present on both the client and server end of the connection. Because only the localhost computer is allowed to use `rndc` in this configuration, this presents no problem. The `rndc` key for the server is stored in the `/etc/rndc.key` file shown above; the key used by the client is stored in the `/etc/rndc.conf` file.

A caching name server is similar in concept to a **forwarding name server**, which forwards all queries to another name server for processing. This allows an administrator to concentrate queries from multiple DNS servers into just a few servers, taking advantage of the cached entries on those servers to reduce response times and lighten the load on your network. Forwarding can be implemented in the options section of the `named.conf` file by specifying the DNS server or servers to which queries should be forwarded:

```
forward first;
forwarders  {
     10.0.5.1;
     10.0.4.1;
}
```

The remaining sections of the `named.conf` file define three zones. A **zone** is a part of the DNS domain tree for which the DNS server has authority to provide information. Including a zone in `named.conf` indicates that information about that zone is provided in the files on the server. Other zones are accessed as described previously, and the results are stored in memory. Part of a zone might be delegated to another name server. For example, if name server B is authoritative for *ibm.com*, it might refer you to another name server for the *research.ibm.com* domain if *research.ibm.com* is not part of the zone of authority for name server B. The format of each `zone` section is shown here:

```
zone "domain-name" IN {
various options
};
```

The `IN` keyword indicates that this refers to an Internet-type zone. Other types of zones exist, but you are unlikely to see them. The three configuration lines you see in the zones defined in `named.conf` above are `type`, `file`, and `allow-update`. The `type` line defines what type of information is provided for the named zone. For the root zone, ".", a hints file is provided. The hints file, given in the `file` line, contains a list of the Internet root servers; we'll look at that shortly. The other two zones are master zones for the given domain. If you had agreed to act as a slave server for a friend, you would copy the friend's zone information file to your server in the `/var/named` directory and include a `zone` section for his or her domain with the `type` set to `slave`. Again, the `file` line defines the local file where a list of information for that domain is stored. Finally, the `allow-update` line defines which hosts can use the `nsupdate` command to remotely make dynamic changes to the DNS information for this zone. By default, this is set to none, meaning that dynamic changes cannot be made.

Both of the master zones in this file refer to localhost: one regular DNS, the other reverse DNS. To support a regular network ID and domain, you could add very similar sections to the `named.conf` file. Here is an example for the network 192.168.24.0, for which *myplace.com* is the domain name. You can name the files anything you choose, but it's traditional to use the domain name and IP address as shown here to avoid confusion when you run a DNS server that holds information for a number of networks.

```
zone "myplace.com" IN {
        type master;
        file "myplace.com.zone";
        allow-update { none; };
```

```
};

zone "24.168.192.in-addr.arpa" IN {
        type master;
        file "24.168.192.in-addr.arpa";
        allow-update { none; };
};
```

 The network IDs used in this chapter are private network IP addresses. None of them should be used for any host that you want to have direct Internet access because these addresses are not routed, as described in Chapter 1.

We turn next to the files referred to in **named.conf**. These are called **zone information files**, because they contain the details about each zone: the information that a DNS query seeks. The first is the file containing a list of root name servers: **named.ca**. The first few noncomment lines of this file are shown here as they appear in Red Hat 7.3:

```
.                            3600000  IN  NS   A.ROOT-
                                                SERVERS.NET.
A.ROOT-SERVERS.NET.          3600000      A    198.41.0.4
.                            3600000      NS   B.ROOT-
                                                SERVERS.NET.
B.ROOT-SERVERS.NET.          3600000      A    128.9.0.107
.                            3600000      NS   C.ROOT-
                                                SERVERS.NET.
C.ROOT-SERVERS.NET.          3600000      A    192.33.4.12
.                            3600000      NS   D.ROOT-
                                                SERVERS.NET.
D.ROOT-SERVERS.NET.          3600000      A    128.8.10.90
.                            3600000      NS   E.ROOT-
                                                SERVERS.NET.
E.ROOT-SERVERS.NET.          3600000      A    192.203.230.10
.                            3600000      NS   F.ROOT-
                                                SERVERS.NET.
F.ROOT-SERVERS.NET.          3600000      A    192.5.5.241
.                            3600000      NS   G.ROOT-
                                                SERVERS.NET.
G.ROOT-SERVERS.NET.          3600000      A    192.112.36.4
```

To explain the contents of the zone information files, let's restate what a DNS server does: a DNS server returns resource records in response to queries from another DNS server or a client resolver. A **resource record** is an information line that defines something about a host on a network that the DNS server knows about. Each resource record has this general format:

item-described   *time-to-keep-cached*   *type-of-record*   *information-sought*

Two types of resource records are used in the `named.ca` file shown above: NS records and A records. An **NS record** defines the authoritative name server for the given domain. An **A record** defines the IP address for the given host. So, taking the first two lines in the file, the authoritative name server for the root domain, ".", is A.ROOT-SERVERS.NET, and the host A.ROOT-SERVERS.NET is at IP address 198.41.0.4. Once cached, both of these pieces of information should be held for 3,600,000 seconds, or about one-and-a-half months. (The IN keyword is used at the beginning to indicate the Internet address type; it is then assumed throughout the rest of the file.)

The IP addresses of the root name servers change over time, so you should update this file occasionally (a quarterly update is usually adequate). Use **dig**, a command-line utility, to ask a DNS server for resource records. The easiest way to get an updated list of root name servers is to use this command, then copy the resulting file to replace your existing list of root servers:

```
dig @a.root-servers.net  .  ns  > /var/named/
    new.rootservers
```

 Domain names can include all letters of the English alphabet, digits 0 through 9, and the dash (-). Upper and lower case never matter when using domain names (unlike most of Linux). Therefore, requesting *ibm.com* is identical to requesting IBM.COM.

Next we look at a master zone file, `localhost.zone`:

```
$TTL    86400
$ORIGIN localhost.
@                       1D IN SOA  @ root (
                                   42          ; serial (d. adams)
                                   3H          ; refresh
                                   15M         ; retry
                                   1W          ; expire
                                   1D )        ; minimum

                1D IN NS    @
                1D IN A           127.0.0.1
```

Understanding zone files can be challenging. You can review the comprehensive documentation on BIND in the directory `/usr/share/doc/bind-9.2.0/arm` (the Administrator's Resource Manual). Even a single misplaced period can prevent a host name from resolving. The first two lines here are directives. The `$TTL` directive indicates that the default Time To Live (store in cache) for all resource records here is 86,400 seconds: 24 hours. This is also indicated by the 1D item (for "one day") in each of the three resource records. The `$ORIGIN` directive provides the domain name to add to any unfinished records.

The **SOA record** (Start-Of-Authority) describes how to use the information provided for this zone. The @ symbol used within a zone information file indicates the root of the zone; in this case, that means localhost. The @ symbol is used again after the SOA keyword, followed by **root**. The word **root** here indicates the email address to which questions should be sent regarding this DNS zone. The format of the email address here is odd, because the @ symbol is already used for something else. The root here refers to a local user account, but if you needed to have a full email address such as *hostmaster@myplace.net*, you would write it as `hostmaster.myplace.net`.

Between the parentheses (across several lines) are numbers that indicate how the information in this file should be transferred to slave servers assigned to handle the zone's DNS information. This exchange of information is called a **zone transfer**. The `refresh` interval (3 hours here) defines how often the slave server checks to see if the master has been updated. If that check fails, the slave retries according to the `retry` interval (every 15 minutes here) until the `expire` interval has passed (one week here). At that point, the slave server stops acting as a secondary source for that zone.

The last number, labeled `minimum` in the comments, is the minimum Time To Live (TTL) for the information in the file. The first number, labeled `serial` in the comments, is used to indicate whether the file has been altered and thus needs to take part in a zone transfer. The `named` daemon checks the serial number to see whether it is a higher number than the last time it checked. If it is, the file is reread. Therefore, every time you make a change to a zone information file, you must update the serial number; if you don't, the update is ignored by the server.

The localhost files are unlikely to ever change, but to make serial number upkeep easy for regular domains, administrators typically use a number like this:

```
2003042300
```

This is year-month-day-00. Each day you can make up to 100 changes in the file, increasing the last two digits each time. If you make a change the next day, the day field changes and you reset the counter to 00. This also helps you see the last time you updated the file.

The NS and A records don't have anything in the first field, so the $ORIGIN directive supplies "localhost." in that field. A name server is defined (@ refers to the system on which this name server is running!), and an IP address for the localhost interface is given.

Next, let's briefly review the reverse DNS file, `named.local`:

```
$TTL    86400
@       IN      SOA     localhost. root.localhost. (
                                1997022700 ; Serial
                                28800      ; Refresh
                                14400      ; Retry
                                3600000    ; Expire
                                86400 )    ; Minimum
```

```
                 IN      NS       localhost.

        1        IN      PTR      localhost.
```

This file also uses a `$TTL` directive. It has the standard format for the serial number and introduces a new resource record type: `PTR`, for "pointer." A **PTR record** "points" to the hostname to which an IP address is assigned; this is used for reverse DNS lookups. Within the current zone, 127.0.0, the host with the IP address "1" has the hostname localhost. Below are a few sample lines from a nonlocalhost domain file. A typical zone information file may consist of hundreds of lines similar to these, with the different hosts and IP addresses on your network.

```
      mail        IN      A        192.168.100.250
      hosta       IN      A        192.168.100.1
      hosta       IN      MX       10 mail.myplace.com.
      hostb       IN      A        192.168.100.2
      hostb       IN      MX       10 mail.myplace.com.
      hostc       IN      A        192.168.100.3
      hostc       IN      MX       10 mail.myplace.com.
      hostd       IN      A        192.168.100.4
      hostd       IN      MX       10 mail.myplace.com.
      hoste       IN      A        192.168.100.5
      hoste       IN      MX       10 mail.myplace.com.
```

The first line in this sample refers to the mail server on our network: *mail.myplace.com*. Information for five hosts is then listed. For each one, an A record defines the hostname's IP address. An **MX record** also defines the mail exchanger for that host. MX records are used by mail transfer agents (MTAs) to find the correct email server to contact when delivering email to a recipient. The 10 before the name of the email server indicates a preference value. You could have multiple MX records for a single host; if one had a 10 and another had a 20 here, the server with 10 would be contacted first; if it were unavailable, the server with 20 would be tried next. For the hosts above, corresponding entries would appear in a reverse DNS zone information file for network `100.168.192.in-addr.arpa.`:

```
      1          PTR      hosta.myplace.com.
      2          PTR      hostb.myplace.com.
      3          PTR      hostc.myplace.com.
      4          PTR      hostd.myplace.com.
      5          PTR      hoste.myplace.com.
```

Another commonly used resource record type is the **CNAME record** (for canonical name), which is used to create an alias for a hostname. For example, suppose you have a single server on your network that runs an FTP server, an email server, and a Web server. You want to use hostnames that correspond to these purposes, even though they all run on the same server. The following lines define an IP address for the main server using an A record, then create aliases for ftp, mail, and www that refer to the main server.

```
main.myplace.com.       IN    A       192.168.100.1
ftp.myplace.com.        IN    CNAME   main.myplace.com.
mail.myplace.com.       IN    CNAME   main.myplace.com.
www.myplace.com.        IN    CNAME   main.myplace.com.
```

Notice that in these lines, full names are used instead of just the hostname. That is, you see *ftp.myplace.com.* instead of just ftp as in the previous examples. You can use either format; the critical point is that the full name includes a period at the end. If no period is included, the server appends the domain name. Therefore, if you specify *www.myplace.com* instead of *www.myplace.com.*, `named` tries to process *www.myplace.com.myplace.com*, and the hostname is not resolved.

CNAME records must refer to a name within an A record, not another CNAME record.

Suppose that you have several Web servers containing identical information, designed to handle a large volume of Web traffic. You can include multiple IP addresses for a single hostname. `named` responds with the first, then the second, and so on, in round-robin fashion. These lines illustrate such a configuration:

```
www.myplace.com.     IN    A    192.168.100.5
www.myplace.com.     IN    A    192.168.100.6
www.myplace.com.     IN    A    192.168.100.7
www.myplace.com.     IN    A    192.168.100.8
```

Table 6-2 summarizes the types of resource records presented in this section. Many others are supported, as well as dozens of options in the `/etc/named.conf` file. Setting up a DNS server can be challenging, but it is an important part of most administrators' work. All users rely on DNS; plus, DNS can consume a lot of network bandwidth and present serious security holes if incorrectly configured, as is often the case on the Internet, unfortunately. To learn more about setting up a DNS server, review the documentation in `/usr/share/doc/bind-9.2.0` or a similar documentation directory on your distribution. Also review the man pages for `named`, `named.conf`, and the related utilities described in the following sections, such as `dig` and `nsupdate`.

Table 6-2   Common DNS resource record types

Resource Record Type	Defines:
A	An IP address for a named host
CNAME	An alias for a hostname, referring it to a name defined in an A record
NS	The authoritative name server for the given domain
PTR	The hostname associated with a given number as part of a network address for a reverse DNS query
SOA	The zone for which this file is authoritative, with zone transfer parameters and the email address of the zone administrator
MX	The mail exchanger: the host running an email server designated to accept email for the named host

Managing the `named` Server

Once you have the `/etc/named.conf` configuration file and the appropriate zone information files set up in `/var/named`, you can start the `named` daemon by entering `/usr/sbin/named`. More likely, you will want to use the script in `/etc/rc.d/init.d`. You can also use the same script to restart the server if you make changes to the files.

The **rndc** utility mentioned previously is provided with the bind package and is used to control it from a command line without reloading. **rndc** can operate over a network connection, but is used only locally by default.

You use the **rndc** command to reload configuration files, write out a status file, or perform other tasks, as described in the man page. The command you are most likely to use is this one, to reload the `/etc/named.conf` configuration file and all zone information files:

```
rndc reload
```

Using `bindconf.gui`

A number of graphical utilities have been developed to help you configure the files described in this section. One of the cleanest is **bindconf**, which is included with Red Hat Linux in the `bind-conf` package. You can start this program by choosing System, then DNS Configuration on the main menu of Gnome. Alternatively, enter `bindconf` at the command line. The main window of bindconf is shown in Figure 6-4. It includes a line for each zone information file.

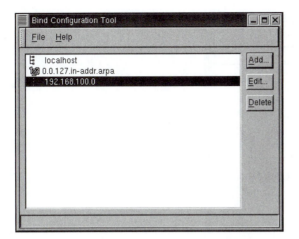

Figure 6-4   The main window of bindconf

From this window you can create a new zone information file by choosing Add. In the window that appears, you select whether to create a regular (forward) DNS master zone, a reverse DNS master zone, or a slave zone. Figure 6–5 shows this dialog box.

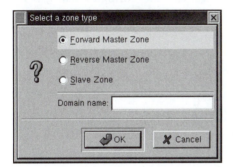

Figure 6-5   The select a zone type dialog box in bindconf

You can edit any existing zone file by selecting it in the main window and choosing Edit. The main editing dialog box is shown in Figure 6-6. For forward DNS zones, this dialog box is labeled Name to IP Translations. The fields in the top part of the dialog box include the SOA record information, but you must manually change the serial number if you make a change. The refresh numbers for zone transfers are accessed via the Time Settings button.

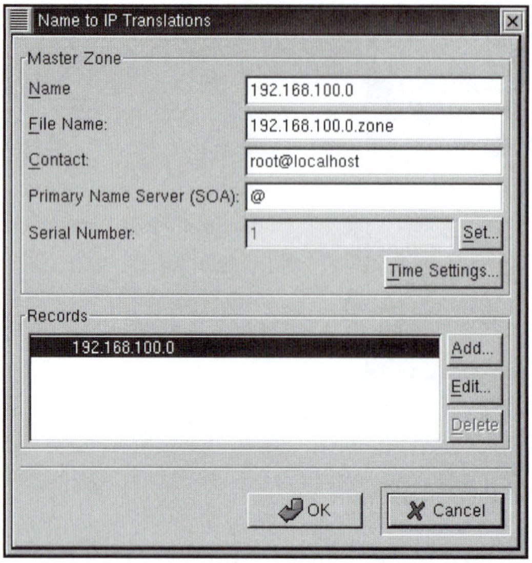

Figure 6-6   Editing forward zone information in bindconf

The bottom part of the dialog box lists hosts that are configured in this file. You can choose Add to include information for another host (see Figure 6-7) or Edit to change the information for a selected host.

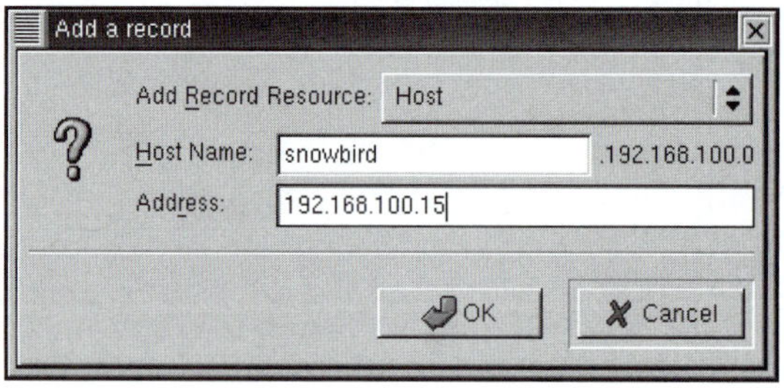

Figure 6-7   Adding a new host for forward resolution in bindconf

If you select a reverse DNS file in the main window of bindconf and then choose Edit, a different dialog box appears, as shown in Figure 6-8. The information here is similar to that used for the forward DNS files. The SOA information is at the top of the dialog box; IP addresses within the network ID and their corresponding hostnames are listed at the bottom of the file.

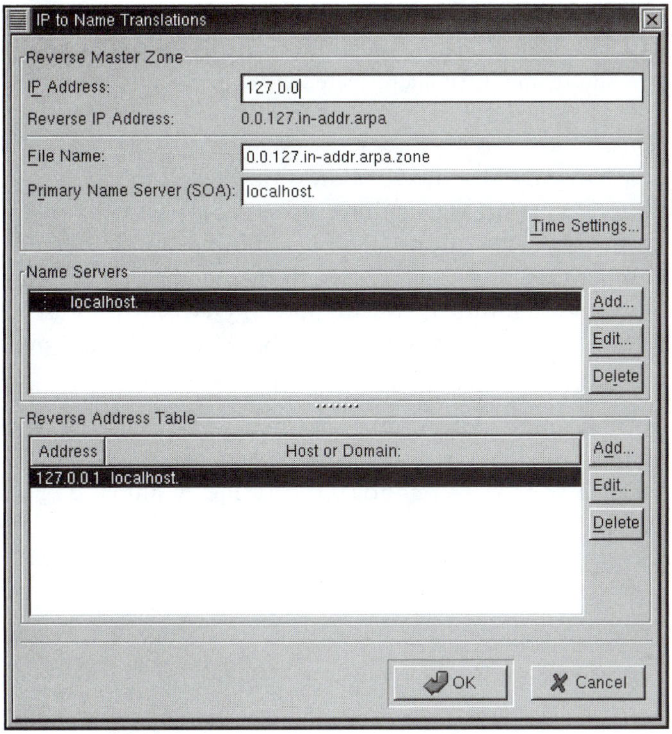

Figure 6-8   Editing a reverse DNS configuration in bindconf

After making any changes with bindconf, choose Apply on the File menu to write your changes to the appropriate zone information files.

Although this is a handy tool for editing zone information and avoids the very real problem of small typing errors causing big headaches for your DNS server, you should also recognize that the tool is of no use unless you first understand DNS. Also, this utility does not let you edit the main DNS configuration file, `named.conf`.

Using Command-Line Utilities

Once you have a DNS server up and running, you normally want to test it to see that it responds as expected to queries. The utilities described here can help you test your own DNS server; they also can help you learn about other DNS servers on the Internet.

> If your name server does not seem to be working properly, one technique is to restart it and then review the messages in the system log: `/var/log/messages`. The `named` daemon writes copious messages when a problem occurs in reading the configuration or zone information files.

Three of the command-line utilities are quite similar: `host`, `nslookup`, and `dig`. All let you ask for DNS information about a specific hostname or IP address. To use the `host` command, enter the hostname or IP address after the command:

```
host www.npr.org
```

You see a brief response showing you the IP address of that hostname. The `nslookup` command is more complete. It can run in interactive mode, with its own command prompt, or directly from the command line using multiple options. The `nslookup` command is not used much today, however. It is still included in most Linux distributions now, but may not be in the future. If you are new to DNS, learn to use `dig` instead of `nslookup`. The options and output from the two programs are quite similar.

The `dig` program lets you extract information from the zone information files of DNS servers for domains you are interested in. You can query for specific types of resource records, and you can direct your query to a specific DNS server, instead of always starting with the server listed in your `/etc/resolv.conf` file. A simple `dig` query looks like this:

```
dig www.npr.org
```

A more complex query looks like this:

```
dig @ns.xmission.com www.xmission.com any
```

This query goes directly to the DNS server *ns.xmission.com*, looking for information about *www.xmission.com*. It returns all types of records for that address, including NS, MX, A, CNAME, and other record types not included in this discussion. The output from the above command is shown here:

```
; <<>> DiG 9.1.3 <<>> @ns.xmission.com www.xmission.com
any
;; global options:  printcmd
;; Got answer:
;; ->>HEADER<<- opcode: QUERY, status: NOERROR, id: 2857
;; flags: qr aa rd ra; QUERY: 1, ANSWER: 2, AUTHORITY: 3,
ADDITIONAL: 4

;; QUESTION SECTION:
;www.xmission.com.            IN      ANY

;; ANSWER SECTION:
www.xmission.com.    3600   IN      MX      10 mail.xmission.com.
www.xmission.com.    3600   IN      A       198.60.22.4

;; AUTHORITY SECTION:
xmission.com.        3600   IN      NS      ns.xmission.com.
xmission.com.        3600   IN      NS      ns1.xmission.com.
xmission.com.        3600   IN      NS      ns2.xmission.com.
```

```
;; ADDITIONAL SECTION:
mail.xmission.com.   3600   IN     A     198.60.22.22
ns.xmission.com.     3600   IN     A     198.60.22.2
ns1.xmission.com.    3600   IN     A     198.60.22.22
ns2.xmission.com.    3600   IN     A     207.78.169.150

;; Query time: 381 msec
;; SERVER: 198.60.22.2#53(ns.xmission.com)
;; WHEN: Sat Apr 20 15:52:12 2002
;; MSG SIZE   rcvd: 188
```

The man page for `dig` describes the command-line options and output in full; but notice some of the features you see here:

- The first line shows the command you entered, so you can see what options created this output.

- A `Question` section summarizes what you asked for.

- An `Answer` section gives you the response data: the records corresponding to the requested domain name.

- An `Authority` section shows you the authoritative name servers for the domain of which the requested host is a part.

- The `Additional` section provides information that `dig` thinks might be useful.

- The summary information at the end shows how long this query took (381 milliseconds), which name server provided the information (including the IP address, port number, and FQDN), along with the precise time of the query.

A utility that goes beyond `dig` and `nslookup` is **nsupdate**. This utility, referred to briefly earlier, lets you update zone information files dynamically at the command line. It is an interactive utility, with a separate command prompt. Two example commands are shown here, to remove all A records for a host, then add a new A record for that host:

```
update delete oldhost.example.com A
update add newhost.example.com 86400 A 172.16.1.1
```

See the **nsupdate** man page for further information on this utility.

You may have a sense at this point that we have only scratched the surface of DNS. Complex configurations, security and performance issues, and dozens of other topics can make DNS administration a full-time job for some networks. The documentation included in `/usr/share/doc/bind-9.2.0/draft` gives you some idea of the expansive nature of DNS. This folder contains working drafts by Internet engineers on topics such as refining DNS used with IPv6 (though IPv6 is already supported in **named**), using new security features such as DNSSEC, and relying on virtual domains to allow non-English speakers to access internationalized domain names without changing the English-only limitations of current DNS.

Figure 6-9 illustrates the relationship between DNS configuration files described in this section. Table 6-3 lists the utilities used to query or update DNS information in Linux.

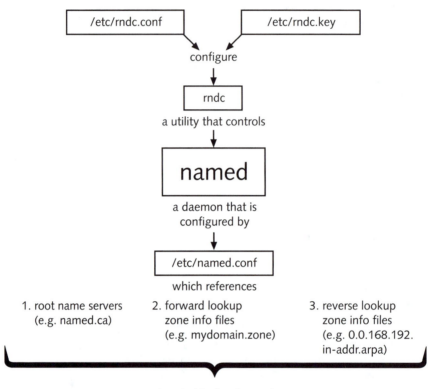

Figure 6-9 DNS configuration files

Table 6-3 DNS utilities in Linux

Utility Name	Description
host	Resolves a hostname into an IP address
dig	Recommended for troubleshooting DNS or doing complex DNS lookups; includes many options for specifying which DNS records are wanted and how to process server responses
nslookup	Similar in functionality to dig, but can be used with command-line options or in an interactive mode
nsupdate	Allows a system administrator to update zone information files remotely (over a network connection)
rndc	Controls the named daemon using command-line parameters
named-checkconf	Checks the validity of the named.conf configuration file

CONFIGURING A BASIC EMAIL SERVER

In Chapter 3 you learned how email delivery on the Internet is structured: a Mail Transfer Agent (MTA) moves mail between servers; the MTA is commonly referred to as the email server. A Mail Delivery Agent (MDA) such as `procmail` examines messages and delivers them to a user's mailbox file (such as `/var/spool/mail/nwells`). A Mail User Agent (MUA) such as Netscape, Kmail, `elm`, or `pine` lets a user view the messages stored in the mailbox and create new messages that are handed to the MTA for delivery to the recipient.

Earlier in this chapter you also learned about a key component of how email servers operate: they use DNS to request the mail exchanger for a recipient. For example, if you send an email message to *quong@teranet.com*, the email server at your site (or at your ISP, if you don't operate your own email server) must somehow find out which email server should receive email destined for *teranet.com*. It does this by making a standard DNS query for *teranet.com*, but once the authoritative DNS server for that domain is found, the email server requests the MX record instead of the A record. The two records may refer to the same server, but more often an organization centralizes mail acceptance in a single mail server. From there, the configuration of the mail server may distribute messages for easier access in a large organization.

Once the correct mail exchanger is located using DNS, your email server can initiate a connection using the SMTP protocol and begin sending all messages destined for any domains that are handled by that mail exchanger.

 The SMTP protocol has been extended since its original introduction, so you may see occasional references to the Extended Simple Mail Transport Protocol, ESMTP. Most administrators just refer to SMTP.

Email Servers

A number of email servers are available for Linux. The most popular are listed here:

- `sendmail`: The most widely known email server in the world; it is estimated that `sendmail` still delivers a large percentage of the world's email. Sendmail has been around for nearly 20 years, but a few years ago, a company was created that sells a commercial version, with graphical development tools, technical support, and other add-ons. You can learn about this at *www.sendmail.com*. The free version is included with every Linux distribution, however. You can learn about the free version at *www.sendmail.org* (or from the documentation included with Linux).

- `Qmail`: This mail server is also quite popular among Linux users. Because of the many security issues that have arisen with `sendmail` over the past decade, Qmail focuses on security. You can learn about `Qmail` at *www.qmail.org/top.html*.

- **Postfix**: This mail server also focuses on security. It is organized as a collection of discrete programs, each performing a separate task, all without root permission on the host. You can learn more about **Postfix** at *www.postfix.org*.

- **Smail**: This is a smaller mail server, based on **sendmail** but without so many features and intended to be easier to configure, using fewer system resources.

The **sendmail** program is installed on Red Hat Linux using three separate software packages. The **sendmail** package contains the **sendmail** daemon and is the only package that is required to use **sendmail**. The other two are **sendmail-cf**, which contains configuration examples and helper programs, and **sendmail-doc**, which contains documentation for the server. You should install all three if you intend to run **sendmail**. The **sendmail-doc** package is not installed automatically; it is located on Red Hat CD 3.

Sendmail is started using a standard script in **/etc/rc.d/init.d**. You can use the **start**, **stop**, **restart**, and **status** commands to control the daemon. The startup parameters of **sendmail** are controlled by information stored in the **/etc/sysconfig/sendmail** file. For example, the parameter **QUEUE=1h** tells **sendmail** to attempt to send out stored messages each hour.

Starting **sendmail** takes a few moments. If the startup script hesitates rather than starting up **sendmail**, check that your hostname is correctly defined in your **/etc/hosts** file. By default, **sendmail** uses this to determine the host on which it is operating, information that it must have.

The operation of **sendmail** is configured using the file **/etc/sendmail.cf**. You should review this file briefly in a text editor, being careful not to change its contents. The **sendmail.cf** file is widely considered to be the single most difficult configuration file to master. You can study the comments in this file and the documentation for **sendmail** to learn how the file is organized and operates; some administration tasks may require you to edit this file directly. The file **README.cf** acts as an online manual for the **sendmail.cf** file. It contains over 3,000 lines of text. In Red Hat Linux, this file is located at **/usr/share/doc/sendmail** after you have installed the **sendmail-doc** package.

Most email administrators prefer to rely on the **m4** program to configure **sendmail**. The **m4** program uses a text file containing configuration parameters and generates a complete **sendmail.cf** file based on those parameters. The m4 parameters are stored in **sendmail.mc**. To create a new **sendmail.cf** file, you edit the **sendmail.mc** file and then execute this command:

```
m4 /etc/mail/sendmail.mc > /etc/sendmail.cf
```

The contents of the **sendmail.mc** file are shown next. Each line here is numbered for reference in the discussion that follows; no line numbers appear in the file itself. The text dnl in the file stands for "delete to new line" and is used to indicate comment lines and also to end each command in the file.

```
1.  divert(-1)
2.  dnl This is the sendmail macro config file. If you make
    changes to this file,
3.  dnl you need the sendmail-cf rpm installed and then
    have to generate a
4.  dnl new /etc/sendmail.cf by running the following
    command:
5.  dnl
6.  dnl          m4 /etc/mail/sendmail.mc > /etc/sendmail.cf
7.  dnl
8.  include('/usr/share/sendmail-cf/m4/cf.m4')
9.  VERSIONID('linux setup for Red Hat Linux')dnl
10.    OSTYPE('linux')
11.    define('confDEF_USER_ID','''8:12''')dnl
12.    undefine('UUCP_RELAY')dnl
13.    undefine('BITNET_RELAY')dnl
14.    define('confAUTO_REBUILD')dnl
15.    define('confTO_CONNECT', '1m')dnl
16.    define('confTRY_NULL_MX_LIST',true)dnl
17.    define('confDONT_PROBE_INTERFACES',true)dnl
18.    define('PROCMAIL_MAILER_PATH','/usr/bin/procmail')
       dnl
19.    define('ALIAS_FILE', '/etc/aliases')dnl
20.    dnl define('STATUS_FILE', '/etc/mail/statistics')dnl
21.    define('UUCP_MAILER_MAX', '2000000')dnl
22.    define('confUSERDB_SPEC', '/etc/mail/userdb.db')dnl
23.    define('confPRIVACY_FLAGS',
       'authwarnings,novrfy,noe xpn,restrictqrun')dnl
24. define('confAUTH_OPTIONS', 'A')dnl
25. dnl TRUST_AUTH_MECH(`DIGEST-MD5 CRAM-MD5 LOGIN PLAIN')
    dnl
26. dnl define('confAUTH_MECHANISMS', 'DIGEST-MD5 CRAM-MD5
    LOGIN PLAIN')dnl
27. dnl define('confTO_QUEUEWARN', '4h')dnl
28. dnl define('confTO_QUEUERETURN', '5d')dnl
29. dnl define('confQUEUE_LA', '12')dnl
30. dnl define('confREFUSE_LA', '18')dnl
31. dnl FEATURE(delay_checks)dnl
32. FEATURE('no_default_msa','dnl')dnl
33. FEATURE('smrsh','/usr/sbin/smrsh')dnl
34. FEATURE('mailertable','hash -o /etc/mail/
    mailertable.db')dnl
35. FEATURE('virtusertable','hash -o /etc/mail/
    virtusertable.db')dnl
36. FEATURE(redirect)dnl
```

```
37. FEATURE(always_add_domain)dnl
38. FEATURE(use_cw_file)dnl
39. FEATURE(use_ct_file)dnl
40. FEATURE(local_procmail,'','procmail -t -Y -a $h -d
    $u')dnl
41. FEATURE('access_db','hash -o /etc/mail/access.db')dnl
42. FEATURE('blacklist_recipients')dnl
43. EXPOSED_USER('root')dnl
44. dnl This changes sendmail to only listen on the
    loopback device 127.0.0.1
45. dnl and not on any other network devices. Comment this
    out if you want
46. dnl to accept email over the network.
47. DAEMON_OPTIONS('Port=smtp,Addr=127.0.0.1, Name=MTA')
48. dnl NOTE: binding both IPv4 and IPv6 daemon to the
    same port requires
49. dnl        a kernel patch
50. dnl DAEMON_OPTIONS('port=smtp,Addr=::1, Name=MTA-
    v6, Family=inet6')
51. dnl We strongly recommend to comment this one out if
    you want to protect
52. dnl yourself from spam. However, the laptop and users
    on computers that do
53. dnl not have 24x7 DNS do need this.
54. FEATURE('accept_unresolvable_domains')dnl
55. dnl FEATURE('relay_based_on_MX')dnl
56. MAILER(smtp)dnl
57. MAILER(procmail)dnl
58. Cwlocalhost.localdomain
```

The default configuration provided with Red Hat Linux provides a workable default sendmail server environment, but you must make a few changes to use it as an Internet email server. The rest of this section describes those recommended changes as well as some of the key features of email servers in general, as implemented in sendmail. Setting up the sendmail.mc file is also described in the README.cf file in /usr/share/doc/sendmail.

Setting up a sendmail configuration file is difficult, but managing any email server is an ongoing challenge because of the nature of the Internet and of email. The configuration file for an email server must contend with issues such as these:

- Many different programs on many types of hosts are creating email messages. All of these messages must be standardized to some degree so that email servers around the world can understand their contents enough to deliver them correctly. This is handled in part by the so-called "rewriting rules" that are a default part of every sendmail.cf file.

- An organization may include numerous SMTP-based email servers, especially if many users run Linux! Yet most organizations want to have a single point (a single address) that manages email reception to avoid naming conflicts and to present a coherent image to the public.

- All users want to send and receive email without restrictions, but **spam** (unsolicited advertisement-related email) has become a problem not only for users but also for email servers. Spam can clog an email server and frustrate users if the administrator doesn't take steps to stem its flow.

- Users want flexibility in how they create and read their email. They want to have access to it from various hosts, they want to have messages they create delivered quickly, and they want to be able to use the program of their choice to work with email. None of these demands are unreasonable, but some require extra work in light of the other issues that face the administrator of an email server.

Before we discuss specific options in the `sendmail.mc` file, consider the following scenario. Suppose you manage the network for a technology company that includes 50 employees, most of whom are very technically savvy and have Linux systems at their desktop. Many users choose to run `sendmail`, because this provides powerful user configuration options. You also have a central email server that is always connected to the Internet. All users receive their email from this server, either by downloading it using POP3 in an email program such as Netscape, or by having the mail transferred in some other way to their system (as described shortly). Figure 6-10 illustrates this scenario.

Now let's review some key sections of the sendmail.mc file as it might relate to this scenario. To begin with, the default settings allow `sendmail` to accept email only from the localhost. This is controlled via the `DAEMON_OPTIONS` directive on line 47 of the file just shown. To make `sendmail` act as a true Internet email server, you must insert `dnl` at the beginning of that line so that other servers can connect to your copy of `sendmail`. If you were configuring Host A in Figure 6-10, you might choose to configure `sendmail` to accept email only from the main email server, using a setting such as this:

```
DAEMON_OPTIONS('Port=smtp,Addr=192.168., Name=MTA')
```

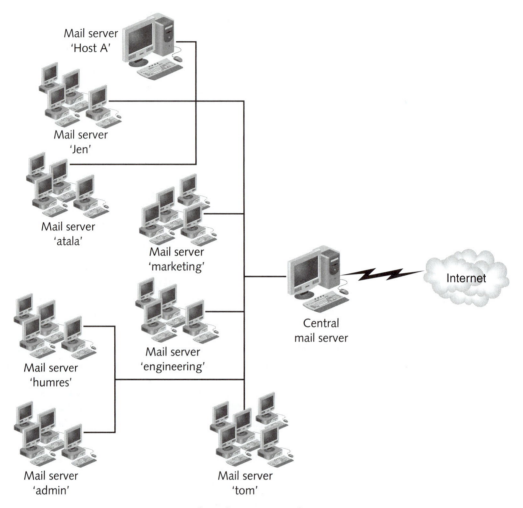

Figure 6-10   A corporate network with many email servers

 None of your changes in `sendmail.mc` take effect until you save the file, run `m4` to create a new `sendmail.cf` file, and restart `sendmail`. Don't do this until you have reviewed all of the information in this section, especially if you are connected to the Internet.

Line 58 in the file indicates which recipient domains `sendmail` accepts email for. You can host email servers for multiple domains by adding names to this option. For example, if line 58 looked as follows, and DNS were configured to list your server in the appropriate MX record, you would be acting as a virtual email server for the four domains listed:

```
Cwmyplace.net myplace.com sllug.org linuxfest.org
```

If you are hosting a number of domains, you can include the following line in the `sendmail.mc` file and list all the domains separately in the file `/etc/mail/sendmail.cw`:

```
FEATURE('use_cw_file')dnl
```

Recall that an email server uses DNS to locate the mail exchanger for a recipient, then hands the message to the `sendmail` daemon on that host, saying in effect, "Here, this is for one of your users." That would be simple enough, because `sendmail` could immediately see whether the hostname of the recipient was a hostname for which it was configured to handle email. However, it doesn't always work that way. In many configurations, a host contacts `sendmail` and says "Here, could you send this to the correct recipient for me?" When `sendmail` tries to deliver a message that didn't originate on the same host where `sendmail` is running, this is called **relaying**. Relaying is useful in the scenario shown in Figure 6-10, where each copy of `sendmail` running at a user's desk should send all its email to the central server for processing. The central server is therefore accepting email that was created on another host and relaying it to its recipient.

The problem with relaying is that people generating spam email (spammers) use it to hide their true locations. They put false information in the headers of their messages and use `sendmail` to relay messages to recipients. One result is that someone could call you and angrily accuse you of sending spam, when in fact your email server was only the last copy of `sendmail` to handle the spam before it was delivered to its recipient. However, `sendmail` can be configured to avoid problems like this. For example, in Figure 6-10, you could choose to relay only messages originating from the same domain as the central mail server. You could relay only messages that came from a host with the same DNS mail exchanger (MX) record as the central mail server. Several other options are available, but these illustrate what is possible. Of course, you might decide to disable relaying altogether. If this is feasible in your situation, then it is the recommended setting. The default setting allows relaying. Line 54 defines this:

```
FEATURE('accept_unresolvable_domains')dnl
```

If you were not working on a network configuration that required such open relaying, you could use the alternative shown on line 55, which causes `sendmail` to accept relayed messages only from hosts that have the same MX record in DNS as the mail server itself. To use this setting, you would change lines 54 and 55 to look like this:

```
dnl FEATURE('accept_unresolvable_domains')dnl
FEATURE('relay_based_on_MX')dnl
```

Looking again at Figure 6-10, you see that each of the hosts running `sendmail` has a separate hostname. When a user creates an email message, its hostname is listed in the From: header of the message. However, the policy of the organization is not to have email coming in to each host individually. It is easier to manage a single email server, so all reply email should come to the central server. You can configure this using two options in `sendmail.mc` that instruct `sendmail` to masquerade as (act as) a specific domain name, even if messages are being relayed from other hosts within your network. This causes everyone who replies to the message to use the name of the central email server, so that all messages come back to the same point. To do this, you would add the following lines to your `sendmail.mc` file:

```
MASQUERADE_AS('myplace.net')
FEATURE('masquerade_envelope')
```

Beyond controlling relaying, a further protection against spam is the access database of `sendmail`. This database defines what to do with messages coming from various addresses. You can specify that the message be discarded without further action, accepted for delivery to the intended user, rejected and a message sent back to the sender, or any of several other options.

To use the access database, place entries in the `/etc/mail/access` file that you want to handle specially. By default, the file contains a listing to indicate that email from local-host should be relayed. (The overall settings of `sendmail` preempt this if you use the relay settings described previously.) Other examples that you could include in the access file are shown here:

```
spammers.net    DISCARD
unbelievableoffer.com    REJECT
```

The first line indicates that any message coming from *spammers.net* is discarded without further action. The second line prevents messages from the named host from being delivered, but a message is returned to the sender stating that the message was not delivered. Several other options are possible. You can also include specific users in this file. For example, if unwanted mail is originating from a particular user account, you can discard that mail with this line:

```
reduceyourmortgagedebt@aol.com    DISCARD
```

After you make a change to the access file, you must convert it to a database format so that `sendmail` can use it. The following command converts the `/etc/mail/access` text file into an `/etc/mail/access.db` database file that `sendmail` can use:

```
makemap hash /etc/mail/access < /etc/mail/access
```

As spam has become a larger problem, email server administrators have taken more heavy-handed measures to protect their users from unwanted email advertising. Many email servers use a **Realtime Blackhole List**. This is a list of sites that are known sources of spam. You can subscribe to one of these services by visiting *mail-abuse.org*. Once you have subscribed, you include the following line in `sendmail.mc` to have email from all domains on the list discarded:

```
FEATURE('dnsbl')dnl
```

The blackhole list is stern. Some domains that generate nonspam messages are listed as well, meaning that you won't get any messages from those domains. Although a blackhole list is an effective way to cut down on the wasted time and offense caused when you face an onslaught of spam, these lists must be carefully maintained or they become dangerous, blocking email you want to receive. Most email servers also support a white list. Messages from a site on the white list are accepted even if the same site is contained on the blackhole list. This lets you override a blackhole list that you are not maintaining yourself.

Using Forwarding and Aliases

In conjunction with the access database described previously, `sendmail` maintains a forwarding database. This lets you set up rules for how a user's email is handled. A table of forwarding instructions is stored in the file `/etc/mail/virtusertable`. This table is useful for sites that accept email for a number of different domains. For example, suppose you agree to act as the email server for a user group with the domain name *sllug.org*. You want email arriving for sllug.org to be redirected to the leader of the organization, who has an individual user account on your system. You could add the following line to the `virtusertable` file to set this up:

```
sllug.org jfreeman
```

Suppose that all email for the support account on *sllug.org* should go to jfreeman, but he has moved his principal email account to a different server. You agree to maintain his email service for a time. The following line forwards all email addressed to *support@sllug.org* to jfreeman's new email address, which is not handled by your email server:

```
support@sllug.org jfreeman@xmission.com
```

After you make changes in the `virtusertable` file, you must update the database using the following command, then restart `sendmail`:

```
makemap hash /etc/mail/virtusertable <
   /etc/mail/virtusertable
```

Forwarding that relies on a single domain name for the incoming message can also be done using two other techniques. The first is the aliases file. An email alias is another name that delivers email messages to a user. This file contains a list of alternate names or email addresses to which email messages might be addressed. Each email alias in this file is followed by text that defines what `sendmail` should do with a message so addressed. For example, suppose that your email address is *kcarver@myplace.net*. Because different companies use specific formats for email addresses, you also want to receive email using the email addresses *kim.carver@myplace.net*, *kim_carver@myplace.net*, and *kimc@myplace.net*. Using email aliases lets you do this if you include the following lines in `/etc/aliases`:

```
kim.carver: kcarver
kim_carver: kcarver
kimc: kcarver
```

In a large company, you would need to be careful about the formats you used, since a person with a similar name might need to use an alias you have created as a real email address. Aliases are also commonly used for assigning topical email to a specific individual. For example, you can define a webmaster alias that sends email to the accounts of Kim Carver and Thomas Jennings, who work at a company that helps manage your Web server:

```
webmaster: kcarver, tjennings@webstuff.com
```

You can include long lists of usernames in the `/etc/aliases` file, you can pipe messages to programs, you can include files containing email addresses, and you can store messages directly to a file, all by varying the format of a line in `/etc/aliases`. Aliases can even be recursive, that is, build on themselves. For example, if you define a `managers` alias that includes five user accounts, you could then specify a `webmaster` alias that went to `managers` and to other user accounts. Aliases are the right tool for creating small mailing lists that don't change membership often. For larger, frequently changing lists, use a mailing list manager such as `majordomo` (described in Chapter 4).

Each time you make a change in `/etc/aliases`, you must run the `newaliases` command to create a database of aliases that `sendmail` can use. This is done automatically each time `sendmail` is started, but you can rebuild the database with `newaliases` at any time without restarting `sendmail`.

Individual users can't alter the `/etc/aliases` file, but they can create a `.forward` file in their home directories. If `sendmail` finds a `.forward` file in a user's home directory, email for that user is processed according to the text in `.forward` instead of simply being sent to the user's standard inbox in `/var/spool/mail`. Common uses of `.forward` include forwarding email to another system when you prefer to receive your email at another host (this method requires you to have a user account on the email server) and piping your messages through a mail filter such as Procmail (described in Chapter 3). If you were on assignment with a subsidiary company for a month, you could include the following line in your `.forward` file:

```
kcarver@myplace_India.net
```

All email that would have been delivered to your mailbox would instead be forwarded to the email address given. What if you had a user account on the central email server in Figure 6-10, used this file in your home directory, and used a forwarding feature in `sendmail` itself? The `sendmail` forwarding feature would forward your mail from the central server to your desktop system before it ever reached your local user account; all the mail would be at your desktop and none would reach you in India.

Watching `sendmail` Work

The `sendmail` daemon creates copious logs of what it does. Each message received and each message sent out are logged along with daemon-specific messages about the server configuration, starting and stopping, etc. These messages are written to the standard system logger, `syslogd`, based on the configuration in `/etc/syslog.conf`. In many

Linux systems these messages are written to `/var/log/messages` by default, along with log messages from many other programs. If you operate a busy `sendmail` mail server, you should alter the configuration of `/etc/syslog.conf` to store messages from the mail facility in a separate file. For example, the default setting in Red Hat 7.3 is to store messages from any mail server in `/var/log/maillog`.

You can also set `sendmail` to generate more or less debugging data in the logs using the `-d` command-line option. See the man page for `sendmail` to learn more about this. (`sendmail.cf` and `sendmail.mc` don't have man pages, but `sendmail` itself does. This man page describes only the startup options for the daemon.)

In addition to learning about `sendmail` activity by reviewing the log files, you can use several other programs that keep you informed about the state of your email server, such as:

- `hoststat`: Displays the status of hosts that have recently sent email to your `sendmail` daemon. By default, information for a host is maintained for 30 minutes.

- `mailq`: Displays a list of messages queued and waiting to be sent out. Messages wait in the queue when sent while you were not connected to the Internet, while `sendmail` waits for a domain name to be resolved, or when they have not been accepted by a remote mail server (by default, `sendmail` tries again later).

- `mailstats`: Displays a summary of the amount of email traffic that `sendmail` has handled. Fields in the output of `mailstats` include messages received, bytes received, messages sent, bytes sent, messages rejected, and messages discarded.

Table 6-4 summarizes the `sendmail` configuration files and utilities that are described in this section.

Table 6-4   Configuration files and utilities for `sendmail`

File or Utility	Description
`sendmail.mc`	A configuration file containing macro definitions used by the m4 program to create a `sendmail.cf` file
`m4`	The conversion utility that converts a `sendmail.mc` file into a `sendmail.cf` file
`sendmail.cf`	The configuration file that defines the operations of `sendmail`
`sendmail.cw`	An additional configuration file that defines the domains for which `sendmail` will accept email messages
`/etc/sysconfig/sendmail`	A system configuration file that defines start-up parameters for `sendmail`; used by the startup script in `/etc/rc.d/init.d`

Table 6-4   Configuration files and utilities for `sendmail` (continued)

File or Utility	Description
`sendmail`	The sendmail daemon or email server (MTA)
`access`	An optional configuration file that defines how `sendmail` should handle email from the domains listed in the file; must be converted to an `access.db` file using the `makemap` utility
`virtusertable`	An optional configuration file that defines how `sendmail` should handle email addressed to user accounts listed in the file; must be converted to a `virtusertable.db` file using the `makemap` utility
`makemap`	Utility to convert plaintext files such as `access` and `virtusertable` into database format files that `sendmail` can process
`aliases`	Lists alternate email addresses and the actual user account or filename that messages to each address should be delivered to
`newaliases`	Utility that converts the `aliases` file into a database format that `sendmail` can process; must be executed after any change is made to the `aliases` file

CREATING A LINUX WEB SERVER

The last networking topic we discuss in this chapter may be the one you are already most familiar with: the World Wide Web. Tim Berners-Lee at the CERN laboratory on the French-Swiss border developed the Web as a way to help scientists exchange data in a variety of different formats. The Hypertext Transport Protocol (HTTP) that he designed focused on real-time exchange of relatively small files between a server and numerous clients. At the time, many data formats were commonly used for information stored on Internet servers. The HTML document description language provided one way to create basic hyperlinked documents for exchange via HTTP-capable servers.

Although the Web was a hit with scientists, the explosive growth of the Web began with the development of a program called Mosaic at the National Center for Supercomputing Applications (*www.ncsa.uiuc.edu*). Mosaic was the first well-known graphical browser, as described in Chapter 3. NCSA also created one of the first Web servers; CERN created another. Today, millions of Web sites are running all over the world. To see more statistics about the Web, visit *wcp.oclc.org*, or visit *www.w3.org* and search on statistics.

A **Web server** in Linux terminology is a daemon that accepts requests via HTTP and responds with the requested files. A basic Web server can be extremely simple in design: it accepts an HTTP command that asks for a file, then it sends that file to the requester. As with other Internet services you have studied, the complexity comes when you begin to add security features, flexible configurations, support for many types of data, and many other features that have led to today's robust, complex Web servers.

Although CERN and NCSA Web servers are still available, the most widely used Web server in the world today is Apache. Apache is included with every standard version of Linux and is installed by default on most of them, often because it is used to provide some of the system documentation. Many other Web servers are available for Linux, some basic and some very complex. A few of them are listed here:

- *Boa* is a small, free Web server designed to be efficient without all the overhead (and features) of a server like Apache. (See *www.boa.org.*)

- *iPlanet* Web server was developed by Netscape Communications and Sun Microsystems. It includes a browser-based administration tool. A free trial version is available for download at *www.iplanet.com.*

- *Servertec iServer* provides features focused on large sites, such as load balancing among multiple Web servers and the ability to interact easily with other types of servers, such as databases. (See *www.servertec.com.*)

- *Stronghold* is a secure server that is appropriate for running e-commerce applications on Linux. It is not free, but is based on Apache and includes source code. Stronghold was developed by C2Net, which is now owned by Red Hat Software. (See *www.redhat.com.*)

- *Zeus* includes a graphical administration interface (like iPlanet) and encryption (like Stronghold). It was designed for ISPs and is considered one of the fastest Web servers. (See *www.zeustech.net.*)

 You can learn about Web server software used around the world by exploring the statistics at *www.netcraft.com*, which claims as of late 2002 to have data on over 38 million Web sites.

Some of the features of Apache that make it popular include:

- A regular development cycle that keeps up with Web technology and provides a very reliable product

- Virtual hosting, which allows a single Web server to provide documents for multiple Web sites (multiple domain names)

- A modular design that lets Web administrators add and remove functionality to meet their site's needs

- Many security options and performance tuning settings

- A broad support base, despite being free software (for example, see *www.apacheweek.com*)

You start Apache from the standard script `/etc/rc.d/init.d/httpd`, but it may be running as part of your default system settings. Apache is not controlled via a superserver, though this used to be a common configuration. Instead, Apache now runs in standalone mode, watching for incoming connections from Web clients (browsers) and starting additional copies of Apache as needed to handle the incoming traffic. The following output shows how many Web server daemons are often running on a Linux system:

```
root     2403  0.0  3.3 46572 6392 ? S     11:46     0:03
  /usr/sbin/httpd -
apache   2488  0.0  3.4 46632 6516 ? S     12:44     0:00
  /usr/sbin/httpd -
apache   2489  0.0  3.4 46632 6516 ? S     12:44     0:00
  /usr/sbin/httpd -
apache   2490  0.0  3.4 46632 6516 ? S     12:44     0:00
  /usr/sbin/httpd -
apache   2491  0.0  3.4 46632 6516 ? S     12:44     0:00
  /usr/sbin/httpd -
apache   2492  0.0  3.4 46632 6516 ? S     12:44     0:00
  /usr/sbin/httpd -
```

Notice that one of the `httpd` processes is owned by root (as indicated by the word **root** in the far left column of the first line); this is the master process. The other processes are owned by user **apache**, a user account that has no access rights outside of the documents designated for the Web server to access. These additional processes were started by the master process to handle incoming requests. (By default, some servers are running even when no requests are pending.)

Apache configuration files are stored in `/etc/httpd/conf`. The documents that the server sends to clients are stored in `/var/www` on Red Hat Linux; other Linux systems may store them in `/home/http` or `/usr/httpd`. The main configuration file, `httpd.conf`, contains hundreds of configuration options, along with comments describing most of them. Each configuration option in this file is called a directive. Whenever you change the configuration file, you should restart Apache by using the script in `/etc/rc.d/init.d`. If you are working with an active Web site, however, restarting the server drops all the current client connections. A better method is to send the master httpd server a "reload" signal using this command:

```
kill -HUP 'cat /var/run/httpd.pid'
```

Because the configuration file contains examples of all the directive types you are likely ever to need for Apache, exploring that file and reading the comments it contains will give you a solid understanding of what Apache is capable of and how to take advantage of those capabilities. The online documentation provided at *www.apache.org* is also worth researching when you have questions about specific directives that you are considering using.

The directives in the first part of `httpd.conf` affect the global operation of Apache. Most are fine with their default values, but a few that are worth noting are mentioned here to illustrate important concepts in Apache configuration. In each case, all the comments that appear alongside the directives in the configuration file have been removed.

A connection to a Web site exists independent of the file being transferred. Apache can keep the connection active (alive) after sending a file, on the theory that a client that has requested one file is likely to request several. By using this **keepalive** feature, the client saves time in requesting additional files, and Apache doesn't have to re-create the connection for each file. Overall performance is better. The following directives control how connections are kept alive:

```
KeepAlive Off
MaxKeepAliveRequests 100
KeepAliveTimeout 15
```

If you anticipate running a publicly available Web server, you should change the `KeepAlive` directive to `On`. The `MaxKeepAliveRequests` refers to the number of requests that a client can make during a single connection; a higher number yields better performance. However, if you have a limited number of connections because your server is overloaded, this directive may prevent someone from connecting to your Web site. The `KeepAliveTimeout` directive indicates a time in seconds that a connection will be maintained without activity. You can adjust this based on how long you think visitors to your Web site pause between viewing one page and clicking on a link to move to the next. You must balance performance from the client's perspective with having idle connections to your Web server.

Apache uses a master server to spawn additional servers that handle client requests, but a series of directives controls how this is done. In general, Apache notes the number of client requests waiting to be handled. If it decides that more copies of Apache are needed, it starts one copy the first second, two the next second, four the next, eight the next, and so forth, until it is starting 32 additional servers per second. This continues until the client demand is met. To control this process, the following directives are used:

```
MinSpareServers 5
MaxSpareServers 20
StartServers 8
MaxClients 150
MaxRequestsPerChild 1000
```

When the genealogy Web site *www.familysearch.org* was first announced, organizers expected less than 1 million hits per day. The actual daily traffic when the site was opened was close to 8 million hits, slowing server performance to a crawl for several days until site administrators could ramp up the hardware to handle the traffic that had materialized immediately upon the site's opening.

The first two directives define the number of spare copies of Apache that are running when they are not needed by pending client requests. Apache always keeps at least `MinSpareServers` running to await new requests. If traffic increases, then drops off, Apache eventually stops all but 20 of the running servers. The `StartServers` number indicates how many copies of Apache should be started immediately when Apache is launched. If you were to stop your server during a heavy load, then restart it, the `StartServers` directive helps it keep up with waiting requests immediately rather than waiting several seconds for the timed increase in server copies.

The `MaxClients` directive imposes a limit on the number of clients that can connect to your server. This keeps Apache from spiraling out of control trying to start new servers to keep up with client demand if the machine's resources simply can't handle the load. You can adjust this number based on the expected traffic and your host's memory, network bandwidth, etc.

`MaxRequestsPerChild` defines how many requests (or connections, if you are using keepalives) a single copy of Apache will process. After that limit is reached, that copy of Apache will be stopped and a new copy started to replace it, if warranted. This is to prevent undetected programming problems (in particular, memory leaks from system libraries) from causing the server to stop functioning after running for a long time. In Linux this not considered a problem, so you could increase this value if you have a busy Web server, or even set it to zero to indicate no limit. Copies of Apache are never stopped just because they have served many requests.

Modules are a key feature of Apache that can seem daunting at first glance. Many features of Apache are implemented as loadable modules; you define what your copy of Apache can do by which modules you select for inclusion. Each module is controlled by various directives that you include in the `httpd.conf` configuration file. Much like the Linux kernel, **Apache modules** can be included when you compile Apache from source code or they can be loaded on the fly as shared objects. This is equivalent to using `modprobe` to load a kernel module, but you must list the modules for Apache in the `httpd.conf` file and include the module itself in a subdirectory. In Red Hat, these modules are stored in `/etc/httpd/modules`. Examples of modules include `mod_userdir` to allow users to have their own home pages in their home directories, `mod_autoindex` to create attractive Web pages automatically from a directory listing, and `mod_log_config` to let you configure exactly what information is logged by Apache. More complex modules, which you won't use by default, include `mod_speling` (that's correct) to spell check URLs so that you are more likely to get the page you intended, a series of `mod_auth` modules to provide authentication for client requests using a variety of methods, and `mod_throttle` to configure usage limits for various classes of incoming users.

The `LoadModule` directive defines a filename for a shared object as well as the programmatic function name of the module. The `AddModule` directive defines a code file for a module. The order in which `AddModule` directives appear is significant, as it indicates the order in which modules are loaded into Apache. If you want to use modules differently than the way they're used in the default Apache configuration, comment or uncomment the `LoadModule` and `AddModule` directives in the default `httpd.conf` file.

You can learn more about all available Apache modules by visiting *modules.apache.org*. This site lists hundreds of modules that you can download to add functionality to Apache. Some of the most important modules are `mod_perl` and `mod_PHP`, which enable Apache to run Perl and PHP scripts without loading a separate Perl or PHP interpreter. These features are so widely used that you see links to separate Web sites for them on the main *www.apache.org* Web site. Adding a Perl or PHP module does make Apache much larger, however.

Several other directives that control overall operation of Apache are described here.

6

- The `User` and `Group` directives define which user and group ID Apache operates under. While the master copy of Apache runs as root, other copies run as the user apache, nobody, or a similar user account. That way, if a browser request should somehow allow unexpected access to the system, that access is limited to what the named user (rather than the root user) could do.

- The `ServerAdmin` directive lists the email address of a contact person who should be listed at the bottom of Apache-generated Web pages. (For example, server error message pages that a user sees when a requested Web page does not exist.)

- The `ServerName` directive defines the domain name to which Apache sends requests among virtual hosts (as described later in this section). This domain name is also reported back to the browser when responding to a request. This gives your site a consistent feel, despite the fact that multiple domain names may resolve to the same IP address.

- The `DocumentRoot` directive defines where documents for the Web server are stored. By default on Red Hat Linux this directory is `/var/www/html`.

Much of the `httpd.conf` file is organized into containers. A **container** is a special type of directive that activates other directives only if a condition is met or only within a particular context. One container example that appears several times in `httpd.conf` is the <directory> container. Each <directory> container starts with a <Directory> line and ends with a </Directory> line, similar to some HTML tags. The container defines how Apache handles requests for files within the named directory. The standard <directory> container for the default document root of Apache is shown here.

```
<Directory "/var/www/html">
    Options Indexes FollowSymLinks
    AllowOverride None
    Order allow,deny
    Allow from all
</Directory>
```

The `Options` line defines what types of files can be accessed in this directory.

- Indexes means that a Web page listing the contents of the directory is generated by Apache if no `index.html` file is available. (The `DirectoryIndex` directive defines the default filename `index.html`, which you can add to or change.)

- `FollowSymLinks` lets Apache follow a symbolic link in this directory to a file in another directory.

- `Includes` would allow Apache to process special statements within the text of files in this directory. These are called **server-side-includes** (or **server-parsed documents**) and allow Apache to alter documents dynamically (as they are requested). This feature can add significantly to the load of a Web server. (It also presents security issues, as do many of the features listed here. See Chapter 12 for more information.)

- `ExecCGI` allows Apache to run a script in this directory and return the output of the script to the requesting browser.

- You could also use the `None` or `All` keywords after `Options` to use all the above (for very open access) or none of the above (for very restrictive access).

The `AllowOverride` line defines which parts of the directory access information defined in this container can be changed if a configuration file called `.htaccess` (by default— you can change this) is present in the named directory. Using `.htaccess` lets you allow multiple users to control their own subdirectories on a Web site, but `AllowOverride` lets you also limit their freedom to choose settings that might endanger the rest of the site. `AllowOverride` can use any of these keywords:

- `FileInfo`, which defines how different data types are handled

- `Options`, as described for the `Options` directive above

- `AuthConfig`, to control the authentication options by which a user must provide a username and password before accessing a file

- `Limit`, which is a separate container that can be included within a <directory> container to limit access to a file to a set of hostnames or IP addresses

- `None` or `All` provides a blanket answer, giving `.htaccess` no ability to change the configuration or letting it set everything differently

The `Order`, `Allow`, and `Deny` directives (`Deny` is not shown above) define which hosts can access files in this directory. `Order` defines which is processed first, `Allow` directives or `Deny` directives. This is similar to what you have learned about the `/etc/hosts.allow` and `/etc/hosts.deny` files. For example, the following lines permit access only by hosts on the 192.168.0.0 network:

```
Order deny,allow
Allow from 192.168.
Deny from all
```

The following lines allow access to everyone except clients from the trouble.net domain:

```
Order allow,deny
Allow from all
Deny from trouble.net
```

Think carefully about what you want to achieve when you set up your access statements, and remember that Apache is not controlled by a superserver, nor does it rely on TCP Wrappers. Besides `httpd.conf`, the only access control mechanism for your Web server are any firewalls that block packets at the network level (as described in the second part of this book).

In `httpd.conf` you see several other examples of <directory> containers, <limit> containers, and other containers to help you understand how these are used. The information in a <directory> container applies to all subdirectories of the named directory unless another <directory> container defines different settings for the subdirectory.

The `Options` field above mentions both server-side-includes and scripts that Apache can execute, returning the output of the script as a document for the browser. Traditionally, scripts were kept in a separate directory that had the `ExecCGI` option set. More common now is the use of the `AddHandler` directive, which lets you specify that Apache should treat a file a particular way based on its file extension. For example, the following two directives define scripts as any file ending with .cgi, and server-side-includes as any file ending with .shtml. Apache processes these files accordingly, no matter where they occur in the directory structure.

```
AddHandler cgi-script .cgi
AddHandler server-parsed .shtml
```

Of course, other factors may also be important. For example, Apache cannot execute a script file if the file does not have the execute file permission (the x bit) set for the class of user as which Apache is running (granting user, group, or other permission to execute the file). Likewise, it is possible to use more advanced directives to limit the type of server-side-includes that Apache processes, beyond simply instructing Apache that .shtml files should be processed.

The version of Apache included with Red Hat Linux includes dozens of directives for **Secure Socket Layer (SSL)** operation, though these are not activated by default. SSL allows a Web server to communicate securely with a browser for e-commerce or similar applications. For more information on the SSL features of Apache, visit *www.apache.org*.

Virtual hosting is the feature of Apache that lets a single copy of Apache serve documents for several Web sites (several domains). For example, if you operated a server for a consortium of schools, you could host the Web sites for all of those schools. The documents for each Web site are stored in a separate subdirectory on the server. Virtual hosting can be name-based or IP-based. In name-based virtual hosting, Apache relies on the server name that the client browser requests. A few browsers may not provide this information in their request, so name-based virtual hosting does not work when such browsers request a document—they receive an unexpected "default" document from the Web server.

IP-based or address-based virtual hosting uses the IP address to determine the Web site that the client browser is trying to access. This is a cleaner solution that works for all browsers, but it means you must assign multiple IP addresses—a scarce commodity—to a single machine.

To succeed at name-based virtual hosting, you must set up your DNS server to refer all the domain names involved to your Web server's IP address. The resource records might look like this:

```
www.college_a.edu.   IN   A   192.168.12.1
www.college_b.edu.   IN   A   192.168.12.1
www.college_c.edu.   IN   A   192.168.12.1
www.college_d.edu.   IN   A   192.168.12.1
```

Within `httpd.conf`, you then specify the directive `NameVirtualHost` with the IP address used for virtual hosting. Apache examines any requests sent to that IP address to see what domain name is requested. You then specify a container such as the following for each of the Web sites that you want to host:

```
<virtualhost 192.168.12.1>
    ServerName www.college_a.edu
    …other directives for this virtual host …
</virtualhost>
```

Any directives you wish can go in the <virtualhost> container. Project 6-4 shows an example with a minimal set of directives to make a virtual Web site look independent and well-configured to a user working in a browser. If a request arrives that does not specify one of the virtual hostnames for which you have defined information, Apache does its best to figure out which document tree to use, either the first listed or the default `DocumentRoot` directive that exists outside of any <virtualhost> containers.

To use IP-based virtual hosting, you must set up the networking interfaces on your server to support multiple IP addresses. If you have multiple Ethernet NICs, each has a separate IP address, but each Ethernet NIC can also have multiple IP addresses using IP aliases, as described in Project 2-5. Once you have set up all the needed IP addresses, DNS should refer each Web site name to the correct IP address, as with name-based virtual hosting, but this time the Web addresses would be different:

```
www.college_a.edu.   IN   A   192.168.12.1
www.college_b.edu.   IN   A   192.168.12.2
www.college_c.edu.   IN   A   192.168.12.3
www.college_d.edu.   IN   A   192.168.12.4
```

The `NameVirtualHost` directive is not used for IP-based virtual hosting. Instead, you simply include the IP address in the <virtualhost> container, as shown here:

```
<virtualhost 192.168.12.1>
     …directives for this virtual host …
</virtualhost>
```

For either type of virtual hosting, you can set up the document tree as you would for a single Web site, by creating a separate directory under `/var/www` for each site.

Another feature of Apache is its ability to act as a **proxy server**, which intercepts requests from clients and forwards them as if they came from the proxy server rather than the original client. When a response comes from a Web server with the requested Web page, the proxy server returns it to the client. This feature lets you implement many types of controls both to protect the security of a network and to limit clients' access to the Web. Most proxy servers are **caching proxy servers**, meaning that they save a copy of any document before passing it back to the client. This enables them to respond immediately if the same document is requested again, without requesting it from the Internet a second time. (Not all documents are cached.)

To set up a proxy server using Apache, you must edit the `httpd.conf` file to include the proxy server module and then set directives to control the actions of the proxy server. The following directives must be included to load the appropriate Apache module and enable it.

```
LoadModule proxy_module modules/libproxy.so
AddModule mod_proxy.c
ProxyRequests On
```

Including the following directives enables document caching in the proxy server by specifying the directory where cached documents are stored and the maximum amount of space that Apache uses for the cache (5 MB here). Many other directives are supported for controlling how documents are cached.

```
CacheRoot "/var/cache/httpd"
CacheSize 5
```

Before you can use a standard proxy server, you must configure your client browser to send requests to the proxy server. A system administrator typically blocks normal Web access with a firewall so that all Web requests must be directed to the proxy server.

In Netscape Communicator, you can set up access to a proxy server by opening the Preferences dialog box under the Edit menu. Choose Proxies under the Advanced item on the left side of the dialog box, select Manual proxy configuration, and then click View to see a dialog box in which you can enter the connection details. If you were using Apache as your proxy server, you would enter the Apache server's IP address in the HTTP field, with 80 in the Port field.

Apache supports many directives that are not discussed in this chapter. All directives are placed in the main configuration file, `httpd.conf`. Table 6-5 lists and describes the directives included in this chapter.

Table 6-5   A selection of Apache directives

Apache Directive (sample values in italics)	Description
KeepAlive *Off*	Sets whether Apache keeps client connections open after responding to a request
MaxKeepAliveRequests *100*	Sets the maximum number of requests from a client via a single connection
KeepAliveTimeout *15*	Sets the length of time in seconds that a connection with a client will be kept open without a request arriving
MinSpareServers *5*	Sets the minimum number of idle copies of Apache to be kept running to handle incoming requests
MaxSpareServers *20*	Sets the maximum number of idle copies of Apache to be kept running to handle incoming requests
StartServers *8*	Sets the number of copies of Apache to start immediately after Apache is launched
MaxClients *150*	Sets the maximum number of clients that can be connected to Apache at the same time
MaxRequestsPerChild *1000*	Sets the maximum number of client requests to which a single copy of Apache can respond before being shut down as a precaution against memory leaks
LoadModule *proxy_module modules/libproxy.so*	Loads code for a shared Apache module
AddModule *mod_proxy.c*	Adds the loaded code for a shared Apache module to the server
User *apache*	Sets the username under which copies of Apache run
Group *apache*	Sets the group name under which copies of Apache run
ServerAdmin *webmaster@mydomain.com*	Sets the email address to be added to Web pages generated by Apache

Table 6-5   A selection of Apache directives (continued)

Apache Directive (sample values in italics)	Description
ServerName *www.mydomain.com*	Sets the servername that Apache associates with Web pages within a given set of documents
DocumentRoot *"/var/www/html"*	Sets the directory where Web pages are located. All client requests are relative to this directory
<Directory *"/var/www/html"*>	Defines characteristics/directives that apply only to files contained in the named directory or its subdirectories
Options Indexes *FollowSymLinks*	Sets access options that apply to Web pages; used within a <Directory> container
AllowOverride *None*	Sets access options that can be overridden by a configuration file located in a subordinate directory
Order *allow,deny*	Defines the order in which the Allow and Deny directives are processed
Allow from *192.168.10.10*	Sets domains or IP addresses from which access is permitted
Deny from *trouble.net*	Sets domains or IP addresses from which access is not permitted
DirectoryIndex	Defines the filenames for which Apache searches as default documents when a client requests a directory name rather than a filename
AddHandler *cgi-script .cgi*	Sets a file extension that has special meaning to Apache, such as an executable script
NameVirtualHost	Sets an IP address for which queries must use settings in a matching <virtualhost> container
<virtualhost *192.168.12.1*>	Sets up a virtual host, with all the directives in the <virtualhost> container applying only to requests to that host
ProxyRequests *On*	Enables Apache proxy server capability
CacheRoot *"/var/cache/httpd"*	Defines the directory where cached documents are stored when Apache is used as a proxy server
CacheSize *5*	Defines the size in MB for the document cache when Apache is used as a proxy server

CHAPTER SUMMARY

❑ Routing tables guide the Linux kernel in sending packets to their final destination on distant networks. These tables can be constructed manually or dynamically with the help of routing protocols.

❑ Interior routing protocols are used within an organization using mathematical algorithms to determine how to route packets. RIP and OSPF are examples of popular interior routing protocols.

❑ Exterior routing protocols are used for routing packets among organizations, based on policy decisions about which specific sources of routing information are to be trusted—and how much. BGP is an example of an exterior routing protocol.

❑ The `routed` daemon implements RIP on Linux. RIP is only appropriate for small networks, but `routed` is easy to use and has no required configuration settings.

❑ OSPF is a highly effective interior routing protocol. It builds a chart of the status of all routers that it knows of, determining the best route based on a complex mathematical algorithm.

❑ The `gated` daemon supports RIP version 2 with classless addressing, OSPF, and BGP on Linux. It must be carefully configured, but provides a powerful, cross-protocol routing engine for dedicated Linux routers.

❑ DNS is an Internetwide information hierarchy used to provide hostname-to-IP-address matching (called forward lookups) and IP-address-to-hostname matching (called reverse lookups, or reverse DNS).

❑ Queries about a given hostname begin with one of the Internet's root DNS servers, unless the host making the query has already cached information about where to find part of such information, such as the location of an authoritative DNS server for the .com domain.

❑ A zone is a part of a domain about which a particular DNS server is authorized to provide information. Most DNS servers provide information on several zones; each zone should have at least one master DNS server and one slave DNS server as a backup. The slave receives updated information from the master via a zone transfer.

❑ Reverse DNS provides a security mechanism that is widely used to prevent unauthorized users from completing queries to various network services. Many servers do not accept a connection if a reverse DNS lookup fails.

❑ Setting up a simple caching name server to forward DNS queries to another name server makes efficient use of network bandwidth for many small networks.

❑ The Domain Name Service (DNS) protocol is implemented in Linux by the `named` daemon, which is part of the BIND collection of programs. The `named` daemon is configured by the `/etc/named.conf` file, which refers to data files typically stored in `/var/named`.

❑ Resource records hold information about a host within a zone that a client can receive through a query. Resource records include A records for an IP address, CNAME records for an alias (alternate name) to the canonical name for a host, PTR records for reverse DNS "pointers" to map an IP address to a hostname, MX records to define a host's mail exchanger, the SOA Start of Authority record, and many others.

❑ The Start of Authority (SOA) record defines how to reach the DNS administrator for a zone. It also includes a serial number to track updated zone information and several parameters governing zone transfers for that zone.

❑ `bindconf.gui` is one of many utilities that let you configure `named`, once you understand the configuration options and structure of the zone information files.

❑ The `host`, `nslookup`, and `dig` commands let you query a DNS server from the command line using numerous options to determine exactly how a DNS server is configured and how default queries function.

❑ The `nsupdate` utility lets you update DNS zone information files over a network, on the fly, if this feature is properly configured in `/etc/named.conf`.

❑ Popular Linux email servers include `sendmail`, Qmail, PostFix, and `smail`. Sendmail is by far the most widely used email server and is available both as free software and as a commercial product.

❑ Startup options for `sendmail` are configured via `/etc/sysconfig/sendmail`, but `sendmail` is most often configured through the `/etc/sendmail.cf` file. Because this file is extremely complex, most email server administrators rely on the `m4` program to create it based on a more general list of features contained in the file `/etc/sendmail.mc`.

❑ Spam is a source of great concern and annoyance to email server administrators. Email servers provide many features to control spam, including relay configuration options, access lists, forwarding features, and Realtime Blackhole Lists.

❑ Aliases are a popular way to redirect email or create small mailing lists via `sendmail`. They are stored in `/etc/aliases` and are activated using the `newaliases` command.

❑ Apache is the most widely used Web server and is included with all standard Linux distributions. It is configured using the `httpd.conf` file.

❑ One copy of Apache is the master server and it controls copies of Apache that handle client requests. Configuration directives define how Apache starts and stops additional copies of itself to manage incoming Web traffic.

❑ Most functions in Apache are performed by loadable modules, configured using directives in `httpd.conf`. Many additional modules are available for special purposes.

❑ Apache uses directives to control access to the server on a per-directory basis, and can also host multiple Web sites using virtual hosting directives.

❑ Apache supports advanced features like virtual hosting and acting as a proxy server.

6

KEY TERMS

A record — A line (a record) within a DNS zone information file that provides the IP address for the given host.

Apache module — Functionality for the Apache Web server that can be independently loaded on the fly as a shared object.

bindconf — A graphical utility used to configure zone information files.

Border Gateway Protocol (BGP) — A widely used external routing protocol.

caching name server — A DNS server that contains no preconfigured information on domains (except localhost), but simply queries other DNS servers and caches the results.

caching proxy server — A proxy server that saves a copy of each Web document before passing it back to the client that originally requested it.

CNAME record — A line (record) in a DNS zone information file that defines the canonical name for a given hostname. In effect, this record creates an alias for a hostname, allowing it to be referenced by multiple names that are resolved to the same IP address.

container — A special type of Apache configuration directive that activates other directives only if a condition is met or only within a particular context.

cost — A measure of how efficient a route is. The route with the lowest cost should always be chosen, other things being equal.

dig — A utility used to query specific DNS servers for specific resource records.

dynamic routing — Collecting and updating routing table information automatically using a routing protocol.

exterior routing protocols — Routing protocols designed for routing packets between networks controlled by different organizations; packets are routed based on administrative policies, often controlled by how much a particular organization's routing information is trusted.

forward lookup — Using DNS to convert a domain name to an IP address.

forwarding name server — A DNS server that forwards all queries to another name server for processing.

gated — The Linux program that implements OSPF, BGP, and RIP v 2 (with classless addressing).

hop — A pass through a router.

host — A utility used to query specific DNS servers for specific resource records.

interior routing protocols — Routing protocols designed for routing packets among networks controlled by a single organization; packets are routed based on mathematical models.

keepalive — Maintaining an active network connection after sending a file, based on the theory that a client that has requested one file is likely to request several.

m4 — A program that converts a text file containing configuration parameters into a complete sendmail.cf file.

master DNS server — The authoritative name server for a zone, typically containing database files that provide IP addresses for hosts within that zone.

MX record — A line (record) in a DNS zone information file that defines the mail exchanger for the named host. MX records are used by mail transfer agents (MTAs) to find the correct email server to contact when delivering email to a recipient.

named — The Linux program that implements the DNS protocol to create a DNS server; part of the BIND collection of programs.

NS record — A line (a record) within a DNS zone information file that defines the authoritative name server for the given domain.

nslookup — A utility used to query DNS servers for resource records.

nsupdate — A utility used to update zone information files dynamically at the command line.

primary master server — *See* master DNS server.

primary server — *See* master DNS server.

proxy server — Software that intercepts requests from Web clients and forwards them as if they came from the proxy server rather than the original client. When a response is received, the proxy server returns it to the client.

PTR record — A line (record) in a DNS zone information file that refers to the hostname to which an IP address is assigned; used for reverse DNS lookups.

Realtime Blackhole List — A list of IP addresses that are known principally as sources of spam and whose messages can be blocked automatically by mail servers such as **sendmail**.

relaying — An email server delivering a message that didn't originate on the same host where the email server is running.

resource record — Information about a host that a DNS server can provide to answer queries. Example resource records include the A record to associate an IP address and hostname, the MX record to define a host's mail exchanger, and the PTR record to associate a hostname with an IP address for reverse DNS lookups.

reverse DNS — Using DNS to obtain the hostname that corresponds to an IP address.

reverse lookup — *See* reverse DNS.

rndc — A control program used to manage the **named** daemon.

root name servers — DNS servers designated as a starting point for DNS queries.

routed — The Linux program that implements the Routing Information Protocol (RIP).

secondary server — *See* slave DNS server.

secondary slave server — *See* slave DNS server.

Secure Socket Layer (SSL) — A protocol that allows a Web server to communicate securely with a browser for e-commerce or similar applications.

server-parsed documents — *See* server-side-includes.

6

server-side-includes — Statements within a text file that are processed on the fly by a Web server when that document is requested.

slave DNS server — A backup to a master DNS server, containing the same database files as the master DNS server.

SOA record — The first line (record) in a DNS zone information file. Defines the Start-Of-Authority for the information in the file, describing how to use the information provided for this zone, including a serial number for updates and refresh periods for zone transfers to slave DNS servers.

spam — Unsolicited advertisement-related email.

spoofing — A technique used by a malicious user to act as another person when contacting a server.

static routing — Assembling a routing table via entries in start-up scripts or by manually entered `route` commands.

virtual hosting — A feature of the Apache Web server that lets a single copy of Apache serve documents for several Web sites (several domains).

Web server — A daemon that accepts requests via HTTP and responds with the requested files.

zone — A part of the DNS domain tree for which a particular DNS server has authority to provide information.

zone information files — The files referred to in `named.conf` that contain detailed information about specific zones: the information that a DNS query seeks.

zone transfer — Exchanging information between a master DNS server and a slave DNS server.

REVIEW QUESTIONS

1. The purpose of a routing protocol is to:

    a. Route packets across multiple network segments.

    b. Facilitate the exchange of routing table entries among routers.

    c. Make static routing easier to configure on multiple hosts.

    d. Avoid the need to use DNS in larger networks.

2. An exterior routing protocol uses _____ to determine how to route packets.

    a. mathematical algorithms

    b. a DNS root server

    c. BGP

    d. policies that may be based on the trust accorded the host providing routing data

3. A primary disadvantage of using RIP as an interior routing protocol for larger organizational networks is that RIP:

   a. can only accommodate a maximum of 15 hops between source and destination

   b. relies on class-based network masks, even in version 2

   c. does not have a long history as a stable protocol

   d. is not as popular as OSPF

4. Explain how the metric differs between OSPF and RIP.

5. Which protocols does `gated` support?

   a. RIP, OSPF, DNS

   b. BGP, RIP, OSPF

   c. SMTP, OSPF, RIP

   d. BGP, OSPF

6. Which statement best describes how a DNS domain name is resolved?

   a. through a recursive tree-walking algorithm starting at a root name server

   b. by relying on cached information stored at multiple DNS servers

   c. because of the master/slave backup relationship of authoritative zone information files

   d. due to the common practice of forwarding queries in order to make the local DNS server more efficient

7. Zone information files are transferred from the primary master server to the secondary server using:

   a. a reverse lookup

   b. spoofing

   c. caching

   d. a zone transfer

8. Which is a validly formed reverse DNS domain name for the network ID 198.165.24.0?

   a. 24.165.198.in-addr.arpa

   b. 0.24.165.198

   c. 198.165.24.0

   d. 198.165.24.in-addr.arpa

9. What is the advantage of using forwarded DNS requests when using a slow Internet connection?

10. Describe the difference between A and CNAME resource records.

11. What is the result of not updating the serial number in an SOA record when making changes to a zone information file?

    a. When **named** is restarted, it will not recognize the updated information.

    b. DNS queries to the master DNS server for the domain cannot produce valid results.

    c. The **rndc** command cannot function properly.

    d. Zone transfers will not update secondary servers, thinking no update is necessary.

12. The **$TTL** directive in a zone information file defines:

    a. the default time to live in a DNS cache for the resource records defined in that file

    b. the Time To Live assigned to the SOA record within that file

    c. the Time To Live for packets used to query that DNS server

    d. the Time To Live for any forwarded queries, if forwarding is enabled in **/etc/named.conf**

13. Multiple MX records assigned to a single hostname indicate that:

    a. The hostname's only valid mail exchanger can be accessed via multiple IP addresses.

    b. Multiple email servers are able to receive messages for users on that host.

    c. The authoritative name server for the hostname has not been correctly defined.

    d. The mail server is likely mentioned in at least one CNAME record.

14. The _____ utility is the preferred tool for querying name servers for administrative or troubleshooting purposes.

    a. **nslookup**

    b. **bindconf**

    c. **dig**

    d. **host**

15. When using the **dig** utility, describe what the "@" symbol before a hostname indicates.

16. The configuration file used by the **sendmail** MTA is:

    a. **/usr/share/doc/sendmail-9.1.3/README.cf**

    b. **/etc/mail/access.db**

    c. **/etc/sendmail.cf**

    d. **/etc/mail/sendmail.cw**

17. Features in a master configuration file are converted to a file that `sendmail` can use via the _____ program.

   a. `m4`

   b. `dnl`

   c. `procmail`

   d. `newaliases`

18. Describe email relaying.

19. Describe the difference between discarding a message and rejecting a message.

20. Modules allow the Apache Web server to:

   a. interact cleanly with the Linux kernel

   b. load and unload functionality by recompiling Apache

   c. use LoadModule and AddModule directives to make new functionality part of Apache

   d. use LoadModule to specify programs that are loaded when a user requests a certain Web document

21. Apache can maintain open network connections with clients, expecting that they will make additional requests. This is called:

   a. load balancing via round-robin DNS lookups

   b. the KeepAlive feature

   c. host-based authentication

   d. virtual connections

22. Server-parsed documents are:

   a. documents stored on the Web server that Apache examines/processes at the moment they are requested by a client

   b. module information files that Apache examines/processes when the server starts up

   c. document files that Apache can pre-load into memory to speed responses to browser queries

   d. another name for virtual-hosted documents

23. Using IP-based virtual hosting requires that you:

   a. Load additional modules in your copy of Apache.

   b. Include all relevant virtually-hosted hostnames in `/etc/hosts`.

   c. Define which remote server holds the document tree for each hosted site.

   d. Configure DNS to refer each domain name to the appropriate IP address configured on your host.

6

24. Name an Apache directive that assists in managing the traffic load on a busy Web server.

25. Which protocol is used for e-commerce applications with Apache?

HANDS-ON PROJECTS

Project 6-1

In this project you set up and test a caching, forwarding name server using the standard packages provided with Red Hat Linux 7.3. To complete this project, you should have Red Hat 7.3 installed, with networking established, root access to the system, and an Internet connection.

1. Log in as root and open a command-line window.

2. Check that the following packages are installed:

   ```
   bind
   bind-utils
   caching-nameserver
   ```

3. Start the name server using the **named** script in /etc/rc.d/init.d.

4. Use this command to query for a domain name. You have not changed your /etc/resolv.conf file, so your previously configured DNS server will still be used.

   ```
   dig www.sony.com
   ```

5. Notice the Query time: and SERVER: lines in the last part of the output of **dig**.

6. Now, try out your caching name server with this command:

   ```
   dig @localhost www.sony.com
   ```

7. Notice the same two lines at the end of the output. How do they differ?

8. Why was the time not faster when the response was already cached at your pre-configured name server?

9. Open the /etc/named.conf file in a text editor.

10. Within the options section near the top of the file, right after the line **directory** **"/var/named"**, insert the following lines. Substitute the IP address of your primary DNS name server at your ISP for the IP address shown here:

    ```
    forward first;
    forwarders {
            198.60.22.2;
    };
    ```

11. Save the file and exit the editor.

12. Run the **named-checkconf** command to see whether any syntax errors were introduced as you edited the configuration file. If so, correct them.

13. Reload the configuration using this command (you may see a warning message about the name key, which you can safely ignore for this project):

    ```
    rndc reload
    ```

14. Select another domain name for testing. You should select one that others in your class have not selected and that you would not expect to have been visited often; a somewhat obscure domain name is better for this test. Use **dig** with your localhost to query for the domain you selected:

    ```
    dig @localhost www.cern.org
    ```

15. Notice how long the query time is, given near the end of **dig**'s response.

16. Perform the same query again. How does the query time differ? Where is the information being taken from? What advantage does forwarding have over simply using a caching name server?

17. If you wish, you can change the /etc/resolv.conf setting of your local system to refer to **127.0.0.1**, so that your local DNS server is always used for name resolution. If you choose to do this, use the following command to make **named** start each time your system is started:

    ```
    chkconfig --level 35 named on
    ```

Project 6-2

In this project you check the contents of remote name servers using the **dig** command. To complete this project, you should have Linux installed (any version that includes the **dig** utility), with networking established, and an Internet connection.

Sometimes the results you receive from a name resolution are unexpected. This can be caused by several problems, such as a poorly configured DNS server, a DNS server without a slave that temporarily goes down, or slow propagation of a change in a DNS file. In this project, you query step-by-step through several name servers to get a complete name resolution. This project uses the sample domain name *ftp.hw.nasa.gov*, but feel free to experiment on any domain name you choose once you understand the process being illustrated.

1. Log in as root and open a command-line window.

2. Query your ISP's name server for the address you are searching for. Instruct the DNS server not to search "down the tree," but to give you only the first piece of information that it has, using the "norecurse" option (to stop recursion) to arrive at the requested domain.

    ```
    dig ftp.hq.nasa.gov NS +norecurse
    ```

3. The result is the address of authoritative DNS servers for the .gov domain, unless the server you queried happens to have cached the authoritative servers for nasa.gov as well. In that case, you might choose to use this command to get the .gov NS records specifically:

    dig gov NS +norecurse

4. From the list of .gov servers, choose three.

5. To each of those three name servers, make the following query to check the next part of the domain. Substitute the actual server names for *gov-ns-server*.

    dig @*gov-ns-server* nasa.gov NS +norecurse

6. Does the ANSWER section of each of the three results match?

7. If so, proceed to the next step. Execute this command three times, using three different NS servers for nasa.gov from the previous responses. (Many domains do not have three name servers, but NASA has a huge network, and so includes numerous name servers.)

    dig @*nasa-ns-server* hq.nasa.gov NS +norecurse

8. Now you see a list of name servers that have information about *hq.nasa.gov* servers, of which *ftp.hq.nasa.gov* is one. Query three of these servers using this **dig** command and see if you get the same result from each one:

    dig @*hq.nasa-ns-server* ftp.hq.nasa.gov

9. Below is the output from the above command (substituting one of the *hq.nasa.gov* name servers in the response to step 9).

```
; <<>> DiG 9.1.3 <<>> @mx.nsi.nasa.gov ftp.hq.nasa.gov
;; global options:  printcmd
;; Got answer:
;; ->>HEADER<<- opcode: QUERY, status: NOERROR, id: 49505
;; flags: qr aa rd ra; QUERY: 1, ANSWER: 1, AUTHORITY:
4, ADDITIONAL: 4

;; QUESTION SECTION:
;ftp.hq.nasa.gov.          IN      A


;; ANSWER SECTION:
ftp.hq.nasa.gov. 86400    IN      A   198.116.65.46


;; AUTHORITY SECTION:
hq.nasa.gov.   86400    IN    NS    ns3.hq.nasa.gov.
hq.nasa.gov.   86400    IN    NS    mx.nsi.nasa.gov.
hq.nasa.gov.   86400    IN    NS    ns1.hq.nasa.gov.
hq.nasa.gov.   86400    IN    NS    ns2.hq.nasa.gov.
```

```
;; ADDITIONAL SECTION:
ns3.hq.nasa.gov. 86400    IN  A   198.116.65.241
mx.nsi.nasa.gov. 3600     IN  A   128.102.18.31
ns1.hq.nasa.gov. 86400    IN  A   131.182.230.28
ns2.hq.nasa.gov. 86400    IN  A   131.182.1.28

;; Query time: 290 msec
;; SERVER: 128.102.18.31#53(mx.nsi.nasa.gov)
;; WHEN: Tue Apr 23 22:09:43 2002
;; MSG SIZE  rcvd: 188
```

10. Look at the SERVER line, third from the bottom. This identifies which name server responded to the query. See if you can locate this address in the ADDITIONAL section.

11. What is the hostname of the responding name server?

12. Look in the AUTHORITY section. Is the responding name server listed as being authoritative for the hq.nasa.gov domain?

13. What does this process tell you about the quality of the information you just obtained? How could you use this process if you were seeing unexpected results from standard DNS operations?

Project 6-3

In this project you experiment with email aliases and **sendmail**. To complete this project, you should have Linux installed, with root access to the system. For simplicity's sake, the directory names referred to are specific to the Red Hat distribution, but most distributions should use the same location for the files named.

1. Log in as root and open a command-line window.

2. View the mail log using this command. This will occupy this text window for the duration of this project:

   ```
   tail –f /var/log/maillog
   ```

3. Use a text editor to add the following lines to the end of the /etc/aliases file.

   supervisor: root

   spam: /tmp/spamcan

4. Save the file, then execute the following command:

   ```
   newaliases
   ```

5. Use a mail program to send a message to the address supervisor. The following command is one way to do this, sending the contents of a text file as the body of the message:

   ```
   mail –s "testing aliases" supervisor < /etc/syslog.conf
   ```

6. Watch the window where the mail log is displayed.

7. When you see a line indicating that your message has been delivered, open an email reading program to see that the message addressed to supervisor was delivered to root.

8. Send another email message to spam. An example command to do this is shown here:

```
mail -s "still testing aliases" spam </etc/syslog.conf
```

9. Watch the window where the mail log is displayed to see when the message has been delivered by `sendmail`.

10. Look in the `/tmp` directory to see whether the `spamcan` file was created.

11. Enter the command **mailstats** to see a summary of activity for your `sendmail` server. Have any messages been discarded (see the **msgsdis** column)? If not, what happened to the message addressed to spam?

Project 6-4

In this project you create a virtual Web site using Apache. To complete this project, you should have Linux installed, with root access to the system. Though the directory names referred to are specific to the Red Hat Linux 7.3 distribution, most other distributions will use similar locations for the files named.

1. Log in as root.

2. Open a browser such as Netscape or Mozilla.

3. Enter the URL **http://localhost** to view the default page provided with Apache.

4. Choose **File**, then **Open Page** from the menu and select the file **/var/www/html/index.html**. How is viewing this file different from viewing the file in Step 3?

5. Create the following directories, which will be used to store documents for the virtual host that you will create: *www.virtualhome.com*.

```
mkdir   /var/www/virtualhome
mkdir   /var/www/virtualhome/html
mkdir   /var/www/virtualhome/logs
```

6. Copy some example HTML files to your document tree. (You can use any html files on your system if you don't have the **bindconf** package installed.) For example:

```
cp -r /usr/share/doc/bindconf-1.6.3/* /var/www/
virtualhome/html
```

7. Change the configuration of your Web server by adding the following lines to the end of the `/etc/httpd/conf/httpd.conf` file. Substitute your own host's IP address for the address in the first line.

```
NameVirtualHost 192.168.100.10
<VirtualHost www.virtualhome.com>
```

```
    ServerAdmin webmaster@virtualhome.com
    DocumentRoot /var/www/virtualhome/html
    ServerName www.virtualhome.com
    ErrorLog /var/www/virtualhome/logs/error_log
    CustomLog /var/www/virtualhome/logs/access_log common
</VirtualHost>
```

8. Start your Web server if it is not running via the script in /etc/rc.d/init.d. If it is running, use the following command to make it reread the configuration file (be sure to use single back quotes where shown):

    kill -HUP 'cat /var/run/httpd.pid'

9. Go back to your browser and load the following URL:

    www.virtualhome.com

10. Why didn't this work?

11. Edit the /etc/hosts file. Add the following line, substituting your own IP address for the one shown:

    192.168.100.10   www.virtualhome.com

12. Return to your Web browser and try the URL again. Why does it work now without restarting the Web server?

13. Open the following file in a text editor to see a record of your browsing on your new virtual Web site. */var/www/virtualhome/logs/access_log.*

Project 6-5

In this project you set up Apache as a caching proxy server. To complete this project, you should have Linux installed, with root access to the system, and an Internet connection. Though the directory names referred to are specific to the Red Hat Linux 7.3 distribution, most other distributions use similar locations for the files named.

In this project you work as a team with another person. Designate one of your hosts as the proxy server. The second host acts only as a client. You need to know the IP addresses of both systems.

1. Log in as root on the server.

2. Open the file /etc/httpd/conf/httpd.conf in a text editor. Search for the following line and remove the comment symbol (#) in front of it:

    ```
    LoadModule proxy_module     modules/libproxy.so
    ```

3. Search for the following line and remove the comment symbol (#) in front of it:

    ```
    AddModule mod_proxy.c
    ```

4. Add the following lines to the bottom of the file. Be certain to use the server's IP address instead of the example.

```
<IfModule mod_proxy.c>
    ProxyRequests On
    <Directory proxy:*>
        Order deny,allow
        Allow from 192.168.100.10
    </Directory>
    ProxyVia On
    CacheRoot "/var/cache/httpd"
    CacheSize 5
</IfModule>
```

5. On the server, open a Web browser and change the proxy server setting to point to your own IP address, port 80. In Netscape or Mozilla, choose **Preferences** on the **Edit** menu. Then select **Advanced**, then **Proxies**. Select **Manual proxy configuration**, then click **View**. Set the proxy for **HTTP**, then click **OK**. Then close the dialog box.

6. Enter a URL to visit, such as **www.yahoo.com**. Why doesn't this URL work?

7. Restart Apache with this command:

   ```
   kill -HUP 'cat /var/run/httpd.pid'
   ```

8. Visit the same site you tried to visit in Step 6.

9. Move to the client system. Open the browser and configure it to use the server as a proxy, just as you did in Step 3.

10. Browse to the same site as in Step 6. Why doesn't it work?

11. Return to the server and change the `httpd.conf` file so that the Allow directive permits access to the client system. You can do this in several ways.

12. Restart Apache.

13. Return to the client system and see whether you can view the site you selected in Step 6. Do you notice it loading faster than it did when you first viewed it on the server?

CASE PROJECTS

A new client has signed up for a consulting contract. The client is an association of small businesses in Fairbanks, Alaska that you met through your work at Snow, Sleet, and Hale. The association has about 50 members, most of whom are family business owners. They want to grow their businesses and are looking for ways that exposure via the Internet can help them. Snow, Sleet, and Hale have agreed with the association to let you place a separate server in their office so that it can hook into the Internet on the office connection (recent oil contracts have led them to install a T3 line).

1. You plan to host a separate domain for each small business that chooses to participate in the association's promotional efforts. For each domain, you want to be able to handle incoming email, provide a Web site and possibly an FTP site for some, and act as a master DNS server for the domain. Describe the configuration issues that you foresee with having up to 50 domains handled on the single server.

2. Describe how you will set up the DNS server for this multidomain host.

3. Several of the small business owners have approached you to ask how they can gather lists of email addresses for people who may be interested in their products or services. We begin discussing related topics in the next chapter, but how do you feel about helping them gather email addresses and sending out their promotional material? What advice would you give them? Would you send them to another "email service bureau" to do the work of mailing? How might your actions affect your relations with the law firm? With the association (your new client)?

6

CHAPTER

7

SECURITY, ETHICS, AND PRIVACY

After reading this chapter and completing the exercises you will be able to:

♦ List security risks typical in modern networked computer systems

♦ Understand how to assess risk and create a security policy

♦ Describe the function of top security-awareness organizations

♦ Outline the role of the government in security and privacy

♦ Locate Linux products designed especially for security-conscious environments

In this chapter, you begin to add the basics of computer security to your knowledge of Linux computer networking. This chapter begins this very large topic by discussing the environment in which system administrators work, the rules they abide by, and the consequences of their actions.

You learn specifically about vulnerabilities of modern networked computer systems. Many of these may be familiar to you because of news stories you have read about computer crimes; others you may not have heard of. Familiarity with these weaknesses will help you understand the broad scope of computer security work.

You also learn in this chapter about organizations that have a keen interest in security. These include professional groups that focus on security education for system administrators, as well as government groups that create policies or enforce laws to make computers more secure.

Finally, you will read about a few specialized versions of Linux that have a particular focus on security. Security-related *utilities*—rather than complete Linux distributions—are the focus of the remaining chapters of this book.

333

INTRODUCING COMPUTER SECURITY AND PRIVACY

To introduce the topics of computer security and privacy, consider a few news stories:

- On November 3, 1988, system administrators all over the United States found that their systems were running abnormally slowly. Eventually, they realized that someone had released a worm into the Internet. A **worm** is like a virus. It is a self-replicating program that invades systems, duplicates itself, and then tries to reach out to infect other systems. This particular event became known as the Morris worm, after its creator, Robert Morris, Jr., then a student at Cornell University. It was the first major security incident that affected the entire Internet, and it scared many people because no one knew how to stop it. Morris had intended no harm, but a programming bug caused his worm to replicate many times faster than expected, slowing Internet systems all over the country to a crawl. Morris anonymously sent out an email describing how to stop the worm, but was eventually apprehended and received a sentence of three years probation and a large fine.

- In early 1998, during one of the more tense moments between India and Pakistan (both of which have nuclear weapons), a group of teens aged 15 to 18 hacked into the computer system of the Bhabha Atomic Research Center in India and intercepted email between the physicists working there. They intended to do the same with a similar facility in Pakistan. The same group penetrated a nuclear facility in Turkey the next day.

- A rash of attacks in early 2000 attempting to shut down the most popular Web sites—Yahoo!, eBay, Microsoft Network, and others—set the technology world on its ear. For several weeks, security experts scrambled to cope with a new type of security problem: a **Denial-of-Service** (DoS) attack, designed to shut down access to an Internet site by overwhelming it with bogus requests (you will learn more about this type of attack later in this chapter).

- In a similar series of incidents later that year, several high-profile Web sites were **defaced** (had the text or images on the home page altered). These sites included NASA, the U.S. Department of Justice, the Central Intelligence Agency, and the White House.

- Kevin Mitnik, who was in the news for a time after being sentenced to six years in prison in 1994 for his cybercrime exploits, has since gained unauthorized access to military sites (including the North American Aerospace Defense Command), financial institutions, and numerous technology companies.

- In March 1997, a programmer in Sweden gained access to the 911 emergency response system in Florida, disabling emergency access for 11 counties. Similar events have occurred in other U.S. states.

- Carlos Felipe Salgado Jr. used a common system-administration technique called sniffing (covered in Chapter 11) to collect over 100,000 credit card numbers from online merchants. He was arrested in June 1997 as he tried to sell them to undercover FBI agents.

Despite all of these hazards, Linux system administration and networking are fascinating topics. With Linux, there are thousands of exciting programs to explore and impressive capabilities with which to complete assignments at work or school. You have a worldwide community of enthusiastic supporters with whom you can learn and share experiences, and you have the operating system source code, which gives you unlimited flexibility in digging into the arcane workings of a modern operating system. Using Linux can be intellectually stimulating and a lot of fun.

But when the discussion turns to security, the tone is unlikely to be light hearted. As the news stories about unauthorized computer access—computer crimes—vividly show, computer security is a serious matter. It suddenly ties the work you do on your Linux server to the entire world, and that world includes far too many people who would use your resources for their own ends.

Computer security is a large and specialized field, separate in many ways from the day-to-day operation of a network server. Security specialists must focus as much on the world outside the computer as on the technology and data they seek to protect. Unfortunate though it seems, security requires you to be paranoid about the world at large, or as you may recall from a once-popular TV show, to "trust no one." The reason is straightforward enough: the more broadly a computer is networked, the more potential for access to that computer, and thus the more anonymous that access may become if not properly controlled. Broad—even anonymous—access represents the power of networked computers, but it also presents an opportunity for those with malicious intentions.

Two terms are commonly used to refer to persons who break into computer systems: hacker and cracker. To Linux enthusiasts and many other technically astute people, the term **hacker** means only a highly skilled technology expert who enjoys learning about the intricate workings of computer systems and software. The term hacker is a compliment, reserved for those whose vast knowledge of a particular area of technology make them invaluable consultants, efficient troubleshooters, and effective programmers when a challenging new project arises.

A **cracker** is a person who breaks the law or ethical standards by accessing computer systems without authorization. Some crackers have malicious intentions and seek to damage or shut down hardware, to corrupt software programs, or to damage or destroy data. Other crackers are not malicious, but only want to test their skills by exploring areas that they are not authorized to enter; they don't intentionally damage systems or data, but they are still breaking the rules. These are the definitions used in this book. You can find nuances of these meanings, of course. Some maintain that a cracker must have malicious intent; for others, the term hacker remains synonymous with criminal mischief.

Crackers form an underground community of Internet users. They use pseudonyms instead of their real names and often form groups bent on achieving a common goal, be it taking down sites with political views opposite their own, or simply having a good time at others' expense. Many crackers are young, from 15 to 18. Older crackers (late 20s or 30s) are more likely to work alone, to have a motivation beyond "let's see what I can get away with," and to have a truly impressive set of technical skills.

What does it mean when you read about someone breaking into a computer system, cracking a system, or, as some publications use the term, hacking into a computer system? It normally means that a user was able to attain remote access to a computer that he or she was not authorized to access. Just as you can use Telnet in Linux to log in to a computer remotely and run commands or view files, nearly all operating systems have programs that permit some sort of remote control or remote access when connected to a network. If the operating system or the program itself is not carefully configured, anyone who knows the software well can gain remote access.

If you like a challenge, this might sound like the ultimate technical thrill seeking: pick a high-profile Web site and see whether you can gain access to the server through the holes in the system administrator's security. Then alter the Web site's home page to show the world what you were able to accomplish. This is exactly what has been done to sites such as the one maintained by the White House.

The fact that is lost on crackers is this: even without malicious intentions, this is not harmless fun. Activities like these have consequences that the crackers may not anticipate: people get fired; billions of dollars are wasted recovering from even "innocent" cracker exploits; participants may be charged fines and have felony criminal records, or may even go to prison. In fact, with the increasingly international scope of cracking activities and of terrorist threats, lives are at stake when crackers start manipulating government and military computer sites. The Government Accounting Office, a research arm of the U.S. Congress, reports that 120 nations have information warfare programs. The purpose of such programs is to exploit vulnerabilities in computer security as a tool of war. The successful attacks on hundreds of (nonclassified) Pentagon servers in February 1998 masterminded by Israeli Ehud Tenenbaum show that the dangers of poor security do not stop at national borders.

Accurate estimates of the damages caused by computer crime are hard to calculate, though useful statistics are available (see, for example, *www.trouble.org/survey/* and the Computer Security Institute's Computer Crime and Security Survey at *www.gocsi.com/prelea11.htm*). Gathering accurate statistics is difficult for several reasons. First, computer break-ins are not always reported, either because they are not discovered or because they are discovered long after the break-in occurred, making prosecution difficult. Second, the company that was broken into may not want to risk negative publicity by reporting the incident; at the very least, they want to avoid inclusion in any statistics related to victimization. Finally, as described in reports by the U.S. Department of Justice, computer crimes are prosecuted using a number of different laws; matching a crime with a law is difficult. Even defining computer crime itself is a difficult task. Which of the following actions do you consider computer crime?

- Breaking into a bank's computer system and transferring funds from a major corporation's account to your own numbered bank account in another country

- Breaking into a bank's computer system and looking up the balances of your employer's bank accounts

- Breaking into a bank's Web server and adding an anonymous note to the bottom of their Web home page

- Breaking into a government or military server and sending email to the system administrator explaining how you were able to break in

- Breaking into a server at your school and changing your grade on a midterm exam

- Breaking into your friend's computer and copying her music files onto your system (without damaging them on her system)

Although the likelihood of prosecution differs in these examples, every one of them could be called a crime if the person whose system you broke into decided to press the issue. In simple terms, **computer crime** is unauthorized access to a computer system.

The Privacy Debate

You may wonder why privacy and ethics are grouped with security in this chapter (and on the SAIR/GNU Linux certification tests). Privacy makes computer security an issue of personal concern. Any personal information stored on a computer is threatened by someone cracking the system where it is stored.

Many books have been written about the immense amount of personal data that is stored for nearly every individual in this country (*Database Nation* by security expert Simon Garfinckel is one good example). The government is naturally a major participant: the Internal Revenue Service has financial data; driver's license divisions have information about you; vital records offices have family information such as birth and marriage records. Some of this data is publicly available, but much is not. Companies also maintain vast databases of personal information to help them market products more effectively. Billions of dollars are spent each year by companies that purchase mailing lists to track your exact spending habits and preferences. For example, anyone can contact a mailing list company and purchase a list of names and addresses for all computer professionals living in zip code 22046 that have an income of at least $80,000 per year, own a home, have at least two cars, two kids, work for the government, and have a college education. If you're willing to pay more, the information you receive can be much more detailed than that.

A great deal of personal information must be stored on computers to make government and businesses function efficiently—we would be annoyed with the results if they stopped doing so. However, because so much information about us is stored on computers, we all have a personal interest in security measures effective enough to prevent someone from stealing our credit card numbers, our medical files, or our military records.

Ongoing debates pit the privacy advocates against those advocating a free flow of information or the need to maintain personal information in government or commercial databases. Who should be able to obtain your credit report (listing all your credit cards, balances, any late payments, loans applied for, mortgages, etc.)? Who should be allowed to obtain your medical records, with or without your permission? Who should be allowed to see copies of your old tax returns? How can a company that gathers information about you use that information?

 Some of the laws regulating privacy issues include the Electronic Communications Privacy Act (U.S. Code, title 18, section 2701) and the Electronic Freedom of Information Act. To see these laws, you can visit *www.law.cornell.edu/uscode* and use the search function or the Title/Section fields halfway down the page.

Laws and government regulations have something to say about who can access your credit records, but when businesses are involved, the answers are uncertain. A company can ask you for information about yourself; once they have that information, do you own it or do they? Can you tell them not to use it for marketing purposes? Can you tell them not to sell it to another company?

 Some people are happy to share basic information about themselves, their preferences, and their habits, either electronically or by regular mail. They like receiving catalogs with products that interest them, and they like getting coupons and special offers. Companies gather and trade personal data primarily for this reason: to get their products to the people most likely to want them.

However, with the growth of the Web, many people became concerned with how their personal information was being used or resold. A company that hadn't made much money selling products on the Web could make a tidy profit by selling information on its customers to other companies. Now every reputable Web site has a link—on either the home page or the page where a user enters personal information, such as a shopping cart page—to the company's privacy policy. A **privacy policy** is a voluntary statement by a company about how it will and will not use data that it collects about users or customers. Figure 7-1 shows a good example of a privacy policy from the site *www.consumerreports.org*. This example is clearly worded and includes a link to the site's public security policy as well (that link appears at the bottom of the privacy policy and is not visible in the figure).

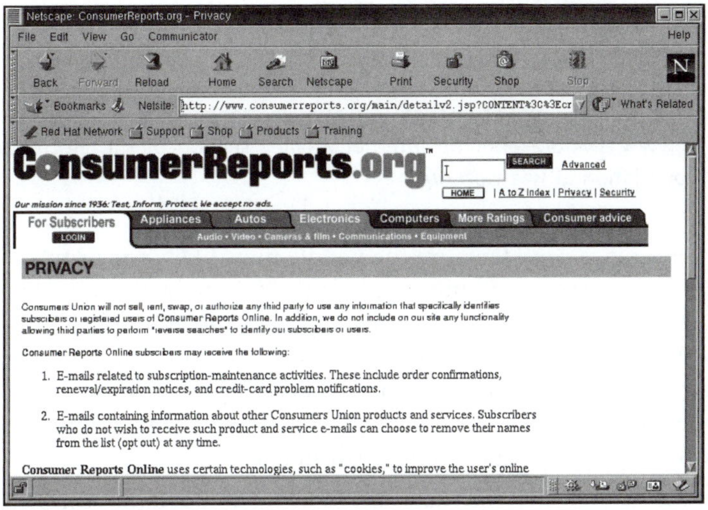

Figure 7-1 A privacy policy

The privacy policy is important to you as the system administrator, because seeing that its terms are carried out may be your responsibility. Privacy policies are usually lengthy, but the sum of their contents is usually similar to one of the following:

- We don't collect or save any information about visitors to our Web site. Nothing but your IP address is logged, and that is used only collectively for statistical purposes in maintaining a viable Web site.

- We collect information in order to complete a sale or register users, but we do not share that information with any other company for any purpose, nor do we use that information to contact you about our products and services.

- We collect information on visitors to our site and use patterns in that information to determine whether you might be interested in some of our other products. If we think you might be interested, we will contact you with marketing information about that product. You can ask us not to contact you if you choose.

- We collect information about you and share that information with our partners who may have products that we think you would enjoy hearing about.

One of the raging debates about privacy (and Internet marketing in general) is whether users should have to opt in or opt out. Using an **opt-in** scheme, you will not receive advertisements unless you specifically say "yes, put me on the mailing list." Much more common is the **opt-out** scheme, in which you receive advertisements (by email, mail, telephone, fax, etc.) unless you contact a company and say "take me off the mailing list." By that time, of course, they may have sold your name to sixteen other companies who don't know that you have opted out. Also note that companies often speak of their "marketing partners." This usually just refers to other companies that have purchased your customer information, thinking that if you bought from company X, you are likely to enjoy their products also.

 If you are interested in privacy issues, visit the Electronic Privacy Information Center at *www.epic.org* and the Internet Privacy section of the Electronic Frontier Foundation at *www.eff.org*.

Lawyers and marketing vice presidents are the people most likely to create a privacy policy. However, because the system administrator is the person with immediate access to data that is collected on an Internet site, he or she plays a role in implementing that policy. As previously mentioned, privacy is the personal aspect of computer security: if you don't use adequate security measures to protect personal information collected by the Internet site you manage, a privacy policy assuring users of your good intentions and plans for their personal information is not worth much.

This places an appropriate burden on you as the system administrator; the system administrator is the person best able to maintain privacy by properly securing the systems on which data is stored.

Ethics and System Administrators

That "burden" brings us to the topic of ethics. Many professionals have a code of ethics: doctors take the Hippocratic oath; government officials must uphold national or state constitutions; lawyers have codes of professional responsibility as well as ethical guidelines. All of these sets of ethical guidelines are voluntary. Though violating them brings no punishment, ethical standards are not the same as laws; ethics revolves around the question of doing the right thing at the right time, for the right reason.

The details of every possible ethical difficulty can't be written out like the laws of the land. Instead, codes of conduct, or ethical guidelines, outline the principles that members of a profession follow. They use those principles to make decisions when difficult situations arise. Ethical codes are based on both philosophy and religion; they are moral guidelines that make society pleasant and livable for everyone. They often play an important role when a great deal of trust is placed in a professional by people who have little or no knowledge of the specialized work of that professional. For doctors and lawyers, this is obvious. For system administrators, it is at least obvious to you, though perhaps not to your employer or to your "customers"—the end users that you support.

The more networked the world becomes—the more dependent on the Internet, on computerized databases, and on digital communications—the more we all depend on the men and women who are the gatekeepers of those systems. Furthermore, the complexity of those systems, like human physiology or the U.S. legal code, is beyond the comprehension of people who are not dedicated to making sense of it. For example, though the president of General Electric has no idea how to maintain a Web site or how to extract statistical sales information from an e-commerce application, the entire company relies on such information.

Consider the privacy policies that are used on Web sites, the information that they safeguard, and the security concerns mentioned above. The person entrusted with the metaphorical keys to all of these critical components of business and government operation is the system administrator. Remember this: trust and power go together. The system administrator is necessarily trusted, because no one else has his or her abilities. Likewise, the position holds a tremendous amount of power—often out of proportion to its salary or prestige. This is because of the information that the system administrator controls. As a system administrator, take the trust of your employer very seriously. The more you validate that trust over time, the more you will find satisfaction in your work and the more you will be rewarded for it. The rewards come in the form of increasing authority or power, more money, expressions of gratitude, or perhaps in forms according to what your employer thinks your contribution deserves.

Note

Not all employers recognize the value of a skilled system administrator, but it is never appropriate to take revenge on a bad employer by violating their trust. You still have responsibilities to internal and external customers, as well as your own integrity, to consider. Move on to another employer if necessary. Your best revenge will be your former employer's difficulty in replacing you.

Very few people set out to act unethically—to break rules of conduct that can lead to embarrassment, loss of position, or even criminal prosecution. However, time pressure and conflicting goals can cause people to make regrettable decisions. Ethics codes were developed to define the role of system administrators in an organization and to increase the respectability and raise standards of behavior in the profession. After all, it is always easier to make a decision before the pressure is on. As you review the ethics codes for system administrators and other technical positions, you should think about difficult situations that might arise and how you would or should respond to them. When challenges do arise, you will already have reasoned out your response and will not be tempted to make a decision you would later regret.

Many professional organizations support system administrators. You are probably familiar already with the SAIR/GNU organization for Linux and Gnu software certification (see *www.linuxcertification.com*) and the Linux Professional Institute (see *www.lpi.org*).

Other organizations are not specific to Linux. The largest professional group for system administrators is the System Administrators Guild (SAGE). SAGE is part of the Advanced Computing Systems Association, which goes by the name USENIX (see *www.sage.org* and *www.usenix.org*). SAGE has thousands of members and sponsors regular technical conferences (with small product trade shows attached) dedicated to current system administration topics on a variety of operating system platforms (though SAGE and USENIX are noted fans of Linux and UNIX generally). The main conference, called LISA, moves to a different city each year. The SAGE Web site referred to above provides details on upcoming conferences.

The SAGE Web site includes the SAGE Code of Ethics, created by Lee Damon, and information about the SAGE Ethics Working Group. Members of SAGE are expected to abide by the ten items in the code, which is reprinted below. (You can find it online at *www.usenix.org/sage/publications/code_of_ethics_newdraft.html*.)

As a member of the international community of systems administrators, I will be guided by the following principles:

1. Fair Treatment: I will treat everyone fairly. I will not discriminate against anyone on grounds such as age, disability, gender, sexual orientation, religion, race, national origin, or any other non-business related issue.

2. Privacy: I will only access private information on computer systems when it is necessary in the course of my duties. I will maintain and protect the confidentiality of any information to which I may have access, regardless of the method by which I came into knowledge of it. I acknowledge and will follow all relevant laws governing information privacy.

3. Communication: I will keep users informed about computing matters that may affect them—such as conditions of acceptable use, sharing of common resources, maintenance of security, occurrence of system monitoring, and any relevant legal obligations.

4. System Integrity: I will strive to ensure the integrity of the systems for which I have responsibility, using all appropriate means—such as regularly maintaining software and hardware; analyzing levels of system performance and activity; and, as far as possible, preventing unauthorized use or access.

5. Cooperation: I will cooperate with and support my fellow computing professionals. I acknowledge the community responsibility that is fundamental to the integrity of local, national, and international network and computing resources.

6. Honesty: I will be honest about my competence and will seek help when necessary. When my professional advice is sought, I will be impartial. I will avoid conflicts of interest; if they do arise I will declare them and recuse myself if necessary.

7. Education: I will continue to update and enhance my technical knowledge and other work-related skills through training, study, and the sharing of information and experiences with my fellow professionals. I will help others improve their skills and understanding where my skills and experience allow me to do so.

8. Social Responsibility: I will continue to enlarge my understanding of the social and legal issues relating to computing environments. When appropriate, I will communicate that understanding to others and encourage the writing and adoption of policies and laws about computer systems consistent with these ethical principles.

9. Quality: I will be honest about the occurrence and impact of mistakes, and where possible and appropriate I will attempt to correct them. I will strive to achieve and maintain a safe, healthy, and productive workplace.

10. Ethical Responsibility: I will lead by example, maintaining a consistently high ethical standard and degree of professionalism in the performance of all my duties.

Other organizations with ethics codes include two engineering groups: the Association for Computing Machinery (ACM, at *www.acm.org*) and the Institute for Electrical and Electronic Engineers (IEEE, at *www.ieee.org*). These organizations focus more on engineering new systems than on managing existing systems, but their sites contain a lot of valuable information. The ethics codes are usually linked from the home page.

One advantage of becoming familiar with a code of ethics geared specifically to system administrators is that it helps you anticipate situations that are most likely to occur in your work as a system administrator, instead of being more generally oriented to good business practices.

 A final comment on the topic of codes of ethics: think of them as minimum standards of behavior in areas that cannot be easily policed. After pondering these codes, decide the personal impact you want to have and how you can achieve your goals.

7

RISK ASSESSMENT AND SECURITY POLICIES

Computer security presents a paradox: the more secure a system is, the less usable it is. No system is totally secure unless it is totally unusable; if someone can gain access, then the wrong person can gain access as well, given the right information. The trick is to make a system both usable and reasonably secure, or, put another way, to make a system highly secure without undue annoyance to authorized system users.

One security method must be debunked at the outset: so-called "security through obscurity." This method says that if no one knows about your server, or your IP address, or what software you're running, then you are safe. However, you cannot hide on the Internet. Computers are too fast, software is too widely used, and some crackers are just too clever. The key to good security is not to hope that no one finds your system's security weaknesses, but rather to eliminate those weaknesses.

 Not all crackers are bright; some use prepackaged software "kits" or scripts created by skilled crackers. These scripts let even neophytes break into systems that have not taken basic security precautions. Such crackers are called **script-kiddies**. They are easy to thwart, though many systems remain vulnerable to their standardized attacks.

Understanding System Vulnerabilities

Crackers can attack different parts of a networked computer system:

- The hardware components
- The software programs
- The data used by the software programs

Of these, the most serious threat is to the data. Hardware can be replaced and software can be reinstalled, but data is the lifeblood of many organizations. Even with a good backup policy in place and an emergency response plan worked out, data losses from cracker attacks can cost a company millions of dollars, because data is generated on the fly and might not be backed up until the end of the day. If you have not taken minimal precautions by regularly backing up your data, a malicious or careless cracker can destroy several years of work in a few minutes.

Crackers have different goals in breaking in to a system:

- Crackers may steal data for their own use, usually trying to avoid detection. This could mean customer sales data, personal information, trade secrets, or similar material. Industrial espionage—though apparently not widely practiced—would use this type of attack. Stolen credit card numbers are another example.

- Crackers may corrupt data, either accidentally as they explore files on a system or on purpose to affect changes in the organization or to damage the creditability or efficiency of the organization. Data corruption may be obvious, as with a defaced Web home page, or it may be intentionally hidden, such as bank account figures changed in a way that is unlikely to be discovered until an audit sometime later.

- Crackers may try to block access to the system, as in a Denial-of-Service (DoS) attack. In such an attack regular users are unable to reach your Web site because it is overwhelmed with Web page requests from a cracker who is trying to cripple your system.

The majority of security incidents result from the actions of users within an organization's network, not from outside attacks. These could be disgruntled current employees trying to wreak havoc or a technical person who tries to explore beyond what has been authorized and instead gets caught.

As you may have learned in discussions of system backup procedures and high-availability computing, any time a computer system cannot be used as intended, it is effectively "down." If a DoS attack or corrupted data make a server unavailable, a cracker has achieved his or her purpose.

Don't confuse high-availability or backup procedures with system security. Security focuses on preventing unauthorized access, which may or may not cause system downtime. (For example, stolen data will not shut down your server.) High-availability hardware and maintenance of good backups help to recover when a security breach causes downtime, but they are also used when hardware failures or natural disasters—unrelated to security concerns—bring down a system.

As with high-availability and backup procedures, security should begin with a careful analysis of the assets you are trying to protect and their value. Consider, for example, the following hypothetical statements that reflect different security concerns:

- A bank manager says: "Our reputation as a secure place to do business electronically is critical to our future. If the public saw a news story that our servers had been broken into, it would be a disaster for us."

- A nonprofit foundation manager says: "Our Web site is a public information service. It doesn't collect any user data, nor is the Web server tied to any other system in our company. If it goes down, we'll look bad to the small number of visitors who were unable to view the site, but nothing beyond that is really at risk, and we can restart the server without much trouble."

- The president of a large insurance company says: "Our Internet servers connect hundreds of our employees to headquarters. If those servers are unavailable, we lose a lot of business because no one can write new insurance policies."

- The founder of an e-commerce company says: "We do business *only* via the Internet. If our servers are unavailable, we lose, on average, nearly $1million per hour, plus we encourage people to shop elsewhere, because we are unavailable: our reputation and future are in jeopardy."

No one wants their system to be broken in to, but you can better judge the appropriate level of effort to put into security measures if you understand the assets that you are protecting, whether they include reputation, revenue generation, secret data, or other factors. Although security by obscurity is never wise, organizations invest differently based on how vigilant they decide to be. For example, the nonprofit foundation in the above examples might decide to place a Web server at an ISP's office (this is called **co-locating** the Web server), and rely on the ISP's security measures to protect the Web server. However, the bank manager—whose security concerns center on keeping the system running and protecting customers' private data—would likely never choose to co-locate a server at a standard ISP.

Wherever they are located, computers are vulnerable to attack using several standard techniques that you should understand in order to consider how you can protect against each one:

- **Password cracking** is a technique in which a cracker obtains a user's password, either by using a program that examines millions of passwords until the correct one is found, or by guessing based on personal knowledge about the user (don't ever use your pet's name as a password). With a valid password in hand, a cracker can log on to your system without any signs of suspicious activity. Chapter 9 describes password security in detail.

- **Trojan horse** attacks occur when you run a program that you obtained from an untrustworthy source or that was installed on your machine by a cracker without your knowledge. The program appears to function normally but actually performs hidden tasks that render your system insecure and allow the cracker to gain access. Email viruses are a common way for Trojan horse programs to enter a computer system, though these viruses themselves are rarely a problem for Linux servers because of the way that Linux multitasking operates. More common on Linux servers are Trojan horses that run with root access, appearing to be valid system utilities.

 If you are not familiar with the term Trojan horse, it refers to the time centuries ago when the Greeks were laying siege to Troy and they built a large wooden horse. They hid their best soldiers inside it and presented the horse as a gift to the Greeks. The Trojans pulled the horse into their fort and were subsequently defeated as a result of this trick. The story is recounted in Homer's *The Illiad* and is the basis of the saying "Beware of Greeks bearing gifts," or as it has been said in this context, "Beware of geeks bearing gifts."

- **Buffer overflow attacks** rely on a weakness in the design of a program. These weaknesses are usually very difficult to find because they are based on complex logic within a large program (such as a DNS server). However, once discovered by a skilled cracker, the buffer overflow is generally not hard to exploit as a security hole, and the cracker may well inform others of the problem. A cracker must find a specific sequence of steps, or specific input to give to a program, so that the program becomes confused and tries to use computer memory inappropriately. The buffer, or memory space, reserved for a part of the program overflows. The result can be corruption of system data, a crashed server, or even direct root access, any of which may be the goal of the cracker.

- Denial-of-Service (DoS) attacks, mentioned previously, try to overwhelm your system so that valid users cannot access it. This is often done by cracking numerous insecure systems and using all of them at the same time to send requests to a server. Services such as DNS and the Web are among those vulnerable to this type of attack. Because a server is designed to accept any incoming connection, this type of attack can be very hard to anticipate and prevent, though features in modern routers and in newer protocols like IPv6 make prevention easier.

After you complete this book, you will not be a security expert, but you will know enough to prevent common security problems from wreaking havoc on your server; you will know enough about how crackers operate to be watchful for new or obscure problems; and you will know where to continue your education about computer security. Security is often divided conceptually into four layers. The remaining chapters of this book follow this model in discussing the technical details of securing your system.

- *Physical security* involves physical access to your Linux server. This topic is not discussed further in this book, but is an important initial step in computer security. Physical access to a server enables crackers to reboot the server using a floppy disk of their own design, actually remove the hard disk, or perhaps to access an open command-line window with root access. Servers should be locked away so that only the system administrator can access the computer.

- *User security*, or *password security* (covered in Chapter 9) means making certain that the person who logs in with a given user account is actually the person authorized to use that account. User security is also concerned with creating appropriate limitations on the activities of authorized users. For example, a user might only be allowed to log in between 9 A.M. and 5 P.M.

- *File security* (covered in Chapter 10) means making sure that files are accessed only by those who are authorized to use them, and that changes to system files do not indicate a breach of security. (For example, a changed system utility file might indicate that a Trojan horse program has been added to the system to replace a valid utility.)

- *Network security* (covered in Chapters 11 and 12) is the broadest security topic because it involves dozens of network services, any one of which may present security challenges. Because many network services have root access in Linux, an insecure configuration can allow outside users to have root access to the server via the network service. You have learned about layers in networking protocol stacks; network security can operate at different layers as well. For example, IP packets can be blocked or allowed using a firewall (see Chapter 11), TCP packets can be controlled using TCP Wrappers (described in Chapter 4), and individual applications may also have their own security mechanism, as the access control mechanisms in the Apache Web server illustrate.

7

Social Security

In one sense, computer security is really about people, about knowing why people act as they do and whom to trust. This is true from the perspective of both the system administrator and the cracker.

The system administrator must watch carefully where he or she obtains the operating system and programs that are run on the server. For all its security features, as detailed in coming chapters, the fact that Linux includes full source code means that a random copy of a Linux kernel taken from the Internet might have been altered by a cracker to permit access via a special "back door" in the source code.

A **back door** is a method of accessing a program or a computer system that is known to its creator but not to other users of the system. It is undocumented and hidden from everyone except the person who created it. For example, a system administrator might create a second account with root access in case the standard root account is disabled by a cracker. Or, a cracker might send out a system administration utility that permits broad access to a host by sending a special code word via the network.

The official site for the Linux kernel source code is *www.kernel.org*. Many mirror sites are maintained around the world. From this site or its mirrors you can download the latest version of Linux or any patches (as described in the next section). Most users prefer to get updates from the vendor from whom they purchased (or downloaded) their copy of Linux. This has the advantage of keeping you in contact with the security bulletins of your vendor and also ensuring that the options set in the kernel closely resemble those you are already using.

Although the Linux kernel is unique among popular operating systems in having full source code available, knowing where your programs are coming from is advisable for any service you intend to run. As a cautionary tale, consider that a few years ago someone broke into the main download archive for a popular FTP server program in Holland and uploaded a corrupted version of the FTP server software. Many people downloaded the compromised software (which would have allowed access to the cracker on any system with that FTP server installed) before the act was noticed.

That was a very unusual circumstance. Generally speaking, downloading server software from its main archive site or a mirror site listed on the main archive site is a very safe way to obtain what you need. Some people consider a Linux vendor such as SuSE, Red Hat Software, or Caldera International a better route because these companies test each product before burning them onto a CD and shipping them. Their Web sites are theoretically still vulnerable to similar attacks when they release updated software via the Web, but apparently no attacks of this type have succeeded.

Either way, the point is to be attentive about where you get the software you run. Be aware that crackers can modify open source software. If they can entice or deceive you into installing it, they have an open door to your systems.

In the next chapter you will learn about encryption technologies. One of these allows programs in rpm package format to be digitally signed using a special numeric key. Software authors or companies (like Red Hat or Caldera) digitally "sign" the rpm files that they distribute. You can use the encryption software described in Chapter 8 to check whether a given rpm file has a valid signature, thereby ensuring that it came unmodified from the organization or person that you think it came from.

Another aspect of computer security from the social perspective is the attitude of the cracker that people are tools. **Social engineering** is the common term used for a cracker manipulating someone to extract needed information about a system. A specific (and all too frequently accurate) example of social engineering occurs when a cracker obtains the name of a user on a system and then calls the user on the phone. The conversation might go something like this:

Cracker: "Hi, this is John down in system engineering. Have you noticed your system slowing down some this morning?" (Because the system is likely to occasionally be slow on many networks, this is a fairly safe line.)

User: "Uh, yeah, a little, I guess. What's wrong?"

Cracker: "We're upgrading the server software and some information in your account appears to have been deleted, but I think if I log in with your regular account name I can recover it."

User: "With my thomasw account?"

Cracker: "Exactly. Can you just spell the password for me so I make sure I get it right?"

Many users, unless instructed otherwise, are helpful and trusting, and offer their password to any stranger over the phone who is bold enough to use such a ruse. Other common social engineering methods are so simple that they have been used in several movies: a walk through an office can yield a harvest of passwords from people who post their password on a slip of paper at their desk so they don't forget it. People also use their child's or pet's name or spouse's birthday as a password. By learning about a target, a cracker may be able to gain access to a server without using any technology tricks.

Once a cracker has gained access to a system using a valid user account, it is much easier to gain root access to the system. The cracker can work without much time pressure, without having all his actions logged (as a Web server or FTP server would do), and often without fear that he will even be noticed unless the cracker is foolish (e.g., he logs on in the middle of the night) or the system administrator is watchful (i.e., she checks the logs carefully using specialized security tools).

Chapter 9 discusses password security in depth, but it begins with educating users and instructing them to take some responsibility for security. No system administrator should ever ask a user for a password. It should never be necessary. As an ethical matter, a system administrator should not know the password of any user, because so many users (foolishly) use the same or similar passwords on their computer at work, their computer at home, their bank account, and numerous other places.

Social engineering lets a cracker play on the ignorance, fear, or trust of users to gain information that he can use to access a computer system. This information might include passwords, dial-up modem phone numbers, numeric access codes, or account usernames.

Creating a Security Policy

In 1998 the consulting firm Ernst & Young conducted a survey of over 4,000 information managers (managers similar in function to system administrators). The survey revealed that over 60% of those surveyed had no written plan to deal with a security "incident" (a break-in). One of your first steps as a system administrator in any organization should be to create a solid security policy if one does not already exist.

As with other policies for backups, disaster recovery, privacy, and the like, creating a security policy forces you to think through thorny issues and difficult decisions before a crisis strikes. It also helps you to prepare your systems and your end users as thoroughly as possible to avert such a crisis. A security policy is a written document that may do any or all of the following:

- Analyze what assets are at risk and need careful protection through computer security.

- Provide statistics to end users regarding the dangers involved in connecting to the Internet. This information may also serve as justification for spending money on security software, security consultants, etc. (The Ernst & Young survey provides some examples. See *www.ey.com/publicate*.)

- Describe procedures to be followed to keep the operating system and network server software upgraded with the latest security patches.

- Outline access levels, specifying which types of employees or outside personnel (such as independent contractors) are to be allowed access to each part of the organization's information systems.

- List specific tasks that need to be completed to make systems secure, such as specific hardware or software to be installed, with a timeline for completing these tasks.

- Compile specific actions to make the system secure after a reboot. If everything is not automated, this would include what scripts must be run, who has the passwords to start the system again, and so forth.

- Describe procedures that all end users should follow to help ensure the integrity of the organization's computer systems and data. This includes such items as password changing policies (for example, minimum lengths, how often they should be changed, and any steps taken to ensure compliance).

- Outline a procedure to follow when an intrusion by a cracker has been detected. Who should be informed, and how should system data subject to corruption or theft be handled?

- Merge the security policies with plans for disaster recovery in case a cracker causes a massive failure.

As with the many other written plans that a good system administrator will create or be familiar with, a security policy puts managers on notice of the dangers that an organization faces. It provides financial justification for the often expensive steps needed to secure information systems. It also prepares the minds of system administrators and users for what is inevitable on any but the smallest networks: someone will try to break in. Watching a break-in or seeing that it has already happened can be paralyzing for an organization that has not planned for it. The reactions range from "shut everything down" to "let's ignore him and hope he doesn't do too much damage while he's in there." Neither route should be part of your security policy document. Instead, prepare your systems and yourself for what may happen, see how you can respond effectively, then follow up and execute the plan you have created.

SECURITY-FOCUSED ORGANIZATIONS

In addition to the professional organizations for system administrators, such as SAGE, organizations that specialize in security can also help you learn more and implement what you learn. They provide a clearinghouse for recent security information. By regularly accessing this information, you lessen the chance that a cracker will be able to use a newly discovered security hole to exploit a weakness in your Linux server.

Upgrading Your Linux System

Your first goal should be to keep your system upgraded using information from security organizations whenever a security issue is discovered. Issues can arise with both the Linux kernel and the programs that run on Linux. Not every upgrade announcement relates to the security of the system; many only affect which hardware devices are supported, or simply add new features or documentation to an existing program. In particular, upgrades to the Linux kernel are rarely done for security reasons. If you manage a Linux system that is running smoothly, you shouldn't feel any need to upgrade the kernel unless a security-specific announcement is made about it.

Most of the software upgrades for security problems come in the form of a patch. A patch doesn't change any of the program features; it only repairs a programming error that lets crackers gain access to your system.

The best way to stay informed about upgrades and patches is to subscribe to the security notification service of a reputable Linux vendor such as Red Hat Software or Caldera International. You will receive emails whenever a security issue arises, describing the issue, what specific program versions are affected, and how to fix the problem. The problem is usually fixed by a patch that you can immediately download. The first part of a security alert that was emailed by Caldera International to all security list subscribers in December 2001 is shown here.

```
Caldera International, Inc. Security Advisory

Subject:            Linux - Local vulnerability in OpenSSH
Advisory number:    CSSA-2001-042.1
Issue date:         2001, December 14
Cross reference:    CSSA-2001-042.0
```

```
1. Problem Description
   This is a revised advisory for the 'UseLogin' vulnerability.
   The original advisory declared the vulnerability as a remote
   vulnerability, which is not the case. The vulnerability
   requires the attacker to have a local account, making it a
   local vulnerability.

   The OpenSSH team has reported a vulnerability in the OpenSSH
   server that allows local users to obtain root privilege if
   the server has the UseLogin option enabled. This option is
   off by default on OpenLinux, so a default installation is
   not vulnerable.

   We nevertheless recommend to our customers to upgrade to the
   fixed package.
```

```
2. Vulnerable Versions
   System                              Package
   -----------------------------------------------------------------
   OpenLinux 2.3                       not vulnerable
   OpenLinux eServer 2.3.1             All packages previous to
   and OpenLinux eBuilder              openssh-2.9p2-4
   OpenLinux eDesktop 2.4              All packages previous to
                                       openssh-2.9p2-4
   OpenLinux Server 3.1                All packages previous to
                                       openssh-2.9p2-4
   OpenLinux Workstation 3.1           All packages previous to
                                       openssh-2.9p2-4
3. Solution
   Workaround
      Make sure that you do not have the UseLogin option enabled.
      In /etc/ssh/sshd_config, the UseLogin option should either
      be commented out, or should be set to "no".
   The proper solution is to upgrade to the latest packages.
```

If you received this email notification, you would follow the instructions given to upgrade your software, typically by downloading a new copy. The exact file you download would depend on the version of Linux you are running. Once the new file was on your system and you had verified that it was trustworthy (as described in Chapter 8), you would need to stop the server (if it was running in standalone mode), upgrade the package, then start the server again.

Upgrades are usually much simpler (and also more secure) when you use a distribution that relies on software packages, such as the Debian package format (deb) or the Red Hat package format (rpm). Linux kernel patches are relatively rare—security holes are not infrequent in some server daemons, but they don't occur much in the kernel itself. When a kernel patch is announced, you must download it as source code, recompile your Linux kernel, then restart your Linux server to activate the new kernel.

The importance of these patches is not lost on Linux vendors. For example, Red Hat Software now has a service called Red Hat Network. You receive a limited-time subscription to this service when you purchase a copy of Professional Red Hat Linux; you can subscribe for longer periods by paying a fee. Red Hat Network informs you of security patches as well as version upgrades to packages you are using by automatically checking the Red Hat Internet site at specific intervals. If you choose to configure this feature, Red Hat Network can automatically download the new software, upgrade the system, and restart the server. This is an excellent way to keep abreast of security upgrades as they are made available—your system would never be subject to security breaches that had been documented but that you had not yet installed. Using a system like Red Hat Network doesn't remove the burden of properly configuring the programs you run. It only means that a break-in is unlikely to be the result of a programming error of which you weren't aware.

Some have suggested that Linux is a less secure operating system because its source code is openly distributed. Nothing could be further from the truth. Because Linux (and hundreds of other programs) provide source code, patches to repair newly discovered security holes are normally available within a few *hours* of discovery. Compare this to the stalling and excuses that some software companies make while they figure out a patch, leaving customers with nothing to do but shut down their servers or hope that crackers don't discover their vulnerability before the patch comes out, perhaps weeks later. Relying on closed source software is nothing but security through obscurity and is a bad bet.

The Security Experts

Two organizations are known as particular bastions of computer security information: the CERT Coordination Center and the System Administration, Networking, and Security (SANS) Institute.

The **CERT Coordination Center (CERT/CC)** is a federally funded software engineering institute operated by Carnegie-Mellon University. It was formerly called the Computer Emergency Response Team and focused on handling computer security incidents; most security experts likely still think of it in those terms. The CERT/CC Web site, *www.cert.org,* maintains lists of security vulnerabilities, alerts, incident reports, and so on. Figure 7-2 shows the home page for CERT/CC and illustrates the types of information the site provides.

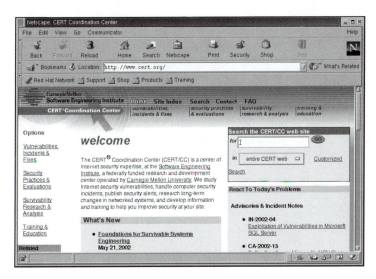

Figure 7-2 The CERT/CC Web site

The **System Administration, Networking, and Security (SANS) Institute** (or simply SANS) is a prestigious and well-regarded education and research organization. Its members include most of the leading computer security experts in the country.

To take advantage of SANS information, start by visiting the Web site at *www.sans.org*. The home page is shown in Figure 7-3. There you can subscribe to mailing lists of security alerts for various platforms. You can also review information about the SANS Storm Center at *www.incidents.org*. This is a statistical summary of what attacks are taking place at more than 3,000 firewalls in over 60 countries around the world. By analyzing these attacks, SANS security experts are able to provide guidance to other network administrators before new attacks become widespread.

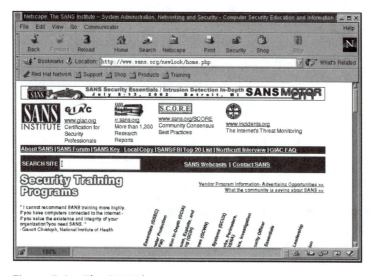

Figure 7-3   The SANS home page

SANS also coordinates with the FBI to provide a Top 20 list of the most widely used strategies being used to attack computer systems. You can review this list to make certain that your systems are protected. For each of the top 20 security issues, the list provides:

- A description of the security issue
- A list of which systems are or may be affected by the issue
- A procedure for determining whether your system is affected
- Steps to protect your system by removing the vulnerability

The first few items on the list are perennial problems that any wise system administrator should avoid: avoid accounts with weak or nonexistent passwords, make sure you have good system backups, and check the default configurations of the network-capable programs you have installed on your system. You can also find more interesting items on the list. A summary of the list, excluding the items that are specific to Windows operating systems, is shown here. The list changes over time, and is current here as of mid-2002.

1. Default installations of operating systems and applications that provide little or no security

2. Accounts with no password or a weak password

3. Nonexistent or incomplete backups

4. Having a large number of open network ports (not blocked by a firewall)

5. Not filtering IP packets for correct incoming and outgoing IP addresses (this is called IP spoofing and is described in Chapters 11 and 12)

6. Nonexistent or incomplete logging of system activity

7. Vulnerable CGI script programs on Web servers

8. Buffer overflow errors in UNIX RPC services

9. Sendmail vulnerabilities

10. Weaknesses in BIND (implemented in Linux by the `named` daemon)

11. Weaknesses in R commands (`rlogin`, `rsh`, and `rcp`)

12. Problems with the LPD printer daemon

13. `Sadmind` and `mountd` (the `sadmind` program mentioned here is not used in Linux, and so would not apply to your Linux servers)

14. Default settings in SNMP network management software that inform a cracker about systems on the network

The information on the SANS Web site is continually updated and includes a number of Linux-specific security resources. Beyond this, SANS maintains a highly regarded hands-on certification program for security professionals: the **Global Information Assurance Certification (GIAC)** program. Related to this effort, SANS focuses a great deal of energy on providing technical conferences in cities around the world. These are amazing conferences, where top security experts teach hands-on courses to network administrators who face security threats each day. Examples of recent course offerings include the following:

- A multiday series on security essentials
- Investigating incidents (break-ins)
- Managerial and legal issues in security
- Network traffic analysis
- Techniques used by crackers
- Protecting the perimeter of your network with firewalls

The SANS conferences are quite expensive (over $2,000 per person), but SANS operates a volunteer program by which you can attend conference sessions for free in exchange for helping produce the conference. See the Web site for details.

 In addition to CERT/CC and SANS, you should review the Web sites *www.securityfocus.com* and *www.securitymanagement.com*. Each contains many additional security resources.

THE U.S. GOVERNMENT AND COMPUTER SECURITY

Because computer security is increasingly viewed as part of our national security, the U.S. federal government continues to increase its involvement with the computer security industry. Two examples of new roles the government is playing are prosecutor of computer crimes and an information clearinghouse to encourage good security practices.

Security and the Law

When crackers began practicing their craft on an unsuspecting world, law enforcement agencies had no laws aimed at stopping them. The FBI tried to rely on fraud statutes (laws) or other statutes related to the damage that the cracker did (such as stealing money by breaking into a bank computer), rather than the specific act of unauthorized computer access.

That situation changed when Congress passed the Computer Fraud and Abuse Act of 1986. This law made it a crime to access a computer without authorization, either for financial gain or to damage U.S. government sites. Various fines and prison terms were the penalties for violating this Act. Additional laws were passed in more recent years to give the FBI and other law enforcement agencies additional tools to stop the damage that crackers were doing. These laws include:

- The Computer Security Act of 1987

- The National Information Infrastructure Protection Act of 1996 (for a good discussion of this law, see *www.usdoj.gov/criminal/cybercrime/1030_anal.html*)

- The Patriot Act of 2002

Prosecuting a cracker is different from prosecuting many other criminals. The person investigating the crime may not have a strong initial understanding of the technology involved and so may not realize what damage has been done; the prosecutor may also be uncertain which law provides the best fit and thus gives the best method of stopping the cracker's activities. These problems are greatly reduced when national law enforcement is involved, as the FBI and others have special units devoted to these types of crimes. Even then, however, the lawmakers can have a hard time keeping up with technology.

Some resources for learning more about these topics are listed here:

- *thomas.loc.gov* (legislative information online through the Library of Congress)

- *www.law.cornell.edu/uscode* (a repository of searchable legal information)

- *www.findlaw.com* (an all-purpose legal search engine)

- *www.senate.gov* and *www.house.gov* (Web sites of the U.S. Congressional houses)

- *www.gsa.gov* (reference site for federal lawyers)

Government Agency Resources

Many different parts of U.S. state and federal governments are concerned with proper information security, despite the fact that such security in other parts of those same governments has proven to be sadly lax, as shown by the many and widely publicized security breaches at government and military sites.

The following list describes some of the key resources for learning about U.S. government involvement with computer security and computer crime.

- The FBI created a National Computer Crime Squad in 1991 to focus on cases involving crackers (they use the term hackers). The FBI maintains extensive online resources related to computer crime. See *www.fbi.gov*.

- The U.S. Department of Justice, Criminal Division, includes a section devoted to Computer Crime and Intellectual Property. This section works with the FBI to prosecute crackers. See *www.usdoj.gov*.

- The FBI also staffs the **National Infrastructure Protection Center (NIPC)**, a clearinghouse for security information, reports, analysis, and legal data related to these topics. See *www.nipc.gov*. The NIPC was formed by the U.S. Attorney General in February 1998 and seeks to protect critical national infrastructures (such as the Internet backbone and telecom networks) from attack by crackers, foreign or domestic. The Center supports law enforcement with investigations of intrusions, counterintelligence missions (when foreign nationals are involved), and training for investigators and security specialists in both government and the private sector. The staff of NIPC comes from the FBI's Computer Investigations and Infrastructure Threat Assessment Center (CIITAS).

- The Department of the Treasury runs the Secret Service and is responsible for protecting the country against counterfeiting and money laundering. It also operates a separate organization dedicated to protecting against financial fraud (which is now typically done using computers). This group is the Financial Crimes Enforcement Network, or FinCEN, which you can learn about at *www.treas.gov/fincen* or via the U.S. Treasury Home Page at *www.ustreas.gov*.

SECURITY-FOCUSED LINUX PRODUCTS

The popularity of Linux, its freely available source code, and the need for increasingly secure networks has led to the development of several security-focused versions of Linux. These versions are also open source, but they add special features to Linux that make it more like the high-grade secure versions of UNIX used by places like the Central Intelligence Agency and some military installations.

 A word to the wise is in order: Don't accept at face value the claims a company makes for the security of its products. Security is a complex topic, one that has produced as many charlatans as it has experts. Even well-intentioned companies may be unaware of the limitations of their claims of "rock-solid, impenetrable security." Keep your skepticism well-sharpened and be prepared to investigate thoroughly.

As one example, consider the experiences of Microsoft. Their Point-to-Point Tunneling Protocol (PPTP), used to create secure networks between different corporate offices, had been widely praised and received awards. It was later examined by security experts who found five separate flaws in its design and referred to its technology as "kindergarten cryptography." Likewise, in the summer of 1999, Microsoft placed online a server running its Web server, Internet Information Server (IIS), and dared people to crack it as a demonstration of their high-quality, secure products. It lasted less than three hours. Many companies have better reputations for security than Microsoft, but be wary and test vendors' claims whenever possible.

One of the undoubted leaders in information security is the National Security Agency (NSA), a group that has concerned itself with computer security for decades (either to prevent it or to promote it, depending on the target). A fairly recent development at NSA is the release of NSA security-enhanced Linux, an experimental version of Linux that adds new levels of security to the Linux kernel. Security-enhanced Linux is not presently a production operating system, but rather a research project. It runs the Linux kernel on top of another kernel (called a microkernel) that allows each process in Linux to be controlled and handled in isolation. This means that if a single program such as a Web server were to be compromised by a security hole, the user could not access any other programs or data on the system. Security-enhanced Linux allows no root user with complete access to the system. Instead, role-based access control ensures that each program is limited to accessing only what it needs.

You can learn more about security-enhanced Linux and download the source code by visiting *www.nsa.gov/selinux/*. The program is provided in the form of patches to a standard Red Hat Linux kernel, with some additional upgrades to utility programs. When you install the program, it modifies an unused part of the Linux hard disk but maintains compatibility with Linux programs. Complete documentation is included on the NSA Web site.

Another version of Linux with a security focus is Trustix Secure Linux (see *www.trustix.net*). Trustix uses a standard Linux kernel, but it is thoroughly configured to be a server with tight security. It does not include a graphical interface, and network services are not enabled by default. Because it generally assumes that you will connect the server to the Internet, a certain level of paranoia is warranted. Many of the precautions and default settings of Trustix are now used by products like Red Hat Linux when you select a server-type installation and specify a high level of firewall protection during installation. Trustix itself is worth exploring because of its design focus on security.

While Trustix is only used by a small group of security-conscious programmers, Red Hat has the resources to update you on any security issues that arise. After experimenting with different systems, you must judge which makes the best use of your time based on the needs of your network and your skill level with different networking and security tools.

Another product that provides a more security-conscious Linux is the Bastille Linux hardening package (to **harden** a system is to make it more secure against crackers). Bastille is a set of scripts that can be run on Red Hat and Mandrake Linux distributions. (Scripts for Debian, TurboLinux, and SuSE are under development.) Bastille scripts examine your installed Linux system, checking for configurations that present a security hazard. The logic in the Bastille scripts is taken from the SANS Web site and a number of reputable books dedicated to Linux security. Figure 7-4 shows a screen from the Bastille program as it examines a Linux system, provides feedback to the user, and modifies the system as directed.

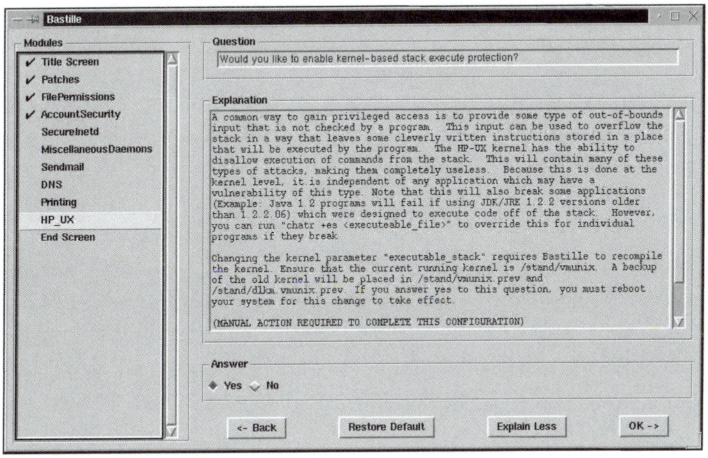

Figure 7-4   The Bastille Linux hardening tool

Using Bastille Linux to harden your Linux system can also help you learn about security, because the Bastille scripts instruct you on the security measures being adopted as your system is reviewed and configuration files are altered. To learn more about Bastille Linux and to download the scripts, visit *www.bastille-linux.org*.

CHAPTER SUMMARY

▫ An amazing number and variety of unauthorized computer access events continually plague network servers all over the world.

▫ Computer security is a serious field that pits crackers against administrators seeking to protect their employers' information assets. It differs from system and network administration generally because it requires the administrator to assume that computer users are malicious.

▫ Computer crime statistics are hard to gather, but billions of dollars are spent annually to recover from unauthorized access; people go to prison for committing computer crimes.

▫ Privacy concerns make computer security a personal issue for anyone using the Internet. A privacy policy is posted on most Web sites and is implemented initially by the system administrator's action or inaction.

▫ System administrators are in a position of great trust and power because of the information they control.

▫ Codes of ethics help system administrators understand professional expectations that can help them create lasting careers and serve both internal and external customers effectively.

▫ Difficult security decisions are best made before a crisis arises, based on a considered long-term view of the consequences of each possible course of action.

▫ Organizations such as SAGE and SANS can help system administrators learn more about security from experts and colleagues.

▫ A proactive approach to security, rather than "security through obscurity," yields the best results in protecting information systems from attack.

▫ Hardware, software, and data are all possible subjects of attack, though data is the most likely target. Methods of attack include a Denial-of-Service (DoS) attack, Trojan horses, buffer overflow attacks, and obtaining passwords.

▫ Crackers may try to steal data, corrupt data, or deny access to your system by legitimate users. Having a written security policy document helps you prepare for all types of attacks by justifying the need for security efforts, informing users of security concerns, and guiding your own actions in defending from or reacting to security breaches.

▫ Social engineering is a potential tool of crackers who contact end users and manipulate them to extract needed information.

▫ You must keep your Linux system upgraded with any security patches to prevent attacks via a known problem with software that you are using.

❒ Many laws now exist to allow prosecution of computer crimes. Many government organizations, led by the FBI, are involved in investigating and prosecuting computer crime.

❒ Security products for Linux may help you improve your security posture, though you must be careful about trusting products that you have not tested.

KEY TERMS

back door — A method of accessing a program or a computer system that is known to its creator but not to other users of the system. It is undocumented and hidden.

buffer overflow attack — A technique for gaining access to a computer system by exploiting a weakness in the design of a computer program. When a cracker follows a specific sequence of steps or provides specific input to a program, the program becomes confused and tries to use computer memory inappropriately. The buffer, or memory space, reserved for a part of the program overflows. The result can be either corruption of system data, a crashed server, or even direct root access.

CERT Coordination Center (CERT/CC) — A federally funded software engineering institute that focuses its attention on computer security issues and provides information to security and system administration professionals around the world; operated by Carnegie-Mellon University.

co-locating — An organization placing a Web server at the office of its ISP, often relying on the ISP's security measures to protect the organization's Web server.

computer crime — Unauthorized access to a computer system.

cracker — A person who breaks the law or ethical rules by accessing computer systems without authorization; called by some a hacker. Some crackers have malicious intentions, others only want to test their skills by exploring areas that they are not authorized to enter.

deface — To alter the text or images on a Web home page.

Denial-of-Service (DoS) attack — A cracker activity that ties up the attacked server or a particular program with so much bogus network traffic that it cannot respond to valid requests.

Global Information Assurance Certification (GIAC) — A hands-on security certification program run by the SANS Institute.

hacker — A highly skilled technology expert who enjoys learning about the intricate workings of computer systems and software. To some people's understanding, a technology expert who maliciously attacks others' computer systems. *See also* cracker.

harden — To make a computer system more secure against cracker attacks.

National Infrastructure Protection Center (NIPC) — A clearinghouse for security information, reports, analysis, and legal data related to these topics. Run by the U.S. government; staffed by the FBI.

opt-in — A marketing scheme in which a user does not receive advertisements unless he or she specifically requests to be added to a list of recipients.

7

opt-out — A marketing scheme in which a user automatically receives advertisements unless he or she asks to be removed from a list of recipients.

password cracking — A cracker activity by which the cracker obtains the password for a valid user account, either by using a program that examines millions of passwords until the correct one is found, or by guessing based on personal knowledge about the user.

privacy policy — A voluntary statement by an organization about how it will and will not use data that it collects about users or customers, often via a Web site.

script-kiddies — Unskilled crackers who use prepackaged software "kits" or scripts created by skilled crackers to break into systems that have not taken basic security precautions.

social engineering — Manipulating someone to extract needed information about a computer system.

System Administration, Networking, and Security (SANS) Institute — A prestigious and well-regarded education and research organization the members of which include most of the leading computer security experts in the country. Also called simply SANS.

Trojan horse attack — A technique for gaining access to a computer system by having a system administrator execute a program that appears normal but which actually creates a security hole for a cracker or destroys data on the host where it is run.

worm — A program that self-replicates and invades networked computer systems. Similar to a virus, but requires less human intervention for continued propagation.

REVIEW QUESTIONS

1. Defacing a Web site refers to:

    a. changing the text or graphics on its home page

    b. attempting to crack it

    c. sending derogatory email to the Webmaster

    d. blocking access to the site for valid users

2. Describe the event in late 1988 that caused many system administrators of Internet servers to begin thinking seriously about security issues.

3. Cracking a system refers to:

    a. gaining unauthorized access to a computer system, usually remotely

    b. giving a password for a system to another user

    c. technical expertise with computers

    d. shutdown of the system

4. Which refers to a reason that accurate statistics on computer crime are hard to gather?

   a. Crackers cannot erase their tracks after gaining access to a system.

   b. Organizations are eager to have the public know that their systems were broken into.

   c. Tracking multiple laws used to prosecute crackers can be very challenging.

   d. Many different groups are attempting to collect these statistics.

5. Malicious intentions are:

   a. part of the definition of a cracker

   b. not required in order for unauthorized access to a computer system to constitute a crime

   c. restricted to those outside a company being attacked

   d. likely limited to older crackers

6. Personal information is often maintained electronically by businesses in order to:

   a. prevent theft of that data by crackers

   b. secure new customers and serve existing customers

   c. avoid the need to maintain a privacy policy

   d. prevent government access to that data

7. Describe the purpose of a privacy policy.

8. An opt-in scheme means that:

   a. A user must request to be included on a marketing list.

   b. A user must ask to be excluded from a marketing list.

   c. A user must read a company's privacy policy for it to be effective.

   d. Government officials intend to participate in a security plan.

9. Ethics codes are:

   a. now upheld as laws in many states

   b. completely voluntary and discretionary

   c. not widely known by members of professional groups

   d. an expectation of professionals who belong to professional organizations

10. Name three professional organizations for system administration and security.

11. A script-kiddie refers to a cracker who:

   a. is young

   b. uses only predefined scripts created by more skilled crackers

   c. gains unauthorized access but without malicious intent

   d. attacks sites without any rational motivation for his choices (such as political motives or a grudge against a certain company)

7

12. To which of the following do crackers present the greatest threat?

    a. data

    b. hardware components

    c. software programs

    d. network connectivity

13. Describe a Denial-of-Service (DoS) attack.

14. Describe a Trojan horse attack.

15. Describe a buffer overflow attack.

16. Suppose that after gaining unauthorized access to a computer, a cracker created a special user account that only he knew about, so that if discovered, he could later log in using the special user account. This would be an example of:

    a. social engineering

    b. a back door

    c. a Denial-of-Service attack

    d. firewalling

17. A security policy document would probably *not* include:

    a. details on the dangers of lax security

    b. procedures to follow in case a break-in were discovered

    c. expectations of all users regarding use of passwords

    d. descriptions of laws under which crackers could be prosecuted

18. Security advisories:

    a. are created by government agencies under authority of the Computer Fraud and Abuse Act

    b. are provided by Linux vendors and security organizations to help system administrators know how and when they need to update their systems to prevent a break-in

    c. are often a tool of crackers seeking to create back doors or Trojan horses

    d. should not be acted on until a security policy document has been revised to include them

19. Name the security certification program developed by the SANS Institute.

20. Name three laws that forbid unauthorized access to computer systems.

21. The National Infrastructure Protection Center is:

    a. a collection of security bulletins created by SANS and CERT/CC in conjunction with Linux vendors

    b. a law designed to protect government computers from crackers who seek financial gain by unauthorized access to computer systems

    c. a division of the U.S. Department of the Treasury that protects against money laundering

    d. an FBI-staffed security resource that helps inform users and system administrators about computer crime and assists with prosecuting those crimes when they occur

22. Which U.S. government agency is primarily responsible for enforcement of computer crime laws?

    a. the FBI

    b. the NSA

    c. the Department of the Treasury

    d. the Secret Service

23. Which U.S. government agency has created publicly available security enhancements to Linux?

    a. the FBI

    b. the NSA

    c. the CIA

    d. the Department of Justice

24. Bastille Linux hardening scripts:

    a. are used by crackers to attack systems using buffer overflow techniques

    b. help system administrators see areas of their system that may be vulnerable to crackers

    c. were created by the NIPC as part of an ongoing program to raise awareness of security issues among government-run Internet sites

    d. are run automatically each time you start your Linux system

25. Computer security for a host is often divided into four areas of concern:

    a. physical, user/password, file, and network

    b. network, firewall, VPN, and tunneling

    c. physical, user, firewalls, intrusion detection

    d. Trojan horse, buffer overflow, password cracking, social engineering

7

HANDS-ON PROJECTS

Project 7-1

In this project you learn how to upgrade a package in which a security hole has been discovered. To complete this project, you should have Red Hat 7.3 installed, with networking established, root access to the system, and an Internet connection. (This project shows how you would upgrade a package if you *did not* have the Red Hat Network automated service described in the chapter text.)

1. Log in as root and open a command-line window.

2. Open a browser and point to *www.redhat.com*.

3. Choose the **Support and Docs** link, then choose the **Errata** link.

4. Click the link for **Red Hat Linux 7.3 (Valhalla)**.

5. Choose **Security Alerts** under Red Hat Linux 7.3. You should now be at *rhn.redhat.com/errata/rh73-errata.html*.

6. Review the list of security advisories published since Red Hat Linux 7.3 was released. Locate the advisory RHSA-2002:105, dated 2002-06-04, and labeled **Updated bind packages fix denial of service attack**. Click on that link.

7. Read about this security hole in the Details section near the top of the page.

8. Under the heading Red Hat Linux 7.3 i386, note the three packages listed: bind, bind-devel, and bind-utils. Click on each of those links in turn and download each rpm file to your Linux system in a temporary directory (such as your home directory or /tmp).

9. Switch to the command line and change to the directory where the three rpm files were downloaded.

10. Use this command to upgrade your system to the new, more secure bind packages:

```
rpm -Uvh bind*
```

Project 7-2

In this project you learn how to upgrade your Linux kernel when a security hole is discovered in it. To complete this project, you should have Red Hat 7.3 installed, with networking established, root access to the system, and an Internet connection. You wouldn't normally upgrade your Linux kernel unless you needed additional hardware support that was only available in a newer kernel or you needed to repair a security hole. This project assumes that you are using Red Hat Linux, which means that rpm files from Red Hat Software can provide a new precompiled kernel. If you are not working with Red Hat Linux or another popular package-based Linux distribution, you may need to download kernel source code from *www.kernel.org* and recompile a new kernel yourself. The last part of this project builds on information at *www.redhat.com/support/docs/howto/kernel-upgrade/*, which you may also find useful.

1. Log in as root and open a command-line window.

2. Open a browser and point to *www.redhat.com*.

3. Choose the **Support and Docs** link, then the **Errata** link for Red Hat Linux 7.3. You should now be at *rhn.redhat.com/errata/rh73-errata.html*.

4. Locate the advisory RHBA-2002:085, dated 2002-05-09, and labeled **Kernel panic on SMP systems with ext3 file systems is now fixed.** and click on that link.

5. Read the details of the security hole that this kernel upgrade fixes, then scroll down to the section labeled Red Hat Linux 7.3 i386.

6. In the command-line window you opened in Step 1, use this command to see what kernel rpms you are using (this varies based on your processor and the options you selected during installation).

   ```
   rpm -qa | grep kernel
   ```

7. Compare the output of the `rpm` command above with the outdated packages listed on the Web site. Note any packages on your system that are outdated by this security hole.

8. Use the following command to see the version of these packages that are installed on your system as well. These packages are tied closely with the operation of the kernel:

   ```
   rpm -q mkinitrd SysVinit initscripts
   ```

9. Visit the FTP site *ftp://updates.redhat.com* and select the links that refer to Red Hat Linux 7.3. You will see kernel rpm files listed in the directory /7.3/en/os/i586 (or for the processor version you installed).

10. Download the rpm files that the previous steps indicate are needed to update your system (both for the kernel and for the kernel support packages, such as `initscripts`). You may find it easier to use an FTP client than a Web browser if you need to download several large files. (If you are working on a slow Internet connection and are not actually maintaining a network server, you may want to merely follow along, as the kernel rpm files are quite large.)

11. Within the directory where you downloaded the new kernel files, use the following command to check that the download worked correctly. A download problem leading to a corrupted kernel rpm could leave you with a system that won't boot:

    ```
    rpm -K --nogpg *rpm
    ```

12. You should see the name of each rpm that you downloaded followed by "md5 OK" to indicate that the download was successful.

13. Unless you are working in a lab where a system crash cannot cause data loss, create a rescue floppy that you can use to boot your system in case of a problem with the kernel upgrade. Use the following command to create it:

    ```
    mkbootdisk --device /dev/fd0 2.4.18-3
    ```

14. Within the directory where you downloaded the files, begin by upgrading the kernel support packages:

    ```
    rpm -Uvh mkinitrd*rpm SysVinit*rpm initscripts*rpm
    ```

15. Next, upgrade the kernel packages:

    ```
    rpm -Uvh kernel*rpm
    ```

16. As noted at the beginning of this project, you are adding precompiled kernels to your system; you are not compiling new source code. To do that, you should refer to more detailed instructions provided by your Linux vendor.

17. If you selected the GRUB boot loader program when you installed Red Hat Linux, you are ready to reboot your system (this was the default choice). If you selected the LILO boot loader during installation, you must update it for the new kernel using this command:

    ```
    lilo
    ```

18. You can now reboot the system. The new kernel will boot. (You can see the version number of the active kernel using the **uname -r** command.)

Project 7-3

In this project you research some aspects of the Computer Fraud and Abuse Act. To complete this project, you should have a browser with an Internet connection.

1. Open a browser and point to *www.law.cornell.edu/uscode*.

2. Scroll down the home page until you locate the section titled "Find US Code Materials by Title and Section."

3. Enter **18** in the Title field and **1030** in the Section field. Then click **Go to title and section**.

4. Statutes are not easy to read, but browse down to subsection (c) and review some of the punishments that crackers face when convicted of a computer crime. What are some of the maximum prison terms mentioned?

5. What are some of the circumstances that the law takes into account when deciding on a punishment? (See, for example, section 1030(c)(2)(b)(i).)

6. Scroll down to subsection (e) and see how "exceeds authorized access" is defined in this law.

7. Go back to the beginning of the page and notice that the law applies to individuals who access a computer without authorization or when their access exceeds their authorization.

8. Notice in subsection (a)(2)(C) that the law refers to computers involved in interstate communication. This is because the U.S. Constitution limits the topics on which Congress can pass laws (though these limits are usually interpreted very broadly). Can you think of examples of computers that are not tied in any way to interstate commerce (business that crosses state borders)?

9. Visit the Web site **www.findlaw.com**.

10. Enter the search query string **Computer Fraud and Abuse Act**.

11. Review the resulting list of items and choose one or two that sound interesting to explore further.

Project 7-4

In this project you research SANS conferences. To complete this project, you should have a browser with an Internet connection.

1. Open a browser and point to *www.sans.org*.

2. Review the list of SANS security conferences that are currently planned. This list may be on the home page, or it may be available by clicking on a link from the home page. The list is a large chart with cities and dates on the left column and conference topics marked within squares across each row.

3. Locate a conference near you that includes the SANS Security Essentials track (most conferences include this track). Click on the link for that city.

4. In the Tracks Offered box on the left side of the page that appears, click the link for **Track 1: SANS Security Essentials**.

5. This is a six-part series (one section is devoted to Windows and one to UNIX/Linux). Scroll down the page and review the topics covered in the different sections of the Security Essentials track. You may want to compare some of the topics listed to those presented later in this book. Not all of the essentials are covered here, both because of space limitations and because the SANS security essentials training assumes that you already have experience working as system administrator.

6. Use the Back button on your browser to return to the description of the conference in the city that you selected. Choose another track that sounds interesting and explore the course offerings for that track. (Some conferences offer only two tracks.)

7. Use the Back button again to return to the conference home page for the city you selected. Under Registration and Tuition information on the left side of the screen, choose the **Tuition Fee Information** link. What are the fees to attend the conference you selected? (Conferences are typically five or six days in length.) How does this fee strike you compared with the value of the conference based on what you have seen on the SANS site? How could you justify such an expense to a manager in order to further your technical training in a work environment?

Project 7-5

In this project you research CERT/CC security advisories. To complete this project, you need a browser with an Internet connection.

1. Point your browser to *www.cert.org*.

2. On the CERT/CC home page locate the search field labeled "for" and enter **bind**, then select **advisories** from the drop-down list labeled "in." x Then click **GO**.

3. Notice that a large number of advisories related to bind are shown. DNS servers (which provide a name service based on the bind protocol) have been one of the major sources of security holes. What reasons can you think of for this?

4. Select one of the advisories listed for bind. Review briefly the Description, Impact, and Solution sections of the document. Does this sound like a problem that might have affected a server that you were responsible for? How would you have learned of this security hole if you had been working as a system administrator?

5. Return to the main page of CERT/CC and search again, this time for **sendmail** in **advisories**.

6. How many sendmail advisories are listed? When was the most recent sendmail problem reported?

7. Return to the main page again and search the **advisories** for **qmail** (another popular mail server).

8. How many qmail advisories are listed?

9. Why might a person choose sendmail when qmail appears to be more secure?

10. Return to the CERT/CC home page. Locate the link on the left column for the **CERT Advisory Mailing list**. Select this link.

11. How can you subscribe to the CERT advisory mailing list so that you receive every new advisory that the CERT/CC issues?

CASE PROJECTS

1. You are working as one of the system administrators for a financial services company, Safety First Financial Services, Inc., which employs 7,000 people. You take care of the computer needs of a group of 75 people. Your supervisor (a non-technical manager) has just called you into his office. An employee in your group has just informed him that another employee has been viewing and storing pornography on his computer at work. Your supervisor asks you to see if this is true without informing the accused person. You can easily check the user's home directory on the server, as well as review logs kept for Internet browsing activity.

   The company has a computer use policy that all employees are to follow. It states specifically that employees cannot visit offensive Web sites and cannot store offensive materials on company computers. However, it also states that the company respects employees' privacy and does not view data stored on their computers or read their email without prior notification and due cause. You are concerned that you might be violating the policy yourself by checking the computer of the accused person as directed, but you also don't want to be in trouble for refusing to do as you are told. If the person is confronted openly, he may erase the offensive files, leaving no basis for disciplinary action or firing, if either became necessary. What should you do? How might you rewrite the company's computer use policy after this incident?

2. Safety First has decided to add a "retirement calculator" feature to their Web site so that users can enter their age, income, and other factors and see how much they should be saving to retire comfortably based on various investment styles and

lifestyle goals. In order to use this free feature, a user must register by providing a name and email address. All the information that a user enters is stored so that he or she can return to the site and change the information to explore new retirement scenarios.

Describe the privacy policy that you would propose for management approval based on the information that you would be collecting for this feature, the expectations of users who use the feature, the needs of the company to market their financial products and services, and other factors you may decide are important. You might decide to visit the Web sites of a few companies to review their privacy policies for ideas. (Examples of financial services companies include *www.etrade.com*, *www.fidelity.com*, and *www.wellsfargo.com*.)

3. You came in to work at Safety First this morning and reviewed your system logs only to discover that a cracker had broken into the retirement calculator Web site during the night and downloaded, as near as you can figure, the registration details and retirement plan summaries (as entered by customers to try out the free retirement calculator) of about 400 customers. What will you do today?

7

8

MAKING DATA SECURE

After reading this chapter and completing the exercises you will be able to:

♦ Explain commonly used cryptographic systems

♦ Understand digital certificates and certificate authorities

♦ Use the PGP and GPG data-encryption utilities

♦ Describe different ways in which cryptography is applied to make computer systems more secure

In this chapter, you learn how information is secured using a variety of encoding techniques that prevent unauthorized users from accessing it. Similar techniques are also used to authenticate users—to guarantee that users seeking access to a system or system resources are who they claim to be.

You also learn about applications that implement these techniques, either directly, by encoding data at your command, or indirectly, by creating a channel for secure communication over which many types of data can be sent.

CRYPTOGRAPHY AND COMPUTER SECURITY

Computer security is about making certain that the only people accessing a given resource (such as a file or a Web site) are those to whom you want to allow access. This is not a new type of problem. More than two thousand years ago, Alexander the Great had the same concern as he tried to send messages about waging battle to commanders in his empire. In the last hundred years, much military, diplomatic, and political intrigue has focused on transmitting information between members of one group without another group being able to intercept or forge that information. The science of encoding data so that it cannot be read without special knowledge or tools is called **cryptography**.

Cryptography is a key part of many applications running on computer networks, though it is usually hidden from view. Networks transmit data through wires that run in and between buildings or wirelessly via radio waves; these may be accessible by unauthorized persons. A person with technical skill and the right equipment can tap into a network connection and see the data being transmitted. This is called **sniffing** the network and is illustrated in Figure 8-1. Programs used to perform this function—called **sniffers**—are used by many system administrators to troubleshoot difficult networking problems. Though crackers use sniffers to gather information from network packets, this is much more difficult if the payload of those packets has been encrypted.

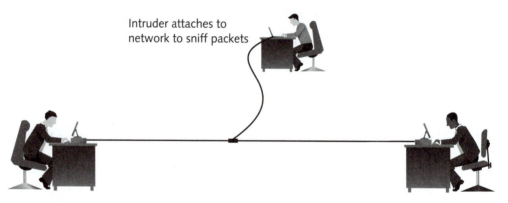

Intruder attaches to
network to sniff packets

Figure 8-1   Sniffing a network connection

Basic Encoding Techniques

The process of cryptography is straightforward. You begin with a message that you want to transmit to another person, called the **plaintext**. Then you apply a technique or rule called a **cipher** to modify the plaintext into something that no longer resembles the plaintext. This process is called **encryption** and the result is **ciphertext**: an encrypted message.

The most elementary example of encryption is letter-substitution. You substitute a different letter of the alphabet for each letter in your message. Suppose that the message you need to encode is:

> ONE IF BY LAND TWO IF BY SEA

You create the following system of substitution—your cipher:

> *Substitute for each letter the letter that follows it in the alphabet*

The result of encoding the above plaintext with this cipher yields the following ciphertext:

> POF JG CZ MBOE UXP JG CZ TFB

While this is certainly unreadable at first glance, it is an easy cipher to break (decode) without knowing the rule by which it was created. To break a letter-substitution cipher of an English plaintext, you would assume that the most frequently occurring letters are substitutions for vowels. Combinations that recur (such as JG and CZ in the above example) must represent common two-letter English words. You can develop more complex letter-substitution rules, but they are all easy to read for an experienced code-breaker. Nevertheless, this simple technique illustrates how cryptography can make data less accessible to someone who does not know how the data was encrypted.

If you are curious and want to experiment with letter-substitution ciphers, you can start with the information that the ten most often used letters in English, from most to least frequent, are ETAONRISHD. Code breakers use databases of letter and word frequency lists. You can use the frequency of occurrence within encrypted text to figure out which letters are substituted for which other letters.

To use letter substitution, the person receiving the ciphertext must know the rule that was used to encrypt the message, or else must figure it out using trial and error, mathematics, or some other technique.

Key Systems

The letter-substitution technique relies on a rule or set of rules for converting plaintext to ciphertext, known as an **algorithm**. Anyone who knows the algorithm you used to encode a message using letter substitution can decode that message. You could also add a level of complexity to the algorithm:

> *Substitute for each letter the letter that follows by X places in the alphabet*

The X in the algorithm is a **key**, a code necessary to encrypt or decrypt (decode) a message correctly using the algorithm. Most keys are numeric. For example, in this cipher, if X=4, the letter A would be converted to E, B to F, and so on. Even if a person knows the algorithm used for the encryption, the message cannot be decrypted without the key. In the case of letter-substitutions, the message is still fairly easy to decrypt using knowledge of the English language, but keys are used in much more complex ciphers with very complex algorithms.

8

Another method of encryption is called the **one-time pad**. This method is as simple as letter-substitution, but it is considered unbreakable using the types of analysis that can break a letter-substitution cipher.

In the one-time pad method, both the person encrypting the message and the person decrypting the message have an identical list of random numbers. The random numbers are the key. To encrypt a message using a one-time pad, the message is converted to numbers (for example, A is 1, B is 2, etc.), then the first random number is added to the first number of the message, the second random number is added to the second number of the message, etc. The resulting encrypted message is a list of numbers that looks random to anyone without the key. The recipient subtracts the random numbers on her list and then easily converts the numeric message into letters (for example, 1=A, 2=B, etc.).

The main problem with the one-time pad technique is getting a list of random numbers to both the message creator and the message recipient. This is an issue with the majority of ciphers: how do you get the key to your partner without its being intercepted? You cannot use the same delivery mechanism for the random numbers as for the encrypted messages (such as a radio signal or the mail), because anyone who obtains the random numbers can easily decrypt the message. A one-time pad was used for years in diplomatic and intelligence circles, where a list of random numbers could be delivered by special courier to the message recipients (such as an embassy in a foreign country). However, in the electronic world there is no efficient and secure way of getting a list of random numbers to a message recipient. If you send the random numbers electronically, they can be intercepted as easily as the encrypted message itself can.

Knowing the algorithm—the cipher—used to encrypt a message should not enable someone to read it. Good security assumes that an eavesdropper knows the cipher; the key, however, must be kept secret.

 Don't confuse compression with encryption. Compression uses a mathematical algorithm to make a file smaller. It has no key, though some compression programs let you add a password to a compressed file. Encryption uses a mathematical algorithm to make a file unreadable without a numeric key. The resulting file may be larger than the original file.

DES

Using computers for cryptography allows you to process very large numbers as part of a cipher. The first widely accepted standard for encryption was developed in the 1970s by IBM and the National Institute of Standards and Technology (NIST, see *www.nist.gov*). This standard is called the **Data Encryption Standard (DES)**. It uses a 56-bit key to encrypt data using various mathematical alterations of the plaintext message. A 56-bit key means that the key to encode any message consists of 56 digits, each of which is a one or a zero. A DES key would look like this:

11001101010011010010100100100100001111101010010110101000

Because each bit can be either one or zero, 56 bits provide for 2^{56} possible keys— roughly 72 quadrillion. Though DES is the most tested and widely used encryption technique in the world, in 1998 John Gilmore and Paul Kocher broke a DES key in 56 hours using a homemade supercomputer with Intel CPUs that they built for $250,000. Their effort was sponsored by the Electronic Frontier Foundation (*www.eff.org*) mentioned in Chapter 7 and by the U.S. government to improve cryptographic methods (since DES was nearly 30 years old). The two winners were awarded a prize of $10,000. Since 1998, the time needed to break a DES key has dropped to below 20 hours.

Getting a DES key to the recipient of a message is still an issue. It is addressed in the following section on Asymmetric Encryption.

DES is being phased out, but is still widely used for certain transactions. This is true for several reasons:

- Relatively few people have the equipment and patience to crack a DES key.

- 20 hours is still a fairly long time in some circumstances. Many transactions require that the information remain unknown for a very short time. For example, a typical Web site sale (e-commerce transaction) or a bank wire transfer requires that the data remain secure only for a few minutes. After that, the key is of no use, since a new key is created for each transaction.

- DES was a widely implemented U.S. government standard—inertia keeps it in place in some cases.

Skipjack and Triple DES

There were several responses to the cracking of DES. In one, DES keys were increased to 1,024 bits, making the key much more difficult to crack. Another response was the creation of a completely different algorithm called **Skipjack**, which uses an 80-bit key, making it more secure than DES. It is also a government-approved standard. But until recent changes, products using a key length over 64 bits could not be exported by any U.S. company, limiting the usefulness of Skipjack. In addition, though it seemed promising, the Skipjack algorithm had not withstood years of testing, as the DES algorithm had.

Another approach was **Triple DES**. This method, which is approved for U.S. government use, still relies on DES, but encodes each message three times using three different DES keys. The recipient must have all three DES keys and decrypt the message three times in the correct order to obtain the original message.

Triple DES is very secure and is considered unbreakable using current techniques and currently available computing power. However, it is not an ideal solution because it is time-consuming and resource-intensive both to encrypt and to decrypt messages. For every block of text (a few lines), Triple DES requires the encrypting computer to perform a series of complex mathematical functions three different times. The message recipient must perform the same functions to read the message.

A government-approved standard for information processing (such as an encryption algorithm) is called a **Federal Information Processing Standard (FIPS)**. The site *www.nist.gov/encryption/* contains information on all FIPS, including those described in this chapter.

Advanced Encryption Standard

Because Triple DES is so computationally intensive, NIST sponsored a competition in 1997 to create a replacement for DES. The winner of that competition was the Rijndael algorithm (pronounced "Rain Doll"), submitted by two Belgians. It is now called the **Advanced Encryption Standard (AES)**.

AES can use three different key lengths: 128 bits, 192 bits, or 256 bits. 256 bits provide roughly 10^{77} possible keys, and NIST expects AES to remain secure for at least 20 more years. AES was approved for use by U.S. government agencies effective May 26, 2002. Government approval means that many other organizations will feel comfortable using AES as well, and you can expect to see many security products in the coming years that support AES. AES does not have the earlier export restrictions affecting algorithms larger than 64 bits. The U.S. Department of Commerce deals with the export of encryption technology. To learn more about AES, see *www.nist.gov/encryption/*.

Several other very good ciphers are commonly used in encryption software. Each has advantages, such as requiring little computing power to decrypt or not being patented (so anyone can use it); and disadvantages, such as making messages much longer after encryption or requiring a lot of computing power (and thus time) to encrypt a message. Some of these ciphers you may hear about are **IDEA**, **Blowfish**, **Twofish**, **RC2**, **RC4**, and **El Gamal**.

Symmetric and Asymmetric Encryption

All of the popular encryption algorithms described thus far—DES, Triple DES, AES, IDEA, Blowfish, El Gamal—use a single numeric key to encrypt and decrypt messages. They are all **symmetric encryption algorithms**, meaning that the same key and the same algorithm are used both to encrypt and to decrypt a message (the algorithm is reversed for decryption). The key used for a symmetric encryption algorithm is called a private key, because it must be kept secret for the message to be secure. For this reason, these algorithms are also called **private-key encryption** techniques.

An **asymmetric encryption algorithm** uses one key to encrypt a message; an additional key is necessary to decrypt it. It is as if you were dropping the message into a box that you lock with one key, but you cannot open the box without another key. The advantage to asymmetric encryption is that you can tell everyone how to encrypt the messages they send you, but only you know how to decrypt them. Because the key that you can reveal to everyone is called the public key and the one you must keep secret is called the private key, asymmetric algorithms are often called **public-key encryption**. This model removes the problematic need to get a symmetric encryption key to another person without it being intercepted by an eavesdropper.

Asymmetric encryption uses only **prime numbers**—those that are evenly divisible only by 1 and the number itself. For example, the number 24 is not prime because it can be factored as $2 \times 3 \times 4$. However, 23 is a prime number; you cannot multiply any two numbers together except 23 and 1 to get 23. Asymmetric encryption takes two very large prime numbers (between 100 and 300 digits each) and combines them using fairly simple mathematical techniques to yield two keys. When one key is used to encrypt data, the other must be used to decrypt the data. The encryption can be done using either the public or the private key; decryption must be done with the opposite key.

Users who regularly rely on public-key encryption maintain a file that contains public keys for use by people that they regularly contact. Some users include their public key in their signature file, so it appears at the end of every email message they send. Others have a Web site that includes a link to their public key so that anyone can download and use it to encrypt or decrypt a message as described above. Some companies also publish a public key on their Web sites. For example, Red Hat Software and most other commercial Linux vendors encrypt or sign software packages so that users can verify that the package actually comes from the vendor and has not been modified.

The distribution of public keys is a major concern to both security experts and privacy advocates (key management and security is discussed at length later in this chapter in the section on GPG). Publicly accessible key servers contain millions of public keys, so you can search for the key of a person you want to contact. One example is *http://www.keyserver.net*. A public key can take many forms, but a typical example resembles the text shown below. This example has been edited to reduce its size. To see examples of active public keys, you can also visit *web.mit.edu/prz/* and choose the link for Phil's Public Keys (Mr. Zimmermann invented PGP, described later, and is a world-renowned cryptography expert).

```
mQCNAiv8ZoAAAAEEAKc4d45hN5qFM79nWGLkrGWputWmtdxJk0BZEbi0kNRbJBC2
p10ASImd//cCDwLR2alBUSt8O2WGik9PBZgthjMOenoDmzKiG8BkE9AFKonyxvD2
lDnqbydXi+YQmOTsWSw4jTTSb3cflhVkf8hVUVpMFQThafV0CmV5hLjHqWbdAAUR
tCJQaGlsaXAgUi4gWmltbWVybWFubiA8cHJ6QGGFjbS5vcmc+iQCVAgUQLB48XPTK
AIGN5yLZAQHWtwP/RBiLPN4dnt8sm9qZtK0HPYV0hfdZ4IiSfR0V52uKKMQsIrBJ
x2c5Z2vurBLeKkh8Oecf/X+Zh2mEenrymR/urBCf8xGQnyTPew4t/3IQ5KXsqi2b
uOTysk9Pkk+cqxZTEXJQWixB3fVKrCkR02xbWcRXQ/pPs0ObOE4VLtQT1G2JAGAC
Od2oMHwGJI4fy8H7SQSVPHV3BlRZpkIou0/vbEZY9b8WlUm9QEETWZEMmKYgHZTb
EzkkFtq0zNqgfsuORoe262c/pbYofNrMmnYok7K3vIAoqbUV6JlRRJ0oo3y+8IMi
                                   fjnNZKfgNpGmJDCMTh8M=Hpg1
```

To understand the usefulness of public-key cryptography, consider these three scenarios:

1. If a person wishes to send you a message, she can use your public key to encrypt the message. You would have made your public key widely available on your Web site or in other publicly accessible locations. You are the only one who can decrypt the message, using your private key, to which only you have access. Thus the person sending you a message knows that you are the only person who can read it. This is illustrated in Figure 8-2. Unfortunately, you have no way of knowing who is sending you the message, because everyone has access to your public key. Though the person may say she is Sally, it may actually be Brutus.

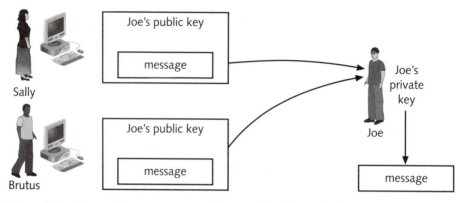

Figure 8-2 Encrypting a message with a recipient's public key

2. To solve this problem, a person could encode a message to you using her private key. You could then be certain that it was from her, because only her public key (which you could find on her Web site or elsewhere) would decrypt the message, as shown in Figure 8-3. Of course, everyone else could also decrypt the message she sent to you.

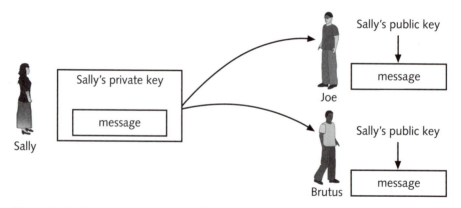

Figure 8-3 Signing a message with your private key

3. To send you an encoded message that only you can decrypt and that you are certain comes from the person who claims to have sent it, a person uses the following steps: First, the person encodes the message using your public key. Then the person encodes it a second time using her private key. When you receive the message, you first decrypt it using the sender's public key. This tells you for certain that the message came from the person who claimed they sent it. Then you decrypt it a second time using your private key and read it, as illustrated in Figure 8-4. Anyone can use the sender's public key and see that the message could only have come from her, but only you can complete the second step and read the contents of the message.

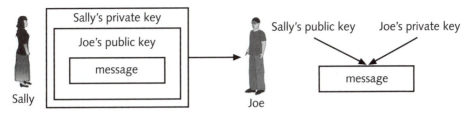

Figure 8-4   Encrypting and signing a document

RSA

The most familiar example of public-key encryption is the **RSA** algorithm, developed by Ronald **R**ivest, Adi **S**hamir, and Len **A**dleman. RSA was the basis for a security product company (see *www.rsasecurity.com*). However, the patent on RSA technology expired in September 2000, so other companies can now use the same techniques in their software. (One that does is PGP, described in the next section.)

RSA technology is used in a number of products from many vendors. RSA Security Inc. uses it for Web server tools, virtual private network (VPN) software (as described in Chapter 11), and for many other situations where high security is needed. RSA technology is used in popular browsers including Netscape and Microsoft Internet Explorer to make Internet transactions secure. This is done in combination with a symmetrical encryption method such as DES.

As with Triple DES and some other symmetric ciphers, encrypting a message using a public-key encryption algorithm requires a lot of computational power. Because of this, most systems rely on a hybrid: they combine a symmetrical key cipher and a public-key cipher. The public-key technology (such as RSA) is used to encrypt the key for a symmetrical cipher so that the recipient can obtain the key and decrypt the rest of the message. Only the symmetrical key requires the more CPU-intensive effort of public-key encryption. This is how browsers handle secure Web transactions, as illustrated in Figure 8-5.

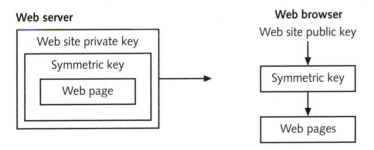

Figure 8-5   A secure Web transaction

SIGNATURES AND CERTIFICATES

Using public-key cryptography to exchange messages has a potential weakness that might have already occurred to you. How do you know that the public key you have for an individual is *really* for that individual? When it comes to cryptography, you really can't take anything for granted, but public-key cryptography also lets you verify the integrity of public keys for individuals or organizations. This is done through the process of authentication, using signatures and certificates.

Authentication is the process of proving to a computer system or another person that you are in fact the person you say you are. In real life, you often authenticate yourself using a photo ID, such as a driver's license. Signatures let you authenticate a public key.

You **sign** another person's public key with your own private key to verify that the key really belongs to that person. Others who get the key can see that you trust it, and so they may decide to trust it, or they may verify its correctness themselves, then add their signature by signing the public key with their private key. A public key that has several signatures from people whom you trust can likely be trusted as a valid public key for the person named as the key's owner. This is illustrated in Figure 8-6.

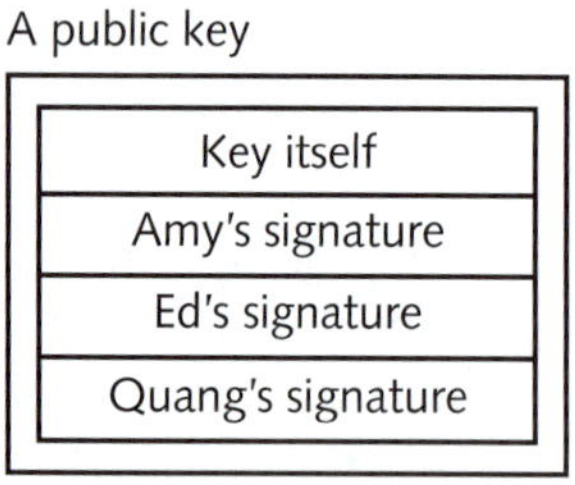

A public key

Key itself
Amy's signature
Ed's signature
Quang's signature

Figure 8-6   Signing a public key to indicate that you trust it to be accurate

 You can verify a key by contacting a person over the telephone if you feel certain you recognize his or her voice. Technical conferences often have key signing parties where you can meet individuals in person and let them verify a public key so that you can communicate securely with them. ("Fingerprints," described below, provide a shorthand method of referring to public keys.)

The personal connections between you and your colleagues, signing keys that you trust and relying on each others' signatures, form a **web of trust**. You must work to expand this web so that the software described later in this chapter—which implements the encryption algorithms discussed—can be truly useful to you.

A distantly related concept uses a very similar term: A **digital signature** is a part of an electronic transaction that gives the transaction the same legally binding effect as a document you had signed with a pen. Such digital signatures are not much used because the laws controlling them are not settled in very many states. One day you may be able to obtain a mortgage or a marriage license without leaving your home or office.

Certificates provide the same type of verification as signatures, but are most often used by organizations engaged in e-commerce. A **certificate** is a numeric code that is used to identify an organization. A certificate is not encryption, it is just a number assigned to you, much like a social security number or a driver's license number. The certificate is signed by a **certificate authority (CA)** who has verified the credentials of the organization presenting the certificate. To obtain a certificate from a certificate authority, you must prove to the certificate authority that you are who you claim to be, as illustrated in the following scenario.

XYZ Corp. wants to do business on the Internet. They approach VeriSign, a large and well-known certificate authority (*www.verisign.com*) and ask for a certificate. VeriSign requires that XYZ Corp. show documents that might include articles of incorporation, names of the corporate officers, various addresses and phone numbers, notarized company letterhead, etc. Once VeriSign determines that XYZ Corp. is a real corporation, it issues a certificate, which XYZ Corp. installs on its Web site. When you try to complete a purchase, the XYZ Web server sends you its certificate. The certificate includes a notation about who issued the certificate. Seeing that the certificate was issued by VeriSign, you trust that the Web site you are visiting (and perhaps giving a credit card number to) is run by a valid corporation that was at least stable enough to get a VeriSign certificate. The more you trust the certificate authority, the more you can be certain that the organization providing the certificate is what it claims to be.

Certificates are used in conjunction with public-key cryptography to prevent certificate forgery. Suppose that a user had done business with XYZ and so had a copy of its certificate. That user could, in theory, set up a Web site and pose as XYZ Corp. You can be certain that only XYZ Corp. sent out the certificate if it was encrypted with the private key of XYZ Corp. and you decrypt it using the public key of XYZ Corp. Figure 8-7 presents such a secure Web transaction with a certificate.

VeriSign sells different types of certificates based on how strongly you prove who you are. Products range from a few hundred dollars to thousands and include features such as business insurance in case of problems with a VeriSign certificate.

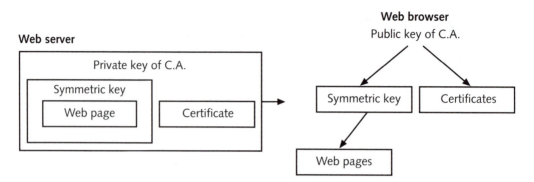

Figure 8-7   A secure Web transaction using a certificate

One practical problem with this system is the identity of the certificate authority. VeriSign has been issuing certificates longer than almost any other company, but should they have a monopoly on a service that every participant in electronic commerce must use? If not, how can a consumer deal with having 500 certificate authorities? Which should be trusted? How can a user know? These issues are not resolved and make the world of certificates somewhat chaotic at this time.

Fingerprints

Public keys and certificates can be hundreds of digits long. A **fingerprint** is a smaller number that is derived from a public key in such a way that it is hard to forge. A fingerprint is created by hashing the key or certificate. A **hash** is the result of a mathematical function (called loosely a hashing function) that converts a large number into a smaller number in a predictable way. If the large number is changed, the smaller number (the hash) will also change. Thus you can compare two hashes of a public key to see whether the key has been modified. Hashes used in this way are also called fingerprints. Two types of hashes are commonly used in computer security: MD5 and SHA-1.

The **message digest hash** (called **MD5**) converts a number of any length (including a large computer file) to a 128-bit number called a checksum. (More generally, a **checksum** is a computed value that helps you verify that a file or transmission has not been corrupted.) Because 128 bits gives just 32 hexadecimal digits, it is fairly easy to compare the MD5 hash of a key or a file with the expected value. The nature of a hash like MD5 means that if the file or key had been altered at all, the resulting hash would also change. Yet it is not possible to extract or derive the original data (the key or the file) by studying the hash.

A simple Linux utility called `md5sum` creates an MD5 hash from any file. The `-c` option of this utility lets you check a list of existing MD5 checksums against files to see whether any do not match. To use this utility to create an MD5 hash of a file, include the filename after the command:

```
md5sum    filename
```

The utility prints the 128-bit MD5 checksum in hexadecimal, as in this example output:

```
15e10987f891132dc13790ba8e71c3a2    timesheet.doc
```

MD5 is used by many Linux vendors to help users make certain that rpm files are not corrupted (either by a cracker or by download errors). You can also select MD5 as a password protection mechanism (using `authconfig` in Red Hat Linux, for example). To perform this check on an rpm file that you have downloaded or have on CD-ROM, run the `rpm` command with the two options `--checksigd --nogpg` (we'll look at the GPG utility shortly). For example, suppose you have downloaded a security upgrade to the `bind` package. The following command will report whether the MD5 checksum stored as part of the rpm file indicates that the file's integrity is intact:

```
rpm --checksig --nogpg bind-9.1.3-6.i386.rpm
```

The output of the command should look like this if the package is intact:

```
bind-9.1.3-6.i386.rpm: md5 OK
```

Another type of hash that is more secure than MD5 is the **Secure Hash Algorithm (SHA-1)**. SHA-1 provides a 160-bit hash of any file or key so that you can check whether the message or key was corrupted during transmission. Fingerprints using this hash are used within the public-key encryption utilities described later in this chapter.

A hash like MD5 or SHA-1 is used when you transmit or receive a block of encrypted text. The hash is combined with a public key to create a signature for the transmission. The **Digital Signature Algorithm (DSA)** is a commonly used standard for doing this.

 The Web page *www.redhat.com/solutions/security/news/publickey.html* includes both Red Hat Software's public key and the fingerprint for that key.

USING CRYPTOGRAPHY IN A BROWSER

The technologies described in this chapter are utilized in a number of software tools, some of which are described later in this chapter and in later chapters. However, the easiest way to see cryptography in action on your computer is to open a browser like Netscape Communicator. Because browsers must deal with encrypted security information from any commercial Web site that you visit, they have well-developed, configurable cryptography features.

Whenever you visit a Web page that has been transmitted to your computer using encryption, you see a small lock or key in the lower left corner of the browser window. Unencrypted pages show this key icon broken into two pieces or show the lock in an unlocked position, as in Figure 8-8. Most encrypted Web pages, such as order-entry screens, shopping carts, account viewing pages, and similar data, appear with a URL that starts with **https**. This indicates that the Web server used an encrypted protocol to transmit the Web page. The encrypted protocol for Web pages is Secure Sockets Layer (SSL), introduced in Chapter 6.

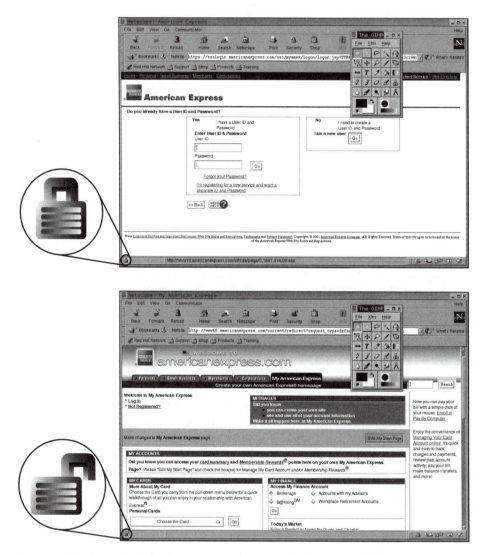

Figure 8-8 Icons to indicate secure and insecure Web pages in Netscape

To see cryptography configuration details in Netscape Communicator, choose Communicator on the menu bar, then Tools, then Security Info. The dialog box shown in Figure 8-9 appears, with a number of links down the left side of the screen. The default page shown, Security Info, displays the security status of the Web page you were viewing when you opened the dialog box. If you were not viewing a secure Web page, this page of the dialog box does not contain much information.

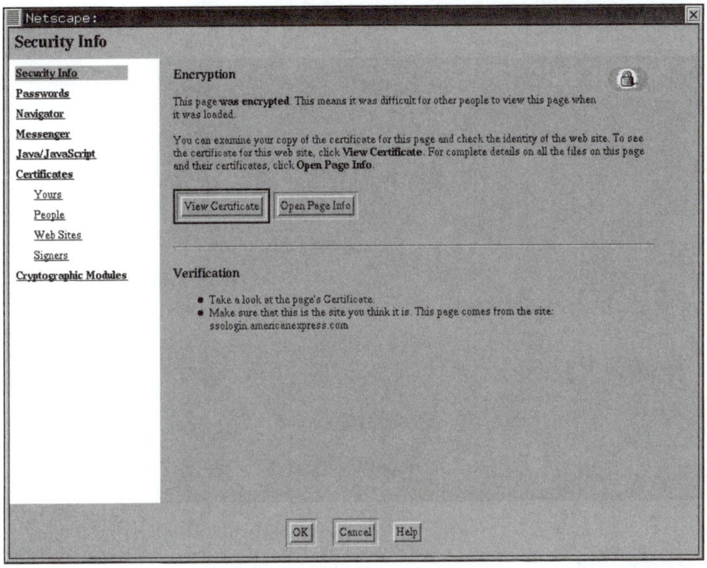

Figure 8-9   The Security Info dialog box in Netscape Communicator

Next, choose Navigator from the list on the left side of the window. You see options for viewing secure Web pages. The last item in the window is a button labeled Configure SSL v3. When you click on this button you see the dialog box in Figure 8-10, which contains many of the terms you have learned already in this chapter.

Netscape supports some encryption algorithms that are not U.S. government-approved (FIPS), not widely used, or older. You can use the Cryptographic Modules link on this page to add security features (such as new encryption algorithms) to Netscape, but this is something that very few users will need to worry about.

The Signers link under the Certificates section on the left side of the Security Info dialog box in Netscape Communicator is shown in Figure 8-11. It lists all the certificate authorities that the authors of Netscape thought you should trust by default. The list includes VeriSign (mentioned above) plus dozens of other companies that issue certificates. If you select one and choose Edit, you see details about that certificate authority.

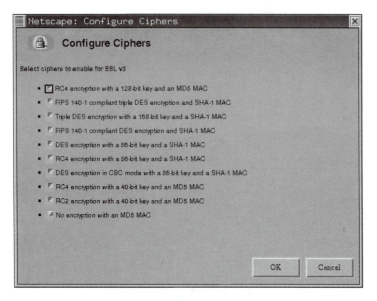

Figure 8-10   Configuring secure Web pages in Netscape Communicator

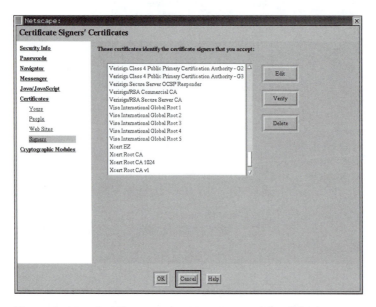

Figure 8-11   Certificate authorities accepted by default in Netscape Communicator

You can delete a certificate authority from the list if you decide you do not trust it; you can also add other certificate authorities if you need to accept a certificate from a secure Web site whose certificate was provided by a company that is not listed in the dialog box by default.

The other pages under the Certificates section of the Security Info dialog box will not list anything unless you have worked with certificates previously. For example, under the subsection labeled Yours, you could view your own certificates. A button labeled Get a Certificate at the bottom of the page also links to a list of certificate authorities from which you can purchase your own certificate.

You don't need a certificate unless you intend to start an e-commerce site or something similar. Having a public key will suffice, and they are free, as described later in this chapter.

Kerberos Authentication

The techniques used by browsers for e-commerce are not sufficient for securing all the different services provided for users on an organizational network. A special type of authentication for organizational networks is **Kerberos**. Kerberos was developed at the Massachusetts Institute of Technology (MIT) and is widely used around the world, but it is not something everyone will want to implement. Kerberos is intrusive, meaning that you must set up all of your other services to work with it. Each of those services must be designed to work with Kerberos, or as MIT says, applications must be "kerberized."

Kerberos secures a network by providing a system that makes users prove who they are before they can use a service (such as a file server or a printer) and also makes services prove who they are. Kerberos uses both public-key cryptography and a symmetric cipher. Signatures and passwords verify actions when users contact a service to perform a task such as printing a document.

For the curious, in Greek mythology, Kerberos is the three-headed dog that guards the entrance to Hades.

A network that uses Kerberos relies on a central Kerberos server on which the private keys of all users and all services are stored. All the users and services whose keys are stored on the Kerberos server constitute the Kerberos **realm**. Kerberos uses the signature techniques described earlier for public key encryption to ensure that only the "right" user or service can decrypt the information that it sends out.

In order to use a service, a user on a Kerberos-aware network contacts the Kerberos server and indicates the action that the user wants to perform. The Kerberos server checks the identity of the user to see whether that action is permitted. If it is, the Kerberos server grants a **ticket**, which contains the following components:

{sessionkey:username:address:servicename:lifespan:timestamp}

The user sends the ticket requesting service to the daemon that the user wants to access; for example, to a print server daemon. The service decrypts the ticket using its private key. Since the ticket was encrypted on the Kerberos server using the service's public key, only the service can decrypt the ticket to see whether it is valid. If it is, the service grants the user access. This is a simplification of the process presented in Figure 8-12, but it illustrates why Kerberos is considered both a valuable security tool and a labor-intensive system to install and maintain.

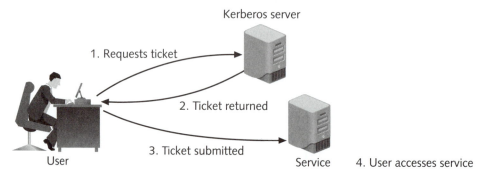

Figure 8-12 The Kerberos ticket–granting process

Linux supports Kerberos, including all of the common services you are likely to need, such as printing, NFS, FTP, r–utilities, and many others. If you are already operating within a Kerberos realm, you can select Kerberos as an option when you install some versions of Linux (including Red Hat Linux 7.3). To set up Kerberos after installation in Red Hat Linux, use the `authconfig` text utility shown in Figure 8-13. This utility has a graphical version that you can start in Red Hat Linux by opening the Gnome main menu and selecting Programs, then System, then Authentication Configuration (see Figure 8-14). You can run this graphical utility with the command `authconfig-gtk`.

 You will see many options in `authconfig` and `authconfig-gtk` that are explained later in this book.

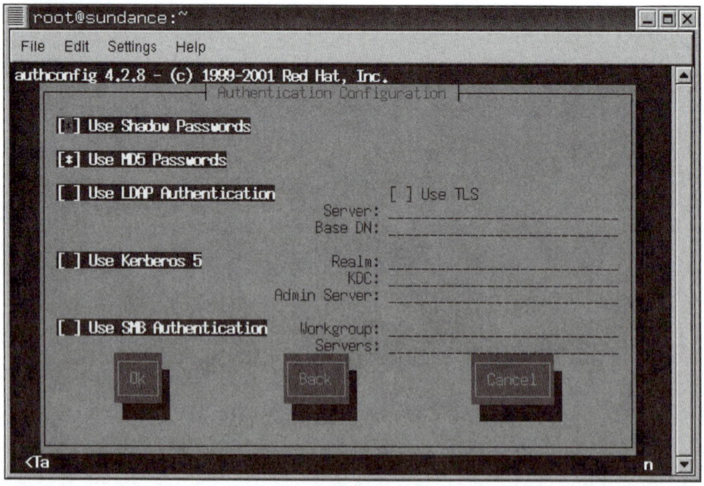

Figure 8-13 The `authconfig` utility in Red Hat Linux

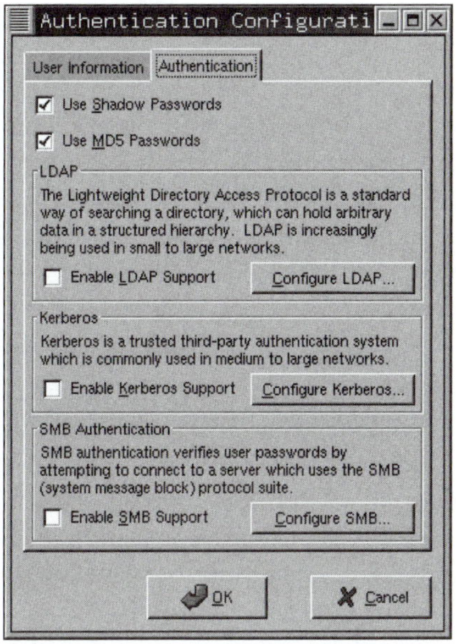

Figure 8-14   The graphical Authentication Configuration utility in Red Hat Linux

For further information on Kerberos, visit *www.kerberos.net*. The FAQ on that site assumes that you are already familiar with much of Kerberos. A good place to start is *http://web.mit.edu/kerberos/www/dialogue.html*, which gives a conceptual outline of the Kerberos ticket-granting process.

USING ENCRYPTION UTILITIES

You use public-key cryptography when you browse secure Web sites, but you can also use it to encrypt email messages or documents before sending them to others.

Pretty Good Privacy (PGP)

The first utility to provide public-key encryption to all comers was the **Pretty Good Privacy (PGP)** program, created by Phil Zimmermann. PGP caused an uproar by making "munition"-grade cryptography—classified by the government as a weapon—available to everyone. Mr. Zimmermann underwent a three-year government investigation because of his desire to make strong encryption (and privacy, in his view) available to everyone with free software.

PGP has not been free since Mr. Zimmermann's company was sold to Network Associates. You can learn more about the products they offer by visiting *www.pgp.com*. Another site that links to many worldwide resources related to PGP is *www.pgp.net*.

Although PGP software was formerly included in every Linux distribution, it has been replaced with another program with similar goals: The Gnu Privacy Guard (GPG) program.

As you learn about GPG in the next section, consider the trade-offs you make with any form of encryption. The more effort you put into securing a document, the more effort it will take an eavesdropper to intercept and read your messages. Some messages are not worth the trouble of using strong encryption techniques, either because their contents are innocuous (e.g., a grocery list) or are only valuable for a very short time (e.g., a financial transaction that must be completed within seconds or the encryption keys become invalid). Yet you must create and maintain the relationships that you need for secure communications so that when you need them, they work effectively—you must create a web of trust appropriate to your circumstances.

Some users working in financial services, or government intelligence, or who are just highly concerned about their privacy, will gladly put the effort into following all the recommendations by security experts for guarding their private keys, signing others' public keys, and otherwise protecting the validity of their security measures. Others do not have such critical information to protect. They assume, perhaps rightly, that no one is likely to spend much time trying to decrypt their messages. You must decide where your security needs fall. All users should be security-conscious, however, and take measures to protect personal data by using secure Internet transmissions, for example, simply because of the number of crackers who are looking for targets for identity theft, credit-card fraud, and similar mischief.

Gnu Privacy Guard (GPG)

Gnu Privacy Guard (GPG) is a public-key encryption utility compatible with PGP in many respects, including the ability to use public keys generated by PGP. PGP uses the patented IDEA encryption, while GPG uses El Gamal and other non-patented algorithms. The GPG package is installed by default on Red Hat Linux 7.3 and is available for all other Linux systems. For many systems you can download a software package in rpm or deb format (see *rpmfind.net*). The package name in Red Hat is **gnupg**. Full information on GPG is provided at the site *www.gnupg.org*.

GPG operates from the command line, though graphical utilities are also available, as described later in this section. You execute **gpg** followed by commands or options given as parameters on the command line. The first step in using GPG is to create a key pair for yourself. A **key pair** is a public key that you can hand out to others and a private or secret key that stays on your system—no one else ever sees it. You create a key pair in GPG using this command:

```
gpg  --gen-key
```

When you execute this command, you must choose which algorithm GPG will use to create your key. The choices are DSA, El Gamal, or both (the default). Choosing the default lets you both encrypt files and sign them. You also select a key size for the DSA algorithm; the 1,024-bit default should be fine for most users. You then select an expiration time. Most key pairs should not have an expiration date, because that would require you to inform everyone who had obtained your public key when it was no longer valid, then redistribute a new public key. For some specialized purposes an expiration time may be a good idea; but generally, choose "key does not expire." You must confirm this choice to continue.

Next you must define a user ID for the key pair. This is like naming the key pair and associating it with yourself. The user ID consists of your real name, your email address, and any brief comment you want to add (such as a nickname, title, or organization name). GPG prompts you for these three items, then creates the user ID in a fixed format. When you have entered these, editing them if needed, you can enter O (for Okay) to continue.

Each key pair is stored on your local hard disk so that it can be used to encrypt and sign files as you use the gpg utility. (The first time you run gpg, it creates directories for the utility to use, then exits. You run the utility a second time to begin creating and managing key pairs.) Because this is highly sensitive information, you should assign a passphrase to your key pair. A **passphrase** is a long password. Anytime GPG needs to access the secret key to encrypt, decrypt, or sign a file, you will be prompted to enter the passphrase. It should consist of multiple words, preferably not all words that can be found in the dictionary. It should be very difficult to guess but easy for you to remember, because *you must remember it* or your key pair becomes useless. Below are two example passphrases to consider. Notice that words are intentionally misspelled, but that patterns are used to help remember the oddities (e.g., the left-to-right progression of the non-letter characters on the keyboard). In the second example, English and foreign words are mixed:

Whan!40@wanters#hav$besized%thy^brow

Trapani~tromps~Siracusa!ogni!!volta!

GPG then generates the key pair. This takes several seconds. While the key is being generated, move your mouse around or play with the keyboard (Shift, Alt, and Ctrl are good choices). This helps to generate the random data in the operating system that GPG needs to create a secure key.

After the key pair is generated, you can view it with the --list-keys command, as shown below.

```
# gpg --list-keys
/root/.gnupg/pubring.gpg
------------------------
pub   1024D/1A949369 2002-05-31
Nicholas Wells (Nick) <nwells@us.net>
sub   1024g/4F0B8B07 2002-05-31

pub   1024D/DB42A60E 1999-09-23 Red Hat,
Inc <security@redhat.com>
sub   2048g/961630A2 1999-09-23

pub   1024D/FF2F845C 2002-06-01
Paula Gutowski <pgutowski@xmission.com>
sub   1024g/0811249D 2002-06-01
```

Notice that only the public key is listed, indicated by pub in the left column. The private key is not shown by the list-keys options. The line labeled sub (for a subordinate key) in the left column is the key for the El Gamal symmetric cipher. The pub key is for public-key cryptography; the subordinate key is for symmetric encryption. GPG will use this process for encrypting a file:

- Encrypt the file using your symmetric key

- Encrypt your symmetric key using the public key of the message recipient

- Sign the resulting ciphertext with the private/secret key of your public-key-cryptography pair so that the recipient can verify that the message could have come only from you

You can export your public key so that others can access it using the `--export` command in GPG. This creates a binary file that you could hand to other people, who then use the `--import` command to add that key to their system, allowing them to send you encrypted messages. The collection of public keys that you have stored on your system is called your **keyring**—it's a file on your system that contains all the keys to which GPG has immediate access.

It's common to use the `-a` option (or `--armor` in long format) to make GPG convert the output to readable characters, which allows you to include your key in an email or printed document.

As an example, suppose you wanted to exchange keys with a friend. You export your public key with the command below, using your user ID to indicate the key that you want to export. You can use your name or email address and GPG will match them with a key on your keyring. The `-o` option indicates the output file where the key will be stored:

```
gpg -o wells.key --export nwells@us.net
```

You then receive a key file from your friend and import it to your keyring using this command:

```
gpg --import thomas.key
```

Now when you list your keys using the `--list-keys` command, the new key is included in the list, and you are able to encrypt messages for that user.

Suppose another user included a key within an email message that she sent to you. She used this command to create the text to paste into her message:

```
gpg -a -o gutowski.key --export pgutowski@xmission.com
```

The text looks something like this:

```
-----BEGIN PGP PUBLIC KEY BLOCK-----
Version: GnuPG v1.0.6 (GNU/Linux)
Comment: For info see http://www.gnupg.org
```

mQGiBDz5HrMRBACT1vx3gG7v6vB6eYZOcHnllf56GWxItWNxCPrc5/BOD+jW80q
qwVAvSUfn/Y+aux0G2p1ypWEsB0GAu3PSeygl11nt0S3AuBP+sPT7IT+W1ZJu2a
wafRa737aHnP4Be8BV0duRff8CmO2ATeklqY57PTvO5PPKcsx4lessXKikZwCgj
hHoqOZRqI1q0Z/wQHJQtoeH678D/1I6kD6bvy2NsAKqZKDy8WMSm9V4+RCAYsMz

```
dUK3mWteM0gkYFJr4dVFtV5rAP164acY2anqzHQ0wig/NZlfUuvOkI/itqitggP
5MTwTwWU3O5slkjkJTGXdxIsRYRR6RPRCDMoEwS/hjQL+sV02b5iM9dmudUJUxA
bgUsWDWQaTA/97G1+hxob0SahM/JDWECj3a1c+wNhoBOawJWPP9zqWaXxU6X/v4
EpzXYC4n9efe2MW8oMzdVyEfEr4HHvpWe3IivWhz5r5e1TGt3dXbp5sxzT4+WBH
oI5qbk60URgv1crrEbhnoaTPyVy0iLHmkOHN76aI4mLGj/k8C5m2L5qjDLQnUGV
0ZXIgR3V0b3dza2kgPHBndXR3Rvd3NraUB4bWlzc2lvbi5jb20+iFcEExECABcFAj
z5HrMFCwcKAwQDFQMCAxYCAQIXgAAKCRBSx7WA/y+EXIbuAJ9WPzfrOu6Uy0Y9x
8KPZXPCkneEjACGgcADA3FeeuamxfZX9CE1+LJj6py5AQ0EPPketxAEAM6zDanG
ygRveThZ+bsOaJI8awGG8rbUSv9h3QnnhEwiDvVwln6OxSi+fJHE5EQCw7E7XUF
7Q6DZZ+pqybe8LPgY0KZytgdj6nivzf6fiLz+iGDjucOKRCMJ8VSDOD4gyilywK
5Ln36gRITahxBphYP66EL3x3K++vopf9hIYj6HAAMFBACjATvzUqkHBgTEqhatq
n6O+kAnnDSkbVJlxkndNKkipyjBqFbcXoBRJpwMA+HNm+xesEeK2zY3WW3g4fT6
/rlmqHQWrqGJUhAB8pKiyMYto8DKyEk5VlkD2IcuyWJ6JwUSFjKzRjp34Ob7Sfu
s+u2cNsp+UWKuSZEUe+2TJo1rgIhGBBgRAgAGBQI8+R63AAoJEFLHtYD/L4RcKT
0An03uYPnqbfCgskKCGhWf5gxoakDzAJ0dIzixzBMx+06Jh2gJuPdT/lhoiJkBo
gQ8+R6zEQQAk9b8d4Bu7+rwenmGTnB55dX+ehlsSLVjcQj63OfwTg/olvNKqsFQ
L01H5/2PmrsdBtqdcqVhLAdBgLtz0nsoJZdZ7dEtwLgT/rD0+yE/lpWSbtmsGn0
Wu9+2h5z+AXvAVdHbkX3/ApjtgE3pJamOez07zuTzynLMeJXrLFyopGcAoI4R6K
jmUaiNatGf8EByULaHh+u/A/9SOpA+m78tjbACqmSg8vFjEpvVePkQgGLDM3VCt
5lrXjNIJGBSa+HVRbVeawD9euGnGNmp6sx0NMIoPzWZX1LrzpCP4raorYID+TE8
E8FlNzubJZI5CUxl3cSLEWEUekT0QgzKBMEv4Y0C/rFdNm+YjPXZrnVCVMQG4FL
Fg1kGkwP/extfocaG9EmoTPyQ1hAo92tXPsDYaATmsCVjz/c6lml8VOl/7+BKc1
2AuJ/Xn3tjFvKDM3VchHxK+Bx76VntyIr1oc+a+XtUxrd3V26ebMc0+PlgR6COa
m5OtFEYL9XK6xG4Z6Gkz8lctIix5pDhze+miOJixo/5PAuZti+aowy0J1BldGVy
IEd1dG93c2tppIDxwZ3V0b3dza2lAeG1pc3Npb24uY29tPohXBBMRAgAXBQI8+R6
zBQsHCgMEAxUDAgMWAgECF4AACgkQUse1gP8vhFyG7gCfVj836zrulMtGPcfCj2
VzwpJ3hIwAoIHAAwNxXnrmpsX2V/QhNfiyY+qcuQENBDz5HrcQBADOsw2pxsoEb
3k4Wfm7DmiSPGsBhvK21Er/Yd0J54RMIg71cJZ+jsUovnyRxOREAsOxO11Be0Og
2Wfqasm3vCz4GNCmcrYHY+p4r83+n4i8/ohg47nDikQjCfFUgzg+IMopcsCuS59
+oESE2ocQaYWD+uhC98dyvvr6KX/YSGI+hwADBQQAowE781KpBwYExKoWrap+jv
pAJ5w0pG1SZcZJ3TSpIqcowahW3F6AUSacDAPhzZvsXrBHits2N1lt4OH0+v65Z
qh0Fq6hiVIQAfKSosjGLaPAyshJOVZZA9iHLslieicFEhYys0Y6d+Dm+0n7rPrt
nDbKflFirkmRFHvtkyaNa4CIRgQYEQIABgUCPPketwAKCRBSx7WA/y+EXCk9AJ9
N7mD56m3woLJCghoVn+YMaGpA8wCdHSM4scwTMftOiYdoCbj3U/5YaIg=
=99xI
-----END PGP PUBLIC KEY BLOCK-----
```

You import that key using the same type of command as before:

```
gpg --import gutowski.key
```

Your keyring contains three keys. Consider now how much you trust that the keys you obtained actually belong to the individuals you think they belong to. Maybe someone forged an email message from gutowski so that you would use the key. That person could intercept your emails to gutowski, read them, re-encrypt them using gutowski's real public key, then forward the message as if it came from you.

Signing a key indicates that you trust that the key really came from its purported owner; for example, you may have talked to the person on the phone to verify the fingerprint of the key or the person might have handed you a copy of the key on a disk. GPG signs your own key on your behalf at the time it is created. You can list the signatures on a key with the `--list-sigs` command.

Considering the two keys added in the above example, Thomas handed you his key in person, so you feel very confident that it really is his public key. You decide to sign it to indicate that trust. Others might obtain his public key from you. If they trust your judgment, they may sign the key also based on your word. To sign the thomas key that you have added to your keyring, use the `--edit-key` command. This starts an interactive interface in which you can use the sign command to add your own signature to the key you are editing, like this:

```
gpg --edit-key thomas@xmission.com
```

The key information for the user ID you entered (thomas@xmission.com here) is displayed, followed by a `Command>` prompt, at which you would enter the command `sign`. You must enter your own passphrase anytime your secret key is accessed, as it must be here to sign Thomas' public key.

The gutowski key, however, you are not so sure of, since it came in email through an insecure Internet connection. To verify it, you print the fingerprint of gutowski's key using this command:

```
gpg --fingerprint pgutowski@xmission.com
```

The output resembles this:

```
pub   1024D/FF2F845C 2002-06-01
Paula Gutowski <pgutowski@xmission.com>
      Key fingerprint = 6FA2 40FA 9213 366D 6C13  3A02 52C7
      B580
               FF2F 845C
sub   1024g/0811249D 2002-06-01
```

Then you call her on the phone. You know where she works, and you know her voice well. You recite the fingerprint over the phone and she verifies that it is correct. Now you feel comfortable signing her key as well.

You can use keys to encrypt documents without having signed them, but signatures indicate that you place a higher level of trust in the key.

To encrypt a document, you specify the recipient and the file to encrypt. The `-o` option gives the filename where the ciphertext will be stored:

```
gpg -o report.gpg --encrypt thomas@xmission.com report.doc
```

It's a good practice to sign files that you encrypt so that the recipient can verify that they came from you. You might use a command to do the following:

- Encrypt a file with a recipient's public key

- Sign the encrypted file with your private/secret key

- Convert the output to a readable format (instead of binary format)

- Store the output in a named file (instead of writing it to the screen)

This command accomplishes all four of these things, using the **-r** option to indicate the recipient instead of adding it after the **--encrypt** command:

```
gpg -o report.gpg -a -r thomas@xmission.com --encrypt
    report.doc
```

 GPG uses not only commands, such as **--encrypt** and **--fingerprint**, but also options, such as **-a** and **-o**. The option should come before the command.

The person who receives the encrypted file can use the following command to decrypt it, assuming that the keyring on his or her system includes your public key if you signed the file and the correct secret key to correspond to the key you used to encrypt the file. The decrypted file is printed to the screen or stored in the file that you indicate with the **-o** option:

```
gpg -o report.doc --decrypt report.gpg
```

GPG includes dozens of other commands and options. Useful documentation includes the GPG man page, a mini-HOWTO document, a user manual, and additional technical reference materials. Some of these are available on your Linux system by default when GPG is installed—for example, the man page and a FAQ document. See **/usr/share/doc/gnupg-1.0.6** in Red Hat Linux 7.3. For other documents, visit *www.gnupg.org*.

To use GPG correctly, you must fully understand the concepts covered in this chapter. Once you do, you can experiment with a graphical interface instead of memorizing all the command-line parameters. Two graphical utilities are the Gnu Privacy Assistant (GPA) and Seahorse. Neither is likely to be included with your Linux distribution, but you can find the source code and (for Seahorse at least) rpm packages for some versions of Red Hat Linux. See *www.gnupg.org/gpa.html* or *seahorse.sourceforge.net*, respectively, for additional information and files to download. Figure 8-15 shows a screen from Seahorse as an illustration of these programs' functionality. Figure 8-16 shows a screen from the Gnu Privacy Assistant.

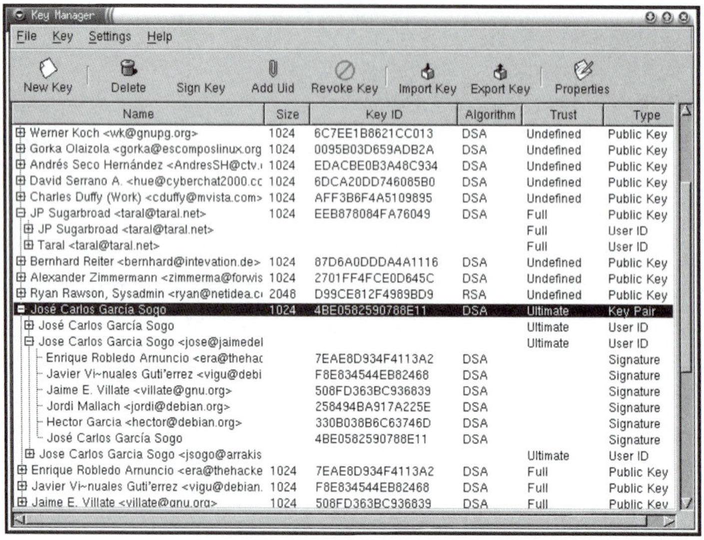

Figure 8-15   The Seahorse graphical interface to GPG

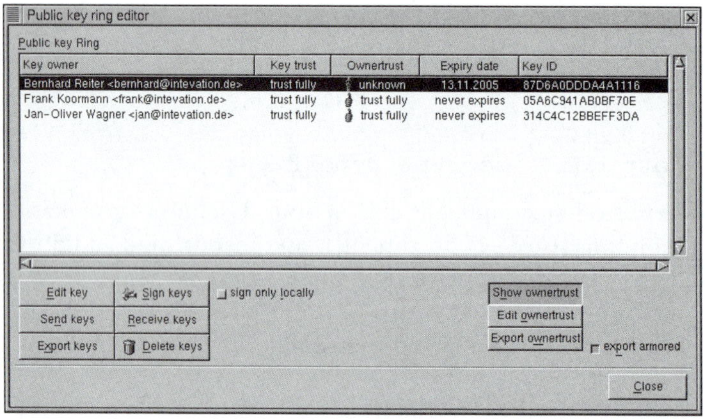

Figure 8-16   The Gnu Privacy Assistant

Many other programs are designed to interact with GPG functionality automatically. For example, several email readers such as `pine`, `elm`, and Kmail can be configured to use GPG in the background to encrypt and decrypt messages automatically based on the email address of the sender or recipient. Modules can also be added to the Mozilla browser to enhance its email in the same way.

OTHER SECURITY APPLICATIONS

GPG is a powerful tool because it lets you manage keyrings with a number of specialized commands and gives you the capability to apply public-key encryption to any file you want to transmit securely. You can send a file encrypted with GPG to a recipient using an insecure network without fear of someone sniffing the network and reading your message. However, keep in mind that GPG is only one of many encryption tools available to Linux users. Many other protocols and utilities use the encryption techniques you learned about in this chapter to provide computer security in a number of different contexts.

Some of these security-related utilities are more specialized. For example, the `rpm` command includes a GPG signature that you can verify to see whether a software package came from Red Hat Software, Inc. without being modified by a cracker. Other utilities are more general-purpose, with the goal of securing all communication between two hosts or two networks, without the need to run a utility like GPG explicitly to encrypt a file.

Without the utilities briefly described in this section, networks would be much more dangerous for businesses and individuals to use because of the technologies available to read other users' packets as they traverse the network. However, using such utilities makes any school-campus or small-business network as secure as U.S. intelligence networks—provided that both the network administrator and the users on the network are willing to follow appropriate steps to create and maintain a secure networking environment.

Whenever you plan for the security of your network, put yourself in a cracker's shoes for a few minutes. How would you try to break into your own network? Where are the weak points? How would you obtain or falsify a key so that you could read messages sent by network users? For example, if a network is built around a public-key encryption system that all users are committed to, a cracker is unlikely to begin by trying to crack a key. Instead, he will try to falsify a key, steal a laptop containing a secret key, or find a disgruntled employee who has some access to the files he wants. By thinking about the weaknesses of your security—technical or human—you can decide in advance how to thwart efforts to exploit them.

RPM Security

Earlier in this chapter you read about using the `rpm` command to check the MD5 signature on an rpm package to verify its integrity. This verifies that the rpm was not damaged during downloading, but says nothing about who created it. To do this, you must add the public key for Red Hat Software from *www.redhat.com/solutions/security/news/publickey.html* and then check the public-key signature of an rpm to verify that the rpm really came from Red Hat. Other companies may use similar techniques; you can obtain their public keys and check the signatures in the same way.

Suppose you had downloaded an rpm package from a Web site that you thought was mirroring official Red Hat packages. A check using the command `rpm -qi` listed the Packager as Red Hat Software. The package was an update to IP Chains, which is used to create firewalls in Linux (as described in Chapter 11). A knowledgeable cracker could wreak havoc on your security by tampering with IP Chains, so you verify that the package was created by Red Hat Software using this command:

```
#rpm --checksig ipchains-1.3.10-15.i386.rpm
ipchains-1.3.10-15.i386.rpm:  md5  gpg  OK
```

The OK output on the second line shows that the file is not corrupted (the MD5 checksum is verified) and that the file was signed by the Red Hat Software private key (the gpg key signature is verified).

The Cryptographic File System

In Chapter 5 you learned about the Network File System (NFS). Though potentially a great convenience for users and system administrators, NFS assumes a network environment in which all users can be trusted. The **Cryptographic File System (CFS)** abandons this assumption, enforcing cryptographic authentication on all users who want to share files across the network. Another group has enhanced the work of the original developer of CFS (Matt Blaze) by making it operate transparently to client users on the network. They have renamed their project the **Transparent Cryptographic File System (TCFS)**. TCFS is still in development; to learn more about it, visit *http://zaphod.redwave.net/linux/tcfs/* and *www.tcfs.it*.

IP Packet Encryption

Encryption can occur at different points in a network transmission. For example, a user could encrypt a file using GPG before attaching the file to an email message. The data is then encrypted from the moment the email client sees it. Conversely, an email server such as `sendmail` could implement a security measure in which it exchanged keys with another `sendmail` server on the Internet and created a secure connection before transferring any email messages.

Beyond the Web (using HTTP and SSL as described previously), very few application protocols have standardized encryption mechanisms. For example, POP3, SMTP, FTP, and NFS do not. Instead, developers have created encryption options at the IP packet level.

IPsec (for Secure IP) is a fairly new industry standard for IP packet encryption. IPsec is supported in Linux, but as a standard, IPsec is still not completely settled—issues remain in areas such as key management and integration with higher-layer protocols. When IPv6 becomes widely used, it will have full support for IPsec. For more information, visit *www.rfc-editor.org* and search for RFC 2401.

A less expansive effort is **Cryptographic IP Encapsulation (CIPE)**, which tunnels IP packets within encrypted UDP packets. CIPE places special effort on being useful immediately (without waiting for complex issues relevant to IPsec to be resolved), and on being compatible with routing techniques used in more complex networks. For details on CIPE, visit *http://sites.inka.de/sites/bigred/devel/cipe.html*.

Secure Shell

The **Secure Shell (SSH)** protocol is probably better known than GPG, though GPG can be used in a broader range of circumstances. The simplest description of SSH is an encrypted version of Telnet—it lets you access a remote host the same way Telnet does, but without the danger that someone sniffing the network can see what you are transmitting. However, such a simple explanation tends to hide the power of SSH; unlike Telnet, SSH has been designed to allow other protocols to ride on top of it (or be encapsulated within it, depending on your preferred metaphor).

For example, protocols like FTP and remote sessions of the X Window System are completely insecure. However, you can start an SSH session and tie an FTP or X session to it, so that all traffic for the FTP or X session is transmitted using SSH—it is completely encrypted.

Like other Linux Internet services, SSH consists of a client utility (**ssh**) and a server daemon (**sshd**). In addition, the SSH package includes utilities to generate keys, and the **scp** program that acts like **rcp**, letting you copy files between any two computers on your network with full encryption. SSH is available as a commercial product—see *www.ssh.com*. Linux distributions rely on the free version of SSH, called **OpenSSH**—see *www.openssh.org*. OpenSSH is installed by default on many Linux systems, including Red Hat Linux 7.3. SSH is described in much more detail in Chapter 11.

Virtual Private Networks

The goal of many system administrators using cryptographic products and protocols is to create a **virtual private network (VPN)**. A VPN is a secure organizational network that uses insecure public networks (such as the Internet) for communications. A VPN takes advantage of the high speed and relatively low cost of Internet connectivity while hiding sensitive data from anyone else connected to the Internet. See Figure 8-17.

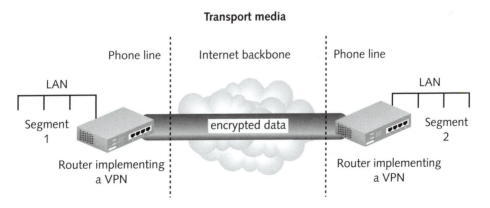

Figure 8-17   A virtual private network (VPN)

VPNs are often created with the aid of specially designed software that integrates many networking functions with cryptographic protocols and system management software. Chapter 11 discusses VPN software in more detail.

Some countries restrict the use of encryption technologies in various ways. For example, citizens of France are not allowed to use public key encryption without special permission. If you intend to move cryptographic products across national borders, you should research what rules apply. The Web site for a package such as OpenSSH contains legal notes on using that package.

Chapter Summary

- Cryptography is the science of encoding data, typically using a key, so that people without the key cannot read the data. Cryptography uses a cipher to encrypt plaintext into ciphertext.

- Cryptography protects computer networks against sniffers, programs that allow crackers to see data passing across a network.

- Many different algorithms are used to encrypt data. These algorithms are either symmetric (using a single key for encryption and decryption) or asymmetric (using two different keys for encryption and decryption). The use of asymmetric algorithms is commonly called public-key cryptography.

- DES was a popular standard algorithm for years. Triple DES and AES have replaced it in many circumstances—both are FIPS (approved for U.S. federal government work). Several other ciphers such as El Gamal, IDEA, and Blowfish are also popular.

- Public-key encryption does not require that you openly exchange a secret key with the recipient of an encrypted message, thus removing a major disadvantage to using encryption on computer networks. Public-key encryption is used to transmit securely the symmetric key with which a document is encrypted.

- RSA is the most familiar public-key algorithm.

- Signatures on a document show that the sender is the only one who could have sent the document; signatures on a public key in GPG indicate that the key is trusted by the signer.

- Certificates are issued and signed by certificate authorities such as VeriSign to vouch for the identity of the organization holding the certificate.

- A hash is a mathematical function that creates a small number from a very large number. Popular hashes are MD5 and SHA-1. A hash is used to create a fingerprint, which lets a user quickly verify the integrity of a public key or other large number or file.

- Browsers such as Netscape and Mozilla use cryptography via the Secure Sockets Layer (SSL) protocol to allow secure e-commerce transactions.

❑ Kerberos provides a network-wide user and service authentication scheme to limit network access to authorized users, but it requires a significant time commitment for configuration and maintenance.

❑ PGP was the first freely available public-key encryption software. It was created by Phil Zimmermann and is now owned by Network Associates, Inc. PGP remains an industry standard on which GPG is based.

❑ The Gnu Privacy Guard (GPG) is a free public-key encryption utility that lets you manage keys and encrypt, sign, and decrypt documents. Graphical utilities can make it easier to work with GPG. Many utilities such as `pine`, `elm`, and Kmail can integrate access to GPG for sending and receiving messages.

❑ Keys should be signed only when the identity of the person providing the key has been ascertained with certainty.

❑ The `rpm` utility can check a public key signature on any package to verify that it came from the person or organization that claims to have created the package.

❑ Other security protocols built on the same principles of cryptography as GPG include IPsec, CIPE, CFS, and TCFS. Many network administrators use technologies like these or specially created software to create a virtual private network (VPN) for an organization that spans multiple offices.

❑ The Secure Shell (SSH) provides encrypted remote access via a utility that functions like Telnet. SSH also lets other protocols work with it to create secure connections for many purposes. Both commercial and open versions of SSH are available.

8

KEY TERMS

Advanced Encryption Standard (AES) — A replacement for DES. The next generation of government-approved encryption standards. Uses the Rijndael algorithm (pronounced "Rain Doll").

algorithm — A set of rules or steps that, when followed, result in a predictable outcome.

asymmetric encryption algorithm — An encryption algorithm in which different keys are used to encrypt and decrypt a message. One is kept secret, one is distributed publicly. Often called public-key encryption.

authentication — The process of proving to a computer system or another person that you are in fact the person you say you are.

Blowfish — A symmetric cipher.

certificate — A numeric code used to identify an organization.

certificate authority (CA) — An organization that issues a certificate to another person or organization after verifying the credentials of the person or organization.

checksum — A computed value that helps to verify that a file or transmission has not been corrupted.

cipher — A cryptographic technique or rule that converts plaintext into ciphertext.

ciphertext — A message that has been encoded using a cipher so that it is no longer readable. The end result of encrypting plaintext.

Cryptographic File System (CFS) — A file-system driver supported by Linux that adds cryptographic features to an NFS-like file-sharing model.

Cryptographic IP Encapsulation (CIPE) — An IP packet encryption protocol. It lacks some features of IPsec but is already fully implemented (while IPsec is not). CIPE operates by tunneling IP packets within encrypted UDP packets.

cryptography — The science of encoding—and trying to decode—data that has been rendered unreadable using special knowledge or tools.

Data Encryption Standard (DES) — The first widely accepted standard for encryption, developed in the 1970s by IBM and the National Institute of Standards and Technology.

digital signature — A part of an electronic transaction that gives the transaction the same legally-binding effect as a document signed with an ink pen.

Digital Signature Algorithm (DSA) — A popular algorithm used to sign encrypted files to verify their origin.

El Gamal — A symmetric cipher used by GPG.

encryption — The process of converting plaintext to ciphertext using a cipher algorithm.

Federal Information Processing Standard (FIPS) — A standard for information processing (such as an encryption algorithm) that has been approved for use by government agencies.

fingerprint — A small number that is derived from a larger number (such as a public key) using a hash. The fingerprint provides a convenient test as to the integrity of the larger number.

Gnu Privacy Guard (GPG) — A command-line public-key encryption utility that is compatible with PGP in many respects.

hash — The result of a mathematical function that converts a large number into a smaller number in a predictable way.

https — A code within a Web page URL that indicates that the page was transmitted over an encrypted connection.

IDEA — A patented symmetric cipher.

IPsec — An industry standard for IP packet encryption. IPsec is supported in Linux, but as a standard, is still not completely settled.

Kerberos — A special type of authentication for organizational networks.

key — A code (usually numeric) that can be used to encrypt or decrypt a message.

key pair — The combination of a public key that can be handed out to others and a private or secret key that remains hidden on a user's system (and is protected with a passphrase).

keyring — The collection of public keys stored on a system; a file containing all of the keys to which GPG has immediate access.

message digest hash (MD5) — A hash that converts a number of any length (including a large computer file) to a 128-bit (32-hexadecimal-digit) number called a checksum.

one-time pad — An encryption method in which a message is converted to numbers, then random numbers taken from a list are added to each part of the message. The recipient must have the same list of random numbers to decrypt the message. Assuming no one else has the list of random numbers, the encrypted message is considered unbreakable.

OpenSSH — A free version of SSH included in most Linux distributions.

passphrase — A long password.

plaintext — A readable message.

Pretty Good Privacy (PGP) — The first utility to provide public-key encryption to all comers. Created by Phil Zimmermann.

prime number — A number that cannot be broken down into factors other than itself and 1. Prime numbers are the core mathematical feature of public-key encryption.

private-key encryption — Encryption using a symmetric algorithm.

public-key encryption — Encryption using an asymmetric encryption algorithm.

RC2 — A symmetric cipher.

RC4 — A symmetric cipher.

realm — Within a Kerberos-enabled network, all the users and services whose keys are stored on the Kerberos server.

RSA — The most widely-known algorithm for public-key encryption. Developed by Ronald Rivest, Adi Shamir, and Len Adleman.

Secure Hash Algorithm (SHA-1) — A hashing algorithm, more secure than MD5, that creates a 160-bit hash of any file or key to help check whether it was tampered with or otherwise corrupted during transmission.

Secure Shell (SSH) — A protocol that provides network connectivity equivalent to an encrypted version of Telnet, plus additional support to allow encryption of other protocols.

sign — To attach your private key to a file to show that the file could only have come from you. Also, to attach your private key to another person's public key to indicate that you trust the validity of that public key.

Skipjack — A government-approved encryption algorithm that uses an 80-bit key.

sniff — To tap into a network connection to read the packets that other users have sent.

sniffer — A software package used to sniff the network.

symmetric encryption algorithm — An encryption algorithm in which the same key is used to both encrypt and decrypt a message (the algorithm is reversed for decryption). Also called private-key encryption.

8

ticket — A set of information provided by a Kerberos server to a user or service that grants the user permission to use the service. A ticket contains the following components: {sessionkey:username:address:servicename:lifespan:timestamp}

Transparent Cryptographic File System (TCFS) — An enhancement to the Cryptographic File System (CFS) that allows it to operate transparently to client users on the network.

Triple DES — A U.S. government-approved encryption algorithm that applies the DES algorithm three times in succession using three different DES keys.

Twofish — A symmetric cipher.

virtual private network (VPN) — A secure organizational network that uses insecure public networks (such as the Internet) for communications.

web of trust — The personal connections between a group of colleagues who have exchanged keys, signed them, and continue to rely on each others' signatures.

REVIEW QUESTIONS

1. Define cryptography.

2. A person using a sniffer would benefit from:

   a. users on the network running unencrypted Telnet sessions

   b. a VPN

   c. the 56-bit key length of a DES cipher

   d. both GPG and PGP

3. Which statement is accurate?

   a. Plaintext and ciphertext differ only in their transmission characteristics.

   b. Cryptography was developed in the 1970s as part of the computer science field.

   c. A cipher is used to encrypt plaintext, yielding ciphertext.

   d. Cipher algorithms cannot use keys if they are to remain secure.

4. For a symmetric cipher to be useful:

   a. The algorithm can be openly known, but the key must remain secret.

   b. The algorithm must be kept secret as well as the key.

   c. The key must be longer than 128 bits.

   d. The government must have approved it as a FIPS.

5. DES is no longer widely used because:

   a. Other ciphers have been better-tested.

   b. DES can now be exported and thus is considered an insecure munition.

   c. Patents make it too expensive to implement on a wide scale.

   d. Its key size is too small, allowing specialized computers to crack a DES key in a relatively short time.

6. Name the three alternatives to DES mentioned in the text.

7. Triple DES is not considered a good long-term cipher choice because:

    a. The creators of the algorithm were not government employees.

    b. Asymmetric ciphers are replacing older symmetric ciphers.

    c. Skipjack is much more secure.

    d. Its use of three DES keys applied sequentially requires too much computing power.

8. Which cipher algorithm does AES use?

    a. Rijndael

    b. Skipjack

    c. Blowfish

    d. El Gamal

9. What standard key lengths does AES support?

    a. 128, 192, and 256 bits

    b. 1,024 and 2,048 bits

    c. 56 bits, three times

    d. 64 bits

10. What is the standard key length for a public key in GPG?

    a. 56 bits

    b. 128 bits

    c. 1,024 bits

    d. 2,048 bits

11. Name five symmetric cipher algorithms.

12. Define the term "prime number."

13. A document is typically both encrypted and signed:

    a. so that it takes twice the computing power to decrypt it

    b. only when the sender does not know the recipient

    c. unless the recipient does not have the private key of the sender

    d. so that only the recipient can decrypt it and the recipient knows that the named sender sent it

14. The most widely known asymmetric encryption algorithm is:

    a. RSA

    b. DES

    c. Triple DES

    d. GPG

8

15. A certificate authority (CA):

    a. issues key pairs that can then be imported into programs such as GPG

    b. can read messages encrypted with certificates that it has issued

    c. issues a certificate cryptographically signed by the CA that indicates the CA's verification of the identity of the certificate holder

    d. signs each Web transaction with its public key

16. A hash and a fingerprint of a public key:

    a. are never used at the same time

    b. are effectively the same thing—a hash of a public key is called its fingerprint and allows easy verification of its integrity

    c. cannot be verified except by the GPG program

    d. provide for symmetric encryption

17. Name two popular hash algorithms.

18. Within a Kerberos _____, the Kerberos server grants _____ to users to access services.

    a. realm, tickets

    b. network, keys

    c. program, ciphers

    d. cipher, hashes

19. Within GPG you must enter a passphrase each time GPG:

    a. decrypts an unsigned document based on the public key of a colleague stored on your keyring

    b. contacts a keyserver

    c. accesses your secret key to encrypt or sign something

    d. only when you initially create your key pair

20. The keyring in GPG is:

    a. The collection of all keys that GPG has access to for encryption or decryption.

    b. The combination of your secret/private key and your public key.

    c. The hash created when you sign another person's public key to verify that you trust it.

    d. Not accessible except through the GPG command-line utility.

21. GPA and Seahorse are:

    a. two symmetric ciphers

    b. two asymmetric ciphers

    c. pseudonyms for the two crackers who broke DES

    d. two graphical utilities that provide GPG functionality

22. Using an `rpm --checksig` command provides:

a. a fingerprint that you can use to send the file to another user securely

b. assurance that the purported packager of an rpm file actually created the file and that it has not been modified

c. access to full GPG functionality from within the package file you are installing

d. a GPG signature check without any MD5 information being provided

23. Name two protocols that encrypt data for network transmission.

24. SSH is commonly used in place of Telnet because:

a. SSH provides a secure communications channel that is immune to sniffing software.

b. Telnet patents do not expire for several more years.

c. SSH is strictly open source and Telnet is not.

d. SSH protocols use a more robust encryption algorithm than that used by Telnet.

25. Moving cryptographic products across national borders requires care because:

a. Language barriers can create unexpected results when signing keys.

b. Different nations use different approved ciphers, which may be incompatible.

c. Taxes on these products can be very high.

d. Laws controlling cryptography vary widely between nations and are taken very seriously.

HANDS-ON PROJECTS

Project 8-1

In this project you decrypt a letter-substitution cipher. To complete this project, you should have a pencil, paper, and some time. You may want to work as a class or in a team so you can more efficiently analyze possible solutions. This type of cipher appears regularly in puzzle books, but this simple cipher provides an excellent chance to understand how more complex ciphers are constructed and how they can be decrypted given patience. Use the hints given in the chapter text about letter and word frequency as you attack this problem. Remember that having a longer message is helpful because it gives you more data to analyze and test your theories as you work out which letter stands for which other letter. For this cipher, each letter represents a single, different letter of the alphabet. Word breaks in the plaintext have been preserved. The ciphertext follows:

```
QCFW OFQFO: R KFIC MCCX GKZJX RX HKC PRDCG ZP HKC JFW
QCBFWHOCXH F GHFHCOCXH ZP HKC FQELHFXH NCXCWFD HKFH
UZL FWC HKC OZHKCW ZP PRIC GZXG JKZ KFIC QRCQ
NDZWRZLGDU ZX HKC PRCDQ ZP MFHHDC. R PCCD KZJ JCFA FXQ
PWLRHDCGG OLGH MC FXU JZWQG ZP ORXC JKRSK GKZLDQ
```

```
FHHCOBH HZ MCNLRDC UZL PWZO HKC NWRCP ZP F DZGG GZ
ZICWJKCDORXN. MLH R SFXXZH WCPWFRX PWZO HCXQCWRXN HZ
UZL HKC SZXGZDPHRZX HKFH OPU MC PZLXQ RX HKC HKFXAG ZP
HKC WCBLMDRS HKCU QRCQ HZ GFIC. R BWFU HKFH ZLW
KCFICXDU PFHKCW OFU FGGLFNC HKC FXNLRGK ZP UZLW
MCWCFICOCXH FXQ DCFIR UZL ZXDU HKC SKCWRGKCQ OCOZWU
ZP HKC DZICQ FXQ DZGH FXQ HKC GZDCOX BWRQC HKFH OLGH MC
UZLWG HZ KFIC DFRQ GZ SZGHDU F GFSWRPRSC LBZX HKC FDHFW
ZP PWCCQZO. - F. DRXSZDX.
```

Project 8-2

In this project you experiment with a hash function to see how changing a large file changes the hash of the file. To complete this project, you should have Red Hat Linux installed.

1. Log in and open a command-line window.

2. Copy the /etc/termcap file to your home directory under the name **test**.

   ```
   cp /etc/termcap ~/test
   ```

3. The **termcap** file, which you just copied and renamed to **test**, has over 17,000 lines of text. Compute an MD5 checksum on the test file using the **md5sum** command:

   ```
   md5sum test
   ```

   (You can also include a regular expression to compute checksums on a number of files with one command.)

4. Open the **test** file in a text editor.

5. Press the spacebar on the first line of the file (or make some other one-character change to the file).

6. Save the file and exit the editor.

7. Run another checksum using **md5sum**:

   ```
   md5sum test
   ```

8. How do the checksums (the hashes) compare?

9. If you have a great deal of time, experiment to find a change that you can make in the test file that will yield the same checksum as the original file did.

Project 8-3

In this project you review Web page security in a browser. To complete this project, you should have Linux installed with a graphical browser and an Internet connection. Netscape Communicator within Red Hat Linux 7.3 is described in the steps for this project, though most browsers will have similar functionality.

1. Log in and launch Netscape Communicator or another graphical browser.

2. Enter the URL **www.americanexpress.com**.

3. Select the link for **My American Express** from the pull-down list on the right side of the home page, then click **Go**.

4. On the My American Express page, choose the **Log In** link. You may have to respond to one or more dialog boxes presented by your browser that inform you of security issues, such as being transferred to another Web server or moving from an insecure to a secure document (or vice versa in other cases). Why does your browser inform you of these things?

5. Notice that the URL has changed to begin with `https` instead of `http`. The small lock icon in the lower left corner of the window is now closed as well.

6. Choose **Page Info** on the View menu.

7. At the bottom of the page that appears, notice the security information. Can you find any of the following on the page?

   ❑ A fingerprint?

   ❑ A certificate authority?

   ❑ A certificate?

   ❑ The owner of the certificate?

   ❑ A cipher name?

   ❑ A key-bit length?

Project 8-4

In this project you use the `gpg` utility to create a key pair and use it to encrypt a file. To complete this project, you should have Red Hat Linux 7.3 installed with the `gpg` utility (which is installed by default). In this project, you work with a partner to share encrypted information. Since you are likely working in a lab environment, do not consider the keys that you create here to be "real" keys that you would distribute to friends outside the classroom. The keys should be discarded after completing the project; you can then create real keys on your personal or office computer.

1. Log in to Linux.

2. Run the `gpg` command for the first time without any parameters. The program creates needed directories.

   gpg

3. Run `gpg` again to generate a key pair for your user account. Use the default values for cipher, key length, and no expiration. Enter your name and lab email address when prompted, and decide on a simple passphrase to protect your private key.

   gpg --gen-key

4. View your public key using the **--list-keys** command.

   gpg --list-keys

5. Export a copy of your public key in binary format. Use your email address as your user ID to specify the key that you want to export (though your keyring contains only one key thus far):

> `gpg -o `*`your_name`*`.key --export `*`your_email_address`*

6. Get the `.key` file you created in the previous step to your lab partner for this exercise, either via a floppy disk or a network connection (you could email it to her, for example).

7. You and your partner should have exchanged files containing your public keys. Import your partner's key into your keyring:

> `gpg --import `*`partner_key_file`*

8. Because the user ID of a key is encoded as part of the key, only the filename is needed, not a user name. Check the list of keys on your keyring again to see that the import function worked.

> `gpg --list-keys`

9. Display the fingerprint/checksum for your partner's key.

> `gpg --fingerprint `*`partner_email_address`*

10. Call your partner on the phone or talk across tables. Have her view the fingerprint for her own key (by specifying her own user ID with the `--fingerprint` command). Review the fingerprint of your partner's key to make certain it is valid.

11. Sign your partner's key by using the `edit-key` command, then the `sign` command. Start with this, substituting your partner's email address where indicated:

> `gpg --edit-key `*`partner_email_address`*

When the command prompt appears, enter

> `sign`

At the Really sign? prompt, type y, then press Enter.

You are prompted for the passphrase you entered in step 3 and your partner's key is signed.

12. Both you and your partner now have a key ring that includes your own key and each other's public key. You can use the text file from the `/etc` directory used here as an example, or you can create or use any file you choose. Encrypt a document to send to your partner using the `--encrypt` command:

> `gpg -a -o message.gpg -r `*`partner_email_address`*` --sign --encrypt /etc/xinetd.d/wu-ftpd`

13. Exchange encrypted files with your partner by FTP, email, floppy disk, or however your choose.

14. Decrypt and review the file you received from your partner:

> `gpg --decrypt message.gpg`

Project 8-5

In this project you use the **rpm** command to verify the signature on an rpm package. To complete this project, you should have Red Hat Linux 7.3 installed, root access to the Linux system, and an Internet connection. You should also have completed Project 8-4 so that GPG is installed and you have an active GPG keyring.

1. Log in to Linux.
2. Open a browser and visit *www.redhat.com/solutions/security/news/publickey.html*.
3. Copy the public key from the Red Hat page.
4. Open a text editor and paste the copied text into the editor window. Save the file as **redhat.key**.
5. Import the Red Hat Software public key using the **--import** command of GPG:

   ```
   gpg --import redhat.key
   ```
6. Verify the import operation by listing all the keys on your keyring:

   ```
   gpg --list-keys
   ```
7. Obtain a copy of an rpm file that was created by Red Hat Software. You can do this by copying an rpm file from the Red Hat Linux CD or downloading a file from the Red Hat Web site. One example would be to visit this page: *http://rhn.redhat.com/errata/rh73-errata-bugfixes.html* and click on the link for updated SANE packages. Within that page, click on the appropriate link to download an updated sane-backends package.
8. Change to the directory where the downloaded rpm package is located.
9. Run the **rpm** command to verify that the package you downloaded was indeed created by Red Hat Software.

   ```
   rpm --checksig package_filename
   ```

8

CASE PROJECTS

1. Using the Web sites mentioned in the chapter text as resources, determine why the Rijndael algorithm was selected for AES and what advantages or disadvantages it has compared to other popular symmetric algorithms that were considered for AES or that were not considered for AES but are in wide use today.

2. Prepare a one-page report on the current issues facing public key infrastructure—the creation and dissemination of trusted public keys to provide privacy and security to citizens around the world. Use the URLs in the chapter text or Internet search engines to begin your research.

3. Suppose you are the network administrator for a company of 400 employees, each of whom works at a computer all day. Would you want to encourage use of GPG as much as possible? Why or why not? How would GPG affect the security of your network operations? What other techniques would you want to consider to enhance network security (many of these are not discussed in detail until later chapters)?

9

USER SECURITY

After reading this chapter and completing the exercises you will be able to:

♦ Follow good password security practices

♦ Understand Linux Pluggable Authentication Modules (PAM)

♦ Use common utilities to promote user security

♦ Set up user access to system administration tasks with sudo

In this chapter you learn about files and utilities related to maintaining secure user accounts. These include the standard password files and utilities, plus a number of other programs that let you see who is logged in to Linux, control user access to system administration activities, and similar functions.

In addition, this chapter describes how to use Linux Pluggable Authentication Modules, which let you control how different programs authenticate users (determine their identity) and authorize them to use different services on Linux.

MANAGING PASSWORD SECURITY

Users can access services on a Linux system in two fundamentally different ways. First, they can use client software that connects to server software running on Linux. The server software must be waiting for the client connection and must accept or reject the connection based on a number of factors. For example, an FTP server might reject a connection request because the client is from a domain that is not permitted FTP access; a Web server might accept a connection but refuse to return the requested Web page because the access required is limited to certain hosts or network IDs. When a person connects to Linux through a network service, access generally consists of limited functionality provided by the server hosting that service. The user does not have broad access to the server, because all the user's actions are carried out by the server. For example, a network user connecting from a Web browser does not have an account on the Linux server, but the Web browser knows how to ask the Web server to do something on the user's behalf. Thus the user's access is limited to the functions performed by the service running on the server.

The second way to access Linux is to log in as a user on that system. To do this you must have a valid user account on the system. That is, you must log in using a user ID listed in the **/etc/passwd** file and enter the password corresponding to that user ID. The following sections outline ways of selecting and managing passwords to enhance security.

Selecting Strong Passwords

Counteracting secret cracker tricks may consume a lot of your time as a system administrator, but a cracker's best bet is simply to obtain a valid password for a user on your system. Then the cracker can log in at his or her leisure without any of the telltale signs of a forced entry that you will be watching for on network services (after reading Chapters 11 and 12). Selecting good passwords and keeping them secure is crucial to good system security. All users need to understand this, and frequently they must have it enforced by rules that a system administrator sets up.

 Crackers sometimes obtain passwords by intercepting network traffic that contains unencrypted passwords. Chapters 11 and 12 describe how to encrypt network traffic to prevent this.

Passwords are sometimes obtained from users by crackers using social engineering tactics such as calling to pose as a system administrator, looking for notes taped to a person's screen or desk, or looking over the shoulder of someone as they type in the password (watching the keyboard, not the screen, as the password does not appear on screen as it is typed). Passwords should not be written down, especially not anywhere near the computer to which they permit access. They must be chosen carefully so they can be remembered without a written aid. However, they should not include easily guessed words or numbers like names of pets, phone numbers, etc.

Passwords are often given out on purpose by a user who is trying to help a co-worker complete some task using his or her account. The other person may then continue to use the password without specific authorization, whenever it is convenient. Or the other person may not be as careful about keeping the password secret as the password owner would be. Users should be taught never to tell anyone their password, and you as system administrator must work to make the system operate in a manner that does not encourage people to give out their passwords. For example, everyone needs to have access to sufficient hardware and software to do their job in a timely manner.

When a user gives out his or her password, he or she violates the idea on which passwords are based: that only a single individual can access the server using a particular user ID and password. Giving out that password also exposes the password's owner to liability for the actions of someone using his or her account. Helping users understand that fact will discourage sharing passwords.

When crackers don't have passwords handed to them on a platter, they may resort to guessing a password based on their knowledge of the account owner. The focus turns from teaching users how to handle their passwords to teaching them what sorts of passwords they ought to use. A skilled cracker has a list of passwords that users regularly rely on when security is not on their mind. These include things such as:

9

- Names of children, pets, or spouse
- Company, industry, or product relating to their job
- Combinations of birthdays of the user or children/spouse
- Commonly used bad passwords like "password," "secret," or the username itself

For each of these, a cracker will try combinations of words, adding numbers, reversing or dropping letters, and trying similar alterations. When users rely on items such as these as the basis of their passwords, guessing the right one does not take a cracker very long. Users should be instructed to use passwords that do not draw on personal information that is readily available; users should also not use a word that can be found in the dictionary. In fact, the best passwords are composed of random letters, numbers, and symbols, but these can be hard to remember without writing them down. Here are some ideas for creating a good password for a Linux user account:

- It must be long enough; a minimum of eight characters should be sufficient in most situations. Passwords of four letters, for example, are easy to crack, no matter how clever they are.
- It should include at least one number (a digit) or one symbol (such as @#$%^&*), and preferably a few of them.
- It could include two or three words separated by one or more symbols or numbers, such as red1*1meat or buda234pest.
- Using multiple words works even better if the words are foreign or altered so that they do not appear in a dictionary. For example, r3d*m3at or rud*muut.

- Using a series of numbers or a pattern of altered letters can make it easier to remember your password. This is especially helpful when you must select a new password frequently and decide to follow your chosen pattern for subsequent passwords. Just make certain the pattern is not obvious to someone who obtains one of your older passwords.

When you use strong passwords like these and avoid being the subject of social engineering, a cracker must resort to a brute force attack to gain entry to your user account. A **brute force attack** means trying all possible combinations until one succeeds in guessing a password. If a cracker can store the encrypted version of your password on the Linux server, he may be able to devote considerable time to a brute force attack. If he must actually attempt to log in each time he tries a password, a brute force attack is not feasible, because any system administrator will notice someone trying to log in unsuccessfully millions of times! A brute force attack can proceed by trying passwords based on a list of words or by trying all possible combinations of letters, numbers, and symbols.

One simple example of a password cracking tool is called **nutcracker**. You can download this program at *linux.tucows.com*. The program is written as a Perl script, so it's slow compared to a program written in C, but it lets you see how a password cracker operates. Some system administrators use a password cracking program to randomly test the strength of users' passwords on the systems they manage, perhaps sending a warning email to users whose passwords were easily broken.

 Be very careful about using a password cracking program in this way! Get the written approval of your supervisor; be certain this does not violate a stated company policy on employee privacy; inform users beforehand that weak passwords will be subject to scrutiny. Avoid the appearance of being a cracker who is trying to pry into personal files, even if you have access to them as root!

The possibility of a brute force attack points out the need to change passwords frequently. Every 30 days is a common security practice, though some organizations require changes weekly. It also shows why the encrypted text of passwords must be safeguarded on each Linux system, as described in the next section on shadow passwords. Finally, a brute force attack is much less likely to succeed when long passwords that include numbers and symbols are used.

To see why such passwords are more effective in resisting a brute force attack, you must review a little math. If you have a four-character password composed only of the 26 capital letters, you have $26 \times 26 \times 26 \times 26$, or 26^4 possible passwords: about 457,000. A fast computer can test that many possible passwords relatively quickly in order to "crack" an unknown password. But what about a password that is six characters long and may include 26 capital and 26 lowercase letters (Linux passwords are case-sensitive), plus 32 possible symbols (such as @#$%) and 10 possible digits? That means that each character of the password has $26 + 26 + 32 + 10 = 94$ possible values. So using six characters yields 94^6 possible passwords: about 690 billion. Using a password cracking tool to guess a password using a brute force attack is very time consuming with so many possible passwords to try. The eight-character recommendation above yields over 6 quadrillion possible passwords. At that point, a brute force attack is only feasible for an organization like the National Security Agency (NSA).

Managing Linux Passwords

Linux includes several facilities for managing passwords that let you enforce security measures such as a minimum number of characters, a maximum length of time a password can be used, and other traits.

When you set up a new user account using the **adduser** or **useradd** command (or a graphical utility), a single line is added to the **/etc/passwd** file. That entry looks like this example:

```
nwells:x:500:500:Nicholas Wells:/home/nwells:/bin/bash
```

The fields on this line are separated by colons. The first field is the username, the second field formerly contained the encrypted password for the user. These days that second field contains nothing but a placeholder, "x". Because the **/etc/passwd** file must be accessed by many different programs, it was considered too dangerous to have the encrypted password accessible to all users on the system; it was becoming too easy to crack passwords. Instead, the encrypted password was moved to a file called **/etc/shadow**, which only the root user could access. Each line in this file also corresponds to a single user account, but the fields are related to password management for that account. Specifically, the shadow password file **/etc/shadow** controls:

- The username to which the entry applies.

- The encrypted password data.

- The last date the password was changed.

- The number of days until the user may change the password again. (Preventing too-frequent password changes thwarts some types of cracker attacks and also prevents overactive users from forgetting their passwords.)

- The number of days until the password must be changed again, at which point it is said to have expired. (Requiring users to update their password regularly is an excellent security practice, though most users hate it.)

- The number of days before the password expires before Linux will warn the user of the upcoming expiration and the need to select a new password.

- The number of days after the password expires that the account will be considered inactive, requiring the system administrator to reactivate the account before a user can log in again.

- The date of the account expiration, either as set explicitly by the system administrator or computed from the last password change, and maximum time for password use.

9

A sample line from /etc/shadow is shown here:

```
nwells:$1$LkrzanmA$/DtzgUGpJa2cTM8rM5WbH1:11844:0:99999:7:::
```

The password data in the second field is encoded by default using MD5 on Red Hat Linux. You can alter this using the **authconf** utility if you choose, in which case DES is used to encode the stored password instead of MD5.

Each user can change his or her password using the **passwd** utility. When you enter this command name, you are prompted to enter your current password (unless you are working as root), then you must enter a new password two times. Nothing appears as you type the new password, so entering it twice helps you verify that you entered what you think you entered. A regular user does not have to specify his or her username when running the **passwd** program. When you are logged in as root, you can change any user's password using **passwd** by adding the username after the command, then entering a new password twice when prompted:

```
passwd nwells
```

The **passwd** utility will perform a few basic checks on the password you enter, based on the configuration of Linux PAM modules described in the next section. However, **passwd** can't prevent you from using poor passwords.

 Although root has access to the /etc/passwd and /etc/shadow files, you should not edit these files directly in a text editor. The danger is too great that you will disable an account (or worse, cause a security hole) because of a typo-graphic error. Instead, use the utilities described below to edit password data.

If you must edit /etc/passwd because the file has become corrupted, use the **vipw** command. This command locks the /etc/passwd file before launching the **vi** text editor. This prevents conflicting edits on systems with multiple system administrators.

Similar to **vipw**, the **vigr** command lets you edit the /etc/group file in which all group membership data is stored on Linux. After you edit the /etc/group file with **vigr**, you may want to run the **grpck** command to verify that all group memberships are valid user accounts and no errors in syntax were introduced by your edits.

The shadow password system located in /etc/shadow is used by default on all major Linux distributions. (You can alter this in the **authconfig** utility of Red Hat if you choose.) The password control information is set using the **useradd** or **passwd** commands. Table 9-1 shows the relevant options for the **passwd** command, and Table 9-2 shows password options you can use with the **useradd** command.

Table 9-1   Command-line options for `passwd`

Command Option	Description
−l	Lock an account so that no one can log in using that username. Use with the −u option.
−u	Unlock an account that was previously locked using the −l option. The password of the account remains intact.
−d	Disable an account. The account must be enabled again by the root user setting a new password.
−n *days*	Set the minimum number of days that the user must wait before changing the password.
−x *days*	Set the maximum number of days that the current password can be used before it must be changed.
−w *days*	Set how many days before the password expiration date the user will be warned (upon logging in) that the password must be changed to prevent the account from locking up.
−i *days*	Set the number of days after an account is locked before it will become disabled (and its password deleted).

Table 9-2   `useradd` command-line options for password control

Command Option	Description
−e *date*	Set an expiration date for the account. At that time, the password will be deleted and the account will be effectively disabled, though the user's files remain intact.
−f *inactive_days*	Set the number of days after an account is locked before it will be changed to disabled (and its password deleted).

An example of a specialized password system is the single-use password suite designed by Bell Communications Research. This suite, called **S/Key**, requires a user to enter a different password each time he or she logs in to the system. It is designed so that the user doesn't have to think of a new password each time, but instead relies on a system-generated password in conjunction with a longer passphrase that the user selects. S/Key is not available on Linux, but a program based on S/Key, called **One-time Password In Everything (OPIE)**, can be compiled for Linux. This suite of utilities was created by the U.S. Naval Research Laboratory based on the S/Key program. You can download UNIX-compatible source code and experiment with OPIE by visiting *www.nas.nasa.gov/Groups/Security/OPIE/*.

USING PLUGGABLE AUTHENTICATION MODULES

The basic UNIX/Linux password architecture described in the previous section includes security that is robust enough for many sites. However it is not robust enough for all sites, nor does it permit much of the flexibility in configuration that other operating systems have offered for a long time. In addition, adding Linux to a network of other systems (such as Windows NT) can place a real burden on a system administrator, who must then keep two sets of configuration files updated with user information, rather than just one.

The **Pluggable Authentication Module (PAM)** architecture was developed by Sun Microsystems. It is now used on virtually every Linux system to provide improved user-level security, flexibility in managing user authentication, and smoother integration between Linux configuration data and user information stored on other systems. PAM is an architecture and set of libraries that let a programmer create a module to perform a specific security-related function, such as testing whether an updated password is too short or whether a user is permitted to log in at a certain time of day. System administrators can select, configure, and then use one or more modules to control the operation of any Linux program that is aware of PAM capabilities. Because PAM has been in widespread use for several years, many programs recognize PAM as a security mechanism.

You may have already seen PAM at work. If you are using a standard Red Hat Linux installation, PAM is configured by default. As one example of its operation, you cannot enter a short word (for example, three characters) when you change your password unless you are root. Instead you see a message telling you that the password is "WAY too short!" and the password is not changed. This message comes from a PAM module (**pam_cracklib**, listed in Table 9-3) that is configured by default in Red Hat Linux to stop users from entering insecure passwords.

To use PAM, you select which PAM modules you want to control the activity of a particular program. You list those modules in a configuration file for that program, with parameters to set how the module behaves. Some examples will help you see how this is done. You'll also get to practice configuring PAM modules in the Hands-on Projects at the end of the chapter.

PAM is configured using either a single configuration file, **/etc/pam.conf**, or a series of configuration files in the directory **/etc/pam.d**. (The person compiling the software selects which configuration style is used.) Red Hat and many other implementations use the directory method because it makes it simple for a software package to add a file to your system in order to configure a newly added program. The **/etc/pam.d** directory contains a file with a name matching the program being configured. For example, the text file **/etc/pam.d/login** configures the **login** program. Each file contains a list of one or more modules that PAM uses when that program is run. The file named **other** is used if a program tries to use PAM but no specific configuration file is found in **/etc/pam.d**. The syntax of each line in a file within **/etc/pam.d** is shown here. Each element is described below:

```
module_type    control_flag    module_path    arguments
```

Be careful working with PAM configuration files. If you were to delete the /etc/pam.d/login file, for example, you would be unable to log in to your system, even as root!

To discuss these elements, it's helpful to have a sample file to review. Below is the default `/etc/pam.d/login` file from Red Hat Linux 7.3. The lines are numbered for reference below; these numbers are not part of the actual file:

```
1 #%PAM-1.0
2 auth       required   /lib/security/pam_securetty.so
3 auth       required   /lib/security/pam_stack.so service=
  system-auth
4 auth       required   /lib/security/pam_nologin.so
5 account    required   /lib/security/pam_stack.so service=
  system-auth
6 password required    /lib/security/pam_stack.so service=
  system-auth
7 session    required   /lib/security/pam_stack.so service=
  system-auth
8 session    optional   /lib/security/pam_console.so
```

The first element on each line is the **module_type**, which defines when the module will be used. Possible types include:

- **auth**: Authentication modules are used to identify a user, normally by prompting for a password.

- **account**: These modules manage the user's account once identity has been established by an **auth** module. These modules typically restrict access, for example, allowing access only during certain times of the day.

- **session**: These modules manage a user's current session, normally attending to tasks that must be completed before a user is allowed to work, such as creating log files or mounting a file system that the user needs.

- **password**: These modules are executed when a user needs to change a password (or other authentication tokens).

 Complete documentation on PAM and individual modules is located in `/usr/share/doc/pam-0.75` on Red Hat Linux 7.3.

When a PAM-compatible program such as `login` or `passwd` is executed, it checks to see which applicable modules are configured for a given task. For example, when a user first logs in, `login` passes control to PAM, which must run all the modules listed as **auth** modules (lines 2, 3, and 4 in the above example file). When multiple modules are listed for a module type, modules are said to be **stacked**. Unless a **control_flag** dictates otherwise, PAM will execute all of the modules in a stack in the order they are listed, and return a result of Access Permitted or Access Denied based on the modules' results.

9

The `control_flag` element determines how PAM processes stacked modules. The `control_flag` has two forms; the older and simpler syntax is still used in most configuration files. It supports four possible values:

- `required`: The module must succeed for the final result to be Access Permitted. Because later modules in the stack are also executed, the user cannot tell which module failed, but the final result will be Access Denied if any required module fails.

- `requisite`: The module must succeed for the final result to be Access Permitted. If a requisite module fails, remaining modules in a stack are not executed; if a requisite module succeeds, remaining modules are also executed.

- `sufficient`: The final result can be Access Permitted even if this module fails, but if this module succeeds, that is sufficient for an Access Permitted result. If a sufficient module succeeds, no other modules are executed; if a previous required module in the stack did not fail, PAM returns immediately with a result of Access Permitted. If a sufficient module fails, later modules are executed without regard to the result of the sufficient module.

- `optional`: The result of an optional module does not affect the final result of a module stack. Optional modules are used to perform tasks such as logging that are not part of determining access but are helpful in system administration or meeting user needs.

Figure 9-1 shows several examples of how these control flags would operate together to determine the final outcome after processing a stack of modules.

As if this system were not sufficiently complicated, PAM also supports another syntax for the `control_flag` element. You can include one or more sets (separated by spaces) of instructions in the format `test=action`. The test is one of 30 codes, such as `user_unknown` or `acct_expired`. The action can be one of six codes such as `ignore`, `done`, or `bad`; or the action can be a number that indicates how many subsequent modules in the current stack should be skipped. Using this format for the `control_flag` lets you create a complex stack of PAM modules and control how they are executed based on the results of previous modules. Standard Linux systems don't implement this more complex system in their default configuration files, but you can read about it in the PAM documentation.

The last two elements in a PAM configuration file are the `module_path` and arguments. The `module_path` is the complete path and module name to be executed. The arguments are information that should be passed to that module as it is executed. Lines 2, 4, and 8 in the sample file on the previous page are examples of lines without any arguments. The other lines (besides 1, which is a comment line) have a single argument for the `pam_stack` module: `service=system-auth`.

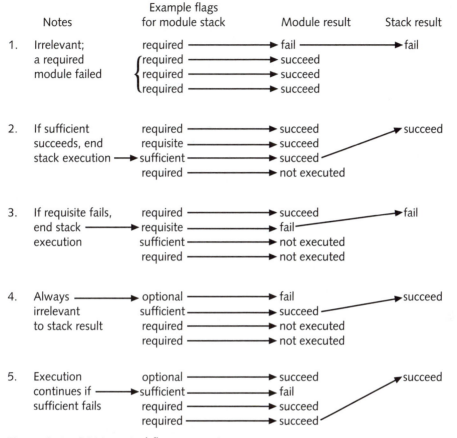

Figure 9-1   PAM control flag processing

The **pam_stack** module is a special module that acts like an "include" file. The service listed after a **pam_stack** module refers to another configuration file in **/etc/pam.d**. All of the modules listed in the named configuration file will be executed at that point. For example, consider the lines above from the PAM login configuration file (again, line numbers are not part of the file):

```
2 auth        required   /lib/security/pam_securetty.so
3 auth        required   /lib/security/pam_stack.so service=
  system-auth
4 auth        required   /lib/security/pam_nologin.so
```

The file /etc/pam.d/system-auth contains these module configuration lines, which are generated automatically by the authconfig utility based on which security measures you select:

```
auth          required       /lib/security/pam_env.so
auth          sufficient     /lib/security/pam_unix.so
   likeauth nullok
auth          required       /lib/security/pam_deny.so
account       required       /lib/security/pam_unix.so
password      required       /lib/security/pam_cracklib.so
   retry=3 type=
password      sufficient     /lib/security/pam_unix.so
   nullok use_authtok md5 shadow
password      required       /lib/security/pam_deny.so
session       required       /lib/security/pam_limits.so
session       required       /lib/security/pam_unix.so
```

Given these two files, the login command would execute these modules—in this order—as part of the login process (the auth stack):

- pam_securetty.so (from /etc/pam.d/login)

- pam_stack.so   (from /etc/pam.d/login—this module only launches the next three)

- pam_env.so   (from /etc/pam.d/system-auth)

- pam_unix.so   (from /etc/pam.d/system-auth)

- pam_deny.so   (from /etc/pam.d/system-auth)

- pam_nologin.so   (from /etc/pam.d/login)

The use of each of these modules is described in Table 9-3. Note that some of these modules support dozens of options. In addition, the file /usr/share/doc/pam-0.75 /html/pam-6.html in Red Hat Linux 7.3 contains reference information for each module, including examples and descriptions of all the supported arguments. These descriptions include information specific to any of the four module types for which the module is supported. For example, the pam_unix module can be used for auth, account, session, or passwd.

 Although you will want to review the PAM documentation to learn about the operation and options supported by each module, reviewing example configuration files and the most commonly used modules will help you understand how you can configure PAM to meet the needs of your own network. Keep in mind that PAM configurations can become quite complicated and that misconfigured systems may allow or prevent access in ways that you had not anticipated. As you learn about PAM, make changes to configuration files one at a time, testing the results after each change to see what happens.

Table 9-3 Commonly used PAM modules

Module Name	Description
path_xauth	Forwards xauth tokens between X client and X server to permit graphical programs to operate with PAM authentication.
pam_deny	Deny access.
pam_permit	Permit access.
pam_ftp	Check whether the user is ftp or anonymous; if so, prompt the user for a password.
pam_group	Grant extended group privileges based on a user's ID.
pam_time	Set limits on when a program can be used. When used with login, this module limits the hours during which a user can log in.
pam_nologin	Permits root access, but permits others access only if no file called /etc/nologin exists on the system. Root can create this file to stop users from logging in for a time while completing system administration work.
pam_securetty	If the user logging in is root, check whether the /etc/securetty file includes the terminal that the user is logging in from, otherwise, do not permit access.
pam_limits	Limit the resources to which a user can have access. This module requires additional configuration, but lets you limit a user's CPU time, number of open files, amount of memory, and many other resources.
pam_env	Set environment variables as part of the authentication process.
pam_warn	Log information as part of the authentication process.
pam_cracklib	Check the quality of a password, for example, rejecting it if it is too short, has been used before, is a dictionary word, or is a minor alteration of the previous password. MD5 password hashing and shadow passwords are implemented through this module.
pam_unix	Performs standard UNIX-style password login authentication. Supports many options.
pam_stack	A special-purpose module that uses modules in another configuration file, as described previously.

Shown below is a sample PAM configuration file for the halt command: /etc/pam.d/halt. (Comment lines have been removed.) This command shuts down all Linux services so that you can safely turn your computer's power off.

When you press Ctrl+Alt+Del to restart or shut down your Linux system, the init program executes a command to restart the system. Typically, the shutdown command is executed (you can see this in the /etc/inittab configuration file). You can also use the commands halt or reboot at the command line to either shut down or reboot your Linux system.

```
auth        sufficient    /lib/security/pam_rootok.so
auth        required      /lib/security/pam_console.so
account     required      /lib/security/pam_permit.so
```

The `auth` stack of PAM modules includes `rootok` and `console`. These modules operate as follows:

1. The `rootok` module checks whether the user who is executing the `halt` command is root (this is normally done by checking whether the User ID is 0). If it is, PAM sees that this condition is sufficient and immediately returns an Access Permitted result, so root can execute `halt`.

2. If the user is not root, the `console` module checks to see whether the user is working at the console (as opposed to logging in via a remote connection of some kind, such as over a network or modem). If the user is on the console, the user can execute `halt`. Otherwise, PAM will deny access and the command will not execute.

Suppose that you let other users sit at the console of your Linux system but they could not log in as root. You don't want them to run the `halt` command. Because the default action of PAM is to deny access if no module specifically permits access, you could make this change so that only root could run `halt` by deleting or commenting out the second line in the above sample file. Then, if the `rootok` module fails (because the user is not root), the `halt` command cannot be run. No other checks will be performed.

Many more PAM modules are available than those listed here, with additional modules in development. For example, PAM modules supporting Kerberos authentication are used if you configure Linux to use Kerberos (using `authconfig` in Red Hat Linux); modules tied to Samba let your users log in to Linux by authenticating to an existing user account on a Windows NT server; multiple database modules let users authenticate based on a user entry in an SQL database; OPIE is supported by a PAM module that is under development. For information on these, see the module listing in the PAM documentation.

SECURITY TOOLS FOR USERS

This section presents a grab-bag of security utilities and related files that system administrators and users should be aware of. Some of these are controlled by PAM modules and are available by default; others are separate packages that you will have to install and configure before using.

Console and Screen Security

It's not uncommon for a user to be running multiple browser windows, a word processor, an email reader, an audio CD player, and maybe one or two other programs, all at the same time. The system administrator might also have a collection of administration utilities running, such as a process monitor, a text editor, and network analysis tool (in addition to Web, email, and the CD player). Linux handles all of this nicely. Shutting down all of these programs and logging out every time you leave your desk for a few minutes would be annoying and unproductive. Yet that is exactly what you should do to protect your system. Otherwise, any employee or visitor in the office who happened by your desk (or was even watching for you to step away for a moment) could review your files, delete something, send himself or herself an email containing your files, or otherwise breach the security of your system. Most security problems arise from other employees, not malicious outsiders.

The solution to this dilemma—waste time logging out or leave your system at risk—is to use a screen locking program. A **screen locking program** disables input from your keyboard and usually clears or hides the screen so that any private information is not visible to passersby. If you are working at a text console (character mode), you can use the **vlock** program to lock the screen you are working with or all of the virtual consoles (typically Alt+F1 through Alt+F6). The **vlock** program is not installed by default on Red Hat Linux, but it is included in the **vlock** package on CD 3 and is available for other Linux versions as well.

After you have installed the package, you can lock your current console at any time using this command:

```
vlock
```

To lock all the consoles (effectively freezing the entire system), use this command:

```
vlock -a
```

You can then only enter either the password for the user you are logged in as, or the root password. Until you do, you can't perform any other task at the console.

 Be certain that the top of your screen doesn't contain any sensitive information; vlock doesn't clear the screen when you execute it.

More likely, you are working in a graphical environment rather than the text-mode console. The **xlock** program has been around for many years to provide the same type of screen locking feature for X Windows. This program is not installed by default on Red Hat Linux, but you can install the latest enhanced version of **xlock** by adding the **xlockmore** package from Red Hat CD 3. You still run the enhanced program with the **xlock** command. (Both **vlock** and **xlock** have a man page describing options that the commands support.) The **xlock** program uses a screensaver that you have configured or else simply blanks your screen. To work again you must enter your Linux password.

One can assume that the **xlockmore** package is not installed by default because most users will rely on the screen saver programs in either Gnome or KDE, both of which include a password option that locks your screen every time the screensaver starts. You can set up the screen saver in Gnome by selecting Programs, then Settings, then Desktop, then Screensaver. The Gnome screensaver dialog box is shown in Figure 9-2. When you select the Require Password checkbox, the screensaver can only be turned off by entering your password.

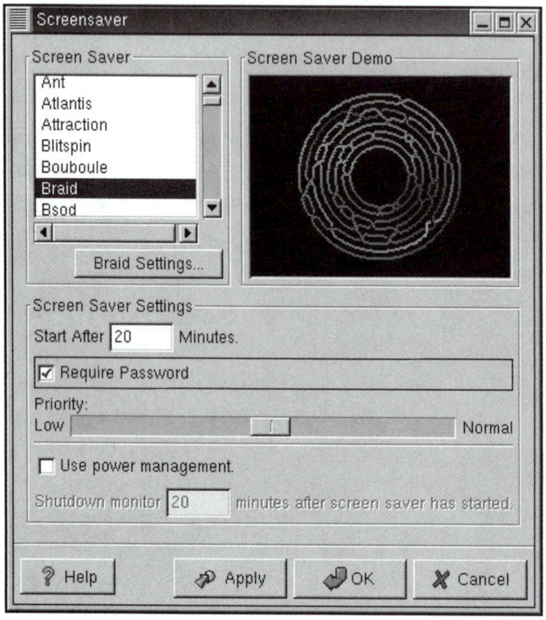

Figure 9-2 Configuring the Gnome screensaver

The KDE screensaver configuration is similar and also includes a Require Password checkbox to lock your screen whenever the screensaver is activated. Figure 9-3 shows the screensaver configuration dialog box for KDE 3.0 in Red Hat Linux 7.3. If you included KDE in your installation, you can open this dialog box via the KDE Menus item in Gnome (or the main menu if you are using KDE as your desktop) by choosing Preferences, then Look and Feel, then Screensaver. If you are running an older version of KDE, such as the one included with Caldera OpenLinux 2.4 or older versions of SuSE Linux, you can open the dialog box by selecting Settings, then Desktop, then Screensaver from the KDE main menu.

The problem with relying on the screensaver is that your screen is locked only after the configured time for the screensaver to activate. If you set the screensaver wait period for 1 minute, you will soon be very annoyed with the ever-present screensaver; if you set it to 15 minutes, your system will be insecure for 15 minutes every time you step away from your desk. (The Test button in the KDE screen saver configuration dialog box does not require you to enter a password to end the test, as some versions of Microsoft Windows do.) Because of this, a good security practice would be to install the **xlockmore** package and get in the habit of entering the **xlock** command just before you walk away from your desk.

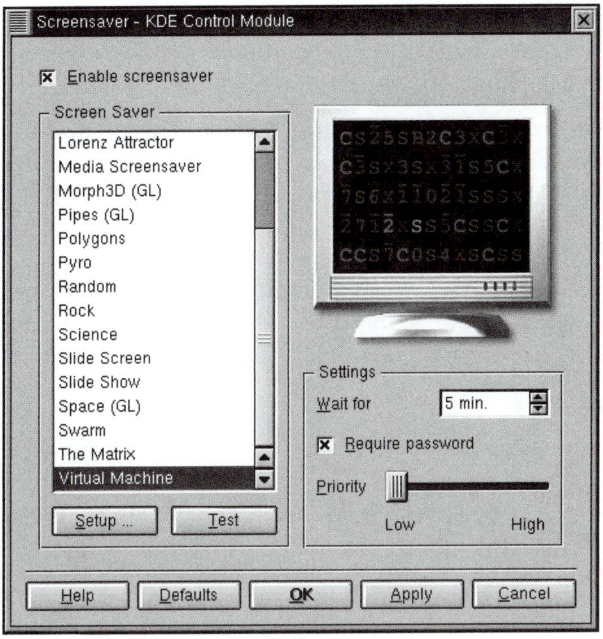

Figure 9-3   Configuring the KDE screensaver

Security Files and Utilities

Linux provides several methods of safeguarding or controlling the login process. Some important methods for system administrators are listed here.

The root user can only log in from terminals that are listed in the file **/etc/securetty**. By default this file contains only the virtual console terminals, such as **tty1**. None of the network or other devices, such as a modem on **ttyS0**, are listed. This means that a user dialing into Linux must log in using a regular user account and then use the **su** command to change to root. You can alter this default by adding a device to /etc/securetty, or by removing some that are already listed, thus limiting the virtual consoles from which root can log in.

If the **/etc/nologin** file exists, only root can log in. No regular users will be allowed to log in. This permits root to perform administrative tasks that would be disrupted by having users working on the system (for example, maintenance of key file systems). The **nologin** file can be empty, but its contents are displayed for any user who tries to log in, so it's a good idea to place an informative message in the file. When you have finished the system administration work, delete **/etc/nologin** to allow users to log in again.

Executable files can have a special file permission set that causes them to take on the permissions of the user who owns the file rather than the user who executed the file. This permission is called the **Set UID bit** (also called **SUID**). You can set it for an executable file using the command **chmod o+s** filename. This is done for some utilities such as **su**, which must have root access to run properly, no matter who invokes it. However, having

9

many files with Set UID is a great security risk, because any user on the system could easily get root access. You can use the `find` command to search for files with Set UID and see whether they look suspicious.

The Linux file systems (both the standard ext2 format and the newer ext3 format used by Red Hat and a few others) support a number of attributes that you can set on any file you choose. To list all the attributes of a file, use the `lsattr` command with the filename:

        lsattr *filename*

To change the attributes of a file, use the `chattr` command with either + or -, followed by the attribute codes you want to add or remove from the file, followed by the filename. For example, to make the file `report.txt` immutable (unchangeable), use this command:

        chattr +i report.txt

Several security-related attributes are listed in the `chattr` man page, but notice also that some of the most interesting ones are not yet supported by the Linux kernel—you can set them using `chattr` and they appear when you use `lsattr`, but they have no effect on how the file is treated. Table 9-4 lists some attributes that are of interest for system security, noting which are not implemented by the Linux kernel.

 Attributes are case-sensitive. For example, `A` and `a` are two different attributes.

Table 9-4   Security-related file attributes

Attribute	Description
a	Append only—A file cannot be changed, it can only be added to.
c	Compression—The file is compressed as it is written to the hard disk and uncompressed each time it is read from the hard disk. *This attribute is not yet supported.*
i	Immutable—The file cannot be changed in any way—including its file permissions—until the root user removes the immutable attribute.
j	Journaling—Changes to the file are specially noted so that if the Linux system is shut down in the middle of the change, the file will not be corrupted. This attribute is only supported by ext3 file systems and is only applicable if the file system is mounted with certain options—see the `chattr` man page for details.
s	Secure delete—When the file is deleted using the `rm` command, the entire file is overwritten by zeros so that no remnants of it remain on the hard disk. *This attribute is not yet supported.* You can, however, use a utility called `shred` to delete files with the same effect.
u	Undelete—When the file is deleted using the `rm` command, its contents are specially marked so that an undelete utility can recover it (until such time as the disk runs low on space or other conditions are met). *This attribute is not yet supported.*

You can use the PAM module `pam_time` with the `login` program to limit when a user can log in to Linux. Similar time restrictions can be enforced in other ways as well. If you are running the standard shell for Linux—bash—you can use the following command to set an environment variable with the number of seconds that the console can sit idle before you are automatically logged out. In this example, the number 600 means that 10 minutes of inactivity will cause the console to be logged out:

```
export TMOUT=600
```

This has value only if you are working in a character-mode console, but it is useful as a backup in case you are called away from your desk suddenly and forget to use `vlock` or log out.

If you are using the tcsh shell, the environment variable to accomplish the same thing is shown in the following example. Note that here the number refers to minutes of idle time, not seconds:

```
set autologout = 10
```

Whichever shell you are using, you should include the appropriate command in `/root/.profile` so that it is executed each time you log in.

Seeing Who Is Using Linux

Linux includes a number of very basic utilities that let you learn about or control user activity on the system. Table 9-5 lists some of these utilities that each system administrator should know how to use.

Table 9-5 Basic security tools for user accounts

Command	Description
mesg	Enables or disables the ability of others users to send a message to your screen using the `write`, `talk`, or (write all) commands. `mesg` alone prints the current status, `mesg` with `yes` or `no` as a parameter either allows or disallows access, respectively.
dmesg	Prints the contents of the kernel ring buffer to standard output (by default the screen). The **kernel ring buffer** is a memory area that holds messages generated by the kernel. When the buffer is full, the oldest message is discarded each time a new message is generated. Using `dmesg` right after booting Linux is a good way to see all the hardware-related messages generated by the kernel. Any user can run `dmesg`.
who	Lists all of the users who are currently logged in on the system. The username and terminal is listed. The `-i` option adds the length of time the user has been idle; the `-q` option prints all logged-in usernames on a single line followed by the number of users logged in. A common use of who is to see who you are logged in as, using the command `who  am  i`.

Table 9-5 Basic security tools for user accounts (continued)

Command	Description
w	Lists all users who are currently logged in with their username and terminal. This is similar to who, but w also includes the remote location from which the user has logged in, if applicable, the command that the user is currently running, the amount of CPU time that the user's current process is using, the amount of CPU time that all the user's background processes are using, and the time the user logged in.
last	Displays a history of user log-ins and log-outs, plus system reboot information. Use the command alone to list all users' activity; add a username as a parameter to list activity for that user; add the word reboot as a parameter to list information about when the system was rebooted.
lastcomm	Displays information about commands that a user has previously executed. This command is part of the process accounting package psacct, which you can search for and download from the *rpmfind.net* Web site.
ttysnoop	Lets a system administrator capture all of the keystrokes and output from another terminal, effectively watching everything that is happening on another user's screen. This package is not distributed with commercial Linux packages, perhaps because it has not been updated in several years. It is still available from *rpmfind.net* or *freshmeat.net*.

Granting Administration Privileges with sudo

Although you must guard the root account of a Linux system with great care, the system administrators and even regular users may occasionally need to perform tasks that only root is allowed to handle. The **sudo** program lets you assign privileges to any user account to execute only specific programs. Examples of how this is useful include:

- The system administrator can complete common system administration tasks without needing to **su** to root.

- Users can mount and unmount floppy disks or CD-ROM discs on systems where they do not have root access.

- Users can kill programs that have crashed or stopped responding.

- Users who don't have root access but manage a particular service (such as printing or Samba) can access the configuration tools for those programs.

The **sudo** command uses the **/etc/sudoers** configuration file to determine which users can perform which tasks. Unfortunately, the syntax of this file can be very complex. If you don't follow the syntax correctly, **sudo** will refuse to execute at all. (Conversely, you may edit the configuration file using correct syntax but without understanding exactly what actions the file will permit, thus creating a security hole.) The man page for sudoers describes the syntax in exhaustive detail. For those new to sudo, skip to the end of the man page and review the examples with explanations instead of wading through the syntax diagrams of all possible configurations. The basic format of a configuration line is:

```
user     host = command_list
```

Part of the power (and possible confusion) of configuring sudo is that you can define aliases by which a single word may represent any of the following:

- A collection of users who are granted permission.

- A collection of hosts on which one or more users' permission is granted.

- A collection of programs for which one or more users is granted permission.

- A set of sudo options that are applied to any of the above collections.

To edit the /etc/sudoers file you must use the **visudo** program. This program prevents conflicts between multiple open files (assuming multiple users have root access to your system) and also checks the syntax of the /etc/sudoers configuration file upon exit. On Red Hat Linux, you must include the path to this command to execute it:

```
/usr/sbin/visudo
```

The default /etc/sudoers file includes sections in which various types of aliases can be listed, plus a couple of examples. Assume, for example, that you want all users to be able to mount and unmount the CD-ROM drive. The following line in /etc/sudoers will permit that:

```
%users  ALL=/sbin/mount /cdrom,/sbin/umount /cdrom
```

The %users refers to a group on your system named users; you must create that group or make certain that all users are members of it for this configuration to work correctly. When used in /etc/sudoers, the ALL keyword always matches, so the host field in this example is not controlled. Finally, the two commands that users can execute are /sbin/mount /cdrom and /sbin/umount /cdrom. A user could execute the mount command like this:

```
sudo /sbin/mount /cdrom
```

After checking the /etc/sudoers file, the sudo command executes the command given as a parameter. For this to work properly, you must have an entry in /etc/fstab so that the /cdrom mount point is defined correctly. Let's assume, for example, that /etc/fstab defines the CD-ROM as being mounted at /mnt/cdrom. Because mount /mnt/cdrom is not listed in sudoers, the user will be unable to mount the CD-ROM. This points out the need to test sudo configurations carefully, not just for syntax (visudo takes care of this), but for actual effect.

Part of the reason for complex sudo configuration options is that sudo can present security dangers if not properly configured. As with other parts of your system, a person should have exactly as much access as his or her job requires, and no more—everything is on a "need to know basis." The particular risk of sudo is that a clever or malicious user will try to use access to a single command to gain access to other commands. Suppose, for example, that you included this line in /etc/sudoers to permit a user to edit the printing configuration file:

```
jamesg    ALL=vi /etc/printcap
```

Once jamesg is in vi, editing this file with root permission, he simply enters :!bash and vi runs a bash command shell—with root permission. This is called **shelling out** of a program. Many programs support shelling out, or at least some limited capacity to execute other programs from within the original program. The sudo program cannot foresee or control all of this; the system administrator must hand out sudo power carefully.

Consider another example: Sarah helps the system administrator with a number of basic Web server administration tasks that require root access. The system administrator creates a subdirectory containing symbolic links that point to the commands that Sarah needs to use and makes the Web user www the owner of those symbolic links. Using /etc/sudoers, the following line grants Sarah access to run any command in that directory on the local machine, all while acting as user www:

```
sarah    myhost = (www) /usr/local/webcommands
```

A single configuration line can assign access to multiple commands, with each assignment pertaining to a different user. By default, a user must enter a password to verify his or her identity before sudo executes the requested command. However, this can be overridden in /etc/sudoers for one or multiple specific commands. Dozens of other options let you control exactly which tasks a user can perform and how the user can perform them.

CHAPTER SUMMARY

◻ A user account provides much fuller access to a Linux system than accessing a network service such as a Web server. The network service runs as a user with very limited permission on the system and cannot execute commands as the network client chooses.

◻ Passwords should be guarded carefully to prevent crackers logging in to a system with the appearance of authorized access. A user should never give a password to anyone.

◻ Good passwords are hard to guess because they are of sufficient length, do not contain dictionary words, and do not relate in a simple or obvious way to personal information about the user.

◻ Brute force password attacks attempt to find a password by trial and error. Many programs exist for this purpose, but success is not really feasible if a password of eight or more characters is used.

◻ System administrators can control how users must manage their passwords using features of the shadow password system, as managed by the passwd command.

❏ A Linux Pluggable Authentication Module (Linux PAM) lets administrators select among many methods of authenticating users and authorizing access. Modules can be configured for independent control of most relevant Linux utilities, such as `login`, `su`, `sudo`, and `halt`.

❏ PAM modules support four types of control: `auth` for authentication, `account` for account management, `session` to initiate or end program use, and `passwd` to change authentication tokens (such as a password).

❏ PAM control flags determine how PAM processes a stack of multiple modules to reach a final determination to permit or deny access. The standard control flags are `required`, `requisite`, `sufficient`, and `optional`.

❏ A second method of specifying PAM control flags lets you test the value of one or more of 30 different parameters and process other PAM modules in the stack based on the result.

❏ The Linux text-mode console can be locked while you are away from your monitor for a moment using the `vlock` command. The `xlock` command provides similar functionality within graphical environments.

❏ Screen saver programs such as those included with KDE and Gnome offer screen-locking capability, but they cannot be activated without letting the requisite time expire for the screensaver to start.

❏ The `securetty` file lists where the root user can log in from; the `nologin` file, if it exists, stops everyone except root from logging in.

❏ File security includes watching for Set UID bits and reviewing the possibility of using file attributes (such as `immutable`) to protect files from alteration.

❏ Users can be logged out automatically after a period of inactivity when an environment variable in the command shell is set.

❏ Simple utilities like `w`, `who`, `last`, and `lastcomm` let users see detailed information about users on the Linux system, including how they are using the system.

❏ The `sudo` program lets a system administrator allow specific users to execute specific commands while acting as another user (including root).

❏ Use of `sudo` is configured by the `/etc/sudoers` text file, which must be edited using the utility `/usr/sbin/visudo`.

❏ Configuration of `sudo` is potentially very complex. Syntax is checked by `visudo`, but other potential security issues mean that administrators should set up and test `sudo` very carefully.

9

Key Terms

/etc/nologin — A file whose existence prevents all users except root from being able to log in. Regular users attempting to log in see the contents of /etc/nologin, if anything.

/etc/passwd — The file in which basic user account configuration data is stored.

/etc/securetty — A file listing all terminals from which root can log in.

/etc/shadow — The file in which users' encrypted passwords and password control data are stored.

/etc/sudoers — A configuration file that determines which users can perform which tasks using the sudo command.

brute force attack — A method of obtaining access to a system by trying all possible combinations until one succeeds in guessing a password.

chattr — A utility used to change the attributes of a file.

control_flag — An element of a PAM module configuration that determines how PAM will process multiple modules in a single stack (e.g., the auth stack).

dmesg — A utility that prints the contents of the kernel ring buffer to standard output (by default the screen). Using dmesg right after booting Linux is a good way to see all the hardware-related messages generated by the kernel.

grpck — A utility that verifies that all group memberships are valid user accounts and that no errors of syntax exist in the /etc/group file.

kernel ring buffer — A memory area that holds messages generated by the kernel. When the buffer is full, the oldest message is discarded each time a new message is generated.

Linux Pluggable Authentication Module (PAM) — A security architecture designed to improve Linux user-level security, add flexibility in how user access is configured, and permit Linux to integrate smoothly with user information stored on other systems.

lsattr — A utility that lists all the attributes of a file.

mesg — A utility that enables or disables other users' ability to send a message to your screen using the write, talk, or wall (write all) commands.

module_type — A characterization of program activity that determines which set of PAM modules will be used to authorize that activity. Possible module_types include auth, account, session, and password.

nutcracker — One of many password-cracking tools.

passwd — Utility used to change passwords or set password control options that are stored in /etc/shadow (such as a maximum use period for each password).

One-time Password In Everything (OPIE) — A single-user password system available for Linux. OPIE was created by the U.S. Naval Research Laboratory based on the S/Key program.

S/Key — A specialized single-use password system designed by Bell Communications Research.

screen locking program — A program that disables input from your keyboard and usually clears or hides the screen so that any private information is not visible to passersby.

Set UID bit — A special file permission that causes executable files (programs) to use the permissions of the user who owns the file rather than those of the user who executed the file. Also called SUID.

shelling out — Starting a command shell from within another program, effectively suspending the first program to execute the shell.

stack — Multiple PAM modules accessed in succession to perform a security check.

sudo — A utility that lets a system administrator assign privileges to any user account so that that user can execute just the programs that the `sudo` configuration specifies.

SUID — *See* Set UID bit.

vigr — A special version of the `vi` editor used to edit the `/etc/group` file.

vipw — A special version of the `vi` editor that should be used anytime you must edit `/etc/passwd` directly (instead of using utilities such as `passwd` or `useradd`).

visudo — A special text editor used to edit the `/etc/sudoers` file; it prevents conflicts between multiple open files and checks the syntax of the `/etc/sudoers` configuration file upon exit.

vlock — A utility that locks a text-mode console screen.

w — A utility that lists all users who are currently logged in with their username and terminal plus additional system usage information.

who — A utility that lists all of the users who are currently logged in on the system.

xlock — A utility that locks a graphical screen.

REVIEW QUESTIONS

1. Describe how logging in to a system with a user account is different from connecting through a Web server.

2. Which of the following is a social engineering method of obtaining a password?
   a. talking your way into an office to deliver a pizza and looking for passwords posted on monitors
   b. guessing at the passwords using a good dictionary
   c. using a cracking program like nutcracker
   d. breaking through a firewall using a combination of knowledge and luck

3. Which action is helpful in creating a good password?
   a. Make the password a single long word found in the dictionary so it will be easy to spell correctly.
   b. Tell the password to a close friend, spouse, or supervisor in case you forget it.
   c. Combine two foreign or altered words with a number or symbol between them.
   d. Include a word with a close relation to the user, such as a pet's name, so it's easy to remember.

4. Using a brute force attack to obtain a password would require:

   a. permission from your target user

   b. that you knew the algorithm used to encode the password

   c. less time than a social engineering method

   d. significant computer processing time

5. Which two files contain user account and encrypted password data on Linux?

   a. `/etc/passwd` and `/etc/group`

   b. `/etc/passwd` and `/etc/shadow`

   c. `/etc/shadow` and `/etc/pam.conf`

   d. `/etc/passwd` and `/etc/vipw`

6. The difference between locking and disabling an account is that:

   a. Locking is temporary and preserves the account password; disabling requires that a new password be set.

   b. Disabling is temporary and preserves the account password; locking requires that a new password be set.

   c. Locking is done through command-line tools; disabling uses a graphical interface.

   d. Disabling leaves an unencrypted password where crackers might obtain it; locking deletes the password entirely and is much safer.

7. Which module performs basic password quality checks, such as forbidding short passwords and dictionary words?

   a. `pam_cracklib`

   b. `pam_limits`

   c. `pam_deny`

   d. `pam_unix_auth`

8. The `auth` keyword in a PAM configuration file refers to:

   a. the module type indicating how the named module is being used

   b. the control flag that defines module interaction with the calling program

   c. the parameters passed to the module

   d. whether users must be authorized in order for the PAM module to be executed

9. Stacking PAM modules refers to:

   a. executing multiple modules of one module type in sequence

   b. the collection of modules of all types listed in a given PAM configuration file

   c. placing PAM data on a fixed memory location where other programs can access it

   d. a user determining the order in which PAM modules are executed to customize login security

10. What is the difference between a `required` and a `requisite` control flag?

11. Two screen-locking utilities are:

   a. `w` and `who`

   b. `vlock` and `xlock`

   c. `mesg` and `dmesg`

   d. `xlock` and `xlockmore`

12. Using a screensaver to lock your screen can be a security problem because:

   a. Some screensavers allow the lock to be broken using a random password.

   b. Xauth tokens may not be processed correctly from remote systems when the screen is locked.

   c. The CPU time used for the screensaver can slow down security mechanisms.

   d. The screensaver does not begin working until you have left your system unguarded for a time.

13. What is the purpose of `/etc/securetty`?

14. What is the purpose of `/etc/nologin`?

15. When the SUID bit is set on a program file, Linux:

   a. makes the file completely unchangeable until root removes that bit

   b. allows only the program owner to execute that file

   c. executes the program with the file permissions of the program file's owner

   d. allows that program to be run only using root permission

16. Two commands used to manage file attributes are:

   a. `w` and `who`

   b. `attrib` and `chmod`

   c. `lsattr` and `chattr`

   d. `mesg` and `dmesg`

17. A file with the immutable attribute set:

   a. makes the file completely unchangeable until root removes that attribute

   b. allows only the program owner to execute that file

   c. does not store any of that program's code or data on the swap partition

   d. allows that program to be run using root permission

9

18. To cause the command shell to automatically log you out if your command line is inactive for a time,

    a. You set an environment variable with the number of minutes or seconds of idle time allowed.

    b. You start the `vlock` or `xlock` program before leaving your console.

    c. You write a small script that checks for activity regularly and executes the `exit` command if needed.

    d. You set up the appropriate configuration file in `/etc/sysconfig`.

19. The `w` command lists information about:

    a. all users currently logged in, with their usernames and additional information about their activities

    b. who is running the program named on the command line as a parameter to `w`

    c. DNS entry information from the appropriate domain registrar

    d. all logged printing activities

20. The contents of the kernel ring buffer are viewed using which command?

    a. `dmesg`

    b. `mesg`

    c. `klogd`

    d. `lastcomm`

21. Which command displays a listing of past system reboots?

    a. `lastcomm --reboot`

    b. `who reboot`

    c. `reboot --history`

    d. `last`

22. The actions of sudo are controlled by the file:

    a. `/etc/sudo.conf`

    b. `/etc/visudo`

    c. `/etc/sudoers`

    d. `/etc/sudo/visudoers.conf`

23. The `viduso` program:

    a. creates default configurations for `sudo` execution by regular users

    b. lets you safely edit the configuration file for `sudo`

    c. must be configured by each user who wants to have access to `sudo` functionality

    d. cannot be accessed without first setting up `/etc/sudoers.conf`

24. Name at least one danger of `sudo`.

25. The more complex of the two methods of setting up PAM control flags lets you:

    a. skip modules based on any of 30 different testable parameters

    b. let users dynamically control which modules are executed

    c. configure PAM in a graphical interface from the Gnome desktop System menu

    d. combine modules of all four types into a single programmable stack

HANDS-ON PROJECTS

Project 9-1

In this project you set password control information for a user account. To complete this project, you should have Red Hat Linux installed with root access and at least one regular user account created. These steps should work on most Linux systems, though some systems may require different commands to configure user accounts and passwords than those shown in this project.

1. Log in using your regular user account to see that it functions correctly.

2. Log in with root access.

3. Look at the entry for your regular user account in the /etc/shadow file. Notice what the first character of the encrypted password is (the first character after the first colon on that line).

4. Lock your regular user account.

    passwd -l *username*

5. Log out and try to log in using your regular user account.

6. Log in as root and look again at the first character in your encrypted password. The "!!" modifies the encryption and makes the password that you enter to log in invalid.

7. Unlock the account.

    passwd -u *username*

8. Check the /etc/shadow file again to see that the !! is gone. You could now log in using the original password.

9. If you are in a lab environment, try using the **-d** option to disable your regular account and then review /etc/shadow again.

    passwd -d *username*

10. Set the minimum days that a password must remain before a user can change it to 100 (this is just an experiment; normally, you would set the minimum at a day or two and the maximum at around 30 to 60).

    passwd -n 100 *username*

11. Can you spot the field where this is stored in /etc/shadow on the line for your regular account?

9

12. Log out and log in again with your regular user account. Try to change your password using **passwd**.

13. Log out, then log in again as root if you wish and change the minimum days between password changes back to 0, which lets you change your password as often as you choose.

Project 9-2

In this project you configure PAM settings for a system utility. To complete this project, you should have Red Hat Linux installed with root access.

1. Log in with root access and open the file **/etc/pam.d/system-auth**.

2. Locate the line on which the **pam_cracklib** module is referenced.

3. Change the retry parameter to **5**, the **type** parameter to **THE**, and add a **minlen** parameter with a value of **12**. The line should look like this:

```
password required   /lib/security/pam_cracklib.so retry=5
type=THE minlen=12
```

(Note that the minimum length value gives "credit" when a password includes a variety of symbols, mixed case, and digits. So a well-formed password would not need to be 12 characters long.)

4. Locate the second line with the **pam_unix** module (of type **password**). Add the parameter **remember=15**. This causes the system to record the previous 15 passwords for each user so that they cannot be used again.

5. Log out and log in using your regular user account.

6. Try changing your password using various lengths and repeating previously used passwords to see how these settings affect what you can do.

Project 9-3

In this project you continue working with PAM by altering the control flag setting for a utility's PAM configuration. To complete this project, you should have Red Hat Linux installed with root access and have just completed Project 9-2. You should only complete this project if you are working in a lab where you are not concerned about the security of your system. In addition, note that changing PAM settings incorrectly can completely lock you out of your system. Follow the steps here carefully and use the virtual consoles to check your work as described rather than logging out of your main working session. (If you do lock yourself out, reboot the system and press "a" at the boot prompt, then add an "S" to the boot parameters to start single user mode. Edit the PAM configuration files to restore their original state and reboot normally.)

1. Log in as root.

2. Edit the file **/etc/pam.d/login**. Change the control flag on the **pam_securetty** line from **required** to **sufficient**.

3. Save the file.

4. Log out and log in again as root. What happened and why?

5. Go back into `/etc/pam.d/login` and change **sufficient** back to **required**.

6. Now edit the `/etc/pam.d/system-auth` file.

7. Just above the lines that begin with **password** insert this line:

   ```
   password    optional    /lib/security/pam_issue.so
   issue=/etc/printcap
   ```

   (You can refer to any brief text file that you choose instead of the `/etc/printcap` file; this file is used simply as an illustration.) Save your changes and exit the text editor.

8. Switch to a free virtual console (for example, press Ctrl+Alt+F5).

9. Log in. Do you see any differences?

10. Switch back to the graphical environment by pressing Alt+F7 (or switch to the virtual console you were previously working in).

11. Open the `/etc/pam.d/system-auth` file again in a text editor.

12. Just above the lines that begin with **auth** insert this line, then save your changes and exit the text editor.

    ```
    auth optional   /lib/security/pam_issue.so
    issue=/etc/printcap
    ```

13. Switch to a free virtual console (for example, press Ctrl+Alt+F5).

14. Log in again by entering your username, but *enter the wrong password*.

15. What do you see?

16. Switch back to the graphical environment or your previous virtual console.

17. Edit the `/etc/pam.d/system-auth` file again and remove the two extra lines you added for this project.

18. Why did the first extra line not have any effect? (See the documentation on the module for the answer.)

19. Why was the optional control flag appropriate here?

Project 9-4

In this project you experiment with screen-locking programs. To complete this project, you should have Linux installed with root access and a copy of the **xlockmore** package, either on CD 3 of Red Hat Linux 7.3 or downloaded from a Web site such as *rpmfind.net*.

1. Log in with root access.

2. Either from Red Hat 7.3 CD 3 or from a download (such as from *rpmfind.net*), install the **xlockmore** package.

   ```
   rpm -Uvh xlockmore-4.17.2-5.i386.rpm
   ```

3. Spend a minute reviewing the `xlock` man page to see what options the program offers.

   ```
   man xlock
   ```

4. Notice that when `xlock` is active, no new network connections are permitted. Why would that be?

5. Start `xlock`. A randomly selected screen saver is displayed.

6. Press a key to see the prompt for the password. Click the icon to continue the screen lock.

7. Press **Alt+Ctrl+F3** to switch to another virtual console.

8. Log in on that console using the same username you used for the graphical environment.

9. Use the `ps` command to see if `xlock` is listed as a process on the system.

   ```
   ps aux | grep xlock
   ```

10. Use the `killall` command to end the `xlock` program.

    ```
    killall -9 xlock
    ```

11. Press Alt+F7 to switch back to the graphical screen.

12. Why is the ability to kill `xlock` in this way not considered a security hazard?

Project 9-5

In this project you experiment with attributes and login control files. To complete this project, you should have Linux installed with root access.

1. Log in with root access.

2. In a text editor, create the `/etc/nologin` file with the following text in it:

   System locked down for maintenance. Please try again in 15 minutes.

3. Save the file.

4. Set the immutable attribute on the file:

   ```
   chattr +i /etc/nologin
   ```

5. Log out.

6. Try to log in now using a regular user account. What happens?

7. Log in as root and delete the file you created:

   ```
   rm /etc/nologin
   ```

8. What happened?

9. Undo the immutable attribute:

   ```
   chattr -i /etc/nologin
   ```

10. Remove the file:

    ```
    rm /etc/nologin
    ```

11. What is the point of having an immutable attribute on a file that only root has permission to alter anyway? Doesn't this just make another step that root has to complete?

CASE PROJECTS

The Managing Partner at Snow, Sleet, and Hale just attended a special conference entitled Computer Security in Law Firms, and your consulting work is about to increase because of the justifiable concern of your client.

1. One of the security systems that is growing in popularity—Kerberos—was mentioned prominently at the security conference. Although Kerberos was not mentioned in the chapter text about PAM modules, Linux PAM actually has very good support for Kerberos. Review the documentation on this feature, located in a separate directory on Red Hat Linux (`/usr/share/doc/pam_krb5-1.55`), plus the information listed under Kerberos at *www.us.kernel.org/pub/linux/libs/pam/modules.html*. Write a one-page summary memo of how PAM implements Kerberos and what benefits or concerns this implementation raises for you. You should target your memo to the Managing Partner, who needs to understand how Kerberos might benefit the organization's LAN but doesn't want too much technical detail.

2. Snow, Sleet, and Hale has several system administrators helping to manage their office networks. Most do not have root access to the Linux servers. Write a list of policy statements regarding the use of **sudo** for these system administrators, who must complete specific networking tasks such as print management, file server maintenance, and email server maintenance. You may want to consult the **sudo** and **sudoers** man pages as well as example security policies that you locate on the Internet.

3. The Managing Partner has asked you to prepare a brief presentation (15 minutes) on the best practices for selecting and protecting account passwords. Your presentation could be a collection of 15–20 slides in a program such as PowerPoint or Corel Presentations. You should include notes for each slide to help you cover important points. Describe both the reasons for your recommendations and the actual techniques that comprise a "good" password.

9

10

FILE SECURITY

After reading this chapter and completing the exercises you will be able to:

♦ Correctly set up special Linux file permissions

♦ Monitor log files to check for suspicious system activity

♦ Automate checks for file integrity and unauthorized modifications

In this chapter you learn how to protect files on your Linux system from unauthorized access. This protection starts with correctly using standard Linux file permissions, but also includes special utilities that watch for problems caused when crackers access your system through a user account that is otherwise valid.

Evidence of crackers' activity often appears in system log files. Several utilities can help you track unexpected messages within log files. Further protection is provided by file integrity checkers, which keep track of suspicious changes to any file, not just within log files.

REVIEWING LINUX FILE PERMISSIONS

Chapter 9 described how to prevent unauthorized users from logging in to your Linux system with a valid username and password, and how to control the actions of authorized users once they are logged in using PAM. Any user who has logged in—with or without authorization—poses a threat to system security chiefly through the ability of such users to view, delete, or create files. The files stored on your hard disks or other storage media contain system configurations that protect your data, keep your server running smoothly, and hopefully prevent unauthorized entry. In addition, those files contain the business and personal data that are the reason for maintaining a system in the first place.

Unauthorized users may want to view files to access data or to see how security settings are configured. They may want to delete data to make it unavailable to you, to disrupt business plans, or to corrupt system configurations. They may want to modify existing files or create new files, either to corrupt your organizational data, to cover signs of their illicit activity in system files, or to establish different security settings that will permit them continued system access.

Your first line of defense in protecting these system and personal or organizational files is careful use of Linux file permissions. Table 10-1 shows these permissions, with the character and number assigned to each when specifying them for the **chmod** command.

Table 10-1 Linux File Permissions

Permission Name	Character Representation	Numeric Representation
Read	r	4
Write	w	2
Execute	x	1

Each permission can be assigned to the owner of the file (designated as user, with **u**), to the group assigned to the file (designated with **g**), or to all other users on the system (designated with **o**). Table 10-2 describes how each permission affects any user with that permission, either for a file or for a directory.

Table 10-2 File Permissions on Files and Directories

Permission	Effect on a File	Effect on a Directory
Read	Read the file (view it)	List the files in a directory
Write	Update or alter the file	Create new files in the directory
Execute	Execute the file	Execute files within the directory

Unfortunately, these permissions are not as sophisticated as those on most non–UNIX operating systems (such as NetWare or Windows NT/2000/XP). For example, on other operating systems you can assign a different set of permissions to each of dozens of users.

However, when carefully used, Linux file permissions can provide an adequate barrier to unauthorized file access.

For any file or directory, standard Linux file permissions are **read** (represented by **r**), **write** (**w**), and **execute** (**x**). Each can be assigned to the owner of a file or directory (represented by **u**, for user), to a group defined in /etc/group (**g**), or to all other users who are logged into the system but who are not the owner or part of the named group (**o**). These form the standard nine permissions that you see when you use the `ls -l` command.

Using these nine permissions can become more complicated than it first seems. It's important that you understand the implications of the file permissions that you assign, either by careful study or by making explicit tests after setting things up. Otherwise you risk creating a set of file permissions that don't prevent access as you suppose they do.

For example, suppose you have two files in a work directory. One is for your use only—no permissions are granted to group or other users. The second file is to be read by other users in a managers group that you have created, so it has group permission set to read (**r**). Because other managers sometimes create files in this working directory, the directory has the execute (**x**) permission set for the group, allowing any member of the group to create files in the directory. The listing for the two files would appear like this (using the `ls -l` command):

```
-rw-------    1 nwells    users   23411 Jun 22 21:40
   private_report
-rw-r--r--    1 nwells    users   21390 Jun 22 21:40
   public_report
```

The listing for the directory would appear like this (using the `ls -ld` command):

```
drwxrwx---    2 nwells    users    4096 Jun 22 21:40 reports
```

Now, suppose that another member of the managers group tries to read the private_report file, using this command:

```
$ less private_report
```

She can't because she does not have read permission; only the owner of the file has it. Suppose she tries to copy a file over it using this command:

```
$ cp public_report private_report
```

Once again, the system reports that this is not allowed, this time because she does not have write permission to private_report, which is required to overwrite the file using copy. However, suppose that she instead uses the **mv** command like this:

```
$ mv public_report private_report
```

This time, the system checks whether she has permission to create or rename files in this directory, which is controlled by the execute permission on the parent directory. In this case, the other manager is part of the group that is granted execute permission,

10

including the ability to create new files in the directory. Because that permission also allows renaming files, the operation is permitted. She has not been able to read `private_report`, but she has erased it. You cannot set up a directory for all members of a group to create and share files without this possibility, but you need to understand that it exists.

Several Linux distributions, including Red Hat, use a technique called **User Private Groups** to enhance file-based security. The idea is this: because every file and directory are assigned both a user (owner) and a group, each with separate permissions, it is more secure to have a group with only a single member, then make that the default group for all files created by that user. To see this in action, create a new user with the `useradd` command, then use the `cat` command or a text editor to look at the `/etc/group` file. You see a group with the same name as the user. No members are listed for the group, but the group number corresponding to the user's name is listed in `/etc/passwd` as the primary group for the user. As a result, any time that user creates a file, the private group—the one with no members—is assigned as the group for that file. This process is reviewed as one of the projects at the end of this chapter.

The paragraphs that follow describe two other group-related techniques to help you manage file security.

Recall that the Set User ID (SUID) bit (which appears as **s** in the Execute bit field for the owner of a file) causes the user who executes a program to assume the permissions of the owner of that file. The SUID bit is necessary for some types of programs, such as the `su` utility. Unfortunately it presents a real security hazard: if crackers are able to set other system files to have the SUID bit active, they may gain root access to the system simply by running a common system utility.

 SUID is considered so dangerous on script files—because they are so easily modified in any text editor—that the Linux kernel will not honor a SUID bit when set on a script file.

You can also add a Set Group ID (SGID) permission to a file or directory. This gives the person who executes a program file the permissions of the file's group while executing the program. Clearly this isn't much use, and you rarely hear of SGID being used on a program file. However, adding SGID to a directory does serve a special purpose.

Consider first that when a user creates a new file, the group assigned to that file is normally the primary group for that user, as defined in `/etc/passwd`. For example, on Linux systems using the User Private Group system described previously, a new file lists the same name as both user and group, a shown in this example:

```
-rw-rw-r--    1 nwells   nwells    3971 Jun 22 21:44 test1
```

You can try this yourself by using the `touch` command to create an empty file and then using `ls  -l` to see the ownership and permissions of the file. However, when you set SGID on a directory, any file that is created within that directory is assigned the group of the directory, rather than the group of the user that creates the file. This is a convenient method for creating a working space for a collection of users who should be allowed to create files and read each others' files, all without need for the system administrator to intervene to permit access to each individual file.

To see how this works, suppose you had already created a group called *managers* with a number of users as members. Then you executed the following commands as root:

```
# mkdir /workspace
# chgrp managers /workspace
# chmod g+rws /workspace
```

Now suppose that user thomas logs in. Within his home directory, he creates a test file and then views its permissions and ownership:

```
$ cd
$ touch test2
$ ls -l test2
-rw-rw-r--  1 thomas   thomas   3971 Jun 22 21:44 test2
```

Then thomas changes to the /workspace directory, creates a test file, and views its permissions and ownership:

```
$ cd /workspace
$ touch test3
$ ls -l test3
-rw-rw-r--  1 thomas   managers 3971 Jun 22 21:44 test3
```

Because the file that thomas created—test3—is owned by the group *managers*, anyone else in the group can read and edit its contents. Files created by any member of group *managers* will have the same characteristics.

A second technique allows you to deny access to members of a group. Remember that the "other" permissions on a file or directory still require that a user be logged in to Linux. So this technique allows you to say "the owner has a certain access level, and everyone else on the system has a certain access level, but the members of this group can't access the file or directory."

To set this up, you might use a series of commands like this, assuming you had created a group called no_finance for whom you wanted to deny access to a particular directory:

```
$ mkdir /finance_data
$ chmod 705 /finance_data
$ chgrp no_finance /finance_data
$ ls -l /finance_data
drwx---r-x 2 nwells no_finance 4096 Jun 22 21:40
finance_data
```

 Recall that the 705 represents the file permissions granted for the user, group, and other categories. The 7 is read, write, and execute for the user; 0 is no rights for the group; 5 is read and execute for others.

10

No member of the `no_finance` group will be able to `cd` into the `/finance_data` directory or list the files it contains. This is effective because Linux computes access rights first by checking whether the user requesting access is the owner and whether the owner's rights permit the access requested. If the user is not the owner, Linux checks to see whether the requesting user is a member of the group assigned to that file or directory. If so, the group permissions of the file or directory are used to assign access (or deny it in this case); the rights assigned to other users are never considered.

USING THE SYSTEM LOG FOR SECURITY CHECKS

System log files are some of the most important files on your Linux system because they may reveal security problems. These files record the activity of programs such as login, FTP, email servers, and many others. System log messages are usually stored in the file `/var/log/messages` on most Linux systems, but you can look in the `/etc/syslog.conf` file to see exactly which log files are used by the system logging daemons. (For example, messages from your email server may be stored in `/var/log/maillog` by default.) In the example lines from `syslog.conf` shown here (taken from Red Hat Linux 7.3), log messages are stored in several different files, depending on which type of program generated the message. The filenames at the end of each configuration line indicate the file where messages are stored. (Some lines have been removed from this listing, but the `syslog.conf` man page describes the format and options used in this file.)

```
.info;mail.none;news.none;authpriv.none;cron.none
        /var/log/messages
authpriv.*                      /var/log/secure
mail.*                          /var/log/maillog
cron.*                          /var/log/cron
uucp,news.crit                  /var/log/spooler
local7.*                        /var/log/boot.log
news.=crit                      /var/log/news/news.crit
news.=err                       /var/log/news/news.err
news.notice                     /var/log/news/news.notice
```

Messages in the system logs are important because they can leave a trail through which you can see evidence of a cracker's attempts to break into your system, or even evidence of what was done after breaking in.

 Skilled crackers will alter log files to hide evidence of their activities. The next section describes how to protect against this.

As an example of how log files can warn you of an impending security crisis, consider what you would think if you found the following message repeated 400 times in succession within `/var/log/messages`:

```
Jun 21 19:42:13 sundance login[1208]: FAILED LOGIN 1 FROM
(null)
        FOR nwells, Authentication failure
```

It's likely that someone is trying hundreds of different passwords to gain access to the system. Admittedly, this would indicate a cracker without much style, but those are the kind you'd prefer to deal with. They're easier to spot before they cause trouble.

In Chapter 4 you learned how you can have the logging daemons store log entries on a remote computer.

A number of utilities can help you watch for log messages that indicate potential security violations. Not all strange log messages come from crackers; some come from valid users who are experimenting with the system or who don't know how to use a program. However, having a utility that brings these to your attention can allow you to protect your system before an attempted break-in succeeds, or to discover and fix things more quickly if a break-in has already occurred.

Rotating Log Files

Log files are an important part of system maintenance and security, but they require regular attention because they can become very large, and old log information is not as valuable as recent log information. The **logrotate** command helps you automate the process of compressing and archiving log files so that the logs never grow unreasonably large, and older log data can be stored in another location—such as on a writeable CD or backup tape—instead of taking up hard disk space. This command is configured on Red Hat Linux 7.3 to run automatically once each day. Once per week, **logrotate** takes the current log files and copies them to another filename. Four weeks worth of messages are saved. When a new week's messages are saved, the oldest messages are discarded. You can see these files in **/var/log/**. For example, if your system has been running for several weeks, you will see **messages** (the current, active log file), plus **messages.1**, **messages.2**, and **messages.3**, the previous three weeks of messages.

The **logrotate** command is executed through the **cronjob** entry stored in **/etc/cron.daily**. The utility itself is configured by **/etc/logrotate.conf** and by the individual files in **/etc/logrotate.d**. For example, configuration for handling the Apache log files is included in **/etc/logrotate.d/apache**. The **logrotate** configuration files support several dozen options. For example, you can have log files compressed, emailed to someone, or rotated when they reach a certain size.

If your Linux system doesn't have **logrotate** available, you could create a script to do log rotation. Note, however, that when you change the name of a file, the program that writes to that file continues writing to it, even with the new name. You must issue a

HUP signal to reinitialize the program so that it will check the filename of the log and start a new log file. For example, the following commands start a new Apache log file:

```
mv /var/log/httpd/access_log   /var/log/httpd/access_log.1
touch /var/log/httpd/access_log
kill -HUP 'cat /var/run/httpd.pid'
```

Tracking Log Files

The programs running on your Linux system are constantly adding to their corresponding log files. For this reason, you don't normally load a log file into a text editor to review it, though you could. The easiest way to view a log file is to either search it using a command like **grep**, or view new messages as they are added, using the **tail** program. The **grep** command would perform a simple search for the word "FAILED" in the system log file:

```
grep "FAILED" /var/log/messages
```

The **tail** program displays the last 10 lines of any text file. You can change the number of lines displayed using the **-n** option. To see the last 20 lines of the system log, with new lines appearing on screen as they are added to the file (specified by the **-f** option), use this command:

```
tail -fn 20 /var/log/messages
```

If you are running Linux with a graphical desktop, you can use the **xlogmaster** program to view several system resources, including the system log file. This simple program is not part of most Linux distributions, but you can download it from *rpmfind.net*. Start the program with the command **xlogmaster** (several command-line options are available, as described in the man page). Figure 10-1 shows the main screen. You can choose one of the buttons on the right side to switch the display window to show different system information.

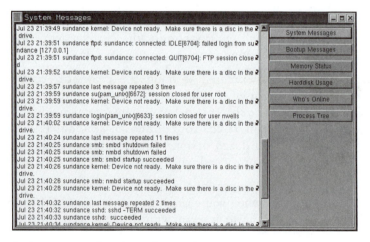

Figure 10-1 The xlogmaster utility

Right-clicking on a line within the display window opens a menu where you can choose Customize Entries to set up how you want xlogmaster to display system data. The customization dialog box is shown in Figure 10-2.

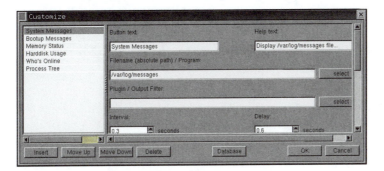

Figure 10-2   Customizing xlogmaster displays

The **logcheck** package does much more than simply display log entries. It checks them hourly for any suspicious entries. If so, those entries are emailed to the root user (or any other account you select). The logcheck package is not part of most Linux systems but is available on *rpmfind.net* and other download sites. When you install the logcheck rpm, a `cron` job file is placed in `/etc/cron.hourly` so that the logcheck program immediately starts running each hour. The script itself is `/usr/bin/logcheck.sh`. You can review this file in a text editor to see how it operates. In summary, logcheck refers to a list of words stored in `/etc/logcheck/hacking`, `/etc/logcheck/violations`, and a couple of other configuration files. When any of those words appears in log entry, logcheck emails root about it. (Change the line `SYSADMIN=root` to alter where emails are sent.)

You don't need to do anything to get logcheck to function once you have installed the package. You may find it helpful, however, to review the contents of the files in `/etc/logcheck` to better understand the types of attacks that logcheck is watching for. You should also review the documentation in `/usr/share/doc/logcheck-1.1.1`. The following list illustrates some of the words that logcheck watches for in system log files. Not all of these will make sense to you, but see how many you can read, and try to understand what a cracker is attempting when such a log message is generated:

- `LOGIN root REFUSED`
- `rlogind.*: Connection from .* on illegal port`
- `rshd.*: Connection from .* on illegal port`
- `sendmail.*: user .* attempted to run daemon`
- `uucico.*: refused connect from .*`
- `tftpd.*: refused connect from .*`
- `login.*: .*LOGIN FAILURE.* FROM .*root`

10

- `login.*: .*LOGIN FAILURE.* FROM .*guest`

- `login.*: .*LOGIN FAILURE.* FROM .*bin`

- `kernel: Oversized packet received from`

- `FAILURE`

- `ILLEGAL`

- `LOGIN FAILURE`

- `LOGIN REFUSED`

- `RETR passwd`

- `RETR pwd.db`

- `ROOT LOGIN`

- `debug`

- `denied`

- `deny`

- `deny host`

 The logcheck utility is based on software originally found in Gauntlet Firewall, from Trusted Information Systems, Inc.

Although you can find logcheck at several download sites, it has been officially absorbed into Psionic Technologies as a commercial product and renamed **LogSentry**. As LogSentry, the latest version of the program has extended capabilities and interacts with Psionic's other intrusion detection products, such as PortSentry and HostSentry. For more information, see *www.psionic.com*.

Another package that performs functions similar to those offered by logcheck/LogSentry is **Swatch**. The Swatch package is not part of most Linux distributions, but you can download it from *rpmfind.net* and other sites. Be forewarned, however, that installing Swatch can be challenging. Swatch is a Perl script that requires you to install several additional Perl modules beyond what you are likely to have installed by default; it also requires you to set up a configuration file to specify which logging messages should trigger a reaction from the utility. (Using logcheck, in contrast, you can simply edit the default configuration files instead of creating your own.)

MAINTAINING FILE INTEGRITY

Although log file maintenance and log analysis tools can help you catch potential intruders, they are not foolproof techniques. Sometimes a skillful cracker will gain sufficient access to your system and the log will not indicate a problem. To see evidence of this more sophisticated type of attack, you need to keep track of the state of important files on your system for any unexpected change.

For example, suppose a cracker were able to gain access to your system and replace your `inetd` superserver daemon with a version that permitted complete access to anyone who telnetted to a particular port and entered a certain password. You would see no evidence of this in the configuration file—it would be built in to the `inetd` program. Or suppose a cracker replaced your `ls` utility with a new version that failed to list any files beginning with a certain code word. This would allow a cracker to store on the hard disk the configuration files used to disrupt your system, without your being able to see them.

Watching for rootkits

Once a cracker has obtained root access on your system, he wants to maintain that access. A cracker typically adds these sort of programs using a **rootkit**, a collection of programs and scripts designed to permit a cracker continued access, even if you discover the original break-in. For example, you might discover that you were using an outdated version of the DNS name server that permitted a cracker to obtain root access. You upgrade the DNS server, so that access point is cut off. However, if the cracker installed a rootkit before you upgraded the DNS server, the cracker will have several more access points that are specifically designed to be much harder to spot. One rootkit, `lrk4`, includes modifications to the programs shown in Table 10-3.

10

Table 10-3   Examples of How Programs are Modified by a rootkit

Program	How Altered
crontab	Hides certain scheduled tasks from its output
du	Doesn't include the size of certain hidden files when reporting disk usage information
find	Doesn't list certain hidden files
ifconfig	Doesn't display network information that would reveal cracker activity
inetd	Permits automatic access on certain network ports (31337 is commonly used)
killall	Doesn't kill certain processes that the cracker uses to maintain access
login	Permits remote login without a password to user root
ls	Doesn't list certain hidden files
ps	Doesn't show certain processes used by the cracker

Dozens of rootkits have been developed and are distributed through Internet sites frequented by crackers. One use of the term script-kiddies (from Chapter 7) is to refer to crackers who use a well-documented security hole in a program like `sendmail`, then install a prepackaged rootkit to maintain unauthorized access to a server.

You can use the **chkrootkit** package to check your system for evidence of a rootkit. This package includes a script that works much like a virus checker, and though it can report the presence of a rootkit, it cannot eliminate one from your system. It examines system binary files to detect evidence of about 30 different rootkits. The chkrootkit package is not included on most Linux distributions, but you can download it through *rpmfind.net*. More useful, however, may be to visit *www.chkrootkit.org*, download the package, and review some of the resource links to see how crackers can exploit rootkits to maintain unauthorized access to your system.

The chkrootkit package includes several programming components that you can add to your own software if you choose. These include **chklastlog** and **chkwtmp**, which check for modifications of the `lastlog` and `wtmp` system files, respectively. These files maintain historical and current data about logins for each user. A rootkit modifies these files to hide their login activity. Another component of chkrootkit, **chkproc**, helps you watch for Linux kernel modules that have been installed as part of a rootkit. These modules, referred to by crackers as **LKMs**, provide complete access to your Linux system and can be very difficult to spot, because you don't have to execute any other programs for them to have their desired effect.

Should you discover a rootkit on your Linux system, consider the following steps:

- If possible, shut down networking on the server until you clean up the problem. On many systems this isn't feasible.

- Back up the entire system, including all the operating system files and all of your data files. You can review these later to track down the cracker for prosecution.

- Rebuild the system, either by updating the specific packages that were damaged, or by reinstalling the entire operating system if necessary.

You can use the `rpm` command to verify the integrity of files in a package. For example, the `ls` command is part of the **fileutils-4.1-10** package on Red Hat Linux 7.3. If you have your original Red Hat Linux CD 1, you can mount it and use this command to verify the integrity of the `ls` command:

```
rpm -Vvp /mnt/cdrom/RedHat/RPMS/fileutils-4.1-10.i386.rpm
```

You may see a few missing language files noted, but if you see something like the following, you know that the `ls` program on your system does not match the `ls` program as originally installed. The rpm man page describes the detail of the `-V` option; each nonperiod character indicates a mismatched attribute between the package file and the program on your system.

```
S.5....T   /bin/ls
```

You could then use this command to update the package:

```
rpm -Uvh /mnt/cdrom/RedHat/RPMS/fileutils-4.1-10.i386.rpm
```

In some cases, you might feel better about a messy situation if you reinstalled the entire operating system and just copied your data files afterwards. This is often quicker initially than checking utilities individually, but remember that you may have a lot of additional work configuring programs after the installation. Since you need to be wary of copying configuration files from the "old" system that you are repairing, consider carefully whether a full reinstall or repairing individual packages is the better choice.

As you read about using the `rpm` command above, you may have wondered, "What if `rpm` is corrupt as well?" It's certainly possible that a rootkit would include a new version of `rpm` that "acted" its part but actually refused to copy over any of the programs that had been modified by the rootkit.

This points out a good way to prepare for a rootkit attack: make a copy of critical utilities such as `ls`, `ps`, `login`, `inetd`, and `find`, placing them on a floppy disk or writeable CD. If you are suspicious about your system, use these utilities to explore your system, not the convenient copies on the hard disk that may have been modified.

If you are able to compile Linux software, consider creating copies of these utilities that are **statically linked**. This means that they are self-contained programs that do not depend on any other system components (called shared libraries) in order to function. The reason for such a procedure is that some rootkits can modify the shared libraries so that any program that uses them has impaired functionality, even though the program itself appears to be unaltered. For example, suppose both the `ls` and `find` commands operate by requesting a list of files from a certain component of a shared library. If that shared library has been altered, the `ls` and `find` commands cannot return accurate results, even though those programs are unaltered.

Using a single-disk version of Linux or a set of miniature Linux utilities is a good way to prepare yourself for emergency system analysis without needing to recompile software. **Tom's Single Disk Linux** is a software package that you can copy to a floppy disk to provide a complete set of standard system utilities. See *www.toms.net/rb*. The **busybox** utility is a single program that performs simplified versions of more than 60 standard utilities such as `ls` and `ps`. (It doesn't support as many command-line options as the full-fledged utilities, but `busybox` is very small.) See *www.busybox.net* or download it from *rpmfind.net*.

Using Integrity Checkers

Although checking your system for a rootkit is a good idea if you suspect that someone has compromised your system's security, a broader and more constant approach is to watch the integrity of files on the system. You learned in Chapters 8 and 9 about using the `md5sum` and `gpg` utilities, plus the `--checksig` option on the `rpm` utility, to validate the integrity of packages. Special file integrity utilities can help you track a large number of files on your system, alerting you to changes that you did not expect.

The best-known integrity checker is **Tripwire**. This program is available in a free version included with many Linux distributions such as Red Hat Linux 7.3 (see *www.tripwire.org*); and a commercial version is also available from *www.tripwire.com* (see Figure 10-3). The Linux version of Tripwire is open source, licensed under the Gnu General Public License, as is the Linux kernel.

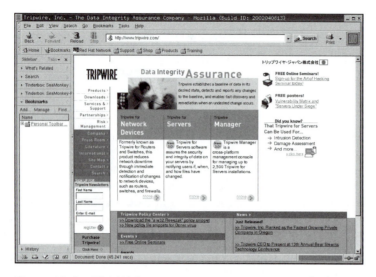

Figure 10-3   The Web site *www.tripwire.com*

To use Tripwire, you start with a system that you trust has not been tampered with—ideally one that you have just installed from CDs, before connecting it to any networks. Tripwire creates a baseline or "snapshot" of your critical system files according to a policy that you can configure. (Example policy configurations are provided to help you get started.) Once the baseline has been established, you run Tripwire at regular intervals to see whether the state of the system has changed. In some cases, the changes will be expected—for example, you may have updated `/etc/passwd` because a new employee started working in your division. When the changes are expected, you can update the baseline in Tripwire so that the changes you approve are not marked as potential problems. However, if there is an unexpected change, you can see immediately which files are affected and take corrective actions. In that case, the information provided by Tripwire can show you where the differences are between the baseline and the current system. This can help you determine how much damage has been done and what the best way to recover the system would be.

Tripwire configuration files are protected by a cryptographic signature based on a passphrase that you provide during the initial setup. The encryption prevents intruders from being able to modify your Tripwire policies, configuration, or reports to hide their activities.

 If you lose your Tripwire passphrase, you must reinitialize Tripwire to establish a new baseline. The Tripwire files cannot be used or recovered without the passphrase.

To set up Tripwire, follow these steps. The first two steps are not necessary on many systems where Tripwire is installed by default (as on Red Hat Linux 7.3).

1. Download the Tripwire rpm from *www.tripwire.org*, *rpmfind.net*, or another well-known download site.

2. Install the Tripwire rpm using a command like:

   ```
   rpm -Uvh tripwire-2.3.1-10.i386.rpm
   ```

3. Edit the Tripwire policy file in any text editor to reflect the needs of your particular Linux installation. The file is `/etc/tripwire/twpol.txt`. In Red Hat Linux 7.3, this file contains a standard configuration for a complete installation of Red Hat Linux. If you use this file without changes but did not install all Red Hat components, expect to see some warnings, because some files are not installed on your system. As you review the policy document, you see hundreds of important configuration files, commands, and system devices listed, with warning levels for each. The policy document uses a complex syntax. You can learn it by reviewing the many comments in the sample file and by reading the `twpolicy` man page. (Enter `man twpolicy`.)

4. Review the contents of `/etc/tripwire/twcfg.txt` to see whether you want to update any basic configuration settings such as the editor and mail server used by Tripwire and directories where Tripwire will look for various system components.

5. Run the configuration script to convert the policy document that you edited into an encrypted rules database that Tripwire will actually use to check your system. The configuration script also lets you select a passphrase and sign the Tripwire files. The command to run the script is:

   ```
   /etc/tripwire/twinstall.sh
   ```

6. When prompted, enter the passphrase (twice) for the sitewide key file. A key is generated. The sitewide key signs the configuration and policy files.

7. When prompted, enter the passphrase (twice) for the local key file. A key is generated. The local key signs the database files and reports that Tripwire generates for your system.

8. When prompted, enter the sitewide passphrase so that Tripwire can use it to sign the configuration file.

9. When prompted, enter the sitewide passphrase so that Tripwire can use it to sign the policy file. The binary file `/etc/tripwire/tw.pol` is created.

10. If you need to update the policy file, make changes in the `/etc/tripwire/twpol.txt` and then use the following command to update the binary `tw.pol` policy file that Tripwire actually uses. (You must enter your site-key passphrase to complete this command.)

    ```
    twadmin -m P /etc/tripwire/twpol.txt
    ```

10

11. The Tripwire documentation recommends that you delete the configuration file `/etc/tripwire/twcfg.txt` after you configure Tripwire using the `twinstall.sh` script. This protects you by stopping intruders from seeing how Tripwire is set up (though relatively little information is contained in this configuration file). If you decide to delete this file, you can recover a new default copy from the Tripwire rpm.

12. Initialize the Tripwire database (create a baseline image of your system) using this command. You must enter the local passphrase to execute this command:

```
tripwire --init
```

If you did not install every package on the Red Hat CDs and are using the default Tripwire configuration files, you will see messages stating "No such file or directory" because Tripwire is looking for files you have not installed. You can ignore these messages for this example. If you were running a production server you would want to either edit the configuration file or install the files and directories that the configuration file refers to.

Depending on the speed of your system and number of packages you have installed, creating the initial Tripwire database can take from 5 to 30 minutes. The result is a database file stored in `/var/lib/tripwire`.

13. Check the integrity of your system on a regular basis. The best way to do this is to include the appropriate Tripwire command in a **cron** job with the `/etc/cron.daily` directory. The command to run an integrity check at any time is:

```
tripwire --check
```

The integrity check also takes several minutes.

14. After running a check, you may determine that the alterations in your system are valid—they were made by an authorized system administrator. You can update the Tripwire database so that those changes don't appear in the next report. To do this, you would determine the name of the database file in the directory `/var/db`, then include that filename in this command:

```
tripwire --update -d filename
```

After you have run an integrity check, you can review the results using the **twprint** command and the name of the results database that was created. Here is one example, though the filename on your system will reflect your hostname and the times you run the Tripwire checks:

```
twprint -m r --twrfile /var/lib/tripwire/reports/sundance-
20030622-142613.twr
```

This command prints the report—which can be quite long—to the screen. You may want to direct the output to a file or an email for later review. The first few lines of a Tripwire report are shown here for reference:

```
Note: Report is not encrypted.
Tripwire(R) 2.3.0 Integrity Check Report

Report generated by:            root
Report created on:              Sat 22 Jun 2002 02:26:13 PM EDT
Database last updated on:       Never
===================================================================
Report Summary:
===================================================================

Host name:                      sundance
Host IP address:                127.0.0.1
Host ID:                        None
Policy file used:               /etc/tripwire/tw.pol
Configuration file used:        /etc/tripwire/tw.cfg
Database file used:             /var/lib/tripwire/sundance.twd
Command line used:              tripwire --check

===================================================================
Rule Summary:
===================================================================

-------------------------------------------------------------------
  Section: Unix File System
-------------------------------------------------------------------
```

Rule Name	Severity Level	Added	Removed	Modified
Invariant Directories	66	0	0	0
Temporary directories	33	0	0	0
* Tripwire Data Files	100	1	0	0
Critical devices	100	0	0	0
* User binaries	66	0	0	1
Tripwire Binaries	100	0	0	0
* Critical configuration files	100	0	0	1
Libraries	66	0	0	0
Operating System Utilities	100	0	0	0
Critical system boot files	100	0	0	0
File System and Disk Administraton Programs	100	0	0	0
Kernel Administration Programs	100	0	0	0
Networking Programs	100	0	0	0
System Administration Programs	100	0	0	0
Hardware and Device Control Programs	100	0	0	0
System Information Programs	100	0	0	0
Application Information Programs	100	0	0	0
Shell Related Programs	100	0	0	0

10

Critical Utility Sym-Links	100	0	0	0
Shell Binaries	100	0	0	0
System boot changes	100	0	0	0
OS executables and libraries	100	0	0	0
Security Control	100	0	0	0
Login Scripts	100	0	0	0
Root config files	100	0	0	0

```
Total objects scanned:  17572
Total violations found:  3
```

As with many complex security tools, learning to use Tripwire effectively requires some research and practice. The man pages for Tripwire (`twprint`, `twadmin`, and `twpolicy`) are a good place to begin. The Tripwire package includes limited documentation. (In `/usr/share/doc/tripwire-2.3.1/` on Red Hat Linux 7.3.) You can also consult the *tripwire.org* and *tripwire.com* Web sites for further information. Because Tripwire is widely used, you can find online discussion groups and hands-on training at security conferences such as those presented by the System Administration, Networking and Security Institute (SANS).

A second file integrity checker is **Samhain**. (Named after an Irish holiday, this is pronounced "sowen.") Although Samhain is similar to Tripwire, it has several potential advantages that turn Samhain into a combination of a file integrity checker, a log file checker, and a network monitor. Key features include:

- Runs as a daemon instead of as a `cron` job, so file changes and login/logout events are noted instantaneously

- Can detect kernel modules that were loaded as part of a rootkit

- Can operate in a client/server environment to provide centralized monitoring of several systems from one location. Network connections are encrypted using 192-bit AES.

- Reports and audit logs are supported.

- Database and configuration files are signed to prevent intruders from altering them.

- Runs on a number of UNIX and Linux platforms so that you can use it across multiple diverse systems

- An HTML status page shows information about any client system being monitored.

Samhain is available from *http://la-samhna.de/samhain/* and from *freshmeat.net*. It runs on numerous versions of Linux and UNIX, so you may have to install the source code rather than simply using an rpm.

As a final tip regarding file integrity, consider installing the `binutils` package. This package is not installed by default on many Linux distributions (it's located on CD 2 in

Red Hat Linux 7.3). It includes more than a dozen utilities useful for exploring the contents of files. For example, the **objdump** command lets you examine the contents of a file byte by byte. The **strings** command lists all text strings within any binary file, including system utilities and shared libraries. To see how **strings** operates, try this command after installing the **binutils** package:

```
strings /bin/ls
```

The output of this command lists all the text that is stored as part of the `ls` command, for example, all the help messages, error messages, and numerous internal items that you never see printed on the command line.

CHAPTER SUMMARY

- ❑ Crackers who break into a system typically want to view or modify the files on that system, either for their own direct use or to cause problems for the organization running the server.

- ❑ Linux file permissions do not allow such sophisticated control as some other operating systems because they only permit assigning rights to a file's owner, a single group assigned to that file, and to all other users on the system.

- ❑ User Private Groups enhance security by creating a group for each new user account. When that user creates files, no other group members will have access to them.

- ❑ Using file permissions can create unexpected results unless you are familiar with their exact consequences. Execute permissions on directories, the SGID bit, and blocking access to a group while allowing access to others are three techniques for using group permissions.

- ❑ Log files are important to system security because they may contain evidence of crackers attempting to break into a system or of actions by programs running on the system that indicate other potential security problems.

- ❑ Rotating logs keeps them to a manageable size and permits easy backup by breaking log entries into groups by date.

- ❑ Running the **logrotate** command as a **cron** job makes automated log rotation easy. This utility uses a configuration file to set up features for log rotation. A simple script can perform basic log rotation if **logrotate** is not available.

- ❑ System services are continually adding lines to the log files. They are often reviewed using not a text editor, but the **grep** search utility or the **tail** program, which displays the last few lines of any text file.

- ❑ The xlogmaster program displays log file and other system data in a graphical window.

- ❑ The logcheck utility package watches log files for specific words and phrases that may indicate a security breach has been attempted or has succeeded. The utility can be customized by altering the words that it watches for as listed in its configuration files.

10

❏ The commercial version of logcheck is called LogSentry and is available from Psionic Technologies. LogSentry works with other security products from the same company, such as PortSentry and HostSentry.

❏ Crackers can hide their activities by replacing system utilities with new versions designed to ignore special cracker-related files or to prevent reporting the crackers processes, networking connections, and similar information.

❏ A rootkit helps a cracker easily install a number of programs on a compromised system that permit continued root access even after the initial security hole has been discovered and fixed. Many rootkits are available. The chkrootkit package can detect many of these, much like a virus detector (but chkrootkit cannot remove the rootkit).

❏ Linux rootkits often include loadable kernel modules (LKMs) that are particularly useful for crackers and difficult to detect without the proper software (such as chkrootkit).

❏ To remove a rootkit, you can reinstall affected programs, or you may choose to reinstall the entire operating system and carefully reconstitute the data on the system. The complexity of your custom configuration settings may determine which is the most efficient use of your time.

❏ A simple step to protect a system from further damage by rootkits is to store statically linked copies of core utilities on a floppy disk or a CD-ROM to use when examining a system that is suspected of harboring a rootkit.

❏ Regularly checking the integrity of system utilities and configuration files will help you identify changes made by unauthorized users. Tripwire is the most widely used utility for checking the integrity of files and directories.

❏ To use Tripwire, you set up a policy text file and a configuration text file, generate policy and configuration binary files with cryptographic signatures, then establish a baseline snapshot of system status. Comparison snapshots are then made at regular intervals to determine whether any critical part of the system has been altered unexpectedly.

❏ Tripwire utilities such as `twprint` and `twadmin` let you maintain up-to-date policy files and manage the reports generated by Tripwire. These reports can be automatically emailed to a system administrator and can also be encrypted to protect them from alteration by a cracker trying to hide his tracks.

❏ Another impressive file integrity-checking package is Samhain. This package provides a client/server model to allow maintenance of multiple servers from a central location. Samhain runs continuously rather than occasionally, as Tripwire does.

❏ The `binutils` package includes several useful utilities for exploring Linux files. The `strings` command is one example; it displays all text strings stored in any binary file.

KEY TERMS

busybox — A utility that performs simplified versions of more than 60 standard system maintenance programs such as `ls` and `ps`.

chkrootkit — A software package that checks for evidence of over 30 different rootkits. This package works much like a virus checker, though it can only report the presence of a rootkit, it cannot eliminate one from your system.

execute (x) — A standard Linux file permission—represented in utilities by **x**—that permits execution of a file as a program or changing the name of a file within a directory (when assigned to that directory).

LKM — A Linux kernel module that has been installed as part of a rootkit.

logcheck — A utility package that checks log files each hour for any suspicious entries.

logrotate — A command to automate the process of compressing, rotating, and archiving log files so that the logs never grow unreasonably large, and older log data can be stored in another location—such as on a writeable CD or backup tape—instead of taking up hard disk space.

LogSentry — The commercial version of the logcheck utility, owned by Psionic Technologies.

objdump — A command that displays the contents of a file byte by byte.

read (r) — A standard Linux file permission (represented in utilities by **r**) that permits reading the contents of a file or listing the files in a directory.

rootkit — A collection of programs and scripts designed to permit a cracker continued access to a compromised system, even after the original security hole that permitted access has been discovered and closed.

Samhain — A file integrity checker that runs as a daemon and supports client/server configurations.

statically linked — A programming technique in which a binary program is self-contained, rather than depending on shared system components in order to function.

strings — A command that lists all text strings within any binary file.

Swatch — A software package that performs log oversight functions, similar to logcheck and LogSentry.

tail — A program to display the last 10 lines (configurable) of any text file.

Tom's Single Disk Linux — A software package that provides a complete set of standard utilities on a single floppy disk.

Tripwire — The best-known and most widely used file integrity checker.

User Private Groups — A security system in which an empty group is created for every user on the system. Files created by a user are assigned to this empty group, meaning that no other users have any default access to the file.

write (w) — A standard Linux file permission—represented in utilities by **w**—that permits modifying a file or creating new files in a directory (when assigned to that directory).

xlogmaster — A program that displays several system resources, including the system log file, in a graphical window.

10

REVIEW QUESTIONS

1. File permissions control access based on user accounts that:
   a. are defined in /etc/passwd
   b. are listed in a TCP Wrappers file or similar security configuration file
   c. are part of /etc/services for all network service requests
   d. need not be logged in before access data

2. Name the three basic Linux file permissions and the three identities to which each can be assigned for a file or directory.

3. A group that has no members but is assigned as the primary group of a single user within is implementing a security feature called:
   a. file integrity checking
   b. denying group access using file permissions
   c. user Private Groups
   d. file attributes

4. Which is never shown as a file permission in the output of ls -l?
   a. x
   b. s
   c. w
   d. u

5. Which controls permission to rename a file within a directory?
   a. the execute permission on the file being renamed
   b. the execute permission on the directory containing the file
   c. the write permission on the directory containing the file
   d. the write permission on the file being renamed

6. Setting the SUID bit on a shell script file:
   a. can only be done while logged in as root
   b. is equivalent to setting the SGID bit on the parent directory of that shell script
   c. cannot be done except when a User Private Group exists for the user that owns the shell script file
   d. will always be ignored by the Linux kernel because it is such a security hazard

7. The _____ file configures system logging; system messages are normally stored in _____.
   a. /etc/syslog.conf; /var/log/messages
   b. /etc/message.conf; /etc/syslog
   c. /etc/log/syslog; /var/log/sysog.messages
   d. /etc/rc.d/init.d/syslog; /var/log

8. Seeing hundreds of FAILED LOGIN messages in the system log probably indicates:

   a. that one of the users has forgotten his or her password

   b. that a cracker is trying a brute force attack to gain access to your system

   c. that the system logging daemon is misconfigured

   d. that the login program PAM modules are misconfigured

9. Because log files can become very large in a short period of time, you should regularly:

   a. Rotate the log files so that old log data can be moved to a storage device or deleted.

   b. Delete the log file and start from scratch every few days.

   c. Configure /etc/syslog.conf to only store the most critical logging messages.

   d. Use a program such as logcheck to inform you of oversized log files.

10. Name three types of messages that the logcheck program watches for in its default configuration.

11. The logcheck program is available commercially as:

    a. LogSentry

    b. HostSentry

    c. LogDaemon

    d. Samhain

12. When rotating log files with your own script instead of the logrotate command, you must:

    a. Keep a detailed record of the rotations in case some of the files are deleted.

    b. Issue a HUP signal to cause the logging daemon to begin using the new file.

    c. Avoid compressing the log files, because this makes them much more susceptible to corruption by crackers.

    d. Configure /etc/syslog.conf to accept your log rotations.

13. List five files that a rootkit might modify, and describe in general terms how each would be modified to protect a cracker.

14. A rootkit is typically distributed through:

    a. a commercial Linux vendor who can sign the rootkit package to verify its integrity.

    b. popular Linux download sites like rpmfind.net

    c. developer sites such as freshmeat.net

    d. cracker sites which are not publicly advertised

10

15. The rpm command can be used to verify the integrity of a program file if:

    a. The md5 fingerprint of the archived rpm file matches the md5 fingerprint of the program file.

    b. You have a CD or verified copy of the downloaded rpm against which to compare the program file.

    c. You have backed up the rpm database to a separate directory.

    d. The `rpm` command is part of the rootkit.

16. To check for evidence of rootkits installed on your system, you can:

    a. Load a kernel module that monitors all network traffic.

    b. Use Tripwire to create a baseline database after a rootkit is suspected.

    c. Use logcheck to see whether a large number of downloaded program files have been modified.

    d. Use chkrootkit to look for signs of altered program files and other indications of a rootkit.

17. With regard to rootkits, an LKM refers to a:

    a. Loadable Kracker-Man, a famous cracker who has created many rootkit packages

    b. the Logged KDE Method of unauthorized access to a remote system

    c. Lame Kode Machine, an acronym for Linux systems that have old versions of popular software (such as bind or sendmail) that allow easy access for crackers

    d. a Linux Kernel Module used for cracker purposes

18. Describe `busybox`.

19. Which command creates an initial database of system files for Tripwire?

    a. `tripwire --init`

    b. `tripwire --check`

    c. `twadmin --init`

    d. `twinstall.sh`

20. Tom's Single Disk Linux can help a system administrator when:

    a. Logcheck indicates that a cracker has attempted to log in multiple times using a bad password.

    b. LogSentry indicates that a cracker has attempted to log in using an unauthorized network service.

    c. A rootkit has corrupted basic system utilities.

    d. File permissions have allowed a user to modify a file unexpectedly.

21. Which command, with appropriate options, displays a formatted report from a Tripwire integrity check?

    a. `twadmin`

    b. `twprint`

    c. `tripwire`

    d. `twrfile`

22. The ability to work over a secure network connection to manage multiple systems at one time is an advantage of:

    a. chkrootkit over Tom's Single Disk Linux

    b. Tripwire over Samhain

    c. logcheck over other binutils programs

    d. Samhain over Tripwire

23. To see all of the text messages stored within any binary program file, you can use

    a. `dmesg`

    b. `strings`

    c. `bin`

    d. LogSentry

24. Using a SGID bit on a directory causes:

    a. users running programs in that directory to have the group permissions of the directory's group

    b. no visible change in permissions, because the SGID bit is so rarely used in Linux

    c. access to be denied when any person not a member of the group assigned to the directory attempts to access a file within that directory

    d. all files created in that directory to be assigned the same group as the directory itself

25. Describe how a cracker attempts to defeat a program such as logcheck.

HANDS-ON PROJECTS

Project 10-1

In this project you explore how User Private Groups affect file permissions on newly created files. To complete this project, you need root access to a Linux system that also has two regular user accounts. (You can create these accounts using the `useradd` command.) This project assumes that your version of Linux implements User Private Groups.

1. Log in as root and open a command-line window.

2. Use **su** to change to one of the regular user accounts.

    `su - username`

10

3. Create a file in the home directory of that user. You can use a command like this one to copy the contents of another text file instead of typing in new material, but don't use the **cp** command, because this will, by default, preserve the permissions of the file you copy. That is not what we want for this project:

    `cat /etc/printcap > ~/file1`

4. Use the **ls -l** command to review the group assigned to this new file and the group permissions.

5. Copy your new file to the **/tmp** directory.

    `cp ~/file1 /tmp`

6. Exit from the **su** command so that you are root again.

7. Use **su** to change to the second regular user account.

8. Go to the **/tmp** directory and find the file you copied there in Step 3. Look at the file using **ls -l**.

9. Can you read the file (using **more**, for example)? Why?

10. What group would your user need to be a member of to have write permission to the file?

11. Exit **su** so you are root again.

12. Review the **/etc/group** file to see which group ID corresponds to the group name for the first regular user account. What members are listed?

13. Use the **vipw** command to review the primary group ID for the first regular user account:

    `vipw /etc/passwd`

    Does this number match the number from the **/etc/group** file?

14. What command could you use to change the permissions assigned to the group when a new file is created?

Project 10-2

In this project you explore the configuration of the **logrotate** command and how daemons access log files. To complete this project you must have the **logrotate** command installed on your Linux system. This project is based on file locations within Red Hat Linux 7.3.

1. Log in as root and open a command-line window.

2. List the message files in **/var/log** and note their names:

    `ls /var/log/mess*`

3. Open the file **/etc/logrotate.conf** in a text editor.

4. Change the configuration of your system to rotate log files every day and to save log files for seven days instead of the default (normally four). (You can review the man page for **logrotate** if you are unsure what keywords to use for these changes.)

5. Save your changes and exit the text editor.

6. What will you see in the `/var/log` file tomorrow?

7. Why might you want to rotate log files more often and save more old log files?

8. Change to the `/etc/logrotate.d` directory.

9. Notice the other daemons that have specific log rotation configurations. Open one or two of these to study their contents briefly.

10. Change now to the `/var/log` directory:

    cd /var/log

11. If your system has been running for several weeks, you saw in Step 2 files such as `messages.1` that are older, rotated log files.

12. If your system is operating in a lab, with no one relying on it for service, continue with the following steps:

13. Change the name of the system log file:

    mv /var/log/messages /var/log/my_message_file

14. Start to view continuously the last 10 lines of this file:

    tail -f /var/log/my_message_file

15. Open another command-line window.

16. In that second window, log in or use the `su` command.

17. Notice that a message appears in the first window. Why is the system log writing to `/var/log/my_message_file` now instead of to `/var/log/messages`?

18. Change back to the first window and press **Ctrl+C** to end the `tail` command.

19. Reinitialize the system logging daemon by sending it a `HUP` (restart) signal:

    kill -HUP 'cat /var/run/syslogd.pid'

    (For some daemons, you might need to create a new, empty log file using the `touch` command. The system logging daemon creates a new `/var/log/messages` file without any action from you.)

Project 10-3

In this project you set up the Tripwire file integrity-checking program on your Linux server. This project does not walk through policy file configuration, however, so it should not be considered as preparing a production server for ongoing file integrity maintenance.

To complete this project you should have Red Hat Linux 7.3 installed, including the Tripwire package (check using `rpm -q tripwire`). You must also have root access and be working on a nonproduction (lab) system. Because this project includes several commands that take from 5-30 minutes to run, you may want to work as a team or split up this project's steps over several days. The files created by each step will remain available for continued use the next day.

10

1. Review the Tripwire policy text file in `/etc/tripwire/twpol.txt`.

2. Review the Tripwire configuration text file in `/etc/tripwire/twcfg.txt`.

3. Run the Tripwire configuration script:

   `/etc/tripwire/twinstall.sh`

4. Enter a site passphrase when prompted.

5. Enter a local passphrase when prompted.

6. Enter the passphrases again as prompted.

7. Initialize the Tripwire database for your system, based on the policy document you reviewed in Step 1. (This command will take several minutes to run; enter the local password when prompted.)

   `tripwire --init`

8. Make a change in your system configuration files by adding a new user (thus altering `/etc/passwd`, a critical configuration file.)

   `useradd my_new_user`

9. Run a Tripwire integrity check. (This takes several minutes.) Redirect the output of the check to a file. (You could also use the `twprint` command to create a report after the fact.)

   `tripwire --check > ~/tw_data.txt`

10. Open the data results file in a text editor.

11. Can you locate the modification in the `/etc/passwd` file? The report likely also shows many other missing files unless you modified the policy document in Step 1 or selected "Everything" when installing Red Hat Linux.

Project 10-4

In this project you create a single-disk version of Linux using a downloaded file. This disk is useful as a rescue disk in many situations, as described in the chapter text regarding rootkits in particular. To complete this project you should have root access to a Linux system with Internet access. You should also have a blank floppy disk.

1. Open your browser and point it to *www.toms.net/rb*.

2. Download a copy of the single-disk Linux archive to your `/tmp` directory by clicking **Download tomsrtbt here**, then **ibiblio** from the list of download sites.

3. In the file list that appears, locate the file named **tomsrtbt**, followed by a version number (which changes from month to month), followed by the file extension **.tar.gz**.

4. Click on that file, and when prompted, save it to `/tmp`.

5. After the download is complete, change to the /tmp file and unpack the archive file you downloaded using this command (substitute the exact filename; the version changes from time to time):

   tar xvzf tomsrtbt-version.tar.gz

6. Change to the directory named **tomsrtbt-*version***.

7. Insert a high-quality floppy disk in the floppy drive. Tom's Single Disk Linux uses a special high-capacity formatting technique that sometimes fails on old, heavily used, or poor-quality disks.

8. Run the installation program:

   ./install.s

9. Follow the screen prompts as needed.

10. Reboot your Linux server using the floppy disk.

11. Use the **ls** command to explore the utilities available on this disk.

12. How could you access your hard disk at this point? How would the utilities on this disk be useful in an emergency? What other utilities might you want to add to this collection?

CASE PROJECTS

You are back as a full-time consultant for Snow, Sleet, and Hale. Management asked their part-time technical help to connect the network to the Internet with the assistance of an ISP, but no security measures were put in place. They want you to set up security measures, but do not want you to shut down the servers or disconnect any networking points, because the employees have become accustomed to Internet access for their legal research.

On your first day setting up security, you install logcheck and several other programs. On your second day, a logcheck report in your email inbox informs you that the following message was logged late last night (long after you had left work):

   ROOT LOGIN

1. What do you suspect has happened? What steps will you take to protect the files on your system? Describe the process you will now go through to eliminate the danger that this message points out.

2. As an ethical and practical matter, what are you going to tell company management? Are you going to shut down the server or break the network connections? What dangers do you face if you do neither?

3. You had not yet installed Tripwire when this occurred, and you are understandably eager to get it running on your server. You are quite concerned about making an initial database on a system that might already have unknown security problems. How will you proceed?

NETWORK SECURITY FUNDAMENTALS

After reading this chapter and completing the exercises you will be able to:

♦ Summarize the types of network security breaches that crackers attempt

♦ Describe how to use special routing techniques to protect local network traffic

♦ Configure a basic Linux firewall

♦ Use networking utilities and techniques that protect network traffic through encryption

In this chapter you begin learning about security tools and methods for protecting networks. After reviewing the ways in which crackers attempt to attack your Linux system, you learn about special routing methods and firewalls that increase network security. The last part of this chapter describes how you can encrypt network traffic using SSH and other security tools.

The main network security features described in this chapter—IP Chains and IP Tables—are part of every Linux kernel. You learn about how to set up these features, and also how to use graphical tools to ease the work of configuration. You also learn about several commercial firewall products.

REVIEWING THREATS TO YOUR NETWORK

Previous chapters have described many of the security threats that any network faces, both from those inside your organization and outside it. A summary of those threats is presented here.

Trojan Horses

Trojan horses are programs concealed within other programs that you intentionally download or install on your Linux system, often from a trustworthy source. However, once installed, the program that "hosts" the Trojan horse appears to do one thing (such as listing files when `ls` is executed), but actually does something else or something in addition (such as accepting any network connection on a certain port or making certain system configuration files visible to crackers). Trojan horse programs are hard to spot before they cause damage to your system unless you use a file integrity program such as Tripwire or Samhain (described in Chapter 10). You can protect yourself against Trojan horses by installing programs only from sources such as your Linux vendor or the official download site for a well-known program and by checking the cryptographic signature or fingerprint on the program before installing it.

Viruses and Worms

Viruses and worms are related security threats designed to replicate themselves once they have been installed on your system. A virus usually tries to replicate as part of another program (for example, as an email attachment), while a worm attempts to infiltrate other systems on its own. Linux is rarely the subject of virus attacks, because programs running on Linux have access to system resources based solely on the user permissions of the person running the program. Unless a program is running as root and is not security-oriented (a rare situation in Linux), a virus can't do much damage. In addition, because Linux lacks support for common viral "carriers" such as Microsoft Word and Excel, few viruses can run on Linux, and those that can have a hard time affecting other programs (unless you run everything as root, which should always be avoided).

Worms pose a greater threat than viruses because they are independent programs, not files attached to other programs or macros. A worm is like an automated cracker: if you protect your system against crackers by regularly updating services like `sendmail` and DNS, the worm will have trouble getting a foothold on your system. Of course, another valid option is to use a program such as qmail or Postfix (in the case of mail servers) instead of `sendmail`, since `sendmail` has a history of security-related problems. Linux supports many powerful programs for each of the popular server functions you might need.

Denial-of-Service (DoS) Attacks

Denial-of-Service (DoS) attacks occur when a cracker tries to overwhelm your system, either causing it to shut down or just making it unavailable to legitimate users. This can be done in several ways. Two common methods are to overwhelm the network connection with traffic and to execute network requests that fill up the hard disk of the targeted server. Because a single machine is unlikely to have the capacity to overwhelm a large commercial server, crackers now rely on **Distributed Denial-of-Service (DDoS)** attacks. In a DDoS attack, a cracker infiltrates many systems (hundreds or thousands, if possible) and installs a program that will execute a DoS attack on an assigned target. The administrators of the affected systems may not even realize that a cracker program has been installed on their systems, because the program doesn't attempt to do anything at the time it is installed. Instead, once many systems have been infiltrated and the DoS program installed, the cracker sends a signal to all of the systems to begin their DoS attack at the same time. With hundreds or thousands of machines from all over the world participating in the attack, a server has a very hard time knowing which packets are part of the attack and which are from legitimate users.

A DDoS attack is hard to plan for and defeat. Nothing on your system is altered, and you have no idea of trouble until the attack commences. At that point, you cannot simply reject packets from a certain computer (as you could with a nondistributed DoS attack) because the attack is coming from a thousand places at once. The IPv6 protocol includes capabilities that make DDoS attacks easier to defeat, but until it is in widespread use, DDoS attacks remain a big concern for commercial Web service providers.

11

Buffer Overflow Attacks

A buffer overflow attack refers to any cracker attack that exploits a programming flaw to cause a network service to shut down, corrupt data, or provide unexpected (and therefore unauthorized) access to a system. Suppose that a program such as an FTP server allocates a block of memory to hold a command such as `ls` that arrives over a network connection. The command normally is terminated by a new-line character. However, if a cracker sends a command that doesn't terminate with a new-line character, but instead continues for thousands of characters, the FTP server software (if it is not well designed) will just keep reading in the command. When the command exceeds the space allocated to it in memory, the FTP server crashes. In some cases, a skilled cracker may be able to include information in the extra-long command that will be written in certain parts of memory to give the cracker unauthorized access.

Buffer overflow attacks are hard to predict. Obviously, if system administrators knew about a potential buffer overflow, they would fix it immediately. When someone discovers how to create a buffer overflow, a race ensues between crackers who want to use it to attack systems and system administrators who want to get a patch—an update—to fix the problem. Good system administrators don't give a cracker much of a chance; they have updates installed the same day they are released, which is usually within two days of the problem being discovered by a group such as SANS or CERT/CC. System administrators who don't pay attention to security let old versions of their network service daemons continue running. Crackers are then free to use well-known buffer overflow attacks against them.

 Other types of programming attacks can also crash a server or permit unauthorized access. Buffer overflow is one category of programming errors that permit an attack, and many others are possible. For example, one attack on older versions of DNS causes the `named` daemon to shut down immediately if it receives a particular request.

Spoofing and Man-in-the-Middle Attacks

Spoofing is the forging of addresses. Crackers use IP spoofing and DNS spoofing. In **IP spoofing**, a cracker modifies the source or the destination address on an IP packet. For example, if a cracker learns your internal IP address, he might send a packet to your firewall from an outside server, but with the source IP address of your internal network. He hopes that your firewall will let the packet through based on the source IP address. A well-designed firewall would not be fooled. (For example, all internal traffic would come through one Ethernet card and all external network traffic through a second Ethernet card.) However, IP spoofing can confuse some programs and should be considered as you plan firewall rules and router designs.

DNS spoofing is pretending that a request comes from a particular host instead of its true host. For example, if security is based on domain names, a cracker might be able to subvert the security setting through DNS spoofing; a packet bears the forged address of an authorized domain. Using reverse DNS lookups can help to avoid this problem, because the cracker will have a hard time actually modifying all of the zone information files on the authoritative DNS server. Recall from Project 6-2 that you can query a series of DNS servers using `dig` to determine the authoritative information for a forward or reverse DNS lookup.

Another attack used with DNS is a **poison cache attack**. A cracker attempts either to block access to your site or to block your access to other sites, by uploading erroneous information into a DNS server's cache. Carefully configuring your `/etc/named.conf` file so that only authorized systems can transfer zone information to your DNS server may be enough to prevent a poison cache attack.

Similar to spoofing attacks, **man-in-the-middle attacks** are those in which a cracker intercepts a communication, reads or alters it, and leads the originator of the packet to believe that the intended recipient has received it. Figure 11-1 shows how this might operate if a cracker obtained a copy of your private key and used it to intercept all traffic between you and a colleague.

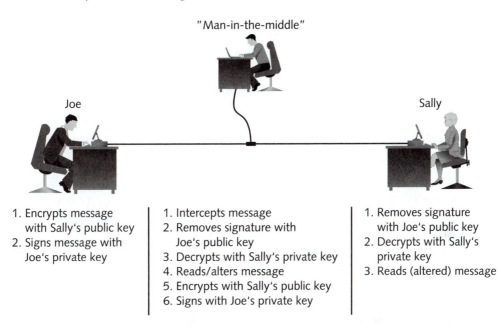

Figure 11-1   Man-in-the-middle attack using a copy of a private key

Another man-in-the-middle attack is **Web spoofing**. In this attack, a cracker deceives a user into linking to the cracker's site when the user thinks he or she is linking to another site. The cracker's server can then begin to intercept every Web request from the user, make the request itself, and alter the response to point all future requests back to the cracker's site. This type of attack is less likely to succeed with the widening use of Java, because Web sites don't rely on simple links that can be easily altered by an intermediate server. Instead, a Java program is more tightly meshed with programming on the originating Web site. If a cracker tries to interfere, the program simply stops working. Nevertheless, Web spoofing may still be an issue under some circumstances.

In discussions of various networking security issues, you will see references to potential man-in-the-middle attacks. This refers to an ongoing concern: a cracker who was able to intercept network traffic should not be able to modify or redirect traffic in such a way as to fool the sender into thinking that the packet was actually received by its intended recipient. For example, a cracker might try to alter header fields in an IP packet to redirect it to a different server, then use IP spoofing so that the return packets appeared to come from the intended recipient of the original packet. Because of man-in-the-middle attacks, some network encryption techniques include a checksum—a cryptographic fingerprint—of the packet header. If any field of the header is modified between the sender and receiver, the fingerprint won't match and the packet can be discarded. Of course, this makes it impossible to use advanced routing techniques such as those described in the next section of this chapter, because they modify IP header fields.

USING ADVANCED ROUTING AND FIREWALLS

You have learned about numerous ways to control access to your system in order to keep crackers at bay. For example, you know that many services use TCP Wrappers through the `inetd` superserver. You can control access to those services by configuring the `/etc/host.allow` and `/etc/host.deny` files. Specific network programs have access control mechanisms. For example, the `wu-ftpd` FTP server supports multiple security directives in `/etc/ftpaccess`; Apache supports similar directives in the `httpd.conf` configuration file. These directives let you specify which hosts can access the Web server; they can be as precise as allowing a certain host to access only a single file. Samba and NFS configuration files also support access control mechanisms.

Using any of these per-service configuration files can protect your computer from intruders that try to gain access to that service. You might think of these as application-specific firewalls. However, the term firewall usually describes controlling network traffic at a lower level in the protocol stack. Recall that you learned back in Chapter 1 about the OSI and Internet networking models, which are shown in Figure 11-2. The middle of the figure shows how different access control mechanisms can protect a network service. A **firewall** typically refers to a packet filter—access control operating at the lowest levels of the networking stack. When a packet of data reaches the higher layers of the protocol stack, there is a much greater chance that it can gain unauthorized access, either through programming errors or configuration errors. A packet filter can examine and discard packets from unauthorized systems before they have a chance to "attack" applications.

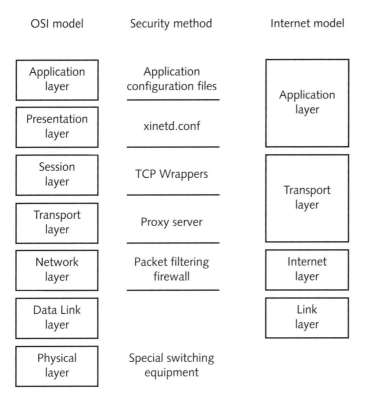

Figure 11-2   Networking models and their access control mechanisms

A traditional firewall relies on rules. A **rule** is a configuration setting that defines certain characteristics of an IP packet and the action to take for any packet that has those characteristics. An example rule might effectively say: "If a packet contains TCP data destined for port 25, and it comes from any address other than network 192.168.125.0/24, then discard the packet." Another way to protect network services and the clients on a LAN is to use advanced routing techniques. These techniques can effectively "hide" LAN clients from crackers on the Internet, even though the clients can still access the Internet.

Networking stacks in Linux are contained in the kernel. This gives Linux great control over network packet management and means that a properly configured Linux firewall or router is all that some networks require. Exceptions occur when you need to control access to many different low-level protocols (such as IPX, SNA, and AppleTalk) and when you want a dedicated router to provide enough capacity for a busy LAN.

11

Advanced routing and firewalls are implemented using the same Linux tools. In the Linux 2.2 kernel (used by Red Hat 7.0 and other Linux distributions released in late 2000 or 2001), the Linux firewall system was called **IP Chains**. In the Linux 2.4 kernel (used by Red Hat 7.3 and other distributions released in 2002 or later), the firewall system is called NetFilter and IP Tables. The 2.4 kernel supports IP Chains as well, but the two systems cannot be used at the same time. In Red Hat Linux 7.3, the IP Chains system is used by default because it is simpler to configure. The sections below describe IP Chains and NetFilter/IP Tables.

 Previous to IP Chains, Linux used a command called **ipfwadm** (for IP firewall administration). An `ipfwadm` command looks similar to a simple `ipchains` command. You will occasionally see references to `ipfwadm` in the documentation on Linux firewall software.

Introducing IP Chains

The IP Chains feature of Linux lets you set up a **chain**: a list of rules for how packets are handled. By default, the Linux kernel includes three chains:

- *Input*: Packets coming from outside the system on which the rule is executed pass through this chain

- *Forward*: Packets coming from outside the system on which the rule is executed and that need to be routed to another computer pass through this chain

- *Output*: Packets coming from within the system on which the rule is executed and that are destined for other systems pass through this chain

The basic operation of an IP Chain is shown in Figure 11-3. Each rule in the chain specifies one or more parameters. If a packet matches those parameters, the packet is handled according to the instruction at the end of the `ipchains` command (the `-j` option, for "jump to"). If the packet doesn't match the parameters in the rule, the next rule is tried. If none of the rules match, a default policy defines what happens to the packet.

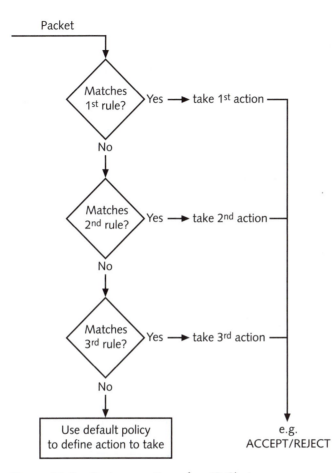

Figure 11-3   Basic operation of an IP Chain

You create and manage rules in these chains using the **ipchains** command. The rules can be simple or complex. A simple rule might indicate that the default policy for the Input chain is DENY, meaning that if an incoming packet is not processed by one of the rules in the chain, it should be rejected with no response sent back to the sender. This rule is shown here:

```
ipchains -P input DENY
```

Rules in an IP Chain can take any of the following basic actions for a packet: Accept, Deny, Reject, and Masquerade (described below). The difference between Deny and Reject is that Reject informs the sender that the packet is being rejected (it sends a "port not reachable" message using ICMP). Deny simply ignores the packet without any feedback to the sender. Much more complex rules than the example above are common. Take this example:

```
ipchains -A input -s 0/0 67:68 -d 0/0 67:68 -p udp -i eth0
   -j  ACCEPT
```

The command above adds a rule to the input chain that says to accept a packet coming from any source IP address and destined for any IP address if it is using UDP, arrives on the eth0 network interface, and uses either port 67 or 68 for the both source and destination addresses.

You can list the rules in all chains using the -L option with the **ipchains** command (the -n option tells the command to go on if IP addresses can't be resolved through DNS):

```
ipchains -n -L
```

Rules are executed in the order that you place them in the chain. For example, suppose you have the following two rules. The first accepts packets from a single network, the second denies packets for all networks.

```
ipchains -A input -s 192.168.10.0/0 -j ACCEPT
ipchains -A input -j DENY
```

As with certain other configuration files that you have seen, the order of the rules is important. If you reversed the above two rules, packets coming from the 192.168.10.0 network would be denied before they could be permitted access by the more specific rule.

> In general, firewall rules should go from more specific at first to more general at the end, with "catch all" rules at the very end so that nothing gets through unexpectedly.

In order for rules in IP Chains to be effective in preventing crackers from accessing your server, they should be in place before networking is activated on your Linux system. Otherwise, a cracker has a small window of opportunity between the time networking is activated and the time the IP Chains rules are activated. On Red Hat Linux, maximum protection is produced by including all of the **ipchains** commands in the file `/etc/sysconfig/ipchains`, then using a script named **ipchains** in `/etc/rc.d/init.d` to execute those commands. If you review the order of execution in the run-level directories (for example, `/etc/rc3.d`) you see that the **ipchains** script is executed before the network script; the IP Chains rules are activated before anyone can reach your system through the network.

During installation of Red Hat Linux, you answer a question about the level of firewall protection that you want to implement. The level that you select—low, medium, or high—determines what **ipchains** commands are executed each time you boot your Linux system. Those commands normally form only the beginning of your firewall; a server connecting an organization to the Internet might use hundreds of **ipchains** commands to set up its network access.

Table 11-1 lists the most commonly used options for the `ipchains` command. All of the options are case sensitive. With the information in this table you should be able to review `ipchains` commands that you find in your default installation and practice new configurations on your network. Refer to the `ipchains` man page for a more complete listing.

Table 11-1   Commonly used options for the `ipchains` command

Option	Description
-A *chain*	Append a rule to the end of the named chain
-D *chain index*	Delete rule number *index* from the named chain
-F *chain*	Flush (delete) all rules from the named chain, or from all chains if no chain is named
-L *chain*	List all the rules from all chains, or from the named chain if given
-P *chain policy*	Set the default policy of the named chain to the named policy
-s *address port*	Define a source IP address against which to compare a packet; you can include a port number after the address to indicate which TCP or UDP port should match the rule
-d *address port*	Define a destination IP address against which to compare a packet; a port number can be included as with the -s option
-i *interface*	Specify the network interface (such as eth0) that a packet must use to match the rule
-p *protocol*	Indicate the protocol field of the IP address that will match the rule; the protocol can be tcp, udp, or icmp (The protocol specification is not case sensitive.)
-j *target*	Define an action for packets matching the packet specifications (such as the -p and -s options); targets can include ACCEPT, DENY, REJECT, MASQ, and a few others

Besides the three chains mentioned—input, forward, and output—you can create your own chains of rules and "call" them like subroutines from within other chains. To use a user-defined chain, you first define it with the -N option, then add rules to it with the -A option. Finally, you can use the -j option within an `ipchains` rule to jump to that chain if the rule succeeds.

Network Address Translation

The IP Chains feature in the Linux kernel also provides special routing functionality. **Network address translation (NAT)** is a routing technique that alters the addresses or other header information in a packet. One popular type of NAT is **IP masquerading**, a type of network address translation in which packets from many computers on a LAN are altered to appear as if they came from a single computer. This technique is very useful for organizational or home networks that connect to the Internet, as shown in the following example (illustrated in Figure 11-4).

- A client on a LAN sends a packet destined for a distant Web server (Server X in the figure).

- The router/firewall that the packet passes through ("Fire" in the figure) removes the source IP address and MAC address of the client and replaces it with the router's IP address and MAC address, then sends the packet on.

- The Web server receives the request as if it came from the router, since that is the source IP address.

- The Web server sends its response to the router's IP address.

- The router receives the response, replaces the destination IP and MAC addresses in the packet with the IP and MAC addresses of the client, and routes the packet to the internal network.

- The client receives the packet from the Web server without any sign that it was intercepted and "masqueraded" by the router.

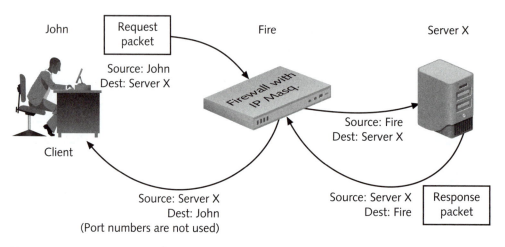

Figure 11-4   IP masquerading

IP masquerading is normally done by using a private IP address such as 192.168.0.0. Using masqueraded addresses provides several benefits compared to having each client access remote sites using its individual IP address:

- Using IP masquerading, a single IP address can permit an entire LAN to connect to the Internet or to larger organizational networks. If more organizations used IP masquerading, the Internet probably would not be running out of IP addresses; a single IP address would suffice where hundreds are now used. Behind the IP masquerading server, the same private IP addresses could be used on every LAN.

- Because only one system is actually sending packets to the remote network (or the Internet), only one connection is required. If your ISP charges per IP address or per account, NAT will save you money; your ISP sees packets coming from only one IP address and, therefore, one user. Some ISPs may have rules about using IP masquerading on your network, because you are obviously likely to generate more network traffic with many LAN clients creating data that a single server sends through the network connection. However, if you are not exceeding your connection limits for time and bandwidth, the ISP shouldn't be concerned.

- IP masquerading acts like a firewall because a remote computer cannot connect to a client within a masqueraded LAN. If you configure the router carefully, IP masquerading effectively hides your entire network.

Alongside the benefits of IP masquerading is one considerable disadvantage. You can "hide" your LAN clients, but this can make some network connectivity unworkable. For example, some network services like FTP, IRC, and streaming audio include lower-layer data in higher layers of the networking protocols. IP masquerading isn't designed to "masquerade" these higher layers where IP and TCP information isn't expected. To make these protocols work through a masquerading server, you must install additional kernel modules for the specific protocols that you want IP masquerading to support. This is not an elegant solution, but it works reasonably well.

To see which protocols older versions of IP masquerading (before NetFilter) support through Linux kernel modules, review the list of modules in `/lib/modules/2.2.16-22/ipv4` on Red Hat Linux 7.0, as an example, or a similar directory, typically within the `/lib/modules` subdirectory. (Things are done differently in the Linux 2.4 kernels, as described below.)

Setting up IP masquerading is very easy; it requires a single rule that says in effect, "any network traffic coming from this network should be masqueraded." Suppose you had a LAN with the network address 192.168.100.0 that you connected to the Internet through a dial-up modem. Using the command below on the server causes all network traffic from the internal network to be masqueraded; all clients on the LAN would then be able to access the Internet (though the ISP would see all traffic as coming from the gateway system). The forward chain is specified because only traffic that is not destined for another server on the local network should be masqueraded.

```
ipchains -A forward -s 192.168.100.0/24 -j MASQ
```

Transparent Proxying

In Chapter 6 you learned how to use an Apache proxy server to "collect" all client requests to Web servers from a LAN in a single server: the proxy server. The proxy then acts in place of the individual clients, making requests to the Web servers that the clients wanted to contact and returning the results to the client. Using a proxy server is very similar to IP masquerading (see Figure 11-5), but the proxy works at the Application level instead of the IP level. Note that port numbers are used in proxy serving, but not in IP masquerading.

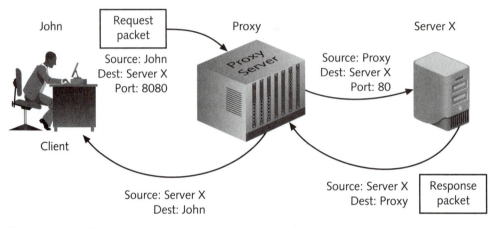

John

Request packet

Source: John
Dest: Server X
Port: 8080

Proxy

Source: Proxy
Dest: Server X
Port: 80

Server X

Client

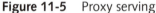

Source: Server X
Dest: John

Source: Server X
Dest: Proxy

Response packet

Figure 11-5 Proxy serving

A proxy server provides security against outside attackers by insulating clients; they don't need an externally accessible IP address. A proxy also lets you control the Web access that clients are permitted. A list of certain Web addresses (such as *www.espn.com*) can easily be blocked so that no one on the network can access those sites. Finally, a proxy can cache the results of Web server accesses to improve performance for all users on the local network.

Apache can act as a proxy server, but the most widely used Linux proxy server is **Squid**. You learn more about Squid in the section that follows. Recall from Chapter 6 that in order to use a Web proxy, you must configure each client on the LAN so that it "knows" it is using a proxy. In many cases (though not in the projects for Chapter 6), you specify a nondefault port for the proxy. For example, instead of letting clients use the default Web port 80, you specify port 8080, 8008, or whatever port you choose. Either way, you must configure each client.

An alternative to this configuration effort is to use the transparent proxy feature of IP Chains and IP Tables. **Transparent proxy** lets you redirect a packet based on the port to which the packet is addressed (see Figure 11-6). Suppose you are running a proxy server such as Apache or Squid on your Linux server, and a browser on your LAN issues a request to a distant Web server. You have not configured the browser to use your proxy server, but the request must pass through a gateway to reach the Internet. Within that router, you configure an IP Chains rule on the Input chain that says, "if any packet comes from another host, is using the TCP protocol, and is destined for port 80 on a remote server, redirect that packet to port 3167 (or whichever port you choose for your proxy server) on the local system." This causes the packet to end up at the proxy server running on the router, even though the client wasn't configured to use a proxy, and the proxy server software took no specific action to get the packet. Instead, the kernel "redirected" the packet. This action was transparent to the client and the proxy server software. A transparent proxy configuration in the Linux kernel therefore acts like an internal IP masquerading feature.

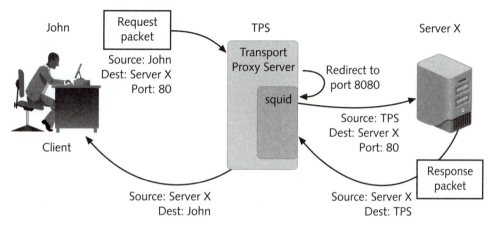

Figure 11-6   Using a transparent proxy

The transparent proxy server retrieves the requested Web page and attempts to return it to the client. The transparent proxy rule intercepts that packet and redirects it to the port on the client that originated the request.

To set up a simple transparent proxy once your proxy server is set up, you can use an `ipchains` command like this:

```
ipchains -A input -p tcp -d 0.0.0.0/0 80 -j REDIRECT 8080
```

The above command inserts a rule in the Input chain that causes any packet destined for port 80 on any system to be redirected to port 8080 on the local system (the one on which the `ipchains` command was executed).

Transparent proxy has some of the same limitations as IP masquerading because of the necessity of a direct connection between client and server for some protocols. In addition, you may want to redirect a number of different protocols or ports using transparent proxy rules and a server such as Squid. Doing so requires additional `ipchains` commands and careful testing.

The Squid server is officially called an "Internet Object cache." This means that it is a caching proxy server for Web requests and other Internet protocols. The proxy support for Web requests works like the proxy feature of Apache described in Chapter 6. Squid is designed for use even on very large servers. It is installed by default on Red Hat Linux 7.3. You can learn about this large and complex program by reading the file `/usr/share/doc/squid-2.4.STABLE6/FAQ.html` in your Web browser. The Squid Web site is *www.squid-cache.org.* This site includes links to documentation, related software, hardware products that are built on Squid, and more.

Graphical Firewall Configuration Utilities

The examples of `ipchains` commands shown so far in this chapter illustrate basic ideas for firewall and NAT configurations, but setting up a robust firewall on a production Linux server is a challenging task. The configuration for every network will be different. Although the syntax of the `ipchains` command can seem obscure, it's not a difficult command to use once you become familiar with the options listed in Table 11-1 and learn how to understand a complex `ipchains` command when you read it. Learning to do this is a key skill for a Linux network administrator.

Nevertheless, Linux supports several graphical tools that you can use to set up a firewall. As with many other graphical utilities, some of these Linux tools are better than others; none provides complete access to `ipchains` functionality; and you need to understand how IP Chains operate before you can do much useful work with the graphical utilities.

There are several great online resources for exploring Linux security-related software. One is *www.linuxapps.com.* Click on Security from the main page and review the dozens of security tools that are listed—about 75 at last count. (Many of these tools are more relevant to the subjects covered in Chapter 12, but packet filtering and firewall tools are also listed.) Another is *www.linux-firewall-tools.com/linux/.* This site lists dozens of sources for downloading software and for study of security topics (both Linux-focused and more general networking security).

Red Hat Linux, like many other Linux distributions, includes basic firewall configuration tools to help new users give their systems some level of protection. When you install Red Hat Linux, you answer basic questions about your network security. These questions are posed using the `lokkit` program, which you can execute at any time from the command line. Use this command:

```
lokkit
```

Figures 11-7 and 11-8 show the two screens that make up this text-mode program. `lokkit` doesn't ask you about "rules," but instead sets up reasonable rules based on how secure you want your system to be and any specific protocols that you want to leave more open. (Remember that "more secure" means "harder to use" if you are in a trusted environment like a testing lab, where you want to run many network services without reconfiguring the firewall for each one.)

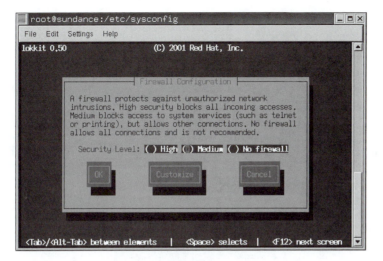

Figure 11-7   The initial screen of `lokkit`

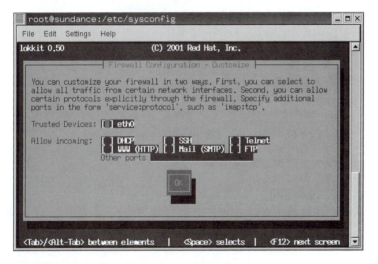

Figure 11-8   The Customize screen of `lokkit`

For the more ambitious network administrator, the **firewall-config** program is also provided on Red Hat Linux 7.3. You can use this graphical program to set up complex firewall rules like those described in this chapter. You won't have much success with this program unless you already feel comfortable with the `ipchains` and `iptables` commands, but using a graphical interface can help you remember the available options and keep track of the rules already included in your chain or table. The program does have minimal online help, but the man pages for `ipchains` or `iptables` are a better resource. To start the program, enter this command:

```
firewall-config
```

You can also choose Programs, then System, then Firewall Configuration on the main menu of Gnome. The main window of the program is shown in Figure 11-9. This window lists all the rules you have created. You can activate or deactivate each one as needed. (Deactivated rules are saved for later use even though they are not part of the kernel configuration.)

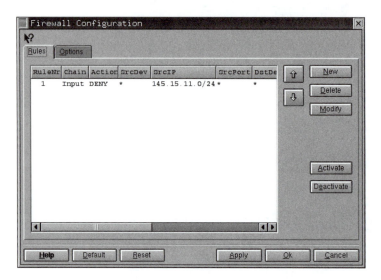

Figure 11-9   The `firewall-config` program's main window

To create a new rule in **`firewall-config`**, choose the New button. A Rule Editor dialog box appears (it's still titled firewall-config). In this dialog box, which is shown in Figure 11-10, you define the network interface, IP addresses, ports, and protocols that you want to control with the rule you are creating. You can also select any existing rule and click the Edit button to use the same dialog box to alter that rule.

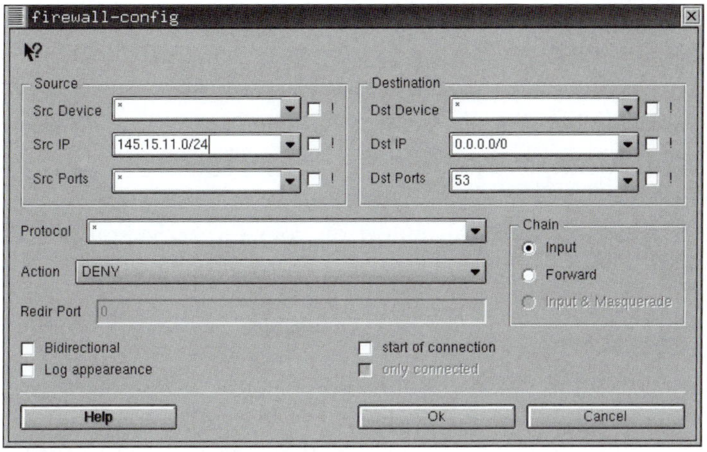

Figure 11-10   Editing a rule in the `firewall-config` program

Several other firewall configuration tools are available for Linux. The Gnome program Firestarter is a good example. It includes a firewall creation wizard to help you set up a basic firewall. Then you can modify those basic rules as needed. You can also watch real-time monitors to see when a packet matches a specific rule. Figure 11-11 shows a sample screen from Firestarter. You can find this program through the download link on *firestarter.sourceforge.net*.

11

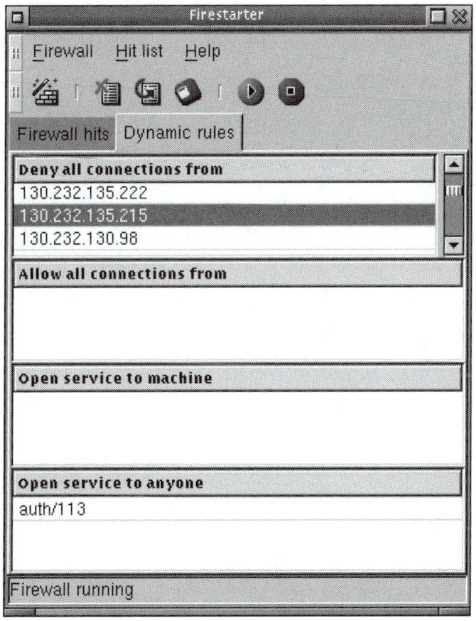

Figure 11-11   Firestarter firewall configuration tool

Another firewall tool is the T.Rex Open Source Firewall. This program features VPN support (described later in this chapter), NAT, proxy services (including Web page caching), workload balancing, and content filtering. For more information see *www.opensourcefirewall.com*.

Mason is a firewall tool that uses a different approach appropriate for less experienced Linux administrators. Instead of defining rules at the outset, you start Mason, then start all the other services that you want to support on your server. Mason prepares a list of rules that intelligently allows only those services and blocks all others. For more information, visit *http://mason.stearns.org*.

KMyFirewall is a KDE-based program that lets you set up a "Personal Firewall" or protect a larger network using IP Tables. It includes a setup wizard for less experienced users, plus a more advanced interface to help you create complex rules. You can save a copy of your firewall rules to a separate file and then use that file to easily configure other firewalls running KMyFirewall where the same rules should be applied. For information, visit *http://kmyfirewall.sourceforge.net*.

One well-regarded firewall configuration utility for Linux is GuardDog. GuardDog can use either a graphical interface (see Figure 11-12) or its own command-line utility. GuardDog's features include:

- A "deny that which is not explicitly allowed" design for more secure systems

- Script-based rules for either `ipchains` or `iptables` to permit import and export of rule sets

- Ability to define firewall "zones": groups of hosts or networks to which rules can be applied

- Categories of protocols for easier decision making

- Connection tracking and logging

- Explicit support for many more protocols than other firewall tools (review your `/etc/services` file). These include X, CORBA, FTP, HTTP, HTTPS, NNTP, POP2, POP3, IMAP, IMAPS, POP3S, ICQ, IRC, MSN Messenger, PowWow, NetMeeting, Gnutella, AudioGalaxy, Real Audio, Diablo II, DirectPlay, Halflife, Quake, QuakeWorld, Quake 2, ping, ICMP Source Quench, ICMP Redirect, traceroute, whois, NetBIOS Name Service, NetBIOS Session Service, DNS, NTP, DHCP, CDDB, finger, telnet, VNC, SSH, PPTP, ISAKMP, Kerberos, auth, klogin, kshell, Telstra's BigPond Cable, XDMCP, SUN RPC, NFS, NIS, LDAP, LDAP-SSL, SMTP, Linuxconf, Webmin, SWAT, Nessus, Line printer spooler, syslog, SOCKS, Squid, pcANYWHERE stat, PostgreSQL, and MySQL.

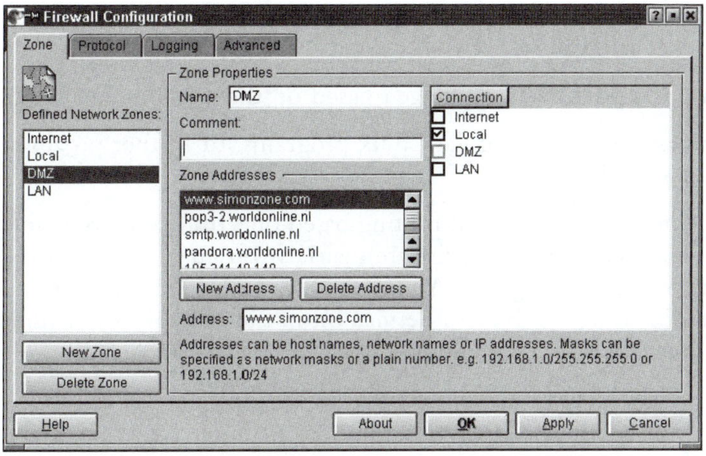

Figure 11-12   The GuardDog firewall tool

Using NetFilter and IP Tables

Now that you are comfortable with IP Chains for basic firewall configurations, IP masquerading, and transparent proxy, you're ready to learn about the latest Linux system that implements firewalling. The newest Linux kernel, version 2.4, includes a completely rewritten packet filtering system called **NetFilter**. NetFilter uses a different architecture than IP Chains, though it includes an IP Chains compatibility system; you can still use all the information that you've just learned (remember that Red Hat still uses IP Chains rules by default). NetFilter offers much more power and flexibility for packet routing by providing "hooks" at five different points in the processing of a network packet. **Hook** is a programming term that refers to the ability to connect another program or list of commands at that point. So, for each of these hooks, you can set up a list of rules that should be executed at that point in the processing of a network packet. The lists of rules associated with the hooks are very similar in function to an IP Chain, and are called **IP Tables**. They contain a list of rules that the kernel uses to examine packets and decide how to process them.

> In Linux documentation and discussion groups (as well as this chapter), you will see the terms NetFilter and IP Tables used interchangeably. Don't be confused; just remember that NetFilter is the system and IP Tables are the rules that you apply within the system.

IP Tables provide much more functionality than IP Chains. This list summarizes the most important additional functionality that IP Tables and NetFilter provide:

- You can act on packets based on their state. This is similar to the "stateful" aspect of the TCP protocol that you learned about in Chapter 1. A packet is part of a larger connection; if you can keep track of information about that connection, you can better decide how to process the packet.

- You can examine and alter just about any header field of a packet. This is called packet **mangling**.

- You can select packets to be logged based on the value of any header field.

- You can pass packets to regular Linux programs for further processing outside the Linux kernel.

- You can implement intelligent routing based on **Quality of Service (QoS)** features. QoS is a networking feature that lets you guarantee bandwidth to certain users or certain programs. A Linux router with QoS capability could be implemented using the Type of Service bit in the IP protocol or using other parts of a packet that you examine using whatever IP Table rules you choose.

Setting up rules using the `iptables` command is similar to using `ipchains`. For example, using the following command on a home computer with a dedicated Internet connection (such as DSL or a cable modem) allows you to connect to anyone on the Internet, but any packets trying to establish a connection to your system would be ignored ("dropped").

```
iptables -A INPUT -p tcp --syn -j DROP
```

Suppose now that you want to allow SSH traffic (as described below) to reach your computer. This will allow you to log in securely to your home computer from remote sites. The following line permits only SSH traffic—it "punches a hole" in the firewall for a single protocol.

```
iptables -A INPUT -p tcp --syn --destination-port 22 -j ACCEPT
```

You would probably want to include both of the previous two examples. First, use the second command to permit SSH traffic, then add the first command so that all other traffic is dropped. Remember that specific rules should come before general rules; the last rules effectively say, "reject anything I haven't specifically allowed before this point."

Options supported by `iptables` are similar to those used with `ipchains`, but some are new. The man page provides details, but you may want to rely on the IP Chains mode of your Linux 2.4 kernel (the default setting in Red Hat Linux 7.3) until you are more familiar with IP Tables. You may also want to use a program such as GuardDog to help you configure a NetFilter firewall.

To determine whether IP Chains mode or the newer IP Tables is currently being used on your Linux system, find out which kernel modules are loaded. If the following command shows that the `ipchains` module is loaded, you are using IP Chains functionality:

```
lsmod | grep ipchains
```

If the above command returns nothing, but searching for iptables is successful, then you are using the newer IP Tables capability. If you use a graphical tool like GuardDog, it will begin by using the method established by the defaults that were configured by your Linux distribution.

```
lsmod | grep iptables
```

Commercial Firewall Products

Previous sections have described a number of security programs that you can download for your Linux server. In addition to free software, many companies have created commercial security products built for Linux. Some of these products will help you secure your existing Linux server; others are intended as complete network firewalls and just happen to be built on Linux. Some are software, but many are separate hardware devices you can add to a network in the same way that you might add a router. A hardware device that is sold specifically to accomplish one purpose or a group of related purposes—such as a firewall, a router, or a VPN, as described later in this chapter—is sometimes called an **appliance**.

When an appliance such as a firewall is built on Linux, it typically uses a standard Linux kernel. The manufacturer may recompile the kernel with different options compared to a standard Linux distribution such as Debian, Red Hat Linux, or SuSE, but the appliance is fundamentally just running Linux. The manufacturer adds value by preconfiguring Linux firewall features such as IP Tables or a network analysis tool (some of these are described in Chapter 12). The following paragraphs mention several commercial products that support or are built on Linux.

Astaro Security Linux is a firewall product that does stateful packet inspection filtering, content filtering, user authentication, virus scanning, VPN with IPSec and PPTP, and more. You can recognize many of the features in this list as coming directly from the list of NetFilter capabilities. The Astaro product includes a Web-based management tool built on the Webmin interface. Though this is a commercial product, Astaro also provides a download version that is free for noncommercial use. Astaro also provides firewall appliances through several partners that built hardware systems. Visit *www.astaro.com* for information.

Another hardware solution built on Linux is the NetMAX VPN Server Suite. For information on this product, visit *www.netmax.com*. Some of the larger firewall companies are also supporting Linux. Search your favorite portal for firewall products online and research the Web sites you find to identify those that mention Linux as the basis of the product or as a supported platform.

11

ENCRYPTING NETWORK TRAFFIC

The routing techniques described in the previous section can help secure your network by isolating clients in a LAN from the Internet at large. Even so, the content of client messages sent through the Internet—and indeed the content of every packet sent on your LAN—is likely to be unencrypted, or plaintext. This means that a person using a network analysis tool (a sniffer) to view all packets on the local network segment could view the data contained in every packet that you send. This is sometimes very useful for diagnosing stubborn networking problems; Chapter 12 describes some popular network administration programs that let you do this. But crackers can use the same programs to look for information to help them gain unauthorized access to your servers.

A recurring theme in this book is the assumption that every unencrypted message that you send might be read by an unauthorized user, either on your local network or on the Internet. Several previous chapters have mentioned the Secure Shell (SSH) as a method of encrypting network traffic. Here we explore that program in more detail and also describe other methods of encrypting network traffic, all designed to make it difficult for someone gathering packets from your network to extract anything useful about you or your organization.

 In addition to introducing the Secure Shell, Chapter 8 described IPsec and Cryptographic IP Encapsulation (CIPE), both of which provide secure network connections by encrypting all traffic through the network. For situations in which the following discussion of SSH doesn't resolve all the security issues, consider using IPsec or CIPE.

Using the Secure Shell

The Secure Shell (SSH) package is a client server protocol similar to Telnet. The SSH application suite includes a client program called **ssh** and a server daemon called **sshd**. A program called **slogin** is also provided; it acts just like **ssh**. The **scp** program is like the **rcp** program; it lets you copy one or more files between two machines on the network. All of these programs use the same encryption techniques that you learned about for the GPG program in Chapter 8: they exchange asymmetric keys to establish the identity of a user requesting a connection and to pass a symmetric session key securely. The symmetric key is then used to encrypt all traffic flowing over the secure shell connection.

The OpenSSH implementation of the SSH is used on most Linux distributions. On Red Hat Linux 7.3 it is installed by default as five separate packages: **openssh**, **openssh-clients**, **openssh-server**, **openssh-askpass**, and **openssh-askpass-gnome**. You can use the **rpm** command to verify that these packages are installed. The OpenSSH Web site has links to source code, packages, and several types of documentation. On Red Hat Linux, the OpenSSH documentation is located at **/usr/share/doc/openssh-3.1p1**, but may not be too helpful until you have figured out the package by other means. The OpenSSH programs also have lengthy man pages that describe both the technology of the programs and the options that each supports. In particular, the **ssh** and **sshd** man pages are useful.

OpenSSH was originally written for the OpenBSD operating system and is now available for many variants of UNIX, Linux, Windows, Macintosh, Java, PalmOS, and others.

The SSH protocol in general and the OpenSSH implementation in particular support two versions. SSH protocol version 1 (SSH1) uses a public key encryption system to authenticate each connection, but it does not support strong encryption of the subsequent network traffic. Current releases of OpenSSH support version 1 for backward compatibility. Previously, SSH2 had stricter licensing provisions than SSH1, but SSH2 can now be freely distributed as part of OpenSSH. SSH protocol version 2 (SSH2) uses a more robust authentication process and also supports strong encryption of all network traffic. Ciphers currently supported include AES (128-, 192-, or 256-bit), 3DES, Blowfish, CAST128, and Arcfour. As you may recall from the discussion in Chapter 8, 3DES is secure but slow, Blowfish is a good choice for a well-tested cipher that is much faster than 3DES, and 192- or 256-bit AES is a highly secure, government standard cipher.

SSH can authenticate a connection in several ways. The least secure, which is not discussed here, is to rely on the r-utilities files, such as `/etc/hosts.equiv` and `~/.rhosts`. (You won't see these files unless you've configured the r-utilities.) The SSH documentation recommends against using the r-utilities method. The second alternative is to rely on user passwords. While using passwords is much better than the **rhosts** method or an unencrypted Telnet session, it still doesn't provide public key authentication of the session.

To use SSH password authentication, make certain that the **sshd** daemon is running on the system to which you want to connect. The **sshd** daemon is configured in the file `/etc/ssh/sshd_config`. The default configuration in Red Hat Linux 7.3 should work fine to get you started. SSH protocol connections use port 22 by default. This port is listed in `/etc/services`, but since **sshd** runs in standalone mode, you won't find any reference to **sshd** in `/etc/xinetd.d` (you might need to check that the **sshd** line is enabled in `/etc/inetd.conf` on some Linux distributions). To check the status of the **sshd** daemon, use the following command:

```
/etc/rc.d/init.d/sshd status
```

If the daemon is running and no firewall is blocking traffic on port 22 between your client and server computers, you should be able to use the following command on the client to connect to **sshd** on the server:

```
ssh -l username server
```

The **-l** option indicates the account ("l" is for "login name") on the server that you want to use to connect. Because the server doesn't know anything about the client at this point, you receive a warning that the server doesn't have a host key for the client. If you are not overly worried about sophisticated crackers, this shouldn't concern you; you can enter the word "yes" to proceed. You are then prompted for the password of the username you entered on the server you entered. At that point you are logged in to the remote system (the system running **sshd**).

11

To use public-key authentication in OpenSSH, you must set up key pairs, much as you did in Chapter 8 when using the GPG utility. The `sshd` server has a server key pair stored in `/etc/ssh`. For example, `ssh_host_rsa_key.pub` contains an RSA-format public key. Both RSA and DSA keys are generated by default in Red Hat Linux 7.3. To create a key pair for your own user account, you must use the `ssh-keygen` program and specify a key type of either RSA or DSA using the `-t` option. The default key length is 1,024 bits, but you can alter that length with the `-b` option (many other options are supported as well—see the man page for `ssh-keygen`). A sample command would look like this:

```
ssh-keygen -t rsa -b 2048
```

After a few moments, the key pair is generated and you are prompted for the file in which the key pair should be saved. If you accept the default by pressing Enter, your private key is stored in `~/.ssh/id_rsa` and your public key is stored in `~/.ssh/id_rsa.pub`. You must also enter a passphrase (twice) to protect this key pair. You may choose to press Enter to leave the key pair unprotected by a passphrase; you can then create scripts that use `ssh` without pausing to request your passphrase. This decision depends on who else is using your computer and how you intend to use `ssh` to access your accounts on remote systems.

 The key pair you generated for OpenSSH is to help you connect to remote computers on which you have a login account. The key pair you generated for GPG is to sign files and communicate with other users via email or other GPG-compatible programs.

Once you have a key pair generated on one account, you should place the public key from that account in the `authorized_keys` file on each system where you want to log in using `ssh`. For example, suppose you have an account named alvarez on your principal computer (call it system1). You also have an account named sarah on a second computer (call it system2) that you want to have secure access to via `ssh`. You could follow these two steps to facilitate that: while logged in on system1 as alvarez, use `ssh-keygen` to generate a key pair; then, using any method you choose (`scp`, FTP, `rcp`, email, or floppy disk), copy the file `/home/alvarez/.ssh/id_rsa.pub` on system1 to the file `/home/sarah/.ssh/authorized_keys` on system2. (This assumes that you used a key type of RSA; if you used DSA, the filename would be `id_dsa.pub`.)

If you have only these two accounts, the `authorized_keys` file will not already exist and you can copy the key file using a command such as this from system1:

```
scp -l sarah ~/.ssh/id_rsa.pub system2:~/.ssh/authorized_keys
```

To complete this command you need to enter your password for the sarah account on system2. If you have multiple accounts and had already created an `authorized_keys` file, you could add another key to the end of the `authorized_keys` file using a command like this one (recall that the `>>` operator appends data to the end of an existing file):

```
ssh -l sarah system2 cat ~/.ssh/id_rsa.pub >>
    system2:~/.ssh/authorized_keys
```

Once you have the public key from one account listed as an authorized user on another account, you can use **ssh** to log in or **scp** to copy files without entering a password. The keys are exchanged in the background to verify your identity.

 If you intend to use the SSH suite on a number of systems, review the **ssh-agent** command. This command provides useful tools for managing key pairs and authentication among multiple SSH-capable systems.

OpenSSH supports a number of very useful features besides replacing **telnet** and **rlogin**. As mentioned in previous chapters, you can use the **ssh** utility to encrypt other network traffic. This lets you create secure connections for protocols that are not inherently secure. One example is the X protocol for serving remote graphical applications, as you learned in Chapter 3. When the **-X** option is added to the **ssh** command, any graphical program (X clients) launched on the remote system is automatically displayed on the system where you executed **ssh**. The **sshd** daemon automatically handles the **DISPLAY** variable, **.Xauthority** cookie-based authentication, and transmission of all X protocol data over the encrypted **ssh** connection. To use this feature, you would follow these steps:

1. Launch a graphical environment on your client system; call it system1.

2. Log in to a remote server using **ssh**. Call it system2. The example command below uses the **-X** option to enable X protocol forwarding over the **ssh** connection, as just described. You could also configure this feature to be used automatically for certain hosts. The **-c** option used here indicates, in order of preference, which cipher you prefer to use. (Note that no spaces are used in the list of ciphers.) The server will select the first listed cipher that it supports.

   ```
   ssh -X -l nwells -c aes192-cbc,blowfish-cbc,3des-cbc
       system2
   ```

3. Once you have a command prompt on system2, enter the command name of a graphical program that you want to run on system2 but display on system1. Don't include any **DISPLAY** variable information; the **ssh** and **sshd** program will handle this.

   ```
   gimp &
   ```

4. The program you launched appears after a moment on system1. Any data that you exchange within the program is encrypted. For example, if you executed a word-processing program on System 2 that was displayed on System 1, all of the document data that you viewed on System 1 would have been encrypted as the X protocol passed it from System 2 to System 1. Figure 11-13 shows how an encrypted remote X connection operates.

11

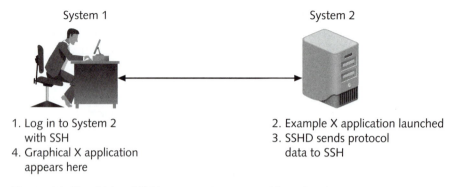

System 1   System 2

1. Log in to System 2   2. Example X application launched
   with SSH   3. SSHD sends protocol
4. Graphical X application   data to SSH
   appears here

Figure 11-13   Using SSH to encrypt a remote X application

Another important feature of SSH is its ability to do **port forwarding**. This is a routing technique that lets you encrypt many other protocols over an SSH connection, much as you can encrypt the X protocol to use a graphical application across the network. Consider the following simple example.

Suppose that you have a large LAN with many Samba servers and you want to use SWAT to manage all of them from a single location called client1. You are concerned, however, about using SWAT in your browser because none of the traffic (including the password you must enter to access SWAT) is encrypted. You can use SSH in this situation by specifying that any traffic on client1 that arrives at port 12345 (you can pick any port with a high number so that it is unlikely to be used) will be forwarded though **ssh** to port 901 (the SWAT port) on the remote server (called server1). The following command initiates that connection:

```
ssh -l nwells server1 -L 12345:server1:901
```

After executing this command to set up a secure communications channel, you can start your browser on client1 and enter the URL *http://client1:12345*. The **ssh** program catches that request and sends it to port 901 on server1, where SWAT is watching for connections. You are then communicating with SWAT over the SSH-encrypted connection. Figure 11-14 illustrates port forwarding. The **-R** option provides a capability similar to this example, but forwards a remote port (e.g. on server1) to a local port (e.g. on client1).

Port forwarding allows you to use almost any protocol you choose securely, including SMTP, FTP, or POP3. With more complex configurations, you can even use **ssh** to tunnel from a remote system through a firewall to an internal server that only permits connections from internal clients.

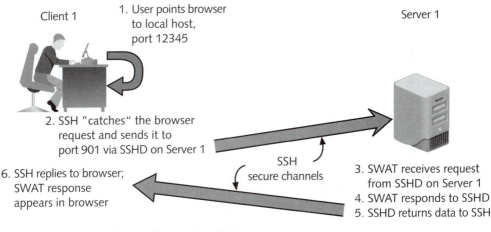

Figure 11-14   Port forwarding using SSH

Other Tunneling Protocols

The concept behind using SSH port forwarding is that you can tunnel an insecure protocol inside a secure protocol. Figure 11-15 illustrates this idea. The secure, encrypted protocol provides shielded transportation; even someone who intercepts the data packets cannot read their contents.

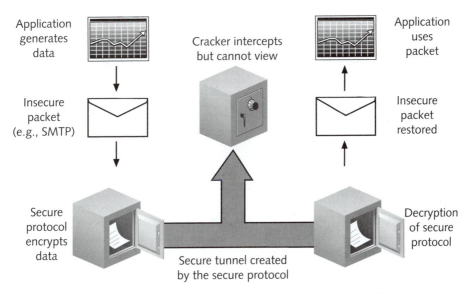

Figure 11-15   Tunneling an insecure protocol in a secure protocol

Several other tunneling strategies are used on Linux. Two of these are the Point-to-Point Tunneling Protocol (PPTP) and `stunnel`.

Using PPTP

The **Point-to-Point Tunneling Protocol (PPTP)** is a standard for creating a virtual private network (VPN—see later in this chapter). Microsoft created PPTP, and many security experts have serious concerns about its viability as a secure protocol. (See, for example, *www.counterpane.com/pptp.html*.) PPTP is supported on Linux, though it is not installed by default on Red Hat Linux.

PPTP uses two communications channels between a client and server. The first is a control channel; the second carries data and can be encrypted. The data channel is simply a PPP channel, with options such as compression and encryption negotiated when the channel is established, based on the capabilities of the client and server systems.

The client portion of PPTP is available for download at *http://pptpclient.sourceforge.net/*. The PPTP server, called Poptop, is located at *www.poptop.org*. The Poptop project is much further along in development than the client project. You can use Poptop to create a Linux-based PPTP server that Windows clients can connect to, as if to another Windows system running PPTP. Windows 95, 98, NT, and 2000 are known to work with Poptop.

Using `stunnel`

The Secure Sockets Layer (SSL) protocol is used on nearly all Linux Web browsers to provide secure transmission of Web data for e-commerce. (SSL is used whenever you see "https" at the beginning of the URL.) This protocol is supported through the `openssl` package. The `stunnel` package lets you use SSL as a transport protocol for other network traffic instead of just HTTP (Web) traffic. Both `openssl` and `stunnel` are installed by default on Red Hat Linux 7.3. You can search *rpmfind.net* for these rpm files if you don't have them already. The following protocols are examples of what you can encrypt using `stunnel`:

- POP3
- IMAP
- NNTP (news)
- SMTP (email)
- PPP

The `stunnel` man page describes various command-line options that `stunnel` supports, but its basic operation is straightforward. You can start `stunnel` from within the `inetd.conf` program to have the superserver launch a service with `stunnel`-encrypted communications. An example command for the last field of the configuration line in `inetd.conf` is shown here. The `-d` option indicates the port that should be used; the `-l` option indicates that the program following is being executed in "inetd mode":

```
stunnel -d 993 -l /usr/sbin/imapd -- imapd
```

If you are using xinetd, as in Red Hat Linux, you can set up a stunnel connection using a separate configuration file for the protocol to be encrypted. For example, to encrypt POP3, you could set up a separate configuration file called /etc/xined.d/pop3-redirect that contains the lines shown below. The server argument shows that xinetd actually launches the stunnel program. The server_args field includes the arguments for stunnel.

```
service pop3
{
      disable    = yes
      socket_type     = stream
      wait            = no
      user            = root
      server          = /usr/sbin/stunnel
      server_args     = -c -r pop3s-server.example.com:pop3s
      log_on_success += USERID
      log_on_failure += USERID
}
```

A final example shows how you can start a standalone program from a command line and have it use encrypted communications via stunnel. The program launched here is the PPP daemon, pppd. Once you establish an encrypted PPP connection using stunnel, all network traffic that uses the PPP connection is encrypted.

```
stunnel -d 2020 -L /usr/sbin/pppd — pppd local
```

11

In this chapter you have learned several methods of encapsulating one protocol within another to create a secure communications channel. For example, you can:

- Use stunnel to encrypt services such as PPP, POP3, and IMAP

- Use PPTP to encrypt a standard PPP channel

- Use SSH to encrypt other protocols such as X, FTP, or POP3

These are useful options to know about, and many Linux users rely on them at some point. However, stacking protocols in this way could be considered a patchwork solution. A better idea is to work on broader network designs that do not require this type of stacking. Technologies such as IPsec and Cryptographic IP Encapsulation (CIPE) can encrypt traffic without the overhead that stacked protocols brings.

Stacked protocols create more network traffic because of the techniques that TCP uses to maintain stable connections. Each packet that TCP transmits must be acknowledged by its recipient. The TCP stack on the transmitting computer adjusts how it transmits based on the acknowledgments it receives from the recipient. For example, if acknowledgments take a long time to return, the sender does not transmit data as fast. This prevents dropped packets and makes better use of network bandwidth. However, when a TCP-based protocol is encapsulated in another TCP-based protocol, the algorithms used to make each of the two connections more efficient can actually work at cross purposes, making the overall connection terribly slow, losing packets, or causing the connection to terminate unexpectedly. This problem is discussed in more technical detail at *http://sites.inka.de/sites/bigred/devel/tcp-tcp.html.*

Creating a Virtual Private Network

Virtual private networks (VPNs) were mentioned in Chapter 8. A VPN allows multiple computers to function as part of a single, secure network when parts of the "private" network are actually separated by a public network such as the Internet. A VPN is like a special application of tunneling, because it lets a group of computers that can be remote to each other act as a single secure LAN by tunneling the traffic through specially configured network connections. You can create a VPN in Linux using any of several strategies. Consider the following examples:

- You want a single file system to be available to users on two separate networks located several miles apart. You would like to use NFS to mount the file system on a remote server so that users in both offices can use it. Instead of paying for a dedicated connection between the offices, you use a fast Internet connection and SSH with port forwarding to establish an NFS mount for the file system. All data passed over the connection (through the Internet) is encrypted by SSH, as represented in Figure 11-16.

- You want to be able to dial in to your office network from home. The system administrator sets up PPTP so that you can establish a PPP connection with all of the transfers between the office server and your home computer being encrypted. No one on the ISP computer (or anywhere else on the Internet) can read the network packets that you send and receive. (Keep in mind the caveats regarding PPTP mentioned previously.) Figure 11-17 illustrates this configuration.

- You need to connect four offices into a single network. The traffic volume is low, but the connections must be secure from eavesdropping. You set up a server in each office with a dedicated dial-up connection to the Internet. The server runs either IPsec or CIPE and includes firewall rules (using either IP Chains or IP Tables) that do not permit any traffic (except for your four offices) into the LAN within each office. All traffic sent out of the LAN is encrypted by IPsec or CIPE and must be destined for one of the other three office network addresses. Figure 11-18 shows this configuration. (Notice that, based on the routing and firewalls described, no one in any of the four offices can send or receive email, browse the Web, or have other access to the Internet. Only packets destined for the other offices are routed.)

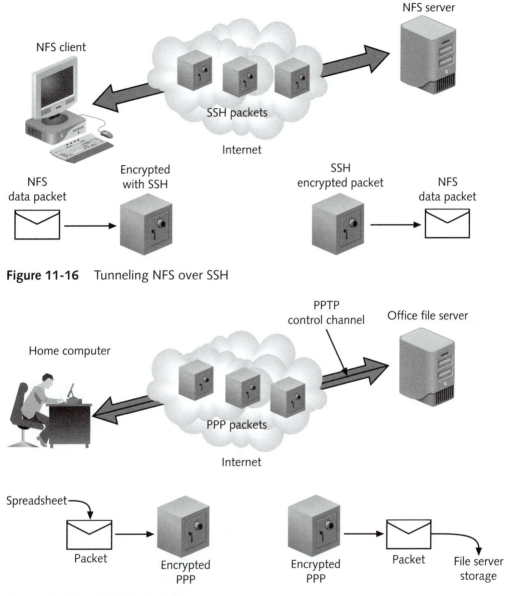

Figure 11-16   Tunneling NFS over SSH

11

Figure 11-17   A PPTP connection via a modem

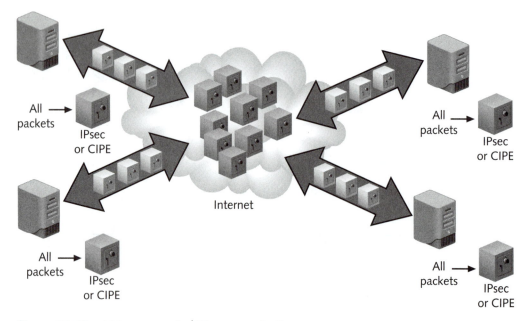

Figure 11-18   Using encrypted IP communications

To learn more about setting up a VPN on Linux, consult the Linux documentation on advanced routing and VPNs available on *www.linuxdocs.org*, *www.linuxhq.com*, or other Linux download sites. Examples of useful resources that you can find on these sites include:

- VPN HOWTO
- VPN Masquerading HOWTO
- Advanced Routing HOWTO
- Linux 2.4 Packet Filtering HOWTO
- Linux Cipe+Masquerading mini-HOWTO

Creating a VPN can be complex, and the dangers of configuration mistakes are usually more serious than mistakes made within your LAN. With a VPN, a mistake can mean that sensitive data from your organization is suddenly visible to anyone on the Internet who knows where to look for it. In addition to using standard Linux software to create a VPN, dozens of commercial VPN products are available to help you along. Some of these are software products, but most are hardware products. A VPN hardware solution (often called a **VPN router**) acts like a dedicated firewall that connects only to another (usually identical) VPN router at the other end of the public network connection. See Figure 11-19. The software on the VPN router encrypts all traffic from the LAN that it is protecting, and also routes traffic between two or more parts of the network as if they were part of a single segment, or a closely allied network.

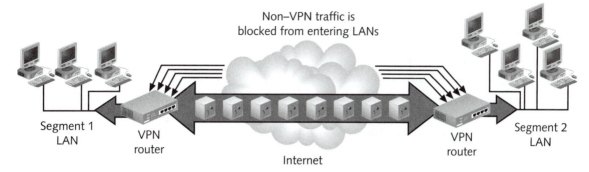

Figure 11-19   VPN routers connecting through the Internet

Configuring Security Services

The browser-based Webmin interface can be used for configuration of system security services and is used by default in Caldera OpenLinux and several other Linux distributions. In previous chapters you have seen how you can configure network cards, DNS, and other features using Webmin. The Webmin Web site (*www.webmin.com*) lists all available Webmin modules. You can download these modules and add them to your Webmin installation. Webmin modules with a security focus are listed in Table 11-2. Besides the security modules listed here, many other Webmin modules that support specific network services (e.g., Apache, NFS, `sendmail`, Qmail, PostFix) will include security options as part of their configuration tools.

Table 11-2   Webmin modules for security management

Webmin Module	Description
Security Sentries	Configure the `portsentry`, `hostsentry`, and `logcheck` utilities (The first two of these are described in Chapter 12)
SSL Tunnels	Set up SSL tunnels (stunnels) to encrypt services such as POP3 and IMAP email
SSH Server	Configure the SSH server (`sshd`)
Squid Proxy Server	Configure the Squid proxy server, including caching options, user lists, and access control lists (who can use which services)
Change Passwords	Change passwords graphically for any user on the system

CHAPTER SUMMARY

- ◻ Trojan horse programs appear to be normal but perform unexpected actions that compromise system security.

- ◻ Viruses and worms are self-propagating security problems. Viruses typically attach themselves to data files; worms work independently of other programs.

❏ Denial-of-Service (DoS) attacks try to block access by legitimate users. Distributed Denial-of-Service (DDoS) attacks use many machines to attack a target and are very hard to defeat.

❏ Buffer overflow attacks rely on a programming oversight to corrupt data or gain unauthorized access by sending unexpected data to a network service.

❏ Spoofing attacks pretend that a packet is coming from a service or location that is not accurate. The man-in-the-middle attack is a concern when someone might be able to intercept and read network traffic.

❏ Firewalls filter data packets based on their source, destination, protocol, or other aspects of the packet's makeup. A Linux firewall is controlled through the Linux kernel, which manages all IP packets entering or leaving the system.

❏ Linux firewalls are created using IP Chains or IP Tables (which are part of the NetFilter architecture). Both let a system administrator add rules to control which packets are accepted or processed and which are discarded.

❏ Rules used by firewalls define characteristics of IP packets and how to handle matching packets. Rules are always executed in the order that they are listed within a chain or table. Advanced rules include special actions such as masquerading and redirecting packets.

❏ IP masquerading is a type of network address translation that lets multiple users access an external network such as the Internet through a single system acting as though it were generating all of the traffic. Transparent proxy lets you redirect packets to different ports.

❏ Programs for setting up and managing firewall rules are included in Red Hat Linux. These include `lokkit` and `firewall-config`. Many other firewall tools are also available for Linux.

❏ IP Tables provide several routing and security features that IP Chains did not include, such as packet mangling and support for Quality of Service/Type of Services flags.

❏ Many commercial firewall products are available for Linux; some are software and some are dedicated security appliances.

❏ The Secure Shell protocol (SSH), implemented in the OpenSSH package, provides an encrypted replacement for Telnet, as well as encrypted communications for many other protocols using the port forwarding feature of SSH.

❏ SSH uses either RSA or DSA public-key cryptography plus a symmetric cipher such as AES. To make the best use of SSH, you generate a key pair using an SSH utility called `ssh-keygen`.

❏ The PPTP protocol was developed by Microsoft to implement a Windows VPN. PPTP uses an encrypted PPP session plus a separate control channel.

□ The `stunnel` package uses the SSL protocol to encrypt other protocols such as POP3 and IMAP (both used for email retrieval). `stunnel` can be used from a superserver or directly on the command line.

□ Tunneling one TCP-based protocol inside another can cause delays and dropped connections because of the way TCP tries to manage each connection.

□ Linux security features can be used to create an effective virtual private network (VPN). Many companies sell dedicated VPN appliances based on Linux.

□ Many Webmin modules are available to help configure security services on Linux.

Key Terms

appliance — A hardware device that is sold specifically to accomplish one purpose or a group of related purposes, such as a firewall, a router, or a VPN.

chain — A list of rules that controls how packets are routed or handled in the Linux kernel.

Distributed Denial-of-Service (DDoS) — A special type of denial of service attack in which a cracker infiltrates many systems and installs a program that will execute a DoS attack on an assigned target at the cracker's command.

DNS spoofing — Pretending that a request comes from a different host than its true originating host.

firewall — A program that filters (blocks) IP packets based on their characteristics, according to a set of rules.

`firewall-config` — A graphical program used to configure IP Chains and IP Tables-based firewalls.

hook — A programming term that refers to the ability to connect another program or list of commands at a certain point of program execution.

IP Chains — The Linux firewalling architecture previous to kernel version 2.4; still supported in 2.4 kernels using a compatibility mode.

IP masquerading — A type of network address translation in which packets from many computers on a LAN are altered to appear as if they came from a single computer.

IP spoofing — A cracker attack in which special low-level software puts any address the cracker selects as either the source or the destination address on an IP packet.

IP Tables — The lists of rules associated with one of the programming hooks provided in the networking stacks by the NetFilter architecture.

`ipchains` — The command used to manage rules within the IP Chains firewall architecture.

`ipfwadm` — A firewall configuration utility in versions of the Linux kernel previous to 2.0.

`lokkit` — A text-mode program that sets up basic firewall rules according to the level of security protection desired.

11

mangling — The ability to alter nearly any aspect of a packet based on any feature of that packet. A feature of NetFilter in Linux 2.4 kernels.

man-in-the-middle attack — A general term for any security attack in which a cracker intercepts communication, reads or alters it, and leads the sender to believe that the information was received by the intended recipient.

NetFilter — The packet filtering and advanced routing architecture in Linux 2.4 kernels.

network address translation (NAT) — A routing technique in which the addresses or other header information in a packet is altered during routing.

Point-to-Point-Tunneling Protocol (PPTP) — A standard created by Microsoft for setting up a virtual private network (VPN). PPTP uses two connections, one for control information and one for data.

poison cache attack — A cracker attack in which a cracker attempts to block access to a site by uploading erroneous information to a DNS server's cache.

port forwarding — A routing technique within SSH that can encrypt many other protocols over an SSH connection by connecting another service's port to the SSH port.

Quality of Service (QoS) — A networking feature that guarantees bandwidth to certain users or certain programs.

rule — A configuration setting that defines characteristics of an IP packet and an action to take for any packet that has those characteristics.

Squid — The most widely used Linux proxy server.

ssh-agent — A part of the SSH suite that helps manage key pairs and authentication among multiple SSH-capable systems.

stunnel — A program that uses SSL as a transport protocol to encrypt other network protocols such as POP3 and IMAP.

transparent proxy — A feature of IP Chains and IP Tables in which a packet is redirected to a different port.

VPN router — A hardware device that acts as a dedicated firewall with VPN capabilities.

Web spoofing — A type of man-in-the-middle attack in which a cracker deceives a user into linking to the cracker's site when the user thinks he or she is linking to another site. The cracker's server then intercepts every Web request from the user and alters the response to point all future requests back to the cracker's site.

REVIEW QUESTIONS

1. A file integrity program such as TripWire can protect against Trojan horse attacks by:

    a. automatically deleting Trojan horse programs

    b. helping you catch unexpected changes to a system utility file that might indicate it had been replaced by a Trojan horse

    c. rejecting packets generated by Trojan horse programs

    d. using programming hooks to inform the kernel of Trojan horse behavior

2. Describe the difference between a DoS attack and a DDoS attack.

3. In a poison cache attack:

   a. Squid or the Apache proxy server are subject to a buffer overflow attack.

   b. Information in memory is corrupted by a virus or worm.

   c. Erroneous DNS entries are included in the cache of a DNS server.

   d. NetFilter must use IP Chains to reject cached packets.

4. Web spoofing is an example of:

   a. a man-in-the-middle attack, because the user thinks she is reaching the intended Web site, but she is not

   b. a Trojan horse attack, because the user's browser doesn't actually attempt to reach the requested site

   c. a worm, because programs on the Web server attempt to infiltrate client sites through the browser

   d. a buffer overflow attack via script programs running on the Web server

5. Linux firewalls consist of _____ organized into _____ or _____ .

   a. commands, packets, datagrams

   b. utilities, secure, insecure

   c. chains, protocols, filters

   d. rules, chains, tables

6. Previous to the introduction of IP Chains architecture, Linux used the _____ command for firewall configuration.

   a. `ipfwadm`

   b. `netfilter`

   c. `ifconfig`

   d. `stunnel`

7. The three default chains used by IP Chains are:

   a. INPUT, FORWARDING, OUTPUT

   b. INPUT, FORWARD, OUPUT

   c. DENY, REJECT, ACCEPT

   d. NETFILTER, IPTABLES, SSH

8. Define the purpose of the following `ipchains` options: `-d`, `-s`, `-p`, `-i`

11

9. The difference between REJECT and DENY is:

   a. DENY informs the sender that the packet was discarded; REJECT provides no feedback to the sender.

   b. REJECT jumps to the next rule in the chain; DENY immediately discards the packet in question.

   c. DENY informs the sender that the packet was discarded; REJECT logs the packet in `/var/log/messages`.

   d. REJECT informs the sender that the packet was discarded; DENY provides no feedback to the sender.

10. IP masquerading is a popular example of:

   a. network address translation

   b. transparent proxy

   c. tunneling TCP through TCP

   d. a new feature that NetFilter introduced to Linux

11. IP masquerading is configured using which option within an `ipchains` command?

   a. `-j MASQ`

   b. `-j REDIRECT`

   c. `-i MASQ`

   d. `-A FORWARD`

12. By using a transparent proxy configuration, a system administrator can:

   a. Securely transmit packets over the Internet using a variety of ciphers.

   b. Hide logging and other security features from users sending packets through a LAN.

   c. Redirect packets destined for a given port on a remote system to a different port on the router.

   d. Cache packets in the router to provide higher performance for all users on the LAN.

13. Name four Linux firewall configuration tools, stating those included with Red Hat Linux.

14. Which is a new feature that NetFilter includes but IP Chains did not include?

   a. routing based on QoS

   b. transparent proxy

   c. IP masquerading

   d. IPsec support

15. Linux is often the basis of dedicated hardware appliances designed as routers, firewalls, or VPNs. True or False?

16. Name two differences between SSH1 and SSH2.

17. If you use **ssh** without first creating and storing a key pair on the remote host:

    a. You are prompted for a password to aid authentication.

    b. The **sshd** program will not permit a connection.

    c. Only the insecure r-utilities method of authentication can be used.

    d. The standard configuration of **sshd** automatically generates a key pair and sends it back to the client.

18. The command to create a key pair for use by **ssh** and **sshd** is:

    a. **gpg**

    b. **ssh-askpass**

    c. **ssh-keygen**

    d. **ssh-agent**

19. Port forwarding with SSH allows you to:

    a. Use SSH to encrypt protocols that use any TCP port.

    b. Use a proxy server to cache packets.

    c. Pass key pairs between hosts that have not previously communicated with each other.

    d. Use SSH within a superserver configuration file, as with **stunnel**.

20. PPTP is a VPN solution that:

    a. was developed by Microsoft and uses separate control and data channels

    b. is considered preferable to IPsec and CIPE

    c. is identical to using PPP over **stunnel**

    d. mimics the features found in hardware VPN devices

21. To create a secure communications channel using **stunnel**, you must:

    a. Generate key pairs and store them on the local and remote systems before using the program.

    b. Configure the SSL feature of your browser so that **stunnel** can recognize your certificate authority.

    c. First use the SSH utilities to establish an encrypted channel, then launch **stunnel** to permit another protocol such as POP3 to use the encrypted channel.

    d. Execute the **stunnel** command from a command line or within a superserver configuration file.

11

22. Describe in detail one method by which that Linux security capabilities can be used to create a VPN.

23. Some experts recommend using _____ instead of _____.

    a. IPsec or CIPE, PPP over SSH

    b. `stunnel`, SSH

    c. PPTP, IPsec or CIPE

    d. `ipfwadm`, NetFilter

24. Name four of the ciphers that are supported by the latest release of OpenSSH.

25. Quality of Service features let a router:

    a. Control how much bandwidth certain users or programs receive on a busy network.

    b. Log information about how well the router is handling a heavy load.

    c. Monitor when someone sends a packet that matches a particular rule in a firewall.

    d. Reset Type of Service bits, which are not supported in modern routers unless they use IPv6.

HANDS-ON PROJECTS

The projects presented here assume that you are working in a lab environment. **If you are working on a production server or one containing any sensitive data, do not attempt the following projects**.

Project 11-1

In this project you explore how the Lokkit firewall configuration tool sets up rules for IP Chains. To complete this project, you should have Red Hat Linux 7.3 installed with root access.

1. Log in as root and start a command-line window.

2. Make a copy of your `ipchains` configuration file.

    ```
    cp /etc/sysconfig/ipchains /etc/sysconfig/ipchains.save
    ```

3. Launch the Lokkit program.

    ```
    lokkit
    ```

4. In the first screen that appears, use the Tab key to highlight the **Medium** security level, then press the **Spacebar** to select it.

5. Use the Tab key to highlight **Customize**, then press **Enter** to select it.

6. Use the Tab and Spacebar keys to highlight and select fields so that your screen looks like the one in Figure 11-20.

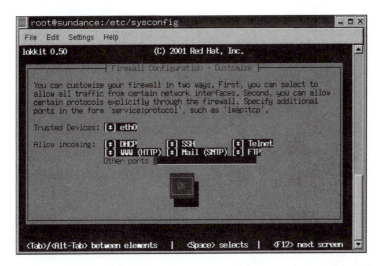

Figure 11-20 The `lokkit` program with a custom configuration

7. Tab to the **OK** button and press **Enter**. The first screen reappears. Tab to **OK** and press **Enter** to save your configuration and close Lokkit.

8. Open the configuration file `/etc/sysconfig/ipchains` in a text editor or view it using the less command:

   `less /etc/sysconfig/ipchains`

9. Notice the lines near the beginning that end with ACCEPT. Can you identify what these lines accomplish by looking at the port numbers that are part of the **–d** field? How important do comments seem in a firewall configuration file?

10. Notice the lines near the end that end with REJECT. What do these lines do? (Note that a representation such as 0:1023 means "all ports between 0 and 1023.")

11. Exit the text editor or `less` command.

12. Launch the `lokkit` program again.

   `lokkit`

13. Use the Tab and Spacebar keys to select the **High** security level. Then select **OK** and press **Enter** to close `lokkit` and save your configuration.

14. View the `/etc/sysconfig/ipchains` file again. What differences do you notice? What single service is permitted to pass through the firewall? (Look for the port number in `/etc/services`.) What interface is permitted broad access?

15. Restore your original ipchains configuration file:

   `cp -f /etc/sysconfig/ipchains.save /etc/sysconfig/ipchains`

None of your changes to the `ipchains` configuration file have taken effect because you did not rerun the `/etc/rc.d/init.d/ipchains` script after changing the file.

Project 11-2

In this project you use `ipchains` commands to block Ping on your system. For this project, you should work as partners with another student or colleague. The two systems mentioned in the steps are your system and your partner's system. To complete this project, you should have two Linux systems with root access. The files described here are taken from Red Hat Linux 7.3 but should be applicable to most versions of Linux.

1. From the first system, `ping` the second system (substituting the IP address of the second system for 192.168.100.6):

   ```
   ping 192.168.100.6
   ```

   Let the `ping` command continue as you complete the following steps.

2. On the second system, see what firewall rules are in effect using this command:

   ```
   ipchains -L -n
   ```

3. Block ICMP packets (which are how Ping operates) by executing this command on the second system:

   ```
   ipchains -A input -p icmp -j REJECT
   ```

4. Notice what has happened on the first system.

5. On the second system, erase all `ipchains` rules from the kernel using this command:

   ```
   ipchains -F
   ```

6. Note how the Ping running on the first system responds. (If Ping has timed out and stopped working, restart it using the command in Step 1.)

7. Use this command to block ICMP packets again. In place of the IP address shown, include the IP address of the first system:

   ```
   ipchains -A input -l -s 192.168.100.5 -p icmp -j DENY
   ```

8. How does the `ping` command on the first system respond?

9. Look in the man page for `ipchains` to see what the `-l` option does in a rule definition.

10. Review the system log file using this command:

    ```
    tail /var/log/messages
    ```

11. Try pinging the second system from the second system (open a second command-line window). Why does this command succeed?

12. Reinitialize your `ipchains` configuration using this command:

    ```
    /etc/rc.d/init.d/ipchains restart
    ```

Project 11-3

In this project you experiment with the `firewall-config` graphical tool. To complete this project, you should have Red Hat Linux 7.3 installed with root access.

1. Log in as root and launch the `firewall-config` program from the Gnome menu or a command line:

   `firewall-config &`

2. Click the **New** button to define a new firewall rule.

3. In the dialog box that appears set these parameters:

   a. In the Src IP field of the Source section, click and enter the network ID for your local network, such as 192.168.100.0/24.

   b. To the right of the Src IP field, click the checkbox next to the "!". This indicates NOT, meaning that any IP that is not from network 192.168.100.0/24 (in this example) will match the rule you are making.

   c. In the Dst Ports field of the Destination section, enter **53**, the DNS port.

   d. In the Action drop-down list, choose **DENY**.

   e. Make sure the **Input** chain is selected in the Chain section.

4. Choose **OK** to save this rule and close the dialog box.

5. You can activate this rule by choosing the **Activate** button in the main dialog box. If you do so, you will erase all existing IP Chains rules and substitute the rules you have defined in the firewall-config program.

6. What is the effect of the rule that you created in this project?

Project 11-4

In this project you configure a key pair and use the `ssh` command. You should work as partners with another student or colleague. The two systems mentioned in the steps are your system and your partner's system. To complete this project, you should have two Linux systems with OpenSSH packages installed. (These are installed by default on Red Hat Linux 7.3.)

1. Log in as a regular user on the first system.

2. Make certain that the necessary SSH packages are installed. (You should have the `ssh`, `sshd`, and `ssh-keygen` programs.)

3. Generate a key pair for your regular user account:

   `ssh-keygen -t rsa -b 2048`

4. Copy the public key you just generated to the list of authorized keys for the other user you are working with.

   `scp ~/.ssh/id_rsa.pub`
   `    user2@system2:/home/user2/.ssh/authorized_keys`

You must enter the password for user2 to complete this command.

5. If user2 already has keys listed in the `authorized_keys` file, this command overwrites them. In that case, copy the keys to a separate file on system2 (for example, you could save them in a file called **saved_key**). Then append that file to the `authorized_keys` file using this command:

    cat saved_key >> /home/user2/.ssh/authorized_keys

6. Now try to log in to system2 from system1 using the **ssh** command.

    ssh system2

7. Why doesn't this work as expected?

8. Try this command to log in:

    ssh -l user2 system2

9. Assuming that you don't always want to enter the login name on the remote system (or that you work with several systems and can't keep track of multiple usernames), review the man page for **ssh** to determine how you can set up the **~/.ssh/config** file so that you don't have to include the **-l user2** parameter when executing **ssh**.

Project 11-5

In this project you build on Project 11-4 to run a graphical program over a secure link using SSH. You should continue to work as partners with another student or colleague. The two systems mentioned in the steps are your system and your partner's system. To complete this project, you should have two Linux systems with OpenSSH packages installed. The first system should be running the X Window System (typically Gnome or KDE).

1. Log in as your regular user account on system1. You should be working in a graphical environment.

2. Launch a graphical program, such as **gedit**, on system2.

    ssh -X system2 gedit &

3. Open a second command-line window on system1 and log in as root.

4. Run the **ps** command to see that the **gedit** program is not running on system1:

    ps aux|grep gedit

5. After reading the next chapter, you can try this project again, using a sniffer to see that any files you open in **gedit** are encrypted as they are transferred over the network.

CASE PROJECTS

1. List the firewall rules that you would want to implement on the main server at Snow, Sleet, and Hale. You can write them out as descriptions rather than `ipchains` commands. For example, one might be "Block all access to our intranet server except from the networks within the organization." The exact rules you think are warranted will depend on how you have designed the network and how concerned you are about different security threats.

2. Pick a few of the rules that you created in the first case and write them out as `ipchains` commands. Review the documentation for IP Chains and for IP Tables to see how you might improve upon your first attempt at creating the needed commands. For example, how might logging or other monitoring help you? What other features seem useful to you?

3. Although the members of the technical committee (a group of partners) at Snow, Sleet, and Hale are impressed with your technical abilities, they are concerned that you have too much to do, overseeing all the other system administrators, implementing Internet connectivity, and now worrying about security configurations. They suggest that instead of configuring all the existing servers, you could just purchase a preconfigured appliance to use as a VPN or firewall. This might allow you to connect the firm's different offices securely and avoid some of the tedium of setting up rules for IP Chains or IP Tables. Go online and research these appliances by searching for appropriate key terms. Many are built on Linux, but not all. Based on your research, write a memo to the technical committee outlining why you might choose to use or avoid such an appliance. Include reasons for both options so that they know you've considered the issues. Spending money on new technology is not a problem for this law firm, though they want to make wise decisions and not waste money on devices that will not help productivity. What will your final decision be about the appliances?

11

12

NETWORK INTRUSION DETECTION

After reading this chapter and completing the exercises you will be able to:

♦ Use network scanning and packet-sniffing utilities

♦ Understand basic intrusion detection systems

♦ Perform automated security audits of your Linux system

In this chapter you learn about the more advanced techniques that crackers use to attack Linux systems and how you can use those same techniques to prepare for and prevent break-ins. Some of those techniques involve special utilities that alert you to signs of cracker activity.

Another way to prevent cracker break-ins is to use security-auditing tools to find weaknesses in your system before a cracker finds them. A security policy is part of security auditing, but the policy should be supplemented by security-auditing utilities, several of which you learn about in this chapter.

SCANNERS AND SNIFFERS

Many previous discussions have shown how crackers might attempt to gain access to your Linux system. In this section you learn two more specific techniques that crackers use to accomplish this:

- **Port scanning**, in which you send packets to a host and gain information about the host from its response. Port scanning normally involves sending packets to many ports or sending malformed packets (as described below) to gain knowledge that the host is not intentionally sharing.

- **Packet sniffing** (also called **network traffic analysis**), in which you examine the headers and data contained within every packet on a network, not just those that are addressed to your own host.

Network administrators disagree about the legitimate uses of these two network activities. An administrator concerned about possible security vulnerabilities on a corporate network is likely to use port scanning to check for security weaknesses. Packet sniffing may serve the same purposes and is certainly valuable when difficult network troubleshooting tasks arise. For example, if the throughput of the network slows down significantly and no one is sure why, the most effective solution is to examine the network traffic to see what is actually happening "on the wire."

So, when are port scanning or packet sniffing considered security audit or troubleshooting tools? When are they considered an attack? When are they merely harmless exploration of the network? The answer depends on who you are and what network you are scanning or sniffing. The documentation for one of the utilities described in the next subsection refers to its use by network administrators or "curious individuals." Many of these individuals see nothing wrong with scanning any system on a publicly accessible network (such as the Internet); others feel the same way only about examining the traffic on their employer's network. Although these activities are not considered illegal (at least no one has yet been prosecuted merely for port scanning or sniffing), you run a serious risk of being fired or expelled if someone finds you scanning systems without notifying the administrator first, or if you are discovered sniffing packets on a network for which you are not the network administrator.

The upshot is this: if you are a network administrator with responsibility for the security of a particular network, feel free to use the tools in this chapter to learn about your network's weaknesses and improve your security. For other networks, ask before you act.

 Regarding the defensive utilities described later in this chapter, a port scan originating from your site may cause your site to be completely blocked from accessing the target of the scan. This may be reason enough to avoid port scans of other networks.

A discussion of these activities is relevant because you, as a network administrator, must actually use these tools. If you don't, you are at a serious disadvantage in securing your networks, because these are the same tools that crackers use every day. To prevent their success, you must plug the holes that these tools locate.

The software described in this chapter is available for many platforms. In fact, a recent survey by a large security consulting firm indicated that 63% of attacks on large corporate networks originated from Windows-based computers.

Port Scanning

A port scan begins with the assumption that the attacker does not know where the vulnerabilities are on your system. A port scan enables the attacker to identify the type of operating system you are running and any network services that might provide access through a more focused attack. You can think of port scanning as a tool for locating chinks in the armor of a host.

The term "attacker" is used in this context rather than cracker because you may port scan your own systems as a test of system vulnerability.

A port scan typically sends packets with the ICMP, UDP, or TCP protocol. TCP is the most popular choice because the header of a TCP packet contains a section devoted to flags, as shown in Figure 12-1. These **flags** are numeric status indications to establish and track TCP connections.

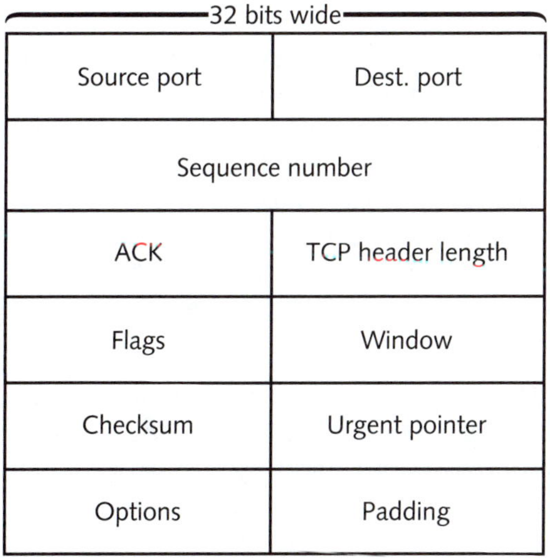

12

32 bits wide	
Source port	Dest. port
Sequence number	
ACK	TCP header length
Flags	Window
Checksum	Urgent pointer
Options	Padding

Figure 12-1 TCP packet header

For example, when your Web browser contacts a Web server, a TCP connection is established. The three-part process of establishing a TCP connection is as follows:

1. The client sends a packet with the SYN flag set. (SYN stands for synchronize.)

2. If the server can accept the TCP connection, it returns a packet to the client with the SYN and ACK flags set. (ACK stands for acknowledge.)

3. The client sends another packet to the server with the ACK flag set (but not the SYN flag).

At this point, the TCP connection is established and either the client or the server can send data to the other and have it processed in an orderly way. In a basic port scan, a port-scanning utility sends packets with the SYN flag set (commonly called a **SYN packet**) to a range of ports on the targeted host. If the host responds with a SYN+ACK packet, the port scanner knows that the responding port can accept connections. Of course, this doesn't mean that the client can actually connect and perform any tasks; that may require that the client be from a particular network address or that it provide a password. However, the port scan has identified a place where the targeted host is listening for network connections.

What would happen if a client sent a packet with the ACK flag set before establishing a connection? Or perhaps all the TCP flags at once? What if sending a SYN packet to a host results not in a SYN+ACK packet from the host, but in an ICMP packet stating that the service is unavailable? This is also useful information for an attacker.

 Sending a packet with all TCP flags set is called an **X-Mas scan**. The name refers to the image of the flags as individual lights. When all the flags are "on," the packet is lit up like a Christmas tree.

An interesting point is that each operating system—often each version of an operating system—responds differently to these nonstandard network activities. For example, if a client sends an ACK packet before establishing a connection, the targeted host may simply ignore it, or may return it with an error message. The flags set on the returned packet vary by operating system. Although the networking standards documents for IP and TCP specify much of the "correct response," many operating systems (particularly Microsoft operating systems) do not adhere to these standardized rules. The result is that a port scanner is often used to identify the operating system of a targeted host. This identification process is called **fingerprinting** the host.

Fingerprinting a host is important for a cracker because it tells him what techniques to use to attack your systems. For example, if he knows you are running a certain version of the Linux kernel, he will also know that if you have not applied a certain upgrade patch, your system is vulnerable to a particular type of attack. Likewise, if he wants to use a certain known weakness in the BIND name server, he knows he may only have one chance to try it. If he knows exactly what software you are running, the attack may succeed (if you haven't upgraded your software to fix security bugs); if he doesn't know what you're running, he may try an attack that fails, but alerts you to his efforts so that you can block further attempts using software such as PortSentry, described later in this chapter.

Port scans sometimes also use ICMP and UDP packets. They do not provide as much information as TCP scans, but under some circumstances they may provide some information when a TCP scan won't provide any. A diligent cracker will try many tactics to find your network's weak spots.

Packets from port scanners typically have a certain "look" because they are malformed; they include unexpected flags or header option fields. They also typically are addressed to ports that are not actively waiting for connections, because an attacker is checking thousands of ports looking for a weakness. The utilities described later in this chapter can watch for port scans by "listening" to all the ports on your system. If they detect packets that appear to come from a port scanner, they may update a firewall in real time to block all access to the scanning client. (You can configure or disable such a response.)

More advanced port-scanning software tries to **randomize** port scans, contacting multiple ports in random order. This can make the scan less easy to recognize and prevent it from triggering a firewall update to block the scanning site. Other specialized tools distribute a scan among many "drone" clients, each of which scans a small range of ports. Because the packets are coming from a large number of sites instead of a single scanning client, the software watching for port scans is less likely to recognize what is happening. The results from all the distributed partial scans are then correlated into a larger picture of the host's vulnerabilities.

Using `nmap`

The most widely used port-scanning utility is **nmap**, the network mapper. **nmap** is a powerful command-line utility that can use a variety of different scanning methods. It also fingerprints hosts using a number of very sophisticated techniques. **nmap** is included with Red Hat Linux and is installed by default in many configurations. You can check for the **nmap** package or install it from Red Hat's CD 2.

To use **nmap**, you specify the type of scan that you want to perform (that is, which packet types you want **nmap** to send out), a set of hosts to scan, and a set of port numbers to scan on those hosts. You can include separate options to fingerprint each host, to provide more verbose output, and to configure things like the timing policy (a more erratic timing policy makes detection of the scan much more difficult).

The home page for the **nmap** utility is *www.insecure.org/nmap*, where you will also find a number of very interesting security-related articles. One of the most valuable is the list of 50 most used security utilities, from a survey of hundreds of network administrators. You can find this list at *www.insecure.org/tools.html*. Several examples of using **nmap** are shown here:

```
nmap -sS www.myplace.net
```

This example performs a port scan using SYN packets (via the -sS option) of the host *www.myplace.net*.

```
nmap -sS -O www.myplace.net/24
```

This example performs a port scan using SYN packets for the entire network on which *www.myplace.net* resides. The /24 is used to identify the network ID from the IP address for *www.myplace.net*. The -O option also attempts to fingerprint the operating system for each host on that network.

```
nmap -sP 192.129.34-74.*
```

This example performs a **Ping scan**, which reports any hosts that are reachable using ICMP echo packets (which are used to "ping" a host). The target here is any IP address beginning with 192.129 and having a third octet of between 34 and 74. This will attempt to reach 40 subnets (74- 34) of 256 hosts each, for a total of over 10,000 hosts. The major options of the **nmap** command are listed in Table 12-1.

Table 12-1   Commonly used command-line options in nmap

nmap Option	Description
-sT	Scan by trying to connect via TCP
-sS	Scan by sending a SYN packet without following up with a connection attempt
-sU	Use UDP instead of TCP to scan ports
-sP	Use Ping (ICMP) to scan ports
-sF	Use the FIN flag in a TCP packet to scan ports
-sX	Use all flags in a TCP packet to scan ports (an Xmas tree scan)
-sN	Use no flags in a TCP packet to scan ports (a Null scan)
-O	Attempt to fingerprint each listed host, reporting the operating system that the host is running (including the version, if known, such as the Linux kernel version or service pack level for Windows)
-p *<range>*	Define a range of ports to scan
-P0	Don't ping hosts as part of the scan
-T *<policy>*	Define a timing policy; the six possible values for *<policy>* are Paranoid, Sneaky, Polite, Normal, Aggressive, and Insane

Using an nmap Graphical Front End

Although **nmap** is not difficult to use, the nmap-frontend package provides a nice graphical interface that is useful both when you are learning to use the utility and when you expect to collect a lot of data that is more easily viewed in a graphical environment. The nmap-frontend package is also installed by default in many configurations of Red Hat Linux 7.3, or you can install it manually from CD 2. Both **nmap** and nmap-frontend are available for many versions of Linux from *rpmfind.net*. However, because the **nmapfe** utility in the nmap-frontend package is written specifically for Gnome desktops, if you're using strictly KDE, you might want to look on *freshmeat.net* or the *apps.kde.com* site for Knmap, KnmapFE, or Qnmap, all of which are KDE-based graphical front ends for **nmap**. As one example, Figure 12-2 shows a view of the Knmap program, which is similar in design to the Gnome program described below. You can learn about Knmap at *http://pages.infinit.net/rewind/*.

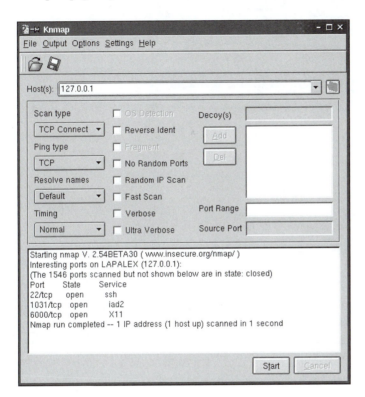

Figure 12-2　The Knmap graphical front end to **nmap**

Both the Knmap program and the Gnome-based **nmapfe** utility included with Red Hat Linux provide graphical access to all **nmap** command-line options. To launch the nmap-frontend graphical utility, enter this command:

```
nmapfe
```

Figure 12-3 shows the main window where all **nmap** activity is displayed. Here you select features for your port scan, then click the Scan button to begin the scan. The output from the scan is shown in the window below the options. Notice that the line just above the output window is a fully formed **nmap** command based on the options you select in the graphical interface. This unusual feature teaches you how to use the command-line utility as you use the graphical front end.

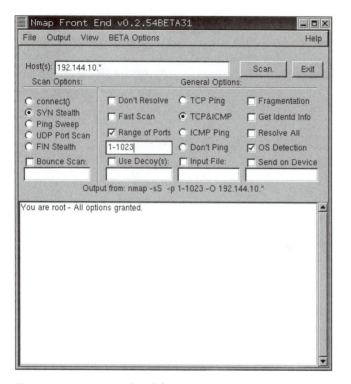

Figure 12-3   A graphical front end to the nmap utility

Many other port-scanning utilities are available. nmap is considered the standard; it also has good documentation and a large and involved developer community. If you are interested in reviewing newer or more specialized port-scanning tools (such as one for performing a distributed port scan as mentioned previously), search for "port scan" on *freshmeat.net*.

Packet Sniffing

A packet sniffer lets you grab and examine any or all of the traffic passing through a network cable or wireless space. Your examination may concentrate on the types of packets being transmitted (the percentage of ICMP, TCP, and UDP packets) or you can examine the payload within individual packets to see what is being sent over your networks. Using the former technique, you can create a statistical picture of your network usage that can be invaluable for planning upgrades, troubleshooting, and providing the best service possible to network users. The latter technique can help you spot security holes, including potentially bad passwords and users who are not following established security procedures.

To understand how a packet sniffer operates, think of the network cable as a stream. Everyone floats their packets down the stream, and each computer plucks from the stream only the packets with that computer's address on them. You can also instruct your computer to make a copy of everything in the stream; any packet that floats by is available. To have an Ethernet card perform this task, the card must operate in a special mode called **promiscuous mode.** You must be logged in as root to use this mode, so all packet sniffers require root access. However, in an office environment, anyone can plug a personal laptop into a wall Ethernet socket and have a full view of the "stream," seeing all network packets on that network segment.

If you are using the encryption technologies as described in previous chapters (including SSH, GPG, and `stunnel`) the data within your packets is quite secure. If you are instead using tools that don't support encryption (and there are many), the data flowing through your network is completely vulnerable to anyone who happens to "plug in." Worse, if any of that data reaches the Internet, it remains completely open to anyone with a packet sniffer who has access to your ISP or an intermediate point on the path to the Internet.

Dozens of packet sniffers and traffic analyzers are available for Linux. Three popular utilities are examined here, but you can find many others by exploring Linux download sites or security Web sites.

IPTraf

The **IPTraf** program is a popular tool for viewing network activity on a LAN. It doesn't display the contents (payload) of packets, but instead displays individual network connections, with protocol and other data for each one. It also displays statistics by protocol, by interface, by hostname, or IP address. You can set up filters to track only certain protocols, certain hostnames, or certain IP addresses. The home page of IPTraf is *http://cebu.mozcom.com/riker/iptraf/*, but it is included on CD 2 in Red Hat Linux 7.3 and on many Linux download sites.

If you download and install IPTraf for a non–Red-Hat Linux system, you may also need to install the `ncurses` package on which the IPTraf interface is built. The `ncurses` package is a programming library that helps programmers easily create text-mode menu-based interfaces. You can see this type of interface in programs such as `authconfig` in Red Hat Linux.

IPTraf is not installed by default in Red Hat Linux. After installing it using the following `rpm` command, you can launch it from any command-line window as shown. (Don't use an ampersand (&) after the command name, because the program needs to take over the command-line window in which it's launched.) Because IPTraf is not a graphical program, you can use it from a text-mode console without running X.

```
# rpm -Uvh iptraf-2.5.0-3.i386.rpm
# iptraf
```

After you press a key to begin, you see the main menu for IPTraf, shown in Figure 12-4. From this menu you can choose to view overall statistics or a live report of connections and packets as they occur. By default, IPTraf uses nonpromiscuous mode, so only traffic originating or destined for the host on which IPTraf is running is included in the reports. This is perfect when IPTraf is run on a server, gateway, or router. You can also choose the LAN station monitor item on the main menu to view summaries of traffic to and from hosts on your LAN. This lets you see which users are consuming all the bandwidth if the network suddenly slows down.

Figure 12-4   The main menu of IPTraf

By choosing Configure on the main menu, you can set up a number of options for how IPTraf processes and displays network information. Figure 12-5 shows this configuration screen. The General interface statistics page shows packet statistics broken down by IP and non-IP categories. The Detailed interface statistics page lists packet volume based on higher-level protocols within IP. For example, the number of packets and bytes for TCP, UDP, and ICMP packets are displayed, both for incoming and outgoing traffic. All of these statistics are updated every few seconds.

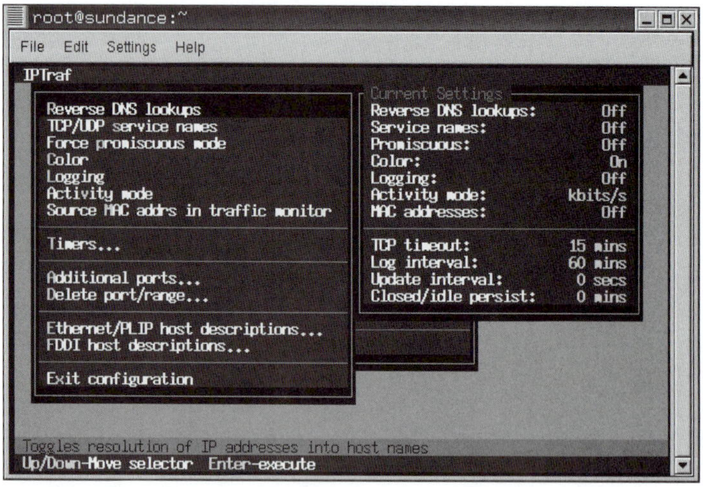

Figure 12-5   The IPTraf configuration screen

The IP traffic monitor selection on the main menu displays a list of connections as they occur, showing the protocol, the flags used to make the connection (recall the TCP flags mentioned in the discussion of port scanning above), and other details. Figure 12-6 shows this screen.

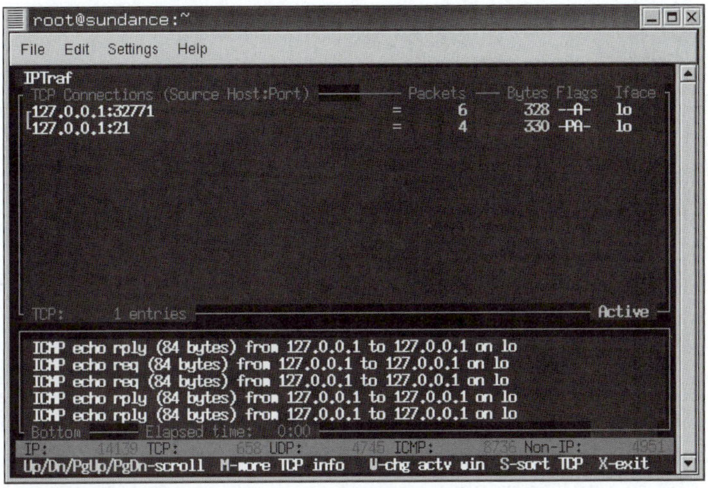

Figure 12-6   The IP traffic monitor screen in IPTraf

`tcpdump`

The **tcpdump** command-line utility provides functionality similar to the IPTraf program, but it also includes more detailed information about packets on your network. Using tcpdump you can examine the headers for each packet and save that information to a file for later analysis. You can also save the data within packets to a file, having tcpdump act as a network sniffer.

You can execute tcpdump from any command line. It supports over twenty parameters to control what information is captured and how it is processed. The simplest example is shown below. This command prints to the screen (STDOUT) all header information for packets with a source or destination IP address matching *www.myplace.net*:

```
tcpdump host www.myplace.net
```

Some of the features that you can add to refine tcpdump actions include the following:

- Use the **-c** option to capture only a given number of packets instead of continuing to capture data until interrupted.

- Decrypt packets using a cipher and key defined on the command line. (Including the key on the command line in this way is not considered very secure, but the feature is supported.)

- Use the **-w** option to write raw packet data to a file rather than processing it at capture time.

- Use the **-r** option to read and process previously saved data from a file.

- Use the **-T** option to limit packets processed to a particular protocol, such as RPC or SNMP.

- Limit the packets being captured to particular protocols, hosts, or networks.

The end of each **tcpdump** command can include an expression that you can make simple or complex, defining characteristics of packets to be captured. You use keywords such as **host**, **port**, **src**, **dst**, and **net** along with specific values required for a packet to be captured by **tcpdump**. For example, if you include the text expression **port 80** at the end of a **tcpdump** command, only packets addressed to port 80 will be captured. Suppose that you include the expression **dst net 192.128.100 and port pop3**. The **tcpdump** command then captures only packets with a destination IP address (using the **dst** keyword) within the network 192.168.100.0 (using the **net** keyword), which also have a port number matching the POP3 service in **/etc/services**.

Many other options are described in the **tcpdump** documentation. As with IPTraf, the more you have learned about TCP and related Internet protocols, the more use a tool like **tcpdump** can be to you for troubleshooting or checking for security holes.

Ethereal

If using **tcpdump** seems uncomfortable, you'll quickly appreciate **Ethereal**, a graphical network traffic analysis tool. Though it's not installed by default on Red Hat Linux, you can add it to your system by installing the following two packages:

ethereal

ethereal-gnome

The first of these packages includes documentation; the second includes the actual **ethereal** program and setup instructions for the Gnome graphical desktop. If you're running other versions of Linux, packaged binaries are also likely to be available for your system. Visit the Ethereal home page at *www.ethereal.com* or your favorite Linux download site (such as *rpmfind.net* or *freshmeat.net*). To start the program, execute this command from any graphical command-line window:

```
ethereal
```

The Ethereal packages also include a text-mode version called `tethereal`. The graphical version is the focus of this discussion.

Before you start working with network traffic in Ethereal, you can configure the system to process only those packets that you are interested in and display them in the way most useful to you. A large network segment can have a tremendous amount of data passing over it each second. You can save yourself a lot of time by focusing your analysis. Ethereal includes several configuration screens. Under the Edit menu, choose Preferences to open a dialog box where you can set up several display options and set specific features for each of the protocols that Ethereal can process. Figure 12-7 shows the screen in which various types of TCP traffic can be color coded to help you spot them instantly on a full screen of information.

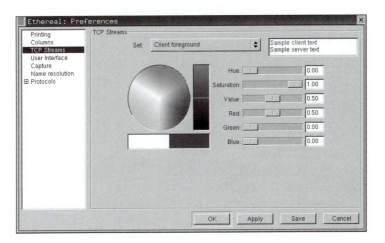

Figure 12-7   Setting color options for TCP packets in Ethereal

Another configuration screen is available via the Protocols item on the Edit menu. This dialog box (shown in Figure 12-8) lets you select or deselect any of the protocols that Ethereal is capable of processing. If you deselect a protocol by deselecting its button in this dialog box, you save the system the time it would take to process those packets, and you save yourself the time of reviewing those unneeded results. As you see how many protocols Ethereal supports, you understand the value of choosing what you want to search for among all the available network traffic on your network.

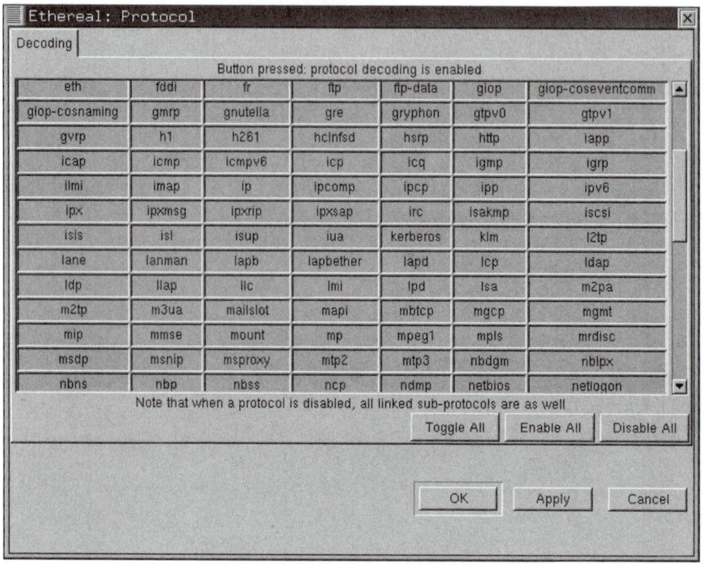

Figure 12-8 Selecting protocols to monitor in Ethereal

You may also want to review the Options item on the Display menu. When you have set up preferences for what data is captured and how it is displayed, choose Start on the Capture menu. A dialog box appears in which you set up how you want the current capture session to operate. A capture session can collect a lot of data; the options in this Start Capture dialog box (shown in Figure 12-9) will help you determine how best to start the capture. If you are experimenting with Ethereal, you may want to check the box for Update list of packets in real time to see what is happening from moment to moment on your network.

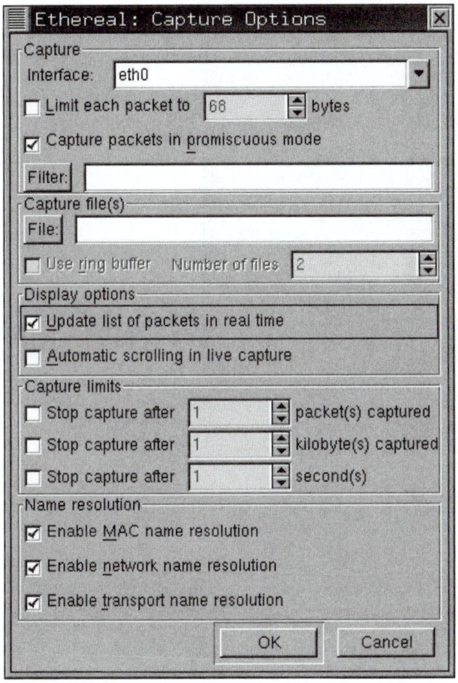

Figure 12-9   Starting a capture in Ethereal

Once a capture is started, you immediately see data filling the main Ethereal window. Figure 12-10 shows a sample capture in progress. The window is divided into three main sections. The top section lists packets. If you are running the capture in promiscuous mode (the default operation), these packets may be passing between any two computers on your network. The line of data in the top window describes the protocol of the packet, when it was sent, the source and destination addresses on the packet, and an additional notes field where Ethereal tells you more about that packet.

No.	Time	Source	Destination	Protocol	Info
41	12.159089	sundance	sundance	TCP	32771 > ftp [ACK] Seq=1423106546 Ack=1436156816
42	12.159378	sundance	sundance	TCP	32772 > 22349 [SYN] Seq=1682151240 Ack=0 Win=32;
43	12.159429	sundance	sundance	TCP	22349 > 32772 [SYN, ACK] Seq=1675189884 Ack=168;
44	12.159481	sundance	sundance	TCP	32772 > 22349 [ACK] Seq=1682151241 Ack=167518986
45	12.159600	sundance	sundance	FTP	Request: LIST
46	12.161448	sundance	sundance	FTP	Response: 150 Opening ASCII mode data connectior
47	12.163449	sundance	sundance	FTP-DAT	FTP Data: 250 bytes
48	12.163707	sundance	sundance	TCP	32772 > 22349 [ACK] Seq=1682151241 Ack=16751901;
49	12.165121	sundance	sundance	TCP	22349 > 32772 [FIN, ACK] Seq=1675190135 Ack=168;
50	12.165363	sundance	sundance	TCP	32772 > 22349 [FIN, ACK] Seq=1682151241 Ack=167!
51	12.165408	sundance	sundance	TCP	22349 > 32772 [ACK] Seq=1675190136 Ack=168215124
52	12.199962	sundance	sundance	TCP	32771 > ftp [ACK] Seq=1423106552 Ack=1436156879
53	12.200171	sundance	sundance	FTP	Response: 226 Transfer complete.
54	12.200337	sundance	sundance	TCP	32771 > ftp [ACK] Seq=1423106552 Ack=1436156903
55	13.000001	sundance	sundance	ICMP	Echo (ping) request
56	13.000062	sundance	sundance	ICMP	Echo (ping) reply

⊞ Frame 1 (100 on wire, 100 captured)
⊞ Linux cooked capture
⊞ Internet Protocol, Src Addr: sundance (127.0.0.1), Dst Addr: sundance (127.0.0.1)
⊞ Internet Control Message Protocol

```
0000  00 00 03 04 00 00 00 00  00 00 00 00 00 00 08 00   ........ ........
0010  45 00 00 54 00 00 40 00  40 01 3c a7 7f 00 00 01   E..T..@. @.<.....
0020  7f 00 00 01 08 00 c9 b7  47 07 df 00 44 8b 33 3d   ......É. G.8.D.3=
```

Figure 12-10   The main window of Ethereal

If you don't set up a filter, either by protocol or by host, the packet list can grow to thousands of lines in a matter of moments.

You can right-click on any line in the top part of the window to see a list of options for processing the selected packet. For example, you can mark a packet for review later on, print its contents, or open one packet in a separate window.

When you select a packet in the top section of the Ethereal window, the middle section contains headers for the selected packet. This section includes *all* the headers from the packet. For example, you can click the small plus sign next to the Ethernet II item in this section to see the Ethernet headers. The line labeled Internet Protocol includes the source and destination addresses for the packet; if you click on the plus sign to the left of this line, you see all the other IP header information for the packet. If you are viewing a TCP packet, you also see a line labeled Transmission Control Protocol that includes the port used by the packet and other relevant information. By clicking on the plus sign next to this line, you can see all TCP header information, including the state of each flag within the packet (recall the brief discussion about TCP flags earlier in this chapter). Figure 12-11 shows this header information section expanded. (You can click and drag the bar between sections in the Ethereal window to resize each section as needed.)

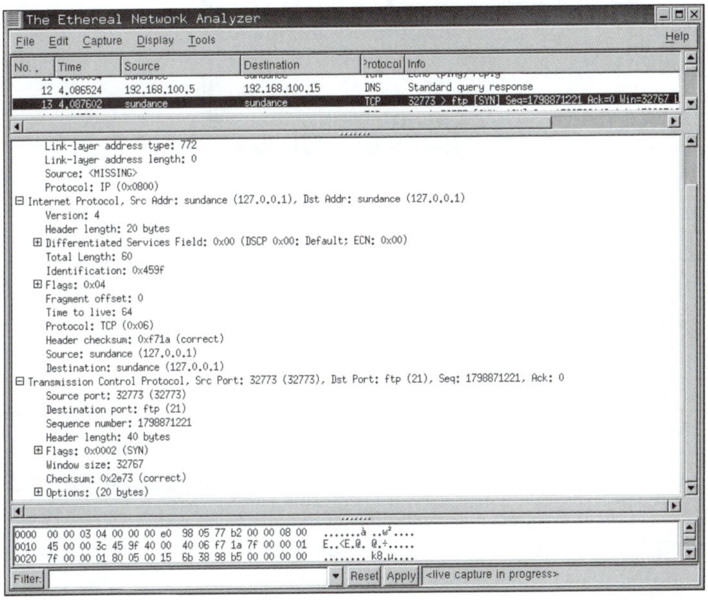

Figure 12-11   Viewing packet header information in Ethereal

The bottom section of the Ethereal window contains the data within the packet—the payload. Packet data is shown in both numeric (hexadecimal) and character formats. This section is where you see peoples' secrets flowing across your screen if they are not using secure protocols. An example of this is covered in the projects at the end of this chapter. Figure 12-12 shows a packet from an FTP connection in progress. Notice that the text the user typed is clearly visible within the packet.

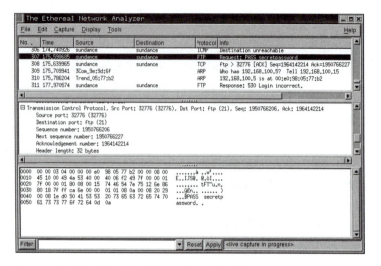

Figure 12-12 Packet data captured in Ethereal

The Telnet protocol is a popular choice when experimenting with a packet sniffer. If you try this, note that Telnet sends each character that a user types as a separate packet. To see the password that a user enters, you'll need to assemble data from a series of packets.

If you wish, you can choose to save data captured by Ethereal to a file. You specify this in the Start Capture dialog box. You can then use the items on the File menu such as Open, Close, and Save As to manage files containing stored packet data from previous captures. Ethereal also includes several statistical tools similar to those offered by IPTraf. For example, you can view graphs of packets received by time unit, or see a percentage breakdown of packets by protocol. This latter feature is shown in Figure 12-13. Here, 100% of the packets are from IP (as opposed to IPX, for example), but within IP, some are TCP and some are ICMP. Further breakdowns by higher-level protocols are also available.

```
┌─ Ethereal: Protocol Hierarchy Statistics ─────────────── □ ▫ × ┐
│ ┌─ Protocol Hierarchy Statistics ──────────────────────────────┐
│ │ Protocol                          % Packets  Packets  Bytes  End Pac │
│ │ ⊟ Frame                           100.00%      319    29954          │
│ │  ⊟ Linux cooked-mode capture      100.00%      319    29954          │
│ │   ⊟ Internet Protocol              94.67%      302    28864          │
│ │      Internet Control Message Protocol  56.74% 181    18104          │
│ │    ⊟ User Datagram Protocol        10.97%       35     3605          │
│ │       Domain Name Service          10.34%       33     3278          │
│ │     ⊟ NetBIOS Datagram Service      0.31%        1      251          │
│ │      ⊟ SMB (Server Message Block Protocol)  0.31%  1   251           │
│ │       ⊟ SMB MailSlot Protocol       0.31%        1      251          │
│ │          Microsoft Windows Browser Protocol  0.31% 1   251           │
│ │       Data                          0.31%        1       76          │
│ │    ⊟ Transmission Control Protocol  26.96%      86     7155          │
│ │       File Transfer Protocol (FTP)  10.97%      35     3373          │
│ │       FTP Data                      0.31%        1      318          │
│ │     Address Resolution Protocol     5.02%       16      902          │
│ │   ⊟ Logical-Link Control            0.31%        1      188          │
│ │    ⊟ NetBIOS                        0.31%        1      188          │
│ │     ⊟ SMB (Server Message Block Protocol)  0.31%  1    188           │
│ │      ⊟ SMB MailSlot Protocol        0.31%        1      188          │
│ │         Microsoft Windows Browser Protocol  0.31% 1    188           │
│ │                                                                      │
│ └──────────────────────────────────────────────────────────────┘
│                         ┌─────────┐
│                         │  Close  │
│                         └─────────┘
└──────────────────────────────────────────────────────────────────┘
```

Figure 12-13   Protocol analysis by percentage in Ethereal

You should become familiar with the use of Ethereal, a powerful tool for network troubleshooting as well as for locating potential security problems. If watching other people's data stream by on your screen for a few minutes doesn't convince you to use encrypted protocols, perhaps nothing else will. Dozens of different packet sniffers are available for Linux. Some are graphical, like Ethereal, or the KDE-based program, `ksnuffle`. Others are text based, such as `ettercap` (see *ettercap.sourceforge.net*). To research what is available, start by searching for "sniff" on *freshmeat.net*.

12

USING INTRUSION DETECTION SOFTWARE

Using a port scanner, installing a rootkit, and performing other intrusive network activities leaves a trace that can be found by a skilled network administrator. Logs sometimes contain the necessary details, but often the intrusion must be seen by monitoring activity in real time. The process of noticing when someone is trying to break into your system (or that they have already broken in) is called **intrusion detection**. This section reviews several software tools that help you track and prevent break-ins by watching for signs of impending attack and, when possible, taking preventive action. This category of software is called **intrusion detection systems (IDS)**.

A port scanner is a popular way for crackers to examine a remote host and determine what methods of attack are most likely to succeed. Network administrators can install a program called **PortSentry** that watches network ports for packets that appear to be port scans, then take action based on a configuration file. PortSentry is free software that you can download from *www.psionic.com*, the company that maintains the `logcheck` program (now called LogSentry). Features of PortSentry include:

- Detects **stealth scans**—port scans that use unexpected flag combinations, including SYN, FIN, none **(null scan)**, and all (X-Mas scan).

- The response based on your configuration can include blocking the scanning system by immediately adding it to a packet filter (such as IP Chains or IP Tables) with the DENY instruction, so that the scanning system will not be able to receive any reply packets of any type from your host.

- Any activity that appears to be a scan is logged so that you can review it. This feature is intended to be used in conjunction with `logcheck`, LogSentry, or a similar program, so that all logged security events are viewed in a coordinated way.

- Systems that have attempted even minimal scanlike activities are recorded by the software so that a port scanner trying to randomize its scan is still likely to be blocked before many ports are contacted.

Several of the programs described in this chapter as well as similar programs you will find mentioned on Linux software archives rely on a programming library called **libpcap**: the packet-capturing library. This library is installed on Red Hat Linux by default. If you are downloading software for other systems and see mention of libpcap or pcap, you may need to find and install that library on your Linux system.

A more complex tool than PortSentry is the **Linux Intrusion Detection System (LIDS)**. LIDS is a challenge to use, but provides a level of protection that's hard to match with other tools. LIDS is based on the premise that the root user in Linux is too powerful. If a cracker gets root access, she can do a great many things to cover her tracks, as well as reading and destroying anything on the system at will. LIDS adds a module to the Linux kernel that blocks access to resources for all users—including root—except as configured by LIDS. Specific features of LIDS include:

- Port scanner detection within the kernel

- Ability to hide files completely or make them read-only, even to root

- Ability to hide processes completely or block which other processes can send signals to them (effectively blocking the use of the `kill` command to stop or restart an application)

- **Access control lists (ACLs)**: data structures that define access to individual directories and individual programs by specific users or groups

- Time-based restrictions: a task can only be performed or a file accessed during specific times during the day (this is similar to features offered by services like Pluggable Authentication Modules, but LIDS performs this directly in the Linux kernel)

To download LIDS, visit *sourceforge.net* and search for LIDS to see a link to the source code. LIDS includes a kernel patch and a set of configuration files that are stored in `/etc/lids`. (These files are completely hidden when LIDS is running.)

Installing and using LIDS requires significant knowledge of the Linux kernel. You can learn about LIDS features and how it operates by reviewing the documentation for the LIDS project, but only experienced Linux users should expect to use LIDS effectively. Because of the complexity of LIDS, you should carefully test the LIDS software before running it on a production server.

Once LIDS is installed, you can start Linux without using LIDS by adding `security=0` as a kernel boot parameter to the LILO or GRUB boot prompt.

After you install LIDS, you configure it by defining ACLs for files and directories and capabilities that processes are permitted. A **capability** is a task that the Linux kernel permits a program to perform. LIDS defines several dozen capabilities as used by a default Linux kernel (the capability concept is part of Linux kernel programming terminology). Examples of capabilities include the ability to send broadcast packets onto the network and the ability to use the **reboot** command. LIDS also adds a few nonstandard capabilities. To define an ACL for a file or directory, or a capability for a process, you use the **lidsadm** command (for "LIDS administration"). This command has a format similar to the **ipchains** command that you've used previously. As with **ipchains** commands, you normally configure a LIDS system by including a number of **lidsadm** commands in the Linux startup files (such as in `/etc/rc.local`). At the end of this configuration loading process, you include the following command to seal the kernel. Once LIDS has sealed the kernel, the LIDS configurations are in effect. No program can then perform any action that is not permitted by your LIDS configuration.

```
lidsadm -I
```

Popular system services may rely on a number of capabilities and other programs to perform their functions. For this reason it's important to read the LIDS documentation carefully and experiment with your own configuration before attempting to run LIDS on a production server.

After the kernel is sealed, you can still alter the configuration of ACLs and capabilities by starting a **LIDS-Free Session (LFS)**. This is a command-line session that is free of LIDS restrictions, so you can do anything you choose, just like root could before you installed LIDS. To start a LFS, use this command:

```
lidsadm -S off
```

You must enter the LIDS password you defined during initial LIDS configuration in order to enter a LIDS-Free Session. Entering an LFS is similar in concept to using the **su** command to gain access to the root user on a standard Linux system. The difference

12

with LIDS is that you must have both the root password and the LIDS password to access resources to which LIDS has restricted access.

A comprehensive program that provides a different level of intrusion detection than LIDS is **Big Brother**. Big Brother uses a client/server model similar in some ways to the Simple Network Management Protocol (SNMP) described in earlier chapters. Big Brother includes a server that gathers data from clients on each host within your network. You can define redundant components to make certain that network status information remains available in the event of failures in one part of the system.

The results from each client are gathered by the server and displayed as a Web page. Color-coded dots identify the status of each service on each host. This lets you immediately see where attention is needed. Some of the 26 standard services that Big Brother manages include:

- DNS
- FTP
- HTTP
- POP3
- SSH
- Telnet

In addition to these services, system resources like disk space, memory usage, and swap space are tracked. You can use the plug-in architecture to develop new modules to help you monitor any part of your system you need to track remotely. For example, if you have database applications running or need to monitor instruments that are feeding data to a remote system, you could write a Big Brother module to help you keep an eye on that service through the Web page of Big Brother on your main server.

Figure 12-14 shows a demonstration Web page from the Big Brother Web site, *www.bb4.com*. You can download Big Brother source code free of charge for Linux and other server platforms. Commercial users need to purchase a license (10% of the price is donated to charity). Clients that can interact with the Big Brother server are available for many platforms, including UNIX, Windows 2000, NetWare, Macintosh, AS/400, and OpenVMS.

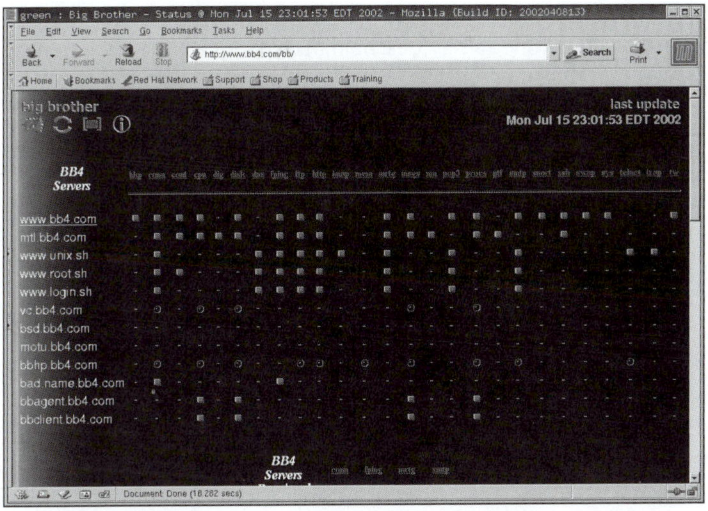

Figure 12-14   A sample of a Big Brother resource management Web page

Big Brother is not as challenging to install as LIDS—you won't need to recompile the kernel. But it will require an hour or two to review the documentation and get the server and a few clients installed and communicating correctly. Big Brother does not detect intruders in the same way as LIDS or PortSentry. Instead, Big Brother informs you if one of your services is no longer operating or otherwise requires attention (for example, if the hard disks on a remote system are almost full). Big Brother works best as part of a set of intrusion detection tools. For example:

- Use **nmap** to carefully scan your system after you have configured it to see whether any security holes are found.

- Use PortSentry (after you've completed your tests with **nmap**) to watch for outside hosts trying to port scan your server. Block these hosts using IP Chains or IP Tables, perhaps with the help of a free commercial firewall configuration and management tool.

- Use LIDS to secure your file system and processes so that anyone who is able to gain unauthorized access will have very limited power, even with the root password.

- Use Big Brother to keep a constant eye on services that you are providing on all of your network servers. If anyone is able to cause a problem despite your other efforts (or just because of a nonintrusive computer error), you will know about it immediately and can take corrective action.

When crackers defaced the Web pages of *USA Today* in July 2002, the fake news stories—including one falsely describing a military attack—were online for 15 minutes before someone alerted the network administrator. The Web site was shut down for three hours while repairs and needed upgrades were made. (The site was running Microsoft's Internet Information Server on Windows 2000.)

SYSTEM SECURITY AUDITS

After you have used one or more of the utilities described so far in this chapter, you might start to feel fairly confident about the security of your Linux system. The best way to test that confidence is to perform a **security audit**, a review or test of how secure your system really is and what needs to be done to improve its security. Such an audit can take many forms. For example, if you work in an organization that has a well-defined security policy, one type of security audit would consist of a careful review of that policy to see where the systems, system administrators, management team, or end users fall short in implementing that policy. This would help to fix procedural problems that might lead to security weaknesses. For example, if management has not fully supported security-related training programs, or system administrators have not installed software that the policy stated was necessary, these things could be fixed before a serious lapse in security occurs.

Another type of security audit is provided by special security-auditing software. These programs use a long list of known security holes, cracker techniques, and networking savvy to poke into every nook and cranny of your networked systems. You receive a detailed report of the problems discovered. Basically, a software security audit performs a systemized attack on your server or servers, letting you know where the weaknesses are. The report might describe such things as:

- You have not upgraded to the latest software for your DNS server. The version you are using is vulnerable to several known attacks.

- You have not turned off email relaying, which can lead to spammers bouncing email off your system.

- Your firewall has not blocked access to several unneeded ports that are commonly used by cracker-oriented software.

- You are providing Telnet service, which is considered an insecure protocol for remote access.

- An attempt to use r-utilities permitted unauthorized access to some files on your system.

- You permit any host to connect and use your X server for remote application display.

- Anonymous users can upload files into your FTP directories.

- File systems have been exported using NFS without any limiting security parameters.

- A recent advisory from CERT has not been implemented on your system.

One of the first security-auditing programs was called the **Security Administrator Tool for Analyzing Networks (SATAN)**. As with many other program names, you can be certain the acronym was chosen first and the full name second, but the name did its job: it created a stir in the news and helped to publicize the need for such a tool. You can review this project at *www.porcupine.org/satan/*, but it is no longer in development and has been superceded by a much stronger program: the **Security Administrator's Integrated Network Tool (SAINT)**.

SAINT is a tool that uses a Web browser interface to manage an "attack" on your network and report to you the vulnerabilities it finds. It is similar to using a port scanner to locate potentially open network ports; SAINT uses different methods and looks for different vulnerabilities than the **nmap** tool. Figure 12-15 shows some of the configuration options you can set up before beginning a security sweep using SAINT.

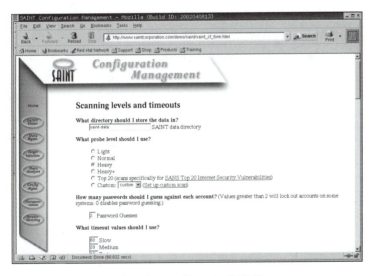

Figure 12-15   Configuring options in SAINT

After auditing (scanning) systems that you have designated, SAINT reports different levels of existing or potential security problems. These are color coded red, yellow, brown, or green. Reported results in SAINT are correlated with the SANS and FBI Top 20 Vulnerabilities list discussed earlier. Figures 12-16 and 12-17 show sample Web pages with summary categories and more detailed results that SAINT has reported after performing a security audit.

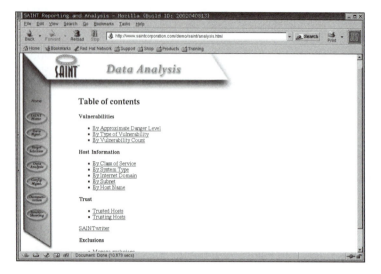

Figure 12-16   Data categories from a security audit using SAINT

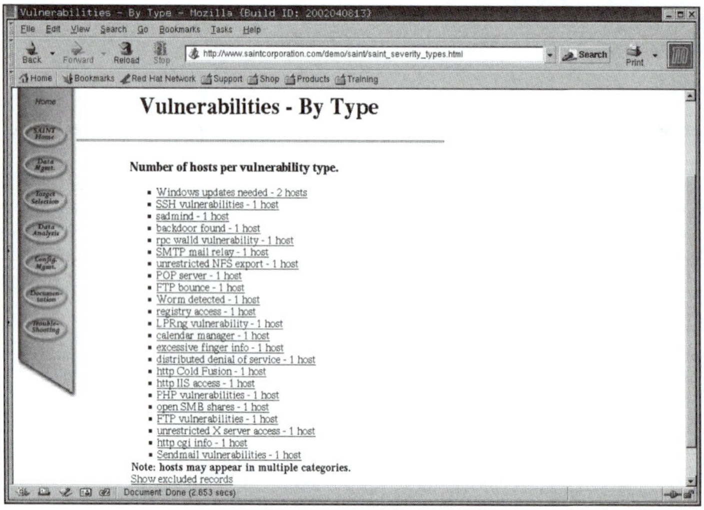

Figure 12-17   Detailed results from a security audit using SAINT

SAINT was formerly a free software project, but as with many of the tools presented in this book, it has been commercialized to some degree. In the case of SAINT, you must purchase a license before you can obtain the software. The Web site does contain quotes from satisfied customers, documentation excerpts, and demos to show you what the product will do. To learn about SAINT, visit the home page at *www.saintcorporation.com*.

One of the benefits of using a popular product like SAINT or `nmap` is that you can be certain hundreds of security experts are focusing their attention on that tool to make it better. Any new security problem that has not been tested by using `nmap` or SAINT soon will be.

Many other security audit tools are available. Some are free, such as the Tiger and SARA projects (see *freshmeat.net*). Others are expensive commercial tools, complete with consulting services and real-time updates when new vulnerabilities are discovered. Several of these commercial products are mentioned in the list of security products at *www.insecure.org/tools.html*.

CHAPTER SUMMARY

- ◻ Port-scanning software lets anyone learn about the potentially vulnerable network access points on any networked computer. Port scans can be done using many techniques, but the goal is always to learn about the host being scanned, such as what programs are listening for traffic on a certain port number.

- ◻ Port scanners use various combinations of TCP flags, UDP packets, and Ping packets to elicit responses that inform the scanner about the services running on the targeted host. Part of the response also permits a good port scanner to identify the type of operating system running on the target.

- ◻ When a host detects that someone is using a port scanner, software such as PortSentry can take action to prevent the completion of the port scan and block all future access by the host performing the scan.

- ◻ The most used port-scanning software is `nmap`. Graphical utilities are available as front ends to `nmap`. Many other port scanners are also available.

- ◻ Packet sniffers use the promiscuous mode of a NIC to capture all data passing through that node of the network, including all headers and payloads (packet data). Ethereal is a powerful and popular graphical packet sniffer.

- ◻ Packet sniffing is just one type—though the most comprehensive—of network traffic analysis. Other programs such as IPTraf help network administrators analyze network traffic patterns based on protocol, point of origination or destination, and other factors.

- ◻ The `tcpdump` program is a very popular network traffic analysis program that captures detailed information about network packets.

- ◻ Intrusion detection systems (IDS) are an important part of modern network security. These software products watch for signs of intruders trying to access your servers and help you respond appropriately.

- ◻ PortSentry is one piece of IDS software that detects port scans from programs like `nmap`. A more comprehensive IDS package is LIDS, which alters the Linux kernel so that even the root user does not have complete access to files and processes. Therefore, even if an intruder gets root access, he or she cannot control the server.

- ◻ Big Brother is a simpler IDS that watches the status of network services on multiple servers through a Web page interface.

12

❐ Security audits using security policies or specialized software can help network administrators see potential security problems and fix them before someone else finds them.

❐ One popular security-auditing software tool is SAINT. Many others are available as well.

KEY TERMS

access control list (ACL) — A data structure that defines the access permitted for individual directories and individual programs.

Big Brother — An intrusion detection program that uses a client/server model to gather network service and host resource data from numerous hosts on a network and report that data in a browser-based interface.

capability — A task that the Linux kernel permits a program to perform, such as the ability to send broadcast packets onto the network and the ability to use the `reboot` command.

Ethereal — A powerful graphical network traffic analysis tool.

fingerprinting — Using the results of a port scan to identify the operating system of a targeted host.

flags — Numeric status indications stored within a packet header that are used to establish and track information about the network communication of which the packet is a part.

intrusion detection — The process of noticing when someone is trying to break into a system or that they have already broken in.

intrusion detection systems (IDS) — A type of software that aids network intrusion detection.

IPTraf — A popular "packet sniffer" program for viewing network activity on a LAN.

libpcap — A programming library used for capturing network packets, required by many network traffic analysis utilities.

Linux Intrusion Detection System (LIDS) — A complex and hard-to-use intrusion detection system that alters the Linux kernel to remove root's comprehensive access to a Linux system.

LIDS-Free Session (LFS) — A command-line session on a system running the LIDS IDS in which LIDS does not affect the permitted actions.

`lidsadm` — The administrative command used to control the LIDS IDS.

network traffic analysis — *See* packet sniffing.

`nmap` — The most widely used port-scanning utility.

`nmapfe` — A utility that acts as a graphical front end to the `nmap` command; requires the Gnome desktop.

null scan — A method of port scanning in which a TCP packet is sent with no flags set.

packet sniffing — A network activity in which the headers and payload of all packets on the network are captured and examined (also called network traffic analysis).

Ping scan — A method of port scanning in which any hosts that are reachable using ICMP echo packets (which are used to "ping" a host) are reported.

port scanning — A network activity in which packets sent to a host are analyzed to learn about that host.

PortSentry — A program that watches network ports for packets that appear to be port scans, then takes action based on a configuration file.

promiscuous mode — A mode of operation for NICs in which any packets that are visible to the NIC are captured and processed, not only those that are addressed to the NIC.

randomization — A method of performing a port scan in which multiple ports are contacted in random order to reduce suspicion.

Security Administrator Tool for Analyzing Networks (SATAN) — One of the first widely known security-auditing programs.

Security Administrator's Integrated Network Tool (SAINT) — A popular security-auditing program that superceded the SATAN program.

security audit — A review or test of how secure a system really is and what needs to be done to improve its security.

stealth scan — A port scan that uses unexpected TCP flag combinations, including SYN, FIN, none (Null scan), and all (X–Mas scan) flags.

SYN packet — A TCP packet sent from a port scanner that has the SYN flag set.

tcpdump — A command-line utility that provides detailed information about packets on a network.

X–Mas scan — A method of port scanning in which all flags in the TCP header are turned on (set).

12

REVIEW QUESTIONS

1. Which statement is true?

    a. A port scanner cannot obtain useful knowledge of a host unless the host responds to a SYN packet.

    b. When a host returns a SYN+ACK packet to a port scanner, this indicates that the sending port can easily be used to gain access to the targeted system.

    c. Even receiving no response at all informs a port scanner about how a targeted host is processing packets sent to a particular port.

    d. Only a null scan should be used on Linux systems.

2. Define an X–Mas scan.

3. Fingerprinting of operating systems is possible because:

   a. Most operating systems do not adhere strictly to the detailed standards for networking protocols.

   b. All operating systems are required to report certain information in the networking packets that they propagate.

   c. Few networks are inherently as secure as network administrators believe.

   d. Most operating systems cannot detect a port scan and so respond with the information necessary to fingerprint the system.

4. Fingerprinting an operating system helps a cracker because:

   a. It defines exactly what software you have installed.

   b. It opens a security-delayed window based on the port being scanned.

   c. It informs the cracker of which vulnerabilities he may be able to exploit on your system.

   d. It doesn't depend on the patches that have been applied to fix existing security holes.

5. A program that defends against a port scanner will attempt to:

   a. Update a firewall rule in real time to prevent the port scan from being completed.

   b. Send back bogus data to the port scanner.

   c. Limit access by the scanning system to publicly available ports only.

   d. Log a violation and recommend use of security-auditing tools.

6. A distributed port scan operates by:

   a. using Denial-of-Service software against a range of TCP ports

   b. having multiple computers each scan a small number of ports, then correlating the results

   c. blocking access to the targeted host by each of the distributed scanning clients

   d. blocking access to the scanning clients by the targeted host

7. An **nmap** command that included the host specification of 192.129.34-35.* would scan how many different hosts?

   a. 512

   b. 2

   c. 256

   d. over 10,000

8. Name three graphical utilities used with `nmap`.

9. One unusual feature of the `nmapfe` program is that it:

    a. only includes a very limited set of functionality compared to the command-line utility

    b. uses the same graphical interface as Ethereal

    c. can be used on both Gnome and KDE desktops without additional software

    d. includes a line illustrating the command-line parameters that correspond to your selections in the graphical interface

10. Which is not a valid reason for using a packet sniffer?

    a. troubleshooting stubborn networking problems

    b. creating statistical data about the protocols being used on your network

    c. auditing security procedures at the managerial level

    d. studying the capacity and bandwidth of the network to plan for upgrades

11. Using a packet sniffer requires root access in Linux because:

    a. Only root should be able to see the payload of other users' packets.

    b. Only root can operate network cards in promiscuous mode.

    c. Any packet available on the network cable requires the root password to access it.

    d. Tools such as `nmap` and Ethereal are always run as SetUID.

12. Which of the following can protect users' data from packet-sniffing software, even on an internal network?

    a. `nmap` and `tcpdump`

    b. SARA or SAINT

    c. IPTraf or PAM

    d. SSH and GPG

13. Which of the following would help you diagnose which user was consuming an inordinate amount of network bandwidth if the network slowed down significantly?

    a. the packet payload section of the Ethereal main window

    b. the timing options in `nmap`

    c. any of the security-auditing tools, particularly a strong commercial tool like SAINT

    d. the LAN station monitor item in IPTraf

12

14. Which `tcpdump` option lets you use data from a previously saved file containing packet data instead of looking at new packets on the network?

    a. `-r`

    b. `-o`

    c. `--old`

    d. `-c`

15. Using a filter or configuration setting to limit which packets are captured by Ethereal is generally a good idea because:

    a. Without an appropriate filter, firewall rules may block the packets that would be most useful in the traffic analysis.

    b. A busy network can generate thousands of packets per second, which may be too much data to easily find what you're looking for.

    c. Only those packets that are included in the filter will be shown on screen; therefore, if a filter is not configured, the traffic needed for the analysis will probably be missed.

    d. Other utilities such as `nmap` and `tcpdump` rely on the filters used by Ethereal to control their interaction with the network administrator.

16. The header information displayed in the middle section of Ethereal includes:

    a. TCP flags

    b. IP source and destination addresses plus TCP flags

    c. application-specific protocol headers plus UDP headers

    d. complete header information for each protocol contained in the packet

17. Describe a possible problem when reviewing Telnet packets in a packet sniffer.

18. Explain the meaning of IDS.

19. Describe how time-based login restrictions are implemented differently in LIDS versus PAM.

20. How is an LFS different from using the **su** command to gain root access?

21. Which would not be part of a security audit?

    a. using a program such as SAINT

    b. checking whether end users were complying with the security policy

    c. reviewing old security advisories on CERT/CC

    d. determining whether system software had been upgraded as required by the security policy

22. Big Brother complements other security tools by:

    a. implementing port scans, security-auditing functions, and packet sniffing in a single program

    b. supporting plug-in modules that also work with SAINT

    c. tracking whether network services and resources on multiple servers are running smoothly or require attention

    d. displaying its results in a color coded Web page format

23. An important benefit of having a program like SAINT only available for a large fee may be that:

    a. Crackers are less likely to use it to identify the vulnerabilities of other users' systems.

    b. Management is more likely to take it seriously as a security tool.

    c. Only such programs are continually enhanced when new security issues arise.

    d. End users will feel more comfortable knowing that commercial tools are being used to protect the network.

24. Describe the function of PortSentry.

HANDS-ON PROJECTS

The projects presented here assume that you are working in a lab environment. **If you are working on a production server or one containing any sensitive data, do not attempt the following projects.**

The steps that follow assume you are working on a network with a 24-bit network ID: network addresses in the example commands use "/24" (based on the CIDR address format). If your network uses a different network ID length, you should modify the "/24" in the commands to match your network ID length.

Project 12-1

In this project you experiment with the **nmap** port-scanning utility. You should work in a lab for this project. In the steps, the hostname *target.edu* has been used; replace this with the IP address or hostname of any single system in your computer lab. To complete this project you should have Linux installed and have root access. The second part of the project requires the nmap-frontend package, which can only be used on Red Hat and other Gnome-compatible systems. *Do not complete this project on a production network; work only in an isolated lab environment.*

1. Use a Ping scan to determine which hosts are "listening" on your local network.

```
nmap -sP target.edu/24
```

12

This scan may take several minutes to complete, depending on the size of your LAN. You see a report listing each system that appears to be running on the network. This gives you the information you need to start reviewing the services offered by each host.

2. Use the following command to fingerprint the OS of one of the hosts in your network and see a list of ports discovered to be open using a basic port scan. (Replace the address shown with an address for a host on your network.) This scan will take a couple of minutes to complete.

   nmap -O 192.168.100.45

3. You would want to try a stealthier scan if you were concerned that the default scan might alert the server to your actions and block your subsequent access. In that case you might try a scan such as this one, which is a null scan. The resulting list should look the same: you see which ports appear to be open, so that you could try to connect to those ports based on the service they are providing to the network.

   nmap -sN target.edu

4. Suppose you knew of a vulnerability in DNS, but didn't know which hosts on the network were running a name server. You could use the following command to scan the DNS port on all systems in your LAN to identify which ones are running a DNS server.

   nmap -sS -p 53 target.edu/24

5. You decide to scan the hosts in the LAN in random order, so you use this command instead:

   nmap --randomize_hosts -sS -p 53 target.edu/24

6. Because you are concerned that someone who may be running PortSentry could block your scans, you decide to slow your scans down in hopes that no one will detect them. Use this command:

   nmap --randomize_hosts -T 0 -sS -p 53 target.edu/24

   When you tire of waiting, press **Ctrl+C** and read the man page for **nmap** to discover how long **nmap** will wait between each packet sent when the **-T 0** timing option is used.

7. Load the nmap-frontend package from Red Hat CD 2 if it is not loaded.

8. Launch the graphical utility:

   nmapfe

9. Use **nmapfe** to complete any three of the six scans given in the preceding steps. You can check your use of the utility by seeing whether the command-line output for **nmap** shown just above the output window matches the command you are trying to duplicate from one of the steps above.

The commands in `nmapfe` may differ slightly from those in steps 1 through 7.

Project 12-2

In this project you research the capabilities of two commercial security tools described in the chapter text. This project requires your successful completion (and comprehension) of the previous project, 12-1, and also that you have a browser with Internet access.

1. Review the types of scans that you performed in Project 12-1.

2. Go to the Psionic Web site at *www.psionic.com* and review the feature lists and any documentation you can find for the PortSentry program.

3. Can PortSentry detect all of the types of scans you performed?

4. Which type of scan mentioned in the chapter text is PortSentry unable to detect?

5. How might a program be designed that would detect such port scans?

6. Go to the SAINT Web page at *www.saintcorporation.com*. Review the feature lists, lists of vulnerabilities, and other information for the SAINT security-auditing program.

7. Does SAINT detect port scans?

8. Can SAINT simulate a port scan?

Project 12-3

12

In this project you use the IPTraf program to view network traffic statistics. You should work with a partner on this project. You will establish network connections with a second system, but all work will be done on one system. (Both you and your partner can perform the steps listed while sitting at your own computer, so long as you permit each other to establish connections as described.) To complete this project you should have Linux installed and have root access. The second system, to which you will make network connections, should permit ping and FTP or Web connections (these are the default settings in Red Hat Linux). Other Linux systems should also support this project, but you must locate and install the IPTraf package. This project is more interesting if several people on your network are working at the same time, so that multiple connections are visible.

1. Log in as root and install the IPTraf package from Red Hat Linux CD 2 if it is not already installed.

2. Start the IPTraf program in any command-line window:

   ```
   iptraf
   ```

3. Press a key to reach the IPTraf main menu.

4. Press **Enter** on the IP traffic monitor menu item.

5. Press **Enter** again to select All interfaces.

6. Open a second command-line window.

7. Use the ftp client command to establish an anonymous FTP connection to your partner's system:

    ```
    ftp partner.lab.edu
    ```

    Use the username *ftp* and your email address to log in so that you have an ftp> prompt.

8. Open a third command-line window and enter a command to ping your partner's system.

    ```
    ping partner.lab.edu
    ```

9. Launch a Web browser and point it to your partner's system or any Web site you choose.

10. Did you notice display action in IPTraf as you completed the previous three steps?

11. Press **X** to exit the IP traffic monitor screen. Choose **Detailed interface statistics** on the main menu. Select the network interface that you have been working with (probably eth0).

12. While you watch the summary statistics, switch to the other programs you have running and download another Web page or enter a command such as `ls` in the FTP client. The ping command should also still be running. Notice how the numbers update each second based on new network traffic.

13. Press **X** to return to the main menu. Choose **LAN station monitor** on the main menu, choose **All interfaces**, and notice which systems are sending out network data.

14. Press **X** to return to the main menu. Choose **Exit** to close IPTraf.

Project 12-4

In this project you experiment with the Ethereal packet-sniffing program. The steps here do not require that you work with a partner. However, you will find experimenting with Ethereal on your own more interesting if others in the computer lab are also working on projects, which makes a variety of network traffic visible to Ethereal. To complete this project you need a Linux system with root access and Ethereal installed. The steps below assume you are working on Red Hat Linux 7.3, though once Ethereal is installed, the steps should be identical for many versions of Linux.

1. Log in as root and make certain the two Ethereal packages from Red Hat CD 2 are installed:

    ```
    ethereal
    ethereal-gnome
    ```

2. Execute a command that will generate ongoing network traffic. You can ping another host on your LAN, start a large Web page download, establish a PPP connection, or start another type of connection such as FTP or SSH. When you establish a connection, network traffic is not constantly flowing, so you may want to switch to the window in which you made the connection and enter a command in order to generate some interesting traffic for analysis.

3. Launch the Ethereal program from any command line while running a graphical environment.

> `ethereal &`

4. Choose **Start** from the Capture menu.

5. Make certain that the correct interface is selected in the top field of the dialog box (normally you would choose the eth0 interface).

6. Under the Display options section, choose **Update list of packets in real time** so that you can see new network traffic on screen as you work.

7. Choose **OK** to begin the capture, then minimize the Ethereal: Capture window.

8. Switch to another screen and launch an FTP session, logging in as an anonymous user with your correct password.

9. Look for a packet labeled with the FTP protocol in the top section of the Ethereal window. See if you can find the packet that contains the password you entered to start your anonymous FTP session. In this case, only your email address is disclosed.

10. Close the FTP session using the **bye** command.

11. Start an SSH session with another host on your LAN that is running `sshd` but which you have not exchanged SSH keys with:

> `ssh -l username partnerhost.edu`

12. Notice the packets listed in the top part of Ethereal as the SSH connection was established (or even if it was rejected because you don't have a valid account on the machine you contacted). See if you can locate the packet that contains the password that you entered within `ssh`.

13. Stop the capture by choosing **Stop** on the Capture menu. The capture may take a moment to finish so that you can access the Ethereal menus to continue.

14. Choose **Display Filters** on the Edit menu.

15. Select the **Add Expression** button in the Display Filters dialog box that appears. A list of protocol components appears.

16. In this dialog box you can set a filter based on any flag or field for any protocol that Ethereal can process (all those listed in this dialog box). Explore some of the protocol options in this dialog box before closing it. Also close the Ethereal: Edit Display Filter List dialog box.

17. Choose **Protocol Hierarchy Statistics** from the Tools menu. Study the resulting percentage breakdowns with different protocol levels represented by indented lines.

18. If there are other users working on your network, continue to explore the Ethereal interface to see how you can process a large number of packets more efficiently by setting up protocol filters, setting values to match for colorization, and using other techniques.

12

CASE PROJECTS

1. One of the biggest legal clients of Snow, Sleet, and Hale is an energy company that runs an oil pipeline across the Alaskan wilderness. Recently, a group of anti-globalization protesters traveled cross-country to a remote part of the pipeline and sabotaged it, then made the resulting oil spill public. Snow, Sleet, & Hale are handling the lawsuit against the protest group for property damage and cleanup costs. At the same time, they are trying to press criminal charges and handle the public relations disaster while the energy company cleans up the oil spill.

   Because of the law firm's involvement and public exposure in this case, protesters from various antiglobalization groups around the world have started attacking the law firm's servers. You have just noticed this activity.

   What do you think the protesters' goals are in attacking the systems? Is it too late to use a security-auditing tool? What possible attacks or vulnerabilities are you most concerned about? Which concern you the least? What actions might you take with your network configurations, services, or daily practices to help you weather this attack? How long would you remain in "siege mode"? What are the main costs and disadvantages of operating in constant expectation of a serious attack? (Consider the benefits and disadvantages to you as system administrator as well as monetary costs to the firm and to end users on the firm's networks.)

2. As it turns out, one of the legal secretaries working in the Fairbanks office is a secret supporter of the largest antiglobalization protest group. Though he doesn't participate in the demonstrations for fear of losing his job, he appears to feel he can contribute to the cause by making your networks more vulnerable to the cyber-attacks.

   What parts of your well-designed security policy will protect your networks from this employee? If he attempts to attack the network from inside the firm, will your safeguards detect his actions and protect against them? How can you protect the networks against internal attackers without excessively reducing ease of use for everyone and without creating a working environment so overburdened with paranoia that no one wants to work at your firm?

3. After the dust settles, the protesters depart, the lawsuits are underway (they won't be over for many years), and your success in dealing with this difficult situation comes to the attention of a number of people through stories in computer trade magazines. As a result, you are asked to join a Presidential Commission run in cooperation with the National Infrastructure Protection Center and the SANS Institute. The Commission will study the current landscape of network security and future trends affecting corporate and governmental risks created by the increased use of networks around the world.

   As an industry luminary, your first task is to prepare brief remarks for a hearing before the Senate Special Committee on Intelligence (see *www.intelligence.senate.gov*).

The Special Committee would like to hear: (a) what you feel should be the greatest network security concerns of corporations and government organizations based on current technologies; (b) what new security-related technologies are in the wings and their possible effects on corporate and government security efforts; (c) how international efforts to standardize security protocols and strengthen encryption technologies may affect the work of the U.S. intelligence community (e.g., the C.I.A.); and (d) what government action, if any, you would recommend to make computer networks more secure in the future. (You may want to review the list of statements made to Congress by the NIPC. See *www.nipc.gov/pressroom/pressroom2.htm.*)

12

APPENDIX

A

LINUX CERTIFICATION OBJECTIVES

This Appendix contains the official testing objectives for the two Linux certification programs that were used in creating this book and its companion volume, *Guide to Linux Installation and System Administration*.

- SAIR/GNU Linux Certified Administrator (see *www.linuxpg.com*)
- Linux Professional Institute Level 1 Certification (see *www.lpi.org*)

Other Linux certification programs exist, including more advanced certifications from each of the two organizations above, a Linux+ certification from CompTIA (see *www.comptia.com*) and the Red Hat Certified Engineer program (RHCE, see *www.redhat.com*). The material in this book and in *Guide to Linux Installation and System Administration*, while not mapped to the objectives for these other examinations, will form a solid foundation for any additional study and practice that may be required to obtain other certifications.

In the descriptions that follow, **Book 1** refers to Course Technology's *Guide to Linux Installation and System Administration* 1st Ed. (ISBN 0-619-00097-X), and **Book 2** refers to this book, *Guide to Linux Networking and Security* (ISBN 0-619-00094-5).

Primary references are highlighted in **bold**.

SAIR/GNU Linux Certified Administrator (LCA) Objectives

The SAIR/GNU objectives appear to be in transition as of this writing. Given the comprehensive nature of the objectives as they currently stand, however, readers of this text should be well prepared for passing the SAIR/GNU exams. Please check the SAIR/GNU Web site to review updates at *www.linuxcertification.com*.

For each objective below, please refer to the Table of Contents and Index of this book and of **Book 1** (*Guide to Linux Installation and System Administration*) for help in locating the desired information. When multiple references are provided for a single objective, and one contains more detailed or precise treatment of the subject, that heading is given in boldface.

Exam 1: Linux Installation and Configuration

Theory of Operation

Objective	Book/Chapter/Section
State the definition, origins, cost, and tradeoff of free software.	**Book 1**, Chapter 1, **The Spirit of Linux** & The Strength of Linux
Compare proprietary versus open source software licenses.	**Book 1**, Chapter 1, The Spirit of Linux
List the GNU public license (GPL) principles.	**Book 1**, Chapter 1, The Spirit of Linux
Describe how to sell free software.	**Book 1**, Chapter 1, The Spirit of Linux
Describe the structural components of Linux.	**Book 1**, Chapter 1, The Strengths of Linux **Book 1**, Chapter 4, *throughout*
Contrast multiuser multitasking versus single-sequential user multitasking.	**Book 1**, Chapter 1, Understanding Operating Systems
Contrast command-line interpreters versus graphical user interfaces with tradeoffs.	**Book 1**, Chapter 5, Learning About the X Window System **Book 1**, Chapter 6, Understanding the Shell
List PC system architecture configuration issues.	**Book 1**, Chapter 2, Preparing to Install Linux
Describe hard disk partitioning strategies.	**Book 1**, Chapter 2, Preparing Your Hard Disk
Contrast video adapter versus monitor capabilities.	**Book 1**, Chapter 5, Running the X Window System
List the network configuration parameters.	**Book 1**, Chapter 2, Preparing to Install Linux

Base System

A

Objective	Book/Chapter/Section
List and give the tradeoff of installation media.	**Book 1**, Chapter 3, Understanding Installation Issues
Explain the Linux device driver lag and give examples.	**Book 1**, Chapter 3, The Installation Process
List the installation steps common to all distributions.	**Book 1**, Chapter 3, The Installation Process
Contrast high volume Linux distributions and give trade-offs.	**Book 1**, Chapter 1, The Spirit of Linux
Install four Linux distributions.	**Book 1**, Chapter 3, The Installation Process and **Project 3-2**
Describe the configuration tools COAS, Linuxconf, and Yast.	**Book 1**, Chapter 7, Using Basic System Administration Tools
List the boot-up sequence, log-in, and shut-down sequence.	**Book 1**, Chapter 4, The Initialization Process
Define "package" and describe how to use it.	**Book 1**, Chapter 4, Managing Software Packages
Describe basic file system principles.	**Book 1**, Chapter 4, Working with Linux Files and Directories **Book 1**, Chapter 8, Maintaining File Systems
Explain the use of mounting versus the use of "mtools" for removable media.	**Book 1**, Chapter 8, Maintaining File Systems
List and describe the role of common directories.	**Book 1**, Chapter 4, Working with Linux Files and Directories
List and describe the use of basic system navigation programs ps, kill, w, etc.	**Book 1**, Chapter 8, **Simple Task Management** **Book 1**, Chapter 10, Managing Processes
Describe the use and misuse of the superuser account.	**Book 1**, Chapter 3, **Starting Linux** **Book 1**, Chapter 8, Administering User Accounts
List the steps in creating a user account.	**Book 1**, Chapter 8, Administering User Accounts
Install, configure, and navigate two X11 window managers.	**Book 1**, Chapter 5, Using Desktop Interfaces

Shells and Commands

Objective	Book/Chapter/Section
Describe shell configuration files.	**Book 1**, Chapter 6, Understanding the Shell
Compare and contrast environmental versus shell variables.	**Book 1**, Chapter 6, Customizing the Shell
Use commands that pass special characters among programs.	**Book 1**, Chapter 7, Using Basic System Administration Tools

Shells and Commands (continued)

Objective	Book/Chapter/Section
Use commands that allow programs to communicate.	**Book 1**, Chapter 7, Using Basic System Administration Tools
Manipulate files and directories.	**Book 1**, Chapter 4, Working with Linux Files and Directories **Book 1**, Chapter 6, Using Text Editors and **Text Processing**
Use the shell for multitasking.	**Book 1**, Chapter 8. Simple Task Management
Describe common shell editing commands.	**Book 1**, Chapter 6, Customizing the Shell
Use the following commands in isolation or in combination with each other: ls, cd, more, less, cp, mv, mkdir, rm, rmdir, ln, head, tail, file, grep, du, df, and zcat.	**Book 1**, Chapter 4, Working with Linux Files and Directories **Book 1**, Chapter 7, Using Basic System Administration Tools
Use the following vi commands i, ZZ, :w! :q!, dd, x, D, and J.	**Book 1**, Chapter 6, Using Text Editors

System Services

Objective	Book/Chapter/Section
List and describe seven tools that provide information on other tools.	**Book 1**, Chapter 1, **Learning More About Linux** **Book 1**, Chapter 7, Using Basic System Administration Tools
Describe and use LILO.	**Book 1**, Chapter 2, **Preparing Your Hard Disk** **Book 1**, Chapter 3,The Installation Process **Book 1**, Chapter 4, The Initialization Process
Install run-time device drivers.	**Book 1**, Chapter 4, The Linux Kernel
Configure a printer capabilities file.	**Book 1**, Chapter 13, Setting Up Printing
Configure a printer filter.	**Book 1**, Chapter 13, Setting Up Printing
Use lpr, lpq, lprm, and lpc to control file printing.	**Book 1**, Chapter 13, Managing Printing
List the sections of the X server configuration file.	**Book 1**, Chapter 5, Running the X Window System
Configure the X server video hardware.	**Book 1**, Chapter 5, Running the X Window System
Contrast xf86config, XF86Setup, Xconfiguator, and SaX.	**Book 1**, Chapter 5, Running the X Window System
Describe five components of the X Window system architecture.	**Book 1**, Chapter 5, Learning About the X Window System
List and give the trade-offs of Afterstep, KDE, Window Maker, FVWM95, Enlightenment, and Blackbox.	**Book 1**, Chapter 5, Using Desktop Interfaces

Applications

A

Objective	Book/Chapter/Section
Describe the general control of X11 desktops.	**Book 1**, Chapter 5, Using Desktop Interfaces
Describe Netscape functions, FTP functions, Telnet functions, and mail functions.	**Book 2**, Chapter 1, Networking Software **Book 2**, Chapter 5, Running an FTP Server **Book 2**, Chapter 3, Web and Email Clients **Book 2**, Chapter 2, Using Basic Networking Utilities
Contrast WYSIWYG versus mark-up word processing.	**Book 1**, Chapter 6, Using Text Editors

Troubleshooting

Objective	Book/Chapter/Section
Describe the cause and solution to read errors.	**Book 1**, Chapter 3, Understanding Installation Issues
Explain why FTP keeps missing certain files in group transfers.	**Book 2**, Chapter 5, Running an FTP Server
Explain the problem and solution when LILO says LI.	**Book 1**, Chapter 3, Troubleshooting a New Installation
Define rescue disk and describe three reasons for using it.	**Book 1**, Chapter 9, Preparing for Emergencies
Explain how to get around a locked-up program.	**Book 1**, Chapter 10, Managing Processes
List eight steps to resolve an unresponsive printer.	**Book 1**, Chapter 13, Managing Printing
Explain why Linux may report the wrong time and describe how to fix the problem.	**Book 2**, Chapter 4, Using Administrative Services
Describe how to reset the console screen,the keyboard repeat rate, and the num lock key.	**Book 1**, Chapter 5, Running the X Window System
Describe the role of system logging and how to use it for troubleshooting.	**Book 1**, Chapter 11, Introducing System Logs

Exam 2: Linux System Administration

Theory of Operation

Objective	Book/Chapter/Section
The student will understand file system structure and hierarchy.	**Book 1**, Chapter 4, Working with Linux Files and Directories
The student will understand file system backup and cron.	**Book 1**, Chapter 14, Back-up Strategies **Book 1**, Chapter 12, Automating Tasks with at and crontab

Theory of Operation (continued)

Objective	Book/Chapter/Section
The student will understand printing and system tuning.	**Book 1**, Chapter 9, Checking File System Integrity **Book 1**, Chapter 10, Managing Memory **Book 1**, Chapter 13, Understanding Linux Printing
The student will understand trouble-shooting and emergency procedures.	**Book 1**, Chapter 9, Preparing for Emergencies
The student will understand system resources.	**Book 1**, Chapter 10, Managing Processes and Managing Memory
The student will understand user profiles.	**Book 1**, Chapter 8, Administering User Accounts
The student will understand RAID.	**Book 1**, Chapter 9, Understanding Redundant Disk Systems

Base System

Objective	Book/Chapter/Section
The student will understand adding and removing a user.	**Book 1**, Chapter 8, Administering User Accounts
The student will understand run levels.	**Book 1**, Chapter 4, The Initialization Process
The student will understand fstab and volume remounting.	**Book 1**, Chapter 8, Maintaining File Systems
The student will understand recompiling the kernel.	**Book 1**, Chapter 4, The Linux Kernel
The student will understand performance and hard disk analysis.	**Book 1**, Chapter 8, Maintaining File Systems **Book 1**, Chapter 9, Checking File System Integrity
The student will understand system shutdown techniques.	**Book 1**, Chapter 4, The Initialization Process

Shells and Commands

Objective	Book/Chapter/Section
The student will understand the role of the superuser.	**Book 1**, Chapter 8, Administering User Accounts
The student will understand motd and the issue with it.	**Book 1**, Chapter 4, The Initialization Process
The student will understand the MS-DOS tools.	**Book 1**, Chapters 4, Working with Linux Files and Directories
The student will understand the ARP/Route precedence.	**Book 2**, Chapter 2, Configuring Networking with Command-Line Utilities
The student will understand Bootp and DHCP.	**Book 1**, Chapter 3, Understanding Installation Issues **Book 2**, Chapter 3, Using DHCP

Shells and Commands (continued)

Objective	Book/Chapter/Section
The student will understand make and touch.	**Book 1**, Chapter 7, Using Basic System Administration Tools
The student will understand CGI scripts.	**Book 1**, Chapter 12, Writing Shell Scripts
The student will understand system status, system message logging, and performance analysis.	**Book 1**, Chapter 10, Managing Processes and Managing Memory **Book 1**, Chapter 11, Introducing System Logs

System Services

Objective	Book/Chapter/Section
The student will understand basic "user" commands.	**Book 1**, Chapter 7, Using Basic System Administration Tools
The student will understand the archive utilities.	**Book 1**, Chapter 14, Using Backup Utilities
The student will understand using fsck and why.	**Book 1**, Chapter 9, Checking File System Integrity
The student will understand process management.	**Book 1**, Chapter 10, Managing Processes
The student will understand printer settings and restarting.	**Book 1**, Chapter 13, Managing Printing
The student will understand the background line printer daemon and the foreground line printer requester.	**Book 1**, Chapter 13, Understanding Linux Printing
The student will understand software packages.	**Book 1**, Chapter 4, Managing Software Packages

Applications

Objective	Book/Chapter/Section
The student will understand AMANDA, ORL's VNC, Mail Exchange, News, and the Apache Web server.	**Book 1**, Chapter 14, Using Back-up Utilities **Book 2**, Chapter 3, Web and Mail Clients **Book 2**, Chapter 6, Creating a Linux Web Server
The student will understand X Windows desktops.	**Book 1**, Chapter 5, Learning About the X Window System
The student will understand benchmarks.	**Book 1**, Chapter 10, Managing Processes

Troubleshooting

Objective	Book/Chapter/Section
The student will understand core dump control.	**Book 1**, Chapter 12, Writing Shell Scripts

Exam 3: Linux Networking

Theory of Operation

Objective	Book/Chapter/Section
The student will understand the basic technology of Internet, Ethernet, and area networks.	**Book 2**, Chapter 1, *throughout*
The student will understand addresses and addressing.	**Book 2**, Chapter 1, Networking Software
The student will understand the protocols.	**Book 2**, Chapter 1, Networking Software
The student will understand DNS, applications, and Internet access.	**Book 2**, Chapter 3, Setting Up Name Resolution
The student will understand broadcasting, address assignment, and multicast.	**Book 2**, Chapter 1, Networking Software
The student will understand the UUCP subsystem.	**Book 2**, Chapter 3, Running Applications Remotely
The student will understand SMB and IPX.	**Book 2**, Chapter 2, Other Networking Protocols [IPX] **Book 2**, Chapter 5, Windows File and Print Integration with Samba [SMB]

Base System

Objective	Book/Chapter/Section
The student will understand networking interfaces.	**Book 2**, Chapter 2, Understanding Network Devices in Linux
The student will understand the ARP and Routing tables.	**Book 2**, Chapter 2, Configuring Networking with Command-Line Utilities
The student will understand firewalls.	**Book 2**, Chapter 11, Using Advanced Routing and Firewalls
The student will understand VPN and proxy servers.	**Book 2**, Chapter 6, Using Advanced Routing and Firewalls
The student will understand IP multicast.	**Book 2**, Chapter 1, Networking Software

A

Shells and Commands

Objective	Book/Chapter/Section
The student will understand basic network configuration.	**Book 2**, Chapter 2, Preparing to Configure Networking
The student will understand how to access, and the importance of, system start-up files.	**Book 1**, Chapter 4, The Initialization Process **Book 2**, Chapter 2, Configuring Networking with Command-Line Utilities
The student will understand UUCP.	**Book 2**, Chapter 3, Running Applications Remotely
The student will understand network troubleshooting.	**Book 2**, Chapters 1, 2, *throughout*

System Services

Objective	Book/Chapter/Section
The student will understand DNS, FTP, and NFS.	**Book 2**, Chapter 3, Setting up Name Resolution [DNS] **Book 2**, Chapter 5, Running an FTP Server [FTP] **Book 2**, Chapter 5, File Sharing with NFS [NFS] **Book 2**, Chapter 6, Setting up a DNS Name Server [DNS]
The student will understand the Internet superserver.	**Book 2**, Chapter 4, The Superservers
The student will understand SAMBA.	**Book 2**, Chapter 5, Windows File and Print Integration with Samba
The student will understand sendmail, smail, and qmail.	**Book 2**, Chapter 6, Configuring a Basic Email Server
The student will understand POP3 and IMAP.	**Book 2**, Chapter 3, Web and Mail clients
The student will understand News, mail list servers, and the Apache server.	**Book 2**, Chapter 4, Understanding Mailing Lists and News Servers **Book 2**, Chapter 6, Creating a Linux Web Server

Applications

Objective	Book/Chapter/Section
The student will understand mail and pine.	**Book 2**, Chapter 3, Web and Mail Clients
The student will understand browsers.	**Book 2**, Chapter 3, Web and Mail Clients

Exam 4: Linux Security, Ethics, and Privacy

Theory of Operation

Objective	Book/Chapter/Section
The student will understand daemons as superusers and the buffer overflow problem.	**Book 2**, Chapter 11, Reviewing Threats to Your Network
The student will understand the protection scheme.	**Book 2**, Chapter 7, Introducing Computer Security and Privacy
The student will understand the access control list.	**Book 2**, Chapter 12, Using Intrusion Detection Software
The student will understand Trojan horses, password weaknesses, and screening IPs.	**Book 2**, Chapter 11, Reviewing Threats to Your Network
The student will understand CERT advisories, daily system checks, and stealth file names.	**Book 2**, Chapter 7, Security-Focused Organizations
The student will understand cert.org and rootshell.com.	**Book 2**, Chapter 7, Security-Focused Organizations
The student will understand intruder detection and removal.	**Book 2**, Chapter 12, Using Intrusion Detection Software
The student will understand user-mode viruses and worms.	**Book 2**, Chapter 11, Reviewing Threats to Your Network
The student will understand Ken Thompson on trusting trust.	**Book 2**, Chapter 7, Introducing Computer Security and Privacy

Base System

Objective	Book/Chapter/Section
The student will understand setting the superuser status from a shell script.	**Book 1**, Chapter 6, Understanding the Shell
The student will understand the importance of the classifications of user, group, and everybody.	**Book 1**, Chapter 8, Administering User Accounts
The student will understand UMASK.	**Book 1**, Chapter 4, Working with Linux Files and Directories
The student will understand shadow passwords, host.allow, and host.deny.	**Book 1**, Chapter 8, Administering User Accounts **Book 2**, Chapter 4, The Superservers
The student will understand the importance of files for logging in as superuser, file transfer as superuser, printer configuration, and system logging.	**Book 2**, Chapter 10, Reviewing Linux File Permissions **Book 1**, Chapter 11, Introducing System Logs **Book 1**, Chapter 13, Managing Printing

A

Shells and Commands

Objective	Book/Chapter/Section
The student will understand the access control list and emulation.	**Book 2**, Chapter 10, Reviewing Linux File Permissions

System Services

Objective	Book/Chapter/Section
The student will understand checksecurity, rotatelogs, quotaon, quotacheck, and sa.	**Book 2**, Chapter 10, Using the System Logs for Security Checks
The student will understand pluggable authentication modules.	**Book 2**, Chapter 9, Using Pluggable Authentication Modules
The student will understand TCP/UDP Wrappers.	**Book 2**, Chapter 4, The Superservers
The student will understand find, its switches, important commands, and their significance.	**Book 1**, Chapter 7, Using Basic System Administration Tools
The student will understand the importance of daily cron checks.	**Book 1**, Chapter 12, Automating Tasks with at and crontab

Applications

Objective	Book/Chapter/Section
The student will understand hidden logfile backup.	**Book 2**, Chapter 12, Using the System Logs for Security Checks

Troubleshooting

Objective	Book/Chapter/Section
The student will understand why setuid shell scripts do not work.	**Book 2**, Chapter 10, Reviewing Linux File Permissions

OBJECTIVES FOR THE LINUX PROFESSIONAL INSTITUTE (LPI) CERTIFICATION EXAMS

The objectives covered here are for LPI Level 1 certification, encompassing two exams:

- 101, General Linux, Part 1
- 102, General Linux, Part 2

The LPI Level 2 certification includes two additional exams:

- 201 Advanced Linux Administration
- 202 Linux Networking Administration

Although the objectives for the Level 2 exams are not given here and were not the focus of this book (or Book 1), you will find that many of the topics addressed in the Level 2 exams are addressed in Book 1 or in this book. See *www.lpi.org* for more information about Level 2 certification.

The numbers associated with these objectives are not sequential because of changes made since the inception of the LPI program. A weight is assigned to each objective. The weights can range from 1 to 10; a higher weight indicates that the topic will be covered by more exam questions. The Web site *www.lpi.org* includes details about the LPI Certification Program. In the sections that follow, **Book 1** refers to Course Technology's *Guide to Linux Installation and System Administration*, 1st Ed. (ISBN 0-619-00097-X), and **Book 2** refers to this volume, *Guide to Linux Networking and Security* (ISBN 0-619-00094-5). Please refer to the Table of Contents and Index of each volume for more precise information. Because this book on networking and security assumes prerequisite knowledge of Linux system administration, the majority of the LPI objectives listed here refer to Book 1.

OBJECTIVES FOR EXAM 101, GENERAL LINUX, PART 1

Topic 1.3: GNU and UNIX Commands

Objective 1: Work effectively on the Unix command line

Weight of objective: 4

Interact with shells and commands using the command line. Includes typing valid commands and command sequences; defining, referencing, and exporting environment variables; using command history and editing facilities; invoking commands in the path and outside the path; using command substitution; and applying commands recursively through a directory tree.

***Book 1**, Chapter 4, Working with Linux Files and Directories*

Objective 2: Process text streams using text processing filters

Weight of objective: 7

Send text files and output streams through text utility filters to modify the output in a useful way. Includes the use of standard unix commands found in the GNU textutils package such as sed, sort, cut, expand, fmt, head, join, nl, od, paste, pr, split, tac, tail, tr, and wc.

***Book 1**, Chapter 6, Text Processing*

Objective 3: Perform basic file management

Weight of objective: 2

Use the basic unix commands to copy and move files and directories. Perform advanced file management operations such as copying multiple files recursively and moving files that meet a wildcard pattern. Use simple and advanced wildcard specifications to refer to files.

Book 1, *Chapter 4, Working with Linux Files and Directories*

Objective 4: Use Unix streams, pipes, and redirects

Weight of objective: 3

Connect files to commands and commands to other commands to efficiently process textual data. Includes redirecting standard input, standard output, and standard error; piping one command's output into another command as input or as arguments (using xargs); and sending output to stdout and a file (using tee).

Book 1, *Chapter 6, Understanding the Shell*

Objective 5: Create, monitor, and kill processes

Weight of objective: 5

Includes running jobs in the foreground and background, bringing a job from the background to the foreground and vice versa, monitoring active processes, sending signals to processes, and killing processes. Includes using the commands ps, top, kill, bg, fg, and jobs.

Book 1, *Chapter 10, Managing Processes*

Objective 6: Modify process execution priorities

Weight of objective: 2

Run a program with higher or lower priority, determine the priority of a process, change the priority of a running process. Includes the command nice and its relatives.

Book 1, *Chapter 10, Managing Processes*

Objective 7: Perform searches of text files making use of regular expressions

Weight of objective: 3

Includes creating simple regular expressions and using related tools such as grep and sed to perform searches.

Book 1, *Chapter 7, Using Basic System Administration Tools*

Topic 2.4: Devices, Linux File Systems, Filesystem Hierarchy Standard

Objective 1: Create partitions and filesystems

Weight of objective: 3

Create disk partitions using fdisk, create hard drive and other media filesystems using mkfs.

Book 1, *Chapter 2, Preparing Your Hard Disk*

Book 1, *Chapter 8, Maintaining File Systems*

Objective 2: Maintain the integrity of filesystems

Weight of objective: 5

Verify the integrity of filesystems, monitor free space and inodes, fix simple filesystem problems. Includes commands fsck, du, df.

Book 1, *Chapter 8, Maintaining File Systems*

Book 1, *Chapter 9, Checking File System Integrity*

Objective 3: Control filesystem mounting and unmounting

Weight of objective: 3

Mount and unmount filesystems manually, configure filesystem mounting on bootup, configure user-mountable removable file systems. Includes managing file /etc/fstab.

Book 1, *Chapter 8, Maintaining File Systems*

Objective 4: Set and view disk quota

Weight of objective: 1

Setup disk quota for a filesystem, edit user quota, check user quota, generate reports of user quota. Includes quota, edquota, repquota, and quotaon commands.

Book 1, *Chapter 8, Maintaining File Systems*

Objective 5: Use file permissions to control access to files

Weight of objective: 3

Set permissions on files, directories, and special files; use special permission modes such as suid and sticky bit; use the group field to grant file access to workgroups; and change default file creation mode. Includes chmod and umask commands. Requires understanding symbolic and numeric permissions.

Book 1, *Chapter 4, Working With Linux Files and Directories*

Objective 6: Manage file ownership

Weight of objective: 2

Change the owner or group for a file, control what group is assigned to new files created in a directory. Includes chown and chgrp commands.

Book 1, *Chapter 4, Working with Linux Files and Directories*

Objective 7: Create and change hard and symbolic links

Weight of objective: 2

Create hard and symbolic links, identify the hard links to a file, copy files by following or not following symbolic links, use hard and symbolic links for efficient system administration.

Book 1, *Chapter 4, Working with Linux Files and Directories*

Objective 8: Find system files and place files in the correct location

Weight of objective: 2

Understand the filesystem hierarchy standard, know standard file locations, know the purpose of various system directories, find commands and files. Involves using the commands: find, locate, which, and updatedb. Involves editing the file: /etc/updatedb.conf.

Book 1, *Chapter 7, Using Basic System Administration Tools*

Topic 2.6: Boot, Initialization, Shutdown, Run Levels

Objective 1: Boot the system

Weight of objective: 3

Guide the system through the booting process, including giving options to the kernel at boot time, and check the events in the log files. Involves using the command: dmesg (lilo). Involves reviewing the files: /var/log/messages, /etc/lilo.conf, /etc/conf.modules | /etc/modules.conf.

Book 1, *Chapter 4, The Initialization Process*

Objective 2: Change runlevels and shutdown or reboot system

Weight of objective: 3

Securely change the runlevel of the system, specifically to single user mode, halt (shutdown) or reboot. Make sure to alert users beforehand, and properly terminate processes. Involves using the commands: shutdown and init.

Book 1, *Chapter 4, The Initialization Process*

Topic 1.8: Documentation

Objective 1: Use and manage local system documentation

Weight of objective: 5

Use and administer the man facility and the material in /usr/doc/. Includes finding relevant man pages, searching man page sections, finding commands and manpages related to one, configuring access to man sources and the man system, using system documentation stored in /usr/doc/ and related places, and determining what documentation to keep in /usr/doc/.

Book 1, *Chapter 1, Learning More About Linux*

Objective 2: Find Linux documentation on the Internet

Weight of objective: 2

Find and use Linux documentation at sources such as the Linux Documentation Project, vendor and third-party Web sites, newsgroups, newsgroup archives, and mailing lists.

Book 1, *Chapter 1, Learning More About Linux*

Objective 3: Write system documentation

Weight of objective: 1

Write documentation and maintain logs for local conventions, procedures, configuration and configuration changes, file locations, applications, and shell scripts.

Book 1, *Chapter 1, Learning More About Linux*

Objective 4: Provide user support

Weight of objective: 1

Provide technical assistance to users via telephone, email, and personal contact.

Book 1, *Chapters 1-14*

Topic 2.11: Administrative Tasks

Objective 1: Manage users and group accounts and related system files

Weight of objective: 7

Add, remove, suspend user accounts; add and remove groups; change user/group info in passwd/group databases; and create special purpose and limited accounts. Includes commands useradd, userdel, groupadd, gpasswd, passwd, and file passwd, group, shadow, and gshadow.

Book 1, *Chapter 8, Administering User Accounts*

Objective 2: Tune the user environment and system environment variables

Weight of objective: 4

Modify global and user profiles to set environment variable, maintain skel directories for new user accounts, place proper commands in path. Involves editing /etc/profile and /etc/skel/.

Book 1, *Chapter 6, Customizing the Shell*

Book 1, *Chapter 8, Administering User Accounts*

Objective 3: Configure and use system log files to meet administrative and security needs

Weight of objective: 3

Configure the type and level of information logged, manually scan log files for notable activity, arrange for automatic rotation and archiving of logs, track down problems noted in logs. Involves editing /etc/syslog.conf.

Book 1, *Chapter 11, throughout*

Objective 4: Automate system administration tasks by scheduling jobs to run in the future

Weight of objective: 4

Use cron to run jobs at regular intervals, use at to run jobs at a specific time, manage cron and at jobs, configure user access to cron and at services.

Book 1, *Chapter 12, Automating Tasks with at and crontab*

Objective 5: Maintain an effective data backup strategy

Weight of objective: 3

Plan a backup strategy, backup filesystems automatically to various media, perform partial and manual backups, verify the integrity of backup files, partially or fully restore backups.

Book 1, *Chapter 14, Backup Strategies*

OBJECTIVES FOR EXAM 102, GENERAL LINUX, PART 2

Topic 1.1: Hardware and Architecture

Objective 1: Configure fundamental system hardware

Weight of objective: 3

Demonstrate a proper understanding of important BIOS settings, set the date and time, ensure IRQs and I/O addresses are correct for all ports including serial and parallel, make a note of IRQs and I/Os, be aware of the issues associated with drives larger than 1024 cylinders.

Book 1, *Chapter 2, Preparing to Install Linux*

Book 1, *Chapter 3, Understanding Installation Issues*

Objective 2: Setup SCSI and NIC devices

Weight of objective: 4

Manipulate the SCSI BIOS to detect used and available SCSI IDs; set the SCSI ID to the correct ID number for the boot device and any other devices required; format the SCSI drive—low level with manufacturer's installation tools—and properly partition and system format with Linux fdisk and mke2fs; set up NIC using manufacturer's setup tools setting the I/O and the IRQ, as well as the DMA, if required.

Book 1, *Chapter 2, Preparing to Install Linux*

Book 1, *Chapter 3, Understanding Installation Issues*

Objective 3: Configure modem and sound cards

Weight of objective: 3

Ensure devices meet compatibility requirements (particularly that the modem is *not a* win-modem); verify that both the modem and sound card are using unique and correct IRQs, I/O, and DMA addresses; if the sound card is PnP install and run sndconfig and isapnp, configure modem for outbound dial-up; configure modem for outbound PPP | SLIP | CSLIP connection; set serial port for 115.2 Kbps.

Book 1, *Chapter 2, Preparing to Install Linux*

Book 1, *Chapter 3, Understanding Installation Issues*

Topic 2.2: Linux Installation and Package Management

Objective 1: Design hard disk layout

Weight of objective: 2

Design a partitioning scheme for a Linux system, depending on the hardware and system use (number of disks, partition sizes, mount points, kernel location on disk, and swap space).

Book 1, *Chapter 2, Preparing Your Hard Disk*

A

Objective 2: Install a boot manager

Weight of objective: 3

Select, install, and configure a boot loader at an appropriate disk location. Provide alternative and backup boot options (like a boot floppy disk). Involves using the command: lilo. Involves editing the file: /etc/lilo.conf.

***Book 1**, Chapter 3, The Installation Process*

Objective 3: Make and install programs from source

Weight of objective: 5

Manage (compressed) archives of files (unpack "tarballs"), specifically GNU source packages. Install and configure these on your systems. Do simple manual customization of the Makefile if necessary (like paths, extra include dirs) and make and install the executable. Involves using the commands: gunzip, tar, ./configure, make, make install. Involves editing the files: ./Makefile.

***Book 1**, Chapter 12, Writing Shell Scripts*

Objective 4: Manage shared libraries

Weight of objective: 3

Determine the dependencies of executable programs on shared libraries, and install these when necessary. Involves using the commands: ldd, ldconfig. Involves editing the files: /etc/ld.so.conf.

***Book 1**, Chapter 4, Managing Software Packages*

Objective 5: Use Debian package management

Weight of objective: 5

Use the Debian package management system from the command line (dpkg) and with interactive tools (dselect). Be able to find a package containing specific files or software; select and retrieve them from archives; install, upgrade, or uninstall them; obtain status information like version, content, dependencies, integrity, and installation status; and determine which packages are installed and from which package a specific file has been installed. Be able to install a non–Debian package on a Debian system. Involves using the commands and programs: dpkg, dselect, apt, apt-get, and alien. Involves reviewing or editing the files and directories: /var/lib/dpkg/*.

***Book 1**, Chapter 4, Managing Software Packages*

Objective 6: Use Red Hat package manager (rpm)

Weight of objective: 6

Use rpm from the command line. Familiarize yourself with these tasks: install a package, uninstall a package, determine the version of the package and the version of the software it contains, list the files in a package, list documentation files in a package, list configuration files or installation or uninstallation scripts in a package, find out for a certain file from which package it was installed, find out which packages have been installed on the system (all packages, or from a subset of packages), find out in which package a certain program or file can be found, verify the integrity of a package, verify the PGP or GPG signature of a package, upgrade a package. Involves using the commands and programs: rpm and grep.

Book 1, *Chapter 4, Managing Software Packages*

Book 2, *Chapter 7, Other Security Applications*

Topic 1.5: Kernel

Objective 1: Manage kernel modules at runtime

Weight of objective: 3

Learn which functionality is available through loadable kernel modules, and manually load and unload the modules as appropriate. Involves using the commands: lsmod, insmod, rmmod, modinfo, and modprobe. Involves reviewing the files: /etc/modules.conf | /etc/conf.modules (* depends on distribution *), /lib/modules/{kernel-version}/modules.dep.

Book 1, *Chapter 4, The Linux Kernel*

Objective 2: Reconfigure, build and install a custom kernel and modules

Weight of objective: 4

Obtain and install approved kernel sources and headers (from a repository at your site, CD, kernel.org, or your vendor); customize the kernel configuration (i.e., reconfigure the kernel from the existing .config file when needed, using oldconfig, menuconfig, or xconfig); make a new Linux kernel and modules; install the new kernel and modules at the proper place; reconfigure and run lilo. N.B.: This does not require to upgrade the kernel to a new version (full source nor patch). Requires the commands: make (dep, clean, menuconfig, bzImage, modules, modules_install), depmod, and lilo. Requires reviewing or editing the files: /usr/src/linux/.config, /usr/src/linux/Makefile, /lib/modules/ {kernelversion}/modules.dep, /etc/conf.modules | /etc/modules.conf, /etc/lilo.conf.

Book 1, *Chapter 4, The Linux Kernel*

Topic 1.7: Text Editing, Processing, Printing

Objective 1: Perform basic file editing operations using vi

Weight of objective: 2

A

Edit text files using vi. Includes vi navigation, basic modes, inserting, editing and deleting text, finding text, and copying text.

***Book 1**, Chapter 6, Using Text Editors*

Objective 2: Manage printers and print queues

Weight of objective: 2

Monitor and manage print queues and user print jobs, troubleshoot general printing problems. Includes the commands: lpc, lpq, lprm and lpr. Includes reviewing the file: /etc/printcap.

***Book 1**, Chapter 13, Managing Printing*

Objective 3: Print files

Weight of objective: 1

Submit jobs to print queues and convert text files to postscript for printing. Includes the lpr command.

***Book 1**, Chapter 13, Setting Up Printing*

Objective 4: Install and configure local and remote printers

Weight of objective: 3

Install a printer daemon, install and configure a print filter (e.g., apsfilter and magicfilter). Make local and remote printers accessible for a Linux system, including postscript, nonpostscript, and Samba printers. Involves the daemon: lpd. Involves editing or reviewing the files and directories: /etc/printcap, /etc/apsfilterrc, /usr/lib/apsfilter/ filter/*/, /etc/magicfilter/*/, /var/spool/lpd/*/.

***Book 1**, Chapter 13, Remote Printing*

***Book 2**, Chapter 4, Using Administrative Services [lpd]*

Topic 1.9: Shells, Scripting, Programming, Compiling

Objective 1: Customize and use the shell environment

Weight of objective: 4

Customize your shell environment: set environment variables (e.g., PATH) at login or when spawning a new shell; and write bash functions for frequently used sequences of commands. Involves editing these files in your home directory: .bash_profile | .bash_login | .profile; .bashrc; .bash_logout; .inputrc.

***Book 1**, Chapter 6, Customizing the Shell*

Objective 2: Customize or write simple scripts

Weight of objective: 5

Customize existing scripts (like paths in scripts of any language), or write simple new (ba)sh scripts. Besides use of standard sh syntax (loops and tests), be able to do things like: command substitution and testing of command return values, test of file status, and conditional mailing to the superuser. Make sure the correct interpreter is called on the first (#!) line, and consider location, ownership, and execution—and suid-rights of the script.

Book 1, *Chapter 12, Writing Shell Scripts*

Topic 2.10: X

Objective 1: Install and configure XFree86

Weight of objective: 4

Verify that the video card and monitor are supported by an X server, install the correct X server, configure the X server, install an X font server, install required fonts for X (may require a manual edit of /etc/X11/XF86Config in the "Files" section), customize and tune X for videocard and monitor. Commands: XF86Setup and XF86Config. Files: /etc/X11/XF86Config and .xresources.

Book 1, *Chapter 5, Running the X Window System*

Objective 2: Setup XDM

Weight of objective: 1

Turn xdm on and off, change the xdm greeting, change default bitplanes for xdm, set-up xdm for use by X-stations.

Book 1, *Chapter 5, Running the X Window System*

Book 2, *Chapter 3, Running Applications Remotely*

Objective 3: Identify and terminate runaway X applications

Weight of objective: 1

Identify and kill X applications that won't die after user ends an X-session. Example: netscape, tkrat, etc.

Book 1, *Chapter 10, Managing Processes*

Objective 4: Install and customize a window manager environment

Weight of objective: 4

Select and customize a systemwide default window manager and/or desktop environment, demonstrate an understanding of customization procedures for window manager menus, configure menus for the window manager, select and configure the desired X-terminal (xterm, rxvt, aterm etc.), verify and resolve library dependency issues for X applications, export an X-display to a client workstation. Commands: Files: .xinitrc, .Xdefaults, and various .rc files.

***Book 1**, Chapter 5, Running the X Window System, and Using Desktop Interfaces*

Topic 1.12: Networking Fundamentals

Objective 1: Fundamentals of TCP/IP

Weight of objective: 4

Demonstrate an understanding of network masks and what they mean (i.e, determine a network address for a host based on its subnet mask), understand basic TCP/IP proto-cols (TCP, UDP, ICMP) and also PPP, demonstrate an understanding of the purpose and use of the more common ports found in /etc/services (20, 21, 23, 25, 53, 80, 110, 119, 139, 143, 161), demonstrate a correct understanding of the function and application of a default route. Execute basic TCP/IP tasks: FTP, anonymous FTP, telnet, host, ping, dig, traceroute, and whois.

***Book 2**, Chapter 1, Networking Software*

***Book 2**, Chapter 2, Configuring Networking Using Command-Line Utilities*

***Book 2**, Chapter 2, Using Basic Networking Utilities*

Objective 2: (superseded)

Objective 3: TCP/IP troubleshooting and configuration

Weight of objective: 10

Demonstrate an understanding of the techniques required to list, configure and verify the operational status of network interfaces; change, view or configure the routing table; check the existing route table; correct an improperly set default route, manually add/start/stop/restart/delete/reconfigure network interfaces; and configure Linux as a DHCP client and a TCP/IP host and debug associated problems. May involve reviewing or configuring the following files or directories: /etc/HOSTNAME | /etc/hostname, /etc/hosts, /etc/networks, /etc/host.conf, /etc/resolv.conf, and other network configu-ration files for your distribution. May involve the use of the following commands and programs: dhcpd, host, hostname (domainname and dnsdomainname), ifconfig, netstat, ping, route, traceroute, and the network scripts run during system initialization.

***Book 2**, Chapter 2, Configuring Networking with Command-Line Utilities*

Objective 4: Configure and use PPP

Weight of objective: 4

Define the chat sequence to connect (given a login example), set up commands to be run automatically when a PPP connection is made, initiate or terminate a PPP connection, initiate or terminate an ISDN connection, and set PPP to automatically reconnect if disconnected.

***Book 2**, Chapter 3, Dial-up Network Access Using PPP*

Topic 1.13: Networking Services

Objective 1: Configure and manage inetd and related services

Weight of objective: 5

Configure which services are available through inetd, use tcpwrappers to allow or deny services on a host-by-host basis, manually start, stop, and restart Internet services, configure basic network services including telnet and ftp. Includes managing inetd.conf, hosts.allow, and hosts.deny.

***Book 2**, Chapter 4, The Superservers*

Objective 2: Operate and perform basic configuration of sendmail

Weight of objective: 5

Modify simple parameters in sendmail config files (modify the DS value for the "Smart Host" if necessary), create mail aliases, manage the mail queue, start and stop sendmail, configure mail forwarding (.forward), and perform basic troubleshooting of sendmail. Does not include advanced custom configuration of sendmail. Includes commands: mailq, sendmail, and newaliases. Includes aliases and mail/ config files.

***Book 2**, Chapter 6, Configuring a Basic Email Server*

Objective 3: Operate and perform basic configuration of Apache

Weight of objective: 3

Modify simple parameters in Apache config files; start, stop, and restart httpd; arrange for automatic restarting of httpd upon boot. Does not include advanced custom configuration of Apache. Includes managing httpd conf files.

***Book 2**, Chapter 6, Creating a Linux Web Server*

Objective 4: Properly manage the NFS, smb, and nmb daemons

Weight of objective: 4

Mount remote filesystems using NFS, configure NFS for exporting local filesystems, start, stop, and restart the NFS server. Install and configure Samba using the included GUI tools or direct edit of the /etc/smb.conf file. (Note: This deliberately excludes advanced NT domain issues, but includes simple sharing of home directories and printers, as well as correctly setting the nmbd as a WINS client.)

Book 2, *Chapter 5, File Sharing with NFS [NFS]*

Book 2, *Chapter 5, Windows File and Print Integration with Samba [smb and nmb]*

Objective 5: Setup and configure basic DNS services

Weight of objective: 3

Configure hostname lookups by maintaining the /etc/hosts, /etc/resolv.conf,/etc/ host.conf, and /etc/nsswitch.conf files, troubleshoot problems with local caching-only name server. Requires an understanding of the domain registration and DNS translation process. Requires understanding key differences in config files for bind 4 and bind 8. Includes commands nslookup and host. Files: named.boot (v.4) or named.conf (v.8).

Book 2, *Chapter 3, Setting up Name Resolution [client]*

Book 2, *Chapter 6, Setting Up a DNS Name Server [server]*

Topic 1.14: Security

Objective 1: Perform security admin tasks

Weight of objective: 4

Configure and use TCP Wrappers to lock down the system, list all files with SUID bit set, determine if any package (.rpm or .deb) has been corrupted, verify new packages prior to install, use setgid on dirs to keep group ownership consistent, change a user's password, set expiration dates on users' passwords, obtain, install and configure ssh.

Book 2, *Chapter 10, Reviewing Linux File Permissions*

Book 2, *Chapter 4, The Superservers*

Objective 2: Setup host security

Weight of objective: 4

Implement shadowed passwords, turn off unnecessary network services in inetd, set the proper mailing alias for root and setup syslogd, monitor CERT and BUGTRAQ, update binaries immediately when security problems are found.

Book 1, *Chapter 4, The Superservers*

Book 1, *Chapter 11, Introducing System Logs*

Objective 3: Setup user level security

Weight of objective: 2

Set limits on user logins, processes, and memory usage.

Book 2, *Chapter 9, Using Pluggable Authentication Modules*

B

COMMAND SUMMARY

This appendix lists alphabetically all commands referred to in this book and in the companion volume, *Guide to Linux Installation and System Administration.* The table below includes:

- Standard command-line utilities.

- Server daemons.

- Many specialized utilities that are part of software packages described in the chapter text (for example, the utilities that are part of the Samba Suite).

- Graphical utilities (using their program name, as they would be launched from a graphical command line).

Configuration files are not included in this table. To learn about any of the server daemons or command-line utilities, use the `man` or `info` command followed by the name of the program. (In some cases, the `man` command refers you to the `info` command for more complete information.) Most graphical programs do not have man pages. For graphical programs, and for many specialized command-line utilities, you can learn more by reviewing the documentation that accompanies the utility. For example, in Red Hat Linux, the documentation for each package is stored as a subdirectory within `/usr/share/doc`.

Table B-1 Command-line utilities, server daemons, and graphical configuration programs

Command Name	Description
alias	Assign a new name to a command.
apropos	See a list of man pages that contain a given keyword.
arp	Display stored MAC-to-IP address mappings that were collected using the Address Resolution Protocol.
at	Set up a one-time task for later execution by the atd daemon.
atq	See the list of jobs submitted to atd using the at command.
atrm	Remove a scheduled job from the queue of jobs to be executed by the atd daemon.
authconfig	Text-mode menu-based configuration tool for setting authentication options in Red Hat Linux.
authconfig-gtk	Graphical configuration tool for setting authentication options in Red Hat Linux.
balsa	Graphical email client (message reader) for Gnome desktops.
bash	The default Linux shell.
batch	Set up a scheduled task for future execution by the atd daemon when the processor load falls below a certain level.
bg	Make the current process a background process within the current shell.
bindconf	Graphical tool for setting up zone information files for the named DNS name server daemon.
busybox	A miniature version of dozens of standard Linux utilities in a single compact binary.
cat	Print the contents of a file or files to STDOUT.
cd	Change the current working directory.
chattr	Change the file attributes of one or more files.
chgrp	Change the group assigned to a file or directory.
chkconfig	Turn a system service on or off in a particular run level, so that the service is activated or not activated when the system boots.
chkrootkit	Checks systems for signs of a rootkit, much like a virus checker.
chmod	Change the permissions assigned to a file or directory.
chown	Change the user (owner) assigned to a file or directory.
clear	Clear the screen.
cp	Copy files or directories from one location or filename to another.
cpio	Back-up utility, similar to tar.
crontab	Submit a script with assigned times for repeated future execution by the crond daemon.
date	Display the system date and current time.
df	Display file system information for all mounted standard file systems (not swap and proc).
dhcpcd	A DHCP client daemon; used to lease network addresses from a DHCP server.

Table B-1   Command-line utilities, server daemons, and graphical configuration programs (continued)

Command Name	Description
dhcpd	The DHCP server.
diald	Daemon that manages dial-up connections (PPP connections), establishing or dropping them as determined by network traffic.
dig	Query a name server for any data the name server maintains in its zone information files.
dmesg	Display the contents of the kernel ring buffer, where certain kernel messages are stored.
du	Display usage information about the size of a directory and its subdirectories.
dump	Back up data in a file system.
echo	Display text to STDOUT.
elm	A text-based email client with a menu-style interface.
emacs	A powerful text-mode editor.
ethereal	Powerful graphical utility for analyzing network traffic, including both header details and packet payload (a sniffer); for Gnome, KDE, or other desktops.
exit	Log out of a session or window.
export	Make an environmental variable available to other processes.
fetchmail	A simple POP3 mail client for Linux.
fg	Move a process to the foreground of the current shell, so that the output of the process is displayed.
file	Display information about the content and file type of a file.
find	Search for a file with certain characteristics and list them or perform other actions on each one.
finger	Network service that provides basic status information via the in.fingerd daemon for any user on a system.
firewall-config	A graphical firewall configuration utility.
free	Display the amount of free memory and swap space, with usage details on each.
ftp	The text-mode FTP client.
ftpshut	Stops the FTP daemon from accepting new connections after the specified length of time.
gated	Dynamic routing daemon that supports RIP, RIP 2, OSPF, and BGP.
gftp	Graphical FTP client in Red Hat Linux.
gpg	Manage public key encryption, including generating and managing key pairs and encrypting or decrypting files.
grep	Search for a pattern using a regular expression within a file, group of files, or other input stream.
grpck	Check the /etc/group file to be certain that all members of groups refer to valid user accounts.

B

Table B-1   Command-line utilities, server daemons, and graphical configuration
programs (continued)

Command Name	Description
gunzip	Uncompress a file that was compressed using gzip.
gzip	Compress a file.
halt	Shut down all processes and halt the system so it can be turned off.
head	Display the first 15 lines of a file.
history	Display recently used commands within the shell.
host	Reports basic DNS information about a hostname, such as its IP address.
hostname	Display the hostname of a system.
httpd	The Apache Web server daemon; more generally, the name used for a Web server daemon.
ifconfig	Use with no parameters to display information on all network interfaces configured in the Linux kernel; use with parameters such as an interface, netmask, and IP address to configure a new interface. System startup scripts are normally used to configure interfaces instead of directly calling ifconfig.
ifdown	A script used to deactivate a networking interface in an orderly way.
ifup	A script used to activate a networking interface in an orderly way.
IglooFTP	Graphical FTP client.
in.fingerd	Server daemon for the finger network service.
in.ftpd	The standard FTP server daemon.
in.telnetd	The standard Telnet server daemon.
in.tftpd	Server daemon for the Trivial FTP protocol.
inetd	A superserver; used to listen to multiple network ports and start the appropriate network services as needed.
init	The master control program in Linux; started by the kernel. All programs are started by either init or one of its children.
innd	The standard Linux news server daemon.
ipchains	Firewall configuration tool for Linux 2.2 kernels; supported in newer kernels for backwards compatibility.
ipfwadm	Firewall configuration tool in old Linux systems.
iptables	Firewall configuration tool in Linux 2.4 kernels.
iptraf	Text-mode menu-based IP traffic analysis and statistics utility. (Not a packet sniffer.)
ipx_configure	Enables or disables automatic IPX configuration via broadcast information from an IPX server on the same network.
ipx_interface	Add, delete, or check IPX configuration information (similar to the ifconfig command for IP).
ipx_internal_net	Configures an internal IPX network (similar to the loopback device for IP).
ipx_route	Manually modify the IPX routing table (similar to the route command for IP).

Table B-1   Command-line utilities, server daemons, and graphical configuration
programs (continued)

Command Name	Description
joe	A full-screen text-mode editor.
kfinger	Graphical finger client for KDE desktops.
kill	Send a signal to a process; often used to end a process.
killall	Send a SIGKILL signal to all processes matching the name given as a parameter.
kmail	Graphical email client (message reader) for KDE desktops.
knode	Graphical newsreader client for KDE desktops.
kppp	Graphical utility for configuring and running a PPP dial-up connection.
krn	Graphical newsreader client for KDE desktops.
last	List the last login time for each user on the system.
lastcomm	List the last command entered by each user on the system.
less	Display STDIN (or a file) one page at a time.
lidsadm	Administrative utility to manage the LIDS intrusion detection system.
ln	Create a link from one file or directory to another (both symbolic and hard links can be created).
locate	Search in the internal index of the file system for any files or directories matching the given string.
logcheck	Automatically watch for suspicious activity in log files and take action when needed, such as emailing root.
login	Log in to the system using a username and password.
logout	End a login session.
logrotate	Rotate logs automatically via a crontab entry.
lokkit	A text-mode menu-based simple firewall configuration utility.
lpc	Control the lpd line printer daemon, setting queuing and printing options for all defined printers.
lpd	The line printing daemon; processes print jobs, including transferring jobs to remote hosts according to /etc/printcap configurations.
lpq	Display print jobs within a print queue.
lpr	Print a file.
lprm	Remove a print job from a print queue.
ls	List the contents of a directory.
lsattr	List the file attributes of one or more files.
lsmod	List all modules that are part of the current kernel.
lynx	A text-based, Web browser.
m4	Utility that converts the macro language of the sendmail.mc file into a standard format configuration file (sendmail.cf) for use by the sendmail email server.
mail	A text-based, command-line email client.
make	Compile or otherwise assemble the source code of a program into a runnable binary file using a Makefile as instructions.

Table B-1   Command-line utilities, server daemons, and graphical configuration
programs (continued)

Command Name	Description
makemap	Converts a text file into a hashed database file for use by the sendmail email server; used with the access and virtusertable files.
makewhatis	Create a database of man pages for use by the apropos command.
man	Display an online manual page for the given command.
mars-nwe	A daemon that emulates NetWare 3.x functionality.
mcopy	Copy a file or files to or from the floppy disk drive.
md5sum	Generate an MD5 hash from a file.
mdel	Delete a file or files from the floppy disk drive.
mdir	List the files on a floppy disk drive.
mesg	Enable or disable on-screen text messages from programs like talk.
mgetty	A terminal management program. (Others include getty, mingetty.) Handles login via a modem or virtual console.
minicom	A terminal emulator for Linux.
mkdir	Create a new subdirectory.
mke2fs	Format a device with the ext2 file system.
mkfs	Format a device with the given file system.
mksmbpasswd.sh	Script to convert existing Linux user accounts to Samba user accounts.
mkswap	Format a device as swap space (virtual memory on hard disk).
modprobe	Manage Linux kernel modules; most commonly used to add a module and any dependent modules to the kernel.
more	Display STDIN (or a file) one page at a time.
mount	Allow access to a named file system via a named directory mount point.
mozilla	Web browser.
mv	Rename or move one or more files or directories.
named	The DNS name server daemon in the BIND package.
named-checkconf	Validates the syntax of the /etc/named.conf configuration file.
neat	Graphical network interface configuration utility for Red Hat Linux.
netconfig	Text-mode, menu-based network interface configuration utility for Red Hat Linux.
netscape	Web browser.
newaliases	Convert the /etc/aliases text file into a hashed database file that sendmail can use for processing email name aliases.
nfsd	Daemon to manage file system requests from mounted NFS file systems.
nmap	Comprehensive port scanning utility.
nmapfe	Graphical front end to the nmap port scanning utility for Gnome desktops.
nmbd	The NetBIOS name server daemon; used as part of the Samba suite to interact with Windows systems.

Table B-1   Command-line utilities, server daemons, and graphical configuration
programs (continued)

Command Name	Description
`nslookup`	Query a name server; similar to `dig`, but this command is not recommended. (Deprecated.)
`nsupdate`	Dynamically updates zone information files for the named daemon.
`ntpd`	The NTP time server daemon. (Named `xntpd` in some versions of Linux.)
`objdump`	Display the contents of a file in any of several low-level formats, such as octal, hex, and ASCII.
`pan`	Graphical newsreader for the Gnome desktop environment.
`passwd`	Set or reset the password for a user account.
`passwd`	Change a user's password.
`pico`	A full-screen, character-mode text editor with on-screen help.
`pine`	A text-based email client with a menu-style interface.
`ping`	Send an ICMP echo packet to see whether a remote can be contacted via the network.
`portmap`	Manages network connections based on the RPC system (such as NFS connections).
`pppd`	The PPP daemon; used for dial-up networking.
`printconf-gui`	Graphical printer configuration tool in Red Hat Linux.
`printtool`	Configure printers in Red Hat Linux.
`procmail`	An email filtering tool (a Mail Delivery Agent).
`ps`	Display information about running processes.
`pump`	A DHCP client daemon; used to lease network addresses from a DHCP server.
`pwd`	Display the current working directory.
`rcp`	Copy one or more files between any two computers on the network that support the r-utilities.
`rlogin`	Log in to a remote host that supports the r-utilities.
`rm`	Delete one or more files or directories.
`rmdir`	Delete an empty directory.
`rndc`	Manages the `named` name server daemon.
`route`	Use with no parameters to display the kernel routing table; use with parameters such as `add -net` to add or remove an entry from the kernel routing table. System startup scripts are normally used to populate the routing table, but some manual reconfiguration with `route` may be needed for complex networks.
`routed`	Dynamic routing daemon that supports RIP and RIP 2 routing protocols.
`rp3`	Graphical utility for establishing a PPP dial-up connection based on a configuration created by rp3-config.
`rp3-config`	Graphical utility for configuring and establishing a dial-up PPP connection.
`rpc.mountd`	Daemon to manage mounting of remote NFS file systems.

B

Table B-1 Command-line utilities, server daemons, and graphical configuration programs (continued)

Command Name	Description
`rpc.rquotad`	Daemon to manage disk storage limits (quotas) for users who have mounted an NFS file system.
`rpc.rstatd`	Daemon to provide statistical data for an NFS file system.
`rpm`	Manage software packages, including installing new packages and verifying the integrity of package files.
`rsh`	Execute a command on a remote computer without logging in and seeing a shell prompt.
`ruptime`	List the uptime for each host on the network that supports the r-utilities.
`rwho`	List users on the local network who are logged on. (Only those supporting r-utilities are listed.)
`sed`	Edit files or STDIN input using patterns and commands.
`sendmail`	Popular MTA (email server).
`shutdown`	Shut down the system, optionally providing a message or delay for users working on the system.
`smbadduser`	Add a user to the /etc/samba/smbpasswd Samba user configuration file.
`smbclient`	Text-mode client for accessed SMB-capable servers (including Microsoft Windows servers).
`smbd`	The SMB server daemon; used as part of the Samba suite to interact with Windows systems.
`smbpasswd`	Updates the password for a Samba user, which is typically stored in the configuration file /etc/samba/smbpasswd.
`smbprint`	Text-mode client for printing to SMB-capable servers (including Microsoft Windows servers).
`sort`	Sort lines in a file according to various options.
`ssh`	The client utility for establishing a Secure Shell encrypted connection to another host.
`ssh-agent`	Manages key pairs for users who use SSH on multiple systems.
`ssh-keygen`	Generates key pairs for use within the SSH suite.
`sshd`	Server daemon to which the ssh utility can make an encrypted connection.
`strings`	Display the readable strings found in any file (including binary files).
`stunnel`	Permits secure network connections of several different protocols (e.g., POP3 and IMAP) using the OpenSSL package that Web browsers use.
`su`	Change to a new user account.
`sudo`	Execute a command with root privileges; edit the permission configuration with `visudo`.
`SWAT`	Browser-based configuration program for the Samba suite.
`swatch`	A log-watching utility.
`syslogd`	The system-logging daemon; operates as configured by /etc/syslog.conf.
`tail`	Display the last 15 lines of a file to STDOUT.

Table B-1 Command-line utilities, server daemons, and graphical configuration programs (continued)

Command Name	Description
talk	A text-based chat client using the talk protocol. Relies on the talkd server daemon.
talkd	The server daemon used for talk-based, text-mode chat sessions.
tar	Create an archive file containing one or more files or directories, optionally compressing them all.
tcpd	The TCP Wrappers daemon; usually called from the inetd superserver; configured by /etc/hosts.allow and /etc/hosts.deny.
tcpdump	Command-line utility for analyzing network traffic.
telnet	Make a remote connection to a system.
tethereal	Text-mode version of the Ethereal network traffic analyzer.
top	Display the processes running on the system sorted with the most processor-intensive task listed first.
touch	Update the last-accessed-time for a file, or create an empty file if the file named does not exist.
traceroute	Determine which routers a packet passes through to reach a destination host.
tripwire	A file integrity-checking program.
trn	A text-mode news reader.
ttysnoop	Capture the output of any tty; useful for teaching situations or spying.
ud	A text-mode LDAP client.
umount	Unmount a file system that is currently mounted as part of the Linux directory structure.
unzip	Uncompress a file that has been created using the zip command.
updatedb	Create an index of the entire file system for use by the locate command.
useradd	Add a new user to the system or modify the parameters associated with a user's account.
uucp	Use the UUCP protocol to transfer files over a dial-up connection.
vi	A powerful full-screen text editor.
vigr	Edit the /etc/group file; used when multiple administrators might be trying to access the file at the same time. Locks the file to prevent conflicting edits.
vipw	Edit the /etc/passwd file; used when multiple administrators might be trying to access the file at the same time. Locks the file to prevent conflicting edits.
visudo	Edit the configuration file that controls use of the sudo command.
vlock	Lock a text-mode virtual console so that the screen cannot be used without first entering the password of the person who used vlock.
vmstat	Display virtual memory (swap space) statistics.
w	List users who are logged in to the system.
wc	Display the number of characters, words, and lines in a file or STDIN input stream.
Webmin	Browser-based, multifunction system administration utility.
who	Display a list of users who are currently logged in.

Table B-1   Command-line utilities, server daemons, and graphical configuration
programs (continued)

Command Name	Description
who	List users who are logged in to the system.
whois	Displays information from the whois domain name database. (Requires Internet access.)
wvdial	Connect to a server using PPP over a modem.
xauth	Manage permission to access an X server from a remote host using the xauth authentication scheme (based on MIT cookies).
xhost	Sets permissions for access to an X server from a remote host using the xhost hostname-based authentication scheme.
xinetd	A superserver; used to listen to multiple network ports and start the appropriate network services as needed.
xload	Display the current processor load from 0% to 100% as a small graphic.
xlock	Lock a graphical screen so that it cannot be viewed or used without first entering the password of the user who started xlock.
xlogmaster	Graphical program to manage log files.
xlsfonts	Graphical utility in which you choose from among installed fonts.
yast	A configuration tool in the SuSE Linux distribution; can be used to configure networking.
zip	Compress one or more files into a single archive (the resulting file is compatible with ZIP files on Windows systems).

Glossary

--display — An option supported by all graphical programs that defines the X server on which the program's output should be shown and from which input should be collected. Overrides the `DISPLAY` environment variable.

.nofinger — A file which, when created in a user's home directory, causes the `finger` program to display no information about that user.

.nwclient — A configuration file used by the `ncpfs` package for client access to NetWare servers.

.plan — A hidden file within a user's home directory, the contents of which the `finger` program displays when queried.

.procmailrc — The configuration file for individual Procmail users. *See also* `/etc/procmailrc`.

.rhosts — A file stored within a user's home directory to determine who is allowed to access that user's account via r-utilities commands such as `rsh` and `rcp`. *See also* `/etc/hosts.equiv`.

.Xauthority — The file that contains tokens (cookies) used by the `xauth` security system for displaying graphical programs.

/etc/host.conf — The file that specifies the order in which the resolver should consult resources to resolve the hostname to an IP address.

/etc/hosts — The file used to store IP addresses and corresponding domain names for hosts, usually those frequently accessed on a local network.

/etc/hosts.allow — Configuration file that defines services and hosts that should be permitted service by TCP Wrappers.

/etc/hosts.deny — Configuration file that defines services and hosts that should be denied service by TCP Wrappers.

/etc/hosts.equiv — A systemwide database of remote hosts and usernames that are permitted to access the host using r-utilities. *See also* `.rhosts`.

/etc/nologin — A file whose existence prevents all users except root from being able to log in. Regular users attempting to log in see the contents of `/etc/nologin`, if anything.

/etc/nsswitch.conf — The file that defines the order in which the resolver and many other programs use various local or network resources to obtain configuration information.

/etc/passwd — The file in which basic user account configuration data is stored.

/etc/procmailrc — The systemwide configuration file for Procmail. *See also* `.procmailrc`.

/etc/rc.d/init.d/network — The main networking control script in Linux. The exact location of this script may vary within different Linux systems, though this is a standard location for it.

/etc/resolv.conf — The file that configures the Linux resolver.

/etc/securetty — A file listing all terminals from which root can log in.

/etc/services — Configuration file that maps service names to port numbers. Used by many programs, including the `inetd` and `xinetd` superservers.

/etc/shadow — The file in which users' encrypted passwords and password control data are stored.

/etc/sudoers — A configuration file that determines which users can perform which tasks using the `sudo` command.

/etc/sysconfig — Directory in which networking configuration files and scripts are stored, specifically in the subdirectory `network-scripts` and the file `networking`.

/lib/modules — Directory in which all of the available kernel modules for Linux are stored.

/var/spool/mail — The default directory for email inboxes on most Linux systems.

access control list (ACL) — A data structure that defines the access permitted for individual directories and individual programs.

Address Resolution Protocol (ARP) — A protocol that broadcasts a message to an entire network segment in order to obtain a host's MAC address.

Advanced Encryption Standard (AES) — A replacement for DES. The next generation of government-approved encryption standards. Uses the Rijndael (pronounced "Rain Doll") algorithm.

afpfs — A software package that lets Linux users access Macintosh resources. This software is still available for download but, because it is not currently being developed, is not supported by the latest Linux kernels (2.4).

agent — An SNMP-aware program running on a host. The client that collects data for analysis and transmission using other SNMP software.

algorithm — A set of rules or steps that, when followed, result in a predictable outcome.

anonymous FTP — Using FTP for public access via a common username, without a user-specific account on the FTP server.

anonymous user home directory — The directory on Linux which anonymous FTP users can access for downloading or uploading files. Typically either /var/ftp or /home ftp.

anonymous users — Users logging in to an FTP server who do not have a regular Linux user account and are thus restricted to a specific area of the file system. *See also* anonymous FTP.

Apache module — Functionality for the Apache Web server that can be independently loaded on the fly as a shared object.

AppleTalk — The networking protocol used by Apple Macintosh computers. AppleTalk is supported in Linux via the Netatalk package.

appliance — A hardware device that is sold specifically to accomplish one purpose or a group of related purposes, such as a firewall, a router, or a VPN.

ARCnet — An older token-passing network technology that has lost a great deal of its former popularity. ARCnet is reliable, but slower than more modern networking technologies like token ring or Ethernet.

A record — A line (a record) within a DNS zone information file that provides the IP address for the given host.

arp — A command that displays or alters the contents of the arp cache. Used mainly for troubleshooting network connectivity.

arp cache — A list of IP address-to-hardware mappings maintained by the ARP protocol to assist in routing packets.

asymmetric encryption algorithm — An encryption algorithm in which different keys are used to encrypt and decrypt a message. One is kept secret, one is distributed publicly. Often called public-key encryption.

Asynchronous Transfer Mode (ATM) — A networking technology used for the Internet backbone or other specialized high-speed networks. It is fast (currently 155 Mb/s with 622 Mb/s under development) but also expensive.

attribute — A discrete data element that is part of an object within a directory service database such as LDAP.

authentication — The process of proving to a computer system or another person that you are in fact the person you say you are.

back door — A method of accessing a program or a computer system that is known to its creator but not to other users of the system. It is undocumented and hidden.

Balsa — A graphical email client (MUA) provided with some releases of the Gnome desktop.

bandwidth — The amount of information that a network technology can transmit; usually expressed in bits per second (b/s).

benchmarking — The process of comparing performance by evaluating it against others performing the same fixed task.

Berkeley Internet Name Domains (BIND) — The name service used by the Internet.

Big Brother — An intrusion detection program that uses a client/server model to gather network service and host resource data from numerous hosts on a network and report that data in a browser-based interface.

bindconf — A graphical utility used to configure zone information files.

bindery — A database of system resources stored on a NetWare server. Versions after NetWare 3 use the newer Novell Directory Service (NDS). *See also* Bindery Emulation.

Bindery Emulation — A system used by versions 4 and above of NetWare to simulate a bindery when the operating system actually uses NDS.

Blowfish — A symmetric cipher.

BOOTP — A protocol used by diskless workstations (prior to DHCP being available) that allowed them to obtain network configuration instructions.

Border Gateway Protocol (BGP) — A widely used external routing protocol.

bridge — A network device used to connect segments so they can share data. A bridge works at the OSI Data Link layer, examining the address of every packet to facilitate network communications.

broadcast address — An IP address in which the host ID consists of all ones that causes the packet to be sent to every host on the named network.

brute force attack — A method of obtaining access to a system by trying all possible combinations until one succeeds in guessing a password.

buffer overflow attack — A technique for gaining access to a computer system by exploiting a weakness in the design of a computer program. When a cracker follows a specific sequence of steps or provides specific input to a program, the program becomes confused and tries to use computer memory inappropriately. The buffer, or memory space, reserved for a part of the program overflows. The result can be corruption of system data, a crashed server, or even direct root access.

bus topology — A network topology design in which computers are connected to a single length of cable.

busybox — A utility that performs simplified versions of more than 60 standard system maintenance programs such as `ls` and `ps`.

C News — A Linux news server program designed for small networks with low newsgroup volume.

cable modem — A device that supports high-speed networking through a cable television connection with the cable TV company acting as the ISP.

caching name server — A DNS server that contains no preconfigured information on domains (except localhost), but simply queries other DNS servers and caches the results.

caching proxy server — A proxy server that saves a copy of each Web document before passing it back to the client that originally requested it.

capability — A task that the Linux kernel will permit a program to perform, such as the ability to send broadcast packets onto the network and the ability to use the `reboot` command.

CERT Coordination Center (CERT/CC) — A federally funded software engineering institute that focuses its attention on computer security issues and provides information to security and system administration professionals around the world; operated by Carnegie-Mellon University.

certificate — A numeric code used to identify an organization.

certificate authority (CA) — An organization that issues a certificate to another person or organization after verifying the credentials of the person or organization.

chain — A list of rules that controls how packets are routed or handled in the Linux kernel.

Challenge Handshake Authentication Protocol (CHAP) — A security method used by PPP. CHAP maintains username and password data locally but never sends it to the remote computer.

chargen — A network testing service provided by `inetd` on port 19. Whenever queried, `chargen` responds with a stream of characters (the standard character set, in numeric order).

chattr — A utility used to change the attributes of a file.

checksum — A computed value that helps to verify that a file or transmission has not been corrupted.

chkrootkit — A software package that checks for evidence of over 30 different rootkits. This package works much like a virus checker, though it can only report the presence of a rootkit, it cannot eliminate one from your system.

cipher — A cryptographic technique or rule that converts plaintext into ciphertext.

ciphertext — A message that has been encoded using a cipher so that it is no longer readable. The end result of encrypting plaintext.

class — A definition for a type of object within a directory service database such as LDAP. The class defines the attributes that an object consists of as well as its place within a directory service tree.

classes of users — The practice of defining groups of potential FTP clients within an FTP server configuration to aid efficient server configuration.

Classless Inter-Domain Routing (CIDR) format — A method of indicating the network prefix length of an IP address by writing it with a slash following the address, e.g. 192.168.14.45/24.

client — A computer or software program that requests information or service from a server and then processes or acts on the information it receives.

client-server — A model of computing in which information is shared between networked systems by multiple clients requesting information from a server.

CNAME record — A line (record) in a DNS zone information file that defines the canonical name for a given hostname. In effect, this record creates an alias for a hostname, allowing it to be referenced by multiple names that are resolved to the same IP address.

coaxial cable (coax) — A network transmission media (a cable) made up of a single thick copper wire encased in thick plastic and foil layers of insulation. Coax is used mostly for video signals, though many people now have Internet access available via a cable modem using coax cable.

collision — When two or more Ethernet packets attempt to use an Ethernet cable at the same time.

co-locating — When an organization places a Web server at the office of its ISP, often relying on the ISP's security measures to protect the organization's Web server.

Common Internet File System (CIFS) — The latest extended version of the SMB protocol, used by recent Microsoft operating systems and provided in Linux via the Samba suite.

common name — The name assigned to a leaf object in a directory service database such as LDAP.

compact news file system (cnfs) — A method of storing newsgroup postings within INN using a single file as a buffer for holding multiple individual postings.

computer crime — Unauthorized access to a computer system.

connectionless — A protocol that sends packets without regard to whether they are correctly received by the destination computer. IP and UDP are examples. *See also* stateless.

connection-oriented — A protocol that keeps track of which packets have been correctly received by the destination computer, resending those that are not received, managing the flow of packets, and reporting errors. *See also* stateful.

console — The SNMP program that collects and analyzes data from SNMP agents on a network.

container — A special type of Apache configuration directive that activates other directives only if a condition is met or only within a particular context.

container object — Within a directory service database such as LDAP, an object that can have one or more subordinate objects "below it" in the data structure. *See also* leaf object.

control_flag — An element of a PAM module configuration that determines how PAM will process multiple modules in a single stack (e.g., the auth stack).

cookie — A token, or long number, used as an identifier by a program such as a Web browser or the xauth X Window System security program.

cost — A measure of how efficient a network route is. The route with the lowest cost should always be chosen, other things being equal.

cracker — A person who breaks the law or ethical rules by accessing computer systems without authorization; called by some a hacker. Some crackers have malicious intentions, others only want to test their skills by exploring areas that they are not authorized to enter.

Cryptographic File System (CFS) — A filesystem driver supported by Linux that adds cryptographic features to an NFS-like filesharing model.

Cryptographic IP Encapsulation (CIPE) — An IP packet encryption protocol. It lacks some features of IPsec but is already fully implemented (while IPsec is not). CIPE operates by tunneling IP packets within encrypted UDP packets.

cryptography — The science of encoding—and trying to decode—data that has been rendered unreadable using special knowledge or tools.

Data Encryption Standard (DES) — The first widely accepted standard for encryption, developed in the 1970s by IBM and the National Institute of Standards and Technology.

datagram — A network packet sent over a connectionless protocol such as UDP.

daytime — A network testing service provided by inetd on port 13. Returns the current date and time in human-readable form.

deface — To alter the text or images on a Web home page.

default gateway — *See* default router.

default route — An IP address configured on a host computer that identifies the computer to which packets should be sent when their network is not known to the host.

default router — The router to which a packet is sent if a host has no idea where else to send it. Also called the *default gateway*.

Denial-of-Service (DoS) attack — A cracker activity that ties up the attacked server or a particular program with so much bogus network traffic that it cannot respond to valid requests.

device driver — Software installed in the Linux kernel that knows how to communicate with a physical or logical device. A logical networking device is used to create a communications channel that any program can use for networking.

Device File System (DevFS) — A system for handling all devices in Linux kernels beginning with version 2.4. This system is a good example of what has always been done with networking devices.

dhclient — One of the most widely used Linux DHCP client daemons.

dhcpcd — One of the most widely used Linux DHCP client daemons.

dhcpd — The most widely used Linux DHCP server daemon.

diald — A program that manages PPP dial-up connections, initiating a connection only when needed by network traffic and disconnecting when the connection is no longer needed.

dig — A utility used to query specific DNS servers for specific resource records.

digital signature — A part of an electronic transaction that gives the transaction the same legally binding effect as a document signed with an ink pen.

Digital Signature Algorithm (DSA) — A popular algorithm used to sign encrypted files to verify their origin.

Digital Subscriber Line (DSL) — A newer digital telephone service that can be added to existing telephone lines in some areas, used for relatively fast Internet connections.

directory service — A database of information about network resources (or other resources) that can be accessed by people throughout a network.

discard — A network testing service provided by `inetd` on port 9. `discard` acts like `/dev/null`. Anything sent to the service is discarded without any processing.

DISPLAY — An environment variable that controls the display of graphical programs in X.

distinguished name (DN) — The complete path to an object within the directory tree, traversing (and naming) all the container objects above that object.

Distributed Denial-of-Service (DDoS) — A special type of denial of service attack in which a cracker infiltrates many systems and installs a program that will execute a DoS attack on an assigned target at the cracker's command.

dmesg — A utility that prints the contents of the kernel ring buffer to standard output (by default the screen). Using `dmesg` right after booting Linux is a good way to see all the hardware-related messages generated by the kernel.

DNS spoofing — Pretending that a request comes from a different host than its true originating host.

domain — A collection of computers, usually on the same network, that can be accessed using a common name.

domain name — A name applied to multiple hosts on the Internet that are referred to collectively, such as *ibm.com* or *utah.edu*.

Domain Name Server or Domain Name Service (DNS) — The software or the computer running the software that provides a name service for network-connected computers. In Linux, a DNS server runs BIND.

dotted-quad notation — A method of writing IP addresses as four numbers separated by periods.

dumb terminal — *See* terminal.

Dynamic Host Configuration Protocol (DHCP) — A protocol that allows a server to hand out IP addresses automatically to clients on a network.

dynamic routing — Collecting and updating routing table information automatically using a routing protocol.

echo — A network testing service provided by `inetd` on port 7. `echo` parrots back whatever it receives.

El Gamal — A symmetric cipher used by GPG.

elm — A powerful text-based email client (MUA) for reading locally stored email folders.

encryption — The process of converting plaintext to ciphertext using a cipher algorithm.

eth0 — The device name in Linux for the first Ethernet card installed in a host.

Ethereal — A powerful graphical network traffic analysis tool.

Ethernet — An international networking standard developed in the 1970s by Xerox, Intel, and Digital Equipment Corporation (now part of Compaq Computer Corp.).

execute (x) — A standard Linux file permission—represented in utilities by **x**—that permits execution of a file as a program or changing the name of a file within a directory (when assigned to that directory).

exportfs — A command used to activate the contents of `/etc/exports`.

exports — The /etc/exports configuration file defining file systems that NFS can make available to other hosts.

exterior routing protocols — Routing protocols designed for routing packets between networks controlled by different organizations; packets are routed based on administrative policies, often controlled by how much a particular organization's routing information is trusted.

Federal Information Processing Standard (FIPS) — A standard for information processing (such as an encryption algorithm) that has been approved for use by government agencies.

fetchmail — A basic POP3 client for Linux.

Fiber Distributed Data Interface (FDDI) — A networking technology that uses fiber-optic cable in a dual ring topology. It is highly reliable, but not installed much now because it is slower and more expensive than newer Ethernet technologies.

fiber optic — A network transmission media (a cable) made of glass or plastic to transmit light signals; it is capable of extremely fast transmission speeds, immune from electromagnetic interference, and highly secure. It is also very expensive to install.

File Transfer Protocol (FTP) — A protocol used to share files between networked computer systems.

finger — A program that provides brief information about a user.

fingerprint — A small number that is derived from a larger number (such as a public key) using a hash. The fingerprint provides a convenient test as to the integrity of the larger number.

fingerprinting — Using the results of a port scan to identify the operating system of a targeted host.

firewall — A program that filters (blocks) IP packets based on their characteristics, according to a set of rules.

firewall-config — A graphical program used to configure IP Chains and IP Tables-based firewalls.

fixed wireless — A wireless network communication technology that relies on small transceivers mounted on buildings; it is normally used to connect multiple offices in the same city.

flags — Numeric status indications stored within a packet header that are used to establish and track information about the network communication of which the packet is a part.

forward — To send a packet onto a different network than the one where it originated.

forward lookup — Using DNS to convert a domain name to an IP address.

forwarding name server — A DNS server that forwards all queries to another name server for processing.

fragmentation — The process of breaking up an IP packet into multiple smaller packets for transmission on a different type of network.

frame relay — A technology used to provide dedicated high-speed Internet connectivity via telephone wires.

ftp — The most common text-based client program for accessing FTP servers.

ftpaccess — The main FTP server configuration file.

ftpshut — A command that causes the FTP server to stop allowing connections.

ftpusers — An FTP server configuration file listing user accounts that are not allowed to log in via FTP.

fully qualified domain name (FQDN) — The complete or official name of a network host including the name of the domain of which the host is a part. More casually, a domain name.

gated — The Linux program that implements OSPF, BGP, and RIP v 2 (with classless addressing).

gateway — Generally, a router that can forward packets to other network segments. Also, the default router that acts as a "gateway" or exit point to reach networks outside of a local segment. Also, more technically, a system that can translate between protocols at the Transport and Application layers of a network.

Gb/s — Gigabits per second. 1 Gb/s is 1,024 Mb/s or roughly a billion bits per second.

getty — A program (and also a type of program) that monitors terminals for activity and processes it, generally to allow a user to log in.

gFTP — A graphical FTP client. Installed by default on many Linux systems.

Gigabit Ethernet — An Ethernet networking technology that can transmit data at either 1 Gb/s or 10 Gb/s.

Global Information Assurance Certification (GIAC) — A hands-on security certification program run by the SANS Institute.

Gnu Privacy Guard (GPG) — A command-line public-key encryption utility that is compatible with PGP in many respects.

grpck — A utility that verifies that all group memberships are valid user accounts and that no errors of syntax exist in the `/etc/group` file.

guest users — Users logging in to an FTP server who have a regular Linux user account, but are restricted in what they can do while logged in using FTP.

hacker — A highly skilled technology expert who enjoys learning about the intricate workings of computer systems and software. To some people's understanding, a technology expert who maliciously attacks others' computer systems. *See also* cracker.

hard mount — A method of mounting an NFS file system that causes NFS to wait indefinitely for the NFS server to respond.

harden — To make a computer system more secure against cracker attacks.

hardware address — *See* Media Access Control (MAC) address.

hash — The result of a mathematical function that converts a large number into a smaller number in a predictable way.

header — Highly structured information within a packet that defines how the network stacks should handle the packet.

header checksum — A numeric code within an IP packet header used to ensure the integrity of the header information.

hook — A programming term that refers to the ability to connect another program or list of commands at a certain point of program execution.

hop — A pass through a router.

host — A utility used to query specific DNS servers for specific resource records.

host — *See* node.

host ID — The part of an IP address that designates the host to which the address refers within a certain network.

hostname – The name assigned to a host on a network.

https — A code within a Web page URL that indicates that the page was transmitted over an encrypted connection.

hub — A device used as a wiring center that allows cables from multiple computers to be concentrated into a single network connection.

IDEA — A patented symmetric cipher.

ifcfg-eth0 — A file, usually located in `/etc/sysconfig/network-scripts/`, that contains information to configure the first Ethernet interface.

ifconfig — The interface configuration utility that configures a networking interface within the Linux kernel or that lists all currently configured network interfaces.

ifdown — Script used to shut down individual networking interfaces. Generally used by other scripts such as `/etc/rc.d/init.d/network` rather than directly by a user.

ifup — Script used to start individual networking interfaces. Generally used by other scripts such as `/etc/rc.d/init.d/network` rather than directly by a user.

IglooFTP — A popular graphical FTP client.

in.fingerd — The Linux daemon that implements the finger protocol (using port 79).

inetd — The most widely used superserver program. *See also* `xinetd`.

init — The master control program that the Linux kernel starts right after the system is started.

INN — The most widely used news server software for Linux. Implemented by the `innd` daemon.

insmod — Command used to install a module into a running Linux kernel. It may include parameters that provide additional information to the module being installed.

Integrated Services Digital Network (ISDN) — A type of telephone service that provides digital signals for higher-speed network connectivity than standard modems.

interior routing protocols — Routing protocols designed for routing packets among networks controlled by a single organization; packets are routed based on mathematical models.

Internet — A collection of many networks around the world that are linked together via high-speed networking connections.

Internet Control Message Protocol (ICMP) — A protocol used by IP to transmit control and error data about IP traffic on a network. Most widely known as the basis of the `ping` utility, which uses ICMP Echo and Echo-request commands.

Internet Mail Access Protocol (IMAP) — A protocol used to interact with a user's email messages that are stored on a remote server, as with many popular Web portals that allow email access via a Web browser.

Internet model — A conceptual model of networking that divides protocols into four layers based on their function. This is the model used by Linux.

Internet Protocol (IP) — The foundation protocol for transporting data across most Linux networks as well as the Internet.

Internetwork Packet Exchange (IPX) — A protocol designed by Novell, Inc., based on an older protocol called the Xerox Network System (XNS) protocol. IPX was the dominant protocol on local area networks for many years and is fully supported in Linux. It uses the network hardware address as a host ID, thus simplifying network configuration.

intranet — A network within an organization that uses Internet standards as the basis for sharing information, usually via Web browsers.

intrusion detection — The process of noticing when someone is trying to break into a system or that they have already broken in.

intrusion detection systems (IDS) — A type of software that aids network intrusion detection.

Inverse ARP (InARP) — A method of using ARP that allows one host to obtain the IP address of another host when it knows the physical address.

IP address class — A grouping of IP addresses. Classes A, B, and C are commonly referred to, each defining a set of networks with a specific maximum number of hosts.

IP addressing — A numbering scheme that allows each computer in the world that wants to use the Internet (or just IP) to have a unique ID number.

IP aliasing — A networking feature that allows a single physical interface to have more than one IP address assigned to it.

IP Chains — The Linux firewalling architecture previous to kernel version 2.4; still supported in 2.4 kernels using a compatibility mode.

IP forwarding — A feature of Linux networking that instructs the Linux kernel to send network packets out on whichever network interface the routing tables dictate. Without IP forwarding, packets arriving on a given network interface can only be sent out on the same interface.

IP masquerading — A type of network address translation in which packets from many computers on a LAN are altered to appear as if they came from a single computer.

IP spoofing — A cracker attack in which special low-level software puts any address the cracker selects as either the source or the destination address on an IP packet.

IP Tables — The lists of rules associated with one of the programming hooks provided in the networking stacks by the NetFilter architecture.

ipchains — The command used to manage rules within the IP Chains firewall architecture.

ipfwadm — A firewall configuration utility in versions of the Linux kernel previous to 2.0.

IPsec — An industry standard for IP packet encryption. IPsec is supported in Linux, but as a standard, is still not completely settled.

IPTraf — A popular "packet sniffer" program for viewing network activity on a LAN.

IPv6 — The new version of IP that uses 128 bits for addresses instead of 32 bits, and adds numerous other features including dynamic configuration capabilities, better security options, and more intelligent packet routing. Using IPv6 requires many changes to other protocols, as well as generally more sophistication in networking hardware and software.

Kb/s — Kilobits per second. 1 Kb/s is 1,024 bits per second.

keepalive — Maintaining an active network connection after sending a file, based on the theory that a client that has requested one file is likely to request several.

Kerberos — A special type of authentication for organizational networks.

kernel modules — Parts of the Linux kernel, such as device drivers, that can be loaded or unloaded while Linux is running using a command such as `modprobe`.

kernel ring buffer — A memory area that holds messages generated by the kernel. When the buffer is full, the oldest message is discarded each time a new message is generated.

key — A code (usually numeric) that can be used to encrypt or decrypt a message.

key pair — The combination of a public key that can be handed out to others and a private or secret key that remains hidden on a user's system (and is protected with a passphrase).

keyring — The collection of public keys stored on a system; a file containing all of the keys to which GPG has immediate access.

kfinger — A graphical version of `finger` (including `talk` protocol capability) for KDE.

Kmail — A graphical email client (MUA) provided as part of the KDE graphical environment.

Knode — A newsreader for KDE.

KPPP — A utility within KDE that allows users to connect to an ISP graphically using PPP.

last mile connection — The connection between a LAN within a home or office and the Internet or other high-speed network.

leaf object — Within a directory service database such as LDAP, an object that cannot have subordinate objects "below it" in the data structure. *See also* container object.

LeafNode — A Linux news server program designed for small networks with low newsgroup volume.

lease — The action a DHCP server takes in assigning an IP address to a client for a specific length of time.

libpcap — A programming library used for capturing network packets, required by many network traffic analysis utilities.

LIDS-Free Session (LFS) — A command-line session on a system running the LIDS IDS in which LIDS does not affect the permitted actions.

`lidsadm` — The administrative command used to control the LIDS IDS.

Lightweight Directory Access Protocol (LDAP) — A protocol for accessing the lightweight directory service.

Linux Intrusion Detection System (LIDS) — A complex and hard-to-use intrusion detection system that alters the Linux kernel to remove root's comprehensive access to a Linux system.

Linux Pluggable Authentication Module (PAM) — A security architecture designed to improve Linux user-level security, add flexibility in how user access is configured, and permit Linux to integrate smoothly with user information stored on other systems.

LinuxConf — The utility that was used in Red Hat prior to version 7.2 to configure networking. Though it is still included in Red Hat, `neat` is now more popular.

ListProc — A commercial mailing list manager (MLM). See *www.listproc.net*.

LISTSERV — The most widely used MLM in the world. A commercial product available from L-Soft (*www.lsoft.com*).

LKM — A Linux kernel module that has been installed as part of a rootkit.

`lo` — Device name of the loopback network device.

local area network (LAN) — A network within a relatively small space such as an office or a building.

local broadcast IP address — The special IP address 255.255.255.255, used to broadcast packets to all hosts on the local network segment.

localhost — The name assigned to the loopback device, corresponding to IP address 127.0.0.1. Often used interchangeably with the term *loopback device*.

logcheck — A utility package that checks log files each hour for any suspicious entries.

`logrotate` — A command to automate the process of compressing, rotating, and archiving log files so that the logs never grow unreasonably large, and older log data can be stored in another location—such as on a writeable CD or backup tape—instead of taking up hard disk space.

LogSentry — The commercial version of the logcheck utility, owned by Psionic Technologies.

`lokkit` — A text-mode program that sets up basic firewall rules according to the level of security protection desired.

loopback address — Any IP address beginning with 127 (127.0.0.1 is normally used). This address is used only within a computer for testing the network stacks. No packet with a 127 address is ever sent out of the local computer.

loopback device — A special "logical" network device used to move packets within a single host. The IP address of the loopback device is 127.0.0.1. Often used interchangeably with the term *localhost*.

`lpd` — The standard Linux print server.

`lsattr` — A utility that lists all the attributes of a file.

`lsmod` — Command used to list the modules that are loaded in your kernel at that moment.

Lynx — A text-based Web browser.

`m4` — A program that converts a text file containing configuration parameters into a complete `sendmail.cf` file.

`mail` — A very basic text-mode email client (MUA) for Linux.

Mail Delivery Agent (MDA) — A program that places email in a user's mailbox so that it can be read. This function is often subsumed by an MTA.

Mail Transfer Agent (MTA) — A program that moves email messages from one server on the Internet to another. Also called an email server.

Mail User Agent (MUA) — A program that displays and manages email messages for a user.

mailing list — A group of users who share information on an ongoing basis via email using special management software.

mailing list manager (MLM) — A software package used to create and manage mailing lists, including collections of user information and the messages those users send.

majordomo — One of the most widely used MLM packages. A free software package consisting of Perl scripts that interact with the `sendmail` email server.

mangling — The ability to alter nearly any aspect of a packet based on any feature of that packet. A feature of NetFilter in Linux 2.4 kernels.

man-in-the-middle attack — A general term for any security attack in which a cracker intercepts communication, reads or alters it, and leads the sender to believe that the information was received by the intended recipient.

map — To create a correspondence between a user ID on an NFS client and user permissions on an NFS server.

mars-nwe — Martin Stovers NetWare Emulator package; software for Linux that provides NetWare server capabilities.

master DNS server — The authoritative name server for a zone, typically containing database files that provide IP addresses for hosts within that zone.

Maximum Transfer Unit (MTU) — The maximum size for a packet on a given type of network.

Mb/s — Megabits per second. 1 Mb/s is 1,024 Kb/s or roughly one million bits per second.

Media Access Control (MAC) address — A unique address assigned to (and programmed into) each Ethernet card in the world.

mesg — A utility that enables or disables other users' ability to send a message to your screen using the `write`, `talk`, or `wall` (write all) commands.

message digest hash (MD5) — A hash that converts a number of any length (including a large computer file) to a 128-bit (32-hexadecimal-digit) number called a checksum.

metaserver — *See* superserver.

metric — A value assigned to a network interface to guide dynamic routing decisions about when to use that interface. A higher metric means an interface is less likely to be used if other interfaces are also available.

mgetty — A version of `getty` adapted to use with modems.

mingetty — A minimalist version of `getty`.

minicom — A terminal emulator program used to connect to a remote computer using a modem.

MIT Magic Cookie — The name given to a cookie used by the `xauth` program for X display authentication.

modprobe — The command to load a kernel module while automatically checking for and loading dependent modules.

module_type — A characterization of program activity that determines which set of PAM modules will be used to authorize that activity. Possible `module_types` include `auth`, `account`, `session`, and `password`.

Mozilla — A very popular graphical Linux Web browser that began as an open source version of Netscape Navigator.

multicasting — An IP addressing system in which one computer can address a packet to multiple specific hosts.

multistation access unit (MAU) — A device that acts like a switch or intelligent hub for a token-ring network, passing the token between computers to facilitate network traffic.

MX record — A line (record) in a DNS zone information file that defines the mail exchanger for the named host. MX records are used by mail transfer agents (MTAs) to find the correct email server to contact when delivering email to a recipient.

name resolution — The process of converting a domain name into a corresponding IP address.

name server — A computer running name service software that can translate from IP addresses to names and vice versa.

name service — An Application-layer software program that lets a computer provide a name and receive back an IP address, or provide an IP address and receive back a name.

named — The Linux program that implements the DNS protocol to create a DNS server; part of the BIND collection of programs.

National Infrastructure Protection Center (NIPC) — A clearinghouse for security information, reports, analysis, and legal data related to these topics. Run by the U.S. government; staffed by the FBI.

ncftp — A text-based FTP client program similar to ftp, but newer and more refined.

ncpfs — A Linux software package that implements NCP and provides a number of NetWare client utilities.

neat — The command-line invocation of the Red Hat Network Administration Tool.

Netatalk — A software package for Linux that allows Macintosh computers to recognize Linux (have it show up on the Mac desktop as an available shared resource).

NetBEUI — A protocol within Windows-based computers that implements NetBIOS functionality.

NetBIOS — A protocol that provides a network name resolution service, similar in concept to DNS. Used by Windows operating systems and provided as part of the Samba suite.

NetFilter — The packet filtering and advanced routing architecture in Linux 2.4 kernels.

NetPerf — A benchmarking package that analyzes networking performance.

NetWare — A network operating system by Novell, an early market leader and still renowned for excellent file and print sharing services.

NetWare Core Protocol (NCP) — A transport protocol used by NetWare for file and print sharing.

network address mask — A series of numbers that looks like an IP address but contains 1s for the network ID portion of the address and zeros for the host ID portion of the address. A network address mask is basically a subnet mask used for classless IP addressing.

network address translation (NAT) — A routing technique in which the addresses or other header information in a packet is altered during routing.

Network File System (NFS) — A protocol used to share file systems on a network.

network ID — The part of an IP address that designates the network to which the address refers.

Network Information System (NIS) — A protocol that lets hosts share configuration information across a network, so that only one master configuration file need be supported for a number of hosts. *See also* NIS+.

network interface card (NIC) — A hardware device used to connect a computer to a network.

Network News Transport Protocol (NNTP) — The protocol used to transport newsgroup messages (postings).

Network Time Protocol (NTP) — A time management and synchronization protocol used by Linux. Implemented by the ntpd daemon.

network traffic analysis — See *packet sniffing*.

nfsd — A daemon that handles file transfers for a mounted NFS file system, based on the settings that the rpc.mountd daemon has validated.

NIS+ — A more advanced version of the NIS protocol. *See* NIS.

nmap — The most widely used port-scanning utility.

nmapfe — A utility that acts as a graphical front-end to the nmap command; requires the Gnome desktop.

nmbd — The daemon within the Samba suite that provides NetBIOS capability to Linux.

node — (1) A data element within a directory service database such as LDAP. Also called an object. (2) A device on the network, such as a workstation, server, or printer.

Novell Directory Service (NDS) — A network resource directory supported by later versions of NetWare but not by NetWare-related Linux tools.

NS record — A line (a record) within a DNS zone information file that defines the authoritative name server for the given domain.

nslookup — A utility used to query DNS servers for resource records.

nsupdate — A utility used to update zone information files dynamically at the command line.

ntpd — The Linux daemon that implements the NTP protocol. *See also* **xntpd**.

null scan — A method of port scanning in which a TCP packet is sent with no flags set.

nutcracker — One of many password-cracking tools.

nwserv.conf — A configuration file used to set up the **mars-nwe** NetWare emulator.

objdump — A command that displays the contents of a file byte by byte.

object — A data element within a directory service database such as LDAP. Also called a node.

one-time pad — An encryption method in which a message is converted to numbers, then random numbers taken from a list are added to each part of the message. The recipient must have the same list of random numbers to decrypt the message. Assuming no one else has the list of random numbers, the encrypted message is considered unbreakable.

One-time Password In Everything (OPIE) — A single-user password system available for Linux. OPIE was created by the U.S. Naval Research Laboratory based on the S/Key program.

Open Shortest Path First (OSPF) — A protocol that automatically fills routing tables with information about how to reach networks.

Open Systems Interconnect (OSI) model — A reference model that divides networking into seven conceptual layers, each assigned a specific task. The OSI model is the basis for much of modern networking theory and system design.

OpenLDAP — The most widely used LDAP server on Linux systems.

OpenSSH — A free version of SSH included in most Linux distributions.

opt-in — A marketing scheme in which a user does not receive advertisements unless he or she specifically requests to be added to a list of recipients.

opt-out — A marketing scheme in which a user automatically receives advertisements unless he or she asks to be removed from a list of recipients.

packet — A small collection of data with identifying information (headers) that is destined for or coming from a network.

packet sniffing — A network activity in which the headers and payload of all packets on the network are captured and examined (also called network traffic analysis).

Pan — A newsreader for Gnome.

Parallel Line Internet Protocol (PLIP) — A protocol that relies on a parallel port to transmit network data, often to connect two computers in a simple, inexpensive network.

parameters — Command-line information provided when loading a kernel module to help the module locate and recognize the hardware it is designed to work with.

passphrase — A long password.

passwd — Utility used to change passwords or set password control options that are stored in /etc/shadow (such as a maximum use period for each password).

Password Authentication Protocol (PAP) — A security method used with PPP. PAP stores pairs of usernames and passwords in a local file and transmits them over the Internet for review by an ISP.

password cracking — A cracker activity by which the cracker obtains the password for a valid user account, either by using a program that examines millions of passwords until the correct one is found, or by guessing based on personal knowledge about the user.

payload — The data that a network packet is transferring. Packets are divided into a header and payload.

peer-to-peer networking — A model of networking in which all computers on the network are *peers* and have the ability to initiate communications, respond to requests for information, and interact with users independent of other computer systems.

pine — A powerful text-based email client (MUA) for reading locally stored email folders.

ping — An administrative utility that uses the Echo and Echo Reply message types within ICMP to test whether a host is reachable and alive (listening to network traffic).

Ping scan — A method of port scanning in which any hosts that are reachable using ICMP echo packets (which are used to "ping" a host) are reported.

plaintext — A readable message.

plug-ins — Programming modules that add functionality to a Web browser, typically the ability to process multimedia formats.

Point-to-Point Protocol (PPP) — A protocol that allows a host to tie directly to a single computer, making a network of two systems. PPP is used most often with a modem providing the underlying physical connection to the second computer.

Point-to-Point-Tunneling-Protocol (PPTP) — A standard created by Microsoft for setting up a virtual private network (VPN). PPTP uses two connections, one for control information and one for data.

poison cache attack — A cracker attack in which a cracker attempts to block access to a site by uploading erroneous information to a DNS server's cache.

port — A number that is associated with a network-capable application.

port forwarding — A routing technique within SSH that can encrypt many other protocols over an SSH connection by connecting another service's port to the SSH port.

port scanning — A network activity in which packets sent to a host are analyzed to learn about that host.

portmap — The program that watches for rpc requests (such as from NFS daemons) and creates the network connections to make them function.

PortSentry — A program that watches network ports for packets that appear to be port scans, then takes action based on a configuration file.

Post Office Protocol version 3 (POP3) — A protocol used to download a single user's email messages that are stored on a remote email server.

Pretty Good Privacy (PGP) — The first utility to provide public-key encryption to all comers. Created by Phil Zimmermann.

primary master server — *See* master DNS server.

primary server — *See* master DNS server.

prime number — A number that cannot be broken down into factors other than itself and 1. Prime numbers are the core mathematical feature of public-key encryption.

printtool — The graphical print configuration tool provided in Red Hat Linux.

privacy policy — A voluntary statement by an organization about how it will and will not use data that it collects about users or customers, often via a Web site.

private-key encryption — Encryption using a symmetric algorithm.

Procmail — A special MDA (Mail Delivery Agent) that filters email messages.

promiscuous mode — A mode of operation for NICs in which any packets that are visible to the NIC are captured and processed, not only those that are addressed to the NIC.

protocol — A formalized system of rules for communication.

protocol stack — The software for maintaining a network protocol. A stack may refer to a single protocol capability or to the collection of protocols supported by a host or server.

proxy ARP — The feature of ARP that allows a host to respond to a request for *another* host's hardware address. Normally, a host only responds to an ARP request if its own information is being requested.

proxy server — Software that intercepts requests from Web clients and forwards them as if they came from the proxy server rather than the original client. When a response is received, the proxy server returns it to the client.

pseudo-terminal — A command-line window acting as a terminal in letting a user interact with a host's resources. These are referred to within Linux as `pty` devices.

PTR record — A line (record) in a DNS zone information file that refers to the hostname to which an IP address is assigned; used for reverse DNS lookups.

public-key encryption — Encryption using an asymmetric encryption algorithm.

pump — One of the most widely used Linux DHCP client daemons.

Quality of Service (QoS) — A networking feature that guarantees bandwidth to certain users or certain programs.

randomization — A method of performing a port scan in which multiple ports are contacted in random order to reduce suspicion.

RC2 — A symmetric cipher.

RC4 — A symmetric cipher.

rcp — A utility that allows a user to copy files between two hosts. Either or both of the hosts can be remote to the host on which `rcp` is executed.

read (r) — A standard Linux file permission (represented in utilities by `r`) that permits reading the contents of a file or listing the files in a directory.

real users — Users logging in to an FTP server who have a regular Linux user account.

realm — Within a Kerberos-enabled network, all the users and services whose keys are stored on the Kerberos server.

Realtime Blackhole List — A list of IP addresses that are known principally as sources of spam and whose messages can be blocked automatically by mail servers such as `sendmail`.

recipe — A formula used by Procmail to filter or examine an email message and take an action if it matches the given criteria.

Red Hat Network Administration Tool — A graphical interface provided in Red Hat Linux that is used to manage hardware devices (the kernel modules used to access them), including parameters needed for each device, plus the network addresses associated with them. It can be started from the command line using `neat`.

relaying — An email server delivering a message that didn't originate on the same host where the email server is running.

remote procedure call (rpc) — A protocol used to allow programs to communicate over a network. rpc acts almost as a superserver, watching for network requests from rpc-capable programs and transferring them to the appropriate transport protocol (such as TCP or UDP).

Request For Comments (RFC) — A document describing a protocol or other technical advance, written by a technical expert and posted on the Internet for review. It then becomes the accepted definition for the protocol or standard it describes.

resolver — The client portion of DNS, which makes requests to a DNS server so that other programs on a host can use the IP address of a named server to make a network connection.

resolving — The process of converting a domain name to an IP address, or vice versa.

resource record — Information about a host that a DNS server can provide to answer queries. Example resource records include the A record to associate an IP address and hostname, the MX record to define a host's mail exchanger, and the PTR record to associate a hostname with an IP address for reverse DNS lookups.

Reverse ARP (RARP) — A method of using ARP that allows a host (generally one that has no local storage, such as a diskless workstation) to retrieve its IP address by sending out its own network hardware address.

reverse DNS — A method of using DNS in which a client sends an IP address to a DNS server and requests the corresponding domain name.

reverse lookup — *See* reverse DNS.

ring topology — A network topology design in which multiple computers are linked into a circular shape.

rlogin — A utility that allows a user to log in to another host, much like the telnet command.

rndc — A control program used to manage the `named` daemon.

root name servers — DNS servers designated as a starting point for DNS queries.

rootkit — A collection of programs and scripts designed to permit a cracker continued access to a compromised system, even after the original security hole that permitted access has been discovered and closed.

route — A command that displays or configures the routing table within the Linux kernel.

routed — The Linux program that implements the Routing Information Protocol (RIP).

router — A device that connects multiple network segments, translating data formats as needed by forwarding packets between segments; also the software program on a computer used for this purpose.

routing algorithm — Software that determines how to process a packet that is sent to the router for forwarding; also called a *routing engine*.

routing daemon — A program that automatically generates routing table entries based on information received over the network via protocols dedicated to routing.

routing engine — *See* routing algorithm.

Routing Information Protocol (RIP) — A protocol that automatically fills routing tables with information about how to reach networks.

routing table — A listing within a router containing network IDs, the network interface by which packets can reach that network, and the IP address of the next router to which the packet should be sent.

rp3 — (for Red Hat PPP) A utility in Red Hat Linux that graphically presents dial-up accounts to permit easy connections using PPP.

rp3-config — A graphical configuration tool in Red Hat Linux that allows users to easily set up dial-up accounts. Typically used together with `rp3`.

rpc.mountd — A daemon used as part of NFS to make new connections, mounting a remote file system after checking relevant permissions to see if the mount is permitted.

RSA — The most widely-known algorithm for public-key encryption. Developed by Ronald Rivest, Adi Shamir, and Len Adleman.

rsh — A utility that allows a user to execute a command on a remote host without logging in to that host.

rule — A configuration setting that defines characteristics of an IP packet and an action to take for any packet that has those characteristics

r-utilities — (for "remote utilities") Programs that allow a user to access remote hosts to run programs, transfer files, or perform other functions within a trusted network.

Samba — A suite of programs for Linux and many UNIX operating systems that permits these systems to support Windows protocols such as SMB, CIFS, and NetBIOS.

Samhain — A file integrity checker that runs as a daemon and supports client/server configurations.

`saucer` — Client software for Linux that is used to browse an LDAP directory service tree.

schema — The collection of all the possible object classes and their attributes that a directory service supports.

screen locking program — A program that disables input from your keyboard and usually clears or hides the screen so that any private information is not visible to passersby.

screen number — A number used as part of the `DISPLAY` environment variable for remotely running graphical programs. Most systems have only a single X Window System session, referred to as screen number 0. The screen number is the second zero (the first is the sequence number) in the standard format `:0.0`.

script-kiddies — Unskilled crackers who use prepackaged software "kits" or scripts created by skilled crackers to break into systems that have not taken basic security precautions.

secondary server — *See* slave DNS server.

secondary slave server — *See* slave DNS server.

Secure Hash Algorithm (SHA-1) — A hashing algorithm, more secure than MD5, that creates a 160-bit hash of any file or key to help check whether it was tampered with or otherwise corrupted during transmission.

Secure Shell (SSH) — A protocol that provides network connectivity equivalent to an encrypted version of Telnet, plus additional support to allow encryption of other protocols.

Secure Socket Layer (SSL) — A protocol that allows a Web server to communicate securely with a browser for e-commerce or similar applications.

Security Administrator Tool for Analyzing Networks (SATAN) — One of the first widely known security-auditing programs.

Security Administrator's Integrated Network Tool (SAINT) — A popular security-auditing program that superceded the SATAN program.

security audit — A review or test of how secure a system really is and what needs to be done to improve its security.

segment — A part of a network whose traffic has been isolated from other parts of the network to improve the efficiency of the network as a whole. Each segment's network traffic is only "seen" within that segment unless it is destined for a host outside the segment.

sequence number — The sequential number of the screen on which a graphical program is displayed. Used as part of the `DISPLAY` environment variable for remotely running graphical programs. Its value is zero (indicated by :0) except on multimonitor systems.

Serial Line Internet Protocol (SLIP) — A protocol that relies on a serial port as the underlying physical connection used to transmit network data, usually over a modem to an ISP.

server — A computer or software program that provides information or services of some type to clients.

Server Message Block (SMB) — The transport protocol used for file and print sharing by Windows systems and the Samba suite.

server-parsed documents — *See* server-side-includes.

server-side-includes — Statements within a text file that are processed on the fly by a Web server when that document is requested.

Service Advertising Protocol (SAP) — A protocol used on IPX networks to distribute information about what network services are available on each server within a network.

session — A connection between two hosts, where the destination host is expecting a stream of packets from the source host.

Set UID bit — A special file permission that causes executable files (programs) to use the permissions of the user who owns the file rather than those of the user who executed the file. Also called SUID.

share — A Windows resource for shared use over a network.

shelling out — Starting a command shell from within another program, effectively suspending the first program to execute the shell.

shielded twisted pair (STP) — A type of network transmission media (a cable) made up of several pairs of wires encased in foil-wrapped insulation to block interference by electromagnetic radiation.

sign — To attach your private key to a file to show that the file could only have come from you. Also, to attach your private key to another person's public key to indicate that you trust the validity of that public key.

Simple Mail Transport Protocol (SMTP) — The protocol by which email is transferred on the Internet.

Simple Network Management Protocol (SNMP) — A protocol designed to provide feedback about how the components of a network are functioning.

S/Key — A specialized single-use password system designed by Bell Communications Research.

Skipjack — A government-approved encryption algorithm that uses an 80-bit key.

slave DNS server — A backup to a master DNS server, containing the same database files as the master DNS server.

SmartList — A free mailing list manager that works in conjunction with `procmail` and `sendmail`.

smbclient — A utility that provides client access to Windows-based hosts or to Samba servers. Part of the Samba suite.

smbd — The daemon within the Samba suite that provides SMB capability to Linux.

smbfs — The file system type designation used to mount a Windows share as part of a Linux file system using the `mount` command.

smbprint — A command within the Samba suite that enables printing to a Windows printer over the network.

sniff — To tap into a network connection to read the packets that other users have sent.

sniffer — A software package used to sniff the network.

SOA record — The first line (record) in a DNS zone information file. Defines the Start-Of-Authority for the information in the file, describing how to use the information provided for this zone, including a serial number for updates and refresh periods for zone transfers to slave DNS servers.

social engineering — Manipulating someone to extract needed information about a computer system.

socket — A communications channel between two applications that need to communicate via a network; created using a protocol such as TCP.

soft mount — A method of mounting an NFS file system that causes NFS to give up on an operation after waiting for a specified time.

source and destination addresses — Fields within an IP packet that indicate the IP address of the computer that created the packet (the source) and the computer to which the packet is being sent (destination).

spam — Unwanted advertisements sent to a large number of email or newsgroup recipients.

spoofing — A technique used by a malicious user to act as another person when contacting a server.

squashing — A security concept used by NFS servers to prevent a user from gaining access to a file system on the NFS server simply by virtue of having the same user ID on the NFS client.

Squid — The most widely used Linux proxy server.

ssh-agent — A part of the SSH suite that helps manage key pairs and authentication among multiple SSH-capable systems.

stack — Multiple PAM modules accessed in succession to perform a security check.

standalone mode — Using a network program without support from a superserver such as `inetd`.

star topology — A network topology design in which multiple computers connect to a single center point, usually a hub or a switch.

stateful — A connection-oriented protocol; one that maintains information about the state of the network transmission so that it can adjust or correct its behavior as needed to ensure success of the overall transmission.

stateless — A connectionless protocol; one that maintains no information about the state of the ongoing transmission that allows it to track packets after each is sent.

static routing — Assembling a routing table via entries in start-up scripts or by manually entered `route` commands.

statically linked — A programming technique in which a binary program is self-contained, rather than depending on shared system components in order to function.

stealth scan — A port scan that uses unexpected TCP flag combinations, including SYN, FIN, none (Null scan), and all (X-Mas scan) flags.

stratum — A layer within the time server structure of NTP.

strings — A command that lists all text strings within any binary file.

stunnel — A program that uses SSL as a transport protocol to encrypt other network protocols such as POP3 and IMAP.

subnet mask — A set of numbers similar in appearance to an IP address that are used to denote how many bits of an IP address are part of the network ID: any bit set (1, not 0) in the subnet mask is part of the network ID; used for class-based IP addressing.

sudo — A utility that lets a system administrator assign privileges to any user account so that that user can execute just the programs that the `sudo` configuration specifies.

SUID — *See* Set UID bit.

supernet — An IP address that would be in one of the classes such as B or C, but whose network mask identifies it as having a smaller network ID (and thus potentially more hosts) than the corresponding class would have.

superserver — A program that listens on multiple network ports and starts appropriate network service daemons when a client connection arrives for that port. Also called a metaserver. The most widely used superserver program is `inetd`.

SWAT — A browser-based graphical configuration interface for setting up and managing the Samba SMB server.

Swatch — A software package that performs log oversight functions, similar to logcheck and LogSentry.

switch — A device used to connect other networking devices (such as hosts or printers) into a larger network using built-in intelligence to decide which network packets should be sent to which parts of the network.

symmetric encryption algorithm — An encryption algorithm in which the same key is used to both encrypt and decrypt a message (the algorithm is reversed for decryption). Also called private-key encryption.

SYN packet — A TCP packet sent from a port scanner that has the SYN flag set.

syslogd — The system logging daemon, which can use port 514 to communicate with syslogd on another system to provide remote logging capability.

System Administration, Networking, and Security (SANS) Institute — A prestigious and well-regarded education and research organization the members of which include most of the leading computer security experts in the country. Also called simply SANS.

T-1 — A high-speed transmission format (1.544 Mb/s) available through your local telephone company, usually for a few hundred dollars per month.

T-3 — A high-speed transmission format (45 Mb/s) available through your local telephone company, usually for several thousand dollars per month.

tail — A program to display the last 10 lines (configurable) of any text file.

talk — A program used with the **talkd** daemon to initiate and manage a real-time typed conversation with another user.

talkd — The daemon that implements the **talk** communication system.

Tb/s — Terabits per second. 1 Tb/s is 1,024 Gb/s or roughly a trillion bits per second.

TCP/IP networking model — *See* Internet model.

tcpd (TCP Wrappers) — An application-level access control (security) program that examines incoming network connections when requested by a superserver, then compares the connection details to a configuration file to determine whether the connection is allowed.

tcpdump — A command-line utility that provides detailed information about packets on a network.

telephony — Technology that lets a computer interact with a telephone in such a way that it can serve as an answering machine, call router, voice recorder, and so forth.

Telnet — A terminal emulator program that allows a user to log in to a remote computer as if sitting at that computer's keyboard.

terminal — A screen and keyboard attached to a computer, usually at a distance from the computer. Multiple terminals attached to the same computer allow multiple people to access the computer at the same time; also known as *dumb terminal*.

terminal emulation — A software program that allows a personal computer (or other intelligent device) to act like a terminal in connecting to another computer.

throughput — The amount of useful payload information that can be transmitted on a network.

ticket — A set of information provided by a Kerberos server to a user or service that grants the user permission to use the service. A ticket contains the following components: {sessionkey: username:address:servicename:lifespan:timestamp}

time — A network testing service provided by **inetd** on port 37. Returns a number corresponding to the current time in a program-readable format, which appears as unreadable characters on-screen.

Time To Live (TTL) — A counter within an IP packet header that determines how many hops (routers) a packet can pass through before being discarded as "destination unreachable."

token — An electronic code that is passed from computer to computer to identify which computer on the network has the right to send out a data packet at that moment. Used by certain types of networks such as token ring.

token ring — A popular networking technology that uses a token—an electronic number that is passed from computer to computer—to identify which computer on the network has the right to send out data at that moment.

Tom's Single Disk Linux — A software package that provides a complete set of standard utilities on a single floppy disk.

topology — A shape or ordering applied to the connections between systems on a network.

traceroute — A command used to list each router (each hop) that a packet passes through between a source host and a destination host.

Transmission Control Protocol (TCP) — A widely used connection-oriented Transport-layer protocol. TCP is the transport mechanism for many popular Internet services such as FTP, SMTP, and HTTP (Web) traffic.

Transparent Cryptographic File System (TCFS) — An enhancement to the Cryptographic File System (CFS) that allows it to operate transparently to client users on the network.

transparent proxy — A feature of IP Chains and IP Tables in which a packet is redirected to a different port.

Triple DES — A U.S. government-approved encryption algorithm that applies the DES algorithm three times in succession using three different DES keys.

Tripwire — The best-known and most widely used file integrity checker.

Trivial FTP (TFTP) — A protocol similar to FTP, but designed for downloading an operating system over a network to boot a diskless workstation. Requires less memory and provides fewer features than standard FTP.

trn — The threaded news reader, probably the most widely used text-mode news reader for Linux.

Trojan horse attack — A technique for gaining access to a computer system by having a system administrator execute a program that appears normal but which actually creates a security hole for a cracker or destroys data on the host where it is run.

trustee — A user who is granted access to a file or directory on a NetWare server.

trustee rights — Access permissions assigned to a file or directory on a NetWare volume.

tunneling — The process of packaging a packet of a given Network-layer protocol within another type of packet from the same layer; for example, IP within IP or IPX within IP.

Twofish — A symmetric cipher.

Type of Service (ToS) — A field within an IP packet used to designate how the packet should be processed (routed). Rarely used at this time.

Unix to Unix Copy (UUCP) — A system used to transfer email between servers via a modem.

Usenet news — Another name for Internet newsgroups.

User Datagram Protocol (UDP) — A fast, connectionless Transport-layer protocol.

User Private Groups — A security system in which an empty group is created for every user on the system. Files created by a user are assigned to this empty group, meaning that no other users have any default access to the file.

uucp — A program that allows users to transfer files between two computers using a modem.

vigr — A special version of the **vi** editor used to edit the **/etc/group** file.

vipw — A special version of the **vi** editor that should be used anytime you must edit **/etc/passwd** directly (instead of using utilities such as **passwd** or **useradd**).

virtual hosting — A feature of the Apache Web server that lets a single copy of Apache serve documents for several Web sites (several domains).

virtual private network (VPN) — A secure organizational network that uses insecure public networks (such as the Internet) for communications.

visudo — A special text editor used to edit the **/etc/sudoers** file; it prevents conflicts between multiple open files and checks the syntax of the **/etc/sudoers** configuration file upon exit.

vlock — A utility that locks a text-mode console screen.

Voice-over-IP (VoIP) — Use of IP as a protocol for transport of digitized voice packets, often as a medium for long-distance telephone calls over the Internet.

volume — A unit of storage in NetWare that is equivalent to a file system in Linux.

VPN router — A hardware device that acts as a dedicated firewall with VPN capabilities.

VT100 — The most widely supported dumb terminal standard.

w — A utility that lists all users who are currently logged in with their username and terminal plus additional system usage information.

web of trust — The personal connections between a group of colleagues who have exchanged keys, signed them, and continue to rely on each others' signatures.

Web server — A daemon that accepts requests via HTTP and responds with the requested files.

Web spoofing — A type of man-in-the-middle attack in which a cracker deceives a user into linking to the cracker's site when the user thinks she is linking to another site. The cracker's server then intercepts every Web request from the user and alters the response to point all future requests back to the cracker's site.

Webmin — A browser-based utility that can manage many system functions, including network configuration. Included by default with Caldera OpenLinux products.

who — A utility that lists all of the users who are currently logged in on the system.

whois — A utility that queries an Internet database to learn about the person who manages a specific domain.

wide area network (WAN) — A network spanning more widely separated geographical locations.

WINS — Acronym for Windows Internet Naming Service, a host locating service for Windows systems, similar in function to a DNS server. The Samba suite can act as a WINS server or client.

wireless LAN (WLAN) — Wireless network designed to be used within a small radius of a central transceiver.

worm — A program that self-replicates and invades networked computer systems. Similar to a virus, but requires less human intervention for continued propagation.

write (w) — A standard Linux file permission—represented in utilities by w—that permits modifying a file or creating new files in a directory (when assigned to that directory).

wu-ftp — The Washington University FTP server. The name of the server daemon is `in.ftpd`.

wvdial — A text-mode utility that allows users to configure and initiate dial-up connections easily using PPP.

X client — A graphical program running on a host. *See also* X server.

X server — The screen where a graphical program is remotely displayed (and the keyboard and mouse of that system). *See also* X client.

X-Mas scan — A method of port scanning in which all flags in the TCP header are turned on (set).

X.500 — A widely known international standard for a directory service.

xauth — A security system for managing the display of graphical programs on remote computers by sharing a numeric token called a cookie; also the program used in Linux to manage this security system and the numeric cookies associated with it.

XDMCP — A protocol that allows remote hosts to use X running on a Linux system to provide a graphical login display.

xhost — A program that can control access by X clients to an X server for display of graphical programs. `xhost` is not a secure system.

xinetd — A superserver with extended configuration options. Standard on Red Hat Linux instead of the more usual `inetd` program.

xlock — A utility that locks a graphical screen.

xlogmaster — A program that displays several system resources, including the system log file, in a graphical window.

xntpd — A daemon used on some Linux systems to implement the NTP protocol. *See also* `ntpd`.

YAST2 — A utility provided in SuSE Linux that includes network configuration tools.

zone — A part of the DNS domain tree for which a particular DNS server has authority to provide information.

zone information files — The files referred to in `named.conf` that contain detailed information about specific zones: the information that a DNS query seeks.

zone transfer — Exchanging information between a master DNS server and a slave DNS server.

Index